Using Mac OS 8.5

Brad M. Miser

que

A Division of Macmillan Computer Publishing, USA
201 W. 103rd Street
Indianapolis, Indiana 46290

Contents at a Glance

P9-BJB-626

I Working with Your Mac

1 Working with Macintosh 3
2 Working with Folders and Windows 35
3 Working with Menus 65
4 Working with the Finder 79
5 Working with Hard Disks, Partitions, and Volumes 111
6 Working with the Apple Menu 123
7 Working witht the Control Strip 143
8 Working with Fonts 151
9 Working with Color and Graphics 161
10 Working with Multimedia 189
11 Working with Mac Applications 237
12 Working with the Mac's Help Systems 275

II Customizing Your Mac

13 Changing the Way Your Mac Looks and Sounds 291
14 Managing Your Mac's Memory 317
15 Managing Your System Folder 335
16 Using Keyboard Shortcuts 367
17 Making Your Mac Do Your Work for You 395

III Using Mac Hardware

18 Understanding and Using Input Devices 423
19 Understanding and Using Output Devices 437
20 Understanding and Using Networking Devices 449

IV Using Your Mac to Work with Others

21 Working with Other Macs 463
22 Working with Windows PCs 489

V Using Your Mac to Surf the Internet

23 Connecting Your Mac to the Net 509
24 Using Email: The Basics 543
25 Using Email: Advanced Techniques 573
26 Browsing the Web: The Basics 597
27 Browsing the Web: Advanced Techiniques 627
28 Reading Newsgroups 661

VI Maintaining, Fixing, and Upgrading Your Mac

29 Backing Up 681
30 Fighting Viruses 701
31 Preventing Mac Problems 713
32 Fixing Mac Problems 745
33 Maintaining Your Mac Through Upgrades 773

VII Using Mac OS 8.5 Appendices

A Installing and Maintaining the Mac OS 805
B Working with PowerBooks 817
C Speaking Essential Mac Lingo 837

Index 863

Using Mac OS 8.5

International Standard Book Number: 0-7897-1614-3

Library of Congress Catalog Card Number: 97-81256

Printed in the United States of America

First Printing: November, 1998

00   99   98   4   3   2   1

Executive Editor
Chris Will

Aquisitions Editor
Chris Will

Development Editor
Marta Partington

Project Editor
Katie Purdum

Copy Editor
Marta Partington

Indexer
Heather Goens

Technical Editor
Lisa Lee

Proofreader
Jennifer Earhart

Layout Technicians
Brian Borders
Marcia Deboy
Susan Geiselman

Cover Designer
Maureen McCarty

Trademarks

Warning and Disclaimer

Contents

I Working with Your Mac

1 Working with Macintosh   3

Mac OS Lives   4

Using the Mac   5
Using Folders and Windows   6
Using Menus   8
Working with the Finder   11
Working with Disks, Discs, Volumes, and Partitions   12
Using the Apple Menu   13
Using the Control Strip   16
Using Fonts   16
Working with Color and Graphics   16
Using Multimedia   17
Working with Applications   18
Finding Help   18

Making Your Mac Your Own   19
Giving Your Mac a Face Lift   19
Not Losing Your Memory   20
Knowing Your System Folder   21
Using the Keyboard   22
Making the Mac Your Slave   22

Working with Mac Hardware   22
Inputting Information to Your Mac   23
Outputting Information from Your Mac   23
Connecting to the World   23

Working with Others   24
Preaching to the Choir   24
Sleeping with the Enemy   25

Surfing the Net   26
Getting Connected   26
Keeping in Touch with Email   27
Walking the World Wide Web   28

Reading News That is Fit to Print—and Some That's Not   28

Maintaining Your Mac   30
Backing Up Isn't Hard to Do   30
Preventing Infection   30
Preventing Trouble   31
Fixing Your Mac   31
Growing Your Mac   32

Using the Appendices   32
Working with the Mac OS Installer   32
Computing on the Move   33
Talking the Talk   33

Understanding this Book   33

2 Working with Folders and Windows   35

Understanding Folder and Windows   36

Working with Mac Windows   39
Using the Keyboard with Windows   41
Setting Finder Window Preferences   42

Working with Folder Windows   45

Working with Folder Views   45
Using Icon Views   46
Using Button Views   47
Using List Views   47
Setting Window Views Preferences   52
Using Hierarchical Folders   56

Working with Pop-Up Windows   57

Working with Spring-Loaded Folders   61

Using Folder Window Features   62

3 **Working with Menus 65**

Understanding Mac Menus 66

Using Mac Menus 68

Working with Contextual Menus 68
  Understanding Contextual Menus 69
  Using Contextual Menus 69
  Adding to Contextual Menus 70

Using the Finder's Unique Menus 72
  Using the Apple Menu 72
  Using the Special Menu 73
  Using the Application Menu 74

4 **Working with the Finder 79**

Understanding the Finder 80

Getting Information About Files and
Folders 83
  Getting General Information for
  Applications and Documents 85
  Getting Sharing Information for a
  Folder 87

Finding Things with the Finder's Find
Command 88
  Finding Files by Attribute 88
  Finding Files by Content 92
  Finding Information on the Internet 95

Working with Aliases 97
  Creating an Alias 98
  Finding an Original for an Alias 98

Setting and Using Favorites 99
  Setting Favorites 99
  Using Favorites 100

Setting Finder Preferences 102

Telling Time with the Clock 104

Taking Out the Trash 107

Saving Energy 108

5 **Working with Hard Disks, Partitions, and
Volumes 111**

Understanding Hard Drives, Volumes, and
Partitions 112

Understanding Drive Terminology 112

Initializing and Partitioning a Hard
Drive 114

Mounting Volumes on the Desktop 119

6 **Working with the Apple Menu 123**

Understanding the Apple Menu 124

Using and Customizing the Apple Menu 126
  Using the Apple Menu 126
  Customizing the Apple Menu 127

Working with Applications and Utilities
on the Apple Menu 130
  Choosing with the Chooser 130
  Calculating with the Simple
  Calculator 132
  Using the Graphing Calculator 132
  Working with the Graphing
  Calculator 134
  Figuring Out Fonts with Key Caps 135
  Taking Notes with Note Pad 136
  Creating Clippings with the
  Scrapbook 136
  Creating Sticky Notes 139
  Playing with the Jigsaw Puzzle 140

7 **Working with the Control Strip 143**

Understanding the Control Strip 144

Using the Standard Control Strip 145
  Collapsing and Expanding the
  Control Strip 145
  Using Control Strip Modules 145

Customizing the Control Strip   146
  Resizing and Moving the Control
  Strip   146
  Using the Control Strip Control
  Panel   147
  Removing Control Strip Modules   148
  Finding and Installing Control Strip
  Modules   148

8 Working with Fonts   151

Using Fonts   152

Understanding Font Types   152
  Understanding Screen Fonts   155
  Understanding PostScript Fonts   156
  Understanding TrueType Fonts   157

Managing Fonts   158

9 Working with Color and Graphics   161

Using Color and Graphics on the Mac   162

Understanding Resolution   162
  Working with Your Mac's Resolution   166
  Understanding Image Resolution   169
  Understanding Imaging Resolution   171

Working with Color   173

Understanding Color   173
  Using Colors on Your Mac   176
  Using ColorSync for Consistent Color
  Across Devices   180

Understanding Graphics   184
  Understanding Raster-Based
  Graphics   185
  Understanding Vector-Based
  Graphics   186

10 Working with Multimedia   189

Using the Ultimate Multimedia Machine   190

Digital Video, Sound, and Animation with
QuickTime   191
  Understanding QuickTime   191
  Playing and Editing QuickTime Movies
  201
  Going Three-Dimensional with
  QuickDraw 3D   219
  Exploring the Digital Frontier   219

Listening and Programming Audio CDs with
the AppleCD Audio Player   219
  Listening While You Work   221
  Creating an Alert Sound from a CD with
  SimpleSound   224
  Programming the AppleCD Audio
  Player   225

Watching and Capturing Video with the Apple
Video Player   228
  Understanding Hardware and System
  Requirements   228
  Understanding Apple Video Player   230
  Watching TV and Movies   231
  Capturing Still Images from Video   232
  Capturing Digital Video   233

Understanding DVD   234

11 Working with Mac Applications   237

Adding and Using Mac Software   238

Assessing Mac Software Requirements   238
  Assessing RAM Requirements   240
  Assessing Disk Space Requirements   242
  Assessing System Software
  Requirements   243
  Assessing Hardware Requirements   244

Installing Mac Software   246
   Using the Easy Install Option   248
   Using the Custom Install Option   249
   Using Other Install Options   250
   Testing Mac Software   250

Registering Mac Software   252

Removing Mac Software   253
   Using Installation Software to Remove
   an Application   254
   Manually Removing an Application   254

Launching Applications   255

Understanding Standard Application
Behavior   258
   Understanding Standard Window
   Behavior   258
   Understanding Standard File Menu
   Items   258
   Understanding Standard Edit Menu
   Items   260
   Understanding Standard Open and Save
   Dialog Boxes   261
   Understanding Navigation Services Open
   and Save Dialogs   263
   Understanding ACTION Files Open and
   Save Dialogs   265
   Setting Application Preferences   267

Moving Information Between
Applications   267
   Cutting and Pasting   267
   Sharing Documents   267
   Drag-and-Drop   268
   Using Desktop Clippings   270

Exiting Applications   272

12 Working with the Mac's Help Systems   275

Finding Help Where You Need It   276

Using the Mac's Help Center   276
   Understanding the Mac OS Help
   Center   277
   Working with the Mac OS Help
   Center   278

Using AppleGuide   280
   Understanding AppleGuide   281
   Working with AppleGuide   281

Using Balloon Help   285
   Understanding Balloon Help   285
   Using Balloon Help   285

Using the Assistants   286

II Customizing Your Mac

**13 Changing the Way Your Mac Looks and
Sounds   291**

Customizing Your Mac Is Fun   292

Customizing the Way Your Mac Looks   293
   Adjusting Monitor Settings   293
   Customizing the Desktop   293
   Changing Icons   298
   Customizing Menus, Highlight Colors, and
   Other Graphic Elements   302
   Customizing Window Options   303
   Customizing Fonts   304
   Customizing Numbers   305

Customizing the Way Your Mac Sounds   306
   Adjusting Sound   306
   Customizing Sound Effects   307
   Customizing the Alert Sound   308
   Customizing Your Mac's Voice   311

Putting It All Together with Themes   313
    Choosing a Theme   313
    Saving Themes   315

14 Managing Your Mac's Memory   317

Understanding Memory   318
    Understanding Physical RAM   318
    Understanding Caches   323

Managing RAM   326
    Managing RAM for the System   327
    Managing RAM for Applications   327

Using RAM Substitutes   330
    Using Virtual Memory   330
    Using Third-Party RAM Extensions   331

Using a Virtual Hard Disk (or RAM
Disk)   332

Upgrading RAM   333

15 Managing Your System Folder   335

Understanding the System Folder   336

Setting the System Your Mac Uses   345

Understanding System Enhancements   347

Managing Your System   348

Manually Managing Your System   349

Using Extensions Manager to Manage Your
System   350
    Using Extensions Manager to Disable
    Extensions, Control Panels, and Other
    System Files   351
    Using Extensions Manager to Define
    Sets   353
    Using Extensions Manager Defined
    Sets   354

Using Extensions Manager to Learn About
Extensions, Control Panels, and Other
System Files   355
    Using Extensions Manager   357

Using Conflict Catcher to Manage Your
System   359
    Using Conflict Catcher to Manage Your
    System   360
    Using Conflict Catcher to Define Sets   361
    Using Conflict Catcher Defined Sets   362
    Using Conflict Catcher to Learn about
    Extensions, Control Panels, and Other
    System Files   363
    Using Conflict Catcher   364

16 Using Keyboard Shortcuts   367

Working with the Keyboard   368

Configuring Your Keyboard   369

Using Predefined Keyboard Shortcuts   370

Creating Your Own Keyboard Shortcuts   372
    Creating Finder Keyboard Shortcuts with
    ResEdit   373
    Adding Keyboards Shortcuts to Applications
    from Within Those Applications   378
    Adding Keyboard Shortcuts to Applications
    with ResEdit   381
    Creating Your Own Keyboard Shortcuts
    with QuickKeys   383

17 Making Your Mac Do Your Work for You   395

Automating Your Mac   396

Scheduling an Automatic Startup or Shutdown
Time   396

Using Startup Items   397

Using Shutdown Items   398

Automating Your Mac with AppleScript   398
   Understanding AppleScript   399
   Using Predefined AppleScripts   401
   Creating Your Own AppleScripts   403

Telling Your Mac What to Do   409

Using QuickKeys to Make Your Mac
Read to You   413

III Using Mac Hardware

18 **Understanding and Using Input
Devices   423**

Working with Input Devices   424

Understanding Connection
Technologies   424
   Understanding Apple Desktop Bus
   (ADB)   424
   Understanding Serial Connections   425
   Understanding Small Computer Serial
   Interface (SCSI)   426
   Understanding Universal Serial Bus
   (USB)   426
   Understanding Other Input
   Connections   427

Working with Mice   427

Working with Keyboards   428

Working with Trackpads   429

Working with Trackballs   429

Working with Joysticks   431

Working with Microphones   431

Working with Scanners   432

Understanding Digital Cameras   434

19 **Understanding and Using Output
Devices   437**

Using Output Devices   438

Using Monitors   438

Using Printers   441
   Installing and Selecting a Printer   443
   Using ColorSync with a Printer   444

Outputting Electronic Documents   445

20 **Understanding and Using Networking
Devices   449**

Connecting to the World   450

Working with Modems   450
   Understanding Modems   450
   Using a Modem   452
   Understanding the Future of Modems
   456

Working with AppleTalk Networks   457
   Setting Up an AppleTalk Network by
   Using Serial Connections   457
   Setting Up an AppleTalk Network by
   Using Ethernet   458
   Configuring an AppleTalk Network   459

Using Other Networks   459

IV Using Your Mac to Work with Others

21 **Working with Other Macs   463**

Understanding How You Can Work with
Other Macs   464

Sharing and Transferring Files   465
   Transferring Files Among Macs   466
   Sharing Your Files with Others   467

Accessing Files That Others Share
with You   479
Working with Files You Share or
Receive   483

Sharing Applications   486

Sharing the Web   486

22 Working with Windows PCs   489

Living in a Windows World   490

Moving Files from PCs to Macs and Back
Again   490
Using Sneakernet to Transfer Files   490
Using Email to Transfer Files   491
Using a Network to Transfer Files   492

Using Windows Files   497
Understanding Windows Files   497
Providing Mac Files for the PC   498
Working with PC Files on Your Mac   499

Running Windows Applications   503
Using Windows Emulators   503
Installing a PC Card in Your Mac   505
Buying a "Real" PC   505

Fighting PC Viruses   506

V Using Your Mac to Surf the Internet

23 Connecting Your Mac to the Net   509

Understanding the Internet—It's Not Just a
Lot of Hype   510
Connecting to the Net with the Mac's
Internet Setup Assistant   510
Understanding Email   510
Understanding the World Wide Web   512

Understanding How the Internet Works   514
Using a Computer and Modem (or
Network)   514

Understanding Internet Service
Providers   515
Understanding Connection Software   516
Understanding Internet Software   516

Understanding Mac OS 8.5's Internet
Software   517

Finding Your Own Path to the Net   519

Connecting Through a Network   520

Connecting To an Existing Internet
Account   524

Connecting Through a Modem and Obtaining
a New Internet Account   530

Finding an Internet Service Provider   531

Using the Internet Connection Wizard   533

Finishing Your Configuration   534

Connecting and Disconnecting with a
Modem   538

Troubleshooting Your Connection
Through a Modem   540

24 Using Email: The Basics   543

Using Email Is Excellent   544

Understanding Addresses   545

Understanding the Anatomy of an Email
Message   546
Understanding the Header   546
Understanding the Body   547
Understanding the Signature   548

Understanding Email Applications   548

Using Microsoft's Outlook Express   550
Experiencing Outlook Express—a Quick
Look   551
Configuring Outlook Express   552

Writing and Sending Email   554
Retrieving and Reading Email   559
Replying to Email   561
Working with Bounced Email   564
Using Contacts   566

Understanding Netiquette   568
Remembering That No One Can See
Your Face   568
Realizing That Nobody Knows Your
Name   569
Understanding Some Dos and
Don'ts   569

Understanding More About Outlook
Express   571

25 **Using Email: Advanced Techniques   573**

Moving Ahead with Email   574

Understanding Email Protocols and
Formats   574
Understanding Email Formats   574
Being Aware of Email Protocols   576

Organizing Your Email   577

Filtering Your Email   579

Searching Your Email   581

Using Multiple Email Accounts   582
Configuring Multiple Email
Accounts   582
Working with Multiple Email
Accounts   583

Using Mailing Lists   584
Using Public Mailing Lists   584
Creating Your Own Mailing List   586

Working with Email Attachments   587
Understanding File Encoding   587
Understanding File Compression   589

Viewing Attachments   591
Receiving Files Attached to Email
Messages   592
Attaching Files to Your Email   594

Updating Outlook Express   595

26 **Browsing the Web: The Basics   597**

Understanding the Web   598

Understanding URLs   598

Introducing Microsoft's Internet
Explorer   601

Understanding the Anatomy of a
Web Page   602

Surfing the Web   604
Browsing the Web   605
Using URLs   605
Setting and Using Favorites   606
Organizing Favorites   609
Getting Info on Favorites   611

Touring Internet Explorer   613
Using the Tool bar   613
Using the Address Bar   614
Using the Explorer Bar   614
Using Status and Security
Information   615
Using the Menu Bar   616

Configuring Internet Explorer
Preferences   616
Setting Your Home Page   617
Setting the Internet Explorer Window
Display   619
Setting Web Content   620

Exploring Your Web History   621

Using Great Web Sites   623

27 Browsing the Web: Advanced Techniques   627

Understanding How the Web Really Works   628
  Understanding HTML   628
  Understanding How a Browser Really Works   629
  Understanding Java   630

Subscribing to Sites   632
  Manually Subscribing to a Web Site   633
  Subscribing to a Web Site While Browsing   635
  Setting Subscription Preferences   636

Browsing a Site Offline   637

Searching the Web   639
  Searching with Yahoo!   640
  Searching with Hotbot   644
  Setting Your Default Search Page   645
  Using the Search Tab to Search   646

Downloading Files   646

Working with Plug-ins   649
  Using Internet Explorer Plug-ins   650
  Installing Internet Explorer Plug-ins   651

Working with Helper Applications   651
  Installing and Using Helper Applications   651
  Configuring the Helper Applications that Internet Explorer Uses   652

Understanding Something About Web Security   654

Speeding Up the Web   655
  Using Contextual Menus   656
  Turning Off Images   657
  Using More Windows on the World   658
  Caching It In   659

Updating Internet Explorer   660

28 Reading Newsgroups   661

Understanding Newsgroups   662

Understanding How Newsgroups Work   663
  Understanding Newsgroup Names   663
  Understanding Newsgroup URLs   664
  Subscribing and Unsubscribing to Newsgroups   664

Reading Newsgroups   666
  Finding Newsgroups   666
  Subscribing to Newsgroups   669
  Reading Newsgroup Messages   671
  Posting and Replying to Newsgroups   673
  Unsubscribing from Newsgroups   676

Using Newsgroups   676

VI Maintaining, Fixing, and Upgrading Your Mac

29 Backing Up   681

Backing Up Can Save You   682

Understanding Backups   683

Defining a Backup Strategy   683
  Deciding What to Back Up   683
  Deciding What Kind of Backup to Make   684
  Choosing a Backup System   685

Choosing Backup Hardware   686
  Backing Up with Tape Drives   689
  Backing Up with Removable Media Drives   690
  Backing Up with CD-R and CD-RW Drives   691
  Backing Up with Hard Drives   692
  Backing Up with Floppy Drives   693
  Deciding Which You Should Use   694

Choosing Backup Software   694
  Creating a Backup   695
  Using Other Backup Software   698

Backing Up Isn't Hard to Do   698

30 Fighting Viruses   701

Protecting Your Mac from Viruses   702

Understanding How Your Mac Might Get
Infected   702

Understanding the Types of Viruses   703

Preventing Infection   703

Identifying Infection   704

Using Anti-Virus Software   705
  Using Symantec Anti-virus for Macintosh
  (SAM)   706
  Using Disinfectant   708

Using Anti-virus Tips   710

31 Preventing Mac Problems   713

Preventing Problems Is Easier Than Solving
Them   714

Maintaining Your Drives   714
  Rebuilding Your Desktop File   715
  Maintaining the Structure of Your
  Disks   719
  Defragmenting and Optimizing Your
  Disks   724
  Cleaning Up Your Drives   727

Maintaining Your System Folder   729
  Cleaning Up Control Panels and
  Extensions   730
  Cleaning Up Other System Files   731

Maintaining Backups   732

  Keeping an Eye Out for Viruses   732

Maintaining Your Hardware   732

Preparing for Trouble   733
  Looking for Trouble   734
  Building a Mac Tool Kit   735

Maintaining Your Records   742

32 Fixing Mac Problems   745

Facing Your Problems   746

Understanding What Could Go Wrong   747
  Being Your Own Worst Enemy   747
  Fighting Bugs   748
  Battling Software   748
  Fighting Viruses   749
  Suffering Hardware Failures   749

Troubleshooting Techniques   750
  Preparing to Troubleshoot   750
  Looking, Listening, and Learning   751
  Solving the Problem   752

Solving Problems   754
  Solving Problems You Create   755
  Fixing Software Problems   756
  Solving "General Weirdness"
  Problems   766
  Solving Hardware Problems   768

Solving the Startup Problem   770

**33 Maintaining Your Mac Through
Upgrades   773**

Improving Your Mac's Software and
Hardware   774

Upgrading Software   774
  Understanding Software Upgrades   775
  Understanding Software Version
  Names   776
  Finding Out About Upgrades   777
  Understanding How to Upgrade   779

Understanding Mac OS Upgrades   780
Knowing That Software Upgrades Aren't
Always Good for You   783
Understanding Why You Shouldn't
Upgrade   784
Answering the Upgrade Question   785
Using Sources of Information on
Upgrades   785
Knowing What to Do If You Do
Upgrade   786
Knowing What to Do If You Don't
Upgrade   787

Understanding Hardware Upgrades   787

Understanding the Hardware Upgrades Your
Mac Can Handle   788
Understanding Active Memory
Upgrades   790
Understanding Storage Memory
Upgrades   793
Understanding Processor Upgrades   796
Upgrading PCI Cards   797
Evaluating Hardware Upgrades   799

VII   Using Mac OS 8.5 Appendices

A   Installing and Maintaining the Mac OS   805

Installing the Mac OS   805
Making Sure That Your Mac Has
Adequate Resources   806
Gathering Resources   806
Plugging in Your PowerBook   807
Recording MacTCP Info, if
Necessary   807
Restarting from an Alternate Startup
Disk   808

Updating System Software   808

Installing Mac OS 8.5   809
Performing a Clean Install   810
Performing an Update to Your

System   815
Installing System Components   815

B   Working with PowerBooks   817

Computing on the Run   818

Managing Energy   818
Putting Your PowerBook to Sleep   820
Reducing Your Processing Power and Other
Advanced Energy Saving Techniques   822
Dimming the Screen   824
Spinning Down the Hard Disk   824
Using a RAM Disk   825
Conditioning Your Batteries   825

Using the PowerBook's Control Strip   826

Using the Track Pad   827

Managing Your Location   828

Synchronizing Files   830

Protecting Your PowerBook   832

Using Your PowerBook as a Hard Disk   834

Networking without Wires   835

C   Speaking Essential Mac Lingo   837

Index   863

About the Author

Brad Miser has been a Mac fan since the late 1980s when he was introduced to MacDraw, Excel, and Word on a Mac SE ("that is a nice
machine, but the screen is so small!"). Since that time, he has been
through lots of hardware and software as well as many "discussions" with
PC users about why they should use a Mac instead of a PC. He has also
spent lots of time helping friends, family, and coworkers (and anyone else
who would listen) learn to use their Macs better. He enjoys all aspects of
the Mac, and particularly likes learning new things about the world's best
computer (which is why he enjoyed writing this book!).

In his "real life," Brad is an engineer who develops technical proposals
for a major aerospace engine company. Additionally, he has authored six
computer books and has been a development, technical, and copy editor
for more than 35 others.

Brad welcomes your comments, criticisms, and suggestions. He'd also
love to hear about your experiences with this book. You can write to him
at bradm@iquest.net.

Dedication

To everyone, young or old, who tries to learn something new

Acknowledgements

One of the hard things about writing a book is that it is impossible to properly express gratitude to all those who helped make the book a reality. It takes lots of hard work by a lot of people to produce a book. And I have certainly had a lot of help with this one. So here it goes, in no particular order...

Special thanks to Marta Partington, who helped focus the vision for this book and made hundreds of improvements in the text itself. Even more important, she is a good friend who listened to me blow off steam when I needed to, and also guided me through the difficult process of making a book.

Thanks to Chris Will, Katie Purdum, and the other good folks at Macmillan Computer Publishing. I really appreciated the opportunity to write this book and all of the work done to get it into the reader's hands.

Thanks to Lisa Lee for catching many of my technical goofs.

Thanks to CE Software, Dantz Corporation, Cassady & Greene, Symantec, Power On Software, and Insignia Software for providing their excellent software for the Mac as well as for this book.

Thanks to my family for enduring my obsession with this book for the past four months. Amy, Jill, Emily, and Grace have patiently put up with me being huddled with my Mac for hours on end.

Thanks to Bat for lots of good questions over the years that helped me know what I needed to talk about in this book. And to Two Dogs (don't ask).

Thanks to my parents who put me in a position to achieve. I owe them a debt that can never be repaid.

And last, but certainly not least, thanks to you for giving this book a chance. I hope it helps you in your Mac life.

Brad Miser
Mooresville, IN
August 1998

We'd Like to Hear from You!

As the reader of this book, *you* are our most important critic and commentator. We value your opinion and want to know what we're doing right, what we could do better, what areas you'd like to see us publish in, and any other words of wisdom you're willing to pass our way.

As the Executive Editor for the [Web development] team at Macmillan Computer Publishing, I welcome your comments. You can fax, email, or write me directly to let me know what you did or didn't like about this book[md]as well as what we can do to make our books stronger.

Please note that I cannot help you with technical problems related to the topic of this book, and that due to the high volume of mail I receive, I might not be able to reply to every message.

When you write, please be sure to include this book's title and author as well as your name and phone or fax number. I will carefully review your comments and share them with the author and editors who worked on the book.

Fax: [317-817-7070]

E-mail: [opsys@mcp.com]

Mail: Chris Will
           Operating Systems
           Macmillan Computer Publishing
           201 West 103rd Street
           Indianapolis, IN 46290 USA

Working with Your Mac

1   **Working with Macintosh 3**

2   **Working with Folders and Windows 35**

3   **Working with Menus 65**

4   **Working with the Finder 79**

5   **Working with Hard Disks, Partitions, and Volumes 111**

6   **Working with the Apple Menu 123**

7   **Working with the Control Strip 143**

8   **Working with Fonts 151**

9   **Working with Color and Graphics 161**

10 **Working with Multimedia 189**

11 **Working with Mac Applications 237**

12 **Working with the Mac's Help Systems 275**

Working with Macintosh

Taking a tour of the Mac OS 8.5 desktop

Learning about the new features for 8.5

Understanding the major areas of your Mac

Understanding this book

Mac OS Lives

According to the press, conventional wisdom, and the PC snobs of the world, the Macintosh has always been on the verge of extinction. Even while admitting that the Mac has the easiest-to-use and most-intuitive interface of any operating system, the Mac's critics proclaimed that the time of doom for Mac users was at hand. The Mac's market share is too small, they said. Retail shops don't carry enough software or hardware for it. People won't continue to support it. No one can compete against Microsoft and Intel. Apple is a floundering entity with a history of poor business decisions and incompetent leadership. The Mac can't survive without clones; the Mac can't survive with clones. It can't survive without Steve Jobs, and now it can't survive with him. The Mac is just another in the long line of extinct platforms, only worthy of consideration by the technology archeologists of the future.

But you know better. The Mac OS lives.

You have chosen to ignore the alarmist cries of the media and PC pundits who are once again claiming that the Mac is not viable. Now in version 8.5, the Mac operating system is more powerful and easier to use than at any time in its history. There are lots of applications and peripherals available for it. There are more Mac users than at any time in the past. The Mac is very much alive.

And Mac OS 8.5 is proof of that. Mac OS 8.5 is a state-of-the-art operating system, and Apple has made substantial improvements even since the release of version 8.0 in 1997.

In this chapter, you will take a whirlwind tour of the world's best operating system. You will learn about the features that are incorporated in it, with special emphasis on the features new to Mac OS 8.5 for those of you who have used earlier versions. You will also find some hints about some of the great things that the Mac OS enables you to do. As you move through this chapter, you will see links to other places in the book where you will get all of the details you need to make the most of your Mac experience. And finally, you will learn how this book was designed and how you can use it to help you grow in Mac knowledge and effectiveness. This chapter is your springboard to exploring the newest and best Mac you have ever seen.

In the following sections, you will learn about the general areas of Mac OS 8.5, and you will see a specific feature or two that should make you excited about this great OS. This chapter is organized to correspond to the rest of the book. Each major section covers a part of the book, while the subsections are related to each chapter. Use this chapter as your map to lead you to the areas that you want to explore first.

Using the Mac

The heart and soul of your Mac, as it always has been, is its desktop. Although there have been thousands of improvements made to the desktop since Apple first introduced it, the Mac desktop, even after more than 20 years, is still where much of the action happens. Figure 1.1 shows an 8.5 desktop.

If you are a current Mac user, or you have used a Mac in the past, you will probably recognize much of what you see, but also note some new and interesting elements. If you are new to the Mac, I will be happy to show you around—don't worry, as powerful as the Mac is, it is also very easy to use.

Of course, there is more to the Mac than meets the eye. Supporting that familiar desktop are all the tools that you need to explore, create, and grow.

In Part I, "Working with Your Mac," you will learn about the fundamental aspects of using your Mac. You will also learn about the Mac OS's new features, and you'll even learn some tips to make you work more effectively.

FIGURE 1.1

The Mac OS desktop is the launching pad for everything you will do on the Mac.

1 Mounted hard disks and volumes

2 Mounted CD-ROM, Zip, and floppy disk

3 Aliases

4 Pop-up window

5 Contextual menu

6 Control Strip

7 Application Switcher

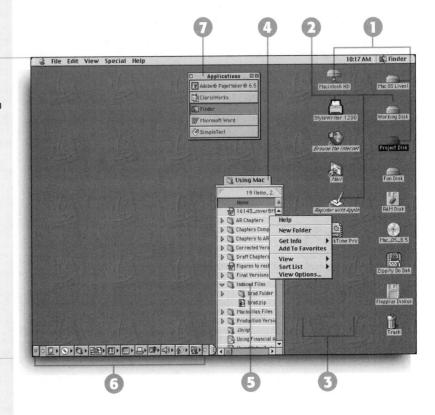

Using Folders and Windows

You will constantly use Mac folders and windows as you work. Everything you work with is displayed in a window or is provided by a folder (even the desktop). With Mac OS 8.5, there are lots of refinements and improvements in the way folders and windows work, and you have more options than ever to make them into what you want them to be.

An innovation in Mac OS 8, pop-up windows are still part of Mac OS 8.5. When you create a pop-up window, it is always available as a tab at the bottom of your desktop (see Figure 1.2). When you click on the tab, the window pops up, and you can work within it (see Figure 1.3). When you are done, it snaps back closed.

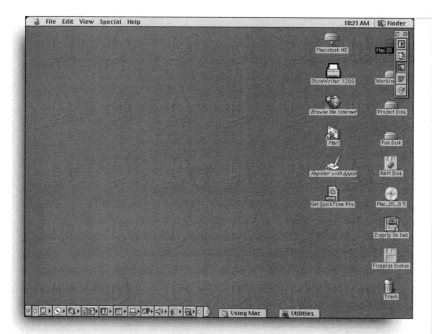

FIGURE 1.2

Pop-up windows provide an easy and fast way to access folders that you frequently use. A pop-up window appears at the bottom of the desktop.

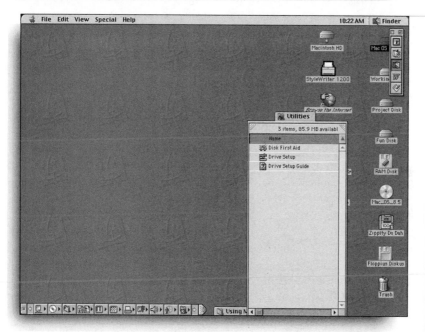

FIGURE 1.3

This window has popped open so that you can use its contents.

New to Mac OS 8.5, the icons at the top of a pop-up window (see Figure 1.2 and Figure 1.3) can be used just like a "regular" folder icon (for example, you just drag the icon to move the folder to another location).

Another interface improvement that was made with Mac OS 8.0, spring-loaded folders open when you drag something onto them. No need to open a folder to put something into it; just drag an item onto a folder, and it opens for you. As you drag an item onto each "level" of a folder, it springs open so that you can quickly reach your final destination, no matter how buried it is. As you move across folders, they automatically close for you. This spring-loaded action works with disks and volumes as well.

You will learn a lot about how to use folders and windows in Chapter 2, "Working with Folders and Windows."

Using Menus

While you view and organize things with folders and windows, you can get your work done by using commands that are on menus. Mac OS 8.5 builds upon the menus in earlier versions.

One of the most powerful interface improvements made in Mac OS 8.0 was the introduction of contextual menus (see Figure 1.4). These are menus that pop up when you activate them (by default you do this by pointing at something, holding the Control key down, and clicking).

> **Contextual menus and applications**
>
> Lots of Mac programs support contextual menus as well. Microsoft does an especially good job of using contextual menus, which is not surprising since they have been a feature of Windows since Windows 95. For example, both Internet Explorer and Outlook Express use contextual menus.

FIGURE 1.4

This is a contextual menu for the desktop.

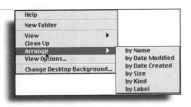

These are called contextual menus because the choices you see depend on the context in which you activate them (for example, you will see a different menu if you Control-click a folder rather than the desktop). You can even modify these menus to suit your needs.

The Applications menu is probably the least understood element of the desktop (see Figure 1.5) since it is related to a fairly difficult-to-understand feature of the operating system, *multitasking*.

FIGURE 1.5

The Applications menu is not easy to understand for some, but once understood, it becomes very useful.

Multitasking is simply your Mac's ability to walk and chew gum at the same time. More meaningfully, multitasking means that your Mac can be doing several things at once. For example, you can have many applications (as much as your RAM will permit) open at the same time, and you can easily and quickly switch between them. And your Mac can do some of its work in the background while you are using it to do something else.

The Applications menu lists all applications that are running on your Mac at any point in time. In Figure 1.5, you can see that there are six applications open. That is the easy part to understand. Now, for the hard part. Applications appear to run in "layers," with one layer seemingly on top of another in a "stack." As you move among applications, you move up and down the stack. If the applications have open windows, this is fairly easy to see (see Figure 1.6).

In Figure 1.6, you can see that SimpleText (the Using English Text-to-Speech window), AppleCD Audio Player, and Calculator are all open and running. You can tell this by seeing the open windows and by seeing them in the Applications menu. Notice, however, that you do not see a window for the other open applications, including Microsoft Word. That is because an open application can be hidden so that its menu bar and any open windows *don't* appear anywhere on the desktop.

True versus cooperative multitasking

The Mac's multitasking capability is not as robust as it might be. It is *cooperative* multitasking in which each application must be written so that it is able to share system resources with other applications. In effect, they must be able to cooperate with each other. This works fairly well, but if one application has problems, it tends to take down the other running applications, too. Under true multitasking (also called pre-emptive multitasking), each application is allotted its own processing resources so that it actually runs independently of the others. True multitasking will come to the Mac with the next major system release, Mac OS X.

FIGURE 1.6

Here three applications have open windows, and you can see one on top of the other.

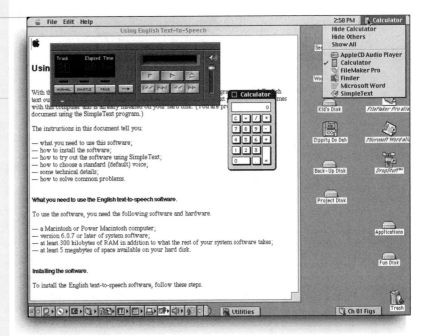

The application that you are using at any given time will be on the "top" of the stack, and its window will be on top of the others. However, it may not have an open window, in which case it can be confusing to know which application you are in.

The Applications menu sports several new features for Mac OS 8.5. One is that the name of the foremost, or active, application is shown at the top of the menu rather that just the icon, as was the case with previous versions (see Figure 1.6). You can also resize the width of the top of the menu so that you can see the whole name of the active application. The most important new feature is that you can tear the menu off so that it becomes a floating palette; then you can click an application to move it to the front (see Figure 1.7).

FIGURE 1.7

With Mac OS 8.5, you can tear the Applications menu off and place it anywhere on your screen.

You will learn all about using the Mac's menus in Chapter 3, "Working with Menus."

Working with the Finder

As with all other versions of the Mac OS, the Finder is the application that controls how everything else on the Mac works. It provides the desktop and manages all other aspects of the system.

The Finder's File menu contains commands that work with, amazingly enough, files. These commands include old favorites such as New, Open, and Page Setup. Some of the other commands are new with version 8.5, such as Add to Favorites, while others were added for version 8.0 (for example, Move to Trash).

The most impressive new Finder feature is the revamped Find command, now called Sherlock (although it still appears as Find on the Finder's File menu). With the Mac OS 8.5's Find command, you can use natural language to search the contents of files in addition to their attributes, such as name and creation date. You can even search the Internet from the Finder (see Figure 1.8). This feature, which Apple calls Sherlock, is one of the most compelling reasons to use Mac OS 8.5. Rather than having to open a Web browser, move to a search page, and then enter your search text (you may have to do this several times to use several different search sites), you can jump to Sherlock, enter your search text, and click Search. Your Mac will do the search and then present the results in a single window.

Natural language?

Being able to use natural language is good because you don't have to worry about proper syntax. For example, you can search for information about using contextual menus by simply entering contextual menus in Sherlock's search dialog.

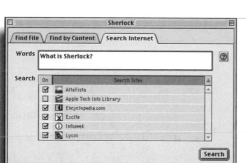

FIGURE 1.8

You can even search the Internet with the Finder's new and improved Find command (now called Sherlock).

Using the Finder's View menu you can change how items on the desktop or within folders appear. You can also clean up a folder on the desktop and set view options. Now Mac OS 8.5 enables you to set global view preferences that are used for every window you open, and you can also set preferences for particular windows.

With Mac OS 8.5, the Finder also enables you to track all of your favorite items so that you can easily move back to them. Once you add something to your favorites, you can jump to it by choosing it from favorites on the Apple menu. You can also choose your favorites from within Open and Save dialogs that use the new Navigation Services feature.

You will explore the Finder in Chapter 4, "Working with the Finder."

Working with Disks, Discs, Volumes, and Partitions

Disks versus discs

You may have noticed that both disks and discs appear in the previous head. Disks usually refer to floppy disks, hard disks, Zip disks, and so on. While discs refer to CD-ROM discs. Is this important? No.

Hard disk versus hard drive

The term hard disk refers to a drive that has a fixed disk; you can't remove it from the drive (not without destroying the drive at any rate). Hard drive means the same thing; the terms are interchangeable.

As in all Mac operating systems, you can mount a wide variety of data storage devices on your desktop (see Figure 1.9). Mounted drives can be any or all of the following:

- **Hard drives**. Hard drives, also called *fixed* drives, have media that can't be removed from the drive. You have at least one internal hard drive, but you may have additional internal or external drives as well.

- **Volumes**. Some of your drives may be *partitioned* into *logical volumes*. Partitioning a drive is simply a way of organizing a drive so that it appears as separate "disks." To your Mac, a partitioned disk behaves just as if it were a physically separate disk, even though it is actually just an electronic construct. Partitioning a large drive provides better performance, but you may want to partition some of your drives as an organizational tool.

- **AppleShare volumes**. If you are on a network, you may have the volumes of other computers or servers mounted on your desktop so that you can access their files as if the volume were installed on your Mac.

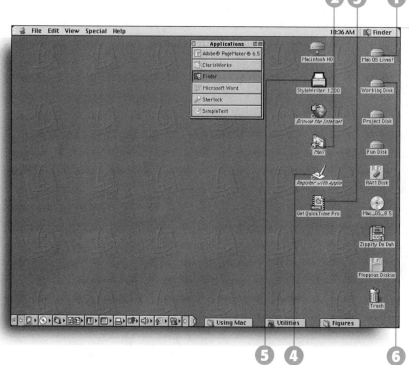

FIGURE 1.9

You can mount disks, volumes, CD-ROMs, DVD-ROMS, floppy disks, Zip disks, as well as any number of other storage devices on your desktop.

1. Hard drive

2. Volume (partition)

3. AppleShare volume

4. Floppy disk

5. Zip disk

6. CD-ROM

Startup disk

Your startup disk—or more accurately, your startup volume since it may or may not be a physical disk—is the one that contains the system software that your Mac is using to operate. This volume is *always* the one located in the top right corner of the desktop. Your startup disk may also be a CD-ROM, Zip disk, or other removable media as well.

The three menus

The Apple, Help, and Applications menus are the only menus that are always available to you, no matter what you are doing.

- **Removable media drives**. Your Mac can work with all sorts of removable media drives, including CD-ROMs, floppy disks, Zip disks, Jaz disks, and so on. These mount on your desktop just as a fixed drive does, except that you can remove the media on which your data is stored.

In Chapter 5, "Working with Hard Disks, Partitions, and Volumes," you will learn more about working with these items, especially how to create and use your own partitions.

Using the Apple Menu

The Apple menu is an extremely useful part of the Mac interface (see Figure 1.10). Since the Apple menu is always available to you, you can use it to access items that you need to use in various situations, such as those times when your desktop is hidden from you. You can easily configure the Apple menu to suit your needs. You can use it to quickly access files, folders, custom scripts, drives, and just about anything else you can think of.

FIGURE 1.10

The Apple menu is one of the most useful interface elements because it is always available to you.

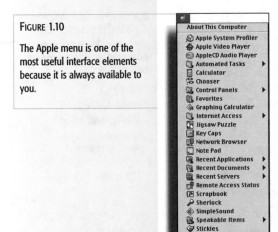

By default, the Apple menu is configured with a number of useful items. These include the following:

- **About This Computer**. This mini-application enables you to set and monitor the RAM used by the various parts of your system.

- **Apple System Profiler**. This application enables you to develop a complete profile of your system. This profile is extremely important when you are doing any kind of maintenance on your Mac, including correcting problems or upgrading your hardware.

- **Apple Video Player**. The Apple video player enables you to watch TV or a VCR if your Mac has a TV tuner card or is an AV capable machine.

- **Apple CDAudio Player**. With this application, you can listen to your favorite music CDs while you work.

- **Automated Tasks**. The Automated Tasks folder contains a number of AppleScripts that you can run to do different tasks.

- **Chooser**. You use the Chooser to select a printer, as well as to connect to a server on your network.

- **Control Panels**. The Control Panels item in the Apple menu is an alias to the real Control Panels folder that is within your System Folder. Since the Apple menu can have hierarchical menus, you can access any control panel from the Apple menu (see Figure 1.11).

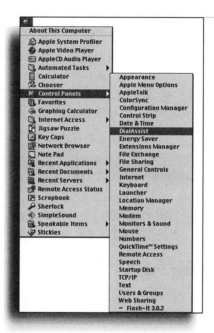

FIGURE 1.11
Using the Control Panels item on the Apple menu, you can get quickly to any active control panel.

- **Favorites**. Favorites are a new feature for Mac OS 8.5. You can add items to your Favorites folder and access them from this selection on the Apple menu, as well as other places.

- **Internet Access**. This item is new for System 8.5. It contains aliases to the various Internet-related functions, such as launching your Web browser, reading email, and so on.

- **Network Browser**. Another new feature of Mac OS 8.5, the Network Browser makes it easier to connect to other Macs on a network.

- **Sherlock**. This item launches Sherlock (called Find on the Finder's File Menu) application.

■ **Remote Access Status**. Under Mac OS 8.5, you can use Remote Access to connect to the Internet, as well as other networks and computers. Remote Access Status is an element of the Remote Access software that you can use to quickly connect and disconnect from the Net.

The Apple menu is so important that Chapter 6, "Working with the Apple Menu," is devoted to it.

Using the Control Strip

The Control Strip was originally intended as an aid for PowerBook users who were pressed for desktop space, and it provides easy access to certain controls (see Figure 1.12). As with contextual menus, you can modify which controls you have access to.

FIGURE 1.12

The Control Strip provides easy access to the controls that you need most frequently.

You will learn how to use and customize the Control Strip in Chapter 7, "Working with the Control Strip."

Using Fonts

Fonts have always been one of the Mac's strengths, and that continues with Mac OS 8.5. Under Mac OS 8.5, there is not a whole lot new about Mac fonts; however, it is still as easy to use and manage Mac fonts as it has been for a long time.

In Chapter 8, "Working with Fonts," you will learn about using Mac fonts.

Working with Color and Graphics

The Mac's graphic capabilities make it the computer of choice for artists, graphics specialists, and publishers. The Mac includes many innovative features that continue to lead the way in the graphics and color management areas. One of the most significant Mac technologies is ColorSync. ColorSync is Apple's color management technology. Its purpose is to enable you to achieve consistent color across all of your key devices, including monitors, printers, and scanners. Color matching, which is the art of trying to get consistent colors, has always been the bane of the printer's existence. With ColorSync, the Mac increases its lead as the best tool for the graphics professional.

In addition to ColorSync, the Color Picker has been further refined and integrated into all aspects of the OS (see Figure 1.13).

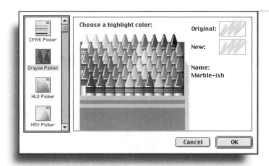

FIGURE 1.13
You use the Color Picker in many areas of the OS, as well as from within applications.

You will get the ins and outs of color and graphics in Chapter 9, "Working with Color and Graphics."

Using Multimedia

The Mac is the premiere multimedia platform. From the advanced capabilities of QuickTime to the Apple Video Player, the Mac can work with, and create, all kinds of media, including video, animation, sound, and any combination thereof. The heart of the Mac's multimedia mind is QuickTime. QuickTime 3 is included with Mac OS 8.5, and it further improves multimedia performance and adds features such as video streaming from the Internet.

QuickTime VR enables you to explore virtual worlds from your desktop. Using QuickTime Pro you can create and edit your own QuickTime movies (see Figure 1.14).

You will learn the ins and outs of multimedia on the Mac, including how to create and edit your own QuickTime movies, in Chapter 10, "Working with Multimedia."

FIGURE **1.14**

You can use QuickTime Pro to create and view your own movies.

Working with Applications

Working with applications is still as easy under Mac OS 8.5 as it always has been. The best new feature for Mac OS 8.5 is the addition of a Navigation Services dialog as the eventual replacement for the outdated Save and Open dialogs (see Figure 1.15). Unlike the Open and Save dialogs, the new Navigation Services dialog can be moved and resized. You can also use it to access recent items as well as your favorites.

You'll read about working with your applications in Chapter 11, "Working with Mac Applications."

FIGURE **1.15**

The new Navigation Services dialog is much more powerful and flexible than the old Open and Save dialog.

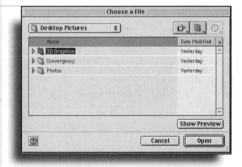

Finding Help

Finding good help on the Mac is a snap. In addition to Balloon Help and AppleGuide, the Mac's Help Center is a hyperlink-based system that you can use to quickly locate the help you need. This system is also integrated with AppleGuide, and can show you how to accomplish specific tasks as well as explain the underlying technologies for those tasks.

Chapter 12, "Working with the Mac's Help Systems," provides help on the Mac's help.

Making Your Mac Your Own

One reason that Mac lovers love their Macs is that it has always been easy and fun to make a Mac reflect *your* personality and the way *you* want to work, rather than forcing you to work the way the machine is set up to work. From themes that enable you to change your Mac's moods as quickly as yours do, to a more powerful AppleScript, Mac OS 8.5 gives you even more control over all aspects of your Mac.

Part II, "Customizing Your Mac," is all about making your Mac what *you* want it to be.

Giving Your Mac a Face Lift

With Mac OS 8.5, you can control lots of things about the way your Mac looks and sounds. You can change the way menus look, which fonts are used, the desktop pattern or picture, the sounds you hear, and even the controls you have in windows. The Appearance control panel enables you to do all this and more (see Figure 1.16).

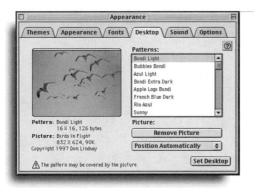

FIGURE 1.16

The Appearance control panel enables you to change almost everything about the way your Mac looks and sounds.

Themes, another new Mac OS 8.5 feature, are collections of preferences (such as menu settings, a desktop picture, and sound effects) that you can create and save (see Figure 1.17). When you switch themes, all of the settings you have defined change in one simple step. You can create complex theme sets and switch among them on a whim.

FIGURE 1.17

Themes make it easy to give your Mac a complete make-over.

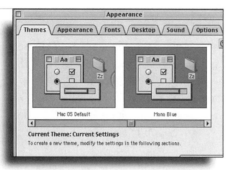

In Chapter 13, "Changing the Way Your Mac Looks and Sounds," you will learn how to use the Appearance control panel and other interface controls to customize your Mac.

Not Losing Your Memory

Understanding and managing your memory is one of the most important things you can do to make your Mac work well. Mac OS 8.5 includes tools that you can use to ensure that your Mac uses its memory wisely, thus maximizing performance and minimizing troubles. There have been some minor changes in the way the Mac OS works with memory under Mac OS 8.5. For example, the RAM allocation fields now appear in their own pane of the Get Info windows as opposed to being just one element on them (see Figure 1.18).

Chapter 14, "Managing Your Mac's Memory," will teach you what you need to know to manage your Mac's memory resources.

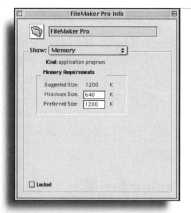

FIGURE 1.18
RAM allocations get their own window pane under Mac OS 8.5.

Knowing Your System Folder

The System Folder contains the software that controls how your Mac looks and acts. The System Folder is as close to being the heart and soul of your Mac as anything could be. You might rightfully say that the System Folder is your Mac. The System Folder can be a scary place when you first look in it, and there have been some new additions to the System Folder for Mac OS 8.5 (see Figure 1.19). For example, the Favorites folder is new, as is the Internet Search Sites folder.

After you read Chapter 15, "Managing Your System Folder," you will be the master of your Mac domain.

FIGURE 1.19
The System Folder can be intimidating, but after you read this book, you won't be afraid anymore.

Using the Keyboard

After all these years, the keyboard is still one of the most important controls you have for your Mac. Once you learn to use it effectively, the keyboard is the fastest way to command your Mac to do your bidding. Mac OS 8.5 comes with lots of predefined keyboard shortcuts, but real power comes when you learn to create and use your own. Chapter 16, "Using Keyboard Shortcuts," will show you how.

Making the Mac Your Slave

Heard a good joke lately?

Well, after you hear your Mac tell you some, you still won't have heard a good joke, but you will enjoy the telling nonetheless.

For me, there isn't much that is more exciting than making my Mac do my work for me (OK, so I don't get out much).

Your Mac can perform complex tasks for you with a click, keyboard shortcut, or even a spoken word. There are several technologies that are part of Mac OS 8.5 that enable you to automate your Mac and do everything from automatically opening a file to performing a complex series of commands with a simple word from you.

With Mac OS 8.5, Apple has revived voice recognition so that you can speak commands to your Mac. AppleScript, the Mac's built-in scripting language, provides lots of predefined scripts that you can use. AppleScript has been improved for Mac OS 8.5, including becoming native for faster scripting and faster running scripts. You can also add a utility, such as the superb QuickKeys to enable you to record your actions and make your own scripts (which you can speak to activate). Automating your Mac is both fun and a work saver—that is a combination that is hard to beat.

You will learn to work smarter, not harder, in Chapter 17, "Making Your Mac Do Your Work For You."

Working with Mac Hardware

You probably will want to do more than your Mac out of the box can. You will want to use hardware to provide more control over your Mac, output your work, and to connect with other users.

In Part III, "Using Mac Hardware," you will learn about some useful hardware that should be part of your Mac.

Inputting Information to Your Mac

There are two basic inputs you need to make your Mac work. The first is control. There are lots of ways to control your Mac. The most common control devices are keyboards and mice, but those are only the beginning. You can also use trackballs, track pads, and other devices to control your Mac.

You also want to input data to your Mac. This data can take many forms, such as the text you type, images you scan, and digital photos that you capture. Again, hardware enables you to get this data into your Mac.

In Chapter 18, "Understanding and Using Input Devices," you will learn about your input hardware options.

Outputting Information from Your Mac

Whatever you do with your Mac, you probably do it for someone else, be it a boss, coworker, customer, or whomever. There are many ways to provide the fruits of your labor to other people. The most obvious is via a hard copy that you print on a printer. But that is only the beginning. You can also output your work to a monitor or maybe to an electronic document, such as a Portable Document File so that people on the Net can read it.

You will learn about your output options in Chapter 19, "Understanding and Using Output Devices."

Connecting to the World

No Mac is an island, and you will want to connect with someone, somewhere, somehow. Whether you use a local network or use a modem, you will learn about some of your connection choices in Chapter 20, "Understanding and Using Networking Devices."

Working with Others

By yourself, you are limited. Combining your work with the works of others expands what everyone involved can do. The sum of the parts can be greater than the whole.

In Part IV, "Using Your Mac to Work with Others," you will learn how to share your work with others, and how to use work that others share with you.

Preaching to the Choir

Even though we Mac users are a small part of the computing community, there are still millions of us who use our Macs in our daily work. You will work with other Mac users in a variety of ways, including sharing files, networking, and so on. While most of the information you share among other Macs users requires little thought on your part, there are situations in which you have to dig a little bit to make things work.

A very powerful feature of the Mac has always been its ability to network with other Macs with no additional software and little additional hardware. You can connect two or more Macs together literally in a few minutes to create a fully functional network across which you can share files, folders, and other resources. Under Mac OS 8.5, File Sharing is even easier. Rather than having to use the Sharing command, now you can access the Sharing controls for an item by choosing the Sharing pane of its Info window (see Figure 1.20).

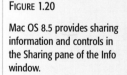

FIGURE 1.20

Mac OS 8.5 provides sharing information and controls in the Sharing pane of the Info window.

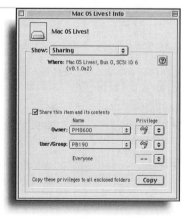

Another very useful addition to the Mac OS, is Mac OS 8.5's Network Browser utility, which makes it very easy to connect to other Macs on your network (see Figure 1.21).

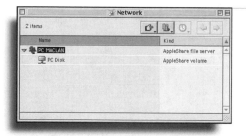

FIGURE 1.21
The Network Browser is a big improvement over the Chooser for connecting to other computers on your network.

You will learn about networking with other Macs and how to work with Mac files that you receive from others in Chapter 21, "Working with Other Macs."

Sleeping with the Enemy

Whether we like it or not, Windows PCs rule the computing world. If you are going to reach out to and work with a large group of people, you need to understand how to live with Windows computers. Fortunately, Mac OS 8.5 provides all the tools you need to peacefully co-exist with your Windows-using friends, coworkers, and anyone else with whom you need to interact.

One of the primary tools that you use to work with Windows files is Mac OS 8.5's new File Exchange control panel (see Figure 1.22).

FIGURE 1.22
The File Exchange control panel provides the tools you need to work with Windows files.

You will learn the fundamentals of living in a Windows-dominated world in Chapter 22, "Working with Windows PCs."

Surfing the Net

The Internet is all the rage. You can't read, see, or hear much of anything without experiencing some reference to the Net. Is all the hype valid? One word: yes. If you aren't using the Internet, you are missing out on the world (literally).

In Part V, "Using Your Mac to Surf the Internet," you will see why your Mac is the ultimate Net surfboard.

Getting Connected

The process of connecting to the Net is not exciting, but what you do once you are connected, what you do with it—email, the World Wide Web, or any of the other services—is very exciting. Getting connected to the Internet is a lot harder than using it, but with the Mac's excellent Internet tools, you can be online in no time. For example, Mac OS 8.5 comes with the Internet Setup Assistant that will walk you through each step you need to do to go online (see Figure 1.23).

FIGURE 1.23

The Internet Setup Assistant will hold your hand and lead you to the promised Net land.

Even if you have never been on the Internet before, you will be able to get on with the information in Chapter 23, "Connecting Your Mac to the Net."

Keeping in Touch with Email

Electronic mail (email) is fantastic. There are few means of having relationships with people that are more convenient, powerful, and inexpensive as email. You can form and maintain relationships with people in the next block or around the world with the same amount of effort and expense.

New to Mac OS 8.5 is Microsoft's excellent Outlook Express email application (see Figure 1.24).

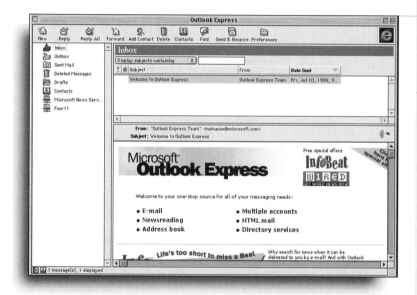

FIGURE 1.24
Outlook Express is a powerful email application with many advanced features.

Outlook Express provides lots of powerful features, and it has an excellent interface. A partial list of some of what you can do with Outlook Express is the following:

- Create and send email
- Read email
- Spell check email you create
- Manage multiple email accounts
- Organize and filter your email
- Send and receive files with your email

You will learn email basics in Chapter 24, "Using Email: The Basics." You will learn to use some of Outlook Express' more sophisticated features in Chapter 25, "Using Email: Advanced Techniques."

Walking the World Wide Web

Netscape

You may have heard of Netscape, or more correctly Netscape Navigator. This is a competitor to Internet Explorer. It used to be the default Web browser that came with the Mac OS, but it has been replaced by Internet Explorer for Mac OS 8.5. However, Netscape Navigator is still included on the Mac OS 8.5 CD-ROM so that you can install it on your Mac and try it for yourself.

When most people think of the Internet, they think of the World Wide Web. And with good reason I might add. The World Wide Web is, well, big. There are thousands and thousands of Web sites that are maintained by every conceivable organization including governments, large businesses, and one-person shops. There also are lots of Web sites created and maintained by individuals to promote a cause or to share an interest. Whatever you can think of, there is a Web site devoted to it.

Once you begin to use the Web, you may wonder how you ever survived without it. Need some information on any topic? Do a quick Web search, and there it is. Need to purchase the newest movie on DVD? Within five minutes, you can have it on its way to you—that even includes time for comparison shopping. Want to visit the Louvre? Fire up your Mac and with light-speed, there you are.

The Mac is an excellent platform from which you can view the Web or even create your own Web pages. For browsing, Microsoft's Internet Explorer is included with Mac OS 8.5. Internet Explorer is a powerful Web browser that offers lots of useful features (see Figure 1.25).

The basics of Web exploration are covered in Chapter 26, "Browsing the Web: The Basics," while you'll learn some tricks of the Web game in Chapter 27, "Browsing the Web: Advanced Techniques."

Reading News That is Fit to Print—and Some That's Not

On the Internet, you can participate in newsgroups, which are electronic discussions on every conceivable topic. You may find that newsgroups are the best thing since sliced bread if you like to hear what other folks all over the world think on any topic you can imagine (and many that you can't imagine).

FIGURE 1.25
Using Internet Explorer, you can crawl the Web like a spider.

You can also use Outlook Express to subscribe to and read newsgroups (see Figure 1.26).

FIGURE 1.26
Outlook Express is also an excellent newsgroup reader.

You'll satisfy your need to read in Chapter 28, "Reading Newsgroups."

Maintaining Your Mac

Like all complex systems, your Mac requires maintenance, some to prevent problems and some to fix problems. Understanding, and more importantly, doing maintenance on your Mac can keep you in business.

In Part VI, "Maintaining, Fixing, and Upgrading Your Mac," you will learn how to prevent lots of problems, and how to solve those that do occur.

Backing Up Isn't Hard to Do

If there is one thing that all computer types say that you should do, but very few actually do, it is backing up. Backing up is vital to protect the enormous amount of time and effort that your work on the Mac entails. With a good back-up system in place, you can quickly and easily recover from almost any situation that arises. Without a good back-up plan in place, you may *never* be able to recover from some problems.

Chapter 29, "Backing Up," is devoted to showing you how to develop and implement your own back-up strategy.

Preventing Infection

Viruses get a lot of press. And they seem to come in waves, with each crest coming about every three months or so. The good news for Mac users is that there are far fewer viruses on the Mac than there are on the PC, and those that do live on the Mac tend to be less destructive. The bad news is that there are Mac viruses, and you need to make sure that your Mac is immune to their attacks.

You can practice safe computing with the tools that came with Mac OS 8.5, but to be as safe as possible, you should buy and use an anti-virus program. In Chapter 30, "Fighting Viruses," you will learn about viruses, and you will learn how to protect your Mac from them.

Preventing Trouble

Who needs more problems in their life? Especially with something as important to our productivity as the Mac. Many Mac problems can be prevented with some simple practices, such as preparing a Mac tool kit and keeping your Mac tuned up.

Mac OS 8.5 comes with several tools that you can use to prevent and solve problems, such as the Apple System Profiler that has been greatly improved for Mac OS 8.5 (see Figure 1.27) and Disk First Aid (see Figure 1.28).

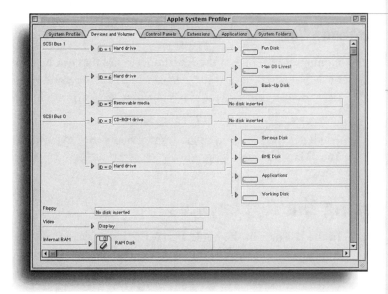

FIGURE 1.27

Apple System Profiler is an important part in your Mac tool kit.

You will learn how to prevent Mac problems in Chapter 31, "Preventing Mac Problems."

Fixing Your Mac

Occasionally, no matter how rigorously you try to defend against them, you will run into a problem that prevents you from doing what you want to do. If you are properly prepared, even the most scary looking problem can be solved quickly, or at least worked around until you can implement a permanent fix.

FIGURE 1.28

You can solve some Mac problems with the tools that came with Mac OS 8.5, such as Disk First Aid.

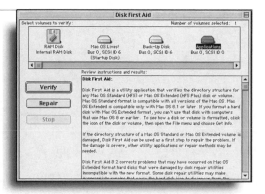

Chapter 32, "Fixing Mac Problems," tells you how to solve problems that you may encounter.

Growing Your Mac

Computers are one of the few things in life that can be continuously improved in terms of performance, stability, and capabilities. You can improve the way your Mac works through both hardware and software upgrades.

You'll get the scoop on upgrades in Chapter 33, "Maintaining Your Mac Through Upgrades."

Using the Appendices

In the last part of the book, Part VII, "Using Mac OS 8.5 Appendices," you'll find an assortment of information that is important, but didn't quite fit elsewhere in the book.

Working with the Mac OS Installer

Whether you are doing a complete Mac OS 8.5 installation, or are simply installing a component or two, learning how to effectively use the Mac OS 8.5 installation CD is a good idea. In Appendix A, "Installing and Maintaining the Mac OS," you'll learn how to do just that.

Computing on the Move

Mac PowerBooks enable you to take your Mac with you. Mac
OS 8.5 provides features and capabilities that are specifically
designed to make your PowerBook capable of everything you
need for mobile computing. In Appendix B, "Working with
PowerBooks," you will learn about the parts of the OS that are
designed to maximize what you do with your PowerBook.

Talking the Talk

Although Macs are as people-friendly as computers get, there is
still a lot of confusing and complicated jargon that people in the
know toss around. Appendix C, "Speaking Essential Mac Lingo,"
will equip you to talk tech with the best of them.

Understanding this Book

Whew. Mac OS 8.5 is a big topic. In fact, it is so big that there
are lots of good books around to help you make the most of it.
Each of these books has its own slant. If you find the one with
the slant that is what you are looking for, you will find it to be
one of the best investments that you can make. If you don't, you
may find it to be a waste of time and money. Here's the slant of
this book.

Using Mac OS 8.5 is about just that. Using the Mac. You won't
find a lot of detailed technical explanations, specifications, or
explanations on the technology or history of the Mac. This book
focuses on practical, and at the same time, fun and productive
ways to use your Mac. You will find discussions that are detailed
enough to equip you to do what you need to do. Typically, you
will find explanations of the underlying technology or software
for a given topic and then you will be able to work through step-
by-steps that enable you to accomplish a specific task. These
step-by-steps are models that you can then apply to your own
projects and requirements. You will often find several different
ways to do specific tasks so that you can use the one that best
suits you.

You will also find lots of ways to make different areas of the OS work with each other, and you will learn tricks and shortcuts that will enable you to work faster and smarter. Plus, you will learn about software and hardware add-ons that are essential to your Mac life.

Throughout the book, you will see sidebars that provide tips, additional information (such as Web site addresses), and even a bit of Mac trivia now and again.

Finally, the chapters have been designed to be self-contained. You can read chapters in any order you like. If a chapter relies on information contained in another chapter, you will see a cross-reference that tells you exactly where to look to find the related information.

So, dive in and start using your Mac right now.

Working with Folders and Windows

Understanding and using the common features of all windows on the Mac

Configuring and using the three types of views for folder windows

Using pop-up windows and spring-loaded folders

Using other window features

Understanding Folder and Windows

If you have worked with a Mac at all, you know that windows are one of the most common elements with which you work. Windows are the, well, window you look through to see whatever you happen to be working with at the time, whether it is a document, folder, drive, control panel, or whatever. Understanding and using windows and folders effectively is important as you use and master the Macintosh.

There are many types of windows and folders with which you can work on the Mac. These include the following:

- Document windows. Whenever you open a document, you will see your data (text, graphic, movie, and so on) in a window. Document windows share many characteristics with the other kinds of windows that you will use. You'll learn about these in the following section. Document windows usually have some special features that are unique to the applications that created them (see Figure 2.1).

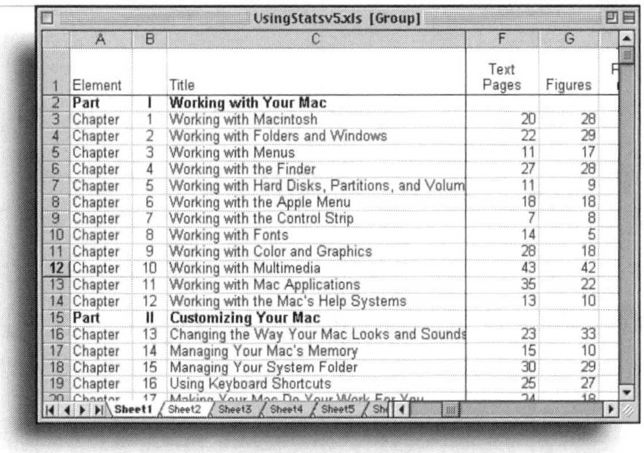

UsingStatsv5.xls [Group]

	Element		Title	Text Pages	Figures
2	**Part**	**I**	**Working with Your Mac**		
3	Chapter	1	Working with Macintosh	20	28
4	Chapter	2	Working with Folders and Windows	22	29
5	Chapter	3	Working with Menus	11	17
6	Chapter	4	Working with the Finder	27	28
7	Chapter	5	Working with Hard Disks, Partitions, and Volum	11	9
8	Chapter	6	Working with the Apple Menu	18	18
9	Chapter	7	Working with the Control Strip	7	8
10	Chapter	8	Working with Fonts	14	5
11	Chapter	9	Working with Color and Graphics	28	18
12	Chapter	10	Working with Multimedia	43	42
13	Chapter	11	Working with Mac Applications	35	22
14	Chapter	12	Working with the Mac's Help Systems	13	10
15	**Part**	**II**	**Customizing Your Mac**		
16	Chapter	13	Changing the Way Your Mac Looks and Sounds	23	33
17	Chapter	14	Managing Your Mac's Memory	15	10
18	Chapter	15	Managing Your System Folder	30	29
19	Chapter	16	Using Keyboard Shortcuts	25	27

FIGURE 2.1

Document windows are what you use to work with data in documents; they sometimes have features particular to the application that created them as this Excel window does.

- Folder windows. When you are viewing files and folder on the desktop, you are using folder windows (see Figure 2.2). (For this discussion, I am lumping volumes, disks, and other containers in to the folder category, since those items are just special types of folders.) Within the folder window category, there are a couple of special types, those being pop-up windows and spring-loaded folders.

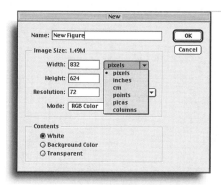

FIGURE 2.2

Folders windows enable you to manipulate files and folders within them.

- Dialog boxes. These special purpose windows are used all over the Mac. They can contain information, buttons, pop-up menus, check boxes, radio buttons, text entry areas, and so on (see Figure 2.3). A dialog box (commonly referred to as a dialog) is used when you need to provide some input or settings for the application or control panel with which you are working. Dialog box windows usually only have a small subset of the features of document and folder windows.

FIGURE 2.3

Dialog boxes are one of the most important interface elements that you use in applications as well as in the Finder (this one is from Adobe Photoshop version 4.0).

Alert windows and dialog boxes

Alert windows and dialog boxes can be somewhat similar in that you can sometimes do something (such as activate a command) from an alert window as you can from a dialog box. You can identify an alert window because it will have an icon that gives you some idea of what the alert window is about. For example, in Figure 2.4, you see an icon that is a triangle with an exclamation point inside it. This is the caution icon, and it means that you need to be careful about what you do next. You will also see a stop sign, which means that you can't do what you are trying to do. There are a few others as well, and they are usually easy to interpret.

- Alert windows. When your Mac wants to tell you something, such as an error has occurred, it displays an alert window (see Figure 2.4). These are often accompanied by a sound or other feedback (such as a flashing menu bar). Alert dialogs usually have an OK button that causes the dialog to go away, although some have a Restart button, which you need to use to restart your Mac.

FIGURE 2.4

Alert windows let you know that something important has happened or that something important is about to happen; in this case, that the items in the Trash are about to be permanently deleted.

The Trash contains 17 items, which use 1.6 MB of disk space. Are you sure you want to remove these items permanently?

Cancel   OK

- Application, control panel, and other special windows. There are certain types of applications that you don't use to create documents, but that have windows associated with them; the Graphing Calculator is an example of this (see Figure 2.5). The Chooser is another special window, as are all control panels (see Figure 2.6). Mostly, these windows have similar features as folder windows and dialog boxes.

In this chapter, you'll learn about the features common to most Mac windows. After that overview of windows, you will learn the details of working with folder windows.

FIGURE 2.5

This Graphing Calculator uses a special window type; while the Graphing Calculator is an application, it does not have documents associated with it.

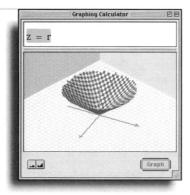

FIGURE 2.6

Control panels, such as the Speech control panel, also have their own windows that work similarly to dialog boxes.

Working with Mac Windows

Many Mac windows share common characteristics. For example, document windows (created by applications) and folder windows (created by the Finder) have many similar features.

Figure 2.7 shows a typical document window while Figure 2.8 shows an example of a folder window.

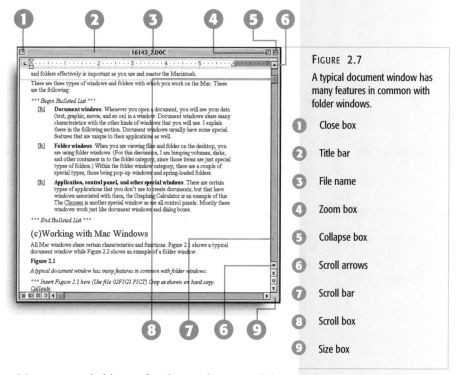

FIGURE 2.7

A typical document window has many features in common with folder windows.

1 Close box

2 Title bar

3 File name

4 Zoom box

5 Collapse box

6 Scroll arrows

7 Scroll bar

8 Scroll box

9 Size box

Since you use a Mac, you probably are familiar with many of the features of Mac windows. Not all windows have all features; the features a window provides depends on the kind of window it is. The following list provides a quick synopsis of some window features that you will use:

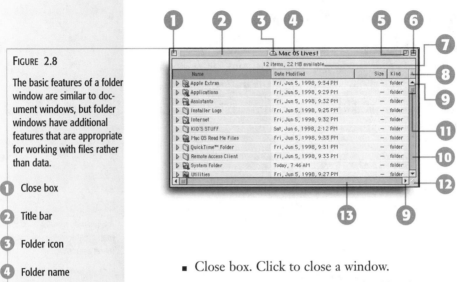

FIGURE 2.8

The basic features of a folder window are similar to document windows, but folder windows have additional features that are appropriate for working with files rather than data.

1 Close box

2 Title bar

3 Folder icon

4 Folder name

5 Zoom box

6 Collapse box

7 Disk information

8 Sort order button (List view)

9 Scroll arrows

10 Scroll bar

11 Scroll box

12 Size box

13 Scroll bar

- Close box. Click to close a window.

- Title bar. Shows the name of the file (document window), folder (folder window), or control panel (control panel window). The active window is indicated by lines in the title bar. The title bars of inactive windows do not have lines.

- Folder icon (folder windows). In folder windows, the folder's icon appears in the title bar, next to the window name. You can use this icon just as you can any other icon (by dragging it to another disk to copy the folder there, for example).

- Zoom box. Resizes the window. Clicking it makes the window its maximum size (document) or shows all of the items in the folder (folder window). Clicking it again restores the window to the size it was when the box was last clicked.

- Collapse box. Clicking this box causes a window to collapse down to its title bar (see Figure 2.9).

- Disk information (folder windows). At the top of each folder window, you will see the number of items that are contained in that window and the amount of free space on the disk that contains that folder.

FIGURE 2.9
This window has been collapsed with the Collapse box.

- List information (folder windows). When you view a folder window in List view, you will see column heads and the sort order button at the top of the window, just under the disk information.

- Scroll arrows. Many Mac windows have vertical and horizontal scroll arrows. Click this to scroll "a little bit" (don't you love some of Apple's terminology?) in the direction of the arrow.

- Scroll bar. The scroll bar represents the entire amount of information contained in a window. Click in the scroll bar above the scroll box and the window will scroll one window up; click below the scroll box and the window scrolls one window down.

- Scroll box. I think a better name for this is the elevator, but that is not what Apple calls it. Anyway, this box represents where you are in the window. Drag it to move up and down in the window.

- Size box. Drag this box to resize a window in either direction.

Using the Keyboard with Windows

When working with windows, don't forget about the keyboard. For example, you can use the following keys to scroll a window:

- Home. This key usually takes you to the top of a document and places your cursor in the first "position" in the window. In a folder window, it takes you to the top of the window.

- End. This key does the opposite of the home key.

- Page up. The page up key scrolls the window up by one page in a document or scrolls by one window's worth of content in folder windows.

- Page down. This does the opposite of page up.

You can do different things with different windows

In the beginning of this chapter, you learned about different windows based on the functions for which you will use them. There are technical differences between the various window types; the terms that are used to describe these differences are a bit scary to look at, but you don't really need to use them much. In case you want to learn about some of the technical differences between the various window types, read the next five side notes. If the technical terms don't interest you, just skip the next five side notes.

Modal windows

Some windows require that you do something with them before you can do anything else, such as switching to a different application. These are called modal windows. Most alert windows are modal, which means that you have to clear them (usually by clicking OK) before you can do anything else.

There are also nonmodal windows. You do things outside a nonmodal window while it is open, such as switching to another open window. Many dialog boxes are nonmodal, as are most document and Finder windows.

Setting Finder Window Preferences

There are several preferences that you can set to determine how Finder windows work. You set most of these by using the Options tab in the Appearance control panel (see Figure 2.10).

FIGURE 2.10

The Options tab of the Appearance control panel enables you to set Finder window preferences.

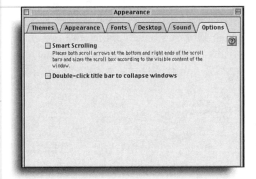

Movable windows

Movable windows are those that you can move around the screen while they are open. Most document and Finder windows are movable; you can move them around while they are open.

As you can probably guess, there are also nonmovable windows. They stay where they are until you close them. Many alert windows are nonmovable. They stay smack dab in the middle of your screen until you close them.

Resizable windows

Resizable windows can be made larger or smaller, both in the vertical dimension and the horizontal. All document and Finder windows are resizable.

Some windows cannot be resized. Most dialog boxes cannot be resized.

These options are the following:

- Smart Scrolling. Traditional Mac windows have a single scroll arrow at each end of the scroll bar. However, you can make it so that windows have both scroll arrows at the bottom or right end of the scroll bar (see Figure 2.11). This makes it easy to scroll in either direction from the same end of the scroll bar. This is a very useful option.

- The traditional scroll box is the same size, no matter how large a window you are viewing. When you use the Smart Scrolling option, the scroll box is proportional to content of a window that is visible. The "smart" scroll box changes size, depending on how much of the window you view (see Figure 2.12). The more of the window's content that you can see at the window's current size, the larger the scroll bars are. The less of a window's content that you can see, the smaller the scroll bars are.

FIGURE 2.11

This window has both scroll arrows at the bottom of the vertical scroll bar and at the right end of the horizontal scroll bar.

FIGURE 2.12

With proportionally sized scroll boxes, the size of the scroll box reflects the proportion of the window's content that you are viewing with the window at its current size (compare the scroll bars in Figure 2.11).

1 Proportional scroll bar

- Collapsing windows. In addition to using the Collapse box to collapse a window to its title bar, you can choose the "Double-click title bar to collapse windows" check box. With this option checked, you can collapse a window by double-clicking its title bar (this does the same thing as the Collapse box). (This is how the original WindowShade control panel worked.)

Floating windows

Floating windows are always in the forefront of the screen no matter what you do. The Control Strip and Application menu are floating windows; when they are open, you can always get to them because they remain "on top" of all other windows. They can't be covered over by other windows.

There is an additional window preference that you can set by using the Sound tab of the Appearance control panel (see Figure 2.13). As you can probably guess, this preference attaches various sounds to different parts of the system. If you choose a Sound track from the pop-up menu and check the Windows check box, you will hear different sound effects when you move, resize, collapse, close, open, or scroll a window.

Figure 2.13

Making noisy windows with the Appearance control panel.

Mix and match

Windows have combinations of these characteristics. For example, many alert windows are modal, nonmovable, and nonresizable. This means that you can't do anything (not even move the window out of the way or make it smaller) except close the window by clicking a button. Document windows are non-modal, movable, and resizable, which means that you can work outside of them (such as moving into another document or application), move them out of the way, and make them larger or smaller.

You don't really need to think about these terms; mostly, you will learn what you can do with certain types of windows, and it will become second nature for you.

Setting window preferences

1. Open the Appearance control panel.
2. Click the Sound tab.
3. Choose a sound track from the Sound track pop-up menu (if you choose None, you won't hear any sound effects).
4. Click Windows to hear window sound effects.
5. Click the Options tab.
6. Check the "Smart Scrolling" check box to have two scroll arrows at the bottom end of the vertical scroll bar and two arrows at the right end of the horizontal scroll bar and to make the scroll boxes proportional.
7. Click the Double-click title bar to minimize windows if you want to be able to collapse windows by double-clicking their title bars.
8. Close the control panel.

Working with Folder Windows

While you are working on the desktop, you will be using folder windows much of the time. (I include volumes and disks as "folders" in this context.) Folder windows have unique capabilities when compared to other kinds of windows (such as document windows). These features fall into the following categories:

- Views. Folder windows enable you to customize the way that the information in those windows appears, as well as what particular data about each file that you see.

- Window management. Folders have navigation and management features that you can use to keep control of your windows, as well as to move up and down through your system.

- Icons. Folders are represented on the desktop by icons. These icons indicate what type of folder is represented by the icon.

SEE ALSO

➤ *To see how to modify a folder's icon, see page 291*

Working with Folder Views

There are three types of views that are available for all folder windows. They are the following:

- Icons. As you no doubt know, the Icon view represents items with icons. You double-click an icon to open it. You can also modify the icons that represent any folder.

- Buttons. Buttons are similar to icons except that to open an item, you single click its button rather than double-clicking its icon.

- Lists. The List view presents the contents of an item in tabular format. This view provides the most information, but may not be quite as nice to look at as icons or buttons. However, in addition to providing the most information about your files, it is also the most efficient view. As you become a more experienced Mac user, you will probably work in the List view more than the others.

Document windows versus folder windows

Although document windows and folder windows share many features, there are some important differences. For example, you can change the view in folder windows, and you can make folder windows into pop-up windows; neither of which you can do with document windows.

Closing with a close box

Some windows (for example, alert windows) don't have a Close box. You close these windows with other things, such as an OK button.

WindowShade

The ability to collapse a window to its title bar was first provided by a utility called WindowShade. It proved to be so popular that Apple purchased the rights to it and incorporated it into the Mac OS. With Mac OS 8, the Collapse box became part of all windows, and the separate WindowShade control panel disappeared forever.

Scroll keys and applications

The action of the scroll keys (home, end, and so on) are controlled by the application that you use them in. Some applications don't provide a function for them. If you press one and nothing happens, that is probably why.

Finder windows?

Finder windows include folder and volume windows.

Document window preferences

Many applications enable you to set the preferences that determine how document windows for that application work and appear. You usually set these preferences with a command called Preferences, Customize, or Options. Each application can provide different preferences that may be different than the preferences you set for Finder windows.

When you have a window open, you can switch among these view types for that window by choosing the view type that you want from the Finder's View menu. Under Mac OS 8.5, you can set global standard view options for each type of view; these standards are then used on every folder except individual folders that you set to have a different set of view options. This feature lets you set default view types for most items; then you can customize the view options for particular folders as you need to.

Using Icon Views

The Icon view is the simplest in many ways, in addition to being the best looking of the three view types. And who doesn't like to see all those pretty icons (see Figure 2.14)?

FIGURE 2.14

The Icon view is not the most useful view, but it is the best looking one.

Stereo sound effects

By the way, the Mac's sound effects are in stereo. Some effects will sound like they are coming from the left, the right, or from both directions.

There isn't a whole lot that you do with icon views; your two options are the following:

- Alignment. You can set the way that your Mac aligns the icons in a window. None means that the Finder will leave icons wherever you place them. Always snap to grid tells the Finder to line up icons according to the invisible grid on the desktop. Keep arranged tells the Finder to arrange icons by the parameters you select; you have a number of options from which to choose (for example, if you choose by Kind, the Finder will group all applications together, all documents together, and so on).

The grid

Your Mac uses an invisible grid on your desktop to locate the items on it. This grid is made up of invisible vertical and horizontal lines that the Finder uses to keep everything lined up nice and neat.

- Icon size. You can choose the size of the icons that are used in a window. Your choices are large, medium, or small.

You can choose among these options by using the Views Preferences window (see Figure 2.15). You will learn more about doing this in a later section.

Using Button Views

The Button view is similar to the icon view except that you single-click a button to open it, rather than double-clicking it as you do with icons. You have similar options for button views as you do for Icon view (see Figure 2.16).

Using List Views

The List view gives you the most information about a window's content, and it also has the most functionality of any of the views. For example, you can choose the information that is provided in the List view, and you can quickly see the contents of any folder. Figure 2.17 shows a typical List view and some of its features.

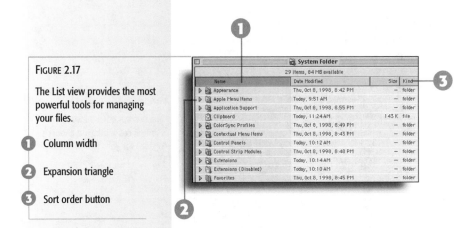

FIGURE 2.17

The List view provides the most powerful tools for managing your files.

1 Column width

2 Expansion triangle

3 Sort order button

Any one out there ever use Launcher?

The Mac OS has had a feature called the Launcher for some time. The Launcher enables you to create a palette of buttons on which you can single-click to open an application or file. (The Launcher has a control panel and a folder called Launcher Items in the System Folder. You show the Launcher with the control panel and place any items that you want on it in the Launcher Items folder.) I don't know if anyone actually has ever used this feature, and while it is still part of Mac OS 8.5, you can do the same thing by simply changing any folder to the Button view. Although the Launcher never really was very useful, it is now even less necessary. My guess is that it will disappear in a future release of the Mac OS.

Views and contextual menu

You can also manipulate the views you use in any window with contextual menus. See Chapter 3, "Working with Menus," for information on using contextual menus.

In any List View, your Mac can display the following columns:

- **File or folder name.** This one is pretty easy because it is simply the name of the file or folder. This is always displayed.
- **Date modified.** This is the most recent date on which the file was modified. A file is modified when you save changes (opening and closing a document without making any changes doesn't change the date modified shown for the file).
- **Date created.** This is the date the file was created. It can also be the date the file was placed on your machine if your Mac doesn't recognize the date attached to the file when you move it onto your Mac.
- **Size.** This is the size of the file. When a file becomes larger than 999 KB, the units become MB. When files get larger than 999 MB, the units change to GB.
- **Kind.** This is the type of file; for example, application, document, control panel, and so on.
- **Labels.** A label is a tag that you can associate with a file. The label consists of a color that is applied to a file's icon and a text label that appears in List views.
- **Comments.** You can enter comments to a file through the Get Info command. The Comments column displays your comments.

- Version. This column shows the version number of the file. This is normally only associated with applications, control panels, extensions, and other software. Although you will occasionally see a document with a version number associated with it, you cannot add a version number to a file without using a utility.

SEE ALSO

➤ *To learn about the Get Info command, see page 83*

Unlike the other two views, the List view offers a number of features that you can use to customize a window's display, as well as the information it contains. The next step-by-steps show you how to do the following tasks:

- Change the width of a column
- Expand a folder
- Sort a list
- Change the labels that you can attach to a file and attach a label to a file

Changing the column width of a column in List view

1. Move the cursor to the right edge of the column that you want to change the width of.
2. When the cursor changes from the arrow to the line with an arrow out of each side of it, click and drag the column to make it the width you want (see Figure 2.18).
3. Release the mouse button, and the column will have the new width.

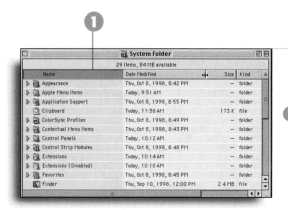

FIGURE 2.18

You can customize the width of any column in any List view.

① When you see this icon you can change a column's width.

Expanding all subfolders

If you hold down the Option key while you click the expansion triangle for a folder, all of the folders within that folder will be expanded at the same time.

4. To resize the columns to their original width, choose Reset Column Positions from the View menu.

Expanding a folder in List view

1. Click the expansion triangle next to the folder you want to expand. The contents of the folder will be displayed; the contents will be indented to the right for each level of folder (see Figure 2.19).

FIGURE 2.19

Expanding a folder in List view shows you the contents of the folder without opening it.

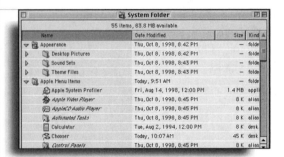

2. Press the Option key and click the expansion triangle to expand a folder and all of the folders it contains (see Figure 2.20).

FIGURE 2.20

If you press the Option key while clicking the expansion triangle, all the folders within a folder will also be expanded.

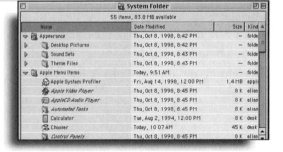

3. Click the expansion triangle again to collapse a folder (press Option while clicking the expansion triangle to also collapse all the folders within that folder).

Expansion triangles

When the expansion triangle is pointing towards the right, you can click on it to expand the contents of the folder. When the expansion triangle is pointing downward, the contents of the folder are expanded; click the expansion triangle to collapse the folder.

Sorting a list in List view

1. Click on the column heading for the column where you want to sort the list. The column heading will be highlighted to show you that this is the criteria used to sort the list, and the list will reorder itself based on the defined criteria for that parameter (for example, from most recent to least recent date modified, largest to smallest size, and so on).

2. Click the Sort order button in the upper right corner of the list area (above the scroll bar) to reverse the sort order (from ascending to descending or from descending to ascending).

Setting labels that you can attach to a file and attaching a label to a file

1. Open the Finder Preferences dialog (choose Preferences from the Edit menu).

2. Click the Labels tab. You will see the Labels Preferences window; for each of the seven label categories, you can set the text and color associated with that label (see Figure 2.21).

Expansion triangles

When the expansion triangle is pointing toward the right, you can click on it to expand the contents of the folder. When the expansion triangle is pointing downward, the contents of the folder are expanded; click the expansion triangle to collapse the folder.

Sorting by menu

To sort a window in List view, you can also choose the Sort List command on the View menu and choose the sort item on the hierarchical menu.

FIGURE 2.21

Using the Labels Preferences window, you can customize the text and color associated with each label.

3. To change a label's color, click the color next to the label text. You will see the Color Picker that you can use to set the color associated with the label (see Figure 2.22).

SEE ALSO

➤ *To learn about the Color Picker, see page 161*

FIGURE 2.22

You can use the Color Picker to change the color of labels.

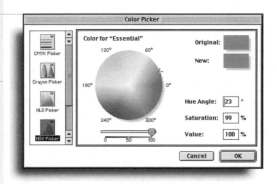

4. Choose the color that you want applied to the label and click OK.

5. Click in the text box and edit the label text.

6. Continue changing labels' text and colors to your heart's content.

7. Close the window when you are done.

8. Select that file or folder to which you want to apply a label.

9. From the File menu, choose Label and then choose the label that you want to apply from the hierarchical menu. The color you selected for your label will be applied to the file's or folder's icon, and the label text you defined will appear in the Label column (see Figure 2.23).

Using labels

One use for labels is to help you organize projects. You can define a label for the project and attach that label to all folders and files that are part of your project. This may help you keep track of your project. For example, you can easily find all the folders and files for your project by using the Find command to find all folders and files on your Mac that have your project's label.

Setting Window Views Preferences

There are two ways to set the views that will be used for your folder windows. You can set views preferences globally or locally. When you set views preferences globally, those preferences will be applied to every window that you open. When you don't want to use those global views preferences for a particular window, you can set preferences locally for that window.

This aspect of the Mac OS can be a bit confusing. To explain it another way, here is the general process you use to determine the views you use for your folders:

1. Set global views preferences for Icon, Button, and List views. These preferences will be applied to every folder window that you open.

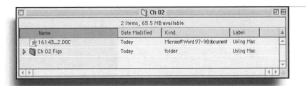

FIGURE 2.23
You can apply a label to any file or folder to help you organize your files.

2. For particular windows in which you don't want to use the global views preferences, set the views preferences for the Icon, Button, or List views for that particular window.

Your Mac calls the global views preferences Standard Views. It calls local preferences View Options.

Setting Standard Views

You can set Standard Views for each type of view. These preferences are then applied to every folder window that you open. For example, you can set Standard Views preferences to set which columns will be shown in a List view. Whenever you choose the List view in any open window, those columns will be shown (you can also set Views Options for any window; for example, in case you don't want those columns shown in a particular window).

Setting Standard Views

1. Choose Preferences from the Finder's Edit menu.

2. Click on the Views tab. You will see the Views Preferences dialog (see Figure 2.24).

The desktop is a window

By the way, the desktop is a folder window and most of the information in this chapter applies to it as well. However, you can't view the desktop in the List view. And the desktop does not have the usual window controls associated with it (such as scroll bars).

FIGURE 2.24
The Views Preferences dialog enables you to set the Standard Views Options for all three views.

3. Choose Icons on the Standard View Options for pop-up menu.

4. Choose the icon arrangement option you want.

5. If you choose the Keep arranged option, choose the parameter by which you want the Finder to arrange icons in the pop-up menu (for example, by kind).

6. Choose the icon size you want by using the radio buttons at the bottom of the window.

7. Choose Buttons from the Standard View Options for pop-up menu.

8. Choose from the options that you see. You have similar options that you use for the Icon view, but you can set them differently for the Button view if you want to.

9. Choose List from the Standard View Options for pop-up menu.

10. Check the Use relative date option if you want the Mac to use "Yesterday" and "Today" instead of yesterday's and today's date.

11. Check the Calculate folder sizes if you want to see how much data folders contain in the Size column in List view.

12. Choose which columns you want the Finder to display (Date Modified, Date Created, Size, and so on). More information is useful, but you have to balance that against the folder width you will need to use to see all of it.

13. Choose the icon size that you want the Finder to display next to the list items with the Icon Size radio buttons.

14. Close the window when you are done.

Setting Custom View Options for a Window

In the previous section, you learned how to set the Standard View options for all of the windows on your desktop. You can also customize the view options for a specific window if the global view options don't make sense for that particular window. After you set a window to use custom preferences, those views will be used each time you view that window.

Folder sizes

Be hesitant to set the Calculate folder sizes option to "on" in the Standard Views preferences for List views. If you do, your Mac has to add up all of the sizes for each file in each folder within the folder you are viewing. If you have more than a few folders within the folder you are viewing, it can take your Mac a while to calculate a size for each folder.

Setting custom view preferences for a window

1. Open a window.

2. Choose View Options from the View menu. You will see the View Options dialog for that window (see Figure 2.25). The options you see will reflect the view that the window was in when you selected View Options (for example, in Figure 2.25, the folder I had selected was in the List view so I saw the List View Options in the dialog).

FIGURE 2.25
You can use the View Options dialog to set custom view options for any window.

3. Set the options just as you did when setting Standard Views preferences for the view type (see the previous section for details). After you change the view settings, the Views text will read Custom and the Set to Standard Views button will become active (see Figure 2.26).

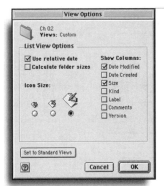

FIGURE 2.26
This folder now has a custom List view.

4. If you want to change the view back to the standard view options for that view type, click the Set to Standard Views button. The custom options will be removed, and the window will revert to the standard view options for that type of view.

5. Close the View Options window by clicking OK. The window will reflect the view options that you set.

Using Hierarchical Folders

Apple menu

In order to see hierarchical folders on the Apple menu, you must turn Submenus on in the Apple Menu Options control panel.

In certain situations, you will see a folder in a hierarchical "view." In this view, items in a folder appear on a pop-up menu that appears next to the folder when you select the folder from a menu. The area in Mac OS 8.5 software in which you will see folders in a hierarchical view is the Apple menu (see Figure 2.27).

FIGURE 2.27

On the Apple menu, you can see folders in the hierarchical view.

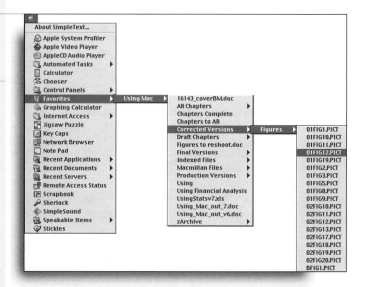

SEE ALSO

➤ *To learn about the Apple menu, see Chapter 6, "Working with the Apple Menu"*

The main benefit of the hierarchical view is that you can easily and quickly move down into a folder to find and open a particular file or folder. The disadvantage is that you cannot select more than one item at a time.

Viewing a folder in the hierarchical view

You can view any folder in the hierarchical view by placing an alias to it on the Apple menu.

Working with Pop-Up Windows

Pop-up windows (introduced in Mac OS 8.0) are a great way to keep files that you frequently use easily accessible. Pop-up windows appear as tabs on the bottom of the desktop. When you click a pop-up window's tab, the window pops open, and you can work within it. When you move out of the window, it pops back to being just a tab (see Figure 2.28).

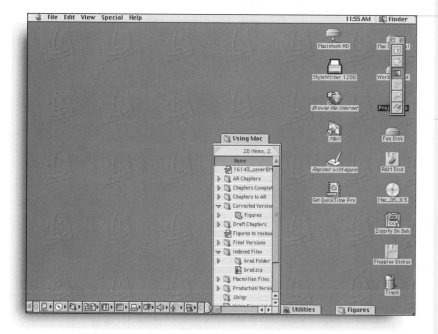

FIGURE 2.28
Pop-up windows appear as tabs across the bottom of your desktop; when you click on a pop-up window, it pops open, and you can work within it.

Pop-up windows have the following features:

- When you drag a file or folder onto a pop-up window's tab, it will pop open so that you can place the folder or file into that folder.

■ You can create pop-up windows in two ways (via the View menu or by dragging a window's title bar to the bottom of the desktop).

■ The folder's icon that appears in the tab works just like an icon in any other view; for example, you can drag it onto a disk to copy the folder there.

■ Pop-up windows can be resized both in width and in the height to which they pop up.

■ If you hold the Command key down and click on the window's title, you will see a pop-up menu showing the folders containing that folder, as well as the folders that the folder you are viewing contains.

Pop-up windows are easy to work with, and they are a great way to access the files within folders that you use frequently.

Setting up and configuring a pop-up window

1. Open a folder or volume (see Figure 2.29).

FIGURE 2.29

This folder is about to become a pop-up window.

Another way to pop

You can also change a window into a pop-up window by dragging its title bar to the bottom of the desktop. When you get close to the bottom of the desktop, the folder will be converted into a pop-up window.

With this method, you can place the pop-up window anywhere along the bottom of the desktop that you like.

You can set the width of the pop-up menu by setting the width of the window that you are changing into a pop-up window. The wider the window you are converting is, the wider the pop-up window's tab will be.

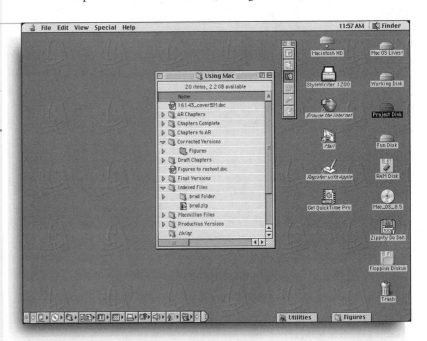

2. Choose as Pop-up window from the View menu. The folder becomes an open pop-up window, located right next to the last pop-window created or close to the left edge of the desktop if there are no other pop-windows (see Figure 2.30).

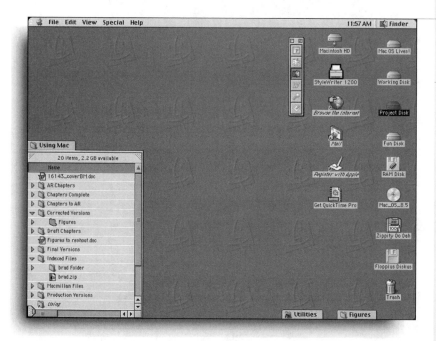

FIGURE 2.30
The Using Mac folder has become a pop-up window.

3. Resize the pop-up window by dragging the handles in the upper left and upper right corners of the window (a pop-up window's handles are diagonal hash marks, see Figure 2.31). Dragging the resizing handles up or down determines how high the window pops up. Dragging them left or right determines how wide a pop-up window will be.

4. Click outside the folder to "pop" it closed (see Figure 2.32).

5. To change a pop-up menu back into a "regular" folder window, drag the tab (not the icon) of the pop-up window up onto the desktop until you see an entire window. The window will now be a "regular" window.

FIGURE 2.31

Resizing the Using Mac folder so that it takes up less space when it is "popped" open.

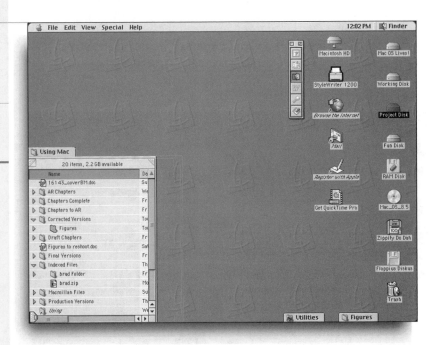

Icons in tabs

The icons you see in the tabs of pop-up windows, and any folder's or volume's title bar for that matter, can be used to move or copy that item. Just use the pop-up window's folder icon as you would any other.

FIGURE 2.32

The Using Mac folder can now be opened by clicking the Using Mac tab.

Or use the menu

You can also choose as Window on the Edit menu to change a pop-up window back into a regular one.

Views options in pop-up windows

All the view options that you have for regular folder windows apply to pop-up windows also (for example, the Icon view).

Expanding files in pop-up windows

In a pop-up window, the expansion triangles work just like they do in the List view.

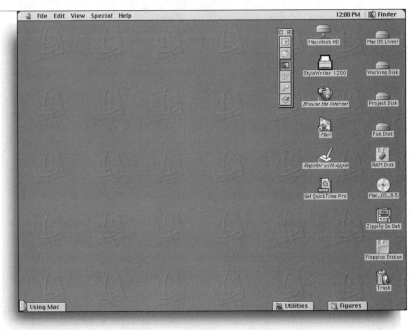

Using a pop-up window is also very easy. Here's how to use them:

- To open a pop-up window, click its tab.
- To close a pop-window, move out of it.
- To place a folder or file within a folder that uses a pop-up window, drag the file or folder into the pop-up window's tab, wait for the window to pop up, and then drag the file to where you want it to be.

Working with Spring-Loaded Folders

Mac OS 8.0 also introduced spring-loaded folders. When you drag a file or folder onto a spring-loaded folder, it springs open, and you can move the folder or file into the folder. This doesn't stop with the first spring-loaded folder you move into either. As you continue to drag items onto folders within a spring-loaded folder, those folders also spring open so that you can quickly move a file or folder into any folder no matter how buried within other folders it is.

One of the good things about spring-loaded folders is that they snap closed once you move out of them so you don't leave a trail of open windows behind you.

You can set the amount of time it takes for folders to spring open after you drag an item onto them.

Setting spring-loaded folder preferences

1. From the Edit menu, choose Preferences.
2. Click the General tab, and you will see the General Preferences window (see Figure 2.33).
3. To turn spring-loaded folders on, check the Spring-loaded folders check box.
4. Use the Delay before opening slider to adjust the amount of time you have to have an item placed over a folder before it springs open.
5. Close the window.

FIGURE 2.33

You can use General Finder Preferences to set the time it takes for spring-loaded folders to spring open.

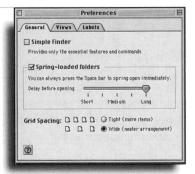

Using Folder Window Features

Folder windows have special navigation, window, and file management features that you won't find with other windows. You can use these features in any of the views, and they work on any open folder window. These features include the following:

- Moving among windows. To move up or down from the folder whose window is open, hold the Command key down and click on the window's title. A menu will pop up that enables you to select any folder within your current folder or containing the current folder all the way up to the startup disk's folder (see Figure 2.34).

FIGURE 2.34

You can command-click on a window's name to move up or down from the current folder.

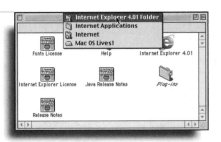

- Opening one folder's window while closing the current window. Sometimes when you are opening folders looking for a particular file, you leave a trail of open windows that may not need to be open (see Figure 2.35). To close the current window while you are opening the next folder, hold down the Option key while opening the next folder. As the folder opens, the window that you are currently in will close. This helps you keep your desktop clean while you are burrowing down into folders.

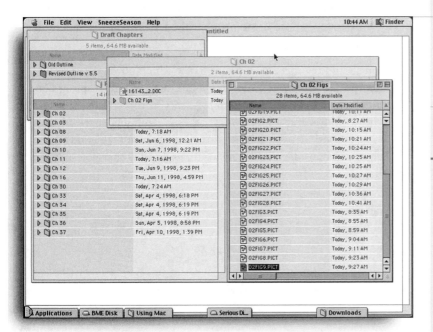

FIGURE 2.35

A trail of opened windows can be a nuisance; you can avoid this by holding Option down when you open the next folder.

Collapsing lots of windows

The Option key also affects the Collapse box. If you hold the Option key down while you click a Finder window's Collapse box, all the open windows will collapse. You can expand all open windows that are collapsed by holding down the Option key and clicking the Collapse box.

- Closing all open windows. You can close all the open windows on your desktop by holding down the Option key and clicking the Close box of one of the open folders.

- Renaming a file. To rename a file, select it and press the Return key (in the List view, you can also select the file and just wait a few moments). When the name is highlighted, you can edit the name of the file. You can change it to anything as long as it is less than 31 characters and there are no other files with that same name.

- Moving around and selecting files and folders in a window with the keyboard. You can use your keyboard to move around within a folder. The Up and Down arrow keys move you in the direction of the arrow. The Tab key moves you to the next file or folder in alphabetical order. Pressing Shift and Tab moves you to the previous file or folder in alphabetical order.

- Selecting files and folders with the keyboard. You can quickly jump to, and select, an item in a window by typing the first few characters of the item's name. You will move to the first item whose name matches the letters you typed, and the item will be selected.

You should try these techniques to see which ones you want to incorporate into your daily Mac use. Doing so will reap big benefits for you because as you use a Mac, you will constantly work with windows and folders. While these techniques may only save you a second or two each, that small difference really adds up when you consider the dozens of times per day that you may use them.

Working with Menus

Understanding the type of menus that your Mac uses

Working with the Mac's menu

Working with contextual menus

Working with the Mac's unique menus

Understanding Mac Menus

One of the major interface elements that you will use while you work on your Mac are menus. These menus come in various formats:

- **Pull-down menus**. These are the most common type of Mac menus, and they appear in almost all applications. In fact, there are standard pull-down menus that are supposed to be included in every application. They include the File and Edit menus. Pull-down menus get their name because you "pull them down" by clicking on them. You can choose commands from the menus in their "pulled down" condition (see Figure 3.1).

FIGURE 3.1

The common pull-down menu is the type you will use most often on the Mac.

- **Pop-up menus**. Pop-up menus are used to provide you with a list of choices that "pop up" when you click on the pop-up menu. From the pop-up, you can choose commands or options (see Figure 3.2). Pop-up menus are most common within dialog boxes, but you see them other places as well.

FIGURE 3.2

Pop-up menus enable you to quickly choose from specific options.

- **Contextual menus**. Another feature introduced in Mac OS 8, contextual menus are pop-up menus that change depending on the context in which they are activated. Contextual menus provide quick and easy access to the most likely commands that you will use in certain situations (see Figure 3.3). Plus, you can customize contextual menus so that the commands you use most are just a click away.

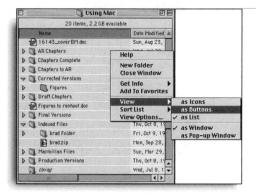

FIGURE 3.3

Contextual menus provide quick access to commands that you are most likely to use in specific situations.

- **Tear-off (floating) menus**. Some menus can be "torn off" the menu bar and become free-floating palettes from which you can choose commands or options. The Application menu in Mac OS 8.5 is an example of a tear-off menu (see Figure 3.4). Many applications also use tear-off menus.

FIGURE 3.4

Tear-off menus can be placed anywhere on your desktop.

- **Unique menus**. There are certain menus that are only available in specific areas. Mac OS 8.5 uses several of these unique menus, including the Finder's View menu (see Figure 3.5).

Tear-off toolbars

Many applications and utilities feature toolbars, which are sets of buttons on which you can click to activate a command. Many toolbars can also be torn off so that they "float" on the screen.

FIGURE 3.5

The commands available on the View menu are unique to the Finder.

Using Mac Menus

Using most Mac menus requires little explanation. To use pull-down menus, you simply click the menu to pull it down, highlight the command you want, and click the mouse button to select a command. To use pop-up menus, you click the menu button and select your choice from the menu that pops up.

Sticky menus were introduced in Mac OS 8.0; this means that pull-down menus stay open without you having to hold down the mouse button, unlike "non-sticky menus" that snapped closed as soon as you let go of the mouse button (this is the way Mac pull-down menus used to work). Note that with Mac OS 8.5, you can no longer turn sticky menus off.

Sticky menus and Windows

Sticky menus were first used in Windows computers, and they still are. This is one of the few features that has appeared on Windows computers before they showed up on the Mac.

Working with Contextual Menus

Contextual Menus (CMs) are one of the most powerful tools on the Mac; they were introduced in Mac OS 8.0 and continue to be integrated in the OS as well as in many applications. CMs provide a pop-up menu of commands that you can easily access by clicking something while holding the Control key down. As their name implies, CMs change depending on the context in which you activate them. For example, when you activate the CM in a window, you will see one set of commands. If you use it on the desktop, you will see another set of choices.

CMs are also extensible, which means that you can add items to CMs to fully customize them for the way you like to work. You can also add new functions to your Mac through CM files.

After you get used to using CMs, you may wonder how you ever got along without them.

CMs and apps

CMs are also supported in many major applications, including Microsoft Office. To see if your favorite applications use CMs, just hold the Control key and click on something in that application. If CMs are supported, you will see one.

Understanding Contextual Menus

Contextual menus are controlled by two items within the System Folder:

- **Contextual Menu Extension**. The CM extension provides CM capabilities to your system. It is installed by default.

- **Contextual Menu Items folder**. This folder, within the System Folder, contains the particular CMs that you will have available. You can add or remove CM files from this folder to change the CMs on your Mac.

To really understand CMs, point to various items on your desktop and within windows and activate their CMs. This will give you a good idea of the CMs that are a part of Mac OS 8.5 by default.

Using Contextual Menus

Using CMs is simple—just point to something, hold the Control key down, and click the mouse button. The CM will pop-up, and you can choose a command from it (see Figure 3.6).

Marking CMs

When you press the Control key and a CM is available, you will notice a small pop-up menu icon by the arrow. If you don't see this, there is no CM available for whatever you are pointing to.

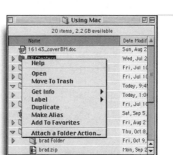

FIGURE 3.6

Contextual menus provide an easy and fast way to access context-specific commands.

Using the desktop contextual menu

1. Move the pointer over an empty space on the desktop.

2. Hold the Control key down and click. You will see a variety of desktop commands, including Help, New Folder, View (with submenus), Clean Up, and so on.

Using CMs within windows is done in the same way.

Using a window's contextual menu

1. Open a window.

2. Hold the Control key down and click. You will see a CM for the window (see Figure 3.7).

FIGURE 3.7

This CM offers a set of commands appropriate for the window.

Adding to Contextual Menus

Contextual menus are extensible; this means that by adding a CM file to the Contextual Menu Items folder, you can add to the commands that you can access via CMs. You can add existing commands to the CM as well as entirely new features. This works similarly to how the Apple Menu Items folder works, except that you can't use aliases. You can obtain CM files from a variety of sources, especially the Internet. One current source of CMs is the following:

http://interdesign.ca/cmcentral/index/html

When I last checked this site, it said that it might go away at some point. If it isn't there, check the Mac software archives for CM files.

SEE ALSO

➤ *To learn where some of the best Mac software archives on the Internet are, see page 639*

To show you how this works by installing StuffItCMPlugin. This plug-in enables you to use a CM to activate Aladdin's StuffIt Engine to compress and decompress files. The process I use in this example is similar for any other CMs that you may want to install and use.

SEE ALSO

➤ *To learn more about file compression, see page 589*

Installing Contextual Menu Add-Ons

Installing a CM add-on requires that you add the CM to the Contextual Menu Items folder and restart your Mac.

Installing StuffItCMPlugin

1. Open the folder containing the CM file you want to install (see Figure 3.8).

FIGURE 3.8
This is the folder for the StuffItCMPlugin.

2. Read any ReadMe or other text files that came with the CM; these can contain important usage information as well as warnings about incompatibilities.

3. Drag the CM file onto the System Folder.

4. Click OK when your Mac asks if it should put the file into the Contextual Menu Items folder.

5. Restart your Mac. Unlike changes to the Apple menu, you need to restart your Mac to make changes to the CM become active.

6. Activate the CM to see the new commands that have been added to it (see Figure 3.9).

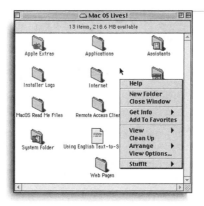

FIGURE 3.9
Compare this to Figure 3.7 to see that there is now an additional item on the Contextual menu (StuffIt at the bottom of the contextual menu).

Using Contextual Menu Add-Ons

Using StuffItCMPlugin to unstuff a file

1. Point to a file that you want to unstuff.

2. Hold Control down and click. You will see the CM with the StuffIt command (see Figure 3.10).

FIGURE 3.10

Using a CM to unstuff a .sit file.

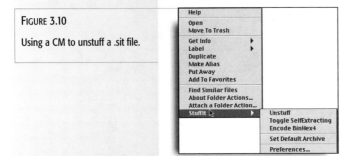

3. Choose Unstuff command from the submenu. The file will be unstuffed.

Using the Finder's Unique Menus

The Finder uses three unique menus to provide certain capabilities and functions; you won't see these menus in any other application. In this section, you will learn about these important menus.

Using the Apple Menu

The Apple menu provides a lot of capability for you, and it is a menu that you can easily customize for your own purposes (see Figure 3.11).

SEE ALSO

➤ *To learn about the Apple menu, see Chapter 6, "Working with the Apple Menu"*

FIGURE 3.11
The Apple menu is extremely flexible, and you can customize it as much as you want to.

Using the Special Menu

Unless you are brand new to the Mac, you have already used commands on the Special menu. The Special commands are fairly important, but most of them are pretty straightforward. The following list is a quick summary of the commands on the Special menu:

- **Empty Trash**. This command deletes the files that are stored in the Trash. One nice-to-know feature of the Trash is that if you hold the Option key while you select Empty Trash, you will delete any locked items that are in the Trash (without using the Option key, you can't empty locked items from the Trash).

SEE ALSO

➤ *To learn more about the Trash, see page 107*

- **Ejecting Disks**. You can use the Eject Disk command, or press Command-E, to eject any removable media that is mounted on the desktop and that is selected. This works with floppy disks, CD-ROMs, Zip disks, and other removable media.

Put that away

You can also use the Put Away command on the File menu (Command-Y) to eject a removable disk. The Put Away command also unmounts any volumes that you are sharing from a network as well.

■ Erasing Disks. The Erase Disk command erases and formats hard and floppy disks. When you choose the Erase Disk command, you have the option of formatting a disk as Mac OS Standard (a Mac disk), DOS (a PC disk), or ProDos (Apple II disk).

SEE ALSO

➤ *To learn more about formatting disks, see page 114*

➤ *To learn more about formatting disks, see page 114*

Go to sleep…

Pressing the Command-Option-Power keys puts your Mac immediately into the sleep mode.

■ **Putting your Mac to sleep**. The Sleep command puts your Mac to sleep. In Sleep mode, your Mac's hard drive stops spinning and the monitor powers down. In Sleep mode, your Mac uses much less power than it does in "awake" mode. And your Mac will be ready for you to use again much faster than if you have to start it up from the shut-down condition. If you are going to be away from your Mac for a while, it is a good idea to put it to sleep.

SEE ALSO

➤ *To learn more about the sleep mode and desktop Macs, see page 108*
➤ *To learn more about the sleep mode and PowerBooks, see page 820*

A fast way to sleep, quit, or restart

If you press the Power key (the key in the upper right corner of the keyboard; it has a small triangle on it), you will see a dialog that enables you to click Restart, Sleep, or Shut Down (the default)—you can also cancel if you need to. The fastest way to shut down your Mac is to hit the Power key and then press Return.

■ **Restarting Your Mac**. The Restart command makes your Mac shut down all running processes and then restart all of its system software. Restarting is also called *warm starting* or *rebooting*. You will need to Restart your Mac occasionally, such as when a program crashes or when you have to restart after making software changes (installing new software for example).

■ **Shutting down your Mac**. You should always use the Shut Down command before turning off the power to your Mac. This command ensures that all of the processes running on your Mac are properly stopped and that the hard drives are ready to stop spinning (the drive heads are parked).

Using the Application Menu

Your Mac is able to *multitask*. What this means is that your Mac can do more than one thing at a time. For example, you can have many applications open simultaneously. This prevents you from having to start and stop one application just because you want to work in another one for a while. Plus, your Mac can do some tasks in the background while you are working within another application.

You use the Application menu to manage all of the open applications that are currently running on your Mac. The Application menu is always available to you; it is the last menu on the far right of the menu bar (see Figure 3.12).

FIGURE 3.12

The Application menu is always ready to use to manage your open applications.

Managing open applications by using the Application menu

1. Click on the Application menu (in the upper right corner of the desktop). You will see a list of the applications currently running on your Mac (see Figure 3.13). The application with the check mark next to it is the one that is currently "on top," or *active*, and its menu bar will be visible. The background applications' names will be grayed out in the menu.

FIGURE 3. 13

The Application menu shows you all of the applications that are open on your Mac.

2. To bring a different application to the front (to work with it), simply choose it from the Application menu (see Figure 3.14). The menu bar will change to the menu bar of the application that you selected, and the application's name and icon will be at the top of the Application menu.

New Application menu feature for Mac OS 8.5

Under Mac OS 8.5, the application's name, as well as its icon, is displayed at the top of the Application menu. (In previous versions of the OS, you would only see the active application's icon.) This helps you more quickly identify the active application.

FIGURE 3.14

Here I am using the Application menu to make SimpleText the active application.

3. If open windows of applications that are in the background distract you, choose Hide others from the Application menu. The other applications will be hidden from view (although they are still running).

4. If you want to move back to the application that was previously active, choose Hide CurrentApplication (where CurrentApplication is the name of the application that is active).

5. To see all the applications that are open, choose Show All.

Also new to Mac OS 8.5 is the ability to customize the Application menu. You can resize the menu to display as much or as little of the active application's name as you would like (if you make it small enough, you will only see its icon). The most significant of these features is the ability to convert the Application menu into a floating menu, or palette. In this mode, the Application menu is called the *Application Switcher*.

It's two tools in one

Even with the Application Switcher open, you can still use the Application menu in the same ways that you can when the Application Switcher is closed.

Customizing the Application menu

1. Resize the menu by dragging the left edge (the hash marks) to the right to make it smaller or to the left to make it bigger.

2. Drag down through the menu to tear it off the Finder's menu bar and make it into a floating window (see Figure 3.15). The active application will be highlighted (SimpleText in Figure 3.15).

FIGURE 3.15

When you "tear off" the Application menu, it becomes a floating window that is always accessible (in this mode, it is called the Application Switcher).

3. To switch to a different application, click its name in the Application Switcher window.

4. To view the Application Switcher in the Icon view, click the window's Zoom box (see Figure 3.16).

Look, it floats!

You can move the Application Switcher around, but it always floats on top of all other open windows. You can collapse it to its title bar by clicking the collapse box.

FIGURE 3.16
You can view the Application Switcher in the Icon view.

5. To toggle the size of the icons, hold the Option key down while you click the Zoom box (see Figure 3.17).

FIGURE 3.17
You can increase the size of the icons in the Application Switcher by holding down the Option key and clicking the Zoom box.

The floating window is always with you

The floating Application Switcher will remain where you last left it, even after you restart your Mac.

Switching Applications with the keyboard

Turnabout is fair play, and Mac OS 8.5 borrows another element from Windows. Holding down the Command key while you press Tab moves down the list of open applications and yo make the next one "down" the list active. Holding down Shift and Command while you press the Tab key moves you in the opposite direction. This is often the fastest way to switch applications because you don't have to take your hands off of the keyboard. In case you are wondering, to do this on a Windows computer, you hold down Alt and press Tab.

Learning to use the Mac's multitasking capability and the Application menu and Application Switcher can save you the time you normally waste opening and closing applications. As long as your Mac has enough RAM to keep the applications you use open at all times, there is really no reason to quit an application. It is much better to simply use the Application menu and Application Switcher to quickly move into the application with which you want to work.

Working with the Finder

Learning about the Finder

Using the Get Info command

Finding files and content on your Mac and information from the Internet with the Find command

Working with aliases and favorites

Using the Trash and clock

Finder quits

The Finder can actually be stopped while your Mac is still running. In fact, in the past, some applications, particularly games (such as Lucas Art's Dark Forces) were able to shut down the Finder and "take over" your Mac. This was because Mac hardware was a bit underpowered for what these applications were trying to do and consequently they needed all of your Mac's resources. With modern Macs, this is no longer necessary.

Control panels and extensions march on

You can see the control panels and extensions that are being loaded as their icons "march" across the bottom of your screen when you start your Mac. You will learn more about control panels and extensions throughout the rest of this book.

Understanding the Finder

The primary piece of software that provides the Mac with its interface and that largely determines how your Mac will work is the Finder. In fact, you can rightly say that the Finder *is* the Mac. There are some parts of the Mac OS that are not specifically part of the Finder, but since the Finder manages the system-level operations of your Mac, and it creates and manages your desktop as well as all processes that are running on your Mac, the Finder is it as far as the OS goes.

The Finder is technically an application. However, you never launch the Finder; rather, it opens when you start your Mac, and it is always running.

The Finder provides the core services that are needed to make your Mac work. And your Mac will run with a plain, vanilla Finder with no "extras" installed at all. The basic Finder is the Mac at its minimum. With the "plain vanilla" Finder, you get the Mac interface, the ability to organize and manipulate files, open windows, work with some devices (such as hard drives and floppy drives), use menus, run applications, and so on. However, the Finder's functionality can be increased through control panels and extensions.

Control panels and extensions are the "extras" that add functionality to the basic OS software that is started when you start your Mac. Control panels and extensions actually modify the system software (which is controlled by the Finder) as it loads so that the functionality of that software becomes available to you. For example, QuickTime (the Mac's multimedia technology which you will learn about in Chapter 10, "Working with Multimedia") is an extension to the Mac OS. When it is installed on your Mac, the Finder is able to use its capabilities to enable you to watch and edit digital video and animation. Your Mac will run just fine without QuickTime installed because it is not a core part of the Finder, but you won't be able to work with multimedia files.

After all of the updates and improvements in Mac OS 8.5, the Finder does more than it ever has. In addition to all of the great folder, window, and menu features you read about in the previous chapters, the Finder provides lots of other features that you constantly use as you work with your Mac. Not only does the Finder enable you to find files, with Mac OS 8.5, you can also find specific content and even search the Internet with it. Beyond the Find feature (Sherlock), there are lots of other interface elements and file and folder management tools that the Finder provides. Learning to use the Finder well will take you a long way toward getting the most out of your Mac.

The following list contains many of the Finder areas and tools that you will use most frequently:

- **Desktop**. In Chapter 1, "Working with Macintosh," you got a quick tour of the Mac desktop, and you learned about some of the most important Mac features, especially the features new for Mac OS 8.5. You will work with the desktop much of the time that you use your Mac. Desktop features are discussed throughout the first two parts of this book.

- **Apple menu**. The Apple menu is an excellent tool that you can use to quickly access *any* folder or file on your Mac. Since it is such a useful feature, Chapter 6, "Working with the Apple Menu" is devoted to the Apple menu.

- **File menu**. The Finder's File menu contains a number of powerful commands that enable to work with files. You'll learn how the most important File commands work in this chapter.

- **Edit menu**. The Finder's Edit menu is useful when you are working with file names, such as when you want to copy a file name into a document. The Finder Preferences command is also located on the Edit menu; you'll see how to set Finder preferences later in this chapter.

- **View menu**. You use the View menu extensively when you work with folders and windows. You can learn how to use the commands on this menu in Chapter 2, "Working with Folders and Windows."

- **Special menu**. The Special menu provides functions that are unique to the Finder. You can learn more about the Special menu in Chapter 3, "Working with Menus."

The Finder does it all

The Finder is involved in just about every operation on your Mac. Whenever you manipulate a file (open, move, save, delete, and so on), open a window, access a device, or anything else, the Finder is the software that makes it happen. Some Finder functions you can use directly (such as the Finder menu commands), while others are working in the background (such as Navigation Services, which enables you to save and open files).

It's quitting time

When a program *hangs*, it just sits there and stops responding to any commands. In order to clear the misbehaving application, the Mac provides a way for you to *force quit* it. To do this, hold down the Option and Command keys and then press the Escape key. This forces an application to stop running. The idea is that you can then move to all of your open applications and save your work before restarting your Mac. You should only force quit as a last resort because it makes your whole Mac unstable and much more likely to hang or crash again. This means that you always need to restart your Mac as soon as you can after you have used the Force Quit command.

Since the Finder is an application, you can force quit it as well. This causes the Finder to quit and then restart. When you are working and the desktop and everything freezes, your last resort should to be force quit. Occasionally, this will work like it is supposed to, and you will be able to move into your applications and save your documents. Much of the time, force quitting the Finder will lock up everything, and you will have no choice but to restart your Mac (which means that you will lose all unsaved changes in any open documents).

Windows 95 and Windows 98 don't have a trash can. They have a Recycling Bin. It works very similarly to the Mac's Trash. Where did the designers of the Windows operating systems get the idea of a recycling bin? I don't know, but I am sure that it wasn't from the Mac's politically-incorrect Trash.

- **Help menu**. The Help menu enables you to get to the three kinds of help that are available for Mac OS 8.5. The Mac's help systems are covered in Chapter 12, "Working with the Mac's Help Systems."

- **File tools**. In addition to the all of the file management capabilities that the Finder provides, it also provides the save and open dialog boxes that you use to create and work with files. New to Mac OS 8.5 is the Finder's Navigation Services feature, which can replace the old Save and Open dialogs.

SEE ALSO

➤ *To learn about the older Save and Open dialogs, see page 261*

➤ *To learn about Navigation services' Save and Open dialogs, see page 263*

- **Organization tools**. These tools include aliases and Favorites that you can use to organize and find files quickly and easily.

- **Clock**. The Finder provides a clock that lives on your desktop. This is an example of an "extra" that is added to the Finder by a control panel. The clock is provided by the Date & Time control panel, which adds the clock feature to the Finder. You will learn how to set and use the clock in this chapter.

- **Application menu**. You can use the Application menu to manage the applications that are open on your Mac.

SEE ALSO

➤ *To learn how to use the Application menu, see page 74*

- **Trash**. One of the most recognized features of the Mac desktop is its Trash. The Trash is a unique folder that has some special features. You will learn to talk "Trash" later in this chapter.

- **Energy control panel**. While the Mac's Trash isn't politically correct, the Energy control panel is. It enables you to set your Mac so that it sleeps after a specified period of inactivity. In the Sleep mode, your Mac uses less energy than it

does when it is "awake." You will learn how to use the
Energy control panel to do your part to save the Earth in
this chapter.

Getting Information About Files and Folders

It is frequently useful to get information about various files,
folders, and volumes that you are using. This information
includes size, where the item resides, when it was created, label
information, naming information, and so on. The information
that you see for any particular item will depend on what kind of
item it is. For example, you will see one set of data for a folder,
another for a document, and still another for an application. A
very important feature of the Get Info command for applications
is to set the RAM allocation for an application.

SEE ALSO

➤ *To learn about allocating RAM for an application, see page 327*

With Mac OS 8.5, the Info command now has a maximum of
three subcommands: General Information, Sharing, and
Memory (see Figure 4.1). The General Information command
does the same thing that the previous Get Info command did (it
provides the general information for folders and files). The
Sharing Information command provides sharing-specific information and controls for an item. The Memory command enables
you to manage an application's memory allocation.

Memory...

You will only see the Memory
command on the Get Info
menu when you have selected
an application.

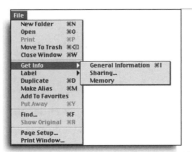

FIGURE 4.1

The Get Info command in Mac
OS 8.5 combines the previous Get
Info command with the Sharing
information function; it also adds
a third option for applications
(Memory).

The information you see with the Get Info command depends on the type of file or folder you have selected. The different types of information you will see are the following:

- **Application information**. There are three areas of information for applications. The first is called General Information and provides data such as the size of the application's file, where it is stored, the dates it was created and modified, the version number, a label, comments, and whether it is locked or not. The second is the Memory Information for the application, which you can view by choosing Memory from the Application pop-up menu. The third area is the Sharing Information, which for applications involves Program Linking.

SEE ALSO

➤ *To learn about working with an application's memory, see page 327*

- **Document information**. When you use Get Info on a document, you can see only one window, which is the General Information window. It provides the same information as the General Information for an application with two exceptions. The version information for a document is always n/a (not applicable). The second exception is that a document's Info window has a Stationery Pad check box that you can use to create a template document.

- **Folder information**. Folder information includes two windows: one for general information and one for sharing. The General Information for folders is similar to applications and documents. It includes: kind (which is always folder for a folder), size, where the folder is stored, when it was created and modified, a label, and comments. The Sharing window enables you to set sharing properties for a folder.

SEE ALSO

➤ *To learn about sharing a folder, see page 467*

- **Volume information**. When used on volumes, the Get Info command (volumes are disks, partitions, and network folders) provides options very similar to those that it provides when the command is used on folders. The differences are that for a disk, the "kind" is disk and the Info window shows the capacity of the disk and how much space is available.

SEE ALSO

➤ *To learn about volumes, see Chapter 5, "Working with Hard Disks, Partitions, and Volumes"*

- **Trash information**. Yes, the good old Trash has its own unique Info window. In it you can see where the Trash is located (which is odd given that the Trash is always on the desktop), whether it contains anything, when the Trash was last modified (by Apple), a label, and the "Warn before emptying" check box. You will learn to use this later in this chapter.

Getting General Information for Applications and Documents

The following step-by-steps show you how the Get Info commands work for applications and documents since they are the items about which you are most likely to want to know. First, you will learn how to get info for an application.

Getting general information for an application

1. Select an application's icon or name in a list.

2. Choose Get Info and then General Information from the hierarchical menu or press Command-I. You will see the General Information window for the application (see Figure 4.2).

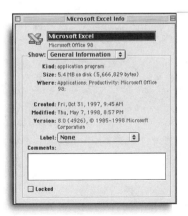

FIGURE 4.2

The General Information window for applications provides some important data, the most important of which is the version information.

3. If you want to rename the application, edit the name at the top of the window.

4. If you want to attach a label to the application, choose it from the pop-up Label menu.

5. If you want to add comments to the application, type in the Comments box.

6. If you want to lock the application so that it cannot be modified, use the Locked check box.

7. Read the various information provided for the application including file size, where it resides, when it was created, and the version number.

Getting info on a document is very similar to getting info for an application. The differences are in the information and options that you will see.

Getting general information on a document

1. Select the document and press Command-I. You will see an information window similar to the one for an application.

2. You can rename the document by typing in the Name field.

3. You can attach a label to it by choosing a label from the pop-up menu.

4. You can add comments to the information window by entering text in the Comments box.

6. You can lock the document so that it cannot be changed by checking the Locked box.

7. You can make the item a Stationery Pad by checking the box. A Stationery Pad is a template that you can use to create other similar documents. When this box is checked and you open the document, it opens as an untitled document formatted like the Stationery Pad, to which you can add your data.

8. Look at the important data for the document, such as creation date and size.

Then there was one

When you choose the Get Info command while you have a document selected, you will see only one choice: General Information. That makes sense because General Information is all you can get for a document.

Getting Sharing Information for a Folder

When you share files on your Mac across a network, you manage the access that people on the network have to folders with the Sharing Information command under the Get Info function.

Getting sharing information for a folder

1. Select a folder.

2. Press Command-I.

3. When the information window appears, choose Sharing from the Show pop-up menu. You will see the Sharing information window (see Figure 4.3).

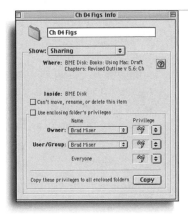

FIGURE 4.3

The sharing function, on the File menu in previous versions of the Mac OS, is now part of the Get Info command. You can use the Sharing information window to set sharing parameters for a folder.

4. Use the pop-up menus and check boxes to set sharing parameters for this item.

SEE ALSO

➤ *To learn about sharing files on a network, see page 467*

5. When you are done, close the information window. The sharing settings will then take effect.

Finding Things with the Finder's Find Command

You have always been able to find files with the Finder's Find application. In Mac OS 8.5, what the Finder can find has been significantly expanded. Previously, you could only use the Find command to find files by their names, creation dates, or other attributes. With Mac OS 8.5, you can still do this, but you can also find files by content (the information that the file contains), and you can also use the Find command to search the Internet.

The way it was

In previous versions of the Finder, you had to hold down the Option key to have the capability to search for creator and file types.

In Mac OS 8.5, the Find File function has been greatly expanded so that it is now quite powerful. In keeping with this power, it has been renamed Sherlock (although it can still be launched by choosing Find from the Finder's File command.) For example, you can save "finds" so that you can rerun them without re-entering all of the search parameters. There are also more parameters to search with, and some that previously required you to press Option to see are now out in the open. For example, the capability of searching for files based on their types and creators is now a
visible option.

Finding files by content is a great help when you know that there is a file on a machine that contains a word, phrase, sentence, or topic, but you can't quite remember what the name of the file is or even when it was created. You can also use the Find by Content feature to locate all of the files on your Mac that relate to a specific topic or concept.

The third major find feature, Internet search, enables you to move directly to the Net to perform a search without having to launch a Web browser. This can be a great time saver and moves the Mac further down the path towards complete Internet integration. You will learn about the Internet in Part V, "Using Your Mac to Surf the Internet," so if you are totally unfamiliar with the Net, you may want to work through that material before you try to use the Search Internet function.

Finding Files by Attribute

Finding files by attributes works similarly to how it always has, but there have been a number of improvements. Specifically, the ability to search for files of specific types or types that were created by a certain application no longer requires that you use the Option key.

Finding files by attributes

1. Choose Find from the File menu or press Command-F. You will see the Find dialog (see Figure 4.4).

FIGURE 4.4

The Find dialog in the Find File mode that enables you to find files by attribute.

2. Make sure that the Find File tab is selected so you see a dialog similar to Figure 4.4.

3. Choose the areas you want to search from the Find Items pop-up menu. You have a variety of choices here that include everything from all the disks accessible on your Mac to just a single volume. Try to narrow the locations to search in order to speed up the process.

4. Choose an attribute to search for from the far left pop-up menu (for example, name or file type).

5. In the center pop-up menu, choose an operator to use (such as "contains" or "is not").

6. Enter the search text in the text box.

7. If you want to add more criteria to your search, click More Choices. You will see another row of search parameters similar to what you saw in steps 4 through 6.

8. Continue to add search criteria until you have covered all of your bases. If you have a complex search, you may end up with a dialog box like that in Figure 4.5. Note that each criteria you choose has its own unique parameters, but they all work similarly; you will see choices in the center pop-up menu that are relevant to the parameter shown in the left pop-up menu.

FIGURE 4.5

This search is probably more complicated than any you will need to do, but it does show you how refined finding files can be.

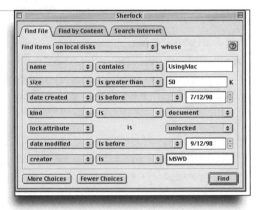

9. When you have defined all of your search parameters, click Find. The search will begin, and when it is complete, you will see the Items Found window (see Figure 4.6). Note that your search parameters are shown in the center of the Items Found window.

FIGURE 4.6

This search found a number of documents that met the search criteria shown in the middle of the window.

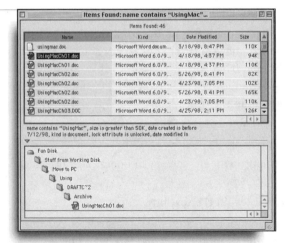

Hiding paths

If you click the downward facing triangle, the pane showing you the path to the file will be closed. Click it again to open the pane.

10. To see where a file is located, select a file and look at the bottom pane of the window, and you will see a complete path to the file.

11. You can move, open, copy, or trash files from the upper window just as if you were using them from the desktop.

12. You can sort the found files in the top pane just like in the Finder (by clicking Size for example).

13. If you want to save this Find so you can run it again at a later date without re-entering all of the search parameters (another feature new to Mac OS 8.5), choose Save Search Criteria from the File menu (or press Command-S).

14. Move to a location where you want to save the Search, name the Search, and click Save.

15. The next time you want to run this Search, choose Open Search Criteria from the File menu.

16. Locate the Search you want to use and click Open. The Search will start, and you will see the results of your Find.

While finding files by attributes is very easy, it is even easier to find files by similarity. For example, you might want to find all of the files whose names contain certain text and that are of a certain type. Rather than having to type all of this data yourself, you can drag and drop a similar file onto the Find dialog and then the parameter that you have selected will be entered in the Find dialog. A quick step-by-step will show you how this works. In this step-by-step, I will search for all documents whose name contains the phrase, "UsingMac," and whose creator is Microsoft Word.

Finding files by name and creator similarity

1. Open Find by choosing it from the File menu or press Command-F. The Find window will open.

2. Choose name for the type of search attribute.

3. Locate a document that contains the name that is similar to the one you are looking for. In this example, I looked for files containing the name, "16143." I found a file called 16143Ch023BM.doc to use as my "model."

4. Drag the model that you found in step 3 onto the Find window. The name will be pasted in the search text box (see Figure 4.7).

5. Leave "contains" as the operator and modify the name to make it general enough for a search (in this case, I removed everything from the name except "16143").

Do it all at once

By the way, you don't have to choose one parameter at a time to extract search criteria. Find will extract whatever information from the model that is needed to match the attribute types that are in the window. For example, if you create a Finder window to search on creator, name, and date modified and then drag a model document onto it, all three fields will be filled in at once.

FIGURE 4.7

I completed this text search box by dragging the UsingMacCh02.doc file onto it.

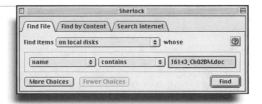

Mix and match

You can use the one-at-a-time approach to extract criteria from multiple documents also. There is no reason to limit yourself to a single model document.

6. Click the More Choices button.

7. Select creator from the Search Attribute pop-up menu.

8. Drag the model document onto the Find window again. This time, MSWD will be entered because the model file was created by Word (see Figure 4.8).

FIGURE 4.8

The Find command extracts whatever parameter you have selected in the pop-up menu from the model document; in this case, it extracted MSWD because the model document was created by Word.

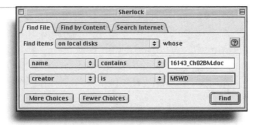

Using Find to determine the file type and creator for a file

Even using the Get Info command, you won't be able to see the file type and creator for a file. However, you can use the Find command to see this information. Simply open Find, open Search attribute of file type and creator, and drag the document onto the Find window. Easy as that, you will see the file type and creator for that document.

Graphics have no content

Note that the search by content only works on text files. You can't use it to search for graphics, even if the graphics contain text.

9. Click Find. The Items Found window will show all documents that meet your criteria.

Finding Files by Content

New to Mac OS 8.5, is the capability to find files by their content. This can be very useful when you know there are files on your Mac that contain certain information, but you can't remember anything about the files, such as their name or when they were created. This is also useful when you aren't sure that there are files on your Mac that contain specific information, but you want to find out.

Finding files by content

1. Choose Find from the Finder's File menu (or press Command-F) or choose Sherlock from the Apple Menu.

2. Click on the Find by Content tab. You will see the Find by Content dialog box (see Figure 4.9). The top pane is where you enter the text you want to search for. In the lower pane, you indicate on which volumes the search is to be done. You also initiate indexing with the controls in the bottom pane.

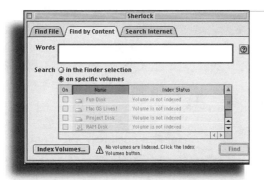

FIGURE 4.9

With Mac OS 8.5, you can search inside files to look for specific content.

Scheduling indexing

Note that you can also schedule indexes to be performed at convenient times, such as when you aren't using the Mac. Use the controls in the Index window to set indexing schedules for all of the volumes that you want to be able to search.

Indexing and multitasking

Indexing is a process that will run in the background. So if you need to index and work at the same time, simply start the index and let it run while you do your work. The index will take longer than it does if it is the only application running, but at least you won't be cooling your heels waiting for it to finish.

3. Before you can perform a Find by Content, you must index any volumes on which the search will be done. The indexing process enables your Mac to "read" all of the files and to build a list of words used in those files. By doing so, it can then tell you which files contain specific words.

4. To index a volume, click Index Volumes.

5. In the Index window, highlight the volumes you want to index (you can tell if a volume is indexed by looking at the Index Status column).

6. Click Create Index. You will see a dialog box warning you that indexing can take a long time; click Create to index a volume. You will see the Indexing Progress window as the Mac indexes all of the files on that volume (see Figure 4.10).

FIGURE 4.10

Indexing a volume can take quite a while so only index those volumes that you need to search.

Indexes aren't forever

Remember that as you add new files to volumes and modify the files that are already there, the index will become out-of-date (you can check an index's date by looking at the Index Status column in the Index dialog). In order to be able to accurately search the volumes, you will need to re-create the index. If you use Find by Content often, you should definitely set up scheduled indexes so that your indexes will always be current.

7. When the index is complete, close the Index dialog.

8. Enter the words or phrases that you want to search for in the Words box. You can use so-called Boolean operators to enter search strings (such as "and" or "or") to attempt to limit the results of your search.

9. Choose the indexed volumes that you want to search on by clicking the On boxes next to those volumes (if a volume isn't indexed, you won't be able to search it).

10. Click Find. In a moment or two, you will see the Items Found window (see Figure 4.11). This window works just like it does for a Find File search except that the files are sorted by the relevance of the search term in the file. For example, a document that contains exactly the same text as your search criteria should rank high on the relevance scale and is your best bet to begin looking for the content.

FIGURE 4.11

The Items Found window shows the files that contain the search text and also ranks them by relevance to it.

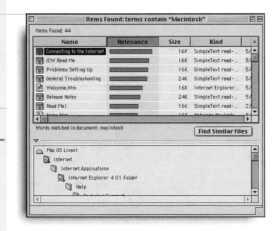

Nobody is perfect

While the Find by Content command is useful, it isn't perfect. You still have to open the files and look for the text. Sometimes you won't even understand why the Mac lists a particular file at all. Still, you will probably end up with what you are trying to find a lot faster than if you arbitrarily opened and closed files.

Drag and drop

As in any of the Items Found windows, you can use files in the Items Found window just like you can in Finder windows. For example, to move an item, simply drag it from the Items Found window to a disk. To open an item, double-click it. To delete it, drag it into the Trash.

11. Open the files and look for the text for which you searched.

12. If you are likely to want to perform this search again, save it by choosing Save Search Criteria from the File menu.

13. When you are done with the find, close the window or press Command-Q to quit.

Finding Information on the Internet

The integration of the Internet onto the Mac is continuing with Mac OS 8.5—you can now use the Sherlock command to search for information on the Internet.

SEE ALSO

➤ *To learn how to connect your Mac to the Net, see Chapter 23, "Connecting Your Mac to the Net."*

➤ *To learn about searching the Web with a Web browser, see page 639*

Using Sherlock to search the Internet

1. From the Finder, press Command-F.

2. Click the Search Internet tab. You will see the Search Internet dialog box (see Figure 4.12).

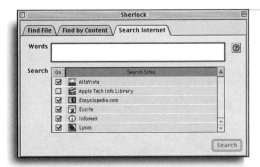

To search the Net

In order to use the Search the Internet feature, you need to have your Mac configured for Net access. See Chapter 23, "Connecting Your Mac to the Net" for help with this.

FIGURE 4.12

This Sherlock feature will search on the checked Web sites for text containing contextual and menus.

3. In the Terms box, enter the text for which you want to search. Again, you can use Boolean expressions in your text strings.

4. In the lower pane, select the sources you want to search by clicking the box next to each source you want to use (see Figure 4.13).

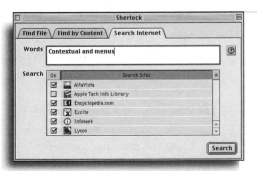

Searching the Web

When you use Find to search the Internet, you are actually searching the Internet via various search sites. You will learn more about these sites in Chapter 27, "Browsing the Web: Advanced Techniques."

FIGURE 4.13

This will look for text containing contextual and menus on the checked Internet search sites.

Drag and drop

As in any of the Items Found windows, you can use files in the Items Found window just like you can in Finder windows. For example, to move an item, simply drag it from the Items Found window to a disk. To open an item, double-click it. To delete it, drag it into the Trash.

5. Connect to the Net by using Remote Access Status (if you have configured your Mac so that it can connect automatically, you can skip this step).

SEE ALSO

➤ *To learn how to configure your Mac for automatic Net connections, see page 534*

6. Click Search. Your Mac will conduct the search. When it is done, you will see a results window similar to the one you saw for a content search. Click on an item to see how relevant it is and to see a link to that information (see Figure 4.14).

FIGURE 4.14

The Items Found window lists all of the information that your Mac found on the sites you selected.

1 Click this link to read the information

2 Internet address of the information

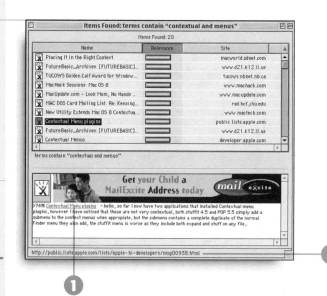

Viva Sherlock!

Mac OS 8.5's capability to search the Net is an excellent feature. It prevents you from having to open a Web browser and moving to specific search sites; you can do your search right from the Mac's desktop. As you conduct lots of Net searches, you will find that Sherlock is a very useful tool.

Saving searches

Remember that you can save your searches. Once you do, you can rerun the search easily. This is useful if you need to periodically look for information on the same topics.

7. Click the link in the lower pane to move to the information that you found (see Figure 4.15).

8. Read the information.

9. Move back to the Items Found window by choosing Sherlock from the Application menu.

10. Refine your search or click on another document link to move there.

11. When you are done, quit Sherlock (if you configure your connection to automatically disconnect after a specified time, you can skip this step).

12. Use Remote Access Status to disconnect from the Net.

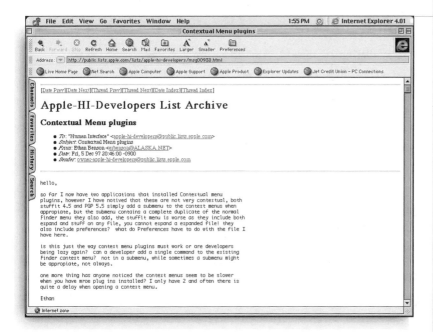

FIGURE 4.15
Clicking on the document link causes Internet Explorer to open on the document that you found in your search.

Working with Aliases

Aliases are a great tool you can use to organize and customize your Mac. An alias is simply a pointer to a file, folder, or volume. Double-click an alias or open it, and the item opens. Aliases are very small, so you can stash them all over your Mac with little storage penalty. Aliases enable you to easily access files, folders, and volumes from the Apple menu, the desktop, within folders, and so on.

The benefit of using an alias, rather than using an item itself, is that you can have multiple aliases that point to the same item, and you can leave the original item where it should reside. For example, you wouldn't want to store a copy of Microsoft Excel in your Apple Menu Items folder in order to be able to access it from the Apple menu. Excel needs several other support files that reside in its folder and moving it to the Apple menu would cause it to be unable to use those files. Instead, you can place an alias of the Excel application on the Apple menu. You could also place another alias to Excel on your desktop.

Alias trivia

While aliases seem like they have always been part of the Mac OS, they weren't introduced to the Mac until System 7. Before that, there was no way to access a file from multiple locations.

Broken aliases

Your Mac will track a file through its alias if you move the original file, and even if you rename it. However, if the file is no longer accessible by your Mac, if you delete it for example, then the alias will be "broken." When you click on a broken alias, you will see a dialog warning you that the original item for that alias cannot be found. Unfortunately, your Mac won't automatically remove aliases for which the original files have been removed from your Mac. You have to do this yourself or use an add-on utility.

Creating an Alias

Creating an alias for any file is simple.

Creating an alias

1. Select the item for which you want to create an alias.

2. Press Command-M. You will see another item with the same name as the original except that the word "alias" has been appended to it and the file name is in italics (see Figure 4.16).

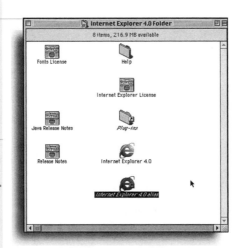

FIGURE 4.16

An alias to Internet Explorer has been created. You can tell that it is an alias because of the word "alias," the file name being in italics, and the arrow in the white box in the icon.

Other ways to create aliases

You can create an alias through the contextual menu. To do so, select a file, press Control, and click the mouse button. Choose Make Alias from the contextual menu.

You can also create an alias by holding the Option and Command keys down while you drag the file for which you want to create an alias. This is especially useful if you want the alias in a different location than the original, which is, of course, almost every time that you want an alias.

Renaming aliases

Just because the Mac tacked the word "alias" onto the end of the alias' file name, there is no reason it has to stay there. You can rename the alias anything you would like—even the same name as the original. The italics help you keep it straight; the Mac always knows which is which.

3. Drag the alias to a convenient location; make as many copies as you need. When you want to access the item, open an alias.

Finding an Original for an Alias

Occasionally, you need to find the original from which an alias was created. This is not hard to do.

Finding the file from which an alias was created

1. Select the alias.

2. Choose Show Original or press Command-R. You will see the original, even if it is deeply buried in layers of folders.

Setting and Using Favorites

Another feature new to Mac OS 8.5 is the addition of favorites to many items. Favorites enable you to quickly and easily move to your favorite items, whether they are files, folders, volumes, servers, and of course, Internet sites. Favorites are similar to aliases in that a favorite is simply a pointer to the original item. When you select a favorite from the Favorites menu, you move to the original item.

Your favorites are stored in the Favorites folder that is in the System Folder. You can access your favorites from the Apple menu, Network Browser, and any Open or Save dialog that uses Mac OS 8.5's new Navigation Services dialog..

When you add something to your favorites, an alias to that item is placed in the Favorites folder. And you can access it through any of the locations listed in the previous paragraph.

You will see Favorites menus in many areas of your Mac, including on the Apple menu (see Figure 4.17).

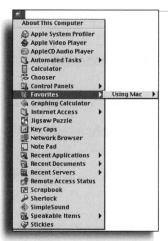

Finding the original with contextual menus

You can also point to an original, hold down the Control key, and select Show Original from the contextual menu.

Favorites equal bookmarks, almost

Favorites are similar to Favorites in the Internet Explorer and Bookmarks in Netscape Navigator Web browsers. You will learn about Web browser favorites in Chapter 27, "Browsing the Web: Advanced Techniques."

FIGURE 4.17

The Favorites folder appears on the Apple menu.

Setting Favorites

As with aliases, there are several ways to add items to your Favorites menu.

Another way to add a favorite

You can also add a favorite to an item by selecting in and choosing Add to Favorites from the Finder's File menu..

Setting Favorite folders

1. Select the item that you want to add to your Favorites folder.

2. Hold down the Control key, click, and choose Add to Favorites from the contextual menu (see Figure 4.18).

FIGURE 4.18

The Photos folder is selected; the Add to Favorites command will add a favorite to this folder in the Favorites folder.

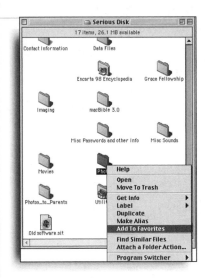

Yet another way

You can also add a favorite to an item by selecting it and clicking the Favorites button from within any Navigation Services dialog (you will see an example of such a dialog in the next section).

Using Favorites

Using favorites is simply a matter of choosing the favorite from one of the locations from which you can access favorites.

Using Favorites on the Apple menu to quickly move to a folder

1. From the Apple menu, choose Favorites.

2. Use the hierarchical menu to select the item that you want to open (see Figure 4.19).

If an application uses Mac OS 8.5's Navigation Services dialog, you can also access your favorites from within Save and Open dialogs.

SEE ALSO

➤ *To learn more about Mac OS 8.5 Navigation Services, see page 263*

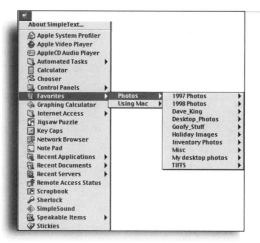

FIGURE 4.19

The Photos folder was added to my Favorites folder and thus can be quickly accessed via the Apple menu.

Using a Navigation Services dialog to access favorites

1. From within an application that uses Navigation Services dialogs (one example is the Appearance control panel), open a file. You will see the Navigation Service's Choose a File (this replaces the standard Open dialog) dialog.

2. Click the Favorites button and choose your favorite from the pop-up menu (see Figure 4.20). If your favorite is a folder, then you will see its contents in the window (which works like a folder window in the Finder). If it is a file, that file will be selected, and you can click Choose to open it.

Navigation Services and Favorites

You can use the Favorites button in any application or dialog that uses Navigation Services, which is new to Mac OS 8.5. Many of the applications that came as part of Mac OS 8.5 (such as Sherlock) use these dialogs. As Apple and other third-party applications are updated, they will also be able to use Navigation Services. So remember that whenever you see a Choose a File or the Navigation Services Save dialog, you can use your favorites.

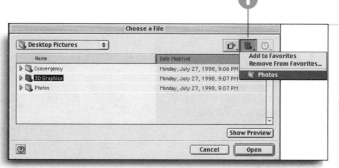

FIGURE 4.20

You can use the Favorites button to quickly access anything that is stored in your Favorites folder.

❶ Favorites button

Setting Finder Preferences

You can set the Finder to work the way you want it to work by setting certain preferences. Using the Preferences on the Finder's Edit menu, there are three categories of preferences that you can set. These are the following:

- **General**. These include Simple Finder and spring-loaded folder controls.
- **Views**. The Views preferences determine how items will appear within folders and volumes as well as on the desktop.
- **Labels**. The Labels preferences enable you to change the labels that you can apply to items in the Finder.

SEE ALSO

➤ *To learn how to set the spring-loaded folder preference, see page 61*

➤ *To learn how to set Views preferences, see page 52*

➤ *To learn how to work with labels, see page 47*

You can also set some general Finder preferences by using the General Controls control panel.

Setting general Finder preferences

1. Choose Preferences from the Edit menu. You will see the Preferences dialog (see Figure 4.21).

Edit menu

The Preferences are the only item on the Finder's Edit menu covered in this chapter. The rest of the Edit commands are pretty basic.

FIGURE 4.21

The Finder Preferences dialog enables you to set General, View, and Label preferences.

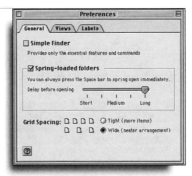

2. Click the General tab so that you can see the options in Figure 4.21.

3. To activate Simple Finder, click the Simple Finder box. However, since Simple Finder reduces the Finder commands that you can use; you should leave this box unchecked unless you are extremely new to the Mac.

4. Close the Finder preferences window.

5. Open the General Controls control panel.

6. Check the Show Desktop when in background if you don't want to see the desktop "behind" the application in which you are working. Seeing the desktop in this way can be confusing to someone new to multitasking and this control provides a way to make it slightly less so.

7. Check the Launcher at system startup box if you want the Launcher to open when your systems starts up.

8. Check the "Warn me if computer was shut down improperly" check box if you want this warning to appear. The Mac tracks how you shut it down. If you turn it off in some way other than using the Shut Down command, the Finder presents a warning dialog explaining that you should use the Shut Down command.

9. Use the Folder Protection controls to prevent changes to the System Folder or to the Applications folder. Checking the check boxes locks those folders so that their contents cannot be changed.

10. Use the Insertion Point Blinking radio buttons to adjust the speed at which the insertion point blinks.

11. Use the Menu Blinking radio buttons to set the number of times that the highlight flashes when you select a command from a menu.

12. Use the Documents radio buttons to determine where the Finder takes you when you open or save a document from inside an application. Your choices are the following: the folder set by the application, the last folder used when you worked in the application, or the Documents folder.

13. Close the General Controls control panel.

Why use Simple Finder?

Simple Finder is supposed to reduce the confusion of using a computer for new users. When Simple Finder is active, the commands listed on the Finder menus are greatly reduced. For example, with Simple Finder, you can't use pop-up windows because the View menu does not have the Pop-up Window command. (If you have pop-up windows open and then switch to Simple Finder, all of the pop-up windows will be converted to regular windows.)

Launcher?

The Launcher is a palette of buttons for your favorite applications or documents. You can click a button to open the related file. The items in the Launcher Items folder in the System Folder are what appear on the Launcher's palette. The Finder's Button view has rendered the Launcher pretty much obsolete. Nonetheless, you can still use it if you want to.

Improper shut down warning

New to Mac OS 8.5, the Mac does more than just tell you that your Mac was shut down improperly. It now runs Disk First Aid the first time you start your Mac after an improper shutdown. Disk First Aid checks for possible damage to your disks caused by the improper shut down. If damage is detected, Disk First Aid will try to repair it before your Mac starts up. While you can cancel this check, it is a better idea to let Disk First Aid do its job.

Telling Time with the Clock

The Finder provides you with a basic clock in its menu bar (see Figure 4.22). You can click on the time to see the current date. You control the clock with the Date & Time control panel.

FIGURE 4.22

You can use the clock to see the current time and date.

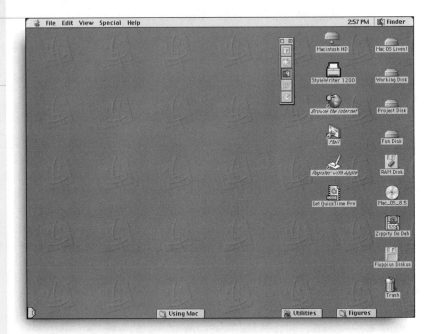

This clock is super

The Mac's clock is based on an old system extension called *SuperClock*. Apple liked it so much that it integrated the clock into the Mac OS.

A new feature for Mac OS 8.5 is the capability to use a Network Time Server to automatically ensure that your clock is synchronized to a time standard that you choose.

Configuring the clock

1. Open the Date & Time control panel (see Figure 4.23).

2. Use the Current Date and Current Time boxes and Format buttons to set the current time and date and the format in which you want these items displayed.

3. Use the Time Zone controls to set the daylight savings options for your area. You can choose a time zone with the Set Time Zone button.

FIGURE 4.23

The Date & Time control panel provides lots of options for your clock, including synchronization with a network server, chimes, and various display options.

4. Check the "Use a Network Server" check box to set your clock by a "standard" clock used on a network server. (See the following step-by-step for details.)

5. You can turn off the clock with Menu Bar Clock radio buttons.

6. Click the Clock Options button to move to set various format options for the clock display (such as the color), as well as Chime Settings (see Figure 4.24). You can also set the font and size that the clock uses.

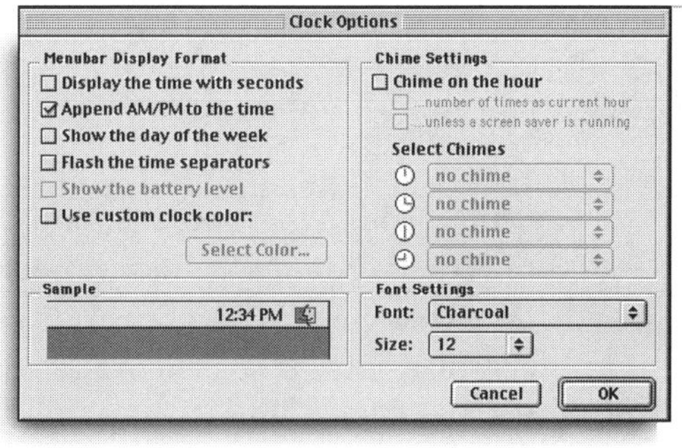

FIGURE 4.24

The Clock Options dialog provides many controls so that you can tweak the clock to your heart's content.

7. Close the Date & Time control panel.

In order to keep your clock synchronized with another clock, presumably a more accurate one, you can set a network time server as your time reference.

Using a Network Time Server

1. Open the Time & Date control panel.

2. Check the "Use a Network Time Server" check box.

3. Click Server Options. You will see the Server Options dialog (see Figure 4.25)."

FIGURE 4.25

The Server Options dialog enables you to select a Time Server to which you can synchronize your Mac's clock.

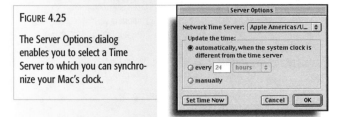

4. Choose the Time Server that you want to use as your time standard from the Network Time Server pop-up menu; Apple provides several for you to use (see Figure 4.26).

FIGURE 4.26

You can choose your Network Time Server from this pop-up menu..

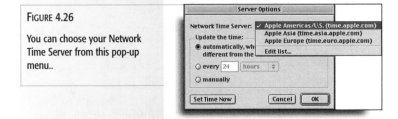

Your own Network Time Server

If you choose Edit List from the Network Time Server pop-up menu, you can add your own Network Time Server to the pop-up menu. You can also edit or remove any that are already listed there.

5. Set the option that you want to use to update the time. You can choose automatically, set a specific interval, or manually. If you choose anything but manually, your Mac will synchronize itself. If you choose manually, you have to use the Set Time Now button.

6. Click Set Time Now to synchronize your Mac's time with the Network Time Server. If your Network Time Server is on the Internet and you need to use a modem to connect to it, your Mac has to dial out and connect to the server before it can update the time. If you haven't configured your Mac for automatic connections to the Internet, you will need to connect to the Internet before you click the Set Time Now button.

7. Click OK to close the Server Options dialog.

8. Close the Date & Time control panel.

Taking Out the Trash

One of the most recognizable features of the Mac is the Trash. Ever since the first Mac was introduced, the Trash has been a part of the Mac experience. The Trash is actually a special folder on your Mac that has certain unique features, those being that you can delete files by placing them in the Trash and then emptying it, and unmounting a network volumes and ejecting disks by dragging them there.

The Trash is pretty easy to work with. Here are some things to keep in mind when working with the Trash:

- If the warning when you empty the Trash annoys you (like it does me), you can turn it off. Select the Trash, press Command-I, and uncheck the "Warn before emptying" check box (see Figure 4.27). The next time you empty the Trash, it will be emptied immediately.

Test

If you don't see any difference in time when you tell your Mac to Set Time Now, it may be that your clock is already synchronized with your Network Time Server. To test your configuration, change your Mac's time so that it is wrong. Then try synchronizing your Mac to the Network Time Server. If you have used a valid Network Time Server, the time on your Mac will be updated.

FIGURE 4.27

If you uncheck the "Warn before emptying" check box, you won't see the annoying warning every time you empty the Trash.

The Mac is intuitive, but…

Once you learn that you can eject a disk a dragging it to the Trash, you don't have trouble with the idea. But it is far from intuitive to do this. Why would anyone think that dragging a disk to the Trash would do anything other than deleting the files on it? I am not sure how this idea became part of the Mac, but it sure is contrary to how intuitive the rest of the Mac is. I guess no one, or no computer, is perfect.

- There are lots of ways to move things into the Trash. You can drag something there. You can select a file or folder and press Command-delete. You can select a file or folder, press Control, click the mouse button, and choose Move to Trash from the contextual menu.

- If you try to Empty the Trash when it contains something that is locked, you will see a dialog box telling you that the locked item can't be deleted. Hold Option while you choose Empty Trash to delete locked items.

- There are also a couple of ways to empty the Trash. One is to select Empty Trash from the Special menu. You can also select the Trash and use the contextual menu to choose Empty Trash.

SEE ALSO

➤ *To learn how to add a keyboard shortcut to empty the Trash, see page 373*

Saving Energy

There are a couple of reasons that you might want to use the energy saving features of your Mac. The most obvious is to reduce the energy that your Mac uses while you are not using it. Another reason is to prevent screen burn-in. Setting your Mac to save energy is simple.

SEE ALSO

➤ *To learn about using energy saving features as part of power management for a PowerBook, see page 818*

Configuring energy saving on a desktop Mac

1. Open the Energy Saver control panel and click Show Details. The window will open to show more options (see Figure 4.28). (Before you customize the energy saver for your Mac, you will see an information dialog when you open Energy Saver. Just click Specify Settings to open the control panel.)

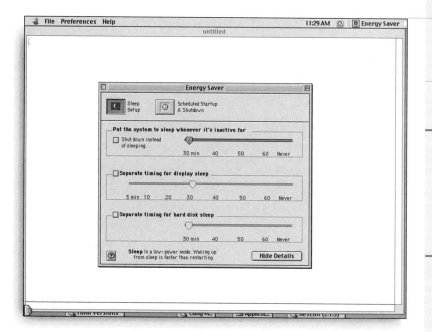

FIGURE 4.28

The Energy control panel makes your Mac politically correct.

Sleep time

If you want the monitor and hard disk to sleep after the same interval, use the top slider and do not check the "Separate timing" check boxes. You can click the Hide Details button to show only one slider.

System sleep

You can't have the hard disk sleep set for less time than the system sleep. If you try to drag the hard disk sleep slider and it doesn't move, drag the system sleep slider to a larger interval.

System shutdown

If you click the "Shut down instead of sleeping" check box, your Mac will turn itself off instead of going to sleep.

Automatic startup and shutdown

If you click the Scheduled Startup & Shutdown button, you can set the times at which your Mac will start itself and shut itself down. This only works for Macs that do not have a "hard" power switch. If your Mac has a hard power switch, you won't be able to see this feature. See Chapter 17, "Making Your Mac Do Your Work For You," for details.

2. You can set a different period of inactivity before the sleep mode activates for the hard disk and monitor. To do so, check the "Separate timing for display sleep" and "Separate timing for hard disk sleep" check boxes.

3. Use the sliders to set the time period after which you want the Mac to go to sleep.

4. Close the control panel. After the specified intervals of inactivity have passed, your Mac will put itself to sleep.

Using the energy saving features of your Mac is more important if you use a PowerBook running on batteries, but since it is easy to configure on a desktop Mac, there is really no reason not to use it. You will save some money in electric bills, protect your monitor from burn-in, and you might even increase the life on some of your Mac's components.

CHAPTER

5

Working with Hard Disks, Partitions, and Volumes

Understanding important hard drive terminology

Initializing and partitioning hard drives

Mounting volumes

Understanding Hard Drives, Volumes, and Partitions

Your Mac's hard drives provide most of the data storage space for your system, and in most situations, a hard drive also contains your system software. Working with hard drives is relatively straightforward, but there is some terminology you need to know, and there are a couple of tasks that you need to be able to do. This chapter begins by explaining the terminology and finishes with the two tasks, which are initializing a drive and mounting volumes.

Understanding Drive Terminology

When working with hard drives, or other kinds of drives for that matter, you need to understand the following terms:

SCSI vs. IDE

In the past, Macs have used two types of hard drives. Small Computer Serial Interface (SCSI, pronounced like something is dirty or scuzzy) was the original protocol that Macs used to communicate with hard drives. Over the years, SCSI has been refined and improved just like other Mac technologies. The benefits of SCSI drives are that they perform better than some other drive technologies. The disadvantage of SCSI drives is that they are more expensive than drives that use other technologies.

In order to reduce the cost of Macs, Apple began using the drive format that is standard on the PC, which is called *Integrated Drive Electronics* or IDE. While this drive format doesn't perform as well as SCSI drives do, it is a lot less expensive and Apple felt that for certain Macs (the low- to mid-range models), IDE made sense.

- **Hard drive**. A hard drive is a fixed media drive, that is the platter on which data is stored within the drive and can't be removed (as opposed to floppy and other removable media drives). You can have one or more hard drives *mounted* on your desktop.

  In the computer world, mounting a drive means to have it available for use. Connecting a hard drive to your Mac is not the same thing as mounting it. In order to mount a drive, you must first connect it to your Mac and then *initialize* it, which means that you'll run software that properly formats the drive. After that is done, you will see the disk on your desktop and, thus, it is mounted.

- **Volume**. Technically, a *volume* is what you actually mount on your desktop. A volume is simply a "space" in which you can write data or from which you can read data. Volumes are not physical entities, but are rather electronic constructs that are maintained by the computers that use them. A hard drive can be a volume, and a network drive on which you have space is also a volume. Also, a single drive can be *partitioned* into multiple volumes.

- **Partition**. Multiple volumes can be created on a single physical drive by partitioning the drive. When you partition a drive, the computer carves out an electronic space on that drive that is capable of storing a specific amount of data. A partition is also called a *volume*.

There are several reasons that you might want to partition a single drive into one or more volumes. One reason is that because of the way the Mac's file structure (under the "regular *Hierarchical File Structure* which you will learn about later in this chapter) works, a smaller volume is more efficient than a larger one. The Mac allocates a certain number of fixed *blocks* in which it stores data. The size of these blocks is related to the size of a volume. The larger the volume, the larger the blocks will be. Since blocks can't contain data from different files, there are lots of partially filled blocks on a disk. The larger these blocks are, the larger the "wasted" space on a volume is. If you partition a large drive into a couple of partitions, it will store files more efficiently, and you will be able to store more data on your system.

The structure that your Mac uses to store data on its disks is called the *Hierarchical File Structure*, or *HFS*. Since Mac OS 8.1, your Mac has also been able to use HFS+. HFS+ does a couple of things for you. First, it eliminates the storage penalty you pay when you have very large volume sizes (the block problem I described earlier). Second, HFS+ enables you to access very large disks. However, in order to use HFS+, a drive has to be reformatted (which you will learn how to do in the next section). And many disk utilities are not yet compatible with HFS+.

Another reason you may want to partition a drive is for organizing purposes. You may want one volume for your applications and system software, another for documents, and yet another for games.

A third reason to partition a drive is that having a drive partitioned makes it easier to do maintenance on the individual volumes.

SEE ALSO

➤ *To learn about maintaining hard drives, see page 714*

Now, USB

For external drives and other peripherals, all Macs used SCSI formats. Until the upcoming iMac. The iMac uses a new interface format called *Universal Serial Bus*, or USB. USB will eventually replace the SCSI interface format on low-end Macs, as well as the Apple Desktop Bus and the serial ports on all Macs. Eventually, the only ports you'll have on a low-end or mid-range Mac will be USB and all your peripherals will plug into the same kind of port. The system will determine what kind of device it is and will work with it accordingly.

For the next year or two, though, SCSI ports will still be included on most Macs. And with such a large installed base of SCSI peripherals, there will be no shortage of support for SCSI devices.

PCs and SCSI

By the way, Windows computers can also use SCSI drives, although they require that a SCSI controller be added to the machine to enable it to recognize the SCSI interface. Most PCs offer SCSI drives as a high-end option.

FireWire

Another communication technology that is beginning to be widely used is called *FireWire*. FireWire is a very high-speed connection technology that is used for data-intense media, such as digital video and other technologies, where it is necessary to move large amounts of data at a high rate of speed. In order to use FireWire, you have to add a FireWire card to your Mac and install the appropriate system software (which is included in Mac OS 8.5 in the Apple Extras folder).

Get on the bus

When talking about SCSI or IDE drives, you will hear the term *bus*. Bus refers to the interface to which devices are attached in order to be able to communicate with the rest of your Mac. You can have more than one bus. For example, some Mac models have an internal SCSI bus that is separate from the external one.

Initializing and Partitioning a Hard Drive

After a drive is installed on your Mac, you need to prepare it for use by initializing and partitioning it (even if you choose to create one volume on it, you still are partitioning it, just with a single volume rather than more than one). You may want to initialize and partition a disk simply to reorganize it. If you are having trouble with a disk and can't fix its problems with less extreme measures, you may have to initialize it to clear its errors. Before you read into the step-by-step, though, I need to cover four important caveats.

The first caveat is that the hard drive must be connected to or installed in your Mac and properly configured for the SCSI or IDE bus. If you have ever used the drive, you know that this disk is properly installed (or at least that it was at one point). If you are installing a new internal hard drive or replacing a current one, make sure that you follow the instructions for your particular Mac model, as well as the instructions that came with the drive.

The second caveat is that before you can initialize and partition the drive on which your system software is located, you need to have another valid startup disk that you can use to start your machine. This may be another hard disk, a Zip disk, or a CD-ROM. Be aware that your hard disk may be partitioned already and your startup disk may actually be a volume on the same disk as the volume that you need to initialize.

SEE ALSO

➤ *To learn the details on finding and using alternate startup disks, see page 740*

The third, and perhaps most important, caveat is that initializing and partitioning a disk **destroys all the data on that disk**. If you are going to initialize and partition a disk that you currently use, you must back up the data before doing so. Because it will all be gone once you do!

SEE ALSO

➤ *To learn about backing up, see Chapter 29, "Backing Up"*

Finally, recognize that there are some down sides to partitioning a drive. The first is that you cannot change the size of a partition without erasing all the data on the *disk* on which the partition lives. If you create partitions that are too small, you will have to go through the entire process again to create larger partitions. For example, if you are going to create a CD-ROM, you might need a partition larger than 650 MB; in fact, it may need to be quite a bit larger to hold the working files you need to create the CD. If your largest partition isn't big enough, you have to go back through the initialization process, which isn't a lot of fun. The same thing can happen if you use partitions to organize your drives. If you create partitions that are too small, you may find yourself violating your organization because your partitions aren't large enough to store all of the files you need to use for your organizational scheme (if you had an application partition that wasn't large enough to store all of your applications, for example).

Initializing and partitioning a hard drive by using Apple's Drive Setup

1. Back up all of the data you want to save on **all volumes** on the disk you are going to initialize and partition.

2. If the disk you are going to initialize contains your system software, restart your Mac by using an alternate startup disk.

SEE ALSO

➤ *To learn about restarting your Mac from an alternate startup disk, see page 740*

3. Copy Drive Setup and the Drive Setup Guide (they are located in the Utilities folder on the disk you installed Mac OS 8.2 on) onto the startup disk that you are using.

4. Launch Drive Setup (make sure that you are not using a copy that is on the disk you are initializing). You will see the Drive Setup window (see Figure 5.1). Drive Setup will look for all the drives available on your system, and they will be listed in the window. Note that you may see some drives that you cannot initialize, such as the CD-ROM drive and Zip drives. These are marked with < >. You can also see the

---

Audio and video

Be particularly careful with the size of your partitions if you plan to work with digital audio and video. These kinds of files are huge and having partitions that are too small may hamper your capability to work with larger audio and video files.

Disks and volumes

How do you tell which partitions are on which disk? Use the Apple System Profiler that is on the Apple menu. When the Profiler is open, click the Devices and Volumes tab. Your Mac will scan your system. When it is finished, you will see a bus and drive tree diagram that shows each disk and all of the partitions on that disk.

Using non-Apple drives

Some non-Apple drives are not compatible with Drive Setup. If you use a third-party drive, make sure that it is compatible with Drive Setup before you try to initialize (you can launch Drive Setup and see if it recognizes the drive or you can check with the drive's manufacturer).

If Drive Setup is not compatible with your drive, then you will need a third-party drive utility such as FWB's Hard Disk Toolkit. Hard Disk Toolkit has long reigned as the supreme disk formatting utility, and it will serve you well if you need it.

Drive Setup Guide

If AppleGuide is not part of your alternate startup disk's system software, the Drive Setup Guide won't work so there is no need to copy it over. You can determine if AppleGuide is installed when you create your alternate startup disk.

bus and ID numbers of all of the drives connected to your system. If you don't see a drive in this window, that means that it isn't installed properly. You have to go back and correct the installation problems before you can use the drive.

FIGURE 5.1

Drive Setup enables you to initial-ize and partition a hard drive.

Get some guidance

Drive Setup comes with a very nice AppleGuide. To get information beyond what this chapter provides, press Command+? to use the Drive Setup Guide.

5. Select the drive that you want to initialize and partition. If it is ready to be initialized and partitioned, you will see a message saying so in the bottom of the window (see Figure 5.1). If not, the software will tell you what needs to be done to make it ready.

6. If you are **sure** that you don't need any data on this drive, click Initialize. You will see the Initialize dialog (see Figure 5.2).

FIGURE 5.2

From the Initialize dialog, you can see that I wasn't kidding about all the data on the disk being destroyed.

7. Click Custom Setup. You will see the Custom Setup dialog (see Figure 5.3). You can see the disk's current name at the top of the window. Just under the Partitioning Scheme pop-up menu, you can see the capacity of the disk.

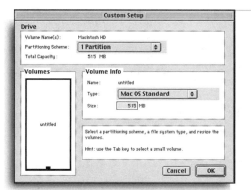

FIGURE 5.3

The Custom Setup dialog is where you define the size of the partitions on the disk.

8. Choose the number of partitions that you want on this disk from the Partitioning Scheme pop-up menu (see Figure 5.4). In the Volumes area, you will see a graphical representation of the volumes with the partitions applied.

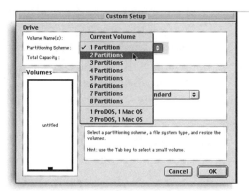

FIGURE 5.4

I chose to make two partitions on this drive.

How many partitions?

While I can't tell you how many partitions you should set up, I can give you some general guidelines. Unless you have a very specific purpose in mind or are working with a small disk, I wouldn't create any partitions smaller than 500 MB. That isn't very large in this day and age. For a 2 GB disk, that means 4 partitions. However, you may want to have a large partition for your applications (750 MB or more), a smaller one for your system software (500 MB), and another large one for your data (750 MB). For a larger disk, you may want larger partitions or to add another partition for games and other nonessential files..

In any case, I'd suggest that you don't create more than 5 partitions on a single disk unless it is extremely large. After a certain point, more partitions become more confusing rather than less.

9. Choose the type of partition that you want from the Type pop-up menu. You have four choices: Mac OS Standard, Mac OS Extended, ProDos, or Unallocated.

10. Enter the size of the partition in the Size box or use the graphical representation of the volumes to adjust the size (drag the handle on the black box around the partition). When you are done, you will see the completed dialog, and you are ready to initialize the disk (see Figure 5.5).

FIGURE 5.5

In this case, I am partitioning a 500 MB drive into a 300 MB volume and a 200 MB volume (this is a small disk in a PowerBook, normally I wouldn't recommend any partitions less than 500 MB).

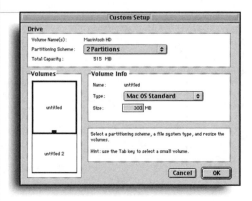

More on partition types

Mac OS Standard uses the Mac's original filing structure, HFS. Mac OS Extended uses HFS+, which is a more modern structure that stores files more efficiently (you can store more data on the same size volume). (I will ignore the other two options: ProDos or Unallocated. If you want one of those, you already know what you are doing!)

The Mac OS Extended (HFS+) type was introduced with Mac OS 8.1, but as of this writing, there are still a lot of disk utilities that are not compatible with it. Also, if you share the drive with others, and they don't have 8.1 or later, they won't be able to mount the drive if you choose HFS+. So if you have an incompatible disk utility such as Norton Utilities for Macintosh version 3.5 or you need to move the disk to other Macs, use Mac OS Standard. If you don't have any incompatible utilities and you are the only one using the drive, choose Mac OS Extended. I am using Mac OS Standard for this example.

Low-level format

There are "levels" of formatting that you can do on a hard drive. Low-level formatting is the most severe, and it recreates the entire data structure of the drive. You normally only use this level when you originally install a disk or when a disk is not working properly. Low-level formats can take a long time.

11. Click OK.

12. In the Initialize dialog, click Initialize if you are sure you want to continue. You will see the Drive Setup window again, and you can see the progress of the initialization and partitioning. If the drive is large and requires a low-level format, this process will take a long time (it can take as much as an hour for a low level format of a 4.5 GB disk, for example). If the disk is small or it does not need a low level format, the process will be done fairly quickly. When it is complete, you will see the partitions listed at the bottom of the Drive Setup window (see Figure 5.6).

13. Quit Drive Setup. You will see the new volumes on your desktop (see Figure 5.7).

14. Select one of the volumes and press Return.

15. Name the volume and press Return.

16. Name the other volumes that you created. The volumes are now ready for your data. If you open them, you will see approximately the amount of free data that you specified for the partition.

FIGURE 5.6

The two partitions have been created (untitled and untitled 2 in the window).

FIGURE 5.7

The two as of yet unnamed volumes.

Mounting Volumes on the Desktop

To use a volume, it must be mounted on your desktop. If the volume is on a hard drive connected to your Mac and initialized, it will automatically be mounted when you start your machine.

If the drive is external, you need to have the power on for that drive before you start your Mac. When your Mac starts up, it scans all of the buses for ready-to-use drives and mounts those on your desktop. If you forget to turn the power on for an external drive, or an internal drive doesn't mount for some reason (this happens very rarely and usually only when you are messing around with alpha or beta software that does things it shouldn't), you can mount a drive and its volumes by using Drive Setup.

Mounting an external or internal drive with Drive Setup

1. Open Drive Setup. You will see a list of all drives on your system.

2. Choose the drive that you want to mount.

3. From the Functions menu, choose Mount Volumes. The volumes on the selected drive will be mounted on the desktop.

Drive overhead

You won't ever get exactly the size of the partition that you set; usually, it is just a tad smaller than what you asked the Mac to create. That is because the structure of the drive itself requires some data to store, thus reducing the amount of free space on that volume. Plus, there are some invisible files on every partition, and they take space to store.

If you want to mount a volume that is located on a server or shared disk to which you have access, you will need to use the Chooser or the Network Browser.

SEE ALSO

➤ *To learn more about using shared volumes, see page 465*

Mounting a volume that is located on a shared disk

1. Choose Chooser from the Apple menu.

2. Click AppleShare. You will see a list of available volumes in the right pane of the Chooser window (see Figure 5.8).

FIGURE 5.8

You can use the Chooser to select a shared volume to mount.

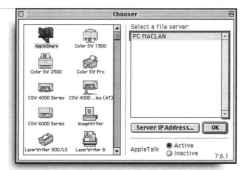

3. Select the volume that you want to mount.

4. Click OK. You will see the Connect to dialog that prompts you for your name and password (see Figure 5.9).

FIGURE 5.9

You can use the Chooser to mount shared volumes on your desktop; in this case, I am mounting a Windows PC disk on my Mac.

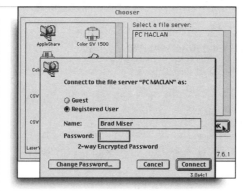

5. Enter your name and password, and then click Connect. You will see a dialog that asks you to choose the items that you want to use. You can also set the Chooser so that the volume is mounted every time that you start your Mac.

6. Click OK.

7. Close the Chooser. The volume will be mounted on your desktop.

You can also mount any drive that you can access on your network more quickly and easily with the Network Browser that is new for Mac OS 8.5. You will learn about the Network Browser in Chapter 21, "Working with Other Macs."

By the way...

You may notice that the server I am using in this example is called PC MACLAN. It is actually a PC running Miramar Systems' Personal MacLAN Connect software. This software enables you to network a PC on your Mac network so that you can share files, printers, and other system resources. If you need to network PCs and Macs together, be sure to check out this software. Miramar's Web site is at http://www.miramarsys.com/.

Working with the Apple Menu

Understanding the Apple menu

Using and customizing the Apple menu

Working with utilities and applications on the Apple menu

Don't see an Apple?

Some customization extensions (such as Kaleidoscope) can change the Apple icon into something different. Or you can change it yourself by using ResEdit. Nonetheless, the Apple menu is still there and works just the same, even if you don't see an apple.

Understanding the Apple Menu

The Apple menu enables you to access any folder, volume, file, or other item on your Mac quickly and easily. The Apple menu is easy to spot; it is always in the upper left corner of the screen no matter where you are working—in an application, on the desktop, in your System Folder, or wherever (see Figure 6.1). Because the Apple menu is always available to you, you can directly access any item that is located on it. Using the Apple menu can make you work with your Mac much more efficiently because you don't waste time moving down into layers of folders looking for a file to open. You just open the Apple menu and everything you need can be right at the tip of your mouse.

FIGURE 6.1

The ever-present Apple menu enables you to quickly access any file, folder, or volume.

About This Computer
Apple System Profiler
Apple Video Player
AppleCD Audio Player
Automated Tasks ▶
Calculator
Chooser
Control Panels ▶
Favorites ▶
Graphing Calculator
Internet Access ▶
Jigsaw Puzzle
Key Caps
Network Browser
Note Pad
Recent Applications ▶
Recent Documents ▶
Recent Servers ▶
Remote Access Status
Scrapbook
Sherlock
SimpleSound
Speakable Items ▶
Stickies

A standard Apple menu is available as soon as you install Mac OS 8.5. It provides quick access to some useful areas and files; it also contains some things that you aren't likely to use that much (don't worry about those, you'll learn how to get rid of them in a moment). In Figure 6.1, you can see that a variety of files, applications, folders, and other items are available to you on the standard Apple menu.

As with a lot of areas of the Mac OS, the real power of the Apple menu comes when you customize it to work the way you want it to. Customizing the Apple menu is easy to do, and in this chapter you'll learn how to do it.

Also notice that some of the items on the Apple menu have a black arrow pointing to the right. As you may know, this means that these are folders in the "hierarchical view" (see Figure 6.2). For example, when you put a folder (or an alias to it) in the Apple Menu Items folder, it becomes a hierarchical folder on the Apple menu. If you choose a folder in the hierarchical view, a menu will appear, providing you with more choices. It's a powerful feature because you can add your own folders to enable yourself to quickly access any item on your Mac.

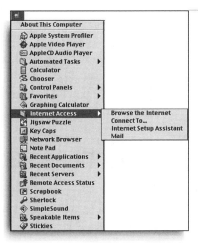

Another nice feature of the Apple menu is the Recent Items folders. These folders track the most recent applications, documents, and servers that you have accessed. You can use these to quickly return to something that you have used recently (you can set the number of items that are tracked).

There are also a number of useful applications and utilities on the Apple menu that you may find yourself using constantly.

The Apple menu is controlled by the following two items:

- **Apple Menu Items folder**. Any files or folders in the Apple Menu Items folder (that is within the System Folder) are what shows up on the Apple menu (see Figure 6.3). Put something in this folder, and it immediately appears on the menu. Take something out of the folder, and it is removed from the menu. It really is that easy.

Adding a project folder to the Apple menu

If you are working on a project that has lots of different folders and files associated with it, consider adding an alias pointing to that folder in the Apple menu. This will put all of your files and folders for that project in one spot, no matter where they are actually located on your Mac.

FIGURE 6.2

Folders on the Apple menu are hierarchical; you can easily access any item in that folder with a submenu.

FIGURE 6.3

The Apple Menu Items folder is located within the System Folder.

■ **Apple Menu Options control panel**. This control panel enables you to turn submenus on or off and to set the number of recently used items that are tracked.

This chapter has two main parts. In the next part, you'll learn how to customize the Apple menu to make it work for you. In the last part, you'll see how the applications and utilities on the Apple menu work.

Using and Customizing the Apple Menu

You can quickly access anything that is on the Apple menu, and since the Apple menu is available all the time, you can always access whatever you have located on it. Even better, customizing the Apple menu is as simple as moving files and folders into the Apple Menu Items folder.

Using the Apple Menu

Using the Apple menu options is as easy as it gets. Just open the menu and choose an item from it to open that item. A couple of short step-by-steps will make the process clear.

One of the most useful items on the Apple menu is the Control Panels folder. By using this, you can access any active control panel quickly and easily.

Using the Apple menu to open a control panel

1. Click the Apple menu icon.

2. Move your arrow to Control Panels. A list of all active control panels will appear.

Control panels on the Apple menu

The Control Panels folder that you see on the Apple menu is actually an alias to the real Control Panels folder that is in the System Folder. This is a great way to access any control panels that are active on your Mac.

3. Highlight the control panel that you want to open.

4. Click the mouse button. The control panel will open.

If you are like me, you will often find yourself reopening a document immediately after you closed it because you forgot to make a certain change. Or you may realize that you need to add some additional information to a document that you worked on a short time ago. Rather than maneuvering back to that file, which may be buried in layers of folders, you can "go back" to your recently used items through the Apple menu (see Figure 6.4). These items can be applications, documents, or shared volumes on a network.

Recent Items folders

Your Mac creates and maintains three recent items folders in the Apple Menu Items folder. There is one folder for each type of recent item (documents, applications, and servers).

FIGURE 6.4
The Recent Items folders, located in the Apple Menu Items folder, enable you to quickly access items that you have recently used.

Using the Apple Menu to open a recent document

1. Open the Apple menu.

2. Point to Recent Documents.

3. Choose a document from the submenu. The document will open.

Customizing the Apple Menu

The basic Apple menu is useful on its own, but the real power of it is that you can customize it to make it contain anything you want. In this section, you'll learn how to make the Apple menu what you want it to be.

Using the Apple Menu Control Panel

The basic settings of the Apple menu are controlled by the Apple menu control panel.

Using the Apple Menu Items control panel

1. Open the Apple menu.

2. Choose Control Panels; then from the submenu, choose Apple Menu Options. You will see the Apple Menu Options control panel (see Figure 6.5).

FIGURE 6.5

The Apple Menu Options control panel enables you to control sub-menus and to set the number of recent items tracked.

Submenus

If you turn submenus off, folders on the Apple menu will act just like regular folders. You will be able to select folders, and they will open, but you won't see their contents in the hierarchical view.

Removing recent items

If you set the number of recent items to zero in the Apple Menu control panel, the Recent Items folders will be removed from the Apple menu.

3. To turn the submenus off, click the Off radio button.

4. Enter the number of recent documents that you want to be available in the Documents box.

5. Enter the number of recent applications that you want to be available in the Applications box.

6. Enter the number of recent servers that you want to be available in the Servers box.

7. Close the control panel.

Adding Items to the Apple Menu

You can easily add items to the Apple menu by manually adding files or by using AppleScript.

Manually adding Items to the Apple Menu

1. To create an alias, select the item that you want to put on the Apple menu and press Command-M.

2. Drag the alias onto the System Folder icon (you may have to drag it across other folders on the way).

3. Wait for the System Folder to spring open and then drag the alias onto the Apple Menu Items folder and release the mouse button. You can now access the item by selecting its alias from the Apple menu.

Using an AppleScript to add something to the Apple menu

1. Select the item that you want to add to the Apple menu.

2. Open the Apple menu, select Automated Tasks, and choose Add Alias to Apple Menu. The script will run and add an alias to the Apple menu.

3. Open the Apple menu to make sure that you see the item you just added.

Removing Items from the Apple Menu

It is just as easy to remove items from the Apple menu as it is to add items to the menu.

Removing items from the Apple menu

1. Open the Apple Menu Items folder (choose it from the Apple menu if you placed an alias to it there).

2. Drag the item out of the folder.

3. Close the Apple Menu Items folder. The item will no longer appear on the Apple menu.

Organizing the Apple Menu

If you add more than a few items to the Apple menu, it can become cluttered, thus making things harder and slower to access. Plus, the menu may get so long that you need to scroll down it to see all of the items on it. Here are some things that you can do to keep your Apple menu organized:

How many recent items is enough?

That all depends on you and how far you want to go back in your list. The trade-off is screen real estate and the ease with which you can choose an item from one of the recent items menus. If you find yourself having a hard time locating something on a recent item menu because there are so many from which to choose, lower the number of recent items you are tracking. If you find that items are dropping off the menus too quickly, increase the number. Personally, I find about 20 for documents, 10 for applications, and 10 for servers works well, so you can use those settings as a starting point if you'd like.

Aliases and the Apple menu

It is almost always better to add aliases to the Apple menu than the actual item itself, especially if the item is not a document. You shouldn't clutter up the Apple Menu Items folder (which is in the System Folder, remember) with a bunch of big files and folders.

What's in a name?

You might want to rename the alias (at least to dump the word alias) so that it makes more sense and the Apple menu is less cluttered looking.

Add Apple Menu Items to the Apple Menu

To make adding things to the Apple menu even easier, consider adding an alias to the Apple Menu Items folder to the Apple menu. Then when you want to add something to the Apple menu, just select Apple Menu Items from the Apple menu and the folder opens for you—no more digging into the System Folder to add files to it.

AppleScript

AppleScript is a powerful scripting language that is built into the Mac. It enables you to automate many repetitive tasks. Your Mac comes with several useful AppleScripts created for you to use, including one that adds the selected files to the Apple menu. I'll cover AppleScript in Chapter 17, "Making Your Mac Do Your Work for You."

More than one

By the way, you can select more than one item before you run this script if you want to. Aliases of all the files you have selected will be added to the Apple menu.

The tilde

The tilde symbol (~) moves an item to the bottom of the menu.

- **Reorder the menu**. Items appear on the menu in alphabetical order. You can tweak the names of the items on it so that they move up or down the list. Adding spaces and other characters to the front of an item's name moves it toward the top of the list. Adding a "z" to the name of an item will move it towards the bottom of the list. This is another advantage of using aliases rather than the original items, in that you can change the alias' name without affecting the original.

- **Use folders**. If you are going to be adding lots of items to the menu, consider using folders to organize these items. For example, if you have a lot of files associated with a particular publication, add an alias to the publication's folder to the Apple menu instead of adding the individual files. Then you can access the files by the alias' submenu while only adding one item to the Apple menu.

- **Add aliases to your volumes to the Apple menu**. This enables you to access any item on those volumes with the hierarchical menus.

- **Remove the chaff**. If there are items on the Apple menu that you don't use very often, consider removing them. The purpose of the Apple menu is to enable you to quickly access your frequently used items, so having it cluttered with a bunch of junk doesn't make sense.

Working with Applications and Utilities on the Apple Menu

There are a number of tools that are installed on the Apple menu by default. In the remainder of this chapter, you'll learn what they are and how to use them.

Choosing with the Chooser

The Chooser is an important utility that you use to choose a printer or to mount a network volume on your desktop. You also use it to turn AppleTalk on or off.

Using the Chooser to select a printer

1. From the Apple menu, choose Chooser.

2. Select the driver for the printer that you want to use in the left pane of the window.

3. In the right pane of the Chooser window, set the options for your printer, such as the port you are using, whether you are using AppleTalk, and if you want Background Printing to be active. If you are using an AppleTalk network to connect to a printer, your Mac will search the network for available printers that use that driver. If you have a printer connected directly to your printer port, you can select the printer port while AppleTalk is turned off. When you are ready to proceed, your Mac will show you the available printer in the upper-right part of the right pane (see Figure 6.6).

FIGURE 6.6

I have used the Chooser to select my DeskJet printer.

4. You can use the Setup button to set parameters specifically for your printer.

5. When you are done, close the Chooser (you will see a warning telling you to open Page Setup from within any open documents to rest the pages). When you print from any application, this printer will be used.

SEE ALSO

➤ *To learn how to use the Chooser to mount a network volume, see page 119*

➤ *To learn more about connecting and configuring a printer, see page 441*

➤ *To learn how to use the Chooser to control AppleTalk, see page 465*

The printer driver controls Page Setup

The options that you see when you use the Page Setup command in any application are determined by the printer driver that you have chosen in the Chooser. Some printer drivers use slightly different dimensions for a page. If you use a different printer driver while designing your document than you do when printing it, the page breaks might be slightly different than you expect. You need to make sure that you have selected the printer driver that you will end up using to print your document when you are designing it.

By the way, this is why you see a warning message when you change printers in the Chooser. Your Mac tells you to choose Page Setup in open applications to force those applications to rebuild pages based on the new printer driver.

Calculating with the Simple Calculator

The Calculator is one of those rare items that has been with the Mac since its inception in 1984. And from the way it looks, you can tell. I have often heard that the Calculator is a way to make your $2,000 Macintosh do *almost* as much as a $1.95 calculator (see Figure 6.7). While the Calculator is very, very basic, it is functional and I have used it myself many times over the years. When you need to do a simple calculation on-the-fly, the Calculator is often the best tool for the job.

FIGURE 6.7

Calculator—it works almost as well as those free calculators that banks give you.

Cut or copy

By the way, you can copy or cut a result from the Calculator's window. Whatever number you see in the window will be copied onto the Clipboard when you choose Copy (Command-C) or Cut (Command-X) from the Edit menu.

Doing simple calculations with the Calculator

1. From the Apple menu, choose Calculator.

2. Use the numeric keypad on your keyboard to do the calculations or use the mouse to click the Calculator's buttons.

3. When you are done, click the Close box.

Using the Graphing Calculator

When Apple introduced the PowerPC processor, it needed a cool application that would show off the PowerPC's computing muscle while being simple enough for potential customers to quickly use. And it would need to be included with the OS so that is would be on every Mac. The result of this quest was the Graphing Calculator (see Figure 6.8). With it, Apple could "wow" people with fairly complex graphs and plots whizzing across the Mac's monitor.

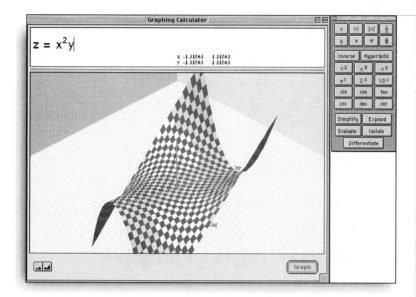

FIGURE 6.8
The Graphing Calculator is what the original Calculator wanted to be when it grew up.

Plotting a Graph with the Graphing Calculator

Contrary to what you might think, you can't calculate with the Graphing Calculator—it should have been called the Graphing tool instead. What it does is to plot equations that you enter. These can be two-dimensional or three-dimensional, as well as various trigonometric functions.

Plotting an equation with the Graphing Calculator

1. From the Apple menu, choose Graphing Calculator.
2. Enter the equation that you want to plot in the top pane of the window. Use the commands on the Equation menu to enter mathematical operators such as exponents and derivatives. You can also use the keypad window by choosing Show Full Keypad or Show Small Keypad from the Equation menu—the keypad provides button access to a variety of commands. You can see the full keypad in Figure 6.8.
3. When you are done entering an equation, click Graph. The equation will be plotted in the lower pane of the window.

A gray Graph button

The Graph button will be grayed out until your equation is both mathematically valid and within the Graphing Calculator's capabilities to handle.

   4. You can rotate the plot by dragging it to see it from various angles.

   5. You can make the plot spin by dragging on the plot and releasing the mouse button.

   6. You can make the plot larger or smaller with the resize buttons in the lower left corner of the screen.

   7. If you want to copy the graph so that you can paste it into another document, choose Copy Graph from the Edit menu.

   8. You can modify your equation and click Graph to see the effect of your changes.

Working with the Graphing Calculator

You may or may not have any use for the Graphing Calculator, but if you do, it is a good tool. Here are some additional hints on how to use it:

- The Graphing Calculator has its own help system. To use it, from the Equation menu, choose Help or from the Help menu, choose Graphing Calculator Help. The Help screen provides help in a variety of areas—click on an area in the left pane, and specific tasks will appear in the right pane (see Figure 6.9). Click on a task to get help with it.

FIGURE **6.9**

The Graphing Calculator provides a fairly extensive help system.

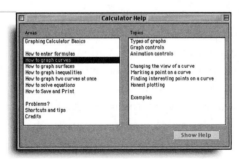

- Use the Demo commands to get a quick overview of how the Graphing Calculator works. You can see demos on specific curves as well as the full demo.

- You can resize the various panes of the windows by dragging the dividers.

- You can move the axes of two-dimensional plots by dragging them.

Figuring Out Fonts with Key Caps

Key Caps is a utility that enables you to locate special characters in the fonts that are installed on your system. For example, if you need to use the Return key symbol, you can use Key Caps to help you find it.

Finding special characters with Key Caps

1. From the Apple menu, choose Key Caps. The Key Caps window will open (see Figure 6.10).

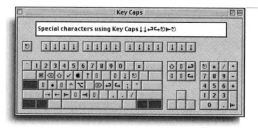

FIGURE 6.10
Using Key Caps to find the Return symbol.

2. Choose the font that you want to work with from the Fonts menu. You will see the font change on Key Caps' keyboard.

3. Look for the symbol you need.

4. If you can't find it, press a modifier key, for example, the Option key. The Key Caps' keyboard will change to reflect the symbols that the modifier key provides.

5. Continue trying keys until you find the symbol that you are looking for.

6. If you can't find the symbol, try a different font.

7. After you find the symbol, you can either repeat the key combination in your working application or simply copy and paste the symbol into your document.

Symbols and fonts

Remember that the symbol depends on the font you are using. If you are using a different font in your working application, the symbol will appear in that font rather than the one you were using in Key Caps. To see the symbol you want, you need to change the font in the working application to be the same one you were using in Key Caps.

Taking Notes with Note Pad

You can use the Note Pad to make simple text notes—it is the electronic equivalent to the paper scratch pad on your desk.

Using Note Pad to create notes

1. From the Apple menu, choose Note Pad. You will see the Note Pad window.

2. Enter your text (see Figure 6.11).

FIGURE 6.11

Using Note Pad to remind myself about something important.

3. To move to the next note, click the bent corner of the note that is in the lower left corner of the window.

4. To move to a previous note, click on the area exposed by the bent corner.

5. To add a note to your pad, from the File menu, choose New Note.

6. To delete a note, choose Delete Note from the File menu.

Setting the font

You can change the font that the Note Pad uses by using the Preferences command (under the Edit menu).

Keeping the Note Pad available

If you find the Note Pad useful, you will probably want it open all the time. You can place an alias to it in the Startup Items folder in your System Folder so that it will open each time your Mac starts up. You can collapse the Note Pad window and drag it to the top of your screen to keep it out of the way.

Creating Clippings with the Scrapbook

The Scrapbook is a good place to store graphics, text, sounds, movies, or other items that you frequently use (see Figure 6.12). The Scrapbook is always accessible via the Apple menu so that you can quickly move to it, grab the item that you want to reuse, and easily paste it into your document. Don't limit your use of the Scrapbook only to still images or text either. It works equally well for sounds, QuickTime movies, and so on.

FIGURE 6.12
The Scrapbook is just what its name implies it is.

Storing something in the Scrapbook

1. From within the document that contains the item you want to reuse, select the item and copy it.

2. Open the Scrapbook by choosing it from the Apple menu. When the Scrapbook opens, you will see a screen that contains some hints on how to use it (see Figure 6.13). At the bottom of the Scrapbook window, it tells you how many items are currently stored in the Scrapbook. It also tells you what type of item is currently displayed and how much space it requires to store. In Figure 6.13, the item in the window is "styled text," and it consumes a whopping 552 bytes of space.

FIGURE 6.13
The Scrapbook is a great place to store items that you want to reuse.

Get rid of the chaff

You can remove anything, including the items in the Scrapbook, by default, by moving to the item's window and choosing Cut or Clear from the Edit menu.

3. Scroll through the Scrapbook by using the horizontal scroll bar at the bottom of the window to see examples of what can be stored in it (see Figure 6.14).

FIGURE 6.14

The Scrapbook can hold a variety of items, including sounds.

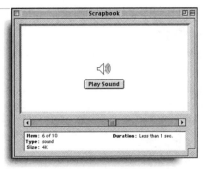

4. Choose Paste from the Edit menu or press Command-V. You will see your item in the Scrapbook (see Figure 6.15). It will always be available there until you remove it.

FIGURE 6.15

I have pasted my company logo into the Scrapbook so that it is easy to paste into other documents on-the-fly.

A better way

Instead of using plain old paste and copy, you can drag and drop items directly to and from the Scrapbook. You can also drag items onto your desktop to make clipping files out of them. It works both ways as long as the application you are working with supports drag-and-drop.

Using an item from the Scrapbook is an easy as putting one in it.

Using an item from the Scrapbook

1. From the document that you want to use the Scrapbook item in, open the Scrapbook.

2. Scroll through the Scrapbook until you see the item that you want to use.

3. Click on the item and drag it onto your document. The item will be pasted into the document (see Figure 6.16).

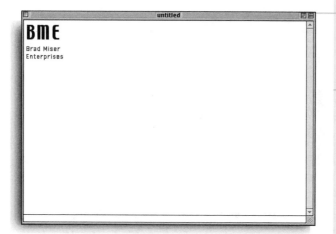

FIGURE 6.16
I just dragged this logo from the Scrapbook onto a SimpleText document.

The Scrapbook is easy to use, and you can work faster with less time wasted recreating items or searching through lots of documents trying to find them. I am sure that you will find your own uses for the Scrapbook, but here are some suggestions on what to store in it to get you started:

- Your company logo
- Your return address
- Your signature block
- Graphics that you use frequently
- Email addresses
- Web site addresses
- A QuickTime movie that you want to reuse in a variety of documents
- Blocks of text that are the same in a variety of documents, such as disclaimers and other legal statements

No dragging here

If the application with which you are working does not support drag-and-drop, you can still use good old copy-and-paste to place something from the Scrapbook into your file.

Creating Sticky Notes

Stickies are the electronic equivalent to the sticky note pads that are so common in offices today (see Figure 6.17). You can create a note and "paste" it on your screen. When you are done, you can close the note to remove it from the screen.

FIGURE 6.17

You can use stickies to leave notes to yourself or others by using your Mac.

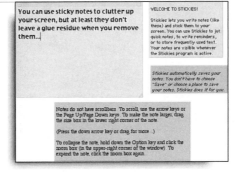

Leaving notes on your screen with stickies

1. From the Apple menu, choose Stickies. You will see some predefined notes appear on-screen. These notes provide some information about how stickies work.

2. Read the sticky notes.

3. When you are done, close them by clicking the Close boxes. You will be prompted to save the text—after you close a sticky, it is gone forever unless you save it. The predefined notes provide good tips on some of the features of sticky notes so you might want to save the text in them for later reference.

4. To create a new note, from the File menu, choose New Note. A blank note window will appear (it has the default font and color settings).

5. Enter your text.

6. Use the Text Style command under the Note menu to set the font and style for the note.

7. Use the Color menu to set the note window's color.

Playing with the Jigsaw Puzzle

This is purely an entertainment application, which you can use to build your own digital jigsaw puzzles. You can create puzzles from your own graphics as well as using the map graphic that Apple provides (see Figure 6.18). When you place a puzzle piece

Defining how your Stickies work

You can use the Preferences command under the Edit menu to define certain aspects of how Stickies works; for example, whether it opens at startup or not.

Stickies are forever

The sticky notes will remain until you quit Stickies—note that sticky notes do not float and may be covered by the front-most application.

in the right place, it automatically snaps into position. You can also choose the size of the puzzle pieces and have the Mac use sound effects.

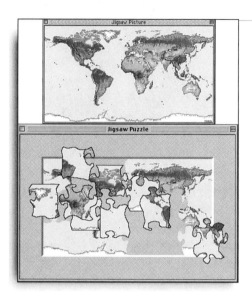

FIGURE 6.18
Jigsaw Puzzle can create a puzzle for your own graphics, or you can build a puzzle from Apple's map graphic.

Now that you have finished this chapter, you may notice that there are several items on the Apple menu that are not covered in this chapter. That is because they are covered in the chapters relating to the items with which you use them. Here are some references that may help you find something not covered in this chapter.

SEE ALSO

➤ *To learn more about the Apple System Profiler, see page 735*

➤ *To learn about the AppleCD Audio Player, see page 219*

➤ *To see how you can use Apple Video Player to watch TV and movies on your Mac, see page 228*

➤ *To learn about AppleScript, see page 398*

➤ *To read about the Internet tools located on the Apple menu, see Part V, "Using Your Mac to Surf the Internet"*

➤ *To learn how you can speak to your Mac (and have it listen), see page 409*

The Apple menu is a very important part of Mac OS 8.5, and if you aren't using it regularly, you should really think about integrating it into your Mac habits. It can save you lots of time and might even help you get your work done more quickly.

Working with the Control Strip

Understanding the Control Strip

Using the Control Strip

Customizing the Control Strip

Understanding the Control Strip

The Control Strip is yet another means to access commands, settings, information, and applications that you frequently use (see Figure 7.1). It appears at the bottom of the desktop as a series of buttons on which you can click to activate whatever the button points to. The Control Strip is installed by default, but the controls you see on it may vary depending on the kind of machine on which it was installed. For example, PowerBook users will see some different buttons on their Control Strips than desktop Mac users will see. These PowerBook-specific modules provide access to commands and applications that are important when using a PowerBook, such as battery monitoring.

SEE ALSO

➤ *To learn about the PowerBook's Control Strip, see page 826,*

You can also customize the Control Strip by adding and removing modules as you do with the Apple menu and contextual menus. Or you can hide the Control Strip or turn it completely off if you don't want to use it.

The Control Strip is made possible by four items, which are the following:

- **Control Strip extension**. This extension provides the software that your Mac uses to make the Control Strip work.

- **Control Strip control panel**. This control panel enables you to show or hide the Control Strip, set a hot key to show and hide it, and set the font and size used on it.

- **Control Strip Modules folder**. This folder contains the modules that are shown on the Control Strip. Just as with the Apple menu and contextual menus, you can add or remove files from this folder to customize the Control Strip.

- **Control Strip Preferences**. This file stores your preferences for the Control Strip, such as where you locate it on the desktop.

The floating Control Strip

The Control Strip floats on top of all other windows so that you can always access it.

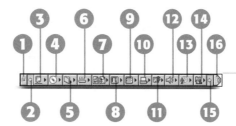

FIGURE 7.1

The Control Strip provides desktop access to a variety of commands, information, settings, and applications.

1 Collapse box

2 Scroll arrow

3 AppleTalk switch

4 Audio CD player

5 File sharing control

6 Hard disk spin down button

7 Location Manager

8 Color depth

9 Resolution

10 Printer selector

11 Remote Access control

12 Volume

13 Sound source

14 Web sharing control

15 Scroll arrow

16 Collapse tab

Using the Standard Control Strip

The Control Strip is a good way to quickly access items that you use frequently. For example, you can quickly change the sound source that your Mac is using by using the Control Strip module rather than having to open the Monitors & Sound control panel.

Collapsing and Expanding the Control Strip

The Control Strip is enabled by default, but you can collapse it if it is getting in your way. Then if you want to use a control on it, you can expand it again.

Collapsing and expanding the Control Strip

1. To collapse the Control Strip so that you just see its "stub," click the very right end of it (see Figure7.2 and Figure 7.3).

Using Control Strip Modules

A couple of quick steps will show you how to use the control modules located on the Control Strip.

Using the Control Strip to change your monitor's color depth

1. Click on the Control Strip button (it looks like a monitor that has stripes of color on it).

2. From the pop-up menu, choose another color depth. Your monitor will be set to that depth.

Another way to collapse the Control Strip

You can also click the Close box on the left end of the Control Strip to collapse it.

FIGURE 7.2

Clicking the collapse tab at the end of the Control Strip collapses it down to a "stub."

1 Click here to collapse the control strip

FIGURE 7.3

The Control Strip is collapsed.

Balloon Help

One area in which Balloon Help can be of help is the Control Strip. Turn on the Balloons and point to the modules for a description of what they do.

The Control Strip CD player

The Control Strip CD player doesn't just provide another way to control the AppleCD Audio Player. It is an entirely different application (or more correctly, it is its own Control Strip module).

Using the Control Strip to listen to audio CDs

1. Click on the Control Strip module with the icon of a CD (not the one that also has a microphone).

2. Choose a command from the pop-up menu (such as a track to play or pause). The action you choose will happen.

Customizing the Control Strip

You can rework the Control Strip in several ways to suit your working style. The simplest of these is to resize it and use its control panel to make changes. You can also add new functions to it by adding Control Strip modules.

Resizing and Moving the Control Strip

You can move the Control Strip around the desktop and change its size (depending on the modules you have installed on it).

Resizing and moving the Control Strip

1. Click the tab at the end of the Control Strip.

2. Drag the end until the Control Strip is the length that you desire. Note that you can't make the Control Strip any longer than the last module that is installed. If you make it shorter than the last module installed, use the left and right arrows to scroll through the modules.

3. To move the Control Strip, press Option and click on the Control Strip, drag it to a new location, and release the mouse button. You are somewhat limited in where you can move it; it has to be anchored on one side of the desktop or the other. If you move it all the way across the desktop, it will flip flop so that the tab is always projecting onto the desktop.

Using the Control Strip Control Panel

You can change several aspects of the Control Strip (including turning it off) by using the Control Strip control panel.

Using the Control Strip control panel

1. Choose the Control Strip control panel from the Control Panels folder on the Apple menu (see Figure 7.4).

2. To remove the Control Strip from the desktop, click the Hide Control Strip radio button.

3. To show it again, click the Show Control Strip radio button.

4. To define a hot key that you can use to hide or show the Control Strip, click the Hot key to show/hide the button.

5. If you don't like the default (Command+Control+S), click the Define hot key button and set a new hot key. When you press the hot key that you define, the Control Strip will be shown if it is hidden, or it will be hidden if it is shown.

6. If you want the Control Strip to have a certain font and size, use the Font Settings controls to set it.

7. Close the control panel.

Moving modules

You can move modules around on the Control Strip (changing the order in which they appear) by holding the Option key down while you drag a module to its new location. (The cursor changes to a closed hand while you hold down the Option key.) The rest of the modules will move to accommodate the new order.

FIGURE 7.4

The Control Strip control panel enables you to adjust the Control Strip.

Control Strip and PowerBooks

In Figure 7.5, you can see some modules that aren't shown in the Control Strip in Figure 7.2. That is because I was using a desktop Mac, and the "extra" modules (such as Media Bay) are only useful on a PowerBook. You'll learn about the PowerBook Control Strip in Appendix B, "Working with PowerBooks."

Removing Control Strip Modules

You can easily remove any Control Strip modules that you don't use.

Removing Control Strip modules

1. Open the Control Strip Modules folder that is within the System Folder (see Figure 7.5).

2. Drag the modules out of the folder and put them in a different folder (you might want to create a folder to store them in rather than throwing them out).

3. Restart your Mac. The Control Strip will reflect your changes (see Figure 7.6).

FIGURE 7.5

You can add or remove Control Strip modules by adding modules to or removing modules from the Control Strip Modules folder.

FIGURE 7.6

The CD Strip and Printer Selector modules have been removed from this Control Strip (compare this to   REF _Ref418141287 * MERGEFORMAT Figure 7.2).

Finding and Installing Control Strip Modules

You can re-install modules you already have or you can add new functions to your Control Strip by adding modules to it. Control Strip modules are available in many places, including the Internet. Here are two addresses of Web sites that contain lots of Control Strip modules that you can download and install:

http://www2.gol.com/users/systma/csm/

http://kissasylum.com/zone/

As an example, I will show you how to install a Control Strip module called BunchOApps, written by Patrick McClaughry. This module enables you to quickly launch applications from the Control Strip. Although the following steps are for this particular module, most Control Strip modules are installed the same way. Use these steps, but use the module you want to install instead of BunchOApps.

Installing the BunchOApps Control Strip module

1. Get a copy of the BunchOApps files and install them on your Mac. Then open the BunchOApps folder (see Figure 7.7).

FIGURE 7.7

The BunchOApps Control Strip module enables you to launch applications from the Control Strip.

2. Read the ReadMe file.
3. Drag the BunchOApps module onto the closed System Folder.
4. Click OK when the Mac asks if it should place the module in the Control Strip Modules folder.
5. Restart your Mac. The Control Strip will now have the new module installed and ready to use (see Figure 7.8).

FIGURE 7.8

The BunchOApps module is now part of this Control Strip.

1 BunchOApps module

If you find yourself wishing that some feature you use regularly had a control strip module for it, it probably does. Do a search on the Internet in your favorite Mac shareware sites to see what modules are available. It is likely that there is one that does what you are looking for. Just install it, and you will able to quickly access that function from the Control Strip.

Working with Fonts

Understanding screen fonts

Understanding PostScript fonts

Working with TrueType fonts

Managing fonts

Using Fonts

Since you work with a Macintosh, chances are that font-handling is part of your work. If you're an art director, designer, or production artist, you probably spend most of your time fussing with the finer points of your layout's type; if you're using office-style applications, like Word and Excel, you routinely generate reports and other mostly-type documents, and you'd like your work to look as good as possible.

The Mac has a long and glorious history of supporting fine typography; in fact, the Mac's early support for typefaces other than the truly monstrous faces cranked out by PCs really made the Mac what it is today. Now, more than a decade later, the Mac remains the best platform for lovers of fine typography.

With power comes complexity. It's fairly easy to install fonts on your Mac—basically, you can just throw them into the System Folder's Font folder—but knowing how fonts work can save you time and frustration. For instance, a document may look fine when you print it out on your laser printer, but when you send it out to a printer or service bureau, the proofs come back with completely different fonts substituted for the ones you used in your document. If you know the basic principles, you won't find yourself at 8PM (again!) waiting for a messenger service to take a disk to your printer's service bureau.

Macs and advertising

The graphics capabilities of the Mac have led to its dominance in the video world as well. When you watch commercials on TV, notice how many of the title bars and other computer elements look like a Mac. The Mac dominates the advertising and video production markets so it is no surprise that the products of these markets reflect their Macintosh base.

More on-screen fonts

Before the advent of TrueType fonts, one of the bad things about screen fonts was that there were only certain sizes available. If you wanted to use a size that wasn't installed, the Mac would do its best to create it for you. But the results were usually very poor. Text looked chunky, and sometimes the results were so bad that you couldn't even read the screen.

ATM

Adobe Type Manager (ATM) is a control panel that enables your Mac to display PostScript fonts on-screen so that they appear smooth no matter what size you use. ATM used to be included in the Mac OS software, but as of the time of this writing, it is not included with Mac OS 8.5. If you use PostScript fonts, you need to get a copy of ATM in order to be able to display those fonts on-screen. You can get a copy of ATM with any Adobe product, including applications and its font management tools.

Understanding Font Types

Mac OS 8.5 supports three basic flavors of fonts. Each has its own strengths and weaknesses. The three font types are the following (listed in increasing order of importance):

- **Screen Fonts**. Screen fonts (also known as bitmap fonts, system fonts, or suitcase fonts) are the fonts that the Mac uses only to display type on-screen. Screen fonts produce mediocre, jagged output when sent to a printer. With Mac OS 8.5, you don't really deal directly with many screen fonts anymore because most fonts you use will be one of the other two types.

- **PostScript Fonts**. Postscript fonts, also known as printer fonts and laser fonts, are used by PostScript printers and imagesetters to create smooth-edged type. The Mac OS (in conjunction with Adobe Type Manager) also uses PostScript fonts to refine the appearance of screen fonts.

- **TrueType Fonts**. TrueType fonts, introduced by Apple as part of System 7, combine properties of both screen fonts and PostScript fonts. Like screen fonts, TrueType fonts can be displayed on-screen; like PostScript fonts, TrueType fonts produce smooth-edged output when printed on a laser printer or imagesetter. One of the great features of TrueType fonts is that you can create sizes "on the fly" so that with a single TrueType font, you have access to an almost unlimited range of point sizes. If you use TrueType fonts exclusively, you don't need ATM.

All active fonts are stored in the Fonts folder that is within the System Folder (see   REF _Ref421154318 * MERGEFORMAT Figure 8.1). Screen and TrueType fonts are stored within font suitcases that are similar to, but not the same as, the old font suitcases. You don't need a utility to move things in and out of one of these suitcases. PostScript fonts are stored loosely within the System Folder. PostScript fonts have an icon that represents the copy that produced it (the PostScript fonts in Figure 8.1 are from Adobe Systems).

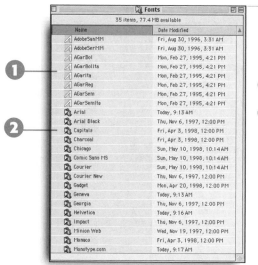

FIGURE 8.1

Having access to lots of fonts can make choosing one a difficult, but fun, process.

① PostScript font

② Font Suitcase

Inactive fonts

As with control panels, extensions, and other system resources, some fonts may be on your Mac, but not active. If a font is not in the Fonts folder, your Mac won't be able to use it. You might want to deactivate fonts in order to reduce the RAM your system needs to run. You'll learn more about managing your fonts later in this chapter.

If you double-click on a suitcase font, you'll find that the suitcase opens to reveal its contents (see Figure 8.2). As with PostScript fonts, screen fonts and TrueType fonts have their own icons. Screen fonts have icons with a single "A" on them—this is because a screen font contains only one point size of that font. TrueType fonts, on the other hand, contain multiple sizes of the font so their icons have multiple "A's" on them. As you can see in Figure 8.2, both screen fonts and TrueType fonts can live in the same suitcase.

FIGURE 8.2

The font suitcase containing good old Helvetica.

1 TrueType font

2 Screen font

If you want to see what a font looks like, double-click its icon (see Figure 8.3). The Finder displays a little window that shows what the font looks like. As you can see in Figure 8.3, the Finder shows a screen font at one size and a TrueType font at several different sizes.

More on suitcases

With Mac OS 8.5, a suitcase window looks and acts like a folder's window, and you can safely treat a suitcase like an ordinary folder. For example, if you want to view the contents of a font suitcase in outline view, simply choose "as List" from the View menu.

FIGURE 8.3

Double-click on a fonts icon to see what the font looks like; the window on the left shows a TrueType font while the one on the right shows a screen font.

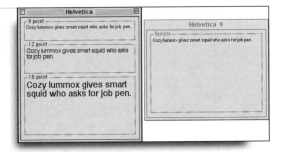

Understanding Screen Fonts

Screen fonts were the first family of fonts to be developed for the Mac—they've been around, in the same form, since the original 128K Macs. Screen fonts are simple, bitmap-based fonts used by the Mac OS to put fonts on the screen.

In a screen font, each character in the font has its own little bitmap image that the Mac throws up on-screen when it needs to display the character.

The great thing about using bitmaps to store a font's characters' shapes is that black-and-white bitmaps are small and simple, so the Mac can handle them quickly. Speed is important, especially when the Mac is routinely called upon to display hundreds of characters simultaneously in every window of text and to quickly update when the user scrolls through the text window. (In the Bad Old Days of 20MHz chips, speed was especially important!)

Because a screen font is essentially a series of pictures, each point size of a typeface is stored in a separate font document. Similarly, each type style—such as italic, bold, and bold italic—is stored in a separate font document.   REF _Ref421156129 * MERGEFORMAT Figure 8.4 shows the window of a typical font suitcase. You can see that there are sizes as well as a bold font. Depending on the number of sizes supported, a typical font suitcase may store dozens of individual font documents.

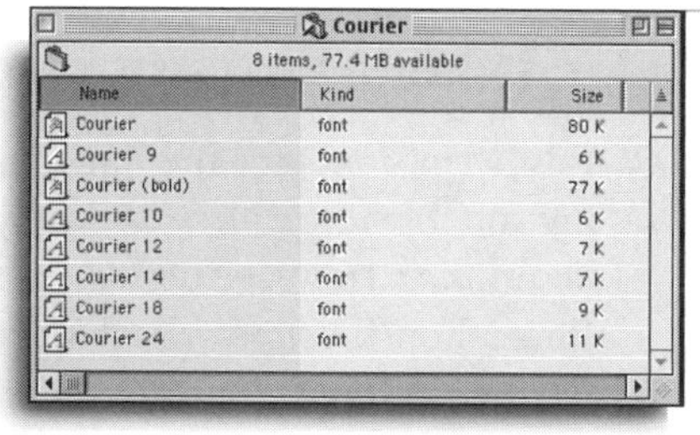

FIGURE 8.4

Each size and style of a screen font requires a separate font document.

There are a couple of good things I can say about screen fonts before we move on to the bad stuff. First, they're very small, so they don't take up a lot of disk space. Also, screen fonts are not protected by copyright laws. If you want to use a new screen font, you can download it from the Web, or copy it from

---

A bitmap by any other name…

"Bitmap" means the same thing that it means in other computer graphics contexts: a bitmap is a matrix, or grid, used to represent an image in digital format. In the case of a screen font, each grid square in the bitmap corresponds to one pixel on-screen, and each square can be either black or white (no gray or color values are allowed).

Speed kills

Before TrueType fonts, the Mac used screen fonts to display information because of the speed with which it could work with them. However, since TrueType fonts can be rapidly scaled between various sizes, screen fonts are not really necessary anymore. In fact, the default font for Mac OS 8.5 is Charcoal, which is a TrueType font.

I don't see any jaggies on my Mac

You may be saying that the fonts on *your* Mac's screen aren't jaggy! They're on-screen so aren't they screen fonts? Yes, they may well be screen fonts. Even so, they may appear smooth for two reasons. One is that you may also have the TrueType font installed. Your Mac will use that to display the font on-screen, and it will look great. The second possibility is that you have Adobe Type Manager installed. ATM uses information from the PostScript version of the font (if available) to *anti-alias*, or smooth the edges of, the type on-screen. If the PostScript version of the font isn't available, ATM can't make a screen font look smooth.

Printing with screen fonts and PostScript

To print a typeface on a PostScript laser printer, you must have the PostScript version of the screen font installed. However, when using a PostScript font, you can't dispense with screen fonts completely; you'll need to install the screen font version of the typeface to display the font on-screen.

Why good screen fonts go bad

Remember, a screen font is essentially a collection of 72 dpi bitmaps; that's just not a lot of resolution. Today's garden-variety printers typically use resolutions of 300 or 600 dpi; imagesetters and direct-to-plate devices use resolutions such as 2700 dpi. A resolution of 72 dpi just isn't very high, especially when you examine it on paper with a sensitive instrument like the human eye.

Using ImageWriters

Screen fonts are perfectly adequate for printing on old dot-matrix printers like the ImageWriter II. (You won't mistake the results for laser printer output, of course.) You'll get the best results from an ImageWriter if ATM is installed.

whomever or wherever you find it. (Unfortunately, the other kinds of fonts *aren't* free.)

Here's the bad news about screen fonts:

- **Screen fonts are jaggy.** There's only so much smoothness that you can achieve with square cells in a square grid and so screen fonts appear to have jagged edges. Technically, this undesirable effect is called *aliasing*; it's also commonly called stair-stepping, for obvious reasons.
- **Screen fonts don't print very well.** If screen fonts are jaggy on-screen, how do they look coming out of a printer? Very lousy, thank you. In fact, in many cases, depending on the application that you're using and your laser printer software, the printer won't even attempt to use a screen font to print. Rather, the laser printer will substitute another font, usually Courier.
- **Screen fonts don't scale very well.** Simple black-and-white bitmaps look bad quickly when you resize them. Screen fonts are black-and-white bitmaps, and they look their best at their original size.

Your main use for screen fonts will probably be for displaying your PostScript fonts. Most other fonts that you deal with will be displayed with a TrueType font which discovered later in the chapter.

Understanding PostScript Fonts

PostScript fonts are the fonts that really made desktop publishing suitable for professional projects. PostScript is a page-description language developed by Adobe Systems, Inc. (those Photoshop/Illustrator/PageMaker folks), and, in short, a PostScript font is a tiny program that a PostScript-savvy laser printer uses to create clean-edged type at any size.

PostScript fonts don't use a bitmap to store the shape of the characters in the font; PostScript fonts store a font as a mathematical description of the font's outline, rather than as a bitmap.

The device that displays or images the font—usually a printer or an imagesetter—calculates where the font's outline lies, and then fills in all of the dots (or pixels, or whatever) inside the outline. Because there's no bitmap involved, PostScript fonts can be printed at any resolution with excellent results. Similarly, PostScript fonts can be scaled to any size without distortion.

Sounds good, doesn't it? Here's the bad news about PostScript fonts: they're complicated. In fact, PostScript fonts are *too* complicated for a Mac to draw on-screen. Every PostScript font is distributed with a screen font "twin." The Mac uses the screen font to display the typeface on-screen. When a document that shows the screen font version of a typeface is sent to a PostScript printer or imagesetter, the Mac (actually, the application that created the document) sends the PostScript font version of the typeface to the printer.

The PostScript fonts for any particular typeface include separate font files for each style (bold, semibold, italic, and so on), but each style only requires one file—there's no need for separate files for each point size. Note also that PostScript fonts always have cryptic one-word names, such as AGarExpSemIta, which corresponds to the font(s) Adobe Garamond Expert Semibold Italic, stored in the Adobe Garamond Expert Set Suitcase.

Understanding TrueType Fonts

It's inelegant and inconvenient to use two fonts—a screen font and a PostScript font—to represent a single typeface. At least that's what the engineers at Apple thought, so when System 7 was unveiled in the early nineties, it included support for a new, Apple-developed font format, called TrueType.

TrueType's greatest strength is that it uses a single font document to display both the typeface on-screen and output the typeface on a printer. Like PostScript, TrueType stores a mathematical description of each character's outline; however, TrueType uses simpler math than PostScript does, so TrueType can be displayed on-screen. Because TrueType fonts are based on outlines, TrueType fonts can be scaled to any size without distortion.

I don't have any PostScript fonts!

If you look for a PostScript font on your Mac, you may not find one. None are installed as part of the Mac OS 8.5 installation. The only way you get PostScript fonts is by adding them. Many applications, especially those from Adobe Systems, come with PostScript fonts, or you can purchase sets of PostScript fonts and add them yourself. If you use PostScript fonts, you need ATM as well. It is usually included with the software that includes PostScript fonts.

Type 1 and Type 3 Fonts

There are actually two kinds of PostScript fonts: Type 1 and Type 3. (No, there's no Type 2.) The difference between Type 1 and Type 3 is pretty technical, and you don't need to worry about it. Some custom icons for PostScript fonts have a tiny 1 or 3 in the icon to indicate which Type of font it is.

The Future of PostScript

The idea that PostScript is too complex to draw on-screen is from an era before today's super-fast Macs and tomorrow's mind-boggling rocket machines. PostScript can be displayed on-screen on a fast enough machine. The engineers at NeXT— such as., the people that Steve Jobs brought with him to Apple to develop Rhapsody and Mac OS X—use *Display PostScript* in the NeXT operating system. It's not too much of a stretch to imagine that someday Macs of the future may use PostScript-based typography on-screen.

No suitcase for you

PostScript fonts can't be stored in suitcases.

Microsoft and TrueType

Actually, the folks at Apple can't claim all the credit for TrueType fonts. Microsoft was also involved in the development of TrueType fonts, and Windows PCs also use them (and no they aren't the same files that Macs use). Whether the drive to develop TrueType was based more on a technical need than a desire to remove Adobe from the font driver's seat is anyone's guess.

Almost perfect

While TrueType can be scaled to almost any size, you may find that some of the smaller sizes are not as clear as their bitmapped equivalents.

TrueType forever!

Unless you have a specific need to work with PostScript fonts and are concerned with obtaining the most sophisticated levels of typographic design, I recommend that you stick with TrueType fonts. They are the easiest to work with, and you are more likely to see on your monitor what you will get out of a printer.

GX

For a while, Apple was pushing QuickDraw GX. GX was a new display technology that could have enabled PostScript or better quality, lots of great new typography tools, and ease-of-use. But applications had to be rewritten to take advantage of it. Since the major producer of applications and fonts that people care about is Adobe, and they have a vested interest in PostScript fonts, no significant applications were ever created to use GX. Thus, it became another one of Apple's promising technologies that never saw the light of day.

TrueType sounds really great on paper, and TrueType *is* really great. However, many Mac folks still use screen font/PostScript pairs, rather than a single TrueType font. Why? There are several reasons:

- Adobe (who invented PostScript) is probably the world's biggest vendor of fonts, and they don't make TrueType fonts. Since Adobe produces the major tools in the desktop publishing and graphics worlds, it makes sense that people would stick with PostScript.

- Some people think that PostScript fonts provide better quality than TrueType fonts. This depends on many factors, including the printer used, so it is not as easy to decide if PostScript is actually better or not. You should try both types to see which works best for you.

- Older versions of many DTP tools don't handle TrueType fonts very well.

- In the early days of TrueType, TrueType fonts often caused imagesetters to crash, costing service bureaus and prepress departments a lot of money.

If you don't use many Adobe products, you are likely to work with TrueType fonts more than any other type. That is good because TrueType fonts provide excellent results, and they are easy to work with. That is a good combination.

Managing Fonts

There are really only two tasks that you need to do to manage fonts on your Mac: installing fonts and removing fonts. Both of these are easy to do.

Installing fonts

1. Look at the font to see what kind of font it is (see Figure 8.1 and Figure 8.2).

2. If it is a TrueType font, drag and drop it onto the System Folder. If it is a PostScript font, make sure that you drag both the PostScript and screen font onto the System Folder.

3. When your Mac asks you if the items should be placed in the Fonts folder, tell it to do so.

4. Restart any open applications to get them to recognize the new font.

Even with today's super-fast Macs, some applications start very slowly if the machine is loaded with many fonts. (SimpleText, Microsoft Word, Adobe Illustrator, and Claris FileMaker are notoriously slow on font-heavy machines.) I recommend that you keep your Fonts folder relatively lean, or use a commercial font management utility (like Symantec's excellent Suitcase) to quickly swap fonts in and out of your Fonts folder.

Uninstalling a font

1. Open the Fonts folder.

2. Drag the font out of the Fonts folder (you should store it in a disabled fonts folder rather than throwing it away in case you ever need to use it again).

When you install Mac OS 8.5, a basic set of TrueType font families are installed by default. Two of these families—Charcoal and Geneva—are, by default, used for things like window title bars and menus, and thus are vital to the operation of your Mac. The other fonts, which include Courier, Times, Helvetica, Symbol, and Palatino, are fonts that are commonly installed on Apple and third-party PostScript laser printers. Strictly speaking, you don't need these fonts, but most documents—including many documents from PCs—specify these fonts, so you should keep them.

If you've installed Microsoft Internet Explorer, you'll find that several TrueType font families from Microsoft—including Arial, Verdana, and Times New Roman—have been installed as well. These fonts are distributed by Microsoft as part of an initiative to make Web typography a little more predictable. You don't need to keep these fonts to run Internet Explorer or other Web browsers, but you may find that pages designed with these fonts look better with them installed.

SEE ALSO

➤ *To see how to set the font that your Mac uses in menus, headings, explanatory text, labels, lists and so on, see page 304*

Installing PostScript fonts

Remember, screen fonts and PostScript fonts are ordinarily installed in pairs; you should have a PostScript font for every screen font. Ordinarily, but not necessarily, all of the screen fonts for a particular font family are stored in a single suitcase. Also remember that PostScript fonts can't be stored in suitcases, and these are stored as separate files in the Fonts folder. Remember that to view PostScript fonts clearly on-screen, you need to install and configure ATM.

Dragging a folder of fonts

Don't drag a folder of fonts onto the System Folder because Mac OS will simply put the folder into the System Folder, rather than installing the fonts. Likewise, don't put a folder of fonts into the Fonts folder; fonts files should be either loose in the Font folder or in Font suitcases.

Font rule of thumb

Basically, if you don't use a font, it is better to deactivate it. Fonts require RAM, and they slow down the speed at which an application works. You can create a folder to store your disabled fonts in and keep them there. When you want to activate a font, it is a simple matter to place it in the Fonts folder. Remember to deactivate it again when you are done with it.

Oh, Chicago!

Chicago used to be the default system font. But is was replaced by the new-font-on-the-block, Charcoal.

Working with Color and Graphics

Learning how color and graphics work on the Mac

Learning what resolution is, why it is important, and how to set the desktop resolution for your Mac

Understanding how color on the Mac works, how to choose colors by using the Color Picker, and how to use ColorSync to get consistent colors across devices

Understanding the two basic types of graphics you use in applications

Using Color and Graphics on the Mac

Because the Mac is the world's premiere graphics-handling computer, thousands of advertising agencies, PR firms, design studios, and digital artists use Macs for graphic design and production. The very first Macs were built from the ground up to be graphics-friendly, and Apple has never wavered in its commitment to this core market. From the early days of MacDraw and MacPaint to today's Photoshop 5, the Mac has always been at the leading edge of graphic arts.

Before you can really understand how to work with graphics on your Mac, however, you need to understand the two basic concepts that affect how your graphics look, both onscreen and when output to a printer. The first concept is *resolution*. The second concept is how your Mac works with color.

Understanding Resolution

Display?

BTW, a display is the same thing as a monitor. "Normal" people often just call it the screen.

Total number of pixels

To determine the total number of pixels that a device can work with, find the area that the device uses. To do this, simply multiply the horizontal number of pixels by the number of vertical pixels. For example, monitors set to work in the 640 x 480 mode can display 307,200 pixels.

Is this important? Not really, since resolution is more commonly described by using the horizontal x vertical convention. But seeing the total number gives you an idea of just how much information your Mac is manipulating. For example, with a large monitor, you might use a resolution of 1,024 x 768, or a total of 786,432 pixels. That is a lot of information, and your Mac has to keep track of each pixel of it!

Resolution can be a difficult topic to get your hands around because the same term is used in different contexts. In order to understand which resolution you are working with, you need to figure what area you are in (for example, on the desktop versus working with a printer). But it is important to take some time to work through the concepts in this chapter. Doing so will help you understand how to use graphics and color effectively, and you will better understand why graphics appear the way they do. You will also learn why the same graphic can look so vastly different, depending on how it is viewed (for example, on your Mac versus on hard copy).

Basically, resolution is a measure of the number of dots with which a device can work (a device means a display, an image capturing, or an output device). On a computer monitor, scanner, digital camera, or other digital imaging device, these dots are called *picture elements*, or more commonly, *pixels*. On printers and other output devices, dots are called, well, dots. That is simple enough, right?

The confusing part of this is that a pixel has no defined physical size. A pixel on one device may appear larger or smaller than a pixel on another device. This is because every device works with its own range of number of pixels that it can display. Some devices display lots of pixels in a given area, while others display fewer. And some devices enable you to change the number of pixels that they display (under some maximum number). Most monitors, for example, can display different numbers of pixels; you set the number that you want to be displayed.

For a display or capturing device, resolution is measured by the total number of pixels that can be displayed or captured. This is indicated by the number of pixels that can be displayed or captured in the horizontal direction and the number of pixels that can be displayed or captured in the vertical direction. For example, a common display resolution is 640 pixels in the horizontal direction by 480 pixels in the vertical direction—in shorthand, this is written as 640 × 480. You will learn about monitor resolution in more detail in the next section, but for now, let me use it as an example to explain how pixels are not a physical entity, but an electronic one.

A monitor has only so much display size; the physical screen of the monitor is fixed. For example, you may have a 15-inch monitor or a 17-inch monitor. These displays use the full physical screen to display the number of pixels they are set to display. For example, if you set the monitor to display at 832 × 624 (or 519,168 pixels), the pixels appear to be a certain size. If you increase the number of pixels displayed to 1,280 × 960 for example (or 1,228,800 pixels), the total number of pixels displayed increases by 709,632 pixels. But the monitor has only so much space in which to display those pixels. The result is that the pixels in the second setting appear to be *smaller* than they were under the first setting; more pixels are displayed in the same screen area. This means that images appear to be larger in the 832 × 624 setting, while you can see a larger area when the display is set at 1,280 × 960.

Figure 9.1 shows a monitor in the 832 × 624 mode, while Figure 9.2 shows the same monitor using the 1,280 × 960 setting. Notice that the windows appear to be smaller in Figure 9.1,

Capturing devices?

By capture device, I mean a device that captures an image. The two main digital capture devices are scanners and digital cameras. Each of these devices is able to capture images with a specified resolution.

Resolution and color depth

The "total" amount of graphic data with which a device can work depends on both the resolution at which it is working as well as the *color depth* (which you will read about a little later in this chapter). These concepts are intimately linked; you can't change one without impacting the other.

while you can see a lot more of the screen in Figure 9.2 (notice that you can see a lot more of the desktop in the background). The point of this example is to show you that a pixel does not have a defined physical dimension, but depends on the settings of the device that is displaying it.

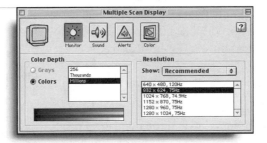

FIGURE 9.1

This is a 21-inch monitor set to display at a resolution of 832 x 624 pixels.

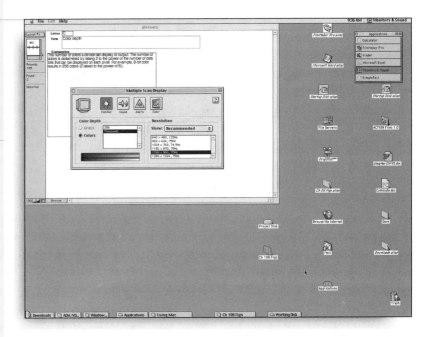

FIGURE 9.2

This is the same monitor and images, but now the monitor is set to display at a resolution of 1,280 x 960 pixels—notice how much more desktop space there is.

So, in addition to the amount of space you have on your desktop, why is resolution important? Because it affects all aspects of how graphics appear onscreen, how they are captured, and how they are printed. The greater the resolution you use, the more information (pixels in this case) can be displayed. The more information that a graphic contains, the more detailed it can be.

The more information a graphic contains (more pixels), the more "horsepower" is required to work with it.

Understanding resolution is also important if you prepare graphics that will be viewed by other people using other Macs. For example, if you design a graphic assuming that your audience has a 21-inch monitor set to $1,280 \times 960$, users who have a 15-inch monitor set to use 640×480 won't be able to see all of your image because you use a larger display image than they are capable of using. If you try to print a graphic using a 300 dpi printer, but you only designed the graphic with 72 dpi, the image won't look as good.

Managing the resolution of your graphics is a vital part of working with graphics on the Mac. Images that don't have sufficiently high resolution won't print properly, or will look bad on a screen-based document, such as a Web page. Images that have a resolution that is too high will waste disk space and imagesetter time, thereby wasting your money.

The last general item you need to understand about resolution is that every device has a maximum resolution at which it can work. For example, a 21-inch monitor may be able to display a resolution up to $1,280 \times 1,024$, but a smaller monitor many be able to display only up to $1,024 \times 768$. Similarly, one digital camera may be able to capture images with a resolution of 640×460 pixels. A camera that can capture images with a resolution of $1,024 \times 768$ will have more detailed images because it can capture more information—more pixels.

When creating Mac graphics, there are at least three kinds of resolutions that you need to think about. These are the following:

- **The resolution of your Mac and its monitor**. Not only do you need to consider the number of pixels (the resolution) that can be displayed by your monitor, but you need to consider the resolution that your Mac is capable of displaying. The amount of information that your Mac can display (its resolution) is determined by the video system it has, including the amount of *Video RAM* installed. I'll show you how to determine your system's resolution in the next section.

Dots per inch

Another measure of resolution is dots per inch (dpi). This indicates how many "dots" of information a device can fit into an inch of length. The more dots per inch that can be used, the higher the detail that can be seen. The resolution of printers is often specified this way; for example, most inkjet printers can print with a resolution of at least 300 dpi.

Maximum resolution

You may be tempted to always use the highest resolution possible so that your images contain as much detail as possible. While this may be your first impulse, life isn't that simple. You must always consider your audience and how your graphic will be delivered to that audience. For example, if you are creating an image for a Web site (which will be displayed onscreen), you don't want a high resolution image. A high resolution image is larger and takes longer to download to the viewer's computer. Plus, a monitor can only display a limited amount of information (compared to a high-resolution printer, for example) so tons of detail in an image designed to be used is "wasted" space. Look for some resolution guidelines later in this chapter.

VRAM

Video RAM, or VRAM, is similar to regular RAM. It is a special area of memory into which your Mac can quickly store information. In VRAM's case, this information is the graphic information that your Mac uses to display an image.

Video cards

Your Mac may have a video card installed in it. If it does, and your monitor is connected to that card, the display capabilities of your system are determined by the video card's specifications, not your Mac's built-in video system. Video cards contain all the hardware needed to display information on your monitor, including the video processor, VRAM, and so on.

Lots of video cards do a lot more than simply display images. Many cards feature 2D and 3D acceleration so that your system draws graphics to the screen quickly. Some cards have TV tuners built in so that you can watch TV on your computer. Others have *digitizing* capabilities that enable you to capture video input (from a video camera or VCR for example) and *digitize* it. You will learn more about these topics in Chapter 10, "Working with Multimedia."

- **The resolution of an image**. The resolution of an image is important because it determines how the media through which you display the graphic (for example, onscreen or hard copy) will display the image. The resolution of an image is simply a measurement of how much information the image contains.

- **The resolution of the imaging device that will be displaying the image**. This means how many dots an imaging device can create per inch of surface (paper, screen, or whatever it is covering with dots).

Working with Your Mac's Resolution

As I said earlier, your Mac's resolution is determined by both its video hardware (VRAM, graphics processor, and so on) and your monitor's capabilities. Your Mac may or may not be capable of displaying a resolution up to your monitor's maximum. All display settings that your Mac uses are determined by the Monitors & Sound control panel (see Figure 9.3). This control panel has four areas: two are devoted to how your Mac displays images, while the other two are devoted to how your Mac uses sound.

FIGURE 9.3

The Monitors & Sound control panel controls the display settings, including resolution, that your Mac uses to display images.

DPI of a monitor

All monitors display 72 dots per inch of viewing area; that is why you won't find a monitor's resolution displayed by a dpi measurement.

Determining the maximum resolution at which you can work is easy to do.

Determining your Mac's maximum resolution

1. Open the Monitors & Sound control panel.
2. Look in the Resolution pane (see Figure 9.3). It lists all of the resolutions that can be used by your Mac *at its current*

color depth (I will explain the link between resolution and color depth in the "Working with Color" section).

3. The maximum resolution of your system is the highest number of pixels that you see on the list; in Figure 9.3, you can see that the maximum resolution for my system is 1,280 × 1,024 pixels (or 1,290,240 total pixels).

Just because your Mac is capable of displaying lots of pixels, you may not feel comfortable working with the maximum amount. Remember that the more pixels that are displayed, the smaller the individual pixels appear to be; with a high resolution, you may find that you have a harder time reading things. For example, if I set my system to its maximum resolution, check out how small things will look (see Figure 9.4). Plus, if you are going to distribute your graphics for onscreen display, you might want to work in a resolution that more closely matches the majority of your intended audience. That way, most people will see your images at the size that you intend for them to see them.

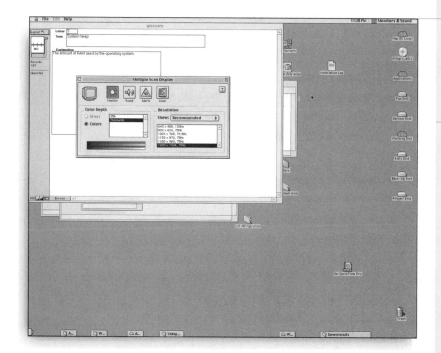

FIGURE 9.4

Using the maximum resolution of your system may not be best for you; look how small things are at the maximum resolution of my system.

Changing your system's resolution is very easy, and you can do it on-the-fly.

Changing your display's resolution

1. Open the Monitors & Sound control panel.

2. Click on the resolution that you want to use.

3. Depending on the resolution you choose, you may see a dialog box asking you to confirm that you want the new setting to be used (see Figure 9.5). If you do, click OK. Your screen will now display according to the resolution you chose.

FIGURE 9.5

When changing monitor resolution, you sometimes see this dialog asking if you really want to choose this resolution.

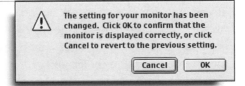

The setting for your monitor has been changed. Click OK to confirm that the monitor is displayed correctly, or click Cancel to revert to the previous setting.

Cancel   OK

That Hz

In Figure 9.3, you may notice the Show pop-up menu, which displays Recommended in the figure. This choice refers to the display frequency that your monitor uses to redraw, also known as "refresh" its screen. In the figure, you can see that resolutions are followed by a comma and then some number of Hz, for example, 832 x 624, 75Hz. In these specifications, Hz stands for Hertz which is a measure of frequency. This number indicates how many times per second that your monitor updates its image. The higher this number, the more often the electron "gun" inside the monitor sprays electrons up and down the inside of your screen (the electrons striking the phosphors on the inside of your monitor is what actually causes images to appear). The higher this number is, the less flicker you will notice in the image. If it gets too low, you will start to notice a flickering of the screen which will lead to poor concentration, headaches, and other problems.

So, how do you know which monitor resolution you should work in? There are several factors that you need to consider, including the following:

- **Your eyesight**. As the resolution increases, the size of everything displayed on your screen decreases. If you increase the resolution enough, you may have trouble reading the smaller text, such as icon labels, that is on your screen. You should choose a resolution that is comfortable for you, remembering that the larger the resolution, the more screen real estate you have.

- **Your working style**. If you are one of those Mac users who likes to keep lots of applications and documents open, then you are likely to want to trade more working room for smaller text and images. If you like to work only in a single application at a time, then a lower resolution may suit you just fine.

■ **Intended use**. Your intended use for the graphic is also an important consideration. If you are creating graphics for others, you really need to think about what kind of resolutions they are most likely to be using. You should shoot for the "lower" end of the resolution scale since you will cover the largest part of the intended audience that way (people who use larger resolutions can easily work with images designed for smaller resolutions, but the reverse is not so true). This is especially important for those graphics that you intend to be viewed onscreen, such as Web pages or electronic documents. Some common resolutions and monitor sizes are in Table 9.1.

TABLE 9.1   **Common monitor sizes and resolutions**

Monitor size	Common Resolution
13-inch	640×480
15-inch	832×624
17-inch	$1,024 \times 768$
21-inch	$1,280 \times 960$

Understanding Image Resolution

Every graphic that you create is developed in a specific resolution, which is not dependent upon the *monitor's* resolution. The resolution of an image is usually measured in pixels per square inch rather than as a horizontal and vertical measurement, as is the case for a monitor's resolution. In a way, this measurement is fictitious: it's easy to resize an image by changing its resolution, or to change an image's resolution by changing its size, without otherwise affecting the contents of the image. It's best to think of image resolution as a measurement of how much information the image contains—how detailed it is, or how many pixels are used to represent a small portion (an inch) of the image.

The higher an image's resolution is, the more detail the image will contain, and the better it will look no matter what size it is

How often should your monitor refresh?

Your monitor is designed to work at certain resolutions and frequencies. These are what you see in the Resolution pane when Recommended is selected. If you choose All from the Show pop-up menu, you will see all of the frequencies that are possible for each resolution.

For most people, a frequency above 70 Hz or so is acceptable.

Is this useful? Not really. I just thought that you might be curious.

What's in a name?

By the way, the name you see at the top of the Monitors & Sound control panel changes depending on the type of monitor you are using. If you have a multi-sync monitor (which is one that can work with multiple resolutions), the name of the window will be Multiple Scan Display. If you have an RGB monitor, it will be called Display.

Changing text size

Of course, you can always increase the size of the font used for icon and folder labels (see Chapter 13, "Changing the Way Your Mac Looks and Sounds" for details). If your desired resolution results in not being able to read the small text, give this a try.

Magnify it

Remember that most applications have an option that enables you to increase the magnification used in a document. You usually have complete control over how large items within a particular document appear. The monitor resolution setting really affects how much screen that you have to work with.

Windows and monitor resolution

Windows PCs can change resolutions just like a Mac can. The standard Windows resolutions are a bit different, though. For example, a common resolution for someone using a 15-inch monitor on a PC is 800 x 600 rather than the Mac's 832 x 624.

viewed at. For example, an image that has 120 pixels per inch will look better when a user zooms in on part of it than an image that was created at a resolution of 72 pixels per inch.

One of the trade-offs is file size. The higher the resolution, the more space it requires to store and the more RAM is required to work with it. Plus, if the image is going to be transmitted via a modem, as it is when it is used on a Web page, size is important. Large files take a long time to transmit.

Deciding what image resolution to use is mainly a trade-off between the quality you need (higher for printed graphics than graphics to be displayed only onscreen), image size (which depends on the medium used to display the graphic), and file size (smaller is better).

Keeping all this straight can be confusing. Since resolution measures an area, the actual size of that area is dependent on the resolution of it. To help you understand this relationship a bit better, take a look at the following calculation.

> If an image's width is 100 pixels and its height is 200 pixels, it contains 20,000 pixels of information.

> If you display it on a monitor that displays 72 pixels per inch, it will be 3.86 square inches in size (that equals 20,000 square pixels divided by 72 pixels per inch times 72 pixels per inch [it is an area]). (For comparison's sake, an 8 × 10 inch image has an area of 80 square inches.)

> If you print the exact same image on a printer that has 300 dots per square inch resolution (without using an application that automatically keeps the image size the same), the image will be only 0.22 square inches (that equals 20,000 pixels divided by 300 dots per inch times two [assuming that the printer has the same resolution in both directions]).

Consider the monitor

Remember that a typical 15-inch monitor running at a resolution of 832 x 624 can display about 100 square inches of inches of information (832 pixels times 624 pixels divided by 72 pixels per inch times 72 pixels per inch [an area]).

What this example hopefully helps you understand is the relationship between image resolution, monitor resolution, and imaging resolution. You need to carefully choose the resolution of your images so that they are appropriate for the media you will use to display those images. For example, you wouldn't want an image to be too small when you print it, nor would you want it to be too large for easy viewing onscreen.

Unfortunately, when talking about resolution, there is still one more twist of which you need to be aware. The issue is this: how does your Mac handle an image that has a higher or lower pixel-to-inch ratio than the monitor? This varies from application to application, but in general the following is true:

- **Layout programs**. Page layout applications, such as QuarkXPress and Adobe PageMaker, and layout program "wannabes," such as Microsoft Word, display the image at its designed-to size. If there are more pixels than the monitor can display in the given size, the application throws away the pixels that it can't use. If there aren't enough pixels, the applications just makes some up, inevitably degrading the image's quality.

- **Web browsers**. Web applications, such as Internet Explorer and Netscape Navigator, display all of the pixels in the image, ignoring the designed-to size of the image.

- **Image editors**. Image editors, such as Adobe Photoshop, enable you to view images at just about any magnification you choose. The image editor will throw away or guess at pixels as needed to display the image at the current screen resolution.

Understanding Imaging Resolution

It doesn't take a genius to understand that you create a graphic for people to look at in order to convey information or to entertain them. There are two basic means by which people will view your masterpiece. One way is through an onscreen presentation; the other is through a printed hard copy.

If you are developing an image for display on a monitor, all you really have to worry about is the image size and number of colors used (which you'll learn about in the next section). Since all monitors have the same resolution, which is 72 dpi, the variables are the physical size of the monitor (the screen area) and how many colors the viewing system will support. Fortunately, since you also use a monitor, these parameters are easy for you to vary to make sure that your image looks good on the monitors of your target audience.

Setting an image's resolution

When you create a new image in many graphics applications (such as Adobe's Photoshop), first, you set the resolution at which you want the image to be created. While it is relatively easy for your Mac to make a higher resolution image into a lower resolution one (since it just has to throw pixels away), trying to increase an image's resolution usually doesn't work because your Mac has to "make up" information to add. The results of this are usually not very good. A rule of thumb is to start with the highest resolution that you think you might need—keeping in mind that the higher resolution you choose, the more computing horsepower will be needed to work with that image. Since you can always reduce the resolution of an image—usually quite easily too—it is better to start on the high resolution side.

Resolution and digital cameras and scanners

The resolution of both scanners and digital cameras are both measured in pixels, just like a monitor. Many consumer-level digital cameras can only capture images at 640 x 480 resolution. That doesn't provide much detail so that images don't look very good when displayed at large sizes on a monitor or when printed on a high-resolution printer. The resolution of cameras is improving and many only slightly more expensive versions have resolutions of 1,200 x 1,000.

The resolution of most scanners is already pretty high, usually in the 1,200 x 1,000 ballpark for a medium-quality scanner.

More on monitor resolution

When referring to monitors, I have used resolution to refer to two different "resolutions." The first kind of resolution referred to the number of pixels that a monitor is able to display–remember that is specified as number of pixels in width by number of pixels in height. The second kind refers to the physical property of all monitors to display 72 dots per inch.

You may be wondering how monitors can display different resolutions if they all display 72 dpi. The answer is that the inch of area gets "smaller" when the resolution increases– well, conceptually anyway. So while a monitor is always displaying 72 dpi, the perceived size of "a dot" that is displayed depends on the monitor's current resolution because the size of the pixels gets smaller. Thus, a higher resolution provides more screen area and images look smaller. A lower resolution provides less screen area and images look larger. This is a bit confusing, but once you think about it a little bit and try changing your system's resolution, you will probably get a handle on this concept.

If your image is to be printed—on an inkjet printer, laser printer, a press, or whatever—you need to be especially concerned about the resolution of the output device. More precisely, you need to make sure that the resolution of the image meets the resolution needs of your imaging device. If your image file doesn't contain enough information, the imaging device will produce a poor, *pixelated* image.

Let me warn you that it can be difficult to calculate to correct resolution for a particular imaging device. Most imagesetters use patterns of dots made up of smaller dots to create gray dots and colors. It would be difficult to cover all of the issues in a single chapter, let alone a few pages, but I can give you the most important, inviolate rule to follow when you're sending images to a printer or service bureau: ask the prepress, technical, or customer-service representative! They know their equipment best, and can give you the best advice.

If there isn't anyone you can ask about what resolution to use, you can look in the manual and other documentation that came with the device to see what its resolution is.

Or, you can use Table 9.2 as a rough guide for the proper resolution to use for common imaging devices. The recommendations are for images at 100% size, and do not apply to images that have been scaled in a page layout program or by other means.

TABLE 9.2   **Suggested image resolutions for various imaging devices**

Device	Suggested Resolution
Monitor (for Web pages and onscreen presentations)	72 pixels/inch
Dot matrix printer	72 pixels/inch
Laser and Inkjet Printers	100-150 pixels/inch (72 pixels/inch may be adequate for comps)
DocuTech%	150 pixels/inch
Imagesetters and direct-to-plate presses	300 pixels/inch

Working with Color

One of the most important factors in any graphic is the colors used in it. The right colors can make an image sing; the wrong colors turn that song into a dirge. Whether you are "color challenged" as I am or you are one of those lucky folks who can sense which colors are "right," you need to have a good understanding of how your Mac works with color. This understanding is especially critical if you are creating graphics for others to view, but it is also important because you work with color constantly even if you aren't creating a masterpiece. For example, the Mac OS 8.5 interface itself makes extensive use of color; the "wrong" colors for you can make looking at your Mac more tiring than it needs to be. You also make use of color within most applications; for example, even Microsoft Word uses color when you use the revisions' tracking feature.

Understanding Color

Ever tried explaining the color of something to someone? No matter how precise you tried to be, it is highly likely that the person you were talking to ended up with a slightly different picture of the color you were describing than the one in your mind. That is because we humans all perceive color slightly differently. Color to us is an abstract concept that can't be described in precise terms.

Computers, on the other hand, are more precise when it comes to color than we are. As with everything else it deals with, your Mac "thinks" about color by using numbers (ones and zeros, to be technical about it).

Your Mac uses two basic techniques to work with color. With one, your Mac specifies a color's coordinates in a *color space*. With the other, your Mac specifies the color's position in a fixed *palette* of colors.

A color space is simply a system that uses a set of three numbers to represent the gamut of possible colors. Many Mac

Not black and white, only shades of gray…

In the following discussion, keep in mind that you can set your Mac in "black-and-white" mode in which it works with shades of gray. You can manipulate the shades of gray just as you do colors. For example, you can set your Mac to use a certain number of shades of gray just as you can set it to use a certain number of colors. Why would you want to work in gray when there is a world of color inside your Mac? You might want to work in the world of gray if you will be printing to a black-and-white (shades of gray actually) printer so that your onscreen image looks more like the printed version. In any case, when I talk about using color, how to set the colors your Mac uses, for example, remember that the same techniques apply when you are working with grays. You can only set your "gray-depth" to 256 shades or less.

Mac palettes won't make your hands dirty

The term palette simply refers to a collection of colors that are used to create an image (remember that everything you see on your Mac is an image, even your desktop). The term comes from the palette used by a painter to hold the paints she uses to create a painting. And the idea of a palette on your Mac is exactly the same—except the Mac's palette is a lot cleaner, and it never runs out of paint.

applications, including Mac OS 8.5, use the *Red Green Blue* (*RGB*) color space, which breaks down colors into their red, green, and blue components. Another common color space, also used by the Mac OS, is *HSB*, which breaks down color into Hue, Saturation, and Brightness components.

The "amount" of each component (red, blue, and green, or hue, saturation, and brightness) in a color is indicated by a number that represents how much of that component is in a particular color. The number for each component can be in the range of zero to 255.

For example, in the RGB color space, "pure" red is represented as (255,0,0), as in the following:

Red = 255

Blue = 0

Green = 0

Using coordinates to specify the color of each pixel in an image enables you to choose each pixel's color from a set of more than 16 million possible colors. This system, sometimes called "true color" or "full color," yields the most natural-looking displays on a monitor, and is the color system used in all serious file formats for color printing.

Unfortunately, providing for 16 million possible colors for each pixel eats up a lot of memory—both the RAM or VRAM memory used by the Mac's video system, and the hard disk memory that is used to store the image. Every pixel requires three bytes of memory to store its RGB value (each byte contains a number for one of the three components, three components require three bytes), and for an image with thousands or millions of pixels, that adds up to a lot of bytes—each of which requires RAM, VRAM, and hard disk space to manipulate.

The extreme resource requirements of color spaces lead to the development of palette-based systems. They solve the resource problem by using a system of abbreviations to store each pixel's color. Let's say an image has a palette of four colors, such as the following:

Why 255?

In case you are wondering, 255 is the maximum value possible for a color's component because it is the largest integer that can be stored in a single byte of computer memory.

color 0 = (0,0,0) (white)

color 1 = (255,255,255) (black)

color 2 = (255,0,0) (red)

color 3 = (0,0,255) (blue)

Rather than having to store three pieces of information for the color of each pixel, your Mac only has to store one piece of data—the number of the color on the palette. This requires a lot fewer resources than storing the numbers of the three components.

The price you pay for the reduced resource requirement is in image quality. Rather than having more than 16 million colors to use, your Mac is now limited to the number on the particular palette you are using (for example, 256 colors). If you have an image that contains thousands of subtly-different colors—as most scanned photographs do—you're going to lose some image quality when you limit the number of colors in the image to a few hundred or a few dozen choices on a palette. Your Mac "forces" all the colors in the image to be those on its palette, resulting in an image that has distorted color when compared to the full-color version. This "forcing" process is actually called *dithering*.

The number of colors on a palette is called its *bit depth*—bit depth refers to how many bits of data are required to store the color for each pixel in an image. The common bit depths and resulting number of colors are shown in Table 9.3.

TABLE 9.3	**Bit depth and number of colors**
Bit Depth	**Number of Colors**
1	2
4	16
8	256
16	65,536
24	16,777,216

Bit depth and number of colors

The number of colors in a palette is determined by raising 2 to the number of bits required to store the data needed to define that amount of color. For example, 8-bit depth results in 256 colors (2 raised to the eighth power).

Setting an image's palette

Many imaging and graphic applications enable you to set the color palette you use to create an image. You need to check the documentation that came with your favorite applications to learn how this works. Because of the variability of how this is done across applications, the remainder of this section deals with managing the color on your system rather than in an image.

Windows palettes

Windows PCs also use color palettes similar to the Mac's. However, the same colors will appear darker on a Windows machine than they do on a Mac (I could draw a conclusion from this, but I will leave that for you to do). If you are designing an image that will be viewed on Windows machines also, try to make the colors a bit lighter than you might choose for images used only on the Mac.

Appeal to the masses

Again, like resolution, if you are developing an image that will be widely distributed (such as on a Web page), you will get a better result if you design your image for the capabilities of the lower end of your target market. For example, if you create an image at the 16-bit color depth, but the bulk of your audience can only use 8-bit color, some of your work will be lost since the viewer's Mac will have to trim the number of colors down. Plus, higher bit-depth images are larger and require more time to download and to display after they are loaded on a machine.

It is always a good idea to take a look at any image you create in a variety of bit depths to make sure that it looks OK in as many situations as possible.

Similar to resolution, there are two areas in which you have to consider bit depth. The first is on your Mac itself. That is, you can set your Mac to display up to a maximum number of colors. The number of the colors that you can have displayed is determined by the combination of your Mac's video hardware (or graphics card), your monitor, and the resolution at which your monitor is set. Depending on your hardware, you may be limited to a fewer number of colors at your system's maximum resolution. If you decrease your resolution, you may be able to increase the number of colors displayed. (Basically, this is a result of your Mac having only so much capability dedicated to displaying pixels. If you ask it to display more pixels, it may have to display less information for each pixel—meaning fewer colors. If you have it display fewer pixels, it may be able to display more colors per pixel.)

The second area in which you need to think about palettes and the number of colors available to your Mac is in images themselves. Just as an image is designed with a particular resolution, it can also be designed by using a particular palette; the larger the number of colors you use for the image, the more resources will be required to open the image. If the person viewing your image has a lower bit depth (number of colors) available, the colors in your image may appear differently than they did to you because his Mac has to substitute colors in the image in order to be able to display them.

Using Colors on Your Mac

As with resolution, you can determine how many colors your Mac uses for its display through the Monitors and Sound control panel. In addition to the color depth, you also can use the Appearance control panel to access the Mac's Color Picker to set highlight colors, as well as the color of some interface elements. The Color Picker is also useful for setting colors within some applications.

Setting Your Mac's Color Depth

Setting the number of colors that your Mac uses is very similar to setting its resolution.

Setting the number of colors displayed on your Mac

1. Open the Monitors & Sound control panel.

2. Click the Monitor button (see Figure 9.6). Depending on your Mac's hardware, in the Color Depth section, you will see color depths from 256 colors to Millions of colors.

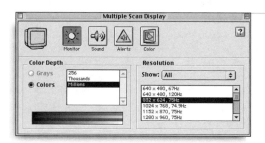

3. Click the color depth that you want. You may see a brief flash as your Mac recalibrates the colors that are being displayed. Your Mac will be capable of displaying up to the number of colors that you choose.

Using the Color Picker to Create and Apply Color

You will likely work with color in a variety of situations. These instances will include when you are working with the desktop as well as from within applications. In Mac OS 8, Apple introduced the Color Picker, which replaced the old color wheel. Color Picker enables you to create custom colors and apply them to interface elements as well as to items within some applications, such as graphic elements and text.

When you access the Color Picker, it opens into a two-pane window (see Figure 9.7). The left pane provides you with various color space choices including: *Cyan Magenta Yellow Black (CMYK)*, Crayon, HSV, HTML, and RGB. The right pane provides the controls you use to make changes to the color.

As you select different color spaces, the controls change to reflect that space. Figure 9.8 shows the controls for the Crayon Picker, while Figure 9.9 shows the RGB Picker controls.

Color depth and resolution, together forever

Remember that your Mac has only so many resources devoted to its display system. If you can't choose the color depth that you want, you will have to choose a lower resolution.

FIGURE 9.6

You can use the Monitors & Sound control panel to set the number of colors used on your Mac.

It looks the same to me

The differences between some color depths can be subtle. For example, if you only have the desktop visible, you probably won't see any difference when you go from Thousands of colors to Millions of colors. However, if you have a full-color photograph open, you will see changes in the colors that are used in the image.

Color depth and games

Games are some of the most demanding applications there are in terms of raw processing power. Because the action is happening fast and furiously, your Mac really works to keep up with all of the movement onscreen. Many games are designed to use a fairly low number of colors, usually 256, to enable mid-level Macs to be able to run them with an adequate *frame rate* (smooth motion as opposed to a flip book effect). Good game programs automatically switch the color depth of your Mac when they are launched and then switch back to the original setting after you quit. Poor programs don't switch back to your original color depth when they quit so you have to do it manually. This is the case for a lot of children's software for some reason.

FIGURE 9.7

The CMYK enables you to customize and apply colors from a variety of color spaces—it is currently using the CMYK color space.

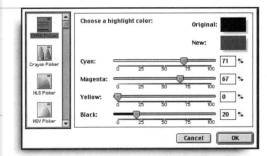

FIGURE 9.8

The Crayon Picker is the most fun to use.

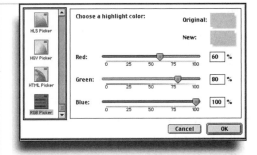

FIGURE 9.9

The RGB Picker is a good choice when you are designing images to be displayed onscreen.

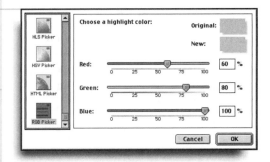

Using these controls, you can create the color that you want to have applied to the item with which you are working.

The nice thing about the Color Picker is that it works the same way no matter where you use it. As an example of how to use it, open the Color Picker and change the color that your Mac uses to highlight items on the desktop.

Creating a custom highlight color by using the Color Picker

1. Open the Appearance control panel.

2. Click on the Appearance tab (see Figure 9.10).

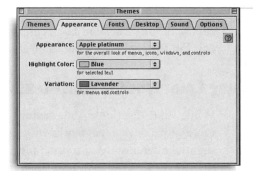

HTML picker

If you are creating graphics for the Web, remember the HTML Picker in the Color Picker. This color space optimizes the color choices so that your images will use standard Web colors and will have colors that are reasonably close to how they look onscreen.

FIGURE 9.10
You can set the Mac's highlight color with the Appearance control panel.

3. Click on the Highlight Color pop-up menu and choose Other.

4. Choose the Crayon Picker color space.

5. Click the crayon showing the color that you want to use. The original color and the new color are shown in the upper-right corner of the screen. The name of the new color is also shown (see Figure 9.11).

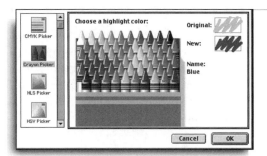

FIGURE 9.11
In this Color Picker dialog, a nice blue has been selected as the highlight color.

Color Picker and video

The eyedropper tool even works on video. So if you have a movie or TV playing in the Apple Video Player, you can click on an image in the video and the Color Picker will grab that color.

6. If you don't see any colors that you like, hold the Option and Command keys down. When you do, the pointer will change into an eyedropper. If you click on a color with the eyedropper showing, the color on which you click will become the new color. You can click on any color that you see (for example, you can pick a color from an image that is open in the background).

7. When the highlight color is just right, click OK.

8. Close the Appearance control panel. Any item you select on the desktop will be highlighted with the color you chose.

The Color Picker works in a similar way wherever you need to choose or create a color. For example, you can use it to create or edit Finder label colors and some applications use it as well.

Using ColorSync for Consistent Color Across Devices

All things ColorSync

Apple maintains a Web site that is dedicated to ColorSync. The address is `http://colorsync.apple.com`.

While your Mac thinks about color by using precise numeric values, each device that works with that color presents it in slightly different ways. For example, a shade of blue may be slightly darker on the monitor than it appears in a printed piece. This discrepancy among the way different devices present color makes it very difficult to achieve the exact color you want.

Color matching is not easy

Matching colors is not easy—even if all of the devices you use implement ColorSync. There is not enough room in this section, let alone this book, to explain color matching technology in detail. The purpose of this section is to explain the basics of ColorSync to you so that you understand how it works and to give you a couple of examples showing how to use it. If you need to achieve professional color matching, you need to do some additional research and learn to fully understand how to use ColorSync with your system and applications.

Traditionally, this problem was solved by making numerous color proof copies. You would get the color close to where you thought it should be and then make a print. If the print wasn't right, which it wasn't, you adjusted the color a bit and tried again. And on it went, until the print looked like you wanted it to—which was different than the color on the monitor. If you sent the piece to an outside printer, you ended up with yet another color. Obviously, this was not an elegant solution at all.

Apple developed ColorSync technology to solve this problem. The purpose of ColorSync is to "match" colors across devices, including monitors, printers, and scanners. Using ColorSync, you can achieve consistent color, regardless of the device being used. This enables you to more efficiently achieve the color you want in the final piece.

ColorSync works by using a *profile* file for each device on with which you want to work; this profile describes the way the device handles color. While ColorSync is built into Mac OS 8.5, you need to add the ColorSync profile for each device that is connected to your Mac. When you use a ColorSync-savvy application, information about each device's profile is embedded into the image that you create. When you work with this image, ColorSync compares the colors of the devices you used (such as a printer) and picks colors that match your target (usually your monitor).

While ColorSync is a very promising solution to a major problem for people who work with color, it is still a relatively new technology. Only recently have major players (such as Adobe Systems) announced support for it. At the moment, ColorSync is implemented in different ways from within different applications, and different printers implement it differently as well. To use ColorSync in more ColorSync-savvy applications, you must choose a source file that you want to use the desired colors first and then choose a target device that contains the colors you want to use. To use ColorSync in general productivity applications, you select the ColorSync option from your printer's Print dialog box.

Understanding ColorSync

ColorSync is implemented in Mac OS 8.5 with the following components:

- **ColorSync control panel**. This control panel enables you to set the default profiles for your system (see Figure 9.12). You can set a System Profile, the RGB Default, CMYK Default, and the Preferred CMM (Color Match Master).

Apple ColorSync profiles

ColorSync profiles for many Apple-produced devices are installed with the ColorSync software.

Digital Color Meter

Mac OS 8.5 comes with the Digital Color Meter application (it is in the Monitors Extras Folder that is within in the Apple Extras folder). This application helps you translate the colors you see on your monitor into industry standard values, such as Pantone. If you need to use industry standard colors, take a look at this application.

FIGURE 9.12

FIGURE 9.12

The ColorSync control panel enables you to select the ColorSync profiles for your system.

FIGURE 9.13

These AppleScripts will help you work with ColorSync; they are located within the ColorSync Extras folder that is in the Apple Extras folder.

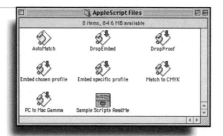

- **ColorSync extension**. The ColorSync extension provides your Mac with the basic ColorSync functionality.
- **ColorSync Profiles folder**. This folder, located within the System Folder, contains ColorSync profiles for the devices installed on your system.
- **ColorSync Extras**. This folder, located on your system startup disk, contains some ColorSync related AppleScripts.

Using ColorSync in a General Application

ColorSync is not only for graphic applications, but you can also apply it in any document that uses color. To do so, you work with the print dialog for your printer.

Using ColorSync with an HP DeskJet printer

1. Open the application containing the image you want to work with (make sure that the document uses color, of course).
2. When you are ready, choose Print.
3. In the DeskJet Print dialog, click Options (see Figure 9.14).
4. In the Options dialog, choose ColorSync from the Color Matching pop-up menu (see Figure 9.15).

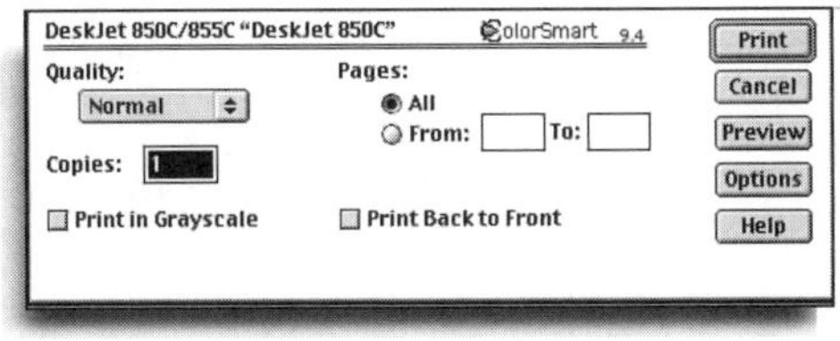

FIGURE 9.14

This figure shows an example of a print dialog with which you can choose ColorSync color matching.

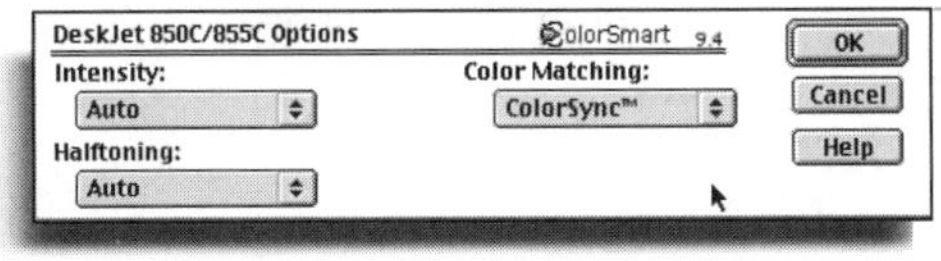

FIGURE 9.15

You can use ColorSync color matching in the DeskJet print dialog.

5. Continue the printing process. When the print job is done, the colors on it should closely match the way they looked on your monitor.

Using ColorSync in a ColorSync-Capable Application

The best image editing application, Adobe Photoshop, has substantial ColorSync capabilities. You can find ColorSync plug-ins for Photoshop on the Apple ColorSync Web site (`http://colorsync.apple.com`). One of these plug-ins enables you to perform a color transformation (based on your target device) on TIFF images while you import them into Photoshop.

Using the ColorSync Import plug-in in Adobe Photoshop

1. Install the ColorSync Import plug-in in the Plug-ins folder in the Adobe Photoshop folder.

2. Launch Photoshop.

3. From the File menu, choose Import; then choose TIFF with ColorSync Profile (see Figure 9.16).

4. Choose the TIFF file that you want to import and click OK.

5. In the ColorSync Import module, click on the Match options that you want (see Figure 9.17). In this example, I have matched the color in the TIFF to my monitor and have chosen the Color LW 12/600 to match the color on printing.

FIGURE 9.16

You can import a TIFF file into Photoshop while correcting the color with ColorSync.

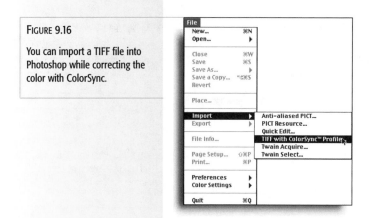

FIGURE 9.17

You can use the ColorSync Import Module to work with ColorSync profiles when you import files.

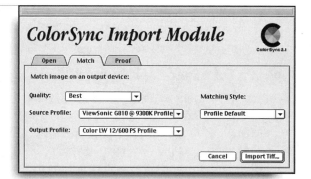

6. Click Import Tiff. The graphic will be opened, and a ColorSync profile will be embedded in it (see Figure 9.18). This will cause the color of the image to be consistent when you output the image—the colors will be the same in the printed version as they are on your monitor.

Understanding Graphics

The last thing you need to know about graphics on the Mac is that there are two main "families" of computer graphic applications: *raster-based* programs and *vector-based* programs. Some graphics programs, and some graphics file formats created by such programs, may not fall neatly into one family or the other, but the difference between the two is essential to understanding how a Mac represents and stores images.

FIGURE 9.18

This image has a ColorSync profile embedded in it.

Understanding Raster-Based Graphics

Raster-based graphics, also commonly called *bitmap images*, break down an image into a grid of pixels. Each pixel is assigned a numerical value that represents the brightness and color value of that pixel. The numerical values are used both to display the image on the Mac's monitor and to store the image on disk.

Raster-based images are great for storing images that contain lots of detail, such as photographs, scans of art, and 3D renderings. *Optical Character Recognition (OCR)* programs that are used to convert scanned paper documents into electronic text documents also usually use a raster-based image as an intermediary form.

The following are the two main down sides to raster-based images:

- **They're big.** Even at the low monitor resolution of 72 dpi, an image that is 100 x 200 pixels will contain 20,000 pixels. If this image is 24-bit or full color, each pixel needs several bytes of memory for display and storage. This is a large amount of information for your Mac to manipulate. And, remember that 72 dpi is a fairly low resolution—certainly too low for printing. A medium-sized color image for use in a real print job may require several dozen MB of storage space.

Raster-based image note

All of the objects in raster-based images are part of the same image; the images are built entirely of pixels. So if you see a line and try to select it, you won't succeed. That line is actually not a line, but a series of pixels. However, some raster-based applications enable you to use layers; layers make it possible to stack objects on top of each other so that they appear to be part of the same image, but are actually separate images "layered." This is good because you can edit the objects on each layer separately.

Raster-based applications

Widely-used Mac graphics programs that manipulate raster-based images are Adobe Photoshop and PhotoDeluxe. Most other image editing applications (as opposed to drawing applications) are also raster-based.

The first raster-based Mac application was the legendary MacPaint.

A vector-based graphic is like silly putty…

Because a vector-based graphic is actually a collection of mathematical equations, it is infinitely scaleable. You don't have to worry about resolution in a vector-based graphic. It depends on mathematical equations for its shape rather than pixels.

Vector-based applications

Commonly-used Mac applications that use vector-based graphics include Adobe Illustrator and Macromedia Freehand.

The most popular vector-based application was MacDraw. It was a simple, but powerful program that was perfect for quick sketches. I still use an old version whenever I want to create an image quickly; it was updated to MacDraw Pro but since has faded into Mac history.

- **They don't scale well.** You can usually reduce the size of raster images fairly successfully, but when you try to scale up a raster-based image, the image quality quickly deteriorates. As I discussed earlier in this chapter, this is because your Mac has to "make up" information to fill in the empty pixels that are added when you increase the image's resolution.

Generally, you will use raster-based graphics for images that are not composed of lines, polygons, and other regular elements. These include photos, complex models, animations, video, and so on.

Understanding Vector-Based Graphics

Vector-based images take a different approach to represent images electronically. Rather than representing a picture as a grid of pixels, a vector-based image represents a picture as a collection of geometric shapes and stores the image as mathematical descriptions of each shape.

I promise that you don't want to see the actual PostScript description of a vector-based image; in fact, even simple graphics are quite complex when you see them in PostScript. However, if the mathematical description for a simple vector-graphic consisting of a line and a "squiggle" were translated into English, it would look something like the following:

```
set the line color to black

set the line weight to 1 pt.

draw a line from point x₁, y₁, to point x₂, y₂ with curvature
c₁

draw a line from point x₂, y₂, to point x₃, y₃ with curvature
c₄

draw a box from point x₄, y₄, to x₅, y₅
```

Although this may seem long-winded, it's much more compact than storing the value of every single pixel in the image. Even better, the size (and quality) of the description doesn't change when you resize the image, even if you scale it from the size of a postage stamp to the size of a billboard.

There's a down side, of course: vector-based images can't handle complexity, especially complexity on the level of a photograph, very well. I'm not saying that you can't create interesting, complex artwork with vector-based images because you can. However, creating a vector-based image that contains as much detail as a photograph would be a monumental challenge.

You should use a vector-based application for simple sketches, floor plans, flow charts, and other graphics for which you need simple geometric shapes.

It's two application in one

There are some applications that can work with both vector-based and raster-based images. Usually, these programs have a separate set of tools for each image type. The most successful of these type of applications was SuperPaint.

10

Working with Multimedia

Using QuickTime to watch digital movies, listen to sound, and see animation

Creating and editing your own QuickTime movies, including multiple-track movies and slide shows

Listening to audio CDs and watching TV and movies on your desktop

Capturing video and sound from both a video source and audio CDs

Understanding DVD

Using the Ultimate Multimedia Machine

Multimedia simply means the combination of various types of media—sound, text, graphics, video, or animation—together into one "experience." In practice, multimedia also refers to any content that uses *dynamic* data to convey information; dynamic data simply means data that changes over time. Although multimedia is one of the most overused buzzwords in the computing world, it is also one of the most compelling reasons to use a computer. Using multimedia makes data come alive, enabling people to better understand it. Equally important, multimedia is *fun*, and, let's face it, in today's high-paced world, most of us can use more fun.

As with graphics, the Macintosh has been at the leading edge of the multimedia world. Since the Mac has always included sound capabilities, it was relatively easy to incorporate sound into documents even with the very first Mac. CD-ROM drives have been standard equipment on Macs for a long time, and unlike many Windows CD-ROMS, most Mac CD-ROMs work flawlessly. And the Mac's superior hardware quality, software, and system integration still make it the best machine for using and creating multimedia.

Mac OS 8.5 includes an excellent multimedia tool kit with which you can view, hear, create, and edit multimedia content. With Mac OS 8.5, you can do the following:

- **Watch, edit, and create digital videos, sound, and animation**. Apple's QuickTime technology is the premiere technology for manipulating, distributing, and displaying time-synchronized data. You can use MoviePlayer to watch videos, animations, and other multimedia files. If you upgrade to QuickTime Pro, you can also edit those files.

- **Listen and capture sound from audio CDs**. The Mac's CD Audio Player provides a sophisticated tool with which you can listen to audio CDs. You can also create custom listening programs that will be remembered each time you play your favorite discs. You can also capture sounds from audio CDs to use as system sounds and in your own projects.

- **Watch TV and movies on your desktop and capture still images and video.** Apple's Video Player enables you to make a Mac (with the required hardware) into a fully-functional entertainment center. Plus, you can capture digital video, images, and sound from your favorite sources to use on your system and in your projects.

Digital Video, Sound, and Animation with QuickTime

Apple's QuickTime is the technology that your Mac uses to handle time-synchronized data. Time-synchronized data simply means data that must be managed so that its components remain "in-time" with each other. For example, when playing a digital video, the video image must remain in synch with the soundtrack. When watching an animation or video, sound effects need to occur at the correct points in the animation or video.

While it is natural to think of QuickTime in terms of video, you should also remember that QuickTime can be used for sound, animation, and other dynamic data as well. And not all components have to be present at all times; for example, you can have a QuickTime movie that consists only of a soundtrack.

You will encounter QuickTime movies in many places, including: interactive games, reference titles, entertainment titles, learning tools, and Web pages.

Understanding QuickTime

QuickTime actually consists of two different "flavors" of technology:

- **QuickTime**. QuickTime is the basic technology through which your Mac manages time-based data. This data takes many forms including video, sound, and animation. Applications can use QuickTime to implement its features.

QuickTime—a rare, Apple-developed standard

Apple's QuickTime has been very successful. So successful, in fact, that it is also a standard on Windows computers as well as Macs. QuickTime movies on Windows will play the same way that they do on the Mac.

QuickTime has also been widely adopted on the Web. Many videos and animations that you will find on Web sites are QuickTime files.

QuickTime and streaming

With QuickTime 3.0, QuickTime movies can now be *streamed*. Streaming means that files can be viewed while they are being downloaded; this makes QuickTime even more valuable for the Web. See Chapter 27, "Browsing the Web: Advanced Techniques," for details.

QuickTime and file formats

QuickTime supports many types of file formats that you are likely to encounter on the Internet as well as on CD-ROMs and other sources of multimedia files (QuickTime Pro supports even more file types than the standard version of QuickTime does). These files can contain all sorts of content, everything from videos to sounds to still images and combinations of all of these. You don't need to be an expert on all these file formats in order to be able to view them. Mostly, you can try them and see what happens.

Some of the more common file types you will use are .mov (QuickTime movie files), MPEG-1 (a video encoding scheme that is used across all platforms), .avi (Windows movie files), and .mid (MIDI music files). MPEG-2 is the encoding system that is used for movies on DVD—if you use a DVD player with your Mac, you will use this file type (although MPEG-2 is not supported by QuickTime yet).

QuickTime on the Web

In order to view QuickTime movies on the Internet, your Web browser needs to have the AppleTalk plug-in installed. You can learn more about this in Chapter 27, "Browsing the Web: Advanced Techniques."

- **QuickTime VR**. QuickTime Virtual Reality (VR) is an amazing technology that enables you to explore virtual worlds. You can move around in those worlds, and you can even closely examine objects in those worlds.

QuickTime is enabled through several control panels, extensions, and other files, including the following:

- **QuickTime Settings control panel**. The control panel enables you to do the basic configuration of QuickTime on your Mac.

- **QuickTime extension**. This extension provides basic QuickTime functionality.

- **QuickTime MPEG extension**. This extension enables QuickTime to open and play movies and images encoded with the *Motion Picture Experts Group (MPEG)* compression scheme. The most common of these is MPEG-1.

- **QuickTime Musical Instruments extension**. This extension enables QuickTime to use MIDI music tracks and to reproduce music provided in the MIDI format.

- **QuickTime PowerPlug extension**. This extension provides PowerPC acceleration for QuickTime.

- **QuickTime VR extension**. This extension enables QuickTime to play QuickTime VR files.

- **QuickTime Preferences**. This preference file stores the settings that you enter through the QuickTime Setting control panel.

There are two applications and one plug-in that are part of the QuickTime package—these are all installed in the QuickTime folder that is installed on your startup disk. The QuickTime viewing tools are the following:

- **MoviePlayer.** You can view all kinds of QuickTime movies through the MoviePlayer application that is part of the QuickTime software. With the QuickTime 3 Pro upgrade of MoviePlayer, you can also do some basic editing of QuickTime movies. (I'll explain features of QuickTime 3 Pro shortly).

- **PictureViewer.** This application enables you to view image files.

- **QuickTime Plugin.** This plug-in enables you to view QuickTime movies from a Web browser. Lots of Web sites contain QuickTime movies so you will use this plug-in frequently.

SEE ALSO

➤ *To learn about using QuickTime on the Web, see page 650*

Version 3.0 of QuickTime is part of Mac OS 8.5. With this version, Apple has added a new scheme for QuickTime distribution. With QuickTime version 3.0, you get a basic set of QuickTime capabilities that enable you to view QuickTime movies. If you want more QuickTime capability, you can upgrade version 3.0 to QuickTime 3 Pro. This version, which costs $29.99, has significantly more features than does the basic version 3.0, included with Mac OS 8.5. I'll explain the differences in these versions and how to upgrade in the later sections in this chapter.

Don't want to pay for QuickTime 3 Pro?

The upgraded "Pro" version of MoviePlayer provides significantly more features than the non-Pro version that is standard with Mac OS 8.5. These features include editing capabilities, as well as the capability to play almost any type of multimedia file. The upgrade to QuickTime 3 Pro is worth the $29.99 cost in my opinion. However, if you can't afford the upgrade, you can get *some* of the features of MoviePlayer Pro by using MoviePlayer 2.5, which was part of the QuickTime 2.5 release. While Apple is no longer distributing this version, you probably have a version of it that came with earlier versions of the Mac OS or with an application that uses QuickTime movies. If you don't want to pay for QuickTime 3 Pro, using the 2.5 version of MoviePlayer is an option. Most of the step-by-steps I'll provide for QuickTime 3 Pro later in the chapter apply to MoviePlayer 2.5.

QuickTime 2.5 survival

When you install QuickTime 3.0, even when it is part of the Mac OS 8.5 installation, it may overwrite earlier versions of MoviePlayer (such as 2.5) if they are located in the QuickTime folder in your startup disk. You should keep 2.5 until you are sure that 3.0 will work for you, or if you don't want to upgrade to QuickTime 3 Pro. Before installing QuickTime 3.0, you should move MoviePlayer 2.5 to a different location on your hard drive or back it up on a floppy.

Understanding QuickTime 3.0

With the base version of QuickTime, you'll get very basic QuickTime capabilities. These features include the following:

- Viewing all flavors of QuickTime movies on and off the Internet
- Working with more than 30 different audio and video file formats
- Doubling the size of movies
- Printing frames of movies

Understanding QuickTime 3 Pro

When you pay for the QuickTime 3 Pro upgrade, you'll get a lot more features, especially editing features. QuickTime 3 Pro provides you with all of the capabilities of QuickTime 3.0, plus many more, including the following:

- Playing full-screen video
- Viewing files in a wide variety of formats
- Editing and saving movies in a variety of formats
- Copying and pasting material from a variety of formats into QuickTime movies
- Preparing QuickTime movies for streaming delivery via the Web
- Using sharpening, color tinting, and embossing filters on movies and images
- Creating slide shows from a series of still images

Understanding QuickTime Specifications and File Formats

As with graphics, there are certain parameters that govern how QuickTime movies appear on your Mac. In order to be comfortable with QuickTime, you should understand some of these basic specifications, including the following:

- **Resolution**. QuickTime movies are composed with specific resolutions, just as still images are. The resolution of QuickTime movies is specified similarly to how the resolution of your monitor is, that being x pixels wide by y pixels high.

  While a QuickTime movie looks best in its default resolution, you can resize it in MoviePlayer. Just as with still images, if you try to increase the resolution of a movie by resizing it, your Mac has to create pixels that aren't really there. This usually makes the movie look pixelated. Making a movie smaller usually does not detract from the way it looks since the Mac only has to remove pixels.

  QuickTime movies created with larger resolution are better because they have a larger image to view and better definition of those images. The trade-off is in the frame-rate at which the movie will play back (covered in a subsequent bullet) and the size of the QuickTime movie file. The larger the resolution, the more information that your Mac has to work with, and thus the harder it has to work to play the movie back and the larger the file sizes will be. Sample resolutions for QuickTime movies are shown in Table 10.1.

QuickTime movies are not official US postage

When QuickTime first appeared on the Mac, Mac hardware was underpowered; thus, the early QuickTime movies had to be pretty small so that playback could even approach smooth motion. The standard resolution for a QuickTime movie in those days was a paltry 160 x 120. This earned QuickTime the label of being "postage stamp" size movies by its critics. A bit of an exaggeration perhaps, but the first QuickTime movies were awfully small. Fortunately, both Mac hardware and QuickTime technology has improved greatly so that QuickTime movies are no longer shipped with magnifying glasses

Table 10.1   Common Resolutions for QuickTime Movies

Resolution	Approximate size on 832 x 624 desktop (21-inch monitor)	Comment
130 x 160	2.75-inch x 3-inch	Size of the QuickTime sample movie that ships with QuickTime
160 x 120	3-inch x 2.75-inch	AKA postage stamp
320 x 240	5.75-inch x 5-inch	A good compromise between viewing size and performance
640 x 480	11.5-inch x 9-inch	Full-screen on smaller monitors (13 - 14 inch)

- **Color depth**. QuickTime movies also contain a specific number of colors, or *color depth*. Just like still images, movies with a larger number of colors require more processing power and larger file sizes. Plus, some Macs are limited in the color depth that they can view so creating a movie in 24-bit color may cause it to look different on those machines that cannot work with that many colors. Therefore, these Macs will have to reduce the number of colors in the movie before the movie is played.

- **Frame rate**. QuickTime movies—just like their analog counterparts—are actually a series of still images that are slightly different from one another. As these images are shown onscreen, you can see the illusion of motion—QuickTime is really just the digital age equivalent of the flip book. The faster these images "flip" on the screen, the smoother and more lifelike the movie appears. The speed at which the movie plays is called the *frame rate*.

As with all other aspects of QuickTime movies, there is a trade-off between the quality of the movie and the resources it requires to be played. The higher the frame rate, the smoother and better the movie appears. However, QuickTime movies with higher frame rates require more processing power to view and the files are larger, thus requiring more disk space and download time.

QuickTime movies can contain multiple *tracks*, where each track contains certain information. For example, a movie can have a video track, a text track, and a soundtrack. You can also have multiple tracks of the same type in a single movie. You can manipulate individual tracks with QuickTime 3 Pro.

QuickTime works with a variety of other file formats, including the following:

- **Digital video**. QuickTime can play QuickTime format files, as well as AVI (Windows video format) and MPEG-1 files.

- **Digital audio**. In addition to all audio formats supported by the Mac, QuickTime also supports formats from other platforms such as .wav and .au.

Speed factors

There are several factors that influence the speed at which QuickTime movies can be displayed. These include processing power, video display hardware, hard disk or CD-ROM speed, and connection speed (for a movie over the Internet).

Everything you need to know about QuickTime

Apple maintains several Web pages dedicated to QuickTime. These pages include software and updates that you can download, information on how QuickTime works, links to QuickTime showcases, and so on. The URL to this site is `http://www.apple.com/quicktime`. The site also has some great samples of QuickTime movies that you can view.

- **Digital image**. Of course QuickTime supports PICT and other Mac graphic formats, but it can also display .bmp (Windows) and JPEG and GIF (image compression formats).

- **Animation**. QuickTime also supports several of the standard animation formats, such as PICS files.

- **Music**. QuickTime can play various music files, such as MIDI. You can also create QuickTime movies from the soundtracks on your favorite audio CDs (with QuickTime Pro).

QuickTime for Windows

The file name extension for QuickTime movies on Windows computers is .mov.

Configuring QuickTime

There are several items that you can configure to affect how QuickTime works on your Mac. All QuickTime configuration is done with the QuickTime Settings control panel.

Configuring QuickTime

1. Open the QuickTime Settings control panel (see Figure 10.1). At the top of the control panel is a pop-up menu from which you can select several options. Each option provides a relevant set of controls in the lower part of the window.

FIGURE 10.1

Using the QuickTime Settings control panel to configure QuickTime.

2. Choose AutoPlay from the pop-up menu. You will see two check boxes; both are related to AutoPlay of CDs when a disc is inserted.

3. Check the Enable Audio CD AutoPlay if you want music CDs to automatically begin playing as soon as they are mounted on the desktop.

AutoPlay virus

There is a nasty virus associated with having AutoPlay active. This virus can cause severe damage to your Mac. If you turn AutoPlay off, the virus cannot affect your Mac. If you don't have any anti-virus software installed and updated on your system, I'd recommend that you leave AutoPlay off. If you have your anti-virus software updated, you probably don't need to worry about the virus. See Chapter 30, "Fighting Viruses," to learn about viruses and how to protect yourself from them.

4. Check the Enable CD-ROM AutoPlay if you want programs on CD-ROMs to automatically launch when the disc is mounted.

5. Choose Connection Speed from the pop-up menu and select the radio button corresponding to the connection type with which you connect to the Net. This setting affects how QuickTime movies are downloaded and played from the Web to your Mac.

6. You can safely ignore the rest of the options for now—except for the Registration screen which I will show you how to use in the next section.

In the previous step-by-step, I skipped several options in the QuickTime Settings control panel because the odds are great that you will have no need for them. But, just in case, here is what they do.

Media Keys enables you to manage your access to protected data files. If you need to get to QuickTime files that are sensitive, you may need to use a password (called a *key*) to be able to access the files. You can use this part of the control panel to set up and manage your keys.

Music enables you to choose a different music synthesizer than the default QuickTime synthesizer. If you are involved in creating MIDI files or using a MIDI instrument, you can use this area to configure the alternate synthesizer.

QuickTime Exchange lets you disable QuickTime's capability to read lots of different file formats that are used on other computer platforms. The only situation in which you might want to disable this is if you have some specialized applications that you want to use to work with these kinds of files. Otherwise, you should leave this enabled, which is the default.

Upgrading to QuickTime 3 Pro

I'd suggest that you don't upgrade to QuickTime 3 Pro right away. Use QuickTime 3 for a while to see if it does everything you need it to do. However, if you have any interest in editing and creating QuickTime movies, I'd recommend that you upgrade. Because when you see some of the neat things you can do in some of the step-by-steps in this chapter, I'll bet that you'll want to upgrade pretty quickly.

Upgrading to QuickTime 3 Pro requires no new software—all you need is an upgrade code. The easiest and fastest way to upgrade is through Apple's Web site at `http://www.apple.com/quicktime`. The cost of the upgrade is $29.99. The upgrade process takes only a few minutes.

SEE ALSO

➤ *To learn how to use a Web browser, see Chapter 26, "Browsing the Web: The Basics"*

➤ *To learn about Web security issues, see page 654*

Upgrading to QuickTime 3 Pro through the Web

1. Use Internet Explorer to move to `http://www.apple.com/quicktime` (see Figure 10.2).

2. Click on the upgrade link. You will move to the Upgrade to QuickTime 3 Pro page.

3. Click the Upgrade Now link. You will move onto the secure upgrade page.

Upgrade by phone

You can also upgrade to QuickTime 3 Pro by calling Apple at 1-888-295-0648.

FIGURE 10.2
Apple's QuickTime Web site is a good place to learn more about QuickTime and to upgrade to QuickTime Pro.

4. Complete the form (see Figure 10.3).

FIGURE 10.3

Ordering the QuickTime 3 Pro
upgrade. is pretty standard stuff.

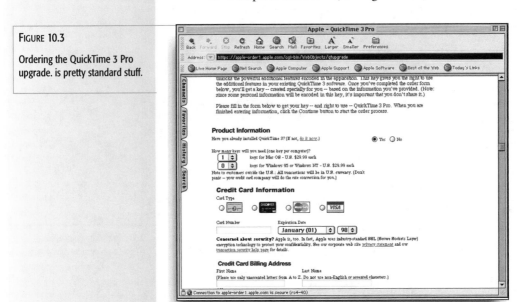

5. When you are done with the form, submit it. Your information will be sent to Apple.

6. Review your order when the review Web page comes up. When everything is OK, click Confirm. After the order process is complete, it will take about a minute for you to see the confirmation page (your key will also be sent to your email address).

7. Print the confirmation Web page for your records.

8. Open the QuickTime Settings control panel (see Figure 10.4).

9. Choose Registration from the pop-up menu at the top of the control panel.

10. Click Enter Registration.

11. Complete the registration information dialog box—here is where you enter your registration number that you received from the upgrade Web site.

12. Click OK. The QuickTime Settings Control panel will confirm that you are now using the Pro version by indicating Pro Player Edition in the QuickTime block.

13. Close the control panel.

14. Put the copy of your registration number in a safe place—it is your proof of registration. Save the email with this number as well. You will need it if you ever reinstall QuickTime.

15. Open the MoviePlayer application. If you don't see the upgrade prompt, you have successfully upgraded to QuickTime 3 Pro.

16. To be even more sure that you have successfully upgraded to QuickTime Pro, open the File menu. If you see the commands in Figure 10.5, you are using QuickTime 3 Pro.

Playing and Editing QuickTime Movies

Using QuickTime is easy, and you can have a lot of creative fun with it—sometimes you might even learn a thing or two. While you need to upgrade to QuickTime 3 Pro to do the really good stuff, you can use the basic version to watch QuickTime movies

What? No movies?

If you don't have any movies on your Mac, use your Web browser to move to `http://www.` `apple.com/quicktime` and download a few movies to try. If you scroll to the bottom of the QuickTime page, you will see the QuickTime Showcase area from which you can view and download movies. Note that if you only click a QuickTime movie from within your Web browser, it will begin playing rather than being downloaded to your Mac. For this example, you should use a movie on your hard drive rather than playing one on the Net.

If you have upgraded to QuickTime Pro, you can download movies from the Internet. To download a movie rather than play it, point to the movie, press Control, click the mouse button, and choose Save As QuickTime Movie from the contextual menu. After the download is completed, you can proceed with the step-by-step. See Chapter 27, "Browsing the Web: Advanced Techniques," for help with downloading files from the Web.

Annoying upgrade message

While I understand why Apple moved to the QuickTime 3 Pro model–previous versions included the full capabilities without additional charge–there is no excuse for the annoying upgrade message that appears the first time you use MoviePlayer each day. The movie is stored on your desktop. Try throwing it out once you have seen it. As I wrote this, Apple was considering changing how this worked.

to your heart's content. In the following sections, you'll learn how to do some basic tasks with QuickTime Pro. Then I'll show you how to do the fun stuff with QuickTime 3 Pro.

Watching QuickTime Movies with MoviePlayer

MoviePlayer is the primary application you use to watch QuickTime movies. With the standard version of MoviePlayer, you can't manipulate movies at all, but for basic viewing, it works.

Watching QuickTime movies

1. Find a movie that you want to watch—you can use the Sample Movie that is in the QuickTime Folder, but that is fairly boring. Find movies on your Mac by using the Finder's Find command to locate movies to watch. Just search for files with the file type MooV. You are likely to find several of them.

SEE ALSO

➤ *To understand how to find files by type, see page 88*

2. Open the movie you want to watch. You will see the MoviePlayer window, which provides all the controls you need to watch a movie, as well as its own set of commands (see Figure 10.6).

3. To start a movie, click the Play button or press the spacebar. While the movie plays, the slider moves to show you where the current point is in the movie.

4. To pause the movie, click the pause button or press the spacebar.

5. To step the movie forward by a frame, click the right-facing step button. To step it backwards, click the left-facing step button.

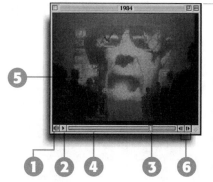

FIGURE 10.6

You can use the MoviePlayer application to watch a QuickTime movie.

1 Volume

2 Play/pause

3 Slider

4 Play bar

5 QuickTime Movie

6 Step buttons

6. To adjust the volume, use the volume slider—click the volume button and the slider pops up. Drag the slider to adjust the volume.

7. To double the size of the movie, from the Movie menu, choose Double Size.

8. When you are done, close the movie or quit MoviePlayer.

Viewing an Image with PictureViewer

PictureViewer is a very simple image viewing utility that is provided with QuickTime. As simple as it is, it can be useful if you come across an image file for which you don't have another viewing application.

Viewing an image with PictureViewer

1. Find an image that you want to view (if you want to download one from the Web, see Chapter 27, "Browsing the Web: Advanced Techniques").

2. Open PictureViewer (it is in the same folder as MoviePlayer).

3. From the File menu, choose Open, move to the image that you want to view, and click Open. You will see the image in the PictureViewer window (see Figure 10.7).

No SimpleText

If SimpleText opens instead of MoviePlayer, quit it and open the movie from within MoviePlayer instead. You can also drag and drop a movie onto MoviePlayer to open it with MoviePlayer.

1984

The movie in Figure 10.6 is a QuickTime version of Apple's famous 1984 commercial, which is one of the most creative and innovative commercials ever made. You might be able to find a copy on the Net if you look for it. It is fun to watch once in a while.

QuickTime everywhere

Many applications can play QuickTime movies, and most of them use controls similar to those that MoviePlayer uses. Some examples include SimpleText, Microsoft Word, Internet Explorer, and many more.

FIGURE 10.7

You can view images in various file format by using Picture-Viewer (it isn't much, but at least it is free).

Blowing it out

If the normal volume adjustment isn't enough for you, hold the Control and Shift keys down when you click the volume slider. You will be able to increase the volume past the normal limit.

Multilingual movies

QuickTime movies can have tracks with different languages. You can select the language track by choosing Choose Language on the Movie menu.

Is there a reason for this?

The reason I have you open an image from within PictureViewer rather than double-clicking it is that you probably have another application that can view images. I want you to try PictureViewer—at least once.

QuickTime VR and Star Trek

QuickTime VR made its first appearance on the Star Trek: The Next Generation Interactive Technical Manual CD-ROM. This disc enabled you to explore the USS Enterprise as if you were actually on it. This disc was, and is, quite popular with fans of both Star Trek and QuickTime VR.

4. Use the commands on the Image menu to resize, rotate, or flip the image.

Experiencing a QuickTime VR World

QuickTime VR enables you to interact with panoramic, virtual worlds. You can move around within a world, and you can even closely examine objects within that world. QuickTime VR is an amazing technology. QuickTime VR is widely used on the Web so there is no shortage of VR worlds for you to explore.

Exploring a QuickTime VR world

1. Find a QuickTime VR world to explore. If you have never used it before, you may not have any QuickTime VR files on your Mac. If you don't, never fear. There are plenty to view on the Web. Go to the QuickTime Web site at `http://www.apple.com/quicktime` and look in the QuickTime Showcase area. There will no doubt be some VR worlds for you to explore (look for files marked with VR). (I am using a QuickTime VR file of the Volkswagen Beetle that enables you to explore the new Bug inside and outside. If you can't find this file, just try any that you do find; all QuickTime VR worlds work in a similar fashion.)

2. Open the QuickTime VR file. If you are using a file stored on your Mac, you will see MoviePlayer. If you are viewing one on the Web, you will just see the movie (see Figure 10.8). When the cursor is over a QuickTime VR movie, it will change into a donut look-alike.

3. To move around the image, simply hold the mouse button down (the cursor will show an arrow to indicate which way you are moving) and move the mouse. The image will move accordingly, and you can explore to your heart's content. Figure 10.9 and Figure 10.10 show various views of the Beetle that I saw by using QuickTime VR.

4. To zoom in on part of the image, hold down the Shift key (see Figure 10.11). To zoom out again, press the Control key.

QuickTime VR is still QuickTime

QuickTime VR files can be viewed with MoviePlayer or the QuickTime plug-in in a Web browser. The difference is in how you control the movie. With a QuickTime VR movie, you can move around in it, while a "regular" QuickTime movie plays in a sequential fashion.

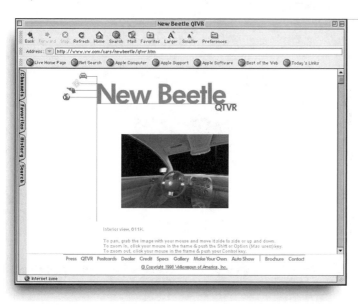

FIGURE 10.8
Exploring a Beetle on the Web with QuickTime VR.

FIGURE 10.9

Here I am exploring the
interior of the VW Beetle with
QuickTime VR.

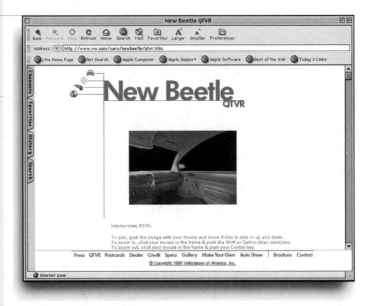

FIGURE 10.10

Now I am looking out the back
window.

Editing Movies with QuickTime 3 Pro

While the standard MoviePlayer application works fine for
watching movies, that is about all you can do with it. If you

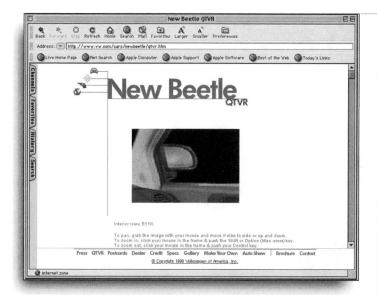

FIGURE 10.11
Here I have zoomed in on the right-side mirror.

upgrade to QuickTime 3 Pro, you will also be able to edit QuickTime movies—this is where the real fun begins. In the following step-by-step, I'll show you how to paste the contents of two movies together to create a new movie. This task shows you the basic editing tools you can use with QuickTime 3 Pro. Editing movies with MoviePlayer is pretty easy because it works just like most other Mac applications. You can select portions of a movie and paste them into other movies, cut them, or duplicate them. Working with QuickTime content is very similar to working with text or graphics.

Editing QuickTime movies with MoviePlayer

1. Launch MoviePlayer. From the File menu, choose New. You will see an empty QuickTime movie (see Figure 10.12).

2. Open a movie from which you want to copy (see Figure 10.13).

QuickTime Pro

Remember that if you haven't upgraded to QuickTime 3 Pro, you won't be able to use MoviePlayer to edit movies.

FIGURE 10.12

Creating a new QuickTime movie–this one doesn't have any content yet.

FIGURE 10.13

This movie is a clip from "Star Trek: The Next Generation."

Copyrights are important

The movies I am using for this example are copyrighted–in this example by Paramount. It is OK for you to play around with them on your own computer for fun, but *don't* distribute any movies that you create from copyrighted material. That is illegal, and it can get you into trouble.

3. To select a portion of the movie, hold down the Shift key and drag the slider (se Figure 10.14). The portion of the movie you select is indicated by the dark section of the play bar.

4. Press Command-C to copy the selection to the clipboard.

5. Move back to the new movie that you created in step 1.

6. Press Command-V to paste the clip into the new movie. The new movie will contain the clip that you pasted into it. Play the clip by pressing the spacebar.

FIGURE 10.14

The dark band in the play bar indicates that that portion of the movie is selected and is ready to be copied.

7. Open another movie and copy a clip from it (repeat steps 3 and 4).

8. Go back into your new movie and move the slider to where you want the next clip to be pasted.

9. Press Command-V to paste the clip in the new movie.

10. Press the spacebar to play both clips—which are now part of the same movie.

11. Keep pasting clips into your movie until it has all of the clips that you want in it.

12. If you want to edit out some of the material, move the slider to the point where you want to begin the cut, hold the Shift key, and drag to select the portion to cut.

13. Press Command-X to remove the selected portion from your movie.

14. Press the spacebar to preview your movie.

15. From the File menu, choose Save As.

16. In the Save As dialog, click the Make movie self-contained radio button, name the movie, choose where you want it to be saved, and click Save. You have created a new QuickTime movie (see Figure 10.15). Hitchcock would be so proud…

When you use resources from one QuickTime movie in another, QuickTime can refer to that information rather than physically placing the material in the movie—this is what happens when you save a movie normally (allowing the movie to depend on the other clip). This is similar to using an alias to a file. The advantage of this is that the movie file will be much smaller since it is storing only the pointer to the material rather than the material itself in the file. The disadvantage is that if you move the movies around, such as when you email them to a friend, the pointer can become invalid, and the movie won't be able to find the referenced material.

If you save a movie with the "Make movie self-contained" button selected, the pasted material is actually stored in the file. This means that the movie does not depend on any references. You can move it wherever you want to, and it will work fine.

Step bars

Remember that you can use the step buttons to move through a clip frame-by-frame. It is sometimes hard to select just the right portion of a movie with the slider. If you hold down the Shift key while you click a step button, you will select the frames that you are stepping through.

Transitions

A transition is the means by which one clip moves into the other. There are lots of different types of transitions that are used when creating videos. The most common is the fade, where one scene gradually fades into the next. There are lots more that are possible, such as spinning transitions, where one clip spins into the next, and shade transitions, where one scene rolls up like a window shade, and so on.

Unfortunately, you can only do one kind of transition with MoviePlayer: the straight cut. This means that one scene ends and the next begins with no transition effect. If you are careful with the clips you paste together and you judiciously use the step button to cut your clips, you can make the transitions work fairly well (remember that if your clip has a soundtrack, it goes along with the video and is cut in the same way).

In order to do more sophisticated transitions, you need to use a full-featured, digital video editor.

FIGURE 10.15

My new movie.

QuickTime 3 Pro

Of course, manipulating tracks only works in QuickTime pro 3 also.

More memory, please

Before you begin editing movies, I suggest that you give MoviePlayer plenty of RAM to work in. I would allocate about 5 MB for it if you can spare that much. See Chapter 14, "Managing Your Mac's Memory," to see how to allocate more RAM to an application.

If you are sure that you won't be moving the clips you are using, use the Save normally option. If you think you might move one or more of the clips, use the Make movie self-contained option.

Adding and Editing Tracks

QuickTime movies can contain different tracks, and those tracks can contain video, text, sound, and so on. You can have multiple tracks in a movie, and you can even have multiple tracks of the same type in a movie, for example, multiple soundtracks. In the next step-by-step, I'll show you how to change the volume of a soundtrack and add a new text track to the movie you just created.

Changing a soundtrack and adding a text track to a movie

1. Open the movie you created in the previous step-by-step.

2. See the tracks the movie has available by opening the Movie menu and choosing Get Info. You will see the Get Info window for your movie (see Figure 10.16). This window provides lots of information about your movie, and there are numerous modes that can provide a variety of information on and control over your movie.

FIGURE 10.16
The Get Info window provides a large amount of information on your movie and lets you do certain tasks with it, such as adjusting the volume of a track.

3. Choose a track to work with from the pop-up menu in the upper left corner of the window (see Figure 10.17). After you select a track, the window will change to reflect information and commands that are appropriate for that track. The Alternate pop-up menu contains another set of contextual commands that enable you to perform different tasks, depending on the track you are working with.

FIGURE 10.17
My movie has three tracks—one video track and two soundtracks.

4. Choose a soundtrack, and from the Alternate pop-up menu, choose Volume (see Figure 10.18). The window will change to show the volume controls (see Figure 10.19).

FIGURE 10.18
You can use the Get Info window to change the volume of a track.

FIGURE 10.19

The volume controls can be used to adjust the sound level of a track.

5. Drag the volume bar to adjust the sound level of the track. You can change the side from which the track plays by dragging the balance bar to the left or right (see Figure 10.20).

FIGURE 10.20

I have lowered the volume of Soundtrack 1 and made it play louder from the right side than the left.

Get Info does more than just get info

The Get Info command in MoviePlayer does a whole lot more than simply getting information about a movie. If you are going to use MoviePlayer, take some time to explore the Get Info command to see what options you have. They all work similarly to the volume adjustment I'll show you in this step-by-step.

Option and the Edit menu

When you hold down the Option key and choose Edit, you will see some new options, including Add and Trim. Add pastes a new track with the selection on the clipboard that runs in parallel with the portion selected in the play bar (whereas paste adds a selection instead of the area selected in the play bar). Trim removes everything from a movie *except* what is selected.

6. Close the Get Info window.

7. Play your movie. You should notice a difference in the way the soundtrack changed sounds.

8. Open SimpleText and create the text for the text track of your movie (see Figure 10.21).

9. Copy the text for your text track to the clipboard.

10. Move back to MoviePlayer and select the area over which you want your text track to be seen (see Figure 10.22).

11. Hold down the Option key, open the Edit menu, and choose Add. The next time you play your movie, when you reach the area that you selected, you will see the text in the new text track (see Figure 10.23).

FIGURE 10.21

I used SimpleText to create a text track for my movie.

FIGURE 10.22

The portion of the movie I selected here is where the text track will be added.

FIGURE 10.23

My movie now has a text track explaining the scene.

Track talk

Unfortunately, with MoviePlayer you have no control over the background color of the text (black), nor can you change the color of the text track (white). However, the text you paste will maintain the formatting you applied in the application you used to create it.

If you want to determine the section of the movie over which the text track is visible, press both the Shift and Option keys when you open the Edit menu. The command will become Add Scaled instead of Add, and the text will be pasted across your selection. For example, if you select the entire movie (Command-A) and use Add Scaled, the text track appears during the whole movie, which looks a lot better than the flashing black text box that occurs when you just use Add.

Tool for the pros

Although MoviePlayer Pro is fun to play with, and you can do some pretty amazing stuff with it, professional video creators and serious hobbyists use more sophisticated tools. One of the most widely used video editing tools on the Mac is Adobe Premiere. There are other more high-end tools available, but those are for the professionals who do serious professional video production.

Tracks are a very powerful feature of MoviePlayer, and I have shown you only a bit of what you can do with them. For example, you can add additional soundtracks, video tracks, graphics, and any other content in the same way that you added a text track. That is the nice thing about QuickTime—it works the same way no matter what kind of data you work with.

Adding Movie Elements to the Mac OS with QuickTime 3 Pro

Another nice thing about QuickTime Pro 3 is that you can add various QuickTime elements to your desktop and interface. In this section, I will show you how you can add a startup sound from a QuickTime movie, create an alert sound taken from a QuickTime movie, and create a movie that plays each time you start your Mac.

Creating a startup sound from a QuickTime movie

1. Open the movie that contains the sound you want your Mac to play when it is ready to be used.

2. From the Edit menu, choose Extract Tracks.

3. Click the soundtrack containing the sound that you want to use and then click Extract. The soundtrack will appear as a new, untitled movie (see Figure 10.24).

4. Play the new movie to hear the soundtrack.

5. Select the portion of the soundtrack that you want to play when your Mac starts (hold the Shift key while you drag the slider or use the step buttons).

6. Hold the Option key down, open the Edit menu, and choose Trim. The movie will now contain only the portion you selected.

7. Play the movie to make sure that it contains the right sound. If it doesn't, undo the Trim and go back to step 5.

8. From the File menu, choose Export.

9. Name the sound.

10. Choose Sound to System 7 Sound from the Export File As pop-up menu.

FIGURE 10.24
The soundtrack I extracted from the movie called Service This! became a new movie containing only that soundtrack.

11. Move to the Startup Items folder (within the System Folder).

12. Click Save. The next time your Mac starts, it will play this sound when the desktop appears.

You can also extract sounds from QuickTime movies to use as alert sounds.

Creating an alert sound with MoviePlayer

1. Open a movie containing the sound that you want as your alert sound.

2. Repeat steps 2 through 10 in the previous step-by-step to create a System 7 sound.

3. Instead of saving the sound in the Startup Items folder, save it to the desktop.

4. Quit all open applications.

5. Drag your new alert sound onto the System file that is within the System Folder.

6. Open the Monitors & Sound control panel.

7. Click the Alerts button.

8. Choose your new alert sound from the Alert Sound list.

9. Adjust the volume of your alert sound with the System Alert Volume slider.

10. Close the Monitors & Sound control panel. Now your Mac will play this sound when it is trying to get your attention.

Creating a Slide Show with MoviePlayer Pro

One of the neatest things you can do with QuickTime 3 Pro is to create a slide show from a series of still images that you have on your Mac. You can even add a soundtrack to your slide show, making it seem really special.

Creating a slide show with a soundtrack

1. Put all of the images that you want to be in the slide show in a single folder.

2. Name the files and add a sequential number at the end of the name (for example, picture1, picture2, and so on).

3. Open MoviePlayer and create a new movie.

4. From the File menu, choose Open Image Sequence.

5. In the open dialog, choose the first image in the series that you want to appear in the slide show and click Open. You will see the Image Sequence Settings dialog (see Figure 10.25).

6. Choose a frame rate from the pop-up menu. This rate determines how long each image stays onscreen. A good value for a slide show is 5 seconds per frame.

7. Click OK. The images will be imported into the movie in order according to the numbers in the names of the files (see Figure 10.26).

8. Press the spacebar to see the slide show. Each image will be shown for the amount of time you set when you set the frame rate. Make a note of how long the slide show plays.

9. From the File menu, choose Save As, name the movie, select either the Save normally or Make movie self-contained option, choose a location, and click Save. Your slide show is now saved as a QuickTime movie.

10. Choose some music for a soundtrack while your slide show plays; insert an audio CD in your Mac that has the music on it that you want to use.

11. From MoviePlayer's File menu, choose Import, open the audio CD, select the track that contains the music that you want to use for a soundtrack, and click Convert.

12. In the resulting Save dialog, name the new soundtrack and click Options. You will see the Audio Import Options dialog (see Figure 10.27).

Other tracks

You can also add a text track or even a voice-over narration track if you want to.

FIGURE 10.27
You can set the time and quality of the music you are importing from an audio CD in the Audio CD Import Options dialog.

13. Choose the settings you want in the top of the dialog. Higher rate and bit size will yield better quality size (as well as larger files), as will stereo.

14. In the bottom of the dialog, set the start and stop times for the music that you want to use. You can either set the start and stop times or drag the sliders. You can choose just part of a track or the whole thing. Your goal should be to have music that plays for about as long as your slide show does.

15. To preview what you have selected, click Play. As the music plays, you can follow the progress of the selection.

16. When you have a selection that you are happy with, click OK.

17. In the Save dialog, click Save. You will see a progress bar as MoviePlayer converts the portion of the audio CD track that you selected into a QuickTime movie. When it is finished, you will see your new movie that contains the music from the CD (see Figure 10.28).

FIGURE 10.28

This QuickTime movie contains the section of the audio CD that I want to use as a soundtrack for the slide show.

18. In your soundtrack movie, select all the music by pressing Command-A and then copy it by pressing Command-C.

19. Move back into your slide show movie and select the portion during which you want the music to play—to select the whole slide show, press Command-A.

20. Hold the Shift and Option keys down, and from the Edit menu, choose Add Scaled.

21. Play the slide show now. You will hear your soundtrack play as the images change.

Problems?

If you have problems converting the movie, make sure that you have plenty of RAM allocated to MoviePlayer. You can also try importing smaller amounts of music at a time—you can always paste them together within MoviePlayer if you have to.

22. View your slide show in all its glory by choosing Present Movie from the File menu and then click play. The images from your slide show will fill your monitor and the music will fill your ears.

23. Save your slide show for posterity. You can always change it by editing it, just as you would any other QuickTime movie.

Going Three-Dimensional with QuickDraw 3D

Another Mac technology that is related to QuickTime is QuickDraw 3D. QuickDraw 3D enables your Mac to display three-dimensional images in those applications that support it. You can also manipulate QuickDraw 3D images by rotating them or moving the perspective towards or away from them. Frankly, there aren't all that many applications that use QuickDraw 3D, but it still can be fun to explore. To learn more about it, open the QuickDraw 3D folder that is in the Apple Extras folder on your startup disk. The folder contains a number of files relating to QuickDraw 3D. You can also explore some QuickDraw 3D models by exploring the 3DMF Models Folder.

Exploring the Digital Frontier

Even though I have shown you a lot of ways to use QuickTime and QuickTime Pro, there a lots of other tools and features that I didn't have the space to show you. With what I have covered, though, you should be able to figure out the rest. In addition to watching QuickTime movies and exploring QuickTime VR worlds, take some time to see what you can create yourself with QuickTime.

Listening and Programming Audio CDs with the AppleCD Audio Player

One of the great things about having a CD-ROM drive in your Mac is that you can listen to audio CDs while you are using the

---

Timing is everything

If you use the Add Scaled command, QuickTime will make your soundtrack play in the time you indicate (by selecting it in the slide show movie), no matter what. If your soundtrack is longer than your slide show, QuickTime will speed up the music so it finishes playing in time—the result may sound like the Chipmunks. Conversely, if your soundtrack is too short, it will be played more slowly to fill up the space.

Making it all work in time

There are two possible solutions to this. The best way is to make sure that your soundtrack is exactly the same length as your slide show. Use the Get Info command on your slide show and choose Time from the Alternate pop-up menu. This will show you exactly how long your slide show lasts. When you convert the soundtrack, choose the same length of time. Then your video track and soundtrack will be the same length, and the music will play as it should.

The other solution is to use Add instead of Add Scaled. This just plunks your soundtrack in and doesn't adjust the length of either track. If your soundtrack is longer than the video track, the soundtrack will continue to play until it finishes, even though the images have stopped changing. If the video track is longer, the last images won't have any sound.

Speakers count

Similar to other stereo and home theater equipment, speakers are the most important factor when listening to music on your Mac. Use a "crummy" pair of cheap speakers, and you will get cheap and "crummy" sound. I recommend that you invest in a good quality set of speakers for your Mac. If you get external speakers (rather than speakers integrated into a monitor), your sound will be better, and you can keep the same speaker set as you replace your Mac or monitor.

Good companies, good speakers

The best names in computer speakers are the same as the best ones for "regular" speakers such as Bose, Boston Acoustics, and so on. Yamaha also makes excellent computer speakers.

Whatever brand you get, make sure that you shell out the extra money for a separate subwoofer. Your system will sound much richer and fuller. This is great for music, and if you play games at all, a subwoofer is a must.

Mac for some task. Work is a lot more pleasant when you can have your favorite tunes playing in the background. And having the controls right on your Mac means you won't have to fool around with a boom box.

The application the Mac OS 8.5 uses to play and control audio CDs is the AppleCD Audio Player. This application provides features that you may not find on even the most expensive component CD players for your stereo system. For example, you can create a program for the CDs that you listen to, and your Mac will remember the program even after you remove the CD. The next time you put that CD in your Mac, your program will play.

The components that enable the AppleCD Audio Player to work are the following:

- **AppleCD Audio Player**. This application, located in the Applications folder installed on your startup disk, controls all facets of playing audio CDs on your Mac. An alias to the AppleCD Audio Player is installed on your Apple menu so that you can always access it.

- **AppleCD Audio Player Guide**. This AppleGuide file provides an extensive help system for playing CDs on your Mac. It is also located in the Applications folder.

- **QuickTime Settings control panel**. You can use this to enable or disable AutoPlay.

- **CDStrip control strip module**. This module enables you to control CD playing by using the Control Strip. It is installed by default.

SEE ALSO

➤ *To learn how to use the Control Strip, see Chapter 7, "Working with the Control Strip"*

- **Audio CD format extensions**. There are several extensions that you need to have installed in order to be able to listen to audio CDs. These include Audio CD Access, Apple CD/DVD driver, and Foreign File Access. These are installed by default.

- **AppleCD Audio Player Prefs**. This preference file is where AppleCD Audio Player stores your custom settings for the AppleCD Audio Player application.
- **CD Remote Programs**. AppleCD Audio Player stores all of your custom CD labeling and programming in this file, which is located in the Preferences folder.

Listening While You Work

In this section, you will learn about AppleCD Audio Player and how to use its controls and options; I'll also include a list of the keyboard shortcuts you can use. Then you'll learn another way to create a custom alert sound from a CD. Lastly, you'll learn how to use AppleCD Audio Player's advanced features, including labeling CDs and creating playback programs.

For the most part, you will use AppleCD Audio Player to listen to audio CDs. This isn't hard to do, but you may not understand all of AppleCD Audio Player's controls just by looking at the application. Figure 10.29 shows the AppleCD Audio Player and includes button labels. In the following list, I'll explain AppleCD Audio Player functions and how they work:

- **CD data**. This area shows you the track you are playing, and depending on the options you have selected, it can show a variety of time-related data on the current CD (see Figure 10.30).

Other CD extensions

Other extensions that you need to work with some CDs (not audio CDs) are High Sierra File Access, ISO 9660 File Access, UDF Volume Access, and Apple Photo Access. These extensions enable your Mac to work with various file formats that you will encounter when you use CD-ROMs. For example, the ISO 9660 File Access extension enables your Mac to mount PC formatted CD-ROMs.

Don't lose this file

If you regularly label and program your CDs, make sure that you back up the CD Remote Programs file. And make sure that you place a copy of this in the Preferences folder whenever you replace your system software. If you don't, you will lose all of your CD customization information, including your programs.

FIGURE 10.29

The AppleCD Audio Player enables you to listen while you work.

1. CD data
2. Options buttons
3. Current CD
4. Volume
5. Play buttons
6. Repeat
7. Expansion triangle

- **Current CD**. This window shows you the CD currently mounted on the desktop. Before you label a CD, you will see Audio CD. If you click this, you can jump to any track on the CD (see Figure 10.31). The check mark indicates which track is playing.

- **Volume**. This slider controls the output level from the CD. Note that it is not the same as adjusting the system volume with the Monitors & Sound control panel; it adjusts only the output level of the CD.

- **Play buttons**. These work just like you probably expect them to. There are buttons for play/stop, pause, eject, skip to next track, move to previous track, scan forward, and scan backward.

- **Normal/Shuffle/Prog**. These buttons control the mode the AppleCD Audio Player is in. Normal plays the CD from the first track to the last. Shuffle plays the CD by randomly shuffling among tracks. Prog plays the program associated with the CD.

- **Repeat**. When this button is clicked, the CD will play continuously, regardless of which mode it is in.

- **Expansion triangle**. When you click this, the AppleCD Audio Player window opens to display the labeling and programming area (see Figure 10.32). What you see will depend on which mode you are in (normal, shuffle, or program).

FIGURE 10.30

You can change the time-related information with this pop-up menu; click the clock button to see it.

FIGURE 10.31

With this pop-up menu, you can quickly jump to any track on the CD.

FIGURE 10.32
This window enables you to label your CDs.

The AppleCD Audio Player also has a few commands on the menu bar. Under the Options menu, there are commands that let you change the colors that are used in the display, set the sound to be stereo or to be played from only the left or right channel, and set the startup CD drive (only useful if you have more than one CD drive).

While you may want to use these buttons and commands, there are keyboard shortcuts that you may find more convenient. These are listed in Table 10.2.

Table 10.2   Keyboard Shortcuts for the AppleCD Audio Player

Keys	Function
Command-E	Eject a disc
Spacebar	Play if paused or stopped, pause if playing
Delete	Stop playing
Right arrow	Jump to the next track
Left arrow	Jump to the previous track
Up arrow	Increase the volume
Down arrow	Decrease the volume
Tab	Move to next track when labeling tracks

Creating an Alert Sound from a CD with SimpleSound

You can use more than one application

You can also use SimpleText or the Monitors & Sound control panel to create an alert sound from an audio CD.

Listening to CDs is great, but how about when you want to use a clip from your favorite CD as your alert sound? No problem. I showed you one way to do that with MoviePlayer. In this section, I'll show you how to do that with AppleCD Audio Player.

Creating an alert sound by using AppleCD Audio Player

1. Open the Monitors & Sound control panel.

2. Click the Sound button.

3. From the Sound Monitoring Source pop-up menu, choose CD.

4. Insert the source CD in your Mac and open AppleCD Audio Player.

5. Use the controls to get to the beginning of the clip that you want to be your alert sound (use scan and watch the timer to help you get to just the right spot) and pause the CD. Make sure that you know how long you want to record.

6. Open SimpleSound (choose it from the Apple menu).

7. Move back to the AppleCD Audio Player and start playing the CD from a few seconds before the clip you want to use starts playing.

8. Move back to SimpleSound.

Recording from the CD

You may want to reduce the CD volume in AppleCD Audio Player just a bit before recording from it so that the recording is not distorted.

9. Click Add, and you will see the Record window that shows the sound from the CD being monitored by the curves emanating out of the speaker icon (see Figure 10.33).

10. When the CD reaches the spot that you want to begin recording, click the Record button. When the clip is done, click Stop.

11. Click Save, name the sound, and click OK. When you move back to the Alert Sounds window, you will see that your new alert sound is highlighted (see Figure 10.34).

Keep it short

Remember that you will hear the entire alert sound every time. Keep your clip short or it will get annoying after the novelty wears off. Alert sounds should be only a second or two long at most.

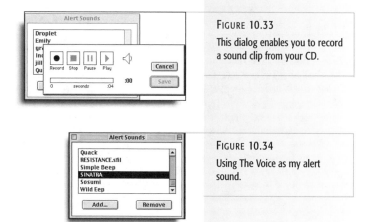

FIGURE 10.33
This dialog enables you to record a sound clip from your CD.

FIGURE 10.34
Using The Voice as my alert sound.

12. Close SimpleSound. The next time your Mac needs your attention, you will hear your clip.

Programming the AppleCD Audio Player

If you are like me, some of your CDs have songs that you don't like very much, and others have songs that you like to hear over and over again. Plus, you may not like to see the same Audio CD and Track 1, Track 2, and so on labels for all of your CDs. With AppleCD Audio Player you can label all your CDs and create custom programs that will play the CD in any order you like (you can also repeat or skip individual tracks). Every time you play a CD for which you have created labels or a program, you will see that information and can use that program.

Labeling and programming an audio CD

1. Insert the CD that you want to work with and open AppleCD Audio Player.

2. Click Normal and click the expansion button to reveal the labeling window (see Figure 10.35).

3. Click the Audio CD at the top of the window and enter the name of the CD.

FIGURE 10.35

When it is in the Normal mode, the lower area of AppleCD Audio Player enables you to label your CD and all of its tracks.

4. Press Tab to move to Track 1 and enter the name of the song on the first track of the CD.

5. Press Tab again to move to the next track and enter its name.

6. Repeat step 5 until you have named all of the tracks on the CD (see Figure 10.36).

FIGURE 10.36

This CD is now labeled; notice that the name of the CD now appears above the play buttons rather than plain old Audio CD.

7. Click the Prog button to move into the program mode (see Figure 10.37). The list in the left pane shows all of the tracks on the disc. The right pane will contain your program.

FIGURE 10.37
Now I am ready to create a custom program for this CD.

8. Drag the first track that you want to play from the left pane and drop it into its position on the right. To remove a track, drag it out of the Playlist window.

9. Repeat step 8 until you have finished with the program (see Figure 10.38).

FIGURE 10.38
When I play this CD in Program mode, the songs will play in the order shown in the right pane of the window.

10. Press the spacebar to play your program.

The labels and program that you create for a CD are stored in the CD Remote Programs file. The next time you insert the CD, you will see the labels, and if you play the disc in the program mode, it will use the program.

Watching and Capturing Video with the Apple Video Player

If your Mac is equipped with the necessary hardware, you can watch TV and movies, capture still images, and create QuickTime movies by using Apple Video Player. This application is similar to the AppleCD Audio Player, but as you can tell from the name, it works with video instead of audio.

Unlike a CD-ROM drive, which almost all Macs have had over the last few years, your Mac may or may not have the hardware needed to be able to use Apple Video Player. In this section, you'll learn how to determine if your Mac has the needed hardware. If it does, I'll show you how to use Apple Video Player to watch TV and movies on your desktop. You'll also learn how to capture still images from video sources. Lastly, you'll see how to capture video and create your own QuickTime movies from your favorite video sources.

Understanding Hardware and System Requirements

In order to be able to use Apple Video Player, your Mac must have the hardware that enables it to convert an analog video signal into a digital one so that it can display on your monitor. For TV or movie viewing, you also need a TV tuner or movie source (such as a VCR). The following list highlights the major components that you need to have as part of your system:

- **Digitizing/video input board**. Video sources from outside your Mac need a way to get into your Mac. The digitizing/video board makes this possible. There are two options for this board. One is a Mac that comes with a board built in or that has a slot with the Apple TV card installed. The second is by adding a video card through your Mac's PCI slots. Here is how to tell if you have a digitizing/video input card on your Mac.

Generalizations

You may find that my descriptions of the hardware you need for video are a bit general. That is because there are literally dozens of ways you can get video into your Mac. Between the various Mac models and the wide variety of video cards available, there is no way that I can provide all the possible specifics. As long as you get a feel for each capability that you need to have and how to tell if your Mac has that capability, that should be sufficient for you to get started.

Watching and Capturing Video with the Apple Video Player

If your Mac has a video-in port or antenna/cable-in port on the back of it (it will probably also have a sound-in right and sound-in left), you have what you need. Look for RCA-style (what most stereo equipment uses) jacks, as well as S-video ports. These kind of jacks are strong indications that you have the needed video hardware in your system.

Some Mac models come with built-in, digitizing capabilities, such as the Power Macintosh 8600. Check your user manual to see if your Mac does.

If you have added a graphics board that has video capabilities, you have what you need as well. Of course, you will know if you have added such a board; or you can look at the back of the machine. If it has an "extra" video out port where the PCI cards are, you *may* have a digitizing board installed. Not all graphics cards have video capabilities, but some do. You will have to figure out what kind of card you have and read the documentation that came with it.

If you can't find any evidence for any of these cases, then you are probably out of luck. To handle video, you will need to add a digital video card. Fortunately, these cards are relatively inexpensive, and a good one will only cost a few hundred dollars. You will need an open PCI slot to install it.

■ **Video source**. The other requirement is to have a video source. Possible sources include a TV tuner with antenna or cable, a VCR, or a camcorder.

If your Mac has a TV tuner, either through an Apple TV card or a 3rd-party video card, then you need to connect that tuner to either an antenna or a cable, just as you do your TV. Depending on the kind of card you have, you may be able to connect a VCR or camcorder though video and audio-in ports.

If your Mac has a digitizer card without a TV tuner, you need to connect some sort of tuner to it for TV or a VCR or a camcorder to be able to input a video signal. Usually, it is a matter of connecting the video device through the video- and audio-in jacks on the back of the Mac. If you

Need a card?

Not all Macs that are capable of having an Apple TV card installed actually have one. You need to check your invoice and user manual to see if your Mac has both the capability and the card. Third-party vendors, such as ATI, sell tuner cards for most desktop Macs. There are also video input cards for PowerBooks (PCMCIA cards).

Apple Video Player and 3rd-party cards

Even if you have a video card, you may not be able to use Apple Video Player. Not all video cards are compatible with it. If not, it is likely that video software was included with your card. If that is the case, see the documentation that came with the card to learn how it works.

connect a VCR to it, you can use the VCR's tuner to watch TV, and you can also watch or capture video from VCR tapes. If you connect a camcorder to the jacks, you can capture taped video or video that is being viewed "live" through the camera.

- **A powerful Mac**. Digital video requires extensive resources to work with. If you are going to capture and digitize video, you need a Mac with a powerful processor, lots of RAM, and lots of disk space. You can get by with a midlevel Mac, but forget trying to use anything with less than a 603 processor and less than 64 MB of RAM. Even a system with 64 MB will be pushed to the limit if you try to capture more than a few seconds of video.

Once you are sure that you have all of the required hardware, connect the video source or antenna or cable to the video- and audio-in jacks on your computer. If you add a 3rd-party video card to your Mac, make sure that you follow the manufacturer's instructions for installation and that any software that came with it is properly installed.

Understanding Apple Video Player

Apple Video Player uses the following files:

- **Apple Video Player application**. This is the software you will use to watch TV or movies or capture images and video. Apple Video Player is located in the Applications folder on your startup disk, and there is an alias to it on the Apple menu.

- **Apple Video Player Guide**. This guide file provides a help system for Apple Video Player that will show you how to make it work for you. This file is located in the Applications folder.

- **TV Tuner Guide Additions**. This is a supplemental guide file for those Macs with an Apple TV card. This file is also located in the Applications folder.

AV hard disk

You may see some hard drives that are called AV drives. What this means is that the drive spins more quickly and has faster access speeds than "regular" drives so they are better able to keep up with the video digitizing process. If you are digitizing video for yourself or for a "low level" video, you don't need an AV drive.

- **Video Startup extension**. This extension enables Apple Video Player to work with your Mac.
- **Apple Video Player Prefs**. This preference file stores your Apple Video Player settings.

Watching TV and Movies

You can use Apple Video Player to watch TV or movies on your desktop—just don't let the boss catch you watching "The X-Files" when you are supposed to be working!

Watching TV or movies on the desktop

1. Launch Apple Video Player. You will see two windows (see Figure 10.39). The left window is the viewing window in which you will see your video source. The right window provides the controls you will use to capture video. If you are using an external video source, such as a VCR, you will have to turn it on before you will see anything.

2. If you use an external video source, you can change the channels by using the controls on that source (such as a VCR). If you are using an Apple TV card, use the remote to change channels.

FIGURE 10.39

It is fun to watch TV and movies on your Mac while you "work."

3. If you are using a VCR or camcorder as a video source, play a tape to see it on your Mac.

4. You can resize the Viewing window by choosing Smallest, Normal, or Largest Size from the Windows menu.

Is this better than my TV?

You will probably notice that the quality of the picture is a lot better than the one on your TV. That is because your Mac uses a digital signal to present the images and sound, and your monitor is a higher-quality device than your TV. When TV technology goes fully digital, its quality may catch up to your Mac, but for now your Mac provides a much higher quality viewing experience than your TV.

No sound?

If you don't hear any sound, but everything is connected properly, you may need to select your video source as the sound input source. Use the Sound button in the Monitors & Sound control panel to do that.

5. If you aren't going to capture images, close the Controls window.

6. When you are done watching, quit Apple Video Player and turn off any external video sources.

Capturing Still Images from Video

Apple Video Player enables you to capture images and video so that you can view them and edit them with other applications such as MoviePlayer.

Capturing a still image by using the Apple Video Player

1. Use the steps in the previous section to watch your source.

2. Open the Controls window by pressing Command-4.

3. Click the camcorder button in the Controls window (see Figure 10.40). You will see the capturing controls for both video and pictures.

4. When your source gets to the image you want to take a picture of, click Freeze. The video will freeze on the image that was playing when you clicked the Freeze button.

FIGURE 10.40

Here I am preparing to capture a still image of the Terminator.

5. If the image is what you want, click Save, name the file, and save it where you want it.

6. Open PictureViewer and then open your captured image to see how it looks (see Figure 10.41).

Video controls

You can control various aspects of the video by using the video controls. To view these, open the Controls window and click the middle button (which looks like a monitor). You can select a video source, as well as adjust various aspects of the picture such as brightness, sharpness, contrast, and color.

FIGURE 10.41
Just hope you don't meet this guy in a dark alley at night, or in broad daylight for that matter.

Capturing Digital Video

The process you use to capture a digital video is very similar to the way you capture a still image.

Capturing video and creating a QuickTime movie

1. Repeat steps 1-3 from the capturing image steps so that the video you want to capture is ready to play.
2. Play the video that you want to capture.
3. Click Record to begin capturing video.
4. When you are done recording, click Stop. You will see a Save As dialog with a preview version of your movie. Click the play button to preview your movie.
5. If your movie is acceptable, name it and save it.
6. Open MoviePlayer and view your movie (see Figure 10.42). You can edit by using the tools you learned about earlier in the chapter.

VCRs are good sources

It is much easier to capture video and still images if you are using a device that you can control as your video source, such as a VCR or camcorder. You can capture live TV, but it is much harder to get what you want since you only have one shot at it.

FIGURE 10.42
I captured a clip of Arnold saying' "Ah'll be back.".

Apple Video Player is not a sophisticated video capture tool so don't expect to create a super high-quality video. Still you can get decent results, especially if you are willing to make some adjustments and make several tries to get it right. The following list includes some tips to increase the quality of your movies:

- Increase the RAM allocation for Apple Video Player.
- Make the size of the window smaller.
- Adjust the compression option by using the Preferences command under the Setup menu.
- Capture short segments of video and paste them together to make longer movies.
- Experiment to your heart's content.

Understanding DVD

Digital Versatile Disc (DVD), or Digital Video Disc (DVD), or whatever the current definition or abbreviation is, is the next big thing in multimedia. Basically, DVD technology can store more than 4 GB of data on a disc that is the same size as a CD-ROM disc; in a short time, that capacity is expected to increase to more than 16 GB per disc. Being able to store such a large quantity of data on a single disc provides the potential for many different kinds of applications.

The primary application for DVD technology at this point is for playback of movies. DVD movies provide digital images and true digital surround sound. The quality of a DVD movie is as much greater than a VHS tape as audio CDs are above cassettes. DVD players are becoming quite popular for home theaters and are making their way to computers.

PCs are now being routinely equipped with DVD drives. These drives can play DVD-ROM discs, as well as the same DVD movies that home theater players can play. At the moment, there aren't many DVD-ROM discs available for the Mac yet, but they are expected to be quite common in the near future. The initial applications are those that cannot fit on a single CD-ROM now, such as Microsoft's Encarta encyclopedia.

In a short time, Macs will be equipped with DVD drives, and they will be as commonplace as CD-ROM drives are now. You will be able to use DVD-ROM software as well as watch DVD movies on your desktop. And DVD drives can read CD-ROM discs, too. While DVD technology is still in its infancy, within a couple of years, it will pretty much replace CD-ROM technology.

DVD movies

There isn't much DVD-ROM software available for any platform, but there are lots of DVD movies available. To play a DVD movie on a Mac, it needs to have a DVD drive, an MPEG-2 decoder (all DVD movies are encoded with MPEG-2), and a playback application. Currently, there are third-party DVD packages for desktop Macs, and you can get an Apple DVD drive and decoder card with GE PowerBooks.

Working with Mac Applications

Assessing Mac software

Installing, testing, and removing software

Understanding standard application behavior

Sharing data between applications

Quitting applications

Adding and Using Mac Software

The software that comes bundled with Mac OS 8.5 is useful, but chances are that you're not going to get all of your work done with SimpleText and the Graphing Calculator. In order to do useful work, you'll need to install and use additional applications and other software on your Mac. For example, you'll probably need a good word processor. If you install new hardware on your Mac, such as a scanner or a drawing tablet, you'll also need to add some new software—extensions, control panels, and applications—in order to be able to use the new hardware. You are also likely to want to add third-party extensions and control panels that add additional functionality to your Mac.

In most cases, installing software on your Mac is simple to do. Basically, there are five steps to a successful installation of a software package:

- Make sure that your Mac has the necessary resources to run the application
- Run the software's installer program or install the software manually
- Test the software to make sure that it runs correctly
- Register the software
- Remove the software after it is no longer needed

After you successfully install software, there are some general ways in which almost all Mac applications work, which are the following:

- Launching
- Working with windows and standard menus and commands
- Sharing data across documents and applications
- Quitting

Removing software is part of the installation process?

You may find it strange that removing software is part of the list of installation steps. This is because you need to remember to remove any software that you no longer use. Unused software still requires precious system resources—such as hard drive space or even RAM (if its extensions or control panels are still active—even if you don't do anything with it. And in a way, removal is the last step of the installation process since all software you install will eventually need to be removed or at least replaced.

Assessing Mac Software Requirements

All Mac software needs certain minimum resources—RAM, hard disk space, system software, and hardware—to work properly.

Before you purchase or install any software package, you should make sure that your Mac has everything it needs to be able to run the software.

There are lots of sources for this information, including the following (listed in order from "best" to "worst"):

- **Demo version**. If you can find a demo version of the software—which is always a good idea to try before you buy it if possible—you can try the software to see how it works on your system. Since you can actually run the software (try before you buy), this is the surest way to tell if your Mac has what it takes to run the software. Plus, you can evaluate the software to see if it really does what you need it to.

- **Reviews**. Software reviews are another good source of information about what is needed to use a particular piece of software. Additionally, you will often find other useful information such as strengths and weaknesses, usage tips, comparisons, and so on. It is always a good idea to try to find a review of software before you buy it. And since most magazines and many Mac Web sites feature archives of reviews, it is usually fairly easy to find a review for a particular piece of software.

- **ReadMe files**. If you're working with unboxed software, such as software distributed via the Web or software from a shareware/freeware collection CD-ROM, you'll usually find information about resource requirements in a ReadMe file that accompanies the software.

- **Sales information**. If you buy your software from a catalog-based store, you can find resource requirements in the description of the software that is in the catalog. If you buy software from a Web site, you'll usually find even more detailed information about requirements than you will find in a catalog.

- **Publisher's Web site**. You can usually find a good description of a software package's resource requirements on the publisher's Web site.

Finding demos

The best place to look for a demo is the Web site of the software publisher. Many companies post demos on their sites that you can download and evaluate.

Mac magazines

The major Mac magazines, such as *MacWorld, MacAddict,* and *MacHome,* all have Web sites in which you can look for and read reviews.

Consider the source

When evaluating the resource requirements of a software package, consider the source of your information. The closer you get to someone making money from your software purchase, the more pressure there is on that "someone" to keep the published resource requirements as low as possible so that the potential market for the software is as large as possible. Software publishers—and hardware manufacturers for that matter—are famous for listing minimum requirements that really push the envelope. There is a fine line between specifying requirements that provide the broadest access to a piece of software (more sales) and having unhappy customers because a piece of software doesn't run very well, even though the minimums are met. Software producers don't always walk on the right side of this line.

Will the real minimum please stand up

Software reviews are great sources for the "real" minimum requirements because the reviewer is supposed to be unbiased—and most of them are. Frequently, you will find the publisher's minimums listed along with the reviewer's caveats about what he believes that you really need to run the software successfully.

Pushing the envelope

In a previous note, I talked about vendors pushing the envelope in terms of specifying minimums that aren't really adequate. Apple has been known to do this, especially in terms of RAM. For a certain period, the Macs that Apple produced came with so little RAM, that you could barely run the system software, not to mention adding applications and other software to the system. When RAM was really expensive, this practice helped Apple keeps its prices down. But the result was that lots of Mac users were suffering with machines that were RAM starved. If your Mac seems like it doesn't work very well, too little RAM is a likely cause of problems. Read Chapter 14: Managing Your Mac's Memory," to learn how to manage the RAM on your Mac.

Virtual memory... like RAM but slower

Be aware that virtual memory causes applications to run much more slowly than they would run if they had real RAM at their disposal. And some applications won't work under virtual memory at all.

- **The box**. Resource requirements are usually printed on the outside of the box that contains the software. If the software comes on a CD-ROM, resource requirements are listed in the jewel case packaging.

- **Documentation**. Ordinarily, you can find information about the resources that software needs in the software's documentation. Of course, to read the documentation, you have to obtain the software. If you have to pay for the software, you don't want to find out this way because it will be too late.

SEE ALSO

➤ *To learn about good Web sites for Mac software related information, see page 623*

Assessing RAM Requirements

Software needs RAM to run, and sometimes it needs lots of it. There are a few relatively slim applications, like SimpleText, which requires only a few hundred Kilobytes of RAM, but most modern desktop applications, such as Microsoft Word, Adobe Photoshop, and Netscape Navigator, require between 10 and 20 megabytes *just to launch the application*.

If your Mac doesn't have enough physical memory to run your application, you're not completely out of luck: you can use the Mac's virtual memory system to use hard disk space as RAM. (This assumes, of course, that you have hard disk space to spare.)

SEE ALSO

➤ *To see how to turn virtual memory on and adjust how much is available, see page 330*

➤ *To understand how to manage the RAM available to your applications, see page 326*

Of course, the Mac OS uses RAM, too. Depending on the way that your system is configured, Mac OS 8.5 demands from 10 to 20 MB or more of your RAM resources. Thus, if you have 16 MB of physical RAM in your machine, chances are that you *can't* run an application that requires more than 3 or 4 MB without turning on virtual memory. Appalling, isn't it?

Fortunately, it is easy to assess how much RAM your Mac has available for applications to run in.

Assessing your Mac to see if it has the RAM needed to run an application

1. Quit all open applications.

2. From the Apple menu, choose About this Computer. You will see the About This Computer window (see Figure 11.1).

FIGURE 11.1

The About This Computer window shows you how much RAM is currently being used.

3. Note how much RAM is allocated to Mac OS (the total length of the bar in Figure 11.1, the shaded part of the bar shows how much is being used at the moment).

4. Note how much memory is available—the Largest Unused Block in the window. This amount is the physical RAM that your Mac has to give to other applications.

5. Determine the RAM minimum required for the software that you are considering by using the sources I described earlier in the chapter.

6. If your unused block number is greater than the software's minimum RAM requirement, you have enough RAM.

7. If your largest unused block is less than the software's minimum, you have several options. One is to rely on virtual memory to cover the RAM shortfall. Virtual memory is much slower than physical RAM; if the software is at all demanding (graphics or a game for example), this is not a good solution. If the application is not processor intensive, and you are only a MB or two short, this might work just

Plug-in RAM

Applications that use plug-ins that extend the program–like Adobe Photoshop and Netscape Navigator–require more memory after the plug-in is installed. For example, Macromedia recommends that you allocate an extra 1 MB to Navigator when you install the Shockwave plug-in. Unfortunately, applications don't necessarily tell you that they need extra memory; rather, they simply crash unexpectedly. See the documentation for your plug-in (rather than the host application) for information about the plug-in's memory requirements.

fine. Another, and probably the best solution, is to add more RAM to your Mac, if possible. Another is to trim the RAM requirements of Mac OS 8.5 to free up more memory. Lastly, find alternative software that doesn't require as much RAM.

Assessing Disk Space Requirements

Programs need disk space. Of course, the amount varies drastically from program to program. Small applications that don't use support or application files might only require a few KB of space, while a large installation, like a Java programming environment, might use more than 100 MB for a full installation of all the software's components.

Ordinarily, large installations are large because they contain a boatload of ancillary files: sample files, templates, tutorial files, documentation files, and so on. If you're short on disk space, you can usually jettison most of the extra stuff by using the Custom Install option or by deleting the extra files after they are installed.

You can determine the disk space requirements of software by checking the sources listed at the beginning of the chapter.

Keep in mind that disk space requirements are approximate, and the same file will use different amounts of space on disks of different sizes. Also keep in mind that Macs with completely full hard disks tend to misbehave; applications may slow down, crash, or generate bizarre error messages if they don't have enough disk space to create temporary work files.

Determining if a volume has enough space available for software installation

1. Decide on which volume you want to install the software.
2. Open the volume's window.
3. Just below the window's title bar, you will see how much free space is on the disk (see Figure 11.2).
4. If the space available is significantly greater than the space requirements of the software, you are set for disk space.

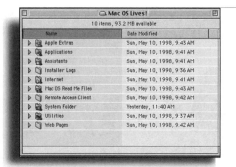

5. If you don't have enough disk space available, you have several options. One is to delete files from the disk to increase the available space. Another option is to use a different disk. Don't forget about removable media drives that you may have. For example, a Zip drive may be fast enough to run certain kinds of applications from. You can consider installing the software on a Zip disk and running it from that. You can also consider adding additional hard disks—either internally or externally. Lastly, you can look for an alternate application that doesn't require as much disk space.

Assessing System Software Requirements

Some applications require that you use a particular version of the OS or that certain Mac OS components are installed. For example, most multimedia applications require that you have QuickTime installed on your Mac.

Determining which version of the Mac OS you are using

1. From the Finder, choose About This Computer. You will see the About This Computer window (see Figure 11.3).

2. Find the version of Mac OS that you are running in the upper right corner of the window.

Since you're using Mac OS 8.5, the latest and greatest version of Mac OS, chances are that you have all of the system software you need to run most applications. However, in some cases the necessary OS components aren't part of the standard Mac OS installation or part of your customer installation. For example, if

Mac trivia

By the way, before Mac clones came onto the scene, this was called, "About This Macintosh." Since Apple never considered Mac clones to be Macs, it changed the name of the window to "About This Computer." It remains to be seen if Apple will change it back again now that the clones are gone.

244

you chose not install the Text-to-Speech component of the OS, and the software requires it, you will have to reinstall that component.

FIGURE 11.3

You can Use the About This Computer window to see which version of the OS is running.

SEE ALSO

➤ *To learn how to install system components, see Appendix A, "Installing and Maintaining the Mac OS"*

Assessing Hardware Requirements

Most software requires certain "levels" of hardware to function. Most frequently, you will need to consider the hardware requirements that specify a minimum processor type and speed. However, there may be other types of hardware requirements as well. For example, if the software is a communications package, it may require that you have a modem. Some games and high-end graphics software require certain video resolutions, which are determined by the video capabilities of your machine.

Assessing your Mac's hardware versus the software requirements

1. Look at the case of your Mac to see which model you have. If it is a Power Macintosh of some kind, you have a PowerPC processor. If it has G3 in the name, you have one of the latest and greatest PowerPC processors.

2. From the Apple menu, choose Apple System Profiler. The Apple System Profiler window will open (see Figure 11.4).

3. In the Hardware Overview section of the Apple System Profiler, locate the name of your Mac's processor and its speed. In Figure 11.4, you can see that my Mac has a PowerPC 604e chip running at 200 MHz.

4. Click on the Devices and Volumes tab. You will see a Devices and Volumes window (see Figure 11.5).

5. Click on the arrow next to the Video line, near the word, "Display." You will see information on your current display settings (see Figure 11.6).

6. Note how many colors you are using, as well as the screen resolution.

7. Compare the software's hardware requirements to the information you found via Apple System Profiler.

8. If your machine meets the hardware requirements, you are ready to go. If your process is older or less powerful than the requirements, you are basically out of luck. Your only option is to upgrade your Mac by either replacing it or upgrading its processor. Or you may be able to find an alternate application that requires less processing power. If you can't display enough colors, try making your screen size smaller and then increasing the number of colors displayed. If you still can't meet the requirements, you may be able to add Video RAM to your machine to boost its display capabilities.

Apple System Profiler is very, very good

Apple System Profiler is a very powerful utility that you will see throughout this book. You should take a few minutes to experiment with it. Whenever you need to know something about your Mac, Apple System Profiler should be the first place you go.

FIGURE 11.5

This window tells you about all of the drives that your Mac can access, as well as information on the video display of your machine.

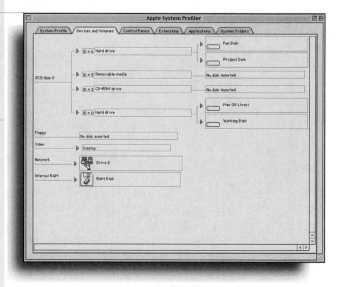

FIGURE 11.6

My machine is currently displaying millions of colors on a screen size of 832 x 624 pixels.

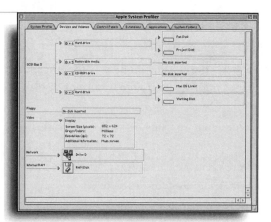

SEE ALSO

➤ *To learn about upgrading your processor, see page 796*

Installing Mac Software

Once you have obtained that new application or other software, you need to get it onto your Mac. In most cases, a trained monkey can install Mac software. If you don't have a trained monkey around, you can even do it yourself.

In the Old Days, users installed Mac applications by dragging the application file or application folder onto the hard disk from the application disk and then dragging any system files—special control panels, extensions, fonts, or other system files required by the software—into the appropriate subfolder of the System Folder. While this was easy enough to do, it required that you find all of the components and make sure that they ended up in the right places. This was sometimes confusing.

Nowadays, most applications are distributed with installer applications. There are many different kinds of installers with many different levels of "smartness," but in most cases, an installer offers the following conveniences:

- It makes sure that you have enough disk space for the installation

- It makes sure that you have the appropriate system software resources

- It puts all special files, such as extensions and fonts, in the right places

- It enables you to choose several different installation options, from a minimal install to a full install

- It offers to register the software electronically

Most installers offer you an Easy Install or a Custom Install. With an Easy Install, the installer picks all of the pieces of the software that will be installed for you—making the process very easy for you. With the Custom Install option, you choose the parts that you want to be installed.

Installers vary from program to program, but they all work fairly similarly. Some of the details depend on the software that you are installing and the installer engine that the publisher has chosen to use. The basic steps are the following:

1. Launch the installer.

Steps no one does

Technically, before you install software, you should run Disk First Aid or some other disk maintenance utility on the disk onto which you are going to install software. And you should also run an anti-virus program on the installer. And you should restart your machine with extensions off.

Do you really need to do all this? That depends. If you are practicing proper Mac maintenance, you should be regularly using a disk repair utility and checking your system for viruses anyway. If you are getting your software from reliable sources, the chances of it containing a virus are pretty slim, and you may or may not need to restart your Mac with extensions off for the installer to work.

2. Choose the drive onto which you want the software installed.

3. Choose Easy or Custom Install.

4. If you choose Easy Install, you must wait until the installer prompts you to restart your Mac.

5. If you choose Custom Install, you must select the components that you want to have installed.

6. Follow the onscreen instructions and restart your Mac when prompted.

Using the Easy Install Option

The details of how installers work varies from program to program. As an example of how easy a typical easy install is, I will walk you through the installation of Adobe's Photoshop (version 4.0) image creation and editing software.

Installing Adobe Photoshop using the easy installer

1. Insert the Photoshop CD.

2. Launch the Install Adobe Photoshop application.

3. Click Continue. The installer window appears (see Figure 11.7). Notice that the installer lists some of the components that will be installed.

FIGURE 11.7

The installer program for most applications looks like the one that Photoshop uses.

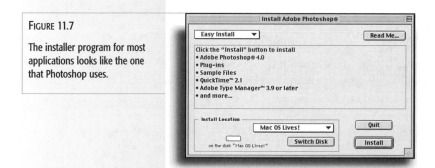

4. Choose the install location (disk) on which you want the software installed.

5. Click Install. You will see a warning that you will need to restart your Mac after the software is installed. This is to activate any system components that need to be installed.

6. Click Continue. (Click Cancel if you need to close applications that have open documents or you can let the installer close them for you.) The installer will begin the installation process. You will see progress windows as it works. When it is done, you will be prompted to restart your Mac. You may also be prompted to register. Most applications feature electronic registration so that you don't even have to fill out and mail a card.

7. Click Restart to restart your Mac. After it starts, you will be able to use the application.

Using the Custom Install Option

Using the Custom Install option of most installers is not much harder than the Easy Install option. The difficulty is that you need to understand a bit more about your Mac and the application to know which parts you need to install. If you feel comfortable with this, then custom installs are normally the better choice.

As an example of how a custom installer works, I will walk you through the installation of Photoshop again, this time using the Custom Install option.

Installing Adobe Photoshop with the custom installer

1. Insert the CD and launch the installer.

2. Click Continue. The installer window will appear (see Figure 11.7).

3. Choose the disk onto which you want the software installed.

4. Choose Custom Install from the pop-up menu. The window will now reflect the Custom Install option (see Figure 11.8).

Check the list

Be sure to take a look through the list of components that will be installed. In this example, you can see that QuickTime 2.1 is going to be installed. The current version of QuickTime is 3.0 so you probably wouldn't want to install an older version of a system component. Sometimes having two versions can cause you problems, or the installer may actually replace a newer version of a component with an older one, which will cause you problems. In the case where the installer is going to use an older version of a system component, you should use the Custom Install option instead.

How to tell which versions you are using

How do you know which versions of system components that you are using? Apple System Profiler. It will tell you the version of each system component that is running on your machine. I'll show you how Apple System Profiler works for this purpose in Chapter 31, "Preventing Mac Problems."

You can also select the component and use the Get Info command, or you can use Extensions Manager or Conflict Catcher. The advantage of using Apple System Profiler is that you can generate a list of all the components at once. Whereas, with the other tools, you have to look at each component individually.

Defaults

Installers always choose your startup disk as the default location onto which to install software. They also always place any system components onto the startup disk's System Folder. If you have multiple startup disks, you may need to run the installer for each of the disks if the application has system components. To do so, you have to start up from the alternate startup disk before running the installer so that the installer will place system components in its System Folder. Installers also default to the Easy Install option.

A benefit of custom installs

One benefit of being able to control which components are installed is that you will better understand what was installed. This will be helpful if you need to manually remove the software for some reason.

Down to the folder

Sometimes when you are choosing a disk to use for the installation, you will be able to select a particular folder into which the software should be installed. This is helpful if you store all of your applications in a specific folder.

Options, options everywhere

You will often see multiple versions of the application you are installing (see Figure 11.8). There are usually three versions. One is only for PowerPC Macs. One is for older, 68K Macs (Macs that use a 68000 series chip). The third is a universal version that contains the code for both versions. It is best to pick a specific version for your Mac because the universal (also known as the fat version) takes up more resources than the other versions do.

5. Choose the components that you want to be installed by checking the boxes next to those components.

6. You can get information about a component by clicking the boxes with an "I" in the center. When you do, an information screen will pop up (see Figure 11.9).

7. When you have finished selecting components, click Install. You will see the warning about having to restart you Mac after the installation.

8. Click Continue. You will see progress windows as the components are installed.

9. When prompted, click Restart to restart your Mac. After the machine starts, you will be able to use the software.

Using Other Install Options

Some software uses customized installers that won't look exactly like the examples in this chapter. Usually, instead of allowing you to choose between Custom or Easy Installs, you will be able to choose among different configurations. One of these is usually called *Typical*. This is equivalent to an Easy Install with a more standard installer. Another option is usually called *Minimal*. This option installs only the files to make the application work—no extras are included. This option is intended for people whose Macs are loaded to the gills already. The third option is called a *Custom* option, which works just like the Custom option in the standard installer.

Testing Mac Software

After you have installed software, you'll need to test your software to make sure that it works. If you're using commercial software, you'll probably need to enter your serial number the first time that you launch it, so be sure that you have it handy.

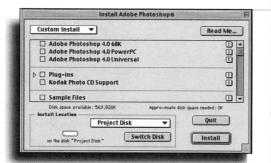

FIGURE 11.8

Custom installs are usually a better choice once you are comfortable with them; this figure shows Photoshop's installer in the Custom mode.

FIGURE 11.9

You can get information on the plug-ins and other components in the installation windows.

Testing newly installed software

1. Launch the application. (If the new software is an extension or control panel, it will be loaded at startup).

2. Open a file to make sure that you can view and edit it. (If the software is a control panel, open it and change some settings.)

3. Make a few changes and save the file.

4. Open it again to make sure your changes were saved.

5. Quit the application.

6. For the first few days after you install new software, pay particular attention to any changes in the way your Mac works. If the software is going to cause you problems, these changes provide important clues as to how to fix those problems later.

Most of the time, the software that you installed will work just fine. If so, you can go on about your business.

If there is a problem, you will usually find out about it the first time that you try to use the software. If there is a problem, it is likely to be one of the following two kinds:

One at a time please

You will have a much easier time diagnosing problems if you install only one piece of software at a time. If you have multiple pieces of software to install, install one and then test it. If it works OK, then install the next one and test it. Continue that process until you have installed all of the software.

Warranty

Note that not registering something in no way limits the warranty on it. While vendors can require that you register your software for technical support, the terms of warranties cannot be legally linked to your completing a registration or warranty card.

- **Machine crash, hang, or failure to start**. If your Mac won't start up or it crashes or hangs when you try to use it, the installer probably installed something that conflicts with some software already on your machine. Ordinarily, application programs don't cause conflicts directly, but if the application uses a custom extension or control panel (or if the software *is* an extension or control panel) you may experience problems.

SEE ALSO
➤ *To learn how to solve software conflicts, see Chapter 32, "Fixing Mac Problems"*

- **Application fails to open**. If your Mac starts, but the newly installed application won't run, you will see a message telling you why. The most common causes are that the software is incompatible with your machine (which is why I spent so much time explaining how to make sure software is compatible with your machine before you buy it). In this case, the only thing you can do is correct the incompatibility or do without the software. Another possibility is that a certain component that the software needs is not active on your machine. In this case, you should also see a message explaining what is needed. If the missing component is part of Mac OS 8.5, use the Mac OS 8.5 CD to reinstall that component. If it is part of the application, use the application's installer to reinstall the missing piece.

Registering Mac Software

Finally, you should register your software. Sometimes, you'll need to send a postcard to the software company. Nowadays, many applications allow you to register quickly via email, and will prompt you to fill out a registration form when you install the software or run the software for the first time.

Here are some reasons to register the software that you just installed:

- You may get email about new releases and bug fixes for the software.

- You may get free stuff (like more software or magazine subscriptions) from the software vendor.

- You'll get much better service from the software vendor when you call for technical support. If you haven't registered, you may not get technical support at all.

- You may get a discount on the next release of the software. In some cases, you might even get discounts on competing software or free updates to the version you registered.

- You're reminding the software vendor that the Mac OS platform is alive and well and that the vendor should continue to support the Mac!

Removing Mac Software

Everything has a limited amount of time in which it is useful—this is especially true in the fast-paced world of computers. All your favorite applications and other software will one day be inadequate for your purposes. Or you may find something that works better. Or you may not need to do a particular task any more. In all of these cases, you should remove software that has become superfluous.

All software—even if you don't use it—requires resources. At the least, it takes up storage space. If it includes extensions or control panels, it also uses valuable RAM. So you should routinely remove software that you no longer use.

Fortunately, removing Mac software is a relatively easy thing to do. It is certainly much easier than it is on the Windows platform, which is why software-removing applications are consistently among the best-selling Windows applications.

Avoiding telemarketers

Most software registration has a box to check if you don't want your contact information provided to other companies. Software and hardware companies routinely sell their mailing lists so I recommend that you check this box unless you enjoy getting called in the middle of dinner with another fantastic offer for something you don't want.

Upgrading software

You will probably upgrade your most useful applications and other software as the software's developer adds new functions, improves its reliability, and so on. Often, in order to be able to use an upgrade installation, rather than a new stand-alone copy of the software, you need to have a previous version of the software installed on your Mac. Upgrade installers will sometimes scan your hard drive to make sure that you have a previous version. If such an installer doesn't find a previous version, it will not run, and you won't be able to use the new software.

It is usually a good idea to leave any software that you are upgrading on your machine until the upgraded version is installed, and you make sure that it is working properly. Then you can go back and remove the previous version.

Gone, but not forgotten

Before you remove an application, make sure that you have the original media. If you don't, make a backup of it. You should always keep copies of your software in case you need it again; for example, you may discover a document you need that was created in that application. Of course, if you sell the software or give it to someone else, you should not keep a copy.

Using Installation Software to Remove an Application

Most Mac installation programs will also remove the software that they install. Usually, this option appears on the same pop-up menu from which you choose the Custom or Easy Install options.

As an example, I will remove Photoshop using its installer.

Removing Photoshop with its installer

1. Launch the installer.

2. Click Continue.

3. Choose Remove from the pop-up menu. You will see the remove software window (see Figure 11.10).

FIGURE 11.10

Most installers will also remove the application that they install; this figure shows Photoshop's installer.

4. Click Remove. The application and its support files should be removed from your Mac.

Manually Removing an Application

Sometimes, using the installer to remove a program doesn't work. Other times, an installer may not include a Remove option. In these cases, you will need to remove the software manually. Or you may want to remove the software manually just to be more sure about what is taken off your Mac. Even removing software manually on the Mac is pretty easy.

Manually removing software

1. Find the software's folder and drag it to the Trash. Make sure that you have a backup of it first!

2. Open the Preferences folder in your System Folder and move any preferences files containing the software's name to the Trash.

3. Look through the Extensions and Control Panels folders for any extensions or control panels associated with the software you are removing.

4. Drag these to the Trash.

5. Look in the System Folder for any loose items associated with the software; throw out any that you find.

6. Use the Finder's Find command to find and delete any remaining items associated with the software.

SEE ALSO

➤ *To learn how to use the Find command, see page 88*

7. Restart your Mac.

8. After it restarts, empty the Trash.

Launching Applications

As with most things on the Mac, there is more than one way to launch an application. In fact, there are many different ways to launch applications under Mac OS 8.5. You can do any of the following:

- Select the application in the Finder and choose the Finder's Open command (press Command-O).

- Double-click the application's icon.

- Single-click an application's button.

- Open an alias to the application.

- Open a document for which the application is the creator.

- Drag and drop a document onto an application's icon.

- Launch the application from within another application. (For example, you can launch a Web browser by double-clicking an URL in the Outlook Express email program. Not every application launches other applications, of course.)

Extensions and control panels

Be careful that you don't throw out system components that your system needs or that other applications use. You should only remove items that were installed as part of the software's installation.

A holding tank…

Rather than moving files directly to the Trash, you may want to create a "holding" folder for them. Instead of moving the files into the Trash, move them into your holding folder. After you have used your machine long enough to be sure that you don't need the software, you can throw your holding folder away and empty the Trash.

- Click the application's button in the Launcher palette. (Assuming, of course, that you use the Launcher.)

- Put an alias into the Startup Items folder so that your Mac opens it when it starts up.

- Launch the application from a script created by AppleScript or other scripting utility.

You have probably used many of these methods to open your own applications. Most of them are very straightforward and require no discussion. A couple of them, though a bit less used, can be effective techniques for you to use.

One of the most powerful methods, yet underused by many Mac users, is to launch an application by drag-and-drop. Macintosh drag-and-drop is a function of the Mac OS 8.5 whereby you move information from one location to another by simply selecting it, dragging it to where you want it to go, and then dropping it. (This works for moving information between programs also, which I'll get to in a moment.)

Drag-and-drop is especially efficient when you want to open a document with an application that wasn't used to create it initially. For example, if you receive a plain text file and double-click it, it will open in SimpleText. If you wanted to open it in Word instead, you can simply drag and drop the document onto Word's icon and Word will be used to open the file. Otherwise, you would have to first open Word, use the Open command, maneuver to the text file, and then open it. Drag-and-drop can help you eliminate a lot of tedious steps.

Launching an application by drag-and-drop

1. Open the Mac OS Read Me Files folder that was installed with Mac OS 8.5. (If you don't have this folder, go ahead and find another text file that you want to open.) Make sure that you can see the About Mac OS 8 file's icon in the folder's window.

2. Open the Applications folder, making sure that you don't cover up the window that you opened in Step 1. Make sure that the SimpleText application icon is visible in the new window (see Figure 11.11).

Drag-and-drop and aliases

By the way, drag-and-drop also works with an alias for an application. For example, you can create an alias to Word and keep that on your desktop. Then you can drop documents onto the alias to open them in Word.

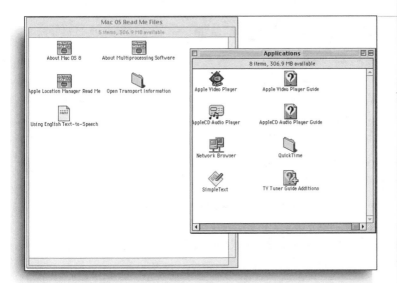

FIGURE 11.11
Using drag-and-drop, you can easily open a specific document with a specific application.

3. Drag the About Mac OS 8 file's icon on top of the SimpleText icon.

4. When the SimpleText icon changes color to show that it is selected, release the mouse button. The document will open in SimpleText. While the document would have opened in SimpleText if you double-clicked on it, this simple example shows you how easy drag-and-drop is to use. It works the same way no matter what application you use.

There are several other less obvious ways to open applications that you should consider. These are the following: by an alias, through the Startup Items folder, and via a script.

SEE ALSO

➤ *To see how to use aliases, see page 97*

➤ *To learn about the Startup Items folder, see page 397*

➤ *To learn about using scripts to open applications, see page 398*

File not recognized

Drag-and-drop won't work if the application doesn't recognize the kind of file that you drag onto its application. For example, if you drag a Microsoft Word document onto Adobe Illustrator, Illustrator will not be launched. In fact, an application's icon won't change color when you drag a file onto it with which it can't work.

Drag-and-drop unstuffing

One of the best uses for drag-and-drop opening of an application is for unstuffing compressed files that you receive via email or that you download from the Web. You can place an alias to the StuffIt Expander utility on your desktop. Whenever you need to unstuff a file, you simply drag and drop it onto the StuffIt Expander's alias. I will explain stuffing and unstuffing files in Chapter 25, "Using Email: Advanced Techniques."

Understanding Standard Application Behavior

One of the things that makes the Mac easy to use is its very predictable consistency of behavior between applications. Just about every application for the Mac uses the same kind of windows, has similar menus, and even similar keyboard shortcuts. After you've spent a little time working with, say, Adobe Photoshop, you'll find that you can make some pretty good guesses about completely different applications—from a Web browser to an accounting package to a drawing program.

Understanding Standard Window Behavior

Almost every application handles windows in pretty much the same way. For example, most Mac applications can open more than one document at the same time, putting each document into an independent window. And most applications provide a Window menu that lets you switch between open documents.

Application windows behave in exactly the same way as folder windows in the Finder. To quickly review the anatomy of a window, look at Figure 11.12 as an example.

Note that each application can add its own items to a window. In Figure 11.12, you can see that Microsoft Word adds some custom navigation tools at the bottom of the scroll bar on the right side of the window, and adds a little toolbar to the bottom-right edge of the window.

Understanding Standard File Menu Items

Every Mac application written according to Apple's Guidelines has a File menu. Nearly every application has some standard commands that you'll find in the File menu, and nearly every application uses standard keyboard shortcuts for these standard commands. Table 11.1 summarizes these conventions.

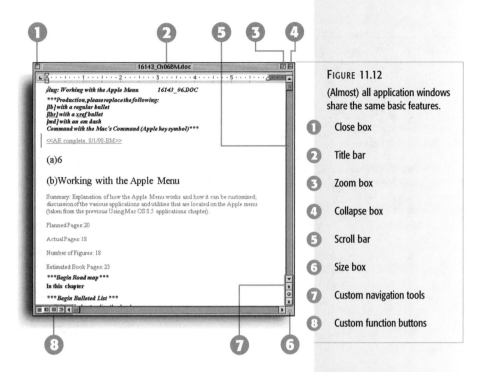

FIGURE 11.12
(Almost) all application windows share the same basic features.

1 Close box

2 Title bar

3 Zoom box

4 Collapse box

5 Scroll bar

6 Size box

7 Custom navigation tools

8 Custom function buttons

Table 11.1 **Common file commands for most applications**

Command	Standard Shortcut	Description
New	Command-N	Creates a new document from scratch. (Some Internet tools open a new connection, or a new browser window, rather than an empty document.)
Open	Command-O	Opens a document that already exists on disk.
Close	Command-W	Closes the current document, *without* quitting the application.
Save	Command-S	Saves all changes to the document. (If it's a new document that you've created from scratch.)
Print	Command-P	Sends the active document to the default printer.
Quit	Command-Q	Closes the current application, closing all windows.

Almost consistent

Not all applications support all of these commands, but most do. For example, some applications don't have a Save command because they continually save files as you work with them (Quicken and FileMaker Pro, for example).

Find and replace

Many applications include a Find (shortcut: Command-F) command on the Edit menu. Find presents a dialog box that helps you search for a particular part of your document. Most word processors, spreadsheets, and text-wrangling applications offer Find; most image editors (like Photoshop and Macromedia Freehand) do not have this feature. Most text applications also enable you to replace any item that you find with something else.

Understanding Standard Edit Menu Items

Almost every application has an Edit menu, and nearly every Edit menu contains the commands (and shortcuts) listed in Table 11.2.

Table 11.2   **Standard Edit commands used in most applications**

Command	Standard Shortcut	Description
Undo	Command-Z	Takes back the last operation performed. The nature of undoable operations varies from application to application; it might include adding text, removing text, positioning an element in a layout program, using a brush or pen stroke in an image-editing application, and so on. Some applications support multiple levels of undo—you can undo several steps back instead of only the most recent one.
Cut	Command-X	Removes the selected object (text, image, layout element, or data record, depending on the application) and temporarily stores the object on the clipboard. (Any object already in the Clipboard is replaced by the newly-cut object.)
Copy	Command-C	Places a copy of the selected object on the Clipboard, leaving the original object untouched. (Any object already on the Clipboard is replaced by the newly-copied object.)
Paste	Command-V	Puts the contents of the Clipboard into the current document. If an object is selected when the Paste command is given, the selected object is replaced by the pasted material.

The Edit menu may contain other commands as well, depending on the particular application. For example, the Preferences command frequently is located on the Edit menu.

Understanding Standard Open and Save Dialog Boxes

There are a few standard dialog boxes that you'll see a zillion times—nearly every application uses standard Apple dialog boxes for common tasks.

Figure 11.13 shows the mother of all dialog boxes: the Open File dialog box (this application calls it the Open publication dialog, but it is the same thing). When you're working with a file that already exists, you can use the Open File dialog box to specify which file you want to open. Individual applications may add their own custom features to the Open dialog box, but almost all applications will offer a box similar to the Adobe PageMaker 6.5 box shown in Figure 11.13.

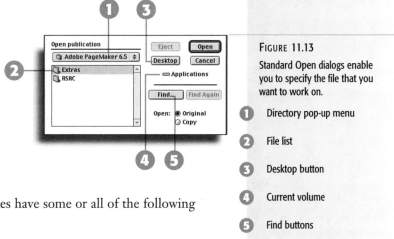

FIGURE 11.13

Standard Open dialogs enable you to specify the file that you want to work on.

1. Directory pop-up menu
2. File list
3. Desktop button
4. Current volume
5. Find buttons

Most Open dialog boxes have some or all of the following features:

- **Directory pop-up menu**. This shows the currently selected folder. If you click the menu, you'll see a list of all of the parent folders (and volumes) of the current folder. You can jump to any folder in the list by selecting the folder's name.
- **File list**. This list shows all of the files in the current folder that the current application recognizes. Since Figure 11.13 is a PageMaker dialog box, the file list won't show, for example, QuarkXPress, Word, or Photoshop files.

- **Desktop button**. This button provides a quick shortcut to the desktop; click it, and the desktop becomes the current folder.

- **Volume icon**. This icon shows you the currently selected volume. This is especially handy when you have similarly named files and folders on more than one volume.

- **Find button**. This enables you to search for files by name, so that you don't need to browse around your disk looking for the file that you want to open.

- **Open options radio buttons**. These enable you to specify whether or not you open the document itself, or a new copy of the document.

There are other things you might see in dialog boxes: common conveniences include preview windows, that let you see what a document looks like before you open it, and file type pop-up menus, which enable you to specify what kind of files are displayed in the file list.

Figure 11.14 shows the Open File dialog's sibling, the Save dialog box (from Adobe Photoshop 4.0.) As you can see, the Save dialog shares much in common with an Open dialog: the Folder pop-up, file list, Volume icon, and Desktop button are still present, and do the same thing that they did in the Open dialog box.

Volume icon

If you click on the volume icon in an open dialog box, you will move up one level in that volume for each click until you reach the desktop.

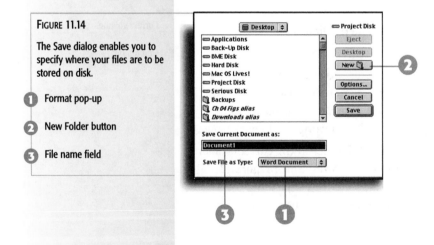

FIGURE 11.14

The Save dialog enables you to specify where your files are to be stored on disk.

1 Format pop-up

2 New Folder button

3 File name field

Save dialog boxes have a few unique tools, including the
following:

- **Format pop-up menu**. This menu enables you to set the
  file format that the application uses to save the file.

- **New Folder button**. This creates a new folder inside the
  currently selected folder.

- **File name field**. This area enables you to enter a name for
  your new file.

Understanding Navigation Services Open and Save Dialogs

While the standard Open and Save dialogs work, they are a pain
in the neck. You can't work outside of them (which from
Chapter 2 you know means that they are modal), you can't move
them, and you can't move to different places on your Mac very
quickly. These dialogs have been around for a long time and
they are showing their old age. Isn't it about time that the Mac
had more modern Open and Save dialogs? Obviously, or I
wouldn't have asked the question.

Mac OS 8.5 provides a new tool called Navigation Services.
Open dialog boxes (sometimes called Find a File under
Navigation Services) and Save dialogs that use Navigation
Services are much improved over the standard versions. Figure
11.15 shows a Navigation Services' Open dialog while Figure
11.16 shows an example of a new Save dialog.

Navigation Services dialogs have many improvements over standard Open and Save dialogs. These include the following:

- **Non-modal, movable, and resizable**. No longer are you
  confined to work within an Open or Save dialog nor do you
  have to endure its size or location. You can resize and move
  these dialogs just as you can Finder windows.

- **List view**. Under Navigation Services, these dialogs have
  features similar to Finder windows in the List view. For
  example, you can sort the files by the columns shown and
  can change the sort order.

FIGURE 11.15

Navigation Services' Open dialogs provide many more features and are easier to work with than the standard Open dialogs.

1 Location pop-up menu

2 Shortcuts button

3 Favorites button

4 Recent button

5 Document type pop-up menu

6 Help button

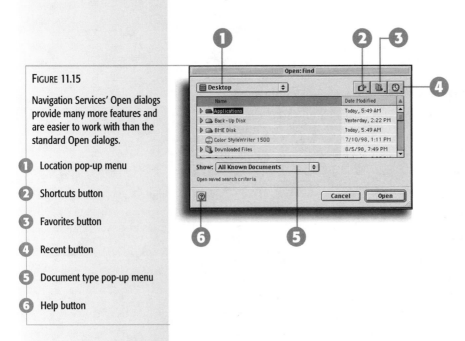

FIGURE 11.16

Navigation Service's Save dialogs are also much more powerful.

1 Location pop-up menu

2 Shortcuts button

3 Favorites button

4 Recent button

5 Help button

6 New Folder button

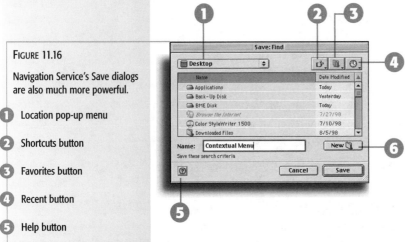

- **Location pop-up menu**. The Location pop-up menu enables you to quickly move up and down your Mac's file structure.

- **Shortcuts button**. Using this button, you can quickly move to any disk mounted on your Mac, including volumes shared across a network.

- **Favorites button**. Clicking this button reveals folders that you have added to your Favorite Items folder so that you can choose them to move quickly into a specific favorite folder.

- **Recent button**. Using this button, you can quickly move back to items you have used recently.

The Navigation Services dialogs are very useful and are a major improvement to the Mac OS. You will find these dialogs in various places in Mac OS 8.5, such as the Find application and when you choose a Desktop Picture in the Appearance application. The bad news is that applications have to be updated in order to use Navigation Services. So until you update your applications, you will have to use the standard versions of these dialogs, unless you use ACTION Files or another utility.

Understanding ACTION Files Open and Save Dialogs

The Navigation Services dialogs are great, but unless the applications you use are updated, they will still use the old, out-of-date Open and Save dialogs. Fortunately, there is an add-on utility that provides enhanced Open and Save dialogs that are every bit as powerful as Navigation Services' dialogs are (they are more powerful in some areas), and all of your applications are able to use them immediately (see Figure 11.17).

Using ACTION files enables you to do the following in Open and Save dialogs:

- Use Finder commands (such as New Folder, Find, and so on) from within the Open and Save dialogs.

- Move easily into any folder on your Mac.

- Use a list of favorite folders and documents in the Open and Save dialogs so that you can move to them quickly.

- Use the list of recent folders and files that ACTION Files tracks for you. This enables you to move back to a recently used item by using one command on a pull-down menu.

Understanding ACTION Files

ACTION Files adds an extension and control panel to your Mac. You can use the control panel (called ACTION Utilities) to control many aspects of the way ACTION Files works. For example, you can set how many recent items that ACTION Files tracks. You can also set ACTION Files so that it doesn't work with a few applications that are incompatible with it, among other things.

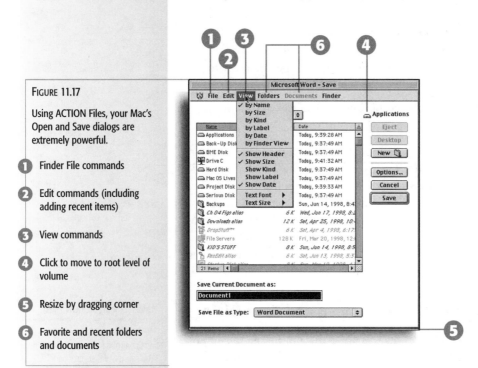

FIGURE 11.17

Using ACTION Files, your Mac's Open and Save dialogs are extremely powerful.

1 Finder File commands

2 Edit commands (including adding recent items)

3 View commands

4 Click to move to root level of volume

5 Resize by dragging corner

6 Favorite and recent folders and documents

Downloading a demo

You can download a fully functional version of ACTION Files from the Power On Web site at http:// www.actionutilities. com. This version is valid for 30 days. You have to pay for a serial number to be able to use it past that time.

Buying a copy

Once you use ACTION Files, I am sure that you will want a permanent copy. You can buy a copy from the Action Utilities Web site for only $39.95. In my opinion, this is an excellent value.

- Move and resize Open and Save dialogs (yes!).
- Create new folders, make aliases, duplicate files and folders, and move things to the Trash.

In my opinion, ACTION Files is one of those few "must-have" pieces of software. A quick example will show you how easy and powerful ACTION Files is.

Using ACTION Files to locate and open a file

1. Choose Open from any application.
2. Choose a favorite or recent folder from the Folders menu.
3. Open the file.

If the file you are opening is located several folders away from where you are currently working, it might take you six or seven mouse clicks to do what ACTION Files enables you to do with one. I don't have the room to cover all the great things that you can do with ACTION Files, but hopefully even this small example has given you some idea of its power.

Setting Application Preferences

Most applications feature a dialog box that allows you to customize the way that the application works. Most modern applications are highly flexible: you can control literally dozens of behaviors.

Although I can generalize that almost all applications will enable you to set your preferences for that application, unfortunately, it's hard to generalize about what an application names its preference-setting command and where the command appears in the application's menu structure. Adobe software usually calls the command "Preferences" and puts it in the Edit menu; Microsoft calls the command "Preferences," but puts it in a Tools menu; Eudora puts it in a Tools menu, but calls it "Settings," and so on. Every application is different.

Preferences for all

Almost every application stores information about preferences in its own preference file in the System Folder's Preferences folder. Some applications, for example, Netscape Navigator, put a whole folder full of stuff in the Preferences folder.

Moving Information Between Applications

Another great thing about the Mac is the way that you can make applications work together. You'll find that you can move data from one application to another easily—say, paste text from a word processor into a page layout program or drag an image from a Web browser straight into an image-editing program.

Cutting and Pasting

One way to move data between applications is the tried-and-true, cut-and-paste method. You can cut (or copy) text from any application, and paste it just about anywhere. If you have used the Mac, you are no doubt very familiar with cutting (or copying) and pasting.

Sharing Documents

Another easy way to move data between applications is to simply open one application's documents with another application. For example, if you create an HTML file by hand with SimpleText, you can open the HTML file with Macromedia Dreamweaver to

Translation

You can use a translator to open a file in an application that is not its creating application. Many applications have a built-in translator. For example, Word can translate and open WordPerfect files.

The Mac OS used to have a built-in translator called MacLinks Plus. It could translate some of the most common file formats into other common formats. However, you were generally better off if you tried to open a file from using an application's translator first, and as of this writing, Apple no longer includes it with the OS anyway.

make quick edits. Similarly, you might save a Web page image to disk by using Microsoft Internet Explorer and then opening the saved image with Adobe Photoshop.

Alas, you can't open just any document with just any application. Every document is marked with tags that indicate which application created the document and what kind of document it is. For example, a document created with Microsoft Word uses the unique creator code MSWD and the document type code WDBN. Applications use these codes to determine which documents they can handle.

Drag-and-Drop

One of the slickest ways to get data from one application to another is to use drag-and-drop. You can select something in one application and drag it onto another window in the same or different application. No need to use the Cut, Copy, or Paste commands; just a quick drag will do the trick. The caveat is that the applications must support Macintosh drag-and-drop in order for this to work. Fortunately, most modern applications do support it.

Moving data with drag-and-drop

1. Open a file that contains the data that you want to copy (see Figure 11.18). This data can be text, an image, sound, a QuickTime movie, or a combination of these. In this example, I am moving a photo of a G3 Mac from Apple's Web site into a new PageMaker document.

2. Open the document into which you want to move the data (see Figure 11.19).

3. Select the data that you want to move.

4. Drag it into the receiving document's window (see Figure 11.20). The image is now in the PageMaker document just as if you had pasted it in.

The tricky part

The tricky part of using drag-and-drop is being able to see all the windows open between which you are going to drag data. Remember to use the resizing boxes so that you can see both windows.

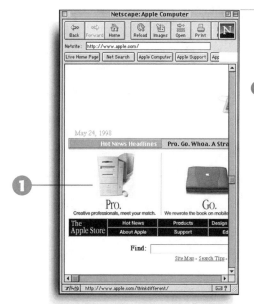

FIGURE 11.18

I want to use an image of the excellent G3 Macs in a PageMaker document.

1 I want to use this graphic in a document.

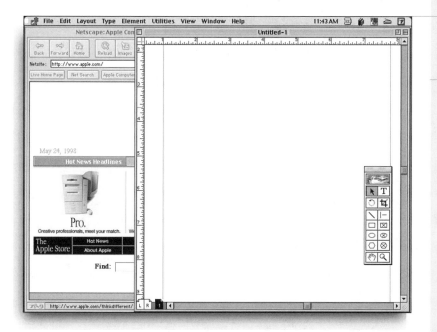

FIGURE 11.19

This new PageMaker document is ready to receive the image.

FIGURE 11.20

I dragged the image from
Netscape Navigator on the left
into PageMaker on the right.

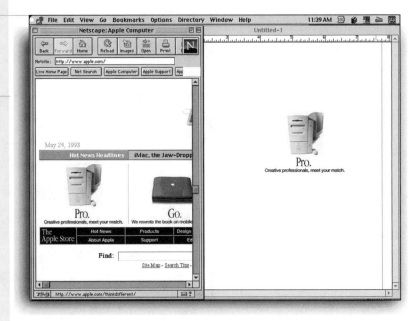

Using Desktop Clippings

Another way to move data is to create desktop clippings of the
data that you want to use. All you have to do is drag data from
an application's window onto your desktop. The Mac will automatically create a clippings file that contains the text, image, or
sound that you dragged onto the desktop. You can open clippings files and drag them into other document windows to place
that data in another document.

Creating and using clippings file

1. Open the document containing the data that you want to
   use. In this example, I will take part of the image that I captured for Figure 11.18 and drag it into a Word document.

2. Select the data that you want to make a clipping from (see
   Figure 11.21). In Figure 11.21, you can see a dashed box
   around my selection.

3. Drag your selection to your desktop. Your Mac will automatically create a clipping file (see Figure 11.22).

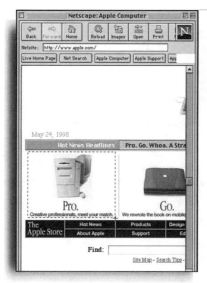

FIGURE 11.21

The dotted marquee indicates that this image is selected.

FIGURE 11.22

The clipping file that was created by the Mac; this icon indicates that the clipping is a PICT graphic.

4. Open the clipping file to view it (see Figure 11.23).

5. Open the document into which you want to place the clipping.

6. Drag the clipping file onto the document's window and release the mouse button. The clipping will become part of the document (see Figure 11.24).

Using clippings to capture information

Another good use for clipping files is to capture email addresses, phone numbers, and other text snippets that you want to save. Just select the text and drag it onto your desktop. The clipping will store the information for you. You can then drag it into another document or view it as a clipping.

FIGURE 11.23

This clipping file contains a picture.

FIGURE 11.24

The clipping file has been dragged onto the Word document.

Exiting Applications

No matter how useful an application is, the time will come when you must quit it. Quitting an application is usually simple: save what you're doing and quit.

Sometimes, however, applications won't respond to your input: the cursor will freeze, or you'll watch a spinning wristwatch for 20 minutes, or the application will otherwise indicate that it doesn't feel like doing anything useful at the moment. Sometimes, the program's aberrant behavior ties up your whole Mac—not just the application that's misbehaving. To make matters worse, because the application won't respond to you, it won't respond to your attempts to quit.

Fortunately, you can force the currently-running application to quit by pressing Command-Option-Esc. The Mac will ask if you really want to quit the application; if you do, the misbehaving application will be forced to quit—sometimes this won't work though and you are forced to restart your Mac. If it does work, I highly recommend that you save your work in other applications and restart your Mac immediately. After a force-quit, the Mac OS is unstable, and will crash sooner or later.

You may be wondering why you should bother to force-quit if you're just going to restart? Why not just reboot the machine and save some time? First, if you have unsaved work in any open applications (other than the misbehaving application), that work will be lost when you reboot. Secondly, doing a sudden, unexpected restart can potentially damage system files or the file structure itself. It's much better to restart gently.

Don't use the force-quit process unless you have no other choice. Nothing good ever comes out of it—except perhaps saving documents opened in other applications.

Working with the Mac's Help Systems

Learning about help systems in the Mac OS

Understanding where and when to use each kind of Mac help

Learning how to use the various kinds of help

Finding Help Where You Need It

As good as Mac OS 8.5 is, not every task that you want to accomplish is obvious. Sometimes, you will need help to do what you want to do. With Mac OS 8.5, Apple has further refined the Mac's help systems. These help systems are the following:

- **Mac OS Help Center**. The Mac OS Help Center has been greatly improved for Mac OS 8.5. The Help Center is a hyperlink-based system, which means that certain keywords are underlined, and you can click on them to move to a related area. The Help Center works just like the World Wide Web does. Help on a specific topic can include additional information on that topic, information on related topics, or an AppleGuide link.

- **AppleGuide**. One of the most innovative help systems ever created, AppleGuide goes beyond being an interactive help system. It is an *active* help system, meaning that AppleGuide literally shows you how to accomplish specific tasks. AppleGuide is still available within applications as it has been in past OS version, but it has also been integrated in Mac OS 8.5. Some links that you click will lead you into an AppleGuide for a task about which you are reading.

- **Balloon Help**. Part of the Mac since System 7.0, Balloon Help provides small "balloons" that provide snippets of information for interface items, menu commands, and other items with which you work.

- **Assistants**. Mac OS 8.5 includes two Assistants. One Assistant helps you configure your Mac while the other helps you configure your Mac to connect to the Internet.

A history of help

Balloon help was introduced in Mac OS 7.0. AppleGuide was introduced in System 7.5. The Help Center and the Assistants were introduced in Mac OS 8. For Mac OS 8.5, the Help Center has been substantially expanded and refined.

Using the Mac's Help Center

The Mac has always been a user-friendly system, which includes its help systems. Mac OS 8.5 continues this tradition. One of the newest help systems on the Mac is its Help Center. The Help Center combines text information with hyperlinks as well as AppleGuide features.

Description: The Help Center is a hyperlink-based system that provides help on many aspects of the Mac OS.

When to use: When you need in-depth information on a topic and help performing a specific task, the Help Center should be your first stop (particularly for those times you need more than a quick blurb on a topic).

Pros: It provides lots of detailed information on the OS, is easy to use, powerful (topic and text searches), and links to AppleGuide.

Cons: It only provides help on the OS so you will need to use a different help system to get help on applications.

The Mac OS Help Center provides the following capabilities:

- **Topic help that you can browse**. You can peruse a variety of help topics. When you find one that interests you, you can click a hyperlink to move into increasing levels of detail on that topic.

- **Text searching for help on specific topics**. You can search for help by keywords. The Help Center will rank resulting hits so that you can look in the most likely topics first, hopefully saving you some time.

- **Links to AppleGuide**. Many task links will lead you into an AppleGuide.

- **Intuitive interface**. The Help Center is very easy to use—if you have used a Web browser, you can use the Help Center. You can move from topic to topic or into the detail on a single topic with a single click.

Understanding the Mac OS Help Center

The following files enable your Mac to provide the Help Center:

- **Help folder**. The Help folder within the System Folder contains all of the files needed for the Help Center. Within this folder are three folders and one file. The Apple Help View folder contains the files associated with the Help View application. The Mac OS Help folder contains the data files the Help Center uses to deliver help. The AppleScript Help folder contains files needed to provide AppleScript help.

The Help Center stands alone

At the moment, the Help Center only provides help with Mac OS topics. Unlike AppleGuide and Balloon Help, you won't find help on your favorite applications or utilities. Hopefully, some day all the Mac's help systems will be a single, integrated system, but for now you have to deal with multiple help systems.

Help on help

In the Apple Help Viewer folder is an AppleGuide for the Help Viewer. So the Mac OS even helps you use the help systems!

More help on the way

While the current Help Center provides only Mac OS 8.5 help, the way Apple has developed the system makes it possible for software developers to add help for their applications. Software developers could provide a folder of their own help files in the Mac's Help folder and provide the links within the application. Then you can access application help in the same manner as Mac OS help.

HTML

HTML, or HyperText Markup Language, is the language of the Web. You will learn more about it in Part V, "Using Your Mac to Surf the Internet."

Web help?

If you have used a Web browser, the Help Center will look very familiar to you. Not only does the Help Center look like a Web browser, it works just like one, too. For example, check out the Forward and Backward buttons at the top of the window.

The Help Center file is another data file that is used by the Help Center.

- **Help Viewer**. The Help Viewer is the application that you use to view the various help pages. It is located in the Apple Help Viewer folder.

- **Data files**. The Help Center uses lots of different data files in order to serve the help pages to you. Some of these are html pages, while others are files unique to the Help Viewer application.

Working with the Mac OS Help Center

As a good help system should be, the Mac OS Help Center is very user friendly. It provides detailed help that is quite easy to access.

Finding help in the Help Center

1. Choose Help Center from the Help menu. You will see the main Help Center screen (see Figure 12.1). You can either search for specific help or use the Mac OS Help links to browse available help topics. In this example, I'll search for specific help on listening to audio CDs.

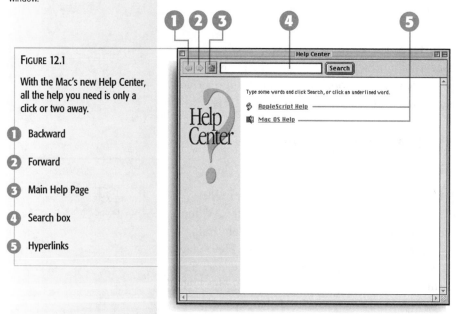

FIGURE 12.1

With the Mac's new Help Center, all the help you need is only a click or two away.

1. Backward

2. Forward

3. Main Help Page

4. Search box

5. Hyperlinks

2. Type "Audio CDs" and click Search. You will see the Search Results screen (see Figure 12.2). The stars next to each title indicate how relevant the Help Center thinks that the item is to your search words.

FIGURE 12.2

This is the help that the Help Center has to offer on using audio CDs.

3. To read a particular help item, simply click on the underlined words. In this case, I clicked on Listening to Music CDs, and the screen in Figure 12.3 appeared.

4. Read the help text.

5. Click links that say they will do something to open the appropriate control (in this example, "Open AppleCD Audio Player for me"). When you click the link, the Help Center opens the Audio CD player. Sometimes, such a link will activate AppleGuide, which will guide you through the rest of the steps you need to take.

6. To move back to earlier screens, click the left arrow at the top of the window.

7. To move forward in the help screens, click the right arrow at the top of the window.

8. To move to the main Help Center page, click the upward pointing arrow.

FIGURE 12.3

The Help Center provides lots of help with audio CDs.

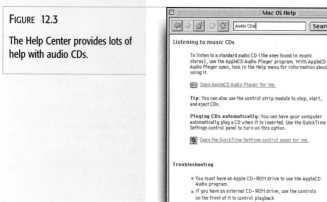

The circle and the stop sign

The red circle with the x in the center is a stop button. It stops any activity that is currently happening in the Help Center. The arrow wrapped in a circle is the Reload button, which reloads a page (to clear an error for example).

9. When you are done getting help, quit the Help Center by pressing Command-Q. Or you can leave it running in the background so that the next time you need it, it will be immediately available.

Using AppleGuide

AppleGuide has been around for a while, yet it is still one of the most powerful and helpful help systems on any computer platform. Mac OS 8.5 continues the Mac's support of AppleGuide. You will also use AppleGuide when obtaining help under the Mac's Help Center.

Description: AppleGuide provides active help; AppleGuide menus appear on the desktop as well as in many applications.

When to use: Use it when you need help on specific topics and tasks for the Mac OS or when you need help from within applications.

Pros: It provides lots of detailed information on many topics; actually walks you through many tasks.

Cons: It's not supported in all applications.

The great thing about AppleGuide is that it explains topics to you *and* then helps you accomplish those tasks by actually performing the steps for you. You can also do topic searches, and you can browse for help. AppleGuide provides help from the desktop as well as from within many applications. It is easy to use, and is one of the most powerful and innovative help systems on any computer platform.

Understanding AppleGuide

Each application that supports AppleGuide comes with its own guide file that lives in the folder with the application (for example, the AppleCD Audio Player Guide file is in the Applications folder with the AppleCD Audio Player). The Mac OS 8.5 files folders that enable AppleGuide are the following:

- **Apple Guide extension**. This extension provides the core AppleGuide services for Mac OS 8.5.

- **Global Guide Files folder**. This folder, located in the Extensions folder, contains the AppleGuide files for some of the system level processes, such as the Color Guide and the Monitors Guide.

- **Application guide files**. There are lots of application guide files installed all over your system, one for each application that uses AppleGuide.

Working with AppleGuide

You can get help from AppleGuide in several ways, including browsing or searching for a topic. After you click a topic on which you want help, AppleGuide begins to display help windows and special marks to show you *what* needs to be done. If you have trouble, AppleGuide performs tasks for you to show you *how* it is done.

Most AppleGuides have three basic modes of operation (see Figure 12.4). You can choose which mode to use by the large buttons at the top of the AppleGuide window. The modes are the following:

Don't move guide files

If you move guide files from the folders containing the application, the AppleGuide will not work for that application.

FIGURE 12.4

Many AppleGuides offer three modes of operation; this Guide is in the Topics mode.

- **Topic**. When you are in this mode, AppleGuide provides you with a list of topics in the left pane and specific questions that you may want to answer in the right pane (see Figure 12.4). Click a question and then click OK to start the guide.

- **Index**. In the index mode, you can see an alphabetical list of index items in the left pane. When you select an item, a list of questions to answer appears in the right pane (see Figure 12.5).

FIGURE 12.5

Using AppleGuide in the index mode enables you to select a topic by alphabetical order.

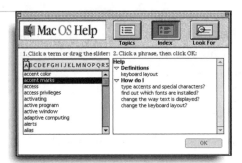

- **Search**. In the search mode, AppleGuide enables you to enter phrases to search for. After you enter a phrase in the left pane and click Search, you will see a list of possible matches for your search phrase in the right pane (see Figure 12.6). Click on a match to start the guide,

FIGURE 12.6
Searching AppleGuide for help with monitors.

While AppleGuide guides you, it prompts you for action with several elements that guide you to a particular menu or command:

- **Coachmarks**. Coachmarks are big red circles that AppleGuide draws to indicate menus that you need to open in order to accomplish a task (see Figure 12.7).

Limited modes

Some AppleGuides only offer one mode. This type usually presents a single pane containing a list of questions that you can click on to get help.

FIGURE 12.7
AppleGuide's hints are not subtle, just look at this coachmark.

- **Underlining**. When you need to make a selection from an open menu, AppleGuide underlines the particular selection you need to choose.

- **AppleGuide windows**. If you have trouble performing tasks, AppleGuide will sometimes open an explanatory window to help you understand what needs to be done.

Using AppleGuide is very straightforward as a simple example will demonstrate.

Finding help with AppleGuide

1. Open an application that has an AppleGuide (try the AppleCD Audio Player on the Apple menu).

2. Choose AppleCD Audio Player Guide from the Help menu (if you are using a different application, look for an AppleGuide command from its Help menu). The AppleGuide window will appear (see Figure 12.8).

FIGURE 12.8

AppleGuide shows you everything you need to know about the AppleCD Audio Player.

Floating windows

AppleGuide windows float, that is they are always foremost on your screen. Sometimes an AppleGuide window will cover the menus or dialogs that you need to complete the task. If that happens, just drag the AppleGuide window out of the way.

3. Click a topic and click OK. You will see an AppleGuide window that contains information for you to read.

4. Follow AppleGuide's instructions to complete the task. When you complete a step described in a window, you need to click the right triangle in the lower right corner of the AppleGuide window to move to the next step. If you have trouble completing a task, look for AppleGuide's marks to guide you.

Using Balloon Help

Balloon Help has been around since Mac OS 7.0, and it is still part of Mac OS 8.5. Balloon Help has its place; it is particularly useful for identifying what unlabeled buttons do (in those applications that support it). Support for Balloon Help has always been spotty, but there are a number of areas of Mac OS 8.5 and some applications that provide it for you.

Description: When you point to certain elements (such as commands and buttons), Balloon Help provides text snippets explaining what the element is used for.

When to use: Use it, when you need to see what a particular button or command does.

Pros: It's quick and easy to use, and a good memory prompter.

Cons: It's not supported in many applications.

Balloon Help can often provide "quick and dirty" information on particular items to which you point. However, be forewarned that many applications do not support it and even when they do, the help offered in the balloons can be weak. In many ways, Balloon Help is the least useful of the ways to get help. In fact, even some of Apple's own software does not offer Balloon Help. Still, there are occasions when Balloon Help can show you what you need to know, particularly if you need a quick reminder as to what a specific button or command does.

Understanding Balloon Help

Balloon Help has no separate files; it is integrated into the OS. This means that it is always on; there is no way for you to disable it.

Using Balloon Help

Using Balloon Help is about as easy as it can be.

AppleGuide support

Not all applications support AppleGuide, but if they do, it will always be available under the Help menu. If you don't see an AppleGuide, you will have to make do with whatever help system is provided with the application. Sometimes, software manufacturers do not use AppleGuide because their products are cross-platform and AppleGuide is only available on the Mac. Rather than developing a help system for each platform, they develop a common help system for all versions of their applications. An example of this is Microsoft. While the help systems in Office for Mac 98 and Office 97 for Windows are slightly different in appearance, the underlying help system is very similar. And, no, Microsoft does not support AppleGuide.

AppleGuide is good, but…

If you try AppleGuide a few times and either don't find it useful or it is not used in your favorite applications, consider disabling it since it does use some RAM if it is enabled. See Chapter 15, "Managing Your System Folder," to learn how to disable extensions.

Getting help with Balloon Help

1. Choose Show Balloons from the Help menu.

2. Point to items for which you want help. If the application supports Balloon Help, a balloon will appear providing an explanation of what you are pointing to (see Figure 12.9).

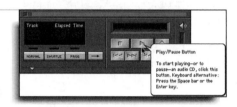

3. Choose Hide Balloons to turn them off.

Using the Assistants

Mac OS 8.5 provides a couple of applications that can help you configure certain settings on your Mac. Cleverly enough, since these applications assist you, they are called *Assistants*.

Two assistant applications are provided with Mac OS 8.5: Mac OS Setup Assistant and Internet Setup Assistant. Mac OS Setup Assistant helps you configure the general settings for your Mac. Internet Setup Assistant helps you configure your Mac to work with an existing Internet account, and you can use it to obtain a new Internet account and configure your Mac to use it.

Description: Mac OS 8.5 comes with two assistant applications that help you configure your Mac. One assistant walks you through the setup of your Mac. The other helps you configure your Mac for the Net.

When to use: Use it when you need to configure the general settings for your Mac or when you need to configure your Mac to connect to the Net.

Pros: It's easy to use.

Cons: It has a limited application.

Balloons and Mac OS

The Mac OS does provide Balloon Help in many areas, but certainly not all of them. It is a good idea to turn balloons on and move your arrow around the desktop to see what help you can find there.

The Finder does provide a basic level of Balloon Help for all software, but the Finder's help is mainly general information about windows and other interface elements (for example, if you point to a title bar in a document's window, Balloon Help will explain what a title bar is).

The Assistants are located in the Assistants folder that is on your startup disk (actually there is only an alias to the Internet Setup Assistant, which is located in the Internet folder).

SEE ALSO

➤ *To learn about the Internet Setup Assistant, see Chapter 23, "Connecting Your Mac to the Net"*

Using the Mac OS Setup Assistant to configure your Mac

1. The first time you start your Mac after installing Mac OS 8.5, the Mac OS Setup Assistant automatically opens (see Figure 12.10). You can also open it at any other time by double-clicking its icon.

FIGURE 12.10

Using Mac OS Setup Assistant to configure a Mac.

2. Click the right-facing triangle at the bottom of the window to begin. From that point on, you enter data and make choices as prompted by the Assistant.

Even after you have configured your Mac and have set it up for the Net, you may still find uses for the Assistants. For example, you can start the Mac OS Setup Assistant up at any time if you want to update your configuration, if you prefer not to use the individual control panels. If you want to add a second Internet account, you can use the Internet Setup Assistant to help you set it up quickly.

Assistants can be helpful

Don't think of these Assistants only when first configuring your Mac. You can use them whenever you need to adjust settings. This will prevent you from having to work with the control panels themselves.

Customizing Your Mac

13   **Changing the Way Your Mac Looks and Sounds 291**

14   **Managing Your Mac's Memory 317**

15   **Managing Your System Folder 335**

16   **Using Keyboard Shortcuts 367**

17   **Making Your Mac Do Your Work For You 395**

Changing the Way Your Mac Looks and Sounds

Customizing your Mac's desktop

Changing icons

Customizing menu bars, system fonts, and other interface elements

Customizing your Mac's sound effects and alert sounds

Putting it all together with themes

Customizing Your Mac Is Fun

One of the most appealing aspects of the Mac has always been the capability to customize it to make it reflect your personality and the way you work. The Mac OS has always included various tools that enable you to change the way your Mac looks and sounds. Mac OS 8.5 is no exception; in fact, there are some extensive improvements in this area. And, let's face it, it is just plain fun to remake your Mac in your own image.

The Appearance control panel was introduced in Mac OS 8.0, but it has been significantly expanded for Mac OS 8.5 (see Figure 13.1). The most significant of these changes is that you can now use *themes* that provide a "look and feel" to your Mac's desktop, as well as the windows, icons, progress bars, sounds, and so on. You can create and save different themes, combining different styles in each of these areas, and you can easily switch between themes to quickly change a number of aspects of your Mac.

FIGURE 13.1

The Appearance control panel provides extensive control over your desktop environment.

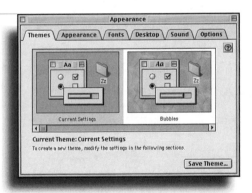

Under Mac OS 8.5, the Appearance control panel enables you to customize the following areas of your Mac:

- Desktop
- Appearance
- Fonts
- Window options
- Sound effects
- Themes

Customizing the Way Your Mac Looks

Almost all Mac users love to tweak their Mac. Whether that means using a great photograph as a desktop, tweaking fonts used in menus, changing the highlight color, or a combination of all of these, Mac users love to make their Macs look unique. After all, you have to spend a lot of time staring at your Mac, it might as well be pleasant for you.

Adjusting Monitor Settings

The fundamental areas to adjust are the color depth and resolution settings of your monitor. Color depth affects the appearance of everything on your desktop because almost everything on the desktop uses color; using a color depth that is inappropriate for the graphics you are working with can make those graphics look poor, or at the least not as their creator intended. Adjusting the resolution of your monitor affects the way graphics appear, and it also determines how much desktop room you have to work in (and simultaneously how large or small objects on the desktop appear).

SEE ALSO

➤ *To learn about color depth and how to set it, see page 176*

➤ *To learn about resolution and how to set it, see page 166*

Customizing the Desktop

One of the most fun things to play around with is the appearance of your desktop. With Mac OS 8.5, you can fill your desktop with either desktop patterns or desktop pictures. Desktop patterns use color and shapes to fill your desktop with (hopefully) pleasing textures and colors. Desktop pictures are photographs that appear on your desktop. If you feel very artistic, you also can combine the two.

Setting desktop patterns and pictures is fun. You can make the argument that having a pleasant desktop will make you work longer and more efficiently, but that is a stretch given the amount of time that you are likely to spend playing around with your desktop!

Patterns everywhere

The Mac has always used desktop patterns. Of course, when the Mac was first created, it was strictly a black-and-white machine, so the possible patterns were somewhat limited. Now, you can use and make intricate patterns.

Where did Desktop Pictures go?

The Desktop Pictures utility in Mac OS 8.0 has been replaced with a tab on the Appearance control panel. You can use this to set either a desktop picture or a desktop pattern.

Desktop photos from the Net

There are lots of images on the Internet that you can download and use as a desktop photo. As long as you use it for strictly personal use, you don't have to worry about copyright issues either. But if the image is part of a shareware collection, make sure that you pay the shareware fee!

Your own desktop photos from CD-ROM

You can also have your photos developed on CD-ROM and then use the digital versions from the CD-ROM as desktop pictures.

Setting the Desktop Pattern on Your Mac

Desktop patterns are somewhat more simple than desktop pictures since they usually involve basic shapes and colors rather than a full-blown image. Desktop patterns consist of smaller "squares" of patterns that are repeated to fill up the entire desktop, much like a quilt is made of "squares" of material. These squares are usually either 16×16 pixels or 128×128 pixels "big." Mac OS 8.5 comes with a large variety of desktop patterns that you can use, or you can create your own patterns to use.

Setting the desktop pattern on your Mac

1. Open the Appearance control panel and click on the Desktop tab. You will see the Desktop Settings window (see Figure 13.2). The window has two panes. In the left pane, you'll see a preview of the pattern that is selected from the list in the right pane. Just below the preview, you'll see the name of the pattern, its size in pixels, and its file size.

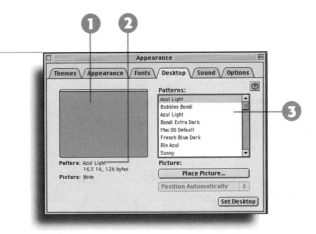

FIGURE 13.2

You can set a desktop pattern with the Appearance control panel.

1 Preview window

2 Pattern name and size

3 Available patterns

2. Use the scroll bar to scroll through available patterns in the right pane.

3. Select a pattern and preview it in the left pane.

4. When you find a pattern that you want, click Set Desktop (see Figure 13.3). The desktop pattern you choose will fill your desktop (see Figure 13.4).

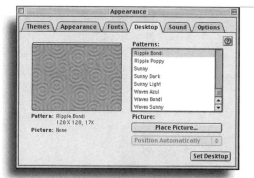

FIGURE 13.3

The desktop pattern Mac OS Default is selected in the available patterns pane and is previewed in the left preview pane.

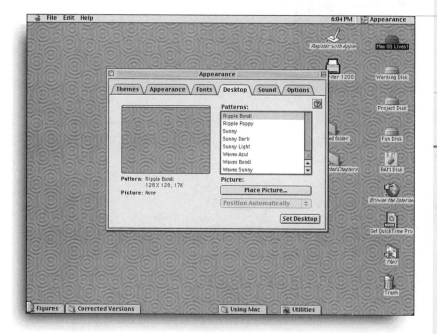

FIGURE 13.4

From this desktop pattern, you can tell which operating system I prefer.

Your own desktop photos from digital cameras or scanners

If you have a digital camera or a scanner, you can create desktop pictures from your own photos. For example, I use a digital camera to take photos during bike tours that I ride. I use these as my desktop pictures. They are a nice reminder of the life that exists away from the keyboard (which is needed, especially in the dead of the Indiana winter!). You can learn about digital cameras and scanners in Chapter 18, "Understanding and Using Input Devices."

5. Close the control panel.

Creating Your Own Desktop Pattern

If you are the artistic type (which I am definitely not, as you can tell from the pattern I created in this section), you can create and use your own desktop patterns.

Creating and using your own desktop pattern

1. Use a graphics program to create a 16 pixel x 16 pixel block (or 128 × 128, as long as it is square, it doesn't matter which). Save the file as a common desktop format, such as PICT (see Figure 13.5).

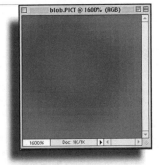

FIGURE 13.5

This pattern was created in Adobe Photoshop and was saved as a PICT.

2. Drag the file you created onto the preview window in the Appearance control panel. You will see your pattern in the window (see Figure 13.6).

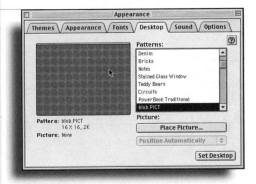

FIGURE 13.6

The file blob.PICT has been dragged onto the preview window; you now see it as a choice in the available patterns pane as well.

3. To apply your new creation to the desktop, click Set Desktop. Your pattern fills your desktop (see Figure 13.7).

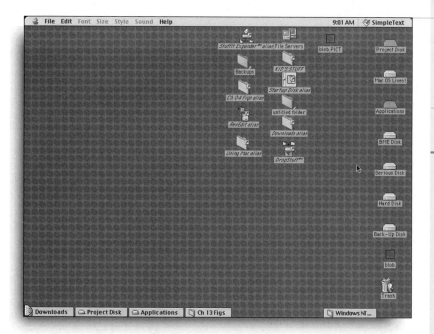

FIGURE 13.7

This pattern looks worse onscreen in color than it does in the book; I warned you that I am not an artist.

Your own desktop photos from digital cameras or scanners

If you have a digital camera or a scanner, you can create desktop pictures from your own photos. For example, I use a digital camera to take photos during bike tours that I ride. I use these as my desktop pictures. They are a nice reminder of the life that exists away from the keyboard (which is needed, especially in the dead of the Indiana winter!). You can learn about digital cameras and scanners in Chapter 18, ""Understanding and Using Input Devices."

Desktop pattern tips

When selecting or creating a desktop pattern, keep the following points in mind. Keep the pattern simple. Complex patterns can interfere with your ability to see things on your desktop. Use only a few colors. Again, too many colors can make your desktop distracting rather than pleasing. Avoid lots of medium-sized graphics in a pattern. If you use a graphic that is about the same size as an icon, you will have an even harder time finding the real icons. Keep the "pattern" graphic significantly smaller or larger than the icon size that you use. You can also use a photo or a part of a photo as a pattern.

   4. Close the control panel.

Setting a Desktop Picture

Desktop pictures are even more fun than desktop patterns. You can make your desktop into anything that you can picture (literally). Photographs of scenery make excellent desktop photos as do photos from special occasions or even special people. Setting desktop pictures is also simple to do.

Setting the desktop picture on your Mac

   1. Open the Appearance control panel and click on the Desktop tab. You will see the desktop settings window (see Figure 13.2).

   2. Click Place Picture. You will see the Choose a File window. The default folder is the Desktop Pictures folder in which there are a number of pictures that you can use.

   3. Select a picture that looks promising (try Golden Poppy).

   4. To see a preview, click Show Preview (see Figure 13.8).

FIGURE 13.8

The Choose a File dialog enables you to preview pictures that you might want to use.

1 Preview of selected file

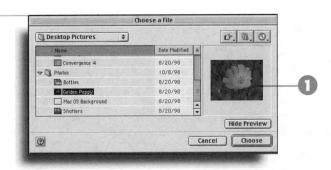

Cut and Paste

You can also select a pattern in your graphics program, copy it, and then paste it in the preview window of the Appearance control panel to apply it. When you do this, your new pattern won't have a name. Choose Pattern Name from the Appearance control panel's Edit menu to give it one.

Choose a pattern

You will find samples of patterns as you travel the Net and use various resources. You can paste these into the Appearance control panel just like you did with your own creation. You can also cut out parts of other graphics (such as photos) to use as a pattern.

Free photos

Mac OS 8.5 comes with a number of pictures that you can apply to your desktop. These are stored in the Desktop Pictures folder that is within the Appearance folder that is within the System Folder.

What is a picture?

A picture can also be a drawing, painting, or even a frame that you capture from video. If you can capture something in an image file, it can be a desktop picture.

---

5. When you find something you like, click Choose. You will return to the Desktop tab of the Appearance control panel.

6. Use the Position pop-up menu to set the position of the photo. Your choices are the following: Position Automatically (the Mac does what it thinks best), Tile (which fills the screen with as many copies of the photo as are needed to fill the desktop), Center (which places one copy of the image in the center of the desktop), Scale (which fills your desktop with the image, but keeps the image to scale), and Fill (which adjusts the photo as needed to fill the desktop).

7. When you are satisfied with the position, click Set Desktop. The desktop picture you choose will appear on the desktop (see Figure 13.9).

Changing Icons

The Mac has been always been known by its icons. They appear everywhere on files, folders, disks, and so on. Everything that appears on your desktop can be represented with an icon. As with most things Macintosh, you can change the icons that are used on your own desktop.

You learned about the Get Info command in Chapter 4, "Working with the Finder," but there is one more trick it does that I saved for this chapter. You can use it to change the icon that is used by the file, folder, or volume for which you are getting information.

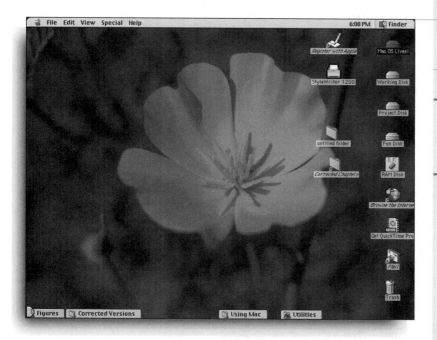

FIGURE 13.9
Ah, that's more like it.

Drag-and-drop

You can also drag a picture file onto the preview window, just as you can do with a pattern.

Picture formats

You can use just about any standard graphic file format as a desktop picture. The formats you can use as desktop pictures include the following: PICT, JPEG, TIFF, GIF, and so on. While you can't use formats that are proprietary to a graphics or image editing application, most of these applications enable you to save files in one of the "standard" graphic file formats.

Picture sizes

The size of the photo you use and the size of your desktop will affect how that image appears. For example, if you use a 640 x 480-sized image on a 832 x 624-sized desktop, it won't fill the screen using the default settings. You can use the Scale and Fill controls in the Desktop tab to fit the picture to the desktop (it will "stretch" a smaller image to fill a larger desktop, for example) in order to make the image look as you want it to (to fill the screen, for example). However, the image will look its best if it is sized properly on its own so that your Mac does not have to "tweak" it to display it.

If you have a small image, you can also tile it to make it fill the screen (although this can give you a headache if it is a complex image).

You can easily copy and paste icons from one file or folder to another. You can also use a graphics program to create your own icons. The main difference between creating icons and other graphics is that icons are small, even at their largest size. Here are some things to keep in mind when you consider creating your own icons:

- **Size does matter**. Icons are tiny images. In fact, you should create icons as images that are 32 pixels wide by 32 pixels high. That is not much room to work with. Even though you can magnify them within your graphics application as you create them, keep in mind that the icon will be 32×32 when it is displayed on the desktop.

- **Copy and create**. You can copy icons from any file, folder, or volume into your graphics program and modify them. No sense in starting from scratch if you don't have to.

- **Previews make great icons**. Some file types, such as graphics and QuickTime movies, enable you to see a thumbnail view of the file as its icon. These thumbnails are particularly good sources of icon material for other files and folders.

Patterns and pictures

If you apply a pattern to your desktop, and then apply a picture over it that does not fill the desktop, you will see the pattern around the edges of your photo. If you center the photo, you can use a pattern to create a nice frame around it.

The first step-by-step in this section shows you how to use cut and paste to swap icons. In the following step-by-step, you will learn how to use icons that you can create in a graphics program.

Changing icons with Get Info

1. Create or find a file, folder, or icon for which you want to change the icon.

2. Select that file or folder and press Command-I. You'll see the info window for that item (see Figure 13.10). In the upper-left corner of the window, you'll see the item's icon.

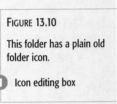

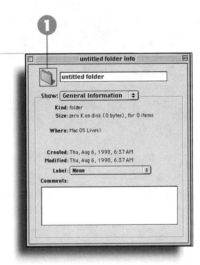

FIGURE 13.10

This folder has a plain old folder icon.

1 Icon editing box

Picture combos

You can also use an image editing program to combine multiple photos into a single desktop image. For example, if you have individual photos of your favorite landmarks, you can paste them all into one image and use that to see all of them at once.

A warning you can ignore

When you set a desktop picture, your Mac warns you that it may cover the desktop pattern. Should you worry? No.

Using your own photos

To use your own photos, either place them in the Desktop Pictures folder or just move to the folder containing them from the Choose a File dialog.

3. Find another icon that you want to use on this item, select it, and press Command-I.

4. Click on its icon to select it and press Command-C to copy it to the clipboard.

5. Move back to the first item's info window.

6. Click the old, boring icon to select it and press Command-V. The icon that you copied will be pasted over the current one (see Figure 13.11).

7. Close the info window. The item will now have the image you pasted as its icon (see Figure 13.12).

FIGURE 13.11

This is the same folder as in Figure 13.10, but notice that it now sports a nice picture as an icon instead of the generic folder.

FIGURE 13.12

This folder now has a nice-looking custom icon.

Copying and pasting icons is all well and good, but who wants to just use someone else's work? You can create your own icons as well.

Creating a custom icon

1. Using your favorite graphics program, create a graphic that is 32 pixels wide by 32 pixels high (see Figure 13.13).

FIGURE 13.13

Unfortunately, my icon art isn't any better than my pattern art was.

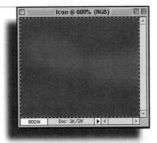

2. When you are done, select your image and copy it to the clipboard.

3. Move to the item for which you want to create a custom icon and open its info window.

4. Select its icon and paste the icon from the clipboard over it. You will see your new icon in the icon editing box.

5. Close the info window. You will see that the item now has your custom icon (see Figure 13.14).

FIGURE 13.14

I am not sure that this custom icon is what anyone would call an improvement, but at least you get the idea.

Customizing Menus, Highlight Colors, and Other Graphic Elements

You can set the appearance of menus, icons, windows, and controls, as well as the highlight color your Mac uses. With Mac OS 8.5, Apple has introduced some new terminology that you should understand:

- **Appearance**. Appearance is the term Apple applies to the general look of menus, icons, windows, and controls.

- **Highlight**. This is the same as in previous versions; it is the color something turns when you select it.

- **Variation**. The variation color is used for emphasis in controls and menus.

Setting these elements is straightforward.

Keep your pictures moving

You can have your Mac randomly select and display a desktop picture so that each time it starts you see a different image on your desktop. This is really neat and is simple to do. Instead of moving a single photo onto the preview window, drag a folder containing photos onto it. Your Mac will randomly choose an image from this folder and display it in the window. Set the desktop picture. The next time you start your Mac, it will select another photo from that folder and display that photo on your desktop. Each time you start your Mac, you are treated to a new desktop image (it randomly selects a photo from the folder you dropped on the preview window).

Setting appearance

1. Open the Appearance control panel.
2. Click the Appearance tab. You will see the Appearance controls (see Figure 13.15).

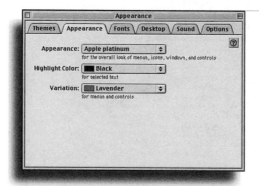

FIGURE 13.15

Setting the Appearance with the Appearance control panel.

3. Choose the Appearance that you want from the Appearance pop-up menu. At the time of this writing, it wasn't clear if more than one Appearance scheme will be provided with Mac OS 8.5. If you only see Apple platinum, then you can't make any other selections. However, there will likely be several appearance schemes from which you can choose; Apple platinum will likely be most moderate choice. The other options will be more "colorful." There are several appearance schemes from which you can choose; Apple platinum is the most moderate choice. The other options are more "colorful."

4. Choose the Highlight color you want to use from the pop-up menu. If you choose Other, you will move into the Color Picker, which you can use to create a custom highlight color.

SEE ALSO
➤ *To learn about the Color Picker, see page 176*

5. Choose the emphasis color for menus and controls from the Variation pop-up menu.

6. Close the control panel. Your new appearance scheme will be applied to the desktop (see Figure 13.17).

Customizing Window Options

The Appearance control panel also enables you to change some standard window behavior with the Options tab.

SEE ALSO
➤ *To learn about window options, see page 42*

Where to get pictures?

If you don't have a digital camera or a scanner, you may wonder where you can get new photos to try. The answer is the Internet (where else?). There are many places from which you can download general images as well as those that are created to be used as desktop pictures.

Dump the picture

You can remove a desktop picture by clicking the Remove Picture button. You will then see the desktop pattern instead.

There is another way

You can also use the resource editing utility, ResEdit, to create your own custom icons for any file, folder, or volume. It isn't terribly difficult to do so, but I don't have room in this chapter to show you how (my editor yells at me when chapters get too long). Check out a good ResEdit book, such as *Zen and the Art of Resource Editing*, to learn about this.

FIGURE 13.16

This desktop has the Gizmo appearance scheme applied; it certainly lives up to its name (this was part of an early beta version of Mac OS 8.5, it may not be part of the final version).

Reverting to the original icon

If you don't like the changes you have made to an icon, you can select it in the Get Info window and press Command-X or choose Clear from the Edit menu to remove the custom icon. The icon will revert to its original one (which is actually stored in the file's resource fork).

Icons, icons everywhere

Just like desktop pictures, you will find collections of icons that you can use with the cut-and-paste method. You can find lots of these at your favorite Mac sites on the Net.

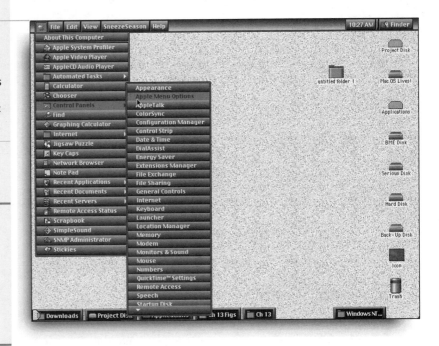

Customizing Fonts

You can also use the Appearance control panel to set the fonts that your Mac uses on the desktop and menus.

Customizing fonts

1. Open the Appearance control panel and click the Fonts tab (see Figure 13.17).

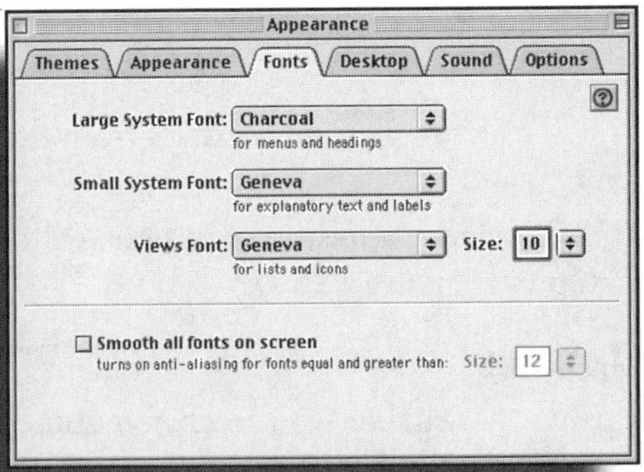

FIGURE 13.17

Using the Fonts tab of the Appearance control panel, you can set the font type and size that your Mac uses.

2. Set the menu and headings font with the Large System Font pop-up menu.

3. Set the font for text and labels with the Small System Font pop-up menu.

4. Set the font used in list views and for icons with the Views Font pop-up menu.

5. Set the size of the font used in List view.

6. If you want the fonts to appear as smooth as possible, check the "Smooth all fonts on screen" check box and set the size that you want your Mac to begin smoothing the fonts.

7. Close the control panel. Your font selections will be used.

Customizing Numbers

You can set the default appearance of numbers on your Mac through the Numbers control panel (see Figure 13.18).

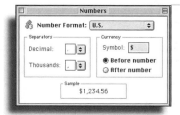

High resolution

If you use a high resolution on your monitor, it makes the items on your desktop seem smaller. If the fonts in the List view get too hard to read, you can use the Appearance control panel to increase their size.

FIGURE 13.18
The Numbers control panel enables you to set the default format of numbers.

Setting the format of numbers on your Mac

1. Open the Numbers control panel.

2. Choose the country format you want to use from the Number Format pop-up menu (you can choose Custom to create your own format).

3. Set the separators that you want to use.

4. Set the currency symbol and location with the Currency controls.

5. Close the control panel.

Font smoothing

Font smoothing, also called anti-aliasing, makes large sizes of fonts look less bitmapped and thus more smooth. Why wouldn't you want this always on? Because it requires "extra" resources for your Mac to smooth fonts. This can slow down the general performance of your Mac when it opens windows and redraws the screen. The surest way to tell if the performance hit is perceptible is to try it and see.

U.S.-centric

If you use U.S. standards for numbers and currency, you don't need to change the settings in the Numbers control panel because they are U.S. standard by default.

Customizing the Way Your Mac Sounds

Changing the way your Mac looks is only half the fun—the Mac is a multimedia machine after all. There are a number of ways that you can use sound on your Mac. In this section, you will learn how to do just that.

Adjusting Sound

You control the basic sound of your Mac through the Monitors & Sound control panel.

Adjusting sound parameters with the Monitors & Sound control panel

1. Open the Monitors & Sound control panel.

2. Click the Sound button (see Figure 13.19).

FIGURE 13.19

Setting sound with the Monitors & Sound control panel.

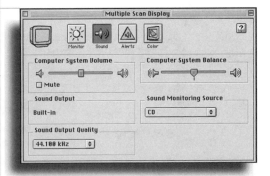

Volume controls

Many applications also have their own volume controls, such as MoviePlayer, AppleCD Audio Player, and Apple Video Player. These volumes "build" off the volume set in the Monitors & Sound control panel. If you can't get enough volume while using an application, check the Monitors & Sound control panel to make sure that the system volume isn't set too low.

3. Use the Computer System Volume slider to set the general volume of your system (or click the Mute check box if you want your machine to be silent).

4. Choose the Sound Output Quality from the pop-up menu. The higher the quality, the more resources are required to play the sound back. Unless your Mac is just limping along, leave this set at its highest setting.

5. Adjust the sound balance between left and right speakers with the Computer System Balance slider.

6. Choose a sound monitoring source with the Sound Monitoring Source pop-up menu. You will see several options, depending on your Mac. These include: CD, which takes input from the CD-ROM drive, Sound in, which takes sound from the microphone, RCA In, which takes sound from an AV board, and None, which disables any sound input. This setting determines what sound is recorded when you use any sound capture utility.

7. Close the control panel.

Customizing Sound Effects

With Mac OS 8.5, you can apply a variety of sound effects to different actions.

Setting sound effects

1. Open the Appearance control panel.

2. Click the Sound tab (see Figure 13.20).

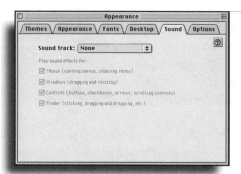

3. Choose a soundtrack from the Sound track pop-up menu. As with the appearance schemes, it wasn't clear which sound effect sets Apple would include with the final version of Mac OS 8.5. With beta versions, the soundtrack choices included Gizmo, High-Tech, and Platinum. The Platinum Sounds sound track will definitely be installed, so you will definitely be able to use it.

4. Check the boxes for the actions for which you want sound effects (Menus, Windows, Controls, or Finder).

5. Close the control panel.

Sound source

You can also select a sound source from the Control Strip module. If you switch between sources regularly, use the Control Strip module because it is the fastest way to do so.

FIGURE 13.20

You can add sound effects to different actions with the Appearance control panel.

A well coordinated Mac

Notice that the available sound-track correlates with the choices you had with the Appearance pop-up menu. These sound-tracks have been designed to "match" the appearance schemes. If you want your Mac to be truly sound-coordinated, select the soundtrack that matches your appearance scheme.

Customizing the Alert Sound

You are probably familiar with the quack, beep, and other alert sounds that your Mac makes when it wants to get your attention. These sounds are fun to play with, and your Mac comes equipped with a number from which you can choose. In this section, you'll learn how to choose an alert sound, how to record your own, and where alert sounds are stored on your Mac.

Setting Alert Sounds

You probably already know how to change your alert sound, but just in case you don't, here's how.

Setting alert sounds

1. Open the Monitors & Sound control panel.

2. Click the Alerts button (see Figure 13.21).

FIGURE 13.21

You can use the Monitors & Sound control panel to set alert sounds.

3. Click the sound you want to use from the Alert Sound window. You are treated to a sample alert.

4. Adjust the sound level of the alert with the slider. This adds to the system lever sound that you set with the Sound button. If you really crank the system volume up and also the alert volume, that quack might knock you out of your seat.

5. Close the control panel.

Recording Your Own Alert Sounds

After a while you may get tired of using the same old alert sounds. If so, add your own. You can record an alert sound from *any* sound source from which you can record. These include audio CDs, the microphone, QuickTime movies, and so on.

There are also several different ways to record alert sounds as well. These include the following:

- Monitors & Sound control panel
- SimpleSound utility
- MoviePlayer (with QuickTime Pro)
- SimpleText

SEE ALSO

➤ *To learn how to record an alert sound from an audio CD, see page 224*

The following step-by-step shows you how to record an alert sound with the SimpleSound, but all the methods work similarly.

Recording and adding your own alert sound by using SimpleSound

1. Open the Monitors & Sound control panel, click the Sound button, and choose the sound monitoring source from the pop-up menu. If you have a microphone on your Mac, use it for this step-by-step by choosing Sound In. If you don't have a microphone, record an alert sound from a CD instead (you can find out how in Chapter 10, "Working with Multimedia").

2. Close the Monitors & Sound control panel.

3. Choose SimpleSound from the Apple menu. You will see the Alert Sounds window (see Figure 13.22).

4. Click Add. You will see the recording tool (see Figure 13.24).

5. Click the Record button and make your sound.

6. When you are done, click the Stop button.

Stating the obvious

Of course you have to have a Mac with a microphone or other sound input to record a sound.

FIGURE 13.22
The Alert Sounds window enables you to record your own alert sounds.

FIGURE 13.23

You will see this recording tool in a number of places, including the SimpleSound utility, SimpleText, and other applications.

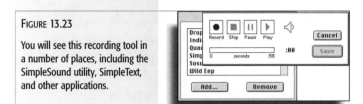

7. Click the Play button to preview your new alert sound. If it isn't good enough, click Record and try again.

8. When you are ready to move on, click Save. In the resulting dialog, name your new alert sound and click OK. When you return to the Alert Sounds dialog box, you will see your new sound added to the list (see Figure 13.24).

FIGURE 13.24

Using SimpleSound, I added a new alert sound, called STOP IT, to my Mac.

9. Close the Alert Sounds dialog. The next time your Mac needs your attention, it will play the alert sound that you just recorded.

Adding Other Alert Sounds

To add a new alert sound, you don't have to record it yourself. You will find lots of sounds on the Net and other places that you can use as alert sounds. The only requirement is that the file be a System 7 type sound. There are lots of those floating around, and there are applications that you can use to convert sounds into System 7 sounds (such as QuickTime Pro, for example).

SEE ALSO
➤ *To learn how to convert a sound into a System 7 sound by using MoviePlayer Pro, see page 214*

Adding an alert sound that you don't record

1. Find the sound that you want to use (see Figure 13.26). Suitable files have an icon with a speaker on it.

Sounds to use?

There are lots of sound formats around that you can use, so how do you know what you can use as an alert sound? Just try double-clicking it. If it plays without launching an application, you can use it as an alert sound. These files have the icon shown in Figure 13.26.

FIGURE 13.25
I recorded this sound in the previous step-by-step.

2. Quit all open applications (otherwise you won't be able to modify the System file which you will learn about in the next section).

3. Drag the sound file into the System Folder; click OK when your Mac asks if it is OK if it puts this file in the System file.

4. Use the Monitors & Sound control panel to choose the new sound as your alert sound.

Beating the System

The System file (which actually is a suitcase) is used to store the sounds that are available as system alerts, as well as the various keyboard layouts that you can use with your Mac. If you open it, you will see the items that are available (see Figure 13.26).

FIGURE 13.26
The System file—also known as the System suitcase—contains your alert sounds and keyboard layouts.

You can see in Figure 13.27 that the alert sound I recorded earlier is in this file. You can manually drag sound files in and out of the System file to install or remove them.

Customizing Your Mac's Voice

Using its Text-to-Speech capabilities, your Mac can read text in a document to you, as well as reading text in alerts and dialog

Text-to-Speech

To have your Mac read to you, you must have installed Text-to-Speech when you installed Mac OS 8.5. If the steps in this section don't work, read Appendix A, "Installing and Maintaining the Mac OS," to learn how to install system components.

boxes. Your Mac has a number of voices that it can use to speak to you. There is just something cool about hearing your Mac speak. Hear it for yourself.

SEE ALSO

➤ *To learn about speaking commands to your Mac, see page 409*

Controlling how your Mac speaks

1. Open the Speech control panel.

2. To make your Mac speak the text in dialogs and alerts, choose Talking Alerts from the Options pop-up menu.

FIGURE 13.27

Your Mac can talk to you; you use the Speech control panel to tell it how and when you want it to talk.

Make your own phrases

If you choose Edit Phrase List and then Add, you can type your own phrase for the Mac to speak. Use the speaker icon to hear your Mac read the phrase, and if you like it, click OK. Your new phrase will appear on the Speak the Phrase pop-up menu.

Both works too

If you have both the "Speak the phrase" and "Speak the alert" check boxes checked, your Mac will first read the phrase and then the text in the dialog.

3. To have the Mac speak a specific phrase for each alert, click the "Speak the phrase" check box and choose the phrase that the Mac should speak from the pop-up menu. Choose Next in the list or Random from the list to have your Mac choose a different phrase each time.

4. To have the Mac speak the text in alert boxes, click the "Speak the alert" text box.

5. Set an interval for the Mac to wait before it begins speaking the alert or text. This interval is the time between the moment when the dialog appears on your screen and when your Mac begins to speak.

6. Set the voice your Mac uses by choosing Voice from the Options pop-up menu; then select a voice from the Voice pop-up menu.

7. Adjust the rate at which the voice speaks by using the slider.

8. Listen to the voice by clicking the speaker icon.

9. When you are done, close the control panel.

Putting It All Together with Themes

Themes, a new feature for Mac OS 8.5, enable you to store all your appearance customizations (appearance of menus, fonts, desktop pictures, sound effects, and so on) in a single place. You can then switch between sets of customizations (themes) by simply changing the theme you are using. Themes enable you to quickly change many aspects of your Mac because you don't have to change all of the individual settings. You can use the themes that came with Mac OS 8.5, and you can create your own themes by creating and saving your own customized appearance settings.

Choosing a Theme

Choosing a theme is simple, and you probably noticed that the Appearance control panel has a Themes tab.

Choosing a theme

1. Choose Appearance from Control Panels on the Apple menu. You will see the Appearance control panel again; this time, click Themes (see Figure 13.28). You will see a list of available themes.

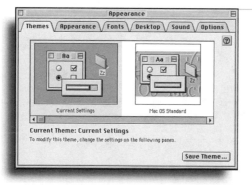

Installing themes

Some themes may not be installed by default when you run the Mac OS Install program. When you open the Mac OS 8.5 CD-ROM, look for a folder called Drag to System Folder. Open this folder and drag all the files you see onto your closed System Folder. When your Mac asks you if it should put these items in the right folder, answer OK. Any themes in this folder will now be available to you in the Appearance control panel. If you don't see this folder on your Mac OS 8.5 CD-ROM, don't worry about it. The themes were probably installed in your System Folder already.

FIGURE 13.28
You can use the Themes pane of the Appearance control panel to set a theme for your Mac.

2. Scroll to the right in the window until you see a theme that you want to try.

3. Click on the theme. Your desktop is transformed from something like that in Figure 13.30 to that in Figure 13.31.

FIGURE 13.29

A desktop with the Mac OS Default theme applied.

More on coordination

The Gizmo Zone theme uses the Gizmo appearance set and the Gizmo Sounds soundtrack to achieve this *delicate* balance of subtle design.

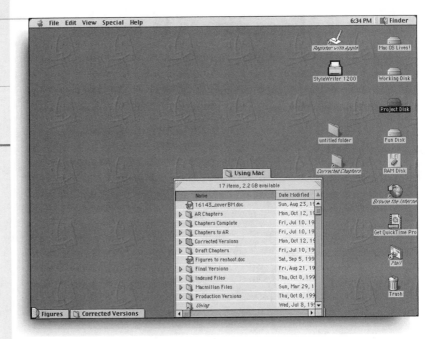

FIGURE 13.30

The same desktop with the Gizmo in the Zone applied.

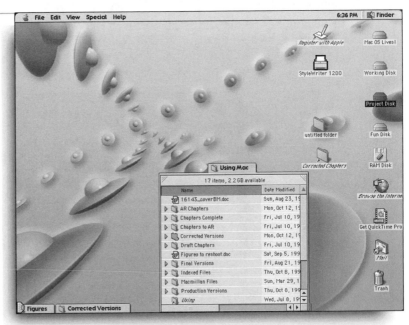

4. Close the control panel.

Saving Themes

You are a Mac user. Why should you use themes created by others? You have to be you, right? With Mac OS 8.5, you can be. Once you have developed a look and feel that you like, you can save all of your settings (appearance, fonts, desktop, sound, and options) as a theme. You can create multiple themes and switch between them whenever the mood strikes.

Creating, saving, and using a custom theme

1. Use the Appearance control panel to adjust any aspect of the interface that you want to (use the previous sections in this chapter to do so).

2. When you have tweaked everything to your satisfaction, click Save Theme.

3. Name your theme and click OK. Your theme will now be part of the available themes list (see Figure 13.32). It will also be applied to your desktop.

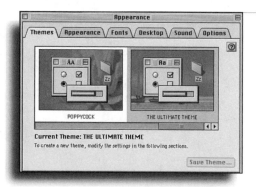

4. Close the control panel and enjoy (see Figure 13.33).

Themes

Eventually, you will be able to find and use themes that other people have created, but that weren't included with Mac OS 8.5. Then you can place theme files in the Theme Files folder that is in the Appearance folder in the System Folder. Once you have done so, you'll be able to choose that particular theme, just as you now use the themes that came with Mac OS 8.5.

Removing themes

You can remove a theme from the list by selecting it and pressing Delete.

FIGURE 13.31
The Ultimate Theme combines the best (or worst?) of everything.

Where did my theme go?

If you open the Themes folder to look for your new theme, you won't see it. It is part of the file called Custom Themes.

FIGURE **13.32**As with the appearance schemes, it wasnít clear which sound effect sets Apple would include with the

Being able to change the way your Mac looks and sounds is one of the most fun parts of using a Mac. With Mac OS 8.5, the amount of control you have over the "personality" of your Mac is even greater than it has been in the past. Even better, themes enable you to make major changes to all aspects of your Mac's appearance with a single mouse click. For those of us who like to customize our Macs, life is good.

Managing Your Mac's Memory

Understanding different kinds of memory

Managing memory allocations

Using RAM substitutes

Using a RAM disk

Physical RAM

Physical RAM refers to the RAM chips that are installed in your Mac. There is also virtual RAM which is a means by which your Mac simulates physical RAM by using its hard disk to store data. Physical RAM is much faster and more reliable than virtual memory.

Types of RAM chips

Although all Macs use RAM, they don't all use the same kind of RAM. As with all other kinds of hardware, the speed and size of RAM chips have increased over the years. There are lots of different types of RAM chips around, and each Mac model uses a specific kind. When looking at RAM chips listed in a catalog or in the specifications for a computer, you will see terms such as SIMM (Single Inline Memory Module), DIMM (Dual Inline Memory Module), and so on.

RAM and your Mac

You don't need to think about the particular kind of RAM chip that your Mac uses beyond ensuring that if you add RAM to your Mac, you get the right type of chip for your particular machine. There are charts and databases that will tell you which kind of chips your Mac uses, but there is an easier way than finding one of those. Simply ask the vendor from whom you purchase the RAM. It should be able to tell you what kind of RAM chips you need. One of the best RAM vendors around is The Chip Merchant at `http://www.thechipmerchant.com`. If you need RAM, this is the place to go.

Understanding Memory

Using a Mac involves using software to control hardware, and the hardware on which you run your software largely determines how well that software works. In order for you to be as productive as possible, both the hardware and software components of your system have to be working in synch or your Mac will not perform the way you want it to.

The most important area of this hardware/software symbiosis is your Mac's memory, particularly its Random Access Memory (RAM). RAM affects everything you do with your Mac. Not having enough RAM installed or not knowing how to properly manage the RAM that you do have will hamper your productivity, not to mention making you frustrated with your machine. Mac OS 8.5 provides several tools that you can use to manage your Mac's memory. Learning to use these tools effectively will help you be more productive and to better know how to prevent or solve lots of problems.

There are other sorts of memory that have an impact on your Mac's performance, such as its processor cache, but you can't control how these areas of memory work. You pretty much use them as they are. The only way to change them is to increase the amount available to your Mac through a hardware upgrade.

In this chapter, you will learn how to manage your Mac's memory resources. But before you get into the "how to," a bit of explanation of "why to" is in order.

Understanding Physical RAM

In a nutshell, RAM is an area in which your Mac stores data that it is working with. Data stored in RAM is only temporary, it is constantly replaced by new, updated information as your Mac continues to work. Think of RAM as your Mac's data holding tank, and you won't be far off.

Fortunately, you don't have to understand all the intricate details of how your Mac works with its RAM. However, in order to be able to effectively manage your Mac's RAM, you do need to have a general understanding of how RAM is used in order to recognize when and why you need to use Mac OS 8.5's memory management tools.

Your Mac works with lots and lots of data. This includes all sorts of data, such as data in documents, the data that makes up an application, and of course, the data that makes up Mac OS 8.5 itself. RAM is the area in which your Mac stores the data while its processor works with that data.

RAM is very fast memory so that your Mac's processor isn't slowed by having to store data to slower media, such as your hard disk. As your Mac reads data from a long-term storage media, such as a hard disk, it loads that data into its RAM and manipulates it. When the processor is "done" with data, it stores it in a long-term memory device such as a hard drive. The Mac is constantly moving data to and from RAM as it moves data to and from the processor.

The more RAM a Mac has, the faster it can provide more data to its processor and the better it performs because the Mac has a larger area in which to store data as it works with it. This also means that your Mac has to spend less time writing data to and reading data from slower devices such as hard or floppy disks.

If the RAM available to your Mac or a particular application is not sufficient for the Mac to load all of the data it needs into RAM, then the Mac or the application becomes slow, unstable, or it won't run at all.

Now that you understand what your Mac uses RAM for, you need to have some idea of how your Mac uses it. Each process that runs on your Mac uses some amount of RAM (remember that RAM is where the data that your Mac's processor is using is stored). As a process is started, your Mac allocates a certain amount of RAM for the data that needs to be stored for that process to run. For example, when you launch an application

ROM?

Another kind of memory that your Mac uses is called Read Only Memory (ROM). You can only read data from ROM (thus the name). Data stored in ROM is physically stored in the memory chip rather than as a temporary electronic construct, as it is in RAM. So you can't change the information that is stored in your Mac's ROM.

ROM is used to store the software that enables your Mac to load its operating system.

such as SimpleText, your Mac devotes a certain amount of RAM to it. The processor stores all of the data needed to run that application in the area of RAM devoted to that application. This area is called the application's *RAM allocation*. Each application on your Mac, including the system itself, must have RAM allocated to it to run.

Think of the RAM on your Mac as a pie. As a process starts up, your Mac takes a piece of the RAM and provides it to that process. When the next process starts, it takes another piece, and so on. Once all of the RAM is allocated (all the pieces of the pie are gone), your Mac cannot start any more processes. If you have ever been unable to open an application and have seen a message saying that there is not enough memory to open it, this is exactly what happened—there was not enough pie for the application you were trying to open.

Unlike a piece of pie, which never can be put back into the pie again, a piece of RAM pie goes back into the pie as soon as the process that was using it stops. Thus, if you see an out-of-memory error message and then quit some other processes (applications for example), you may be able to open that additional application since more RAM will now be available to be allocated to it.

The amount of RAM allocated to an application greatly affects how that application works in terms of speed and stability. Starve an application for RAM, and it becomes slow, unstable, or limited in what it can do. Give that same application plenty of RAM, and it will hum along.

Also understand that RAM must have power to it in order to store data. When the power to RAM goes away, so does any data stored there. Unlike long-term media, such as hard drives, RAM has no media on which to hold data without power. This is why you must save a document to a hard disk or other media in order to be able to access it again. If you were to leave that document only in RAM, it would disappear as soon as you quit the creating application (when an application is quit, your Mac removes its RAM allocation and so there is no RAM "room" for that data that makes up that document). Whenever the power to your Mac stops (such as in a restart or when you shut down the Mac), everything in its RAM is "wiped clean."

Batteries included

Since all its RAM is wiped clean when you turn it off, you may be wondering how your Mac "remembers" certain things, such as the time. There is a small area of RAM in which your Mac stores certain information such as the time, date, and other parameters that need to be retained when your Mac's power is off. This RAM is called Parameter RAM or PRAM. A battery in your Mac keeps power flowing to your Mac's PRAM even when the Mac is turned off so that the data stored in PRAM is always available.

The most important rule when it comes to RAM is this: more is better. To run Mac OS 8.5 and an application or two, you might be able to get by with 32 MB of RAM. You will be better off with 64 MB or more. If you plan on doing heavy graphics or video work, you will need 126, 256, or even more RAM.

Use the following step-by-step to see how much RAM your Mac has.

Assessing the amount of RAM in your Mac and understanding how it is allocated

1. Start your Mac.

2. When the desktop appears, choose About this Computer from the Apple menu (see Figure 14.1).

FIGURE 14.1

You can use the About This Computer window to learn about your Mac's RAM usage.

3. In the middle left side of the window, you will see three measures of memory. Built-in Memory is the total amount of physical RAM installed in your Mac. Virtual Memory is a kind of substitute RAM that you will learn about shortly. The Largest Unused Block is the amount of RAM that is currently available to be allocated to other processes.

4. In the lower pane of the window, you can see the current allocation of your Mac's RAM. One item you will always see is the Mac OS allocation. The Mac OS requires its own RAM allocation, and if your Mac is running, some amount of RAM is dedicated to the OS. The length of the bar indicates how much memory is allocated to a particular process, while the shaded part of the bar shows how much of that allocated space is currently being used.

5. Now open an application. In this example, I opened
SimpleText. Look at the About This Computer window
again (see Figure 14.2). You can see that SimpleText has
been allocated an amount of RAM, and if you don't have
many documents open, it is probably not using all of the
RAM allocated to it.

FIGURE 14.2

When SimpleText was launched,
RAM was allocated to it (the size
of its RAM allocation is indicated
by the length of the bar next to its
name).

6. Now open more applications. As you do, each will be allocated an amount of RAM (you will learn how to set these
allocations later in this chapter). After you have opened several, look at the About This Computer window one more
time (see Figure 14.3). You will see that each application has
its own RAM allocation.

FIGURE 14.3

Each of these applications is open
and has been allocated some
RAM.

7. Close the About This Computer window.

Now that you have a good grasp of RAM and how your Mac
uses and allocates it, you may wonder why you need to worry
about it. There are several reasons you need to be aware of
RAM and how it is used on your Mac. These include the
following:

- **RAM is scarce**. Unless your Mac has lots of RAM in it, you have to be cognizant of how much RAM is being allocated so that you can be sure you have enough to do what you want to do.

- **Applications need different amounts of RAM**. All applications, as well as Mac OS 8.5 itself, need RAM to run. Sometimes you have to adjust the amount of RAM available to an application in order to make it work properly or to lower its RAM allocation so that you can also run other applications at the same time.

- **Lots of problems are caused by lack of effective RAM management**. These problems include unexpected quits, failure of applications to do what they are supposed to do, sluggish performance, and so on. Understanding how RAM works will help you prevent, or at least minimize, these problems.

SEE ALSO

➤ *To learn more about RAM management's role in correcting problems, see page 754*

Later in this chapter, you will learn techniques to manage your Mac's RAM.

Understanding Caches

Another kind of temporary memory that your Mac uses to temporarily store data is called a *cache*. There are two kinds of caches that your Mac might use to process data: an inline or backside processor cache and a disk cache.

Understanding Processor Caches

An inline cache is a special portion of memory that is located on the same card with the processor. It functions sort of like RAM, but it is more closely integrated into the processor. The processor can store data in the cache for even faster access. Doing so speeds up the computer, as compared to the same computer without an inline processor cache. There are two basic types of this kind of cache. One is an inline cache, while the other is a backside cache. The difference is how the cache memory is installed. Inline caches are the older arrangement. Backside caches are newer and faster. But either will make a Mac significantly faster.

There are no controls associated with a cache—your Mac either has one installed, in which case it is on and functioning, or it doesn't have a cache. If your Mac doesn't have a cache installed, it may have an open cache slot, in which case it is possible to add a cache card. If there isn't a cache slot, your Mac can't use a processor cache.

Determining if your Mac has a cache

1. From the Apple menu, choose Apple System Profiler.

2. In the Apple System Profiler window, look in the Memory overview section (see Figure 14.4). If your Mac has a cache installed, you will see its information (type and size) listed.

Does size matter?

Compared to RAM and other memory areas, processor caches are relatively small. Most Macs that use a processor cache have either 512 KB or 1 MB of cache memory.

FIGURE 14.4

This Mac has a 1 MB L2 cache installed.

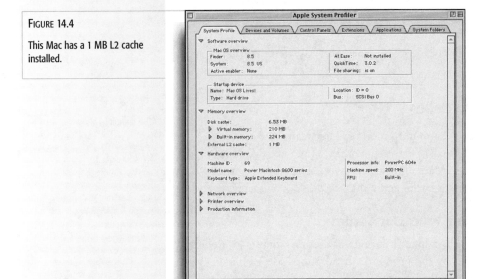

L2 cache?

The L2 in L2 cache stands for Level 2, which is the same thing as an inline processor cache.

3. If you don't see any cache information, check the documentation for your Mac to see if you have a cache slot available. If so, you can consider buying and installing a cache card to

make your Mac work faster. If you don't have a cache slot, there is no need to worry about it.

4. Close the Apple System Profiler.

Understanding Disk Cache

The disk cache is an area of RAM that your Mac can use to temporarily store, or cache, data that it would otherwise write to a disk. A disk cache speeds up the computer because writing to and reading from RAM is much faster than reading from and writing from a disk. You can set the amount of RAM set aside for a disk cache, but Mac OS 8.5's default setting will probably be sufficient for you.

The disk cache adds to the RAM requirements of your system software, so you don't want a disk cache that is too large. You just want enough to speed up your Mac a noticeable amount while not cutting into the available RAM too much. So, how much is that? This is one of the ongoing debates among Mac users. Some claim you only need a few hundred KB of disk cache. Others claim that you need as much as 50 KB per 1 MB of real RAM. How much disk cache you should set really depends on your particular system. If you have a fast hard drive, but not much RAM, you might want a very small disk cache. If you have lots of RAM, but a slow drive, then you might want a larger disk cache. The only real way to tell is to change the setting until you notice a positive or negative difference.

Setting a disk cache

1. Open the Memory control panel (see Figure 14.5). The amount of default disk cache that your Mac has set is shown in the upper right corner of the window. In Figure 14.5, the default was set at more than 7 MB. That is probably a lot larger than it needs to be.

2. If you don't want to use the default amount of disk cache, click the Custom setting radio button.

3. Click Custom in the warning dialog that appears.

4. Click the arrow buttons to adjust the amount of RAM to be set aside for the disk cache (see Figure 14.6).

Source of cache

If you need to add a new, or upgrade your old, cache card, a good source to purchase cache cards is The Chip Merchant (`http://www.thechipmerchant.com`). Refer to the documentation that came with your Mac to see how to install it.

The default

Your Mac will set a default value for disk cache for your machine. This is a good place to start your experimentation. Add some more and see if you notice a difference. Make the disk cache smaller and see if the machine seems to be working more slowly. Keep adjusting it until you think you have the best balance of performance and RAM use.

The default value is based on the amount of RAM installed on your Mac. If you add RAM to your Mac, the default amount of disk cache will increase.

FIGURE 14.5

The Memory control panel enables you to manage how your Mac works with its memory resources, including its disk cache.

FIGURE 14.6

In the Memory control panel, the disk cache has been reduced to slightly more than 5 MB.

5. Close the control panel.

6. Restart your Mac to enable the new disk cache.

7. Experiment to see what effect the change had on the performance of your Mac. Continue experimenting until you have the correct setting for your machine. If you get too far from the default value, you might want to double-check what you have done. That value should be in the ballpark of what you need.

Managing RAM

You need to understand how to manage the RAM on your Mac for the following reasons:

- **Performance improvements**. By setting the RAM allocations properly for your system and applications, you can make your Mac operate up to its potential.

- **Problem solving**. Lots of problems are related to improper RAM allocations. You need to know how to adjust RAM when you experience trouble.

- **Capability improvements**. With proper RAM management, you may be able to do more with your Mac. For example, if you understand how to adjust the RAM allocations for your applications, you may be able to run more applications at the same time.

There are two general areas in which you need to manage RAM: the system and applications.

Managing RAM for the System

If you have read any of the other chapters of this book, you have seen that the Mac is loaded with extensions and control panels that add additional functionality to your Mac. While this is good, each control panel and extension you add to the system increases the amount of RAM that the system is allocated when your Mac starts. Since the amount of physical RAM your Mac has is fixed, this necessarily means that the amount of RAM free for applications to run is less.

You can turn system components off to reduce the RAM required for your system to run. Activating system components increases the RAM required for the system to run. A general rule is that you should turn off all system components that provide functionality that you don't use in order to maximize the RAM available for the applications that you want to run.

SEE ALSO

➤ *To understand the components of your system software and to learn how to enable or disable system components, see Chapter 15, "Managing Your System Folder"*

Managing RAM for Applications

As you learned earlier in this chapter, each application that runs on your Mac is allocated a certain amount of RAM in which it runs. You can set this allocation. Providing enough RAM for an application ensures that it works as well as it can. Starving an

How much RAM is enough?

You may be wondering how much RAM you should have in your Mac. Generally, you should have as much as you can afford up to your Mac's maximum amount. Fortunately, RAM prices have fallen drastically in the last few years so you can often fill your Mac's RAM slots for only a few hundred dollars.

Getting memory

To see an application's memory requirements, you can also select the application, press Command-I to open the info window, and choose Memory from the Show pop-up menu.

The numbers don't always add up

As you use the About This Computer window, you may notice that the RAM values shown in the lower pane don't always exactly match the settings for an application in the application's info window. Nor does the total RAM allocation of all the open applications plus the Unused Block amount add up to exactly the amount of RAM installed in your Mac. All of the numbers are only approximations and depend on the amount of memory fragmentation there currently is on your machine among other things. I wouldn't worry about the exact numbers; just use the window to get a good general idea of how your RAM is being allocated.

If you notice that the free memory on your Mac is decreasing each time you open and then close applications, your memory is becoming fragmented. The only way to clear the fragmentation is to quit all your applications and restart your Mac.

application for RAM results in poor performance, bugginess, and other problems.

When dealing with the RAM allocation for an application, you will see the following categories of memory requirements:

- **Suggested Size**. All applications are designed to run in a certain amount of RAM, which is called the Suggested Size. This amount is set by the publisher, and you cannot modify it, which doesn't matter since it is simply a reference point anyway. This is the value of RAM allocation in which the publisher believes that the application will work properly.

- **Minimum Size**. This is the minimum amount of RAM that has to be available so that an application can open. You can set this value, and depending on how you set it, an application may work fine with the minimum allocation, or it may be buggy or not function at all.

- **Preferred Size**. This is the maximum amount of RAM that will be allocated to an application when it is opened. You can also set this value.

The trade-off when allocating RAM is performance versus available RAM. The more RAM you allocate to an application, the better it will work (to a point of course). The less you allocate, the worse its performance will be. And the effect on RAM is the opposite; the more you allocate to one application, the less that is available for other applications to use.

Adjusting an application's RAM allocation

1. Select the application for which you want to adjust the RAM allocation.

2. From the File menu, choose Get Info and then Memory from the hierarchical menu. You will see the Memory pane of the info window for that application (see Figure 14.7).

3. Open the application.

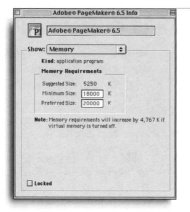

Figure 14.7
The RAM allocations for
PageMaker are shown in the
Memory pane of its info window.

4. Choose About This Computer from the Apple menu. Notice that the amount of RAM allocated to that application is between its Minimum Size and its Preferred Size. (Remember that the amount allocated is the total length of the bar across from that application in the About This Computer window.)

5. Quit the application (you can't adjust the RAM allocation for an application while it is open.)

6. Check the About This Computer window again. You will see that the application you closed has disappeared from the lower pane, and its RAM has been added to the Largest Unused Block amount.

7. Move back to the application's info window.

8. Use the Preferred Size field to increase the application's Preferred Size by 5 MB or so if you have that much more free space available. Increase the Minimum Size by a similar amount.

9. Open the application.

10. Move back to the About This Computer window and notice that the bar showing the RAM allocation is longer than it was before. This means that your Mac is giving this application more RAM room in which to work.

11. Close all the open windows.

Another advantage of lots of RAM

If you have lots of RAM on your Mac, you can keep most of the applications you use running all the time. This keeps you from having to launch and quit them as you use different documents. This limits RAM fragmentation.

Cutting back on RAM

You can decrease the RAM allocation for an application by reducing the sizes instead of increasing them. However, you should leave the Minimum Size at least as large as the Suggested Size or else you risk problems. Some applications will work fine for you with a lower Minimum value than the Suggested Size. Others will behave quite poorly. Some applications occasionally have the Minimum Size set lower than the Suggested Size by default. It is not a bad idea to check an application's RAM allocation after you first install it to see how much RAM it will be allocated.

Using RAM Substitutes

You can't always have enough physical RAM to do what you want to do. Sometimes, you can't afford to add more RAM to your Mac. Other times, all of your RAM slots may be full. Occasionally, your Mac can't even hold enough RAM to get the job done. In these cases, you can supplement the physical RAM on your machine or maximize the way in which it is used by using RAM "substitutes." However, none of these substitutes are as good as physical RAM. You should have as much physical RAM as you can and only use the substitutes as you have to.

Using Virtual Memory

Virtual speed

Using virtual memory, your Mac writes to the hard drive instead of to RAM. The faster the hard drive you use, the faster the virtual memory will be. But even with the fastest disks, virtual memory is still much slower than physical memory.

Your Mac can write temporary data to a hard disk instead of RAM when it runs low or out of physical RAM. This kind of memory is called *virtual memory*. It is virtual because it is not actually RAM, but it acts like it is—except a lot slower. While using a disk is much slower than using RAM, it at least enables you to do things that you wouldn't be able to do if your Mac didn't have sufficient RAM. Besides slowing the speed at which your Mac operates, the other down side of virtual memory is that the amount of disk space that you allocate for virtual memory will not be available to use to store data on the disk.

Still, if you need to add some cushion to the physical RAM on your Mac so that you don't have to suffer the "not enough memory" error messages, using virtual memory can be a workable solution.

Increasing available RAM by setting virtual memory

Lots of disk space

You should realize that on the hard drive you use for virtual memory, your Mac sets aside an amount equivalent to the *total* RAM amount. If you have the total RAM amount set to 100 MB, for example, your Mac will declare 100 MB of space on the virtual memory drive to be off-limits for other purposes.

1. Open the Memory control panel.

2. Click the Virtual Memory radio On button.

3. Select a hard disk to use in the Select Hard Disk pop-up menu. This is the disk to which the temporary data will be written. The control panel tells you how much space is available on the selected disk and how much RAM you have built-in (see Figure 14.5).

4. Click the arrow buttons next to the After restart box to adjust the total amount of RAM available to your Mac; this number includes the physical RAM that you have installed (see Figure 14.8). Your only limit is the amount of free disk space on the disk you have selected. Remember that this amount of space will be unavailable for "regular" disk duties.

FIGURE 14.8
You can set the amount of virtual memory that your Mac uses with the Memory control panel.

5. Close the control panel.

6. Restart your Mac to activate the virtual memory. With virtual memory, your Mac will use all of its physical RAM first before using the virtual memory. The only penalty you pay for using virtual memory is that the amount of space you set aside on your disk for virtual memory will not be available for data storage. If you are low on disk space, set virtual memory low or turn it off.

7. Open the About This Computer window to verify that the amount of RAM available to your Mac has been increased. Check the Virtual Memory line to see how much virtual memory is being used.

8. Close the window.

Another benefit of virtual memory

You may have noticed in the Memory pane of the info window for applications that having virtual memory off actually increases the memory requirements for an application. That alone is a good reason to leave virtual memory on.

Using Third-Party RAM Extensions

There are several third-party software packages that provide an alternative to Mac OS 8.5's virtual memory scheme. These software use different sorts of algorithms and techniques to provide extended RAM capacity to your Mac. The most popular of these utilities is Connectix' RAMDoubler.

These utilities provide more efficient virtual memory than the Mac OS 8.5's virtual memory. They also don't suffer as much of a performance hit as the virtual memory used by Mac OS 8.5. However, you have to purchase these utilities. And since they use extensions and control panels, you will have more compatibility problems than you will with Apple's virtual memory scheme. However, if your Mac is severely short of RAM, this kind of utility can be helpful (assuming that you can't add more physical RAM).

Using a Virtual Hard Disk (or RAM Disk)

A RAM disk is the opposite of virtual memory. Rather than using a hard disk to simulate RAM, you can use RAM to simulate a hard disk. The advantage of a RAM disk is that it is very fast, and it also uses much less power than a spinning hard disk. This makes RAM disks ideal for PowerBook users as well as for those applications that constantly write to and read from a hard disk (such as a Web browser).

You define a RAM disk, and when you restart your Mac, you will have a simulated disk mounted on the desktop. You can use this disk just as you would a hard drive. Of course, data on RAM is not permanently stored as it is on a hard disk. If something happens before you save the data to a disk (such as a crash), you will lose all of the data on the RAM disk.

Sharing and RAM disks

If you have file sharing on, you must stop it before you can make changes to an existing RAM disk.

SEE ALSO

➤ *To learn about using a RAM disk to speed up Web browsing, see page 659*

➤ *To learn about using a RAM disk on a PowerBook, see page 825*

Creating a RAM disk

  1. Open the Memory control panel.

  2. Click the RAM Disk On radio button.

  3. Use the slider to set the percentage of your RAM that you want used as a RAM disk (see Figure 14.9). Note that the RAM you use for a RAM disk will not be available for your system to work with.

FIGURE 14.9

This RAM disk will be about 17 MB.

4. Close the control panel.

5. Restart your Mac. After it restarts, you will see the RAM disk mounted on the desktop (see Figure 14.10). You can use the disk as you would a physical disk. Be aware that you need to save any files that you store on the RAM disk to a real disk before you shut down your computer. Otherwise, you will lose any data stored on the RAM disk (since it is actually RAM storing the data, the data is erased when power is removed from the RAM).

RAM disks and PowerBooks

On PowerBooks and some other Macs, you will see a "Save on Shutdown" check box in the Memory control panel. If you check this box, your Mac will save everything on your RAM disk to the hard disk before it shuts down. When you restart, your Mac will restore the RAM disk to its condition before you shut down the Mac.

FIGURE 14.10

This isn't a real disk; it is a virtual disk that is actually RAM.

Upgrading RAM

One of the best things you can do for your Mac is to make sure that your Mac has plenty of physical RAM. While telling you how to upgrade the RAM in your Specific Mac is beyond the scope of this book, it isn't hard to do. Here are the general steps you need to follow:

Dumping the RAM disk

To get rid of the RAM disk, you need to turn it off in the Memory control panel and restart your Mac.

Chip source

A great source for RAM as well as advice on what chips you need and how to install them is The Chip Merchant. You can contact The Chip Merchant at `http://www.thechipmerchant.com`.

1. Read the documentation that came with your computer to learn about its RAM configuration and the specifications for the RAM chips it uses.

2. If your Mac can use more RAM than it has installed, obtain more RAM chips. If there aren't any empty RAM slots in your machine, you may need to replace some existing chips with chips of a higher capacity. Make sure that the chips you obtain are compatible with your Mac.

3. Install the RAM in your Mac. Usually this is easy to do and simply requires that you open the case and install the chips in the open slots (or replace the chips currently installed). Make sure that you follow the instructions in your documentation.

4. Close up your Mac. If you installed the RAM properly, when you start it, you will be able to use the new RAM.

Learning to effectively manage your Mac's memory is one of the most important things you can do to make the most of your Mac. Adding physical RAM to your Mac is the best management tool of all.

Managing Your System Folder

Understanding the System Folder

Setting the startup system

Knowing when you need to manage your System Folder

Manually managing your system

Using Extensions Manager to manage your system

Using Conflict Catcher to manage your system

Understanding the System Folder

The System Folder is the heart of every Mac. The software in this folder determines how your Mac works as well as how it looks and sounds. It provides everything from the desktop that you see to the underlying system management processes that you don't. While you can often use a Mac for a long time without ever opening the System Folder, understanding the System Folder and knowing how to manage it is very important to be able to get the most out of your Mac.

In previous chapters, you learned a great deal about how to work with lots of the software that is in the System Folder. Examples include the Appearance, General Controls, QuickTime Settings, and other control panels as well as folders such as the Fonts and Contextual Menu folders and even the System file. While it is more important that you understand and use these parts of the system, there are other items within the System Folder that you should also understand. In order to get the most out of your Mac, you need to be comfortable with the System Folder and understand the various items contained within it. You also need to know how to manage your own System Folder so that you can make your Mac be what you want it to be. That information is the essence of this chapter.

Until you understand the System Folder, it can be intimidating—it has lots of folders and loose items within it (see Figure 15.1).

If looking at Figure 15.1 scares you, don't worry. If you have read through the previous chapters, you already understand the most important parts of this folder, and you know how to make your system work the way that you want it to.

Through the rest of this chapter, you will get a good overall view of the System Folder, and you will learn how to configure the System Folder to suit your own purposes.

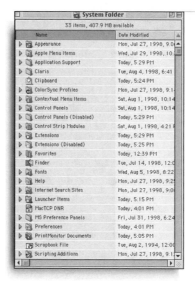

FIGURE 15.1

Your System Folder—not as scary as it looks.

Shared libraries

As you work with your Mac, you will hear the term *shared libraries*. These are "pieces" of computer code that programs use for various reasons. Shared libraries can be shared across different applications. Some applications store these shared libraries in the Application Support folder, while others have them "hanging loose" in the System Folder. You don't need to do anything with shared library files. In fact, if you move them out of the System Folder, the application that needs them probably won't work.

Microsoft's Office 98 for Mac has a unique capability to reinstall these libraries as needed so that if something should happen to one of Office's shared libraries for some reason, Office can "repair" itself and you can keep working.

To get started on the road to System Folder enlightenment, take a quick tour of your System Folder. The important folders and files in your System Folder are the following:

- **Appearance folder**. The Appearance folder, new for Mac OS 8.5, contains subfolders that store various customization information for the "look and feel" of your Mac's desktop (see Figure 15.2).

FIGURE 15.2

The Appearance folder contains files that you can use to customize the appearance of your Mac.

SEE ALSO

➤ *To learn about the Appearance folder, see page 293*

- **Apple Menu Items folder**. This folder contains the items that appear on your Apple menu.

SEE ALSO

➤ *To learn about the Apple menu, see Chapter 6, "Working with the Apple Menu"*

- **Application Support folder**. Many applications use files that are best stored within the System Folder; examples of these include custom dictionaries, import filters, help systems, and the like. In previous versions of the Mac OS, these application specific files were stored within folders for that application (or for the company that developed the application). If you had a lot of applications, you had a lot of these application folders cluttering up your System Folder. Under Mac OS 8.5, these items can be stored in the Application Support folder to prevent the proliferation of application folders within your System Folder. Not all applications will "follow the rules" and store their files in this folder, but at least it is available. You probably won't have much reason to poke around in this folder, but at least you know it exists.

- **Clipboard file**. The Clipboard file is where information that you cut or copy is stored. You can open the Clipboard to see what is stored there (see Figure 15.3). At the top of the window, you will see what the item on the Clipboard is, such as a picture, sound, or text. The Clipboard mainly works in the background, but if you ever need to see what it contains, you can always choose Show Clipboard from the Finder's Edit menu to see what it contains.

FIGURE 15.3

My Clipboard shows the screen-shot that I took for Figure 15.2.

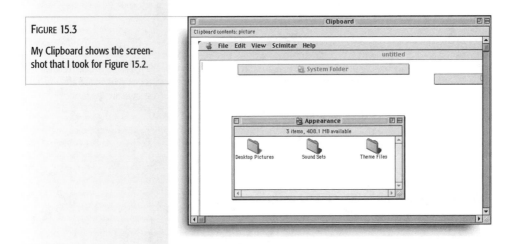

- **ColorSync Profiles folder**. ColorSync is the technology that enables your Mac to achieve consistent color across different devices, such as monitors, printers, and scanners. In order to use ColorSync, each device has a profile that describes how it applies color. Your Mac uses these profiles to achieve color consistency for that device when compared to the other devices that your Mac uses. The profiles that are available for your Mac to use are stored in the ColorSync Profiles folder.

SEE ALSO

➤ *To learn about ColorSync, see page 180*

- **Contextual Menu Items folder**. This folder contains the items that appear on your Mac's contextual menus.

SEE ALSO

➤ *To learn about contextual menus, see page 68*

- **Control Panels folder**. This folder contains your active control panels. You will learn more about this later in this chapter.

- **Control Panels (Disabled) folder**. Extensions Manager and other control panel and extension manager applications create this folder to store items that have been disabled. If you open this folder, you will see all of the extensions and control panels that are installed on your Mac, but not in use. You will learn more about this later in this chapter.

- **Control Strip Modules folder**. This folder contains the items that you see on your Control Strip.

SEE ALSO

➤ *To learn how to use and customize the Control Strip, see Chapter 7, "Working with the Control Strip"*

- **Extensions folder**. This folder contains the Extensions that are active on your machine.

- **Extensions (Disabled) folder**. This folder is analogous to the Control Panels (Disabled) folder.

- **Favorites folder**. You can use favorites to move quickly to your favorite items. When you use the Add to Favorites command, an alias to the item you have selected is placed in the Favorites folder. An alias to this folder is on the Apple menu for quick access.

SEE ALSO

➤ *To learn how to use favorites, see page 99*

- **Finder file**. This file is the piece of software that manages everything on your Mac. You don't really need to know anything else about it other than that you can't open it, and if the correct version isn't present, your Mac won't start up.

- **Fonts folder**. This folder contains all of the fonts that are available to you.

SEE ALSO

➤ *To learn about fonts, see Chapter 8, "Working with Fonts"]*

- **Help folder**. This folder contains reference files for the various help systems that are part of Mac OS 8.5 (see Figure 15.4). These systems include the Mac OS Help hyperlink-based system, as well as the AppleScript Help system files.

FIGURE 15.4

This folder is home for the help files that your Mac needs to help you help yourself.

SEE ALSO

➤ *To learn about using the Mac's help systems, see Chapter 12, "Working with the Mac's Help Systems"*

- **Internet Search Sites folder**. In Mac OS 8.5, you can use the Finder's Find command to search the Internet. The sites that you can search are contained in this folder as .src files (see Figure 15.5). If you want to make more sites available for these finds, you can add additional .src files to this folder for each site you want to be able to search.

FIGURE 15.5
If you use the Finder Find command to search the Internet, you will be able to search the sites with .src files in the Internet Search Sites folder.

SEE ALSO

➤ *To learn how to search the Net from the Finder, see page 95*

- **Launcher Items folder**. The Launcher is a palette on which you can place buttons that can be clicked once to open the item to which the button points. Because you can view any Finder window by using buttons with Mac OS 8.5, there isn't a whole lot the Launcher can do for you. If you use the Launcher, you can place aliases to items that you want to appear on it in the Launcher Items folder.

- **MacTCP DNR file**. MacTCP enables your Mac to "speak" Transmission Control Protocol/Internet Protocol (TCP/IP). TCP/IP is the language that all computers on the Internet must be able to speak. The Mac TCP DNR file stores certain information that your Mac needs to connect to the Net. Since you can't open it, there isn't any reason to mess around with it. If you happen to delete it for some reason, your Mac will create another one automatically.

- **MS Preference Panels folder**. Under Mac OS 8.5, Microsoft applications are the default Internet applications installed on your Mac. The configuration preferences that you set for these applications are controlled by the various panels that are contained in this folder (see Figure 15.6). You can double-click these files to open a particular preferences area in the Configuration Manager window (see Figure 15.7).

FIGURE 15.6

The panels stored in this folder enable you to set preferences for various aspects of the Microsoft Internet software that is part of Mac OS 8.5.

FIGURE 15.7

Double-clicking a preference panel opens the Configuration Manager window and enables you to set the preferences for that area (General Email settings in this figure).

SEE ALSO

➤ *To learn about configuring your Mac to connect to the Net, see Chapter 23, "Connecting Your Mac to the Net"*

■ **Preferences folder**. Each application with which you work creates a preference file that contains any settings that you customize. This customization information is stored in a preference file. All preference files are stored within the Preferences folder. Since every application, and most control panels and extensions as well, create a preference file the first time you open them, it doesn't take long until you have lots of individual preference files in the Preferences folder. In fact, even before you have used any applications, Mac OS 8.5 creates a lot of preference files (see Figure 15.8).

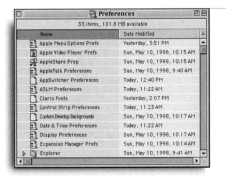

FIGURE 15.8
Even before you do much of anything, there are a lot of preference files in your System Folder.

- **PrintMonitor Documents folder**. Your Mac uses this folder to store documents that it is printing. When you open the PrintMonitor, you will see the queue of documents that are being printed. These documents are temporarily stored in this folder—once a document finishes printing, it is removed from this folder.

SEE ALSO
➤ *To learn more about installing and using a printer, see page 441*

- **Scrapbook File**. The Scrapbook File is a file that you can use to hold items that you frequently use.

SEE ALSO
➤ *To learn how to use the Scrapbook, see page 136*

- **Scripting Additions folder**. This folder contains software that is used in conjunction with AppleScript. AppleScript enables you to automate repetitive tasks.

SEE ALSO
➤ *To learn more about AppleScript, see page 398*

- **Scripts folder**. Individual AppleScripts are stored in this folder. You can use these scripts when creating your own AppleScripts.

SEE ALSO
➤ *To learn more about AppleScript, see page 398*

Easy to create, but hard to remember to get rid of

You should be aware that when you throw out an application and its folder, any preferences file that it creates will remain in the Preferences folder. While preference files are typically small (10 KB or less), there is no reason to keep a preference file for an application that you no longer use. It is a good idea to look in the Preferences folder every so often and delete any preference files that you find for which you no longer use the application.

Going back in time

If you have tweaked the preferences of an application so much that you can hardly use it any more, delete its preference file. The next time you open the application, it will look like it did the first time that you opened it. And you can begin tweaking it all over again.

- **Shutdown Items folder**. Placing an item in this folder causes your Mac to open that item when you shut down your machine.

SEE ALSO

➤ *To learn more about using this folder, see page 398*

- **Shutdown Items (Disabled) folder**. This folder works similarly to the way the other (Disabled) folders work. When you use Extensions Manager or another utility to disable a shutdown item, it is moved into this folder.

- **Startup Items folder**. You can use this folder to make your Mac open any file or folder when it starts up.

SEE ALSO

➤ *To learn more about using this folder, see page 397*

- **Startup Items (Disabled) folder**. You can probably guess what this one is for.

- **System**. The system file contains sounds, keyboard items, and other files that your Mac uses.

SEE ALSO

➤ *To learn about adding sound files to the system, see page 311*

- **System Extensions (Disabled) folder**. Does this one sound familiar? It should. This folder is very similar to the Extensions (Disabled) folder. Why is it here? There are certain pieces of software that act just like extensions, but are stored loosely in the System Folder rather than in the Extensions folder. The MacTCP DNR file is one example of this kind of file—and it is likely the only one you will see. If you use Extensions Manager to disable MacTCP DNR—or any other similar "extension"—it is moved into this folder.

- **Text Encodings folder**. Your Mac is multilingual, and can be made to "speak" many languages; the files in the Text Encodings folder enable your Mac to work with a variety of languages. Take a look inside the folder to see how worldly your Mac really is (see Figure 15.9).

Packing a suitcase

The System file—not to be confused with the System Folder—is a type of file called a *suitcase*. A suitcase is a file that is a container for other files. In previous versions of the Mac OS, fonts and other items were also stored in a suitcase rather than in folders. As the Mac OS has progressed, the number of suitcases has been reduced. Now only fonts and the System are stored in suitcases. Suitcases are somewhat harder to work with than folders so that is a good thing.

Does your Mac have bugs?

The debugging utility called MacsBug uses another one of these "extensions" that is not stored in the Extensions folder.

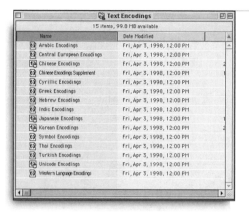

FIGURE 15.9
Your Mac is multilingual.

While the preceding list of "stuff" in your System Folder is long, it may or may not contain everything that you actually see in your own System Folder. Applications can add additional folders to the System Folder, and if you do a custom installation of Mac OS 8.5, you may see fewer—or more—things in your own System Folder. At any rate, you should feel comfortable with what you find in there, and hopefully, you'll know where to go in this book for additional information on any listed item.

Setting the System Your Mac Uses

The System Folder that your Mac uses to start up is the one that determines how your Mac works and looks. There are certain situations in which you may want to be able to choose from among a variety of System Folders for your Mac to use. For example, if you share a Mac with children, you may want to create a System Folder tailored to them. Or, if you have major problems with your current System Folder, you may need to be able to start up from another System Folder so that you can fix your original one.

Before you get into the nuts and bolts of setting the active System Folder, the following list includes some points that you need to keep in mind:

Lots of startup disks

Note that in the Startup Disk control panel, you see all the volumes on any disk that contains valid system software. Not all of the volumes you see in the control panel have a valid System Folder on them. Make sure that you choose a volume with valid system software.

Using other media to startup

If you have a removable disk or CD-ROM containing valid system software mounted on your desktop, you can select it as your startup disk.

- A volume can contain only a single System Folder.
- A physical drive can be partitioned into multiple volumes, each of which can contain a System Folder.
- The volume containing a viable System Folder (one from which your Mac is capable of starting up) is called the startup disk, even if the volume is actually a partition on a drive.

SEE ALSO
> *To learn how to create an alternate startup disk containing a viable System Folder, see page 740*

You use the Startup Disk control panel to set the startup disk that your Mac uses to startup.

Setting the startup disk

1. Open the Startup Disk control panel (see Figure 15.10). The current startup disk is highlighted.

FIGURE 15.10

The Startup Disk control panel shows you all the volumes on disks that contain valid System Folders.

Invalid system software

If, for some reason, the System Folder on the startup disk you have selected in the Startup Disk control panel becomes invalid (your Mac can't start up from it), your Mac will search other disks and volumes for a valid System Folder. It will start up from the first valid System Folder that it finds.

2. Choose the startup disk that you want your Mac to use the next time it starts up.
3. Close the control panel.
4. Restart your Mac. The volume you selected will now be the startup disk.

SEE ALSO
> *To learn how to start up from CD-ROMs and other removable media drives, see page 740*

Understanding System Enhancements

Extensions and control panels are "pieces" of software that add functionality to your Mac. Mac OS 8.5 comes with a number of extensions that are installed; some are installed by the Easy Install option, while others are installed if you use custom installation options when you install the system software. There are also literally thousands of third-party extensions and control panels that you can add to your Mac to make it work better for you.

SEE ALSO

➤ *To learn about installing Mac OS 8.5 extensions and control panels, see Appendix A, "Installing and Maintaining the Mac OS"*

Extensions and control panels both modify your system (thus adding functionality) when your Mac starts. As your Mac works through the start-up process, it loads each extension and control panel (which you can see as their icons march across your screen). These items then become part of the operating system.

The good thing about control panels and extensions is that they add functionality to your Mac, thus enabling it to do more. The down side is that control panels and extensions add to the RAM requirements of your system, and they can cause your system to be more unstable than it might be without them.

The main difference between extensions and control panels is the level of control they provide. Extensions are either on or off; you don't have any control over how extensions work. If you don't like the way an extension is working, your only choice is to disable it. Control panels, on the other hand, provide controls that you can use to change how the added functions work.

From the earlier tour of the System Folder, you saw that extensions and control panels were stored in individual folders.

A full list of all of the available extensions and control panels would be longer than this chapter, but some of the types of extensions that you may end up using are the following:

Your Mac knows best

When you install the system software, the installer program checks to see on what kind of Mac the software is being installed. Some extensions (some of the system enablers for example) will only be installed on certain kinds of machines.

Extensions and control panels

Many control panels also have corresponding extensions (or extensions have corresponding control panels, depending on how you look at it). For example, it takes both a control panel and an extension to enable contextual menus. The extension provides the basic functionality while the control panels enables you to modify how that function works.

■ **System software**. The Mac OS contains a number of Apple extensions and control panels that provide core functions of the system. Examples include AppleGuide, Contextual Menus, the Control Strip, Application Switcher, and so on.

■ **Hardware drivers**. Many hardware devices require a *driver* to work properly (or at all). A driver is simply an extension that enables your Mac to communicate with the device in a language that it understands. There are driver extensions for printers, scanners, some removable media drives, and so on.

■ **Technology enablers**. Some extensions and control panels add a technology to your Mac. Examples of these kind of extensions are QuickTime (which enables your Mac to work with time synchronized data such as digital video), AppleScript (which enables you to automate your Mac), and Open Transport (which is the technology that you use to communicate across networks, including the Internet).

■ **Application support**. Many applications require specific extensions or shared libraries in order to run. These are installed during the software installation process. If you look through the System Folder and Extensions folder on your Mac, you will likely see some shared libraries and extensions from Microsoft and other third-party software developers. Some applications also install support files in the System Folder, such as help files, dictionaries, and so on.

■ **Third-party extensions and control panels**. There are thousands of third-party extensions and control panels that add unique features and functions to your Mac. You can add extensions to change the interface, add new functions, or to improve functions that are already there.

Technology enablers

The more technical term for a technology enabler is Application Programming Interface (API). APIs are available to applications so that they can make use of that technology. For example, to use QuickTime, applications use the QuickTime API.

Not all software in the System Folder loads at startup

While all active extensions and control panels load into the operating system during the start-up process, some software in the System Folder does not. For example, shared libraries are not loaded during the start-up process. They are loaded as needed by the applications that use them.

Managing Your System

Now that you understand the System Folder and the items it contains, you need to understand the situations in which you need to manage it. Here are three possible situations in which you may need to use the tools and techniques described in this chapter to manage your System Folder:

- **You are having unexplained crashes, hangs, and other problems**. One likely cause of these problems is conflicts between various extensions and control panels that are installed in your system. As part of the troubleshooting process, you need to know how to enable and disable extensions and control panels.

SEE ALSO

➤ *To learn more about troubleshooting and correcting problems, see page 750*

- **You are doing something that requires intensive system resources**. Some tasks will tax your Mac's limits. For example, if you record or edit digital video on your Mac, you need to eliminate all extraneous activity so that all of your Mac's resources are devoted to the digital video application. You can accomplish this by disabling all unneeded extensions and control panels. Some of the more advanced games also benefit from having the Mac to themselves.

- **Your Mac is always at its limit**. If your Mac doesn't have much RAM in it or if its processor is slow, you may want to disable extensions and control panels to reduce the RAM requirements of the OS, thus increasing the RAM available for your applications.

Fortunately, you can use the same tools and techniques to manage your system regardless of the reason you are managing it.

Manually Managing Your System

The most basic way to manage your system is to manually drag items in or out of their folders within the System Folder. While this is easy enough to do, I don't recommend this method because keeping track of the extensions and control panels that are in your System Folder—as well as those that aren't—can be messy. It is easy to lose track of what is installed and what isn't. But, if you want to try this method, be my guest.

While the following step-by-step uses an extension, you can use the same process to disable controls panels and other system files. You just have to open the appropriate folder and drag the item out of its folder.

Disabled folders

If you have opened Extensions Manager or another system management utility, you will see several (Disabled) folders within your System Folder. You can use these to store your disabled items.

Why you have to restart

When enabling or disabling extensions and control panels, you always need to restart your Mac for your changes to take effect. That is because extensions and control panels are "patched" into the system software as it loads. So changes that you make to the Extensions and Control Panels folder don't make immediate changes in the system since that software is already part of the system that is running. After you disable an extension, it won't be loaded the next time the system is started. And only then will you see the results of the changes you make.

Your Mac is smart

Your Mac can recognize extensions, control panels, fonts, and other system files and automatically put them where they belong. Just drag the file onto the closed System Folder and the Mac will ask you if it should put the extension, control panel, or other file where it belongs. No need to even open the individual folders.

Spring-loaded folders

Remember that if you want to put a file in a folder that is within the System Folder, you can also drag it over the System Folder and wait for the folder to spring open. Then you can easily and quickly move items into the Extensions or any other folder.

Manually disabling an extension

1. Open the Extensions folder.

2. Drag the extension that you want to disable outside of the Extensions folder. You may want to create a "holding" folder for these disabled extensions in case you want to re-enable them later.

3. Restart your computer. The extension will no longer be loaded during the start-up process.

Manually enabling a system element is as easy as disabling one was.

Manually enabling an extension

1. Drag the extension into the Extensions folder.

2. Restart your Mac. The extension will be loaded during the start-up process and will be part of the system.

Using Extensions Manager to Manage Your System

While you can do things the hard (manual) way, why would you want to when the Mac OS provides a good tool that will help you manage your system much more easily and effectively? This tool is Extensions Manager (see Figure 15.11).

Extensions Manager has been part of the Mac OS for some time, and as with most parts of the system, it has undergone many improvements through the various versions of the OS.

Now in version 4.0.3, Extensions Manager, offers several great features that will help you manage your system. Extensions Manager enables you to do the following tasks:

- **Turn individual system items on or off**. This makes enabling and disabling items much easier and more convenient than the manual method. You may also need to do this when you are troubleshooting problems.

SEE ALSO

➤ *To learn how to use Extensions Manager during the troubleshooting process, see page 756*

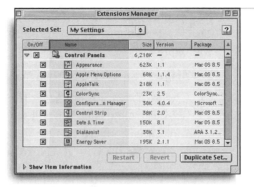

FIGURE 15.11
Extensions Manager enables you to control which extensions and control panels are loaded into your system during startup, thus enabling you to fine-tune your Mac.

- **Create sets of extensions, controls panels, startup items, shutdown items, and other System Folder items**. These sets enable you to quickly and easily switch between Mac configurations. For example, if you use your Mac to record digital video, you should define a set of extensions and control panels so that only the items you need to record the video are active. This minimizes background activity so that your Mac will do a better job on the video. Another example might be when you want to play a graphic and processor intensive game. You can create a minimum set of extensions and control panels so that the game will have a maximum amount of system resources to use, thus making the game's performance better.

- **Identify information about the extensions and control panels in your system**. The names of many extensions and control panels are somewhat obtuse, and you may have no idea what the item does from its name. With Extensions Manager, you can obtain a description of each item's purpose as well as its version number, size, and other such information.

Using Extensions Manager to Disable Extensions, Control Panels, and Other System Files

Your primary use of Extensions Manager will be to enable and disable particular items that you need or don't need. You may want to do this for performance reasons—the fewer components

Another piece of shareware is assimilated

Extensions Manager began its life as shareware created by Ricardo Batista. Version 3.0 of Extensions Manager was added to Mac OS 7.5. Extensions Manager 4.0 was included with Mac OS 7.6.

Extensions Manager consists of an application and an extension

Extensions Manager is an application, even though it is located in the Control Panels folder. There is also an Extensions Manager extension. The purpose of this extension is to enable you to open the Extensions Manager application by holding the spacebar down while your Mac starts up.

(extensions, control panels, and so on) that are loaded into your Mac's system, the faster it will run and the less RAM the system will require to operate.

Disabling an item using Extensions Manager

1. Choose Extensions Manager from the Control Panels folder on the Apple menu. You will see the Extensions Manager window (see Figure 15.12). Across the top of the window, you can see the On/Off control as well as various data for each item (name, size, version, and so on). This window works just like a folder in list view in the Finder. For example, you can re-sort the list by clicking in the column name, and you can hide the contents of a folder by clicking the hide triangle.

FIGURE 15.12

When you open Extensions Manager, you will see the control panels and extensions that are installed on your Mac.

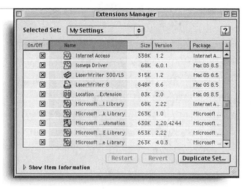

What's in the package?

The far right column in the Extensions Manager window is the Package column. Many technologies and third-party software contain several extensions and control panels. These items can be identified by the package name of which they are part. For example, in Figure 15.12, you can see that many of the items are part of the Mac OS 8 package. This means that they are part of the standard installation. In the figure, you can also see that there are files associated with Internet Access and the ARA client. The package information can help you identify all of the component parts associated with certain software so that you can more easily disable (or enable) all of the pieces that make up the package.

2. Scroll down the window to see which items are active in your system. Notice that you can see the following folders within the Extensions Manager window: Control Panels, Extensions, Shutdown Items, Startup Items, and System Folder. Each of these are the same folders that are within your System Folder.

3. To disable a particular item, click the On/Off box. Any item is active if the box is checked; it is inactive if the check box is empty. For this example, I have disabled the extensions associated with certain printers that I don't use (see Figure 15.13).

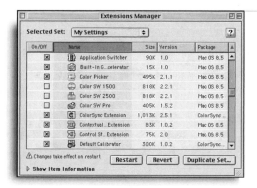

FIGURE 15.13
By unchecking the On/Off box,
you can enable/disable an item;
in this case, I have disabled the
Color StyleWriter extensions.

4. To enable an item, click a blank check box.

5. Continue enabling and disabling items until you have your system the way you want it.

6. Quit Extensions Manager.

7. Restart your Mac. You always have to restart your Mac after making any changes to the extensions and control panels that are loaded in the system during startup.

Using Extensions Manager to Define Sets

While it is useful to be able to enable and disable individual items, you may want to keep various configurations of extensions and control panels handy so that you can easily switch between them. As you probably can guess, Extensions Manager makes it easy to do this. These configurations are called *sets* in Extensions Manager lingo. You can define and save multiple sets; changing configurations is then as easy as simply selecting another set and restarting your Mac.

Defining sets with Extensions Manager

1. Open Extensions Manager.

2. Choose New Set from the File menu.

3. In the resulting dialog box, name the set you are about to define and click OK (see Figure 15.14). Notice that the name you choose now appears in the Selected Set pop-up menu (see Figure 15.15).

Careful...

Be careful that you understand what something does before you disable it, especially if it is an extension provided by Apple as part of Mac OS 8.5. If you disable something without knowing what it does, you may find that some very important feature is no longer available. Some extensions are even required for your Mac to work. For example, your system will not start up without the Appearance control panel being enabled. Unfortunately, Extensions Manager will not tell you which ones are vital to your Mac's existence.

Get them all

When you are disabling an item, make sure that you disable all of the items that may be associated with that item. For example, many extensions also have an associated control panel. You need to disable both items since one won't work without the other anyway. Use the item names and the Package column to figure out which items are related.

Using Extensions Manager during startup

To open the Extensions Manager during startup, hold the space-bar down while you start your Mac. Extensions Manager will open, and you can manipulate system files. When you close the Extensions Manager window, the start-up process starts over by using the most recent Extensions Manager settings.

FIGURE 15.14

Naming a new set of extensions and control panels in Extensions Manager.

FIGURE 15.15

Sets that you define are available in the Selected Set pop-up menu.

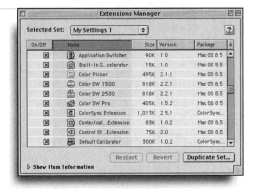

Where have all the little files gone?

You may wonder what happens to extensions and control panels when you disable them. Remember that Extensions Manager creates "disabled" items folder for each category within your System Folder and moves disabled items into these folders. For example, disabled extensions are moved to the Extensions (Disabled)folder. Then when your Mac restarts, the items are not loaded into the system since they are no longer in the proper folders. Do you really need to know this? Not really since Extensions Manager handles all of the moving for you.

4. Disable the items that you do not want to be loaded during system startup.

5. Enable the items that you do want to be loaded during system startup. Note that Extensions Manager continually saves sets that you define as you go. There is no need to save a set once you have created it.

6. When your configuration is complete, click the Restart button to restart your Mac. When the machine restarts, the set you defined will determine what items are loaded into the system.

Using Extensions Manager Defined Sets

The purpose of defining sets is so that you can easily switch between configurations. Using sets is almost trivially simple.

Changing your System Folder by using sets

1. Open Extensions Manager.

2. Choose the set that you want to use from the Selected Set pop-up menu.

3. Restart your Mac. The set that you selected will be loaded during startup.

Using Extensions Manager to Learn About Extensions, Control Panels, and Other System Files

One of the more confusing things about extensions, control panels, and other system files is figuring out what individual files do. You can look at the names; they sometimes will tell you what the item is about, or at least what it is related to. However, the names of these items are sometimes confusing and frequently downright baffling. Fortunately, with Extensions Manager, you don't have to rely on the names alone (don't forget about the Package column). Extensions Manager provides some additional information for most of your extensions and control panels.

Notice that I wrote *most* rather than all. Software has to be written in such a way that it provides the information that Extensions Manager passes onto you. If it doesn't, Extensions Manager won't be able to help. Fortunately, almost all extensions and control panels provide this information nowadays.

Why do you care about what specific extensions and control panels do? Because you want to know what they do before you disable or enable them. If you don't know what something does, turning it off can be problematic. While the function you lose may be irrelevant to what you are doing, it may provide a vital function that may not be obvious. Turning it off may prevent you from doing something important (such as being able to start your Mac at all).

Using Extensions Manager to get information on items

1. Open Extensions Manager.

2. Click the triangle next to Show Item Information. The Extensions Manager window will expand, and you will see another area at the bottom of the window (see Figure 15.16).

FIGURE 15.16

Expanding Extensions Manager's window provides an area that you can use to view information about specific items.

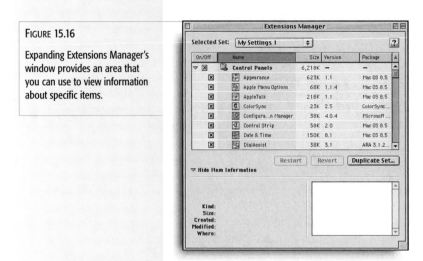

3. Choose an item in the Extensions Manager window. You will see various information about that item in the lower pane (see Figure 15.17). This information includes the name, version, what kind of software the item is, its size (storage size, not RAM requirements), when it was created, when it was modified, and where the item is stored. The most useful information provided is a description of what the item does, which is located in the lower-right pane of the Extensions Manager window.

FIGURE 15.17

Using Extensions Manager to get information about the Appearance control panel.

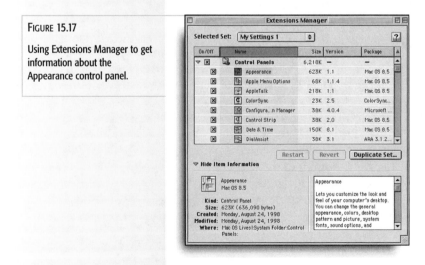

4. To hide the information pane, click the triangle next to Hide Item Information.

5. When you are done, close Extensions Manager.

Using Extensions Manager

Extensions Manager is a fairly powerful utility that enables you to really take control of the software that is loaded into the operating system during startup. While you have learned the basics in the previous step-by-steps, there are more features that you should be aware of. Here are a few tips that will help you explore more of Extensions Manager's features:

- You can change the views of the Extensions Manager window by using the View menu. View as Folders shows the items in the folders in which they are stored. View as Packages shows the items in the packages groups (see Figure 15.18); this view is particularly useful when you want to disable or enable all of the files associated with a particular technology. View as Items shows the items with no folders or other organization applied (except that provided by the list columns).

Apple help

You can reach technical information and help on Apple software (including Extensions Manager) from Apple's Web site located at: http://www.apple.com.

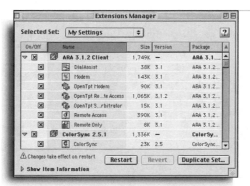

FIGURE 15.18
Viewing Items as Packages can be very helpful when you are trying to enable or disable all of the items associated with a particular technology.

- Save Set as Text (under the File menu) enables you to generate a text list of all of the items in your System Folder (see Figure 15.19). This listing can be useful when you are trying to troubleshoot your Mac or when you want to know what version of each item you are using.

FIGURE 15.19

Generating a list of items in a text file can be useful when you are troubleshooting your system.

The text file is a mess

While the text file listing your items is easy to create, it is a mess. The formatting does not make it easy to read, and everything is all squished together. However, you can open it in your favorite word processor and clean it up rather easily. If you use Microsoft Word, for example, you can easily convert the listing into a nice, neat table.

A better way

A better way to get configuration is to use Apple System Profiler on the Apple menu.

- You can quickly turn all items on or off by using the All On or All Off command on the Edit menu.

- You can add the Type and Creator columns to the Extensions Manager window by choosing Preferences from the Edit menu and then clicking the check boxes for the information that you want to add (see Figure 15.20).

FIGURE 15.20

Adding the Type and Creator columns can sometimes provide useful information, but most likely you will be better off leaving this information hidden.

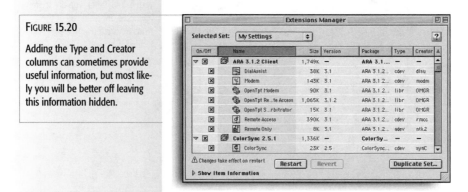

- The Revert button enables you to go back to the settings that were in effect when you opened Extensions Manager. Any changes you have made in the current session will be lost if you use this button.

- To make a new set that is based on an existing set, use the Duplicate Set button. This creates a copy of a set to which you can make changes and quickly create a new set. This is very useful if one of your sets is "close" to a new set that you want to create.

- If you click on the Select Set pop-up menu, you will see two predefined sets: Mac OS 8.5 Base and Mac OS 8.5 All (see   Figure 15.21). The Mac OS 8.5 Base set turns on only those items that your Mac needs to start up. The Mac OS 8.5 All turns on all items that were installed as part of Mac OS 8.5. Unlike that All On command, it does not turn on any third-party items that you may have installed.

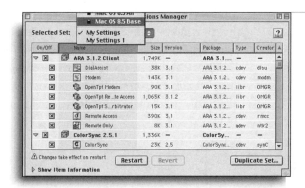

FIGURE 15.21
These two Mac OS predefined sets can help you get back to standard Mac OS configurations.

A word about naming

When you view the list alphabetically, you may notice that some items do not appear to be in alphabetical order. That is because the Mac treats certain symbols as part of an item's name. For example, if an item's name begins with a space, it will appear at the top of a view that is sorted by Name. If it begins with another symbol, such as a tilde, it will move to the bottom of the list.

Items are loaded into the system in the order that they appear in an alphabetical list. Sometimes it is necessary to load certain items before others for functionality reasons or to prevent conflicts. For example, Extensions Manager's name actually has a space in front of it. This makes its extension load before any of the other items so that it can be opened during the startup process.

Using Conflict Catcher to Manage Your System

While Extensions Manager is a pretty good tool, there is a much better one available. It is Cassady and Greene's Conflict Catcher. Conflict Catcher does everything that Extensions Manager does plus lots of other useful things. For example, Conflict Catcher can automate the troubleshooting process by automatically enabling and disabling items for you. It also provides live links to the creators of items so that you can quickly move to related

Demo

You can download a demo version of Conflict Catcher from Cassady and Greene's Web site located at `http://www.casadyg.com`. I recommend that you get a demo and try Conflict Catcher for yourself.

Web sites for additional information as well as to download updates to the various software installed in your system.

SEE ALSO

➤ *To learn how Conflict Catcher's automatic troubleshooting process works, see page 763*

The basic system management tasks that you do with Conflict Catcher are similar to those of Extensions Manager. It is just that Conflict Catcher does them better, and it does more.

Using Conflict Catcher to Manage Your System

Just as you can with Extensions Manager, you can use Conflict Catcher to disable or enable individual files.

Using Conflict Catcher to disable system files

1. Open Conflict Catcher by using the menu that it installs on your desktop (see Figure 15.22). The Conflict Catcher will open (see Figure 15.23). Conflict Catcher has a three-pane window. The left pane is the information pane (you will use that in a moment). The top-right pane lists the items in your System Folder. Active items are highlighted in the Conflict Catcher window. Inactive items are not. The lower-right pane shows the groups of system files that relate to a particular technology (such as QuickTime).

FIGURE 15.22

Conflict Catcher installs a menu on your desktop so that you can access it quickly and easily.

Conflict Catcher and Extensions Manager

Notice that as soon as you install Conflict Catcher, it disables Extensions Manager. There is no reason to have both utilities active, and at least one reason not to. Conflict Catcher will conflict with Extensions Manager during the start-up process.

2. Click on an item to disable it. The highlight will go away.

3. When you are done disabling items, close Conflict Catcher. You will be prompted about saving the changes in a set. Click No.

4. Restart your Mac. When it restarts, the items you disabled will not be loaded.

FIGURE 15.23
Conflict Catcher looks similar to
Extensions Manager, but it is
more powerful.

Enabling a system file is also easy.

Enabling a system file by using Conflict Catcher

1. Open Conflict Catcher.
2. Click an unhighlighted item to re-enable it.
3. Close Conflict Catcher.
4. Restart your Mac. The items you enabled will be loaded into the system.

Using Conflict Catcher to Define Sets

As with Extensions Manager, you can define sets of system files so that you switch among configurations quickly.

Using Conflict Catcher to create system configurations

1. Open Conflict Catcher using the Conflict Catcher menu.
2. From the Sets menu, choose Create Set. You will see the Create Set dialog (see Figure 15.24).
3. Name the set and choose the other options. For example, using the Set control pop-up menu, you can determine which files are affected by the set. You can also set a startup sound for each set by using the Startup Sound pop-up menu. There are several more options in the dialog, but these are sufficient for most sets.
4. Click OK.

FIGURE 15.24

You can create custom system configurations with Conflict Catcher's Create Set dialog.

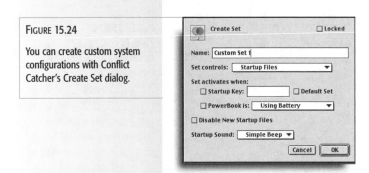

5. Enable and disable system files to create your custom set. You can use the Group Links in the lower pane to enable or disable groups of files.

6. When you are finished with your set, close Conflict Catcher.

7. Answer Yes when you are prompted to save changes.

8. Restart your Mac. As your Mac restarts, you will see the name of your set appear at the top of the screen. You will also hear the sound you associated with that set. When you Mac restarts, the system files that you enabled in your set will be loaded into the system.

Using Conflict Catcher Defined Sets

Conflict Catcher adds your defined sets to its menu so that changing configurations is even easier than it is with Extensions Manager. You don't even need to open Conflict Catcher, you can simply use its menu.

Using Conflict Catcher sets

1. From the Conflict Catcher menu, choose the set that you want to be active (see Figure 15.25).

FIGURE 15.25

Conflict Catcher makes it extremely easy to change your system configuration.

2. Restart your Mac. The set you choose will be active.

Using Conflict Catcher to Learn about Extensions, Control Panels, and Other System Files

In addition to the kind of information that you can get using Extensions Manager, Conflict Catcher also enables you to contact the software's publisher as well. This makes updating your system files easy, not to mention being able to get help more quickly.

Learning about system files using Conflict Catcher

1. Open Conflict Catcher (see Figure 15.26).

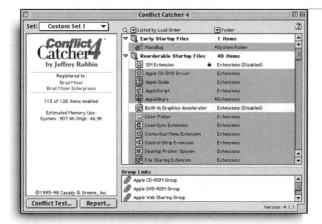

Your Mac tool kit

Conflict Catcher should be part of your Mac tool kit. You can purchase a copy from your favorite retailer or from Cassady and Greene's Web site. It costs $79.95, which is a bargain in my opinion.

FIGURE 15.26

The left pane of Conflict Catcher provides room for extensive information about each system file.

2. Click in the far left column next to the system file about which you want information (the column has a magnifying glass at the top). Information about that item will be displayed in the left pane (see Figure 15.27). Notice that there is also contact information for the publisher at the bottom of the pane. This includes live Web links. If you click on one of these links, you will move directly to that site.

3. When you are done getting information, close Conflict Catcher.

FIGURE 15.27

The information about Apple's
File Sharing Extension is displayed
in the left pane of the Conflict
Catcher window.

Using Conflict Catcher

Conflict Catcher is a very powerful utility for both system management and troubleshooting and fixing problems. The following list includes some additional features of Conflict Catcher and
a few tips on how to use them:

- You can edit the information provided for a file by clicking
  the pencil cursor that appears over the information window
  while you have a file selected. You will see a field in which
  you can enter comments about a file (see Figure 15.28). Your
  text will appear at the bottom of the window.

FIGURE 15.28

Conflict Catcher enables you to
annotate your system files.

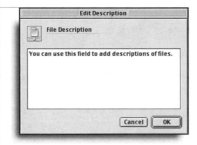

- You can change the order that the files are listed in the right pane by using the pop-up menus indicated by the downward-facing arrows at the top of the window.

- You can use the commands on the Sets menu to edit existing sets as well as to create new ones.

- The Preferences command on the Edit menu enables you to customize the way Conflict Catcher works.

- The Web menu provides a quick way to get to some great Mac-related Web sites. Just choose a site from the menu (see Figure 15.29).

FIGURE 15.29

Conflict Catcher provides links to some great Mac Web sites.

- Conflict Catcher provides a complete set of menus and commands that you should explore to realize the full power of Conflict Catcher. You can also use Conflict Catcher's help system to explore its capabilities.

Using a system management tool such as Conflict Catcher enables you to better understand your system, control how it operates, and solve any software conflict problems that arise. You should actively manage your System Folder to ensure that your Mac works as good as it can at all times.

Using Keyboard Shortcuts

Configuring a keyboard

Understanding and using predefined keyboard shortcuts

Creating keyboard shortcuts with ResEdit

Creating keyboard shortcuts with an application's customization tools

Creating keyboard shortcuts with QuickKeys

Working with the Keyboard

Even with all of the great desktop management tools included as part of Mac OS 8.5, the old-fashioned keyboard is still one of the best tools you can use to do your work quickly and efficiently. Using the keyboard to activate commands is faster (especially once you memorize your most frequently used shortcuts) because you don't have to take the time to remove your hand from the keyboard, grab the mouse, move the pointer to the top of the screen, open a menu, make a choice, and then move your hand back to the keyboard. You can use just a few keystrokes to accomplish lots of the tasks that you need to do.

Mac OS 8.5 provides lots of predefined keyboard shortcuts for you to use, and using these in addition to your mouse will dramatically increase your working efficiency. However, you can do even more by creating your own custom keyboard shortcuts. There are several ways to create or modify your own keyboard shortcuts, three of which are the following:

- **ResEdit**. The hardest way requires that you use a resource editing tool, Apple's ResEdit (which is freeware). By using ResEdit, you can add your own keyboard shortcuts to the Finder, as well as other applications. ResEdit is not only fun, but you can also learn a lot about how the Mac works by using it. A warning, though, that ResEdit is not the easiest tool in the world to use.

- **Applications' own tools**. Many applications enable you to customize the keyboard shortcuts for that application from within the application. The benefits of using these customization tools is that you don't need any additional software, and it's usually fairly easy to do. The disadvantage is that you need to set the keyboard shortcuts for each application individually.

- **QuickKeys**. The easiest and more powerful way is to use a keyboard shortcut/macro utility. In this chapter, I'll show you how to use CE Software's QuickKeys, which I have used for many years, and I can't imagine using a Mac without it. QuickKeys provides the best of all worlds. It is easy to use and provides much more power and flexibility than the

Keyboard shortcuts everywhere

Mac OS 8.5 provides lots of keyboard shortcuts that you can use while working with the Finder. Applications also provide their own keyboard shortcuts that you can use when you are working with that application. If an application is properly designed, many of its shortcuts will be the same as those for the Finder (such as Command-V for paste).

You can also create your own keyboard shortcuts that can work with the Finder and with applications.

other options. The only down side is that QuickKeys is a commercial piece of software so that you have to buy a copy of it. However, once you use it to customize the way your Mac works, you'll also wonder how you ever got along without it.

You can use any or all of these methods. Try them and see which is best for you—it is likely that you will continue to use more than one technique depending on your working style.

Before I get into the details of using and creating keyboard shortcuts, though, I'll show you how to configure the keyboard itself.

Configuring Your Keyboard

Using a keyboard is pretty easy—you just plug it in, turn the Mac on, and begin typing, right? The answer is: yes, it is that easy; however, there are a couple of adjustments that you can make to the way your keyboard works. You do this through the Keyboard control panel.

Changing the keyboard setup

1. Open the Keyboard control panel (see Figure 16.1).

FIGURE 16.1

The Keyboard control panel enables you to set the language configuration of your keyboard, the key repeat rate, and the key delay.

2. To use a different language, select it from the Script pop-up menu.

3. To change the keyboard configuration to one appropriate for a country other than the U.S., click the box next to that country in the list.

4. Use the slider to set the Key Repeat rate. The repeat rate is how fast a letter will be typed while you hold down a key.

5. Use the other slider to set the Delay Until Repeat; this delay is the time between when you press and hold a key down until the letter begins to repeat.

6. Close the control panel.

Modifier keys

All keyboard shortcuts require that you use one or more modifier keys in conjunction with a letter, number, or function key. A modifier key simply tells your Mac that you want to do something other than enter the character normally associated with that key. The Mac's modifier keys are: Shift, Ctrl, Option, and Command.

Using Predefined Keyboard Shortcuts

With Mac OS 8.5, there are lots of predefined keyboard shortcuts that you can use to quickly and easily accomplish tasks. Table 16.1 shows some of the more useful keyboard commands for the Finder; some of these commands are also useful within applications (such as the editing commands). Learning to use these can save you the time and effort you might otherwise spend reaching for the mouse.

TABLE 16.1   **Useful Keyboard Commands**

Key command	Function Name	Purpose
Command+N	New	Creates a new folder on the desktop Creates a new document from within an application
Command+O	Open	Opens whatever is selected
Command+P	Print	Prints
Command+delete	Move To Trash	From the desktop, moves selected files to the Trash
Command+W	Close Window	Closes a window Closes a document if the only window is open for the document
Command+I	Get Info	Opens the Get Info dialog for the selected folder or file
Command+D	Duplicate	Creates a duplicate of the selected file or folder
Command+M	Make Alias	Creates an alias of the selected file
Command+Y	Put Away	Ejects a selected disk Moves selected servers into the Trash to remove them from the desktop

Key command	Function Name	Purpose
Command+F	Find	Opens the Finder's File command
Command+R	Show Original	Locates the original item from which an alias was created
Command+Z	Undo	Undoes the last action
Command+X	Cut	Removes the selected data and places it on the Clipboard
Command+C	Copy	Copies the selected data and places it on the Clipboard
Command+V	Paste	Places data from the Clipboard into a document at the current location
Command+A	Select All	Selects all items in a window
Command+E	Eject	Ejects any selected removable media
Command+?	Help	Opens the Help Center
Power Key	(Mac off)	Start up if the Mac is off
Power Key (Mac on)	Restart, Sleep, Shut Down dialog	Causes a dialog to appear that has Restart, Sleep, and Shut Down buttons on it
Command+Control+ Power Key	Warm restart	Restarts your Mac; only use this method as a last resort (when your Mac is locked up, and you can't do anything else)
Command+Option+ Power Key	Sleep	Causes Macs to go into sleep mode
Command+Option+ Esc	Force quit	Forces the active application to quit: use this only as a last resort If the Force Quit works, immediately quit all applications and restart your Mac
Command+	Stops process	Causes some processes to be interrupted
Tab	Move cursor	Advances the cursor one field or changes the selected button in most dialog boxes
Arrow keys	Select a file	Selects the icon appropriate for the key (for example, the file immediately above the current position for the up arrow key)

continues...

Power key to start

While the Power key is on all keyboards, it doesn't work in the same way on all Macs. If your Mac has a "hard," or external, power switch, usually located on the front of the CPU, the Power key will not cause it to start or to shut off all power. You have to use the external power switch to start your Mac and to turn off all power.

However, on Macs with external power switches, pressing the Power key will bring up a dialog in which you can click Shut Down to shut down your Mac. You still have to turn the external switch off to stop all power to the Mac.

Models with external power switches include the Power Mac 6100 models.

Keyboard shortcuts in applications

Most applications also have a number of predefined keyboard shortcuts. To find out what they are, peruse the menus and commands that you use. The predefined keyboard shortcuts will be listed next to the commands on the menus.

That's not all folks

Table 16.1 does not list all of the keyboard commands, and there are others that require that you use the mouse in combination with them. You can access the Mac OS Help system to see more (go to the Working Smarter screen and click Keyboard shortcuts).

TABLE 16.1   Continued

Key command	Function Name	Purpose
Return	Edit file name	Highlights a file's, folder's, or disk's name and enables you to edit it
Command+right arrow	Expand folder	Expands the contents of a folder in List view
Command+left arrow	Collapse folder	Collapses the contents of a folder in List view
Letter keys	Select name	In lists, selects the item in the list that begins with the letters typed
Command+D	Desktop	Moves to desktop
Up and Down arrows	Move up or move down	In open and close dialogs, moves the selection up or down
Command+Shift+3	Desktop screenshot	Captures a screenshot of the entire desktop
Command+Shift+4+ caps lock	Window screenshot	Captures a screenshot of a window

While using keyboard shortcuts may not come naturally to you, it is worth your time to learn to use them. They save a tremendous amount of time; it is a lot faster to press two or three keys than to move your mouse up to a menu. Plus, you may place less strain on your lower arm by using the mouse a bit less.

Creating Your Own Keyboard Shortcuts

The predefined keyboard shortcuts enable you to quickly do lots of tasks, but to really make the most of using the keyboard, you can customize keyboard shortcuts for the tasks that are important to you. And by using a keyboard shortcut/macro utility, you can even assign tasks that ordinarily require multiple steps to a single keystroke combination.

The techniques you can use to create your own keyboard shortcuts are summarized in Table 16.2.

TABLE 16.2   Techniques You Can Use To Create Your Own Keyboard Shortcuts

Technique	Advantages	Disadvantages
Use ResEdit	ResEdit is freeware, good learning opportunity to see how Mac software works	Difficult interface, resources are confusing to use, no consistency across applications, can only do single commands, can munge files so they become unusable
Use an applications' own customization	No additional cost, easy to use	Keyboard shortcuts apply tools only to individual application, need to use different tools in each application, can't work across applications, can't create keyboard shortcuts for the Finder
Use QuicKeys or other macro/ keyboard shortcut tool	Easy to use, maximum flexibility, can create consistent set of keyboard shortcuts across applications including the Finder, can easily create complex macros using many applications	Cost of software

Creating Finder Keyboard Shortcuts with ResEdit

All Mac files, including applications, have two sides, or in the correct technical lingo, *forks*. One of these forks, called the *resource fork*, contains all the resources used by that application. Resources include the icons used to represent that application and its documents, the menus you see, and so on. Part of these resources are the predefined keyboard shortcuts that you can use in that application (and that you see in the application's pull-down menus). The Finder also has a resource fork.

The other fork is the data fork, and it contains the actual data that is in the file.

Some documents files don't have resource forks, while some applications don't have data forks. Some files have both forks.

Finding software

When you are looking for a piece of software such as ResEdit, the place to start your search is Mac OS 8.5's Sherlock feature. This enables you to search lots of sites on the Internet at the same time, all from the Finder. For example, I was able to find a place to download ResEdit in less than two minutes by using Sherlock. This is very powerful. See Chapter 4, "Working with the Finder," for details.

Your first warning

And now a warning that you will see again: never use ResEdit on your only copy of a file—always make a copy of a file before using ResEdit on it. If you don't make a copy and then mess up the file, you may render the file unusable.

You can use Apple's ResEdit program to modify the resource fork of any Mac file. For example, you can change the predefined keyboard shortcuts in an application, and you can add keyboard shortcuts for those commands that do not have predefined keyboard shortcuts.

Before I get into the step-by-step to show you how to add custom keyboard shortcuts using ResEdit, I need to make a couple of points. First, using ResEdit is not terribly easy. It has a confusing interface and some of what it does is not easy to understand. Second, using ResEdit takes you into the inner workings of your Mac. If you mess something up and you haven't taken the appropriate precautions, you can cause yourself all sorts of problems, the worst of which is your Mac not being able to start up.

The bottom line is that if you aren't fairly comfortable working with somewhat complicated and intimidating "innards" of the Mac and its software, you will be better off by skipping ResEdit and using QuickKeys instead. In fact, even if you are comfortable with this area of your Mac, you will be better off using QuickKeys. But it can be fun to use ResEdit, and you will learn about how your Mac works.

You can use ResEdit on both the Finder to add keyboard shortcuts to the Mac OS or to add keyboard shortcuts to your favorite applications. In the following step-by-step, I'll show you how to add a keyboard shortcut to the Finder so that you can empty the Trash from the keyboard. Using ResEdit to add keyboard shortcuts for other Finder commands is similar.

When you open ResEdit, you will see a lot of resources that the Finder uses to present different parts of its interface. When you double-click a resource, ResEdit opens an editor for that type of resource. Some editors are relatively easy-to-use while others are a bit more difficult. The Finder command's menu resources fall into the latter category. But, you won't really need to understand the details to add keyboard shortcuts to the Finder. Just follow the next step-by-step, and it will work just fine.

Adding a keyboard shortcut to empty the trash using ResEdit

1. Open the System Folder, find the Finder file, and make a copy of it. Drag the copy to your desktop. Make sure you name it so that you know it is the copy (see Figure 16.2).

FIGURE 16.2

I used the clever name, "Finder Copy" to make sure I knew that this was my working copy of the Finder.

2. Launch ResEdit and click to clear the splash screen (see Figure 16.3). You will see the open file dialog.

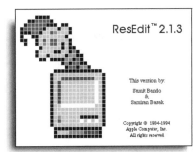

FIGURE 16.3

ResEdit's splash screen features the famous ResEdit clown (I guess that is because using ResEdit is as fun as going to the circus).

3. Maneuver to your copy of the Finder and open it. You will see a window that makes perfect sense to you (see Figure 16.4). Actually, it looks about as confusing as it actually is. Fortunately, to do what you are going to do, you don't need to understand everything that you see.

4. Find the icon resource labeled fmn2 and double-click it to open its editor (see Figure 16.5).

The second and final warning

If you open the Finder that is in your System Folder with ResEdit and mess it up, your Mac won't restart. Then you will have to start up from an alternate disk and replace the messed-up Finder with a working copy. If you don't have a valid alternate startup disk, you will be out of luck. Make a copy of the Finder before you open it with ResEdit.

Drag-and-drop

Don't forget that you can also open the Finder copy by dragging and dropping it onto ResEdit's icon. Of course, you don't get to see the clown if you do this.

FIGURE 16.4

The meaning of this ResEdit window is easy to see (Not!).

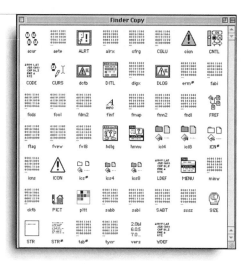

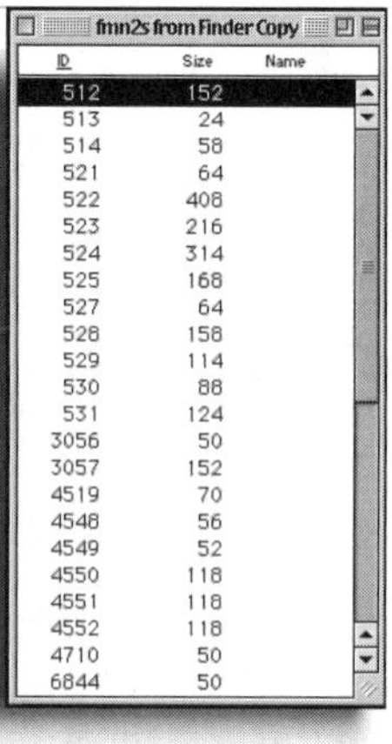

FIGURE 16.5

These are the resources that the Finder uses to create its menus.

What is the meaning of this?

In Figure 16.4, each of the icons that you see represents some aspect of the Finder's resources. For example, the icon labeled ALRT defines the alert messages that the Finder uses to tell you when something is wrong. The CURS icon contains the various cursors that the Finder uses (such as the clock, hand, spinning wheel, and so on). With ResEdit, you can open and change any of these resources.

When the Finder needs one of these resources, it refers to it by the numbers you see when you open a particular resource. Note that most of these resource icons contain lots and lots of individual resources.

You will have to explore on your own to find out what each icon means, or you can read a good ResEdit book.

5. Find the resource with the ID of 525 and double-click to open it in an editor (see Figure 16.6). This may look a bit confusing, but once you see what you are going to do, you will get the hang of it. Notice the Special menu's commands that are written in the right-hand column. If you look closely, you may notice that several have a letter that is two spaces before the command name. That is the keyboard shortcut for that command.

FIGURE 16.6

Here are the menu keyboard shortcuts for the Finder's Special menu.

Not all resources are the same

Note that not all applications store the same resources in the same areas. Just because you find the Finder's keyboard short-cuts in the fmn2 resource with the ID number 525, doesn't mean that you will find the resources for the keyboard short-cuts in another application, for example, Adobe Photoshop, in the same place. Sometimes you have to hunt around inside a file to find the resources that you want to change. For example, most applications store their key-board shortcut resources in the MENU resource, which has a much better editor.

6. Locate the Empty Trash command that starts on the sixth line down from the top of the window.

7. Put your cursor right after the first character in the sixth line.

8. Delete the first character in the sixth line and type T.

9. Quit ResEdit and save your changes.

10. Open the System Folder and drag the original Finder to another location; for now stick it in the Trash, but don't empty the Trash (you won't be able to do this even if you try since the Finder is in use).

11. Drag your edited copy of the Finder into the System Folder and rename it so that its name is just Finder.

12. Restart your Mac.

13. Open the Special menu to see your new keyboard shortcut for the Empty Trash command (see Figure 16.7). The next time that you need to empty the Trash, just press Command-T.

One last, really final warning

Before you do step 10, make sure that you have a valid startup disk that you can use in case something you did messed up the Finder. If you don't, and the Finder was munged when you used ResEdit on it, your Mac may not be able to start up from the current startup disk. See Chapter 31, "Preventing Mac Problems," to learn about creating and using an alternate startup disk.

FIGURE 16.7

Using ResEdit, I have added a keyboard shortcut so that I can empty the Trash by pressing Command-T.

Duplicate keyboard shortcuts

Be careful that you don't add a keyboard shortcut that is already used for another command. This can cause you problems.

Battling applications

One of the problems with using applications' predefined keyboard shortcuts and using their keyboard shortcut customization tool is that keyboard shortcuts are not necessarily consistent across different applications. While most applications have the same keyboard shortcuts for the "basics" (such as Copy and Paste), often they use different keyboard shortcuts for similar tasks. This can really be confusing as you try to remember which application uses which shortcut.

If you use a keyboard shortcut/macro utility, you can make all your keyboard shortcuts consistent across applications since you are using a single tool to create all of your shortcuts.

To add other keyboard shortcuts for Finder commands, explore the other resources within the fmn2 resources until you see the command to which you want to add a keyboard shortcut. Then follow the previous step-by-step while substituting the other command for Empty Trash and another keyboard shortcut for Command-T.

Adding Keyboards Shortcuts to Applications from Within Those Applications

Most applications allow you to add or modify keyboard shortcuts from within the application. For example, in Microsoft Office, you can assign a keyboard shortcut to any command; you can also modify or remove any predefined keyboard shortcuts.

Applications enable you to do this is various ways, but the general process that you follow is:

1. Choose the application's customization or preferences command.

2. Choose the command to which you want to assign a shortcut.

3. Press your shortcut keys to associate them with the command.

Using an application's own tools to add keyboard shortcuts is useful, easy, quick, and you don't have to use any outside software. Be aware that the Finder doesn't have any tools to enable you to do this directly, thus the need for ResEdit or a keyboard/shortcut macro utility. The most significant disadvantage is that it is either difficult or impossible to work *across* applications. By that I mean that it is difficult to assign keyboard shortcuts for a series of steps (a macro) for which you use several applications (I'll show you how to do this with QuickKeys in the next section). Another disadvantage is that not all applications have the capability to customize keyboard shortcuts, and so for those applications, you must use a utility of some sort. Still, for fast and dirty keyboard shortcut customization, you should check to see if your favorite applications enable you to create your own keyboard shortcuts.

In the following step-by-step, you'll see an example of how one application, Microsoft Word 98, enables you to customize its keyboard shortcuts.

Creating a keyboard shortcut in Microsoft Word 98

1. Launch Word.

2. From the Tools menu, choose Customize.

3. In the Customize dialog, click Keyboard. You will see the Customize Keyboard window (see Figure 16.8).

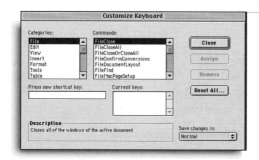

FIGURE 16.8

Word's Customize Keyboard window enables you to add your own keyboard shortcuts or modify Word's predefined shortcuts.

4. In the Categories pane, select the category of the command to which you want to assign a keyboard shortcut. The commands listed in the Commands pane will change to reflect the category selected in the left pane.

5. Choose the command to which you want to apply a keyboard shortcut in the Commands pane. For this example, I chose the Category Format and the Command DemoteList (which demotes a selection one level), as you can see in Figure 16.9. If no keyboard shortcut is displayed in Current keys area, there is currently no keyboard shortcut assigned to this command. If there was one, you would see it listed in this area.

6. Press tab to move into the Press new shortcut key box.

7. Press the key combination that you want to use to activate the command. It helps if you choose something that you can remember easily, which is easier said than done. You can try any combination of the modifier keys and numbers, letters, or functions keys.

All commands

When you first open the Customize Keyboard window, all of Word's commands are listed in the Commands pane. You can skip selecting a category if you want and instead simply scroll through all of Word's commands. However, Word has a lot of commands so that may take a while. It is better to pick a category if you can, although sometimes that isn't easy.

Word 98 has a lot of keyboard shortcuts

If you happen to choose a keyboard shortcut that Word already has assigned to a command, you can either replace Word's default keyboard shortcut or change yours.

FIGURE 16.9

I am going to apply a keyboard shortcut to the DemoteList command.

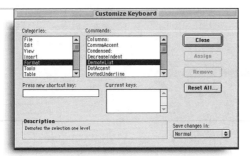

8. When you are satisfied with your new keyboard shortcut, click Assign. The new keyboard shortcut will be moved into the Current Keys area (see Figure 16.10).

FIGURE 16.10

I assigned the keyboard shortcut Command-Option-Control-D to the DemoteList command (unfortunately, a poor dialog design cuts off the keyboard shortcut so that you can't see the whole thing).

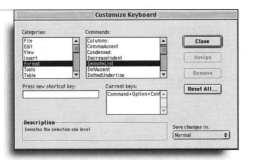

9. Click Close. The dialog will disappear. From now on, when you press your new keyboard shortcut, the command will be activated.

While the preceding step-by-step used Word 98, most applications have similar tools that enable you to define keyboard shortcuts. (All of the Microsoft productivity applications use the exact same process as Word 98.) To see how you can do this in your other applications, check the applications' help features, such as their AppleGuide. Search for keyboard shortcuts or keyboard customization.

Changing a Word keyboard shortcut

You follow a similar process to change any of Word's default keyboard shortcuts. When you select a command that has a keyboard shortcut assigned to it, you will see the keyboard shortcut in the Current Keys pane. If you select the keyboard shortcut and click Remove, the keyboard shortcut will be deleted. If you enter a new keyboard shortcut and click Assign, the keyboard shortcut will be assigned to the command. Yes, you can have more than one keyboard shortcut assigned to the same command.

Adding Keyboard Shortcuts to Applications with ResEdit

If your favorite application doesn't have a tool by which you can customize its keyboard shortcuts, you can use ResEdit to do so. Fortunately, modifying keyboard shortcuts for most applications by using ResEdit is easier than it was for the Finder.

In the next step-by-step, I'll add a keyboard shortcut to the SimpleText application's Extended style command. You can follow similar steps with other applications to add your own keyboard shortcuts to them.

Adding keyboard shortcuts to an application by using ResEdit

1. Make a copy of the application's file. Again, if you mess up your original application by using ResEdit on it, you may not be able to run the application.

2. Open the *copy* of the application (in this case, SimpleText) in ResEdit. You will see SimpleText's resources (see Figure 16.11).

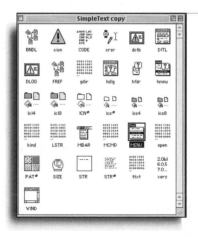

FIGURE 16.11
Opening SimpleText in ResEdit reveals its resources.

3. Find and open the MENU resources (see Figure 16.12).

4. Open the Style menu by double-clicking it. You will see its editor (see Figure 16.13).

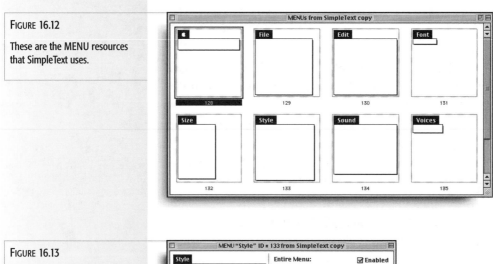

FIGURE 16.12

These are the MENU resources that SimpleText uses.

FIGURE 16.13

The Style menu in SimpleText can be edited with this window.

5. Choose the command to which you want to add a keyboard shortcut; in this case, Extended, which applies the extended font style. When you do so, the right pane of the editor changes to reflect the options appropriate for that command (see Figure 16.14).

FIGURE 16.14

Using the options in the right pane of the window, you can assign various properties to the Extended command, including a keyboard shortcut.

6. In the Command-Key box, enter the shortcut key, in this case, E.

7. Quit ResEdit and save your changes.

8. Launch the application that you just modified with ResEdit.

9. Check the command to which you assigned the keyboard shortcut to see your keyboard shortcut (see Figure 16.15).

FIGURE 16.15

The Command-E keyboard shortcut will now cause selected text to be styled with the Extended style.

10. If everything works with the modified application, throw away the original and rename the copy with the original's name (for example, change SimpleText copy to SimpleText).

Creating Your Own Keyboard Shortcuts with QuickKeys

I saved the best for last. The best tool for creating your own keyboard shortcuts is a keyboard shortcut/macro utility. Using such a utility, you can automate your Mac so that almost any series of repetitive tasks can be accomplished with a simple keyboard shortcut. And creating a keyboard shortcut for a single command or task is so easy that it is almost trivial. Plus, you can create shortcuts across applications, enabling you to do steps by using different applications with a single shortcut. You can also standardize your shortcuts so that the same shortcuts do the same thing no matter what application you are using—including the Finder. No other method can match that.

The potential uses for this kind of utility are limitless. Almost anything that you can do with your Mac can either be fully automated, or at least greatly simplified, by using keyboard shortcuts and macros. If you can define each step of a task, you can automate it. It is that simple.

Macro?

A *macro* is simply a series of steps that can be repeated by your Mac. A macro can be anything from two commands joined together to a complex series of dozens of tasks. A macro is actually a simple program that tells your Mac what you want it to do, in the order in which you want the steps to happen. For example, you can define a macro that connects you to the Internet, checks your email, and then moves to your favorite Web site.

You can make macros as simple or as complex as you need to get your work done quickly and easily. Any tasks that are repetitive in nature are excellent candidates for a macro. You will learn more about macros in Chapter 17, "Making Your Mac Do Your Work For You."

So, what's a script?

A *script* is basically the same thing as a macro—it is a series of defined steps that result in a task being accomplished. The terms are basically interchangeable.

Keyboard shortcuts or menus

In this chapter, I'll focus on creating keyboard shortcuts, but with QuickKeys you can just as easily create your own custom menus containing your macros. You can also create icons that you can double-click to run your macros. Custom menus and icons are ideal for those macros that you may not use every day and so don't want to memorize a keyboard shortcut for, but still want to run easily and quickly.

QuickKeys sets

Another good feature of QuickKeys is that you can define sets of keyboard shortcuts and macros for various applications, or you can define sets that work everywhere on your Mac. This provides maximum flexibility for you; you can choose exactly where and when you want your macros and keyboard shortcuts to work.

In this section, I'll focus primarily on creating simple macros and keyboard shortcuts. In the next chapter, I'll show you how to create more complex macros by using a couple of different tools.

SEE ALSO

➤ *To learn more about QuickKeys, see page 413*

➤ *To learn about creating and using macros with AppleScript, see page 398*

One of the best keyboard/macro utilities for the Mac is CE Software's outstanding QuickKeys. I have used QuickKeys for a number of years, and it is an indispensable part of my daily Mac life. It has saved me literally hundreds of hours over the years, not to mention enabling me to concentrate on the more important parts of my work, such as creating content, rather than mundane and repetitive tasks, such as applying formats to my documents.

If I tried to list all of the things that you can do with QuickKeys, I would quickly fill up the rest of this chapter. The following examples are a *brief* list just to give you some ideas:

- **Create keyboard shortcuts**. Obviously, QuickKeys wouldn't be in this chapter if it couldn't do this. QuickKeys excels at creating keyboard shortcuts for any menu item or command.

- **Create macros**. You can record all the steps needed to accomplish a task and create a keyboard shortcut to automate that task. You can also define these steps directly within QuickKeys as well.

- **Mount drives and volumes and choose printers**. You can easily mount any drives or volumes that you access over a network, again with a keyboard shortcut. You can also quickly choose any printer that you can use.

In the remainder of this section, I'll show you how QuickKeys works as examples for several of the kinds of tasks listed in the previous bulleted list.

Adding a keyboard shortcut to empty the Trash by using QuickKeys

1. Open the QuickKeys menu that is installed on your Mac when you install QuickKeys (see Figure 16.16).

FIGURE 16.16

The QuickKeys menu provides access to the functions and tools you need to create and manage your macros and keyboard shortcuts.

2. Choose Record One Shortcut.

3. Open the Special menu and choose Empty Trash. The command will be recorded, and you will see the QuickKeys menu editor (see Figure 16.17).

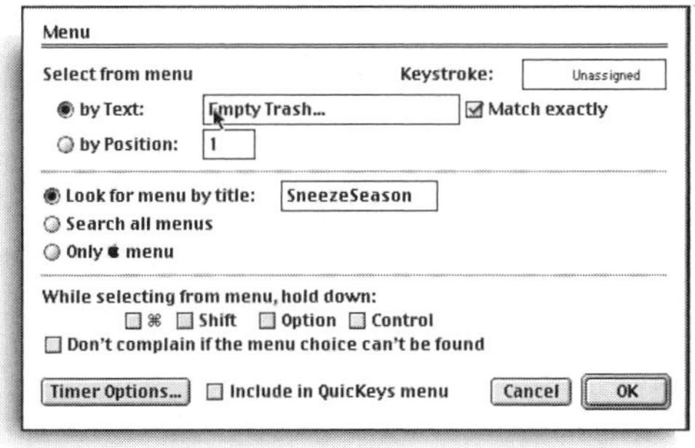

FIGURE 16.17

The QuicKeys menu editor enables you to fine-tune your keyboard shortcut.

Try before you buy

CE Software provides a functional demo of QuickKeys that you can download and use to see how useful QuickKeys is for yourself. To get the demo, use your Web browser to go to `http://www.cesoft.com` to download the demo. See Chapter 27, "Browsing the Web: Advanced Techniques," for help with downloading and using files from the Web.

4. Move to the Keystroke box and enter your keyboard shortcut. In this example, I pressed Command-T to create my keyboard shortcut to empty the Trash.

5. Click OK. You will see the QuickKeys Editor (see Figure 16.18). You can see the keyboard shortcut that you just created.

FIGURE 16.18

The QuickKeys editor is where you manage all of your QuickKeys macros and keyboard shortcuts.

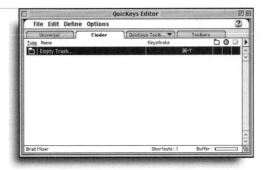

QuickKeys works in gray

When recording a keyboard shortcut or macro with QuickKeys, you can even choose to record commands that are grayed out in menu bars. This is essential because not every command that you want to record for your macros and keyboard shortcuts will be available when you are recording a keyboard shortcut. For example, if your Trash is empty when you create an Empty Trash keyboard shortcut, the command will be grayed out. But QuickKeys can choose it anyway.

More on QuickKeys sets

In this example, the keyboard shortcut was stored in the Finder set since that is the only place the command makes sense. If it was a broadly applicable command that you use in many applications, you could store it in the Universal set so that it would always be available.

6. Close the QuickKeys window. Your keyboard shortcut is now active. That was more than a little bit easier than using ResEdit, wasn't it!

From the previous example, you can see that creating a keyboard shortcut for a single menu choice is trivial with QuickKeys. It requires just a few seconds, a mouse click or two, and a few keystrokes. As good as it is to be able to create these kinds of keyboard shortcuts, QuickKeys' real power comes in creating macros that perform multiple-step tasks for you with a simple keyboard shortcut or menu selection.

In the next step-by-step, I'll show you a macro I used to print the screenshots you have seen throughout this book. While this macro may seem a bit complex at first, it really isn't all that hard to create, and it saves me lots of time and effort. Hopefully, this example will get you thinking beyond creating keyboard shortcuts for simple menu selections. The macro I will create does the following tasks:

- Opens the selected file in Photoshop
- Adds a text block containing the figure's filename
- Changes the orientation of the figure from portrait to landscape
- Changes the scale to 90 percent
- Prints the figure
- Closes the file, but doesn't save the changes
- Selects the next figure in the folder

Each of these steps requires several actions to complete, but with QuickKeys, I can do them all with a single keyboard shortcut.

Sometimes, you need to use a couple of macros together. For example, for the following example, I wanted to use Photoshop to print my screenshots. However, the screenshots are all PICT files with the creator code of ttxt, which my Mac opens in SimpleText instead of Photoshop. This made creating a macro to open files sequentially from within Photoshop harder since it wasn't the creating application for those files.

What was I to do? Well, using ResEdit, you can change the creator of a file so that a different application will open when you open the file. In this case, I created a macro using QuickKeys that would replace the files' original creator (ttxt which is the creator code for SimpleText) with Photoshop's creator code (8BIM). I ran that macro on a folder full of figures to change them all to Photoshop files. After that was finished, I could easily open them in Photoshop and this made the printing script much easier. Sometimes, it helps to make several individual macros rather than one "super-macro." Another advantage of doing this is that you can use the pieces in other macros that you create later.

Creating a keyboard shortcut to print figures

1. Open the folder containing the figures that you want to print. In this example, I am using the folder that contains the figures for Chapter 3 (see Figure 16.19).

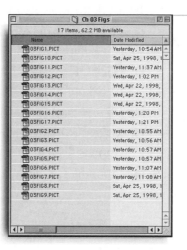

FIGURE 16.19

The macro will add the filename and print all of the figures in a folder in the format required by the publisher of this book.

Editing macros

By the way, you can always edit any macro that you record just in case some of the recorded steps aren't quite right. Using QuickKeys editor is fairly straightforward, and once you use it a time or two, you will see how to edit your own macros.

2. Open Photoshop and create a new file. You will use this to set the text format of the figure's filename that you will add to the print.

3. Choose the text tool and add some text in the format in which you want your filename to appear. Since Photoshop keeps the same text formatting until you change it, this step ensures that all of the filenames will be printed in the same format. In this example, I used Helvetica in 48-point size and bold because I wanted people to easily see the filename.

4. When you have set the text format, close the file (no need to save changes).

5. Move back to the Finder and select the first file that you want to print.

6. Start QuickKeys recording your macro by choosing Record Sequence from the QuickKeys menu. QuickKeys will begin to record your actions.

7. Press Enter so that the filename is in the edit mode and you can copy the name to the Clipboard.

8. Press Command-C to copy the filename to the Clipboard.

9. Press Command-O to open the selected file. The file will open in Photoshop.

10. Move into the center of the figure, near the bottom (the text tool should still be selected from your preparation in steps 2 and 3).

11. Click the mouse button to enter the Type Tool dialog.

12. Press Command-V to paste the filename in the Type Tool (see Figure 16.20).

13. Click OK to close the Type Tool. The filename will now be pasted onto the figure (see Figure 16.21).

14. Choose Page Setup from the File menu.

15. Make the desired changes (in this case, changing the orientation and scale) and press Return to close the dialog.

16. From the File menu, choose Print.

Keyboard shortcuts within keyboard shortcuts

While you are recording, you can still use keyboard shortcuts, for example, Command-P to print.

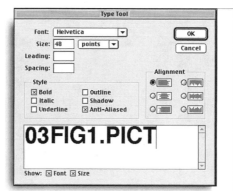

FIGURE 16.20
In this step, I am pasting the figure's filename into Photoshop's Type Tool.

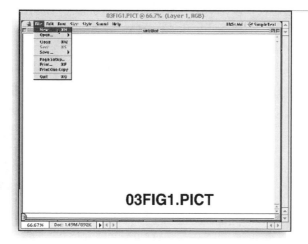

FIGURE 16.21
The figure now has the filename pasted into it.

17. In the Print dialog, set your print options and press Print. Your document will be printed.

18. Press Command-W to close the document, but don't save changes. (In this case, I didn't want the filename to actually be part of the file, it was just for the hard copy.)

19. Choose Finder from the Application menu to move back to the Finder.

20. Press the Down arrow to select the next file in the folder. This step starts the process over again so that you can make a repeating script.

21. Choose Stop Recording from the QuickKeys menu. You will see the QuickKeys Sequence Editor(see Figure 16.22).

FIGURE 16.22

The QuickKeys macro editing dialog contains the script that you just recorded.

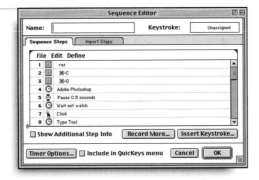

22. Enter a name for your macro, press Tab, and then press a keyboard shortcut for this macro (the Keystroke field needs to be highlighted). In this case, I used Shift-Option-Control-P.

23. Click OK to close the QuickKeys Sequence Editor.

24. Click the Close box in the QuickKeys Editor to exit QuickKeys.

25. Test your macro by selecting another file in the folder and pressing your keyboard shortcut. If it works as you want it to, you are all set. If not, you may need to go back and edit it in the QuickKeys Editor. Keep tweaking it until it works correctly.

SEE ALSO

➤ *To learn more about using the QuickKeys editor, see page 413*

26. After the script works properly, you can add a sequence control so that you can set the number of times your macro runs. To get started, choose QuickKeys from the QuickKeys menu. The QuickKeys Editor will open.

27. Double-click your macro. The Sequence Editor will open (see Figure 16.23).

FIGURE 16.23
QuickKeys' Sequence Editor
enables you to edit each step of
your macro.

1 Step arrow

28. Move the step arrow to the very top of the macro, before step 1.

29. From the Define menu, choose Extensions, Sequence Tools, and Repeat.

30. In the Repeat Extension dialog, click the Begin Repeat radio button, check the "Display dialog box asking how many times to repeat" check box, and click OK to close the window. This tells the macro to start repeating here, and also tells it to ask you how many times it should repeat.

31. Move the step arrow all the way to the bottom of the macro, below the last step.

32. From the Define menu, choose Extensions, Sequence Tools, and Repeat. You will see the Repeat Extension dialog again.

33. This time, click the End Repeat radio button and click OK. This tells the macro where to stop repeating.

34. Click OK to close the Sequence Editor.

35. Close QuickKeys.

36. Try your macro again. This time you will be prompted to input how many times the macro should repeat (see Figure 16.24). When you enter a number and click OK, the macro will run the number of times you input. This makes it easy to print a whole folder of files; just input the number of files in the folder at the prompt.

FIGURE 16.24

When prompted by this dialog, you can tell the macro how many times to repeat itself.

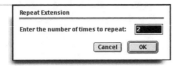

Getting your own QuickKeys

After you try the QuickKeys demo, you can purchase a full version by checking your favorite software retailer or buying it directly from CE Software at 1-800-523-7638 or from its Web site at `http://www.cesoft.com`.

While this may seem like a complicated process at first, once you are comfortable with QuickKeys (which doesn't take very long), you can create such a macro in just a few minutes. And it can save you hours of repetitious and time-consuming steps.

In the next step-by-step, I'll create a keyboard shortcut to mount a network drive on the desktop. This macro eliminates a number of steps that you have to do to mount a drive manually.

Creating a keyboard shortcut by using the Chooser to mount a network volume

1. From the QuickKeys menu, choose Record Sequence.

2. From the Apple menu, choose Chooser. You will see the Chooser window (see Figure 16.25).

FIGURE 16.25

Using the Chooser you can select AppleShare and then choose an AppleShare volume while QuickKeys records your steps.

Mounty

QuickKeys does have a function called Mounty that is supposed to enable you to create a keyboard shortcut to mount a network drive. But I have had some trouble getting it to work properly. So I use the method in this step-by-step, which is just as easy and works every time.

3. Click AppleShare.

4. Click the volume that you want to mount on your desktop and then click OK.

5. Enter your network name in the Name box and your password in the Password box (see Figure 16.26).

Connect to the file server "PC MACLAN" as:

○ Guest
◉ Registered User

Name: Brad Miser

Password: ●●●

2-way Encrypted Password

Change Password...   Cancel   Connect

3.8b2c1

FIGURE 16.26

This dialog enables you to log into an AppleShare volume.

6. Click Connect.

7. In the next window, make sure that the Save My Name and Password button is selected (if it isn't choose Pause Recording from the QuickKeys menu, click this button, and then choose Pause Recording again).

8. Click OK.

9. Close the Chooser.

10. From the QuickKeys menu, choose Stop Recording. You will see the Sequence Editor containing your new macro (see Figure 16.27).

Macros and applications

Some applications also provides tools that you can use to create macros with other applications. Some of these macro tools are quite elaborate. For example, Microsoft Office uses its own programming language to enable you to create macros. Fortunately, you can also record your steps so that you don't have to learn the language in order to create basic macros. Another example is FileMaker Pro, the dominant Mac database application (which is the second most popular database on the PC as well). It uses its own scripting tool to enable you to create macros that will automate fairly complex tasks.

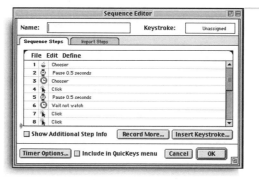

Sequence Editor

Name: [   ]   Keystroke: Unassigned

Sequence Steps   Import Steps

File Edit Define

1   Chooser
2   Pause 0.5 seconds
3   Chooser
4   Click
5   Pause 0.5 seconds
6   Wait not watch
7   Click
8   Click

☐ Show Additional Step Info   Record More...   Insert Keystroke...

Timer Options... ☐ Include in QuicKeys menu   Cancel   OK

FIGURE 16.27

The Sequence Editor shows your newly recorded macro.

11. Name the macro and assign a keyboard shortcut.

12. Click OK to close the Sequence Editor.

Position counts

In a macro, if you select something with the mouse rather than with a key combination, you are using relative positioning. QuickKeys records where on the screen you clicked rather than what you clicked on. If the item you click moves from the time that you recorded your macro, it may not work properly. Usually, this isn't a problem because most windows and dialogs will return to a default position so that the relative positioning works just fine.

However, it is best to use the keyboard to choose things while you are recording, if possible. For example, instead of clicking OK, press Return if the OK button is selected.

13. Close QuickKeys.

14. Unmount the volume that you mounted while creating the macro.

15. Test your macro. If it works, the volume should be mounted. If not, go back and tweak the macro until it works properly. When you want to mount this drive in the future, just use your keyboard shortcut. No need to mess around with the Chooser yourself.

From these examples, you can see how powerful QuickKeys is. If you do repetitive steps (and since you use a Mac, trust me, you do), QuickKeys will make you much more productive, and you will also enjoy your work more because you can focus on the fun part rather than the drudgery of choosing commands and clicking the mouse. Who can argue with that result?

17

Making Your Mac Do
Your Work for You

Automatically starting up and shutting down your Mac

Automatically opening a file on startup or shutdown

Automating your Mac with AppleScript

Using voice recognition to speak commands to your Mac

Automating your Mac with QuickKeys

Automating Your Mac

The reason you use a Mac is to do better work faster and enjoy the creative process more than you would doing things without a Mac. The Mac can do a lot of the drudgery associated with any task, leaving you free to concentrate on the form and content of what you are doing. Mac OS 8.5 includes a number of features to take your Mac's ability to do work for you even further. You will be even better off if you use a macro utility (such as CE Software's excellent QuickKeys that you will learn more about in this chapter) to really put your Mac to work.

With Mac OS 8.5 and a macro tool, you can automate just about any repetitive task that you do with your Mac. A lot of what you do on your Mac can be automated, including almost everything that you can do with the keyboard or by choosing commands from menus. Automating your Mac will make you even more efficient, and it can be a lot of fun watching your Mac do your work for you.

Scheduling an Automatic Startup or Shutdown Time

Not all Macs are included

If your Mac has a hard power switch on the front of its case (for example, the Power Mac 61XX models), automatic startup and shutdown won't work. If you aren't sure if you have a hard power switch, try setting a startup or shutdown time; your Mac will tell you if it won't work.

You can automate the two most basic tasks that you do with your Mac: turning it on or off. By using the Energy Saver control panel, you can set the times at which your Mac turns itself on and shuts itself down. No more waiting for the system to start up in the morning!

Scheduling a startup and shutdown time

1. Open the Energy Saver control panel.
2. Click the Schedule Startup & Shutdown button. You will see the Schedule Startup & Shutdown window (see Figure 17.1).

FIGURE 17.1

Using the Schedule Startup & Shutdown window, you can have your Mac turn itself on and off.

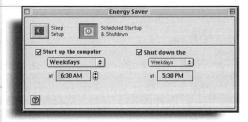

3. To set a startup time, click the Start up the computer check box, set the day from the pop-up menu, and enter the startup time.

4. To set a shutdown time, click the Shut down the computer check box, set the day from the pop-up menu, and enter the shutdown time.

5. Close the control panel. Your Mac will now start up and shut down at the specified times.

Using Startup Items

You can have your Mac automatically open files, folders, and even servers for you each time that it starts up. You make this happen by placing an alias to the item that you want opened in the Startup Items folder that is in the System Folder. Startup items are great if you always use one or more applications or documents because you can easily have your Mac open those items every time that you start up. No more spending lots of time opening the same items day after day. Just put an alias in the Startup Items folder and your Mac will open it for you.

Making something open at system startup

1. Make an alias of the item that you want to open when you start your Mac.

2. Drag the alias to the Startup Items folder that is in the System Folder. The next time you start your Mac, the item will be opened automatically.

The Startup Items feature can be a great relief from the tedium of opening the same files every day. Following are some ideas that you may want to use on your Mac:

- Open documents and applications that you open every day, such as databases or contact managers.

- Open your email program and Web browser so that they are always open and ready to use.

- Make your Web browser's Home page a favorite news site and then place an alias to the Web browser in the Startup Items folder; then you can get your morning news as soon as your Mac starts up.

Energy saving and PowerBooks

PowerBooks use a slightly different interface for the Energy Saver control panel. I was using a desktop Mac during this chapter. If you are using a PowerBook, see Appendix B, "Working with PowerBooks," for the details on saving energy on a PowerBook.

Alphabetical Mac

The items in both the Startup and Shutdown folders open in alphabetical order. You can use this to your advantage. For example, you may want to have your Mac play a sound when it has completed the start-up process so that you don't have to sit there and watch it. Just name the alias of the sound that is in the Startup Items folder so that it appears last in a list sorted by name. It will be opened after everything else has.

- Play a sound so that you know when your Mac is ready to work.
- Open a server or group folder.
- Open a project folder that you will use throughout the day.

Using Shutdown Items

Shutdown Items work in the same way that Startup Items do, except that they open during shutdown rather than startup (I bet you figured that one out on your own). There may be items that you want to open every time that your Mac shuts down. For example, you may have a back-up script that you want to run every time you quit work for the day. Or perhaps you have a QuickTime video that you want anyone working on a Mac to see before they quit (perhaps the sign-out procedure for your office). Or, maybe you want the Mac to play a certain sound each time it is shut down. The Shutdown Items folder in your System Folder makes these tasks very easy to do.

Making something open during shutdown

1. Make an alias of the file that you want to open when your Mac shuts down.

2. Drag the item into the Shutdown Items folder in the System Folder. The next time you shut down your Mac, the item will run if it is a scripted item or will play if it is a movie or an animation.

Automating Your Mac with AppleScript

AppleScript is the Mac's built-in macro/scripting technology. AppleScript is very powerful, and you can create *very* sophisticated macros with it. AppleScript is widely used in the publishing industry because there are lots of tasks that are repetitive in the publishing process.

Don't get carried away

Remember that every application you open will use part of the RAM available. If you open lots of applications every time you start your Mac, there may not be enough RAM left to work with anything else. Plus, the more applications that open when your Mac starts up, the longer the startup process will take.

Restarting

Note that items in the Shutdown Items folder are also opened when you shut down during a Restart as well as when you shut down your Mac.

Be nimble, be quick

If you place an alias to a "static" document, such as a text document, it will simply flash open when the shutdown process begins. Unless the document requires some time to run (such as a script, movie, or sound), placing it in the Shutdown Items folder doesn't do much good.

Your Mac comes with everything you need to run predefined AppleScripts and to create your own scripts as well.

Understanding AppleScript

Mac OS 8.5 comes with the following components that enable AppleScript:

- **AppleScript extension**. This is the extension that enables AppleScript on your Mac.

- **AppleScriptLib**. This is a library file that is installed in your Extensions folder. It is necessary for PowerPC native applications to use AppleScript.

- **Scripting Additions folder**. This folder is located in the System Folder and contains some additional scripts that you can use and incorporate in your own scripts.

- **Scripts folder**. This folder is also located in the AF. It contains more scripts, such as scripts for folder actions. These are primarily for you to incorporate in your own scripts.

- **Speakable Items and More Speakable Items folders**. These folders contain more AppleScripts. Using PlainTalk, you can speak the names of the scripts in the Speakable Items folder to run them. You will learn how to use this in a later section of this chapter.

- **Speech control panel**. The Speech control panel enables you to control aspects of how your Mac uses voice recognition as well as text-to-speech, such as the voice it uses to talk to you.

- **AppleScript folder**. This folder, which is installed in the Apple Extras folder that is installed on your startup disk, contains several files related to AppleScript, including the Script Editor.

- **Script Editor**. This is the application that you use to create and edit AppleScripts.

Macros and scripts

As you learned in Chapter 16, macros and scripts are really the same thing– a series of steps that your Mac will perform on command. Macros and scripts can be as simple as choosing a command from a menu to as complex as performing a series of tasks covering dozens of steps.

- **AppleScript Guide and AppleScript Help**. AppleScript comes with an AppleGuide to help you use AppleScript. This guide is stored in the AppleScript folder. The AppleScript Help folder works with the Mac's Help Viewer to provide help through the Mac's Help Center.

- **Automated Tasks and More Automated Tasks folders**. These folders contain predefined AppleScripts that you can run. The folders are in the AppleScript folder, and there is an alias to the Automated Tasks folder on the Apple menu.

While Mac OS 8.5 comes with everything you need to create your own AppleScripts, many Mac users will be better off using one of the third-party macro applications available for the Mac such as QuickKeys (which you will learn about later in this chapter) and Westland Software's OneClick. This is because of some inherent limitations of AppleScript, which include the following:

- **Not all applications support AppleScript**. If an application does not have AppleScript support built into it, AppleScript will not work with that application. Fortunately, many major applications do support it so this may not be an issue for you.

- **AppleScript recording is not as reliable as it should be**. You are most likely to create macros by recording them. AppleScript's recording technology doesn't work as well as that of other macro utilities, such as QuickKeys.

- **AppleScript's scripting language is not trivial to learn**. While the AppleScript language is much simpler than many other scripting and programming languages, it does require substantial effort to understand and be able to use effectively.

Nonetheless, even if you choose not to use AppleScript to create your own scripts, you can still use the predefined AppleScripts that come with Mac OS 8.5, as well as those you will find on the Net and in other locations.

Scripts are applications

AppleScripts are actually applications—so you can place them in the Startup Items and Shutdown Items folders to launch them automatically.

AppleScript is accelerated

With Mac OS 8.5, AppleScript is fully native and runs faster on Macs with PowerPC processors (all Macs that can run 8.5).

Using Predefined AppleScripts

Mac OS 8.5 comes with a number of AppleScripts that you can use to quickly accomplish certain tasks. Just to give you some idea of the predefined AppleScripts available to you, here is a partial list of them; you should explore the folders listed previously to see all of the AppleScripts that are ready for you to use:

- **Add Alias to the Apple Menu**. When you select a file or folder and run this script, an alias to that file or folder is placed on the Apple menu.

- **Share a Folder**. This script turns on file sharing for a folder.

- **Start File Sharing and Stop File Sharing**. These scripts start and stop File Sharing.

- **Synchronize Folders**. When you select two folders and run this script, it makes their contents the same (it copies files and folders from one to other, and vice-versa).

- **Change View to pop**. When you select a window and run this script, it changes the view of the window to pop-up.

- **Empty the Trash**. You can probably guess what this script does. It is in the Speakable Items folder so using Speech Recognition, you can literally tell your Mac to take out the Trash.

Since AppleScript are applications, you can double-click an AppleScript to run it, choose it from the Apple menu, you can activate it by dragging and dropping a file on the script's icon, and if you use Speech Recognition, you can speak its name to run it (as long it is located in the Speakable Items folder). Each script works slightly differently, depending on what a particular script is designed to do. For example, some scripts work on files and folder so you need to have something selected when you launch the script. Others work on windows, so you need to have a window open. A quick step-by-step will show you how AppleScripts work in general. You can use the Add Alias to Apple Menu AppleScript to quickly add an alias to the selected item to the Apple menu.

AppleScripts, AppleScripts, everywhere

As you can tell from the list of AppleScript items in this chapter, these scripts are scattered all about your Mac. It will be worth your time to explore those folders to see what scripts you might find useful.

Using an AppleScript to add an alias to the Apple menu

1. Select the item that you want added to the Apple menu.

2. From the Apple menu, open the Automated Tasks folder and choose Add Alias to Apple menu. The script will run, and you will see confirmation that the item was added to the Apple menu (see Figure 17.2).

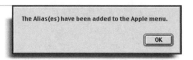

FIGURE 17.2

This dialog confirms that the script ran successfully and the item you selected in now on the Apple menu.

3. Click OK to clear the confirmation message.

4. Open the Apple menu and see that the item you selected appears on it.

You can see from this simple example that AppleScript can save you lots of time. Think about all of the steps you would have had to perform yourself to add an alias to the Apple menu. These steps are the following:

1. Select the item.

2. Create an alias to it.

3. Open the System Folder.

4. Drag the alias you created into the Apple Menu Items folder.

5. Close the System Folder.

With the AppleScript, you can do the same task with one menu selection and a press of the Return key.

Just because a script may be stored in a certain folder, there is no reason it has to remain there. You can move AppleScripts around to suit yourself. For example, there are lots of great AppleScripts in the Speakable Items folder, and you can use them even if you don't want to use PlainTalk. You can run them as you do any script. You can even place them on the Apple menu by selecting them and running the Add this to the Apple Menu script!

Creating Your Own AppleScripts

You can create your own AppleScripts to do many of the tasks that you need to do to complete your work. There are two basic ways that you can create an AppleScript. One is to record your actions in a script (which you can edit as needed). The other is to use the AppleScript language to write a script. You can do both of these by using the Script Editor application.

Before you try to do so, however, you need to make sure that the applications that you need to do the tasks that you want to script are AppleScript-savvy. If they are, you can use AppleScript to control them. If they aren't, you will have to use another macro or scripting tool.

An AppleScript-savvy application has a dictionary of AppleScript commands that it supports. If an application does not have such a dictionary, then you will need to use another scripting tool with it.

Determining if an application is AppleScript-savvy

1. Open Script Editor (it is in the AppleScript folder). You will see the Script Editor window (see Figure 17.3).

FIGURE 17.3

You use Script Editor to create and edit AppleScripts.

2. From the File menu, choose Open Dictionary.

3. Move to the application (or an alias to it) and click Open. The dictionary for that application will open. In Figure 17.4, you can see that the Apple Video Player does support AppleScript because there is a suite of AppleScript commands associated with it (the Apple Video Player Suite). When you select a command in the left pane of the dictionary window, you will see an explanation of the command and its syntax in the right pane.

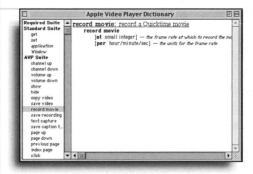

FIGURE 17.4

Apple Video Player is AppleScript-savvy; you can tell by the commands list in its dictionary.

If you cannot open the application's dictionary (you can't see the application in the Open Dictionary's Open dialog), it does not support AppleScript and you will not be able to create AppleScripts to work with it.

4. Close the dictionary window.

5. Quit Script Editor.

If the applications you need are AppleScript-savvy, then you can use AppleScript Editor to record, create, and edit a script. Explaining the details of creating AppleScripts is beyond the scope of this book, but the following step-by-step will give you some idea of how to use the AppleScript Editor.

While going over the details of creating AppleScripts is beyond what I have room to cover here, a quick step-by-step will show you that using AppleScript is relatively easy, and you will also learn how to use an application's dictionary to see what commands it will support.

In the following step-by-step, I will create a script that opens Internet Explorer and moves to Apple Computer's Home page. This is a very simple script, but it will save you several steps regardless. Before this script will work for you, your Mac must be connected to the Net.

SEE ALSO

➤ *To learn how to connect your Mac to the Net, see Chapter 23, "Connecting Your Mac to the Net"*

➤ *To learn how to use Internet Explorer and the Web, see Chapter 26, "Browsing the Web: The Basics"*

More about AppleScript

If you want to learn how to create and edit AppleScripts, locate a copy of *The Tao of AppleScript,* published by Hayden Books.

The steps you need this script to do are the following:

1. Open Internet Explorer.

2. Move to Apple's Web site which is at `http://www.apple.com`.

These are simple steps, yet creating an AppleScript will enable you to do them more quickly and easily than you could do them manually.

Creating an AppleScript to move to Apple's Web site

1. Open Script Editor. You will see an empty script window (see Figure 17.5).

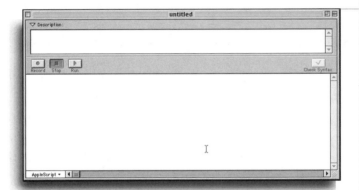

FIGURE 17.5

When you open Script Editor, you will see an empty script window, ready for your masterpiece.

2. From the File menu, choose Open Dictionary. Maneuver to the Internet Explorer application and open it. You will see its dictionary window, which shows you the commands that you can use in a script. When you choose a command in the left pane, the syntax and variables you can use are shown in the right pane (see Figure 17.6).

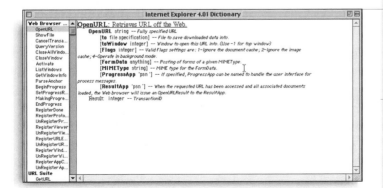

FIGURE 17.6

Using Internet Explorer's AppleScript dictionary, you can see the AppleScript commands that it supports.

3. In the Description window at the top of the Script Editor window, type a description of what the script does (see Figure 17.7).

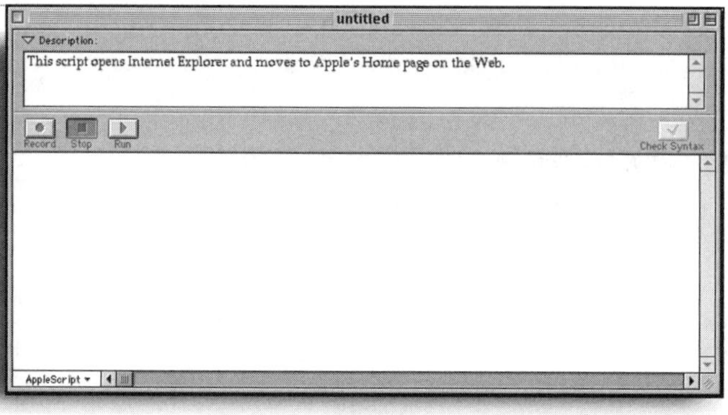

FIGURE 17.7

It is a good idea to add descriptions of what your scripts do in case anyone else should ever need to use them.

untitled
▽ Description:
This script opens Internet Explorer and moves to Apple's Home page on the Web.
● Record ■ Stop ▶ Run   ✓ Check Syntax
AppleScript ▼

AppleScript syntax and commands

AppleScript syntax and commands, like those I used in the script created in this section, are not something you will know intuitively. They have to be learned. One of the best ways to learn general AppleScript commands (as opposed to specific commands in applications) is to use the Script Editor to record actions (such as opening an application) and then look at the commands it recorded. You can also look in the AppleScript help that is part of Mac OS 8.5. If you decide that you really want to get into creating AppleScripts, you will need a book that explains its commands to you.

You can also visit the AppleScript Web site at `http://www.applescript.apple.com`.

4. Choose Save As from the File menu. The Save dialog will appear.

5. Ensure that Compiled Script appears in the Kind pop-up menu.

6. Name your script and save it (I called it, "Apple Home page").

7. Tab into the lower pane of the Script Editor window, which is the area in which you enter the script.

8. Type the following, *Tell application "Internet Explorer 4.01"*. The nice thing about AppleScript is that it is a natural English language. Tell means what you think it does. Your Mac tells the application Internet Explorer to do something.

9. Press Return to move to the next line.

10. Type *Activate*. Activate causes an application to open.

11. Press Return to move to the next line.

12. Type *OpenURL "http://www.apple.com"*. If you open Internet Explorer's AppleScript dictionary, you will see this command and the syntax it uses. It tells Internet Explorer to open a particular URL (see Figure 17.6).

13. Press Return to move to the next line.

14. Type *end tell*. (Don't include the period.) This command
tells the AppleScript that the action that you started with
the tell command ends here. Your script should look like
Figure 17.8.

FIGURE 17.8
This script is ready to be checked
for syntax errors.

15. Click the Check Syntax button to make sure that your script
is valid. When it is done, your script will have formatting
applied (such as the bold on the tell command (see Figure
17.9). If an error is found, go back and make sure that you
typed the script exactly as I did.

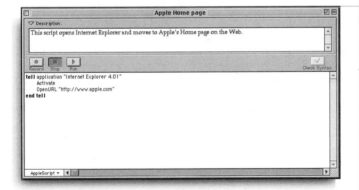

FIGURE 17.9
AppleScript properly formats your
script when you check its syntax.

16. Save your script.

17. Now connect to the Net (if you have configured Remote Access to allow Internet applications to connect automatically, you can skip this step). When you are online, move back to the Script Editor.

SEE ALSO

➤ *To learn how to configure Remote Access, see page 534*

18. Back in the Script Editor, click the Run button. You will see Internet Explorer launch and move to the Apple Home page (see Figure 17.10).

FIGURE **17.10**

You can move to this Web site with a single click of the mouse.

19. Move back to Script Editor and choose Save As.

20. This time, choose Application from the Kind pop-up menu. This will enable you to run the script by opening the file (rather than having it open in Script Editor).

21. Check the Never Show Startup Screen check box (if you don't, you will see a dialog containing the description you entered and will have to press Return to run the script).

22. If you want to save the script as a script, give the application a new name. Otherwise, replace the script with the application. (You can edit the application by opening it from within the Script Editor.)

23. Quit Script Editor. You will see that your new script has the icon that indicates it is an application (see Figure 17.11).

FIGURE 17.11

This script is an application—you can tell by the square behind the scroll.

24. Test your new application. Quit Internet Explorer and then double-click your saved script. Internet Explorer will open and move to the Apple Web site. You can launch your application to do this in any number of ways, such as from the Apple menu, by double-clicking it, and even by speaking its name (you will learn how to do this in the next section).

While AppleScript is relatively easy to use given its power, unless you are prepared to learn its scripting language and you are sure that applications you need are AppleScript-savvy, you will probably be better off just running AppleScripts or making edits to existing scripts. This is not a bad thing since there are so many readily available AppleScripts with Mac OS 8.5 as well as on the Net. You can then use a macro utility, such as QuickKeys, to create your own scripts.

Telling Your Mac What to Do

This section will probably make you smile more than any other in the whole book. There is something totally cool about speaking to your Mac and having it do what you say, answer a question, or even tell you a joke.

Consider the task

Creating a script that does more than a few simple commands does take some time and effort. Consider the tasks for which you might create scripts. If you only do the task once-in-a-while and creating the script will require lots of effort, you may be better off doing the work manually. The best candidates for scripts are those that you do at least somewhat frequently and that require repetitive steps (choosing commands, switching applications, and so on).

The purpose of scripting is to save time and effort in the long run. You need to balance the time and effort needed to create, edit, and test the script versus the time and effort savings that you will get from using it.

Before you speak

In order to be able to speak commands to your Mac, the Speech Recognition (English Speech Recognition in the case of U.S. users) software must be installed on your Mac. It is not installed by default. If you did not choose to install it when you originally installed Mac OS 8.5, see Appendix A, "Installing and Maintaining the Mac OS," for information on how to install Mac OS components.

Speaking extensions

Speech-to-text and voice recognition are enabled by two extensions: Speech Manager and Voice Recognition.

A live mic

In order for your Mac to hear you, you must have the microphone selected as the sound input source. To do so, open the Monitors & Sound control panel, click the Sound button, and choose External Mic from the Sound Monitoring Source pop-up menu; then close the control panel.

Changing the face of your Mac

You can change the character you see in the left pane of the feedback window as well as the feedback sound you hear by choosing Feedback from the Options pop-up menu. You can choose Voice from the Options pop-up menu to change the voice your Mac uses to speak to you.

Mac OS 8.5 includes PlainTalk, which enables your Mac to speak to you (and read to you) and to listen to your spoken commands, pretty much like the computers on *Star Trek* do. Well, perhaps not *quite* that good, but PlainTalk is very cool nonetheless. Even though it is tremendously fun, using voice commands will also help you work faster and better.

Before you can speak to your Mac, you need to have a PlainTalk-compatible microphone installed.

If you have a PlainTalk-compatible microphone and a Mac capable of running Mac OS 8.5, you are all set to speak.

Basically, you can speak the name of anything in the Speakable Items folder (an alias to this folder is on the Apple menu) and that item will open. If it is an AppleScript, the script will run. If it is an alias to a folder, the folder will open, no matter how deeply it is buried. If it is a document, the document will open. Getting interested now?

The first task to do is to configure your Mac to receive commands.

Configuring your Mac to receive commands

1. Open the Speech control panel.

2. Choose Speakable Items from the Options pop-up menu. You will see the Speakable Items window (see Figure 17.12).

3. Click the On radio button. Another window will appear, and you will hear your Mac say that Speakable Items is ready (see Figure 17.13). This window provides feedback for you while you are using voice commands. It will always be open while Speakable Items is on.

4. From the Options pop-up menu, choose Listening. You need to tell your Mac when it needs to listen to your commands. You can do this two ways. One is to define a key that you must press for your Mac to listen to you. The other is to define a name for your Mac that you speak before each command. For this example, I use the second option and name my computer, Mac.

FIGURE 17.12

You can use the Speech control panel to turn on voice recognition.

FIGURE 17.13

When you see this window, your Mac is ready to listen to you.

5. Click the "Key(s) toggle listening on and off" radio button.

6. In the Name field, enter Mac. The name or key you choose will be shown under the character in the left pane of the feedback window.

7. Leave the Name is pop-up menu set to Required before every command.

8. Close the control panel.

Now the fun begins. Open the Speakable Items folder to see the commands you can speak to your Mac. Try the following step-by-step to see (hear) how it works.

Ordering your Mac around

1. Say the following to your Mac (use the name you gave it if you didn't use Mac), "Mac, what day is it?" Your Mac will show you what it thinks you said in the feedback window and then answer your question (see Figure 17.14). If it didn't hear you (your question wasn't repeated in the feedback window), try again. Make sure that you use your Mac's name so you get its attention. (If you choose to require that you press a key before a command, you need to press that key before you speak.)

FIGURE **17.14**

This Mac is listening to my every word.

2. Now say, "Mac, tell me a joke." It will. Remember that you have to answer with a "Mac" each time your Mac responds to you.

3. Move back to the application you created with AppleScript and select it.

4. Say the following, "Mac, make this speakable." Your Mac will respond with, "Apple Home page is now speakable." You have just made your script a speakable item.

5. Now say to your Mac, "Mac, Apple Home page." Your script will be launched, and you will move to the Apple Home page. This is way cool.

As you can tell, any item that you add to the Speakable Items folder becomes speakable. Here are some ideas for things you may want to add so that you can speak them:

Change the name to change the command

You can change the command you speak to activate any Speakable Item by changing the name of the script. You will still see the original name of the script in the feedback window when it runs though.

- **Folders**. Place aliases of folders in the Speakable Items folder. When you say the folder's name, it will open.

- **Scripts**. Any AppleScripts you use can be placed in this folder so that you can speak their names.

- **Control panels**. If you need to open a control panel quickly, place an alias to it in the Speakable Items folder.

- **Documents**. Say the name; open the document.

- **Applications**. Ditto.

Lots of great scripts

Make sure that you check out all of the folders listed earlier to see all of the scripts that came with Mac OS 8.5. There are quite a number of very useful ones.

As you can tell, anything you place in this folder will be opened when you speak its name.

A downside

One downside to using Speakable Items is that the microphone ties up the sound source. So you can't use voice recognition while you listen to CDs, for example, because you can only be using a single sound source at a time.

Using QuickKeys to Make Your Mac Read to You

QuickKeys is a very powerful macro and scripting utility that enables you to easily automate tasks. The advantages of QuickKeys compared to AppleScript are the following:

- **QuickKeys works with almost all software**. There may be a few control panels or extensions that conflict with QuickKeys, but applications do not have to support QuickKeys for it to work with them. You can use QuickKeys with everything that you do on your Mac.

- **QuickKeys recording is very reliable**. You can easily create even complex macros by recording your actions. You can edit these recorded macros, and you can add steps to them with the QuickKeys Editor.

- **QuickKeys is easy to use**. QuickKeys is a very intuitive utility. You don't have to learn complex syntax and commands.

There are two disadvantages of QuickKeys when compared to AppleScript. The first is that you have to purchase it (it doesn't cost all that much so this isn't a major disadvantage). The second is that QuickKeys can't create scripts that are as complex as those you can create with AppleScript. If you have to do lots of file manipulations and perform complex tasks that you can't easily define, QuickKeys may not be able to create the scripts that you need. However, for many Mac users, QuickKeys is a better choice due to its power and ease-of-use.

SEE ALSO

➤ *To learn more about QuickKeys, see page 372*

QuickKeys is a utility that has broad applications and once you begin using it, you will find all sorts of ways that it can help you work faster and smarter. As an example of how you might use QuickKeys to make your Mac work for you, I will show you how to create a macro that makes your Mac read to you.

More Speakable Items

The scripts in the folder More Speakable Items have to be moved to the Speakable Items folder before you can speak their names to run them.

Try before you buy

CE Software provides a functional demo of QuickKeys that you can download and use to see how useful QuickKeys is for you. To get the demo, use your Web browser to go to `http://www.cesoft.com` to download the demo. See Chapter 27, "Browsing the Web: Advanced Techniques," for help with downloading and using files from the Web.

More Mac trivia

SimpleText used to be called TeachText in the olden days. If you use some very old software or you have had your Mac for a long time, you may still have a copy of the TeachText versions. It didn't have as many features as SimpleText does; for example, you couldn't have more than one document open at a time.

Mac OS 8.5's Text-to-Speech technology enables your Mac to speak text. Within a Text-to-Speech-savvy application, you can choose Speak commands to have your Mac read to you. Even if your favorite application does not support Text-to-Speech, you can use SimpleText to have your Mac read to you.

SimpleText is a basic word processor that Apple includes as part of the Mac OS 8.5 installation. Its primary function is to enable you to read the ReadMe files that come with most applications and other software. However, there are lots of other ways to use SimpleText, as well. For example, you can use it to view PICT graphics (a common Mac graphic format), QuickTime movies, and other files for which you may not have the creating applications. Another good feature of SimpleText is that it supports Text-to-Speech.

Before you jump into creating a script, it is a good idea to work through the steps that you need to do to accomplish a task. By doing so, you will be able to record the script more effectively and thus it will require less editing.

The first task in preparing your script that will make your Mac read to you is to explore how SimpleText uses Text-to-Speech to read documents.

Having your Mac read to you with SimpleText

1. Open a Read Me or other text file (you can find some in the Mac OS Read Me Files folder that is on your startup disk; for example, the About Mac OS 8 file). The document will open in SimpleText.

2. From the Sound menu, choose the voice that you want your Mac to use to read to you (see Figure 17.15).

3. Choose Speak All (Command-J).

Proofreading

When you are proofing a document, it is often a good idea to read the document aloud. It is even better if you have someone else read it to you. That is where SimpleText comes in. You can use SimpleText to have your Mac read almost any text document to you. Even if you create the document outside of SimpleText, you can copy and paste the text into SimpleText and have it read to you as you follow along in the creating application. This is very cool.

The mysterious Contents menu

When you open some SimpleText documents, you may see a new menu called Contents (see Figure 17.15). SimpleText documents can be created so that they have a hot-linked list of contents (click on a title to go to that section). This list of contents appears under the Contents menu. While you can use a Contents menu with SimpleText, you can't create one in your own SimpleText documents. You need other software to do that.

FIGURE 17.15

Your Mac can speak with many voices.

4. When you want your Mac to stop speaking, press Command-. or choose Stop Speaking from the Sound menu.

Now that you see how SimpleText works with Text-to-Speech, work through the steps needed to have it read text that is not in a SimpleText document.

Proofing a document with SimpleText

1. Open the document that you want to proof. It doesn't matter which application opens, you can use any text processing application.

2. Copy the portion of the document that you want your Mac to read to you.

3. Open SimpleText and create a new document.

4. Paste the text that you copied in step 2.

5. Choose Speak All or press Command-J. Your Mac will begin to read your document to you.

6. Choose Stop Speaking if you want the Mac to stop before the end of the text (for example, when you hear something that needs to be fixed).

7. Move back to the creating application and correct the problem.

Giving your Mac voice

The Mac's Text-to-Speech capability is part of the standard installation. However, if you chose not to install the Text-to-Speech software, you won't be able to use SimpleText to have your Mac read to you. If you don't see the Voices or other Sound commands, refer to Appendix A, "Installing and Maintaining the Mac OS," to see how to add the Text-to-Speech component.

Mac Voices

If you are going to have your Mac read to you on a regular basis, you should experiment with the different voices that are available. Some of them may suit your listening style better than others. To do so, open the Speech control panel and choose Voice from the Options pop-up menu. You can choose from a variety of voices, and you can vary the rate at which the voices speak.

Other word processors

Your regular word processor may support Text-to-Speech. If it does, there is no reason to paste the text into SimpleText.

8. Repeat steps 2 through 7 as needed.

9. When you are done, quit SimpleText.

The previous two step-by-steps are the major tasks that you will need to accomplish to create your script. The next step is to map out the major steps that your script will have. These are the following:

1. Copy text that you want read to you to the Clipboard (you want the script to begin with the copy command so that you can use the script with any selected text in any application).

2. Create a new SimpleText document.

3. Paste the text on the Clipboard into the SimpleText document.

4. Have your Mac read the document.

Now you are ready to create the QuickKeys macro.

Creating the macro to have your Mac read selected text to you

1. Open SimpleText.

2. In a text document, select some text. It doesn't have to be in SimpleText, it can be any text in any document. The script will actually begin with the Copy command so that you can use it from any application.

3. From the QuickKeys menu, choose Record Sequence. QuickKeys will go into the record mode and will record each step that you do.

4. Copy the selected text (press Command-C).

5. Switch to SimpleText.

6. Create a New Document (press Command-N).

7. Choose Paste to paste in the text that is to be read (press Command-V).

8. From the Sound menu, choose Speak All. The Mac will begin to read the document.

9. From the QuickKeys menu, choose Stop Recording. The QuickKeys Sequence Editor window will open (see Figure 17.16).

FIGURE 17.16

The QuickKeys Sequence Editor enables you to create and edit scripts.

1   Step arrow

10. Name the script, perhaps something creative such as "Read to me."

11. If you want to use a keyboard shortcut to activate the command, tab to that field and press the key combination that you want to use. The one assumption that was made while recording the script was that SimpleText was open (remember that you opened it before you started recording the script). In order for the script to work, SimpleText needs to be running. Now you will add a step to your recorded script to make sure that it is running.

12. Move the step arrow to after the first step in the script, which should be the Copy command.

13. From the Define menu, choose File Launch.

14. In the Open dialog, move to SimpleText, select it, and click Open. You will see the File Launch window that will show SimpleText as the name of the file to be launched.

15. Click OK. This step will now appear just after the Copy command and will ensure that SimpleText is open when the script continues (see Figure 17.17). The other thing that QuickKeys records is that the new window you created in SimpleText is called untitled 2. QuickKeys will stop the script just after the step in which the new document is created and will wait until it sees a window named untitled 2. Since the new window you create with the script won't be called that, you have to get rid of this Wait step.

FIGURE 17.17

Opening SimpleText is now the
first step of this script (compare
step 2 in this figure with step 2 in
Figure 17.16).

Using the Read to me script

Don't think about using this script
just for text documents you are creating. You can use it in email, Web
pages, ReadMe documents, or
wherever else you can select and
copy text.

16. Select the Wait step (number 6) and press Command-X to
remove it from the script.

17. Add the script to the QuickKeys menu by checking the
Include in QuickKeys menu check box.

18. Click OK to close the Sequence Editor. Make sure that the
Read to me script is listed under the Universal tab. If it isn't,
select it, press Command-X, click the Universal tab, and
press Command-V. This will ensure that this script is always
available (see Figure 17.18).

FIGURE 17.18

Placing a script under the
Universal tab makes it available
from anywhere on your Mac.

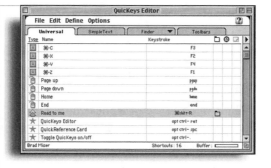

Getting your own QuickKeys

Once you try the QuickKeys demo,
you can purchase a full version by
checking your favorite software
retailer or buying it directly from CE
Software at 1-800-523-7638 or from
its Web site at
http://www.cesoft.com.

19. Click the Close box to close QuickKeys. Now test the
script.

20. Open a text document and select some text.

21. Press your keyboard shortcut for the macro or choose it from the QuickKeys menu. You should see QuickKeys working through the steps it recorded. If the script works correctly, you will hear your Mac read the text you selected to you. If it doesn't work, figure out where it is going wrong by running the script and determining the step at which it stops working correctly. Go back into the Sequence Editor and look at the steps before the one where QuickKeys stops working properly. Use QuickKeys' tools to edit the script as needed. You may need to walk through the steps yourself *exactly* as they are in QuickKeys to figure out where it is wrong. Continue editing and testing the script until it works the way you want it to.

Hopefully, this example has sparked your interest in using QuickKeys. If so, download the demo version and give it a try. You won't regret it. It is fun to make your Mac do your work for you.

Speaking QuickKeys

You can make any QuickKeys an icon on which you can double-click to run the script. This enables you to create Speakable Items out of QuickKeys scripts just as you can with AppleScripts. To do so, from within the QuickKeys Editor, choose the script. From the File menu, and then choose Make Icon. Choose where you want the QuickKeys icon to be stored, click the "Save Shortcut Data in QK Icon" check box and click Save. Move back to the Finder, select the icon you just created, and say, "Mac, make this speakable." Your Mac will add this to the Speakable Items folder. To activate this QuickKeys script, simply speak its name. Cool.

You can use this technique to make *any* menu item or series of items from any program into a Speakable Item.

Make them work together

You can also make scripts from different utilities work together. For example, you can create a QuickKeys script that connects you to the Internet. From within that script, you can have it launch your Apple Home page script by using the Launch File step and choosing the Apple Home page script. Then you can connect to the Net and move to the Apple Home page with a spoken word, menu choice, or keyboard shortcut.

PART

III

Using Mac Hardware

18   **Understanding and Using Input Devices 423**

19   **Understanding and Using Output Devices 437**

20   **Understanding and Using Networking Devices 449**

Understanding and Using Input Devices

Understanding connection technologies

Working with mice, keyboards, and trackballs

Understanding scanners and digital cameras

The mighty iMac

The first Mac, unveiled in 1984, was ahead of its time in many ways, not the least of which was the now-familiar graphical user interface that we have come to know and love. In 1998, Apple unveiled another revolutionary iMac. In addition to having a low price point, the iMac offers advanced features. Some of these have been well received by the media and computing pundits, such as the elimination of the ADB port in favor of the Universal Serial Bus (USB) port. Others have not been so well received, such as the lack of a floppy drive. No matter how it is eventually received by the computing public, the iMac provokes a strong reaction. Whether it will be as successful as the first Mac remains to be seen.

Check your monitor

If you have an Apple AV monitor, it may have one or more ADB ports on it. These are useful in that they are often more conveniently located than those on the Mac itself, and depending on the number of ports provided on the monitor, you may be able to connect more ADB devices than you can without an AV monitor.

Modems and ADB

Some modems draw their power from the ADB port on your Mac rather than having a dedicated power source. Such modems provide a pass-through connector that attaches between your keyboard's connector and the Mac's ADB port.

Working with Input Devices

Whatever you use your Mac for, you need to give it commands, and you need to input information into it. This information takes many forms, and there is a hardware device for each one of them. These devices include control devices, such as a mouse, and data input devices, such as a digital camera. Some devices are both for control and data input, such as the keyboard. While you can get by with the two standard input devices that are part of every Mac system (the mouse and keyboard), you will probably benefit from adding and using other input devices as well.

Understanding Connection Technologies

Before you can know what is required to add a hardware device to your Mac, you need to understand the different ways that devices use to connect to and communicate with your Mac. In technical-speak, the way in which a hardware device connects to and communicates with your Mac is called the *interface*.

An interface is simply a connection between two or more devices through which data passes so that the two or more devices can communicate with one another. There are hundreds of interfaces inside and outside of your Mac. At each point where there is one device (be it a RAM chip, processor card, a hard disk, and so on), there is an interface. Fortunately, the only interfaces that you have to think about are those between your Mac and any hardware devices that you connect to it or install inside it.

The Mac uses several different types of interfaces to connect with hardware devices. In this section, you will learn about the major interfaces through which input devices connect to your Mac.

Understanding Apple Desktop Bus (ADB)

The Apple Desktop Bus was part of the very first Mac, and has continued to be part of every Mac until very recently (the iMac is the first Mac that doesn't have an ADB port). The ADB provides the interface to your primary control devices, such as the keyboard and mouse. Normally, there is one ADB port on the back of your Mac and another on your keyboard. You plug your keyboard into the Mac and your mouse into the keyboard. You also use ADB ports to connect other control devices, such as trackballs and joysticks.

A few Macs have multiple ADB ports on them, but most only have a single ADB port, and you must attach all ADB devices to that one port in a "chain." ADB connectors are round and contain four pins and a large plastic locating pin.

There are two primary things that you need to keep in mind about ADB. The most important is that you should *never* connect or disconnect an ADB device while your Mac is turned on. This can lead to very severe problems and can destroy your Mac. The other thing is that if you purchase a Mac in the future, you may or may not use ADB devices. Although the iMac does not have an ADB port, it is unclear if Apple will eliminate the ADB ports on all Macs. They will probably remain on new Macs until Apple moves to the next generation of Macs. Once that happens, all Macs will use USB devices instead of ADB devices.

Understanding Serial Connections

While ADB ports are used primarily for control devices, serial ports are used primarily for data input and output. The two most common devices that use serial ports are modems and printers, although some other devices use serial connections as well (such as certain digital cameras and personal digital assistants like the PalmPilot).

Most Macs have two serial ports—one is labeled with the printer icon and one is labeled with a phone receiver (which is the symbol for the modem port). Serial connectors are round and have eight pins, which are arranged differently than the ADB's pins (so don't try to cram a connector of one type into the port of another).

Adapters for ADB

Just as soon as a new connection technology is implemented, adapters are produced that enable devices using the older technology to be used on newer machines and to enable newer devices to be used on older machines. The ADB-USB transition is no exception. If you have a Mac with USB ports, you can purchase an adapter that will enable you to use your older ADB devices with it. If you have a Mac with ADB ports, you can purchase an adapter so that you can use newer USB devices with it.

Multiple serial ports

Sometimes you need more than two serial ports. For example, you may want to connect a modem, printer, and digital camera to your Mac at the same time. If you don't want to have to unplug one device to connect another (it is a good idea to power down your Mac before you connect or remove serial devices), you can add devices that provide additional serial ports for your Mac. You plug these devices into one of your Mac's serial ports, and then you can plug multiple serial devices into that serial port multiplier. Datatek makes a simple mechanical serial port multiplier that enables you to connect two serial devices to it. You have to use a physical switch to change between the two devices connected to it. There are other serial multipliers that sense which device is communicating and use an electronic switch to connect that device to your Mac.

Serial connections are also on their way out. Eventually, they will also be replaced by USB ports.

Understanding Small Computer Serial Interface (SCSI)

Small Computer Serial Interface (SCSI which is pronounced Scuzzy) is used for a number of purposes both inside and outside of your Mac. Inside your Mac, it is the interface through which many Macs communicate with SCSI hard drives, CD-ROM drives, and Zip drives that are installed internally. Outside of your Mac, you use SCSI ports to connect a variety of devices, including data storage devices (such as hard disks and tape drives) and input devices (such as a scanner).

If your Mac has one, the SCSI port is the largest one on it. Its cables are thick and the rectangular connectors have 25 pins. PowerBooks use a special compact SCSI connector that is square, and the pins are packed quite densely.

SCSI has a couple of primary benefits. One is that it is a relatively fast interface, which makes it good for communicating large amounts of data (disks and scanners). The second is that you can chain SCSI devices together. This enables you to connect multiple devices to your Mac's single SCSI port (there are different limits as to the number of devices that you can connect on a single bus, but that depends on the configuration you are using—a typical limitation is seven devices).

The external SCSI interface will disappear on some Macs (for example, the iMac has no SCSI port), but it will remain on others.

Understanding Universal Serial Bus (USB)

The idea behind the Universal Serial Bus is that there are too many confusing (and competing) ways to connect devices to your Mac. Rather than dealing with ADB, serial, SCSI, and other interfaces, why not have a single interface to which you can connect any of these devices? Then let the Mac deal with figuring out what kind of device you have connected and let it figure out how to configure itself to use that device. This is precisely the idea behind USB. Eventually, you will connect all of your external devices to the USB ports. The Mac will recognize the device and will handle all the details.

USB is relatively fast, and you can chain multiple devices to it. You will use USB for almost all of the devices that you connect to future Macs, including disks, scanners, modems, keyboards, trackballs, and so on. For example on the iMac, which is the first Mac to use USBs, you can plug your keyboard into the USB port and then plug your mouse (also USB) into the keyboard. There will also be USB hubs that will attach to a single USB port and enable you to plug multiple USB devices into them.

Clearly, USB is the interface of the future for most hardware that you will connect to your Mac.

Understanding Other Input Connections

The following are a few other types of input interfaces that you may or may not have on your Mac:

- **Sound input**. All Macs have a sound input jack to which you can connect a PlainTalk-compatible microphone.

- **RCA jacks**. If your Mac has an Audio Visual (AV) or graphics card that enables it to receive video and audio input from external sources (such as a VCR or camcorder), then you will have sets of RCA jacks on your Mac. You can use the input jacks to watch TV or movies on your Mac and to record output from the external devices.

- **S-video**. If you have an AV Mac or a third-party video card, you may have an S-video port. S-video provides a higher quality connection than RCA jacks.

Working with Mice

When the Mac was first introduced, its mouse separated it from all the computers that came before it, and those that came after it, for a long time. Until Windows and other platforms adopted the mouse as their primary input devices, the Mac and its mouse really stood out from the crowd.

Putting some fire into it

Another interface that will become more important in the future is called *Firewire*. Firewire is a very high-speed interface, which is about four times as fast as the fastest SCSI. It will be used to connect devices that move large amounts of data, including hard drives and digital video cameras. In a year or two, you can expect to see Firewire ports on mid-level and high-end Macs.

Windows has better mice

As much as it pains me to admit it, Windows has better mice than Macs do. That is because Windows mice have two buttons. This is useful in a number of situations, but the most significant is when you are using contextual menus. When you want to activate a contextual menu in Windows, you simply click the right mouse button. That works better than the Mac on which you have to hold the control key down and click the mouse button. Maybe Apple will adopt the two-button mouse some day (why should Windows be the only OS that "borrows" from others?). There are two button mice available for the Mac, as well as trackballs and other devices that feature more than a "mouse" button, but I think Apple should adopt the two-button mouse as standard equipment.

If you have used a Mac, you are no doubt familiar with a mouse so there is not much that needs to be said about it, except that you can configure your Mac to customize the way it works.

Setting your mouse's behavior

1. Open the Mouse control panel (see Figure 18.1).

FIGURE 18.1

You can use the Mouse control panel to change the way your mouse works.

2. Set the tracking speed with the radio buttons. This setting determines how fast the cursor moves relative to how fast you move the mouse.

3. Set the double-click rate with the radio buttons. This changes the rate at which you need to click the mouse button to register a double-click.

4. Close the control panel.

Working with Keyboards

As with the mouse, if you have used a Mac, then you have used a keyboard so there isn't much you need to know, except that you can configure your keyboard.

Configuring your keyboard

1. Open the Keyboard control panel (see Figure 18.2).

FIGURE 18.2

Using the Keyboard control panel, you can customize your keyboard.

2. If you have other languages installed with your system, you can choose a script to use from the Script pop-up menu.

3. Choose the country standard keyboard that you want by checking the box next to that country's name.

4. Set the key repeat rate with the Key Repeat slider.

5. Set the time that you have to hold a key down until the letter is typed again by using the Delay Until Repeat slider.

6. Close the control panel.

SEE ALSO

➤ *To learn how to use your keyboard more effectively and efficiently, see Chapter 16, "Using Keyboard Shortcuts"*

Working with Trackpads

A trackpad performs the same functions as a mouse. The difference is that the motion is communicated by you moving your finger on top of the trackpad to move the cursor rather than by moving the device itself as you do with a mouse. You can click the "mouse button" by tapping directly on the trackpad or by clicking the button located next to the trackpad. PowerBooks have integrated trackpads, and you can add an external trackpad to desktop Macs if you want to.

SEE ALSO

➤ *To learn how to configure a PowerBook's trackpad, see page 827*

Working with Trackballs

Trackballs are really upside-down mice. Instead of the ball being inside the body, the ball is on the outside of a trackball and you move just the ball (when you move a mouse, you are actually moving the ball that is inside the mouse to move the cursor). Trackballs have a number of advantages over mice. Since you don't actually move the trackball itself, it takes up less space than does a mouse. And you don't have to lift it up to move it when you run out of desk space. Since your hand remains stationary, you don't rub the sensitive areas of your wrist across the edge of your desk, which can lead to damage of the tissues in your fore-arm. Trackballs also have more than one button, and you can program the other buttons to perform various functions. For example, you can set a button to add a modifier key to the click so that you can bring up contextual menus with a click instead of having to hold down the Control key while you click. And track-balls can move the cursor both faster to cover more screen real estate and more slowly to give you more precise control than a mouse.

One of the best trackballs is Kensington's Orbit (see Figure 18.3). The Orbit has two buttons that you can program, and you can even have those buttons perform different functions depending on the application that you are using. This is managed through the excellent Kensington MouseWorks software (see Figure 18.4). For example, I have my Orbit set to click the left button as a standard single-click and the right as a double-click, and both as a control-click for contextual menus.

FIGURE 18.3

The Kensington Orbit is one of the best trackballs available.

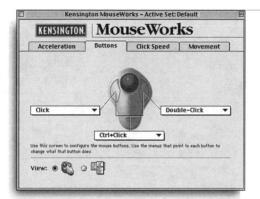

FIGURE 18.4
You can define various actions
and settings for the Orbit with
the Kensington MouseWorks
application.

Working with Joysticks

If you play games, particularly flight simulators, a joystick is a
good addition to your Mac. Joysticks give you more realistic and
fun play. Thrustmaster makes excellent flight simulator joysticks
while Gravis makes good general gaming joysticks.

Working with Microphones

If you want to record your own Alert or other sounds, you need
a microphone. In order to use Voice Recognition, you need a
PlainTalk compatible microphone (see Figure 18.5). Most Macs
come with a PlainTalk microphone, or you can order one from
Apple. Some Apple monitors have PlainTalk-compatible microphones built-in. All modern PowerBooks have PlainTalk-compatible microphones built in to their cases.

SEE ALSO
➤ *To learn how to record your own Alert sounds, see page 308*
➤ *To learn how to use voice recognition, see page 409*

Digital tablets

Another input device that is
popular with artists and others
who need to draw precisely
on-screen are tablets. These
provide a pen-based input
mechanism that enables you to
draw with a stylus as you would
a pen on paper.

FIGURE 18.5

A PlainTalk microphone enables you to speak commands to your Mac.

Desktop pictures

You can also use a scanner to convert your favorite photos into desktop pictures so that you can see them while you work on your Mac. See Chapter 13, "Changing the Way Your Mac Looks and Sounds," for information about desktop pictures.

Working with Scanners

A scanner enables you to convert hard copies of photographs, drawings, sketches, and text documents into digital format so that you can work with them in your favorite applications. Scanners used to be the domain of graphics professionals, but in recent years, prices have dropped so that almost anyone can afford to have a scanner. Scanners are useful in many ways, including the following:

- **Making your photographs digital**. You can use digital photos in lots of different projects including static documents, QuickTime movies, and so on. Using a scanner actually produces better images than most digital cameras do, with only slightly more work.

- **Using optical character recognition on text documents**. You can scan text documents onto your computer and use *Optical Character Recognition* (OCR) to convert those documents into editable text.

- **Scan other artwork**. You can scan any artwork that you find, such as ads or drawings that you have. You can use these digital images in your own projects.

- **Create digital records**. You can scan important documents and save them on your computer for quick and easy access.

When choosing a scanner, there are several important factors that you need to consider. These include the following:.

- **Resolution**. As with everything else in the graphics arena, resolution is very important. The higher the resolution capabilities of a scanner, the higher the quality of images you will be able to create. A mid-range resolution for a scanner is 600×1200. This will give more than satisfactory results for all but the most demanding professional user.

- **Compatibility**. You need to make sure that the scanner you buy is compatible with your Mac. This includes the interface it uses (SCSI or USB) as well as the software that comes with it (the driver and applications).

- **Price**. Scanners vary significantly in price, but paying more won't necessarily get you a scanner that works any better. For a mid-range scanner, you should expect to pay $300 or less.

UMAX Corporation makes very good, but inexpensive, scanners, such as the SE-6 (see Figure 18.6).

> **ColorSync compatibility**
>
> For best results, you want to choose a scanner that uses ColorSync technology so that colors will be consistent across all of your devices. See Chapter 9, "Working with Color and Graphics," for information about using ColorSync.

FIGURE 18.6
The UMAX SE-6 is an excellent and affordable scanner.

It is pretty easy to get a decent quality scan, but there are a lot of details that you will need to learn if you want to get the best possible quality with the smallest possible file size. The following step-by-step is typical of the steps you can use to scan a photograph (the details will depend on the scanner and software that you use).

Scanning a photograph

1. Turn on the scanner and place a photograph on its scanning bed (see Figure 18.6).

2. Open the scanning application that came with the scanner.

3. Choose the size and resolution of the scan (you choose lower resolutions for on-screen images and higher for print versions).

4. Preview your scan and make any needed adjustments to the scanned area.

5. Scan the image.

6. Open the image in an image editing tool such as Photoshop to touch it up as needed.

Autoscan

Some scanner software includes an autoscan feature that will set almost all of the parameters for you.

Understanding Digital Cameras

Digital cameras are the next step in the evolution of imaging technology. It is likely that some day all cameras will be digital. There are many advantages to digital cameras; these include the following:

- **No film**. The best thing about a digital camera is that you don't need any film. All the images are stored electronically so there is no processing required.

- **No cost per shot**. Since each image is digital, you can easily shoot more photos than you would with a film camera and simply delete any images that you don't want to keep. You don't have to worry about wasting film.

- **Speed**. Using a digital camera is faster than using a film camera. You can connect a digital camera to a Mac and quickly download the images and immediately take a look.

With many digital cameras, you can view the images on a TV as well.

- **Easy to manipulate**. After the images are on your Mac, you can use an image editing application to modify the images as much as you want to.

With these advantages, you may wonder why digital cameras haven't already sent film cameras into the oblivion of technological history. There are three primary reasons:

- **Cost**. Digital cameras are still very expensive to purchase relative to film cameras. A fair-quality digital camera can cost upwards of $700 while you can buy an excellent film-based camera for less than $250.

- **Quality**. Mid-level and lower digital cameras produce images that are not nearly as crisp and sharp as film-based cameras. In order to get a digital camera that produces results comparable to the quality of a mid-level 35 mm camera, you will have to pay thousands of dollars. Images from digital cameras tend to be grainy or blurred and many have poor color results. This situation is changing rapidly. The third generation digital cameras have made quantum leaps in image quality; however, they still have a way to go to match film-camera's cost/quality ratio.

- **Technology barriers**. To use a digital camera, you really need a computer on which to store and manipulate images. Many people still do not have computers, and many of those that do are fearful of using technology to replace something that is as user-friendly as film-based cameras.

Progress marches on, and there is no doubt that within a couple of years, digital cameras will have matched and bested their film-based counterparts in terms of cost, features, and quality. Once the prices of these units reach the consumer level, you can expect digital cameras to take over.

It's two cameras in one

Digital video cameras are also now available. They offer benefits that are similar to those of digital still cameras, and they have similar drawbacks (not the least of which is the expense—a good-quality digital video camera is more than twice as expensive as its analog counterparts). One of the neat things about a digital video camera is that you can use it for both video *and* still images. No more having to choose which camera to take with you!

With a FireWire-equipped Mac and a digital video camera, you can have a near-professional video studio on your desktop. You can use a digital video camera even if your Mac doesn't have a FireWire card, but moving those huge digital video files back and forth will take a while.

Understanding and Using Output Devices

Using monitors

Using printers

Creating electronic documents with PDF

Using Output Devices

Seeing the results of what you do on your Mac is the point of it all, isn't it? There are a number of ways that you can provide your handiwork to the world. You can design your work to be viewed onscreen or you might want to kill some trees and print your work. For each method, there is a class of hardware devices or software that you can use to output the results of your labor. In this chapter, you will get an overview of the three most common output methods that you will use. These are the following: onscreen on your monitor, as a hard copy from printer, or as an electronic document that you can distribute over the Internet or on a CD-ROM (or even floppy disk)..

Using Monitors

The primary way that your Mac communicates with you is via a monitor. You constantly use the monitor as you work with your Mac. It is important that you understand your monitor choices so that the way you work is made as efficient and effective as possible. Monitors have the following basic characteristics:

- **Display type**. There are two options in the way a monitor displays information. With a Cathode Ray Tube (CRT) type of monitor, information appears on the screen as the result of an electron gun spraying electrons against the inside of the monitor screen, which is covered with phosphors that glow when struck by electrons. The other choice is a Liquid Crystal Display (LCD), which uses a liquid-based display medium. This technology enables the viewing area to be very thin, which is why all laptops are equipped with LCD displays.

  The image quality of both types of displays is very good. Until recently, the cost of LCD displays has prevented their use except where nothing else will work because of size limitations, such as a laptop. Recently, the cost of LCD monitors has decreased so that you can now get somewhat affordable LCD screens for desktop machines as well.

Although the cost difference is still prohibitive for most people, the advantage of LCD screens is their "thinness." A comparably-sized LCD display will be much smaller and lighter than one that is CRT-based. And a high-quality LCD screen will have a sharper and more vibrant picture than its CRT cousin.

- **Display size**. This is the most important factor when considering a monitor. There are various sizes of display area available. The most common are 15-inch, 17-inch, and 21-inch. With display size, bigger is better. You should get a quality monitor in the largest size that you can afford.

- **Dot Pitch**. On CRT monitors, the electron gun sprays electrons on metallic grid on the inside of the glass. The smaller the distance between the holes in this grid is, the more fine an image the monitor can display. Monitors with smaller pitches are better than those with larger pitches, all other things being equal. Typical pitch sizes range from 24 mm to 28 mm.

Beyond connecting a monitor to your Mac, there isn't all that much to do as far as working with a monitor goes, except for setting the resolution and color depth it displays, as well as the ColorSync profile that it uses.

SEE ALSO

➤ *To learn how to set the resolution that your monitor uses, see page 166*
➤ *To learn how to set the color depth that your monitor uses, see page 176*

ColorSync is the technology that ensures that the color is consistent between all peripherals that use ColorSync, including monitors, printers, scanners, and so on.

SEE ALSO

➤ *To learn more about ColorSync, see page 180*

When you install a monitor, you should obtain and install the ColorSync profile for it. (If you use an Apple monitor, the ColorSync profile is part of Mac OS 8.5.) If the ColorSync profile did not come with the software included with your monitor, check with the manufacturer of your monitor to see if a ColorSync profile is available.

Size does matter

To create the ultimate amount of desktop space, consider adding a second monitor to your system. With the Mac OS, you have always been able to have two monitors working at the same time. You can display different portions of the desktop in each monitor. For example, you can display the document on which you are working on one monitor and all of the tool bars and palettes that you use on another.

To have multiple monitors, you need to install a graphics/video card for the second monitor. You will then have one connected to your Mac's video port and the other connected to the graphics card that you install in your Mac.

By the way, until Windows 98, there was no way to support multiple monitors on the same Windows computer.

Configuring ColorSync for a monitor

1. If you have a non-Apple monitor, check with its manufacturer to see if it has a ColorSync profile for your monitor. Most monitor makers do have ColorSync profiles; the best place to find them is the monitor manufacturer's Web site. Place the profile for your monitor in the ColorSync Profiles folder within the System Folder, and you will be able to choose it from the pop-up menu (see Figure 19.1).

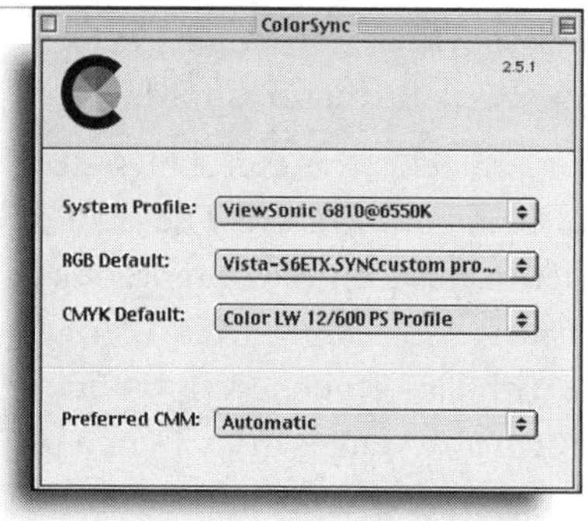

FIGURE 19.1

ColorSync enables you to make the colors on your peripheral consistent.

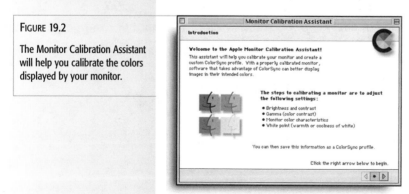

2. Open the Monitors and Sound control panel.
3. Click the Color button.
4. Click the ColorSync Profile for your monitor. (This is the same as the profile set with the ColorSync control panel.)
5. If you want to calibrate your monitor, click the Calibrate button and follow the instructions provided by the Monitor Calibration Assistant (seeFigure 19.2).

FIGURE 19.2

The Monitor Calibration Assistant will help you calibrate the colors displayed by your monitor.

6. Close the control panel.

Using Printers

There are many different printers that are available for Mac OS 8.5 computers. There are four basic categories of printers available based on the technology that a particular printer uses to imprint the paper:

- **Inkjet**. Inkjet printers spray small dots of ink on the paper to form images and text. All inkjet printers now sold are color. Inkjet printers produce excellent quality text and good-to-excellent quality graphics. You can also buy inkjets that are network ready, but their relatively slow speed does not make them the best choice for a network printer. But for personal printers or those that are shared by only a few people, inkjets are hard to beat. A good quality inkjet printer costs less than $400 so it is an excellent value. The best inkjets are made by Hewlett-Packard and Epson.

- **Laser**. Laser printers produce superb quality for both text and graphics. They are also very fast and are the best choice for network printing. The lower-end laser printers are affordable enough to be a good choice for a personal printer. Unfortunately, almost all laser printers are black-and-white only.

- **Color laser**. Color laser printers produce excellent text and graphics and also have color capability. Unfortunately, color laser printers are very expensive, and are not likely to be an option for you unless high-quality color printing and network support is needed.

- **Other printers**. Above color laser printers are dye-sublimation and other higher-quality printers that are used in graphic design and other high-end businesses.

Once you have a printer, there are two ways that you can connect it to your Mac: directly or through a network. To connect a printer directly to your Mac, you simply attach the printer cable to the printer port on your Mac. How you connect a printer to your network depends on the kind of network you are using. If you are using an AppleTalk network, you can attach an

Other networks and printers

There are other network options, such as Novell, but I assume that if you are using a Novell or other network, you have a system administrator who sets up the printers on the network.

AppleTalk connector box to the printer. If you are using an Ethernet network, you can attach a cable from the nearest router or print server to your printer. In either case, the printer will show up in the Chooser as a network resource.

Your printer driver determines the features that you will be able to use from the Print dialog in any application. Some of the features you may be able to choose include the following:

- **Background printing**. If your printer is capable of background printing (most printers are), the printing process happens in the background while you can work in the foreground.

- **Desktop Printing**. If you use an Apple printer, or a non-Apple printer that can use the Apple LaserWriter driver, you can use desktop printing. With desktop printing, an icon of your printer is installed on your desktop (see Figure 19.3). When you want to print a document with that printer, you can drop the document on the printer's icon to print it. You can also open the printer to manage the documents in the print queue; for example, you can remove a document from the queue or reorder documents that are being printed.

FIGURE 19.3

You can use desktop printing icons to print documents and to monitor the status of print jobs in process.

- **Print quality**. Some printers enable you to choose print quality to conserve toner or ink during draft printing.

- **Print in grayscale**. If you are using a color printer, you can choose to print it in grayscale to save your color ink.

- **Print back to front**. When you print a document, it typically prints with the first pages coming out first. This usually results in the document being backwards when you pick it up. If you choose the back to front option, the printer starts from the back of the document so that when you pick up your print job, it will be in the proper order.

- **Print Preview**. Print Preview enables you to see your document as it will be printed. This is useful if your application does not have a Print Preview mode.

- **ColorSync settings**. If you are using a color printer, you can choose which color matching technology that you want to use, for example, ColorSync or the color matching technology that is part of your printer's driver.

Installing and Selecting a Printer

Once you have a printer connected to the network, or connected directly to your Mac, every printer needs a *driver* in order to communicate with your Mac. If you have an Apple printer, the driver you need is installed as part of Mac OS 8.5. And many non-Apple printers (especially laser printers) can use the Apple LaserWriter driver. Otherwise, you should have received a driver when you purchased your printer.

SEE ALSO

➤ *To learn how to install system components (including printer drivers) with the Mac OS 8.5 installer, see Appendix A, "Installing and Maintaining the Mac OS"*

Installing a printer driver and configuring a printer works similarly no matter what kind of printer you use. As an example, the following step-by-step configures a DeskJet printer on an AppleTalk network.

Installing a printer driver for an HP DeskJet printer and choosing it in the Chooser

1. Run the installer for the printer you want to install.

2. When the installer is done, restart your Mac.

3. When the Mac restarts, open the Chooser and select the driver that you installed.

4. If you are using a network, such as AppleTalk, your Mac will scan the network for available printers that use the driver you have selected. When it finds them all, it will display the available printers in the right pane of the Chooser window (see Figure 19.4). If you have the printer directly connected, choose the port to which it is connected (printer or modem).

Apple's LaserWriter driver is a good driver

If you use a laser printer, even if it isn't made by Apple, you might be able to use Apple's LaserWriter driver with it (you can install it with the Mac OS 8.5 installer). The LaserWriter driver is an advanced driver that provides lots of good features, and Apple is continuously updating it. If you have a laser printer, try using the LaserWriter driver with it. To do so, install the driver (it is installed by default), open the Chooser, and click on the LaserWriter driver in the left pane of the Chooser window. If your printer is connected, and it can use the LaserWriter driver, you will see your printer in the right pane of the window. Select it to use it as your printer. If you can't see your printer with the LaserWriter driver selected, but you can with your printer's driver selected, then you can't use Apple's LaserWriter driver.

Desktop printing

Desktop printing is a nice feature, but unless you use an Apple printer, or a printer that can use an Apple driver, you can't use it.

FIGURE 19.4

Using the Chooser to select a printer driver.

5. Choose the options that you want your printer to use, such as Background Printing.

6. Close the Chooser. You will see a warning that says you have changed the printer driver, and you need to choose Page Setup in all open applications. Click OK to clear the warning.

7. When you choose Print from within an application, you will see the Print dialog for the printer driver that you have chosen (see Figure 19.5).

FIGURE 19.5

This Print dialog is determined by the print driver chosen in the Chooser.

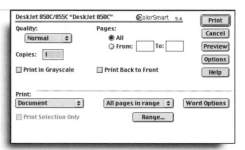

Printing features

You won't see the same printer options in the Print dialog in all applications. Applications can implement their own features in the Print dialog. For example, you won't see all of the options in Figure 19.5 in the Print dialog in SimpleText.

Using ColorSync with a Printer

ColorSync also works with your printer if you have a ColorSync profile for your printer. (If you don't receive a ColorSync profile with your printer, contact the printer's manufacturer.)

To use ColorSync with your printer, install the ColorSync profile for your printer in the ColorSync Profiles folder that is in your System Folder.

After the profile is installed, you need to select it in the ColorSync control panel.

Choosing a printer ColorSync profile

1. Open the ColorSync control panel.

2. Choose your printer's ColorSync profile from the RGB Default pop-up menu if you use a three-color printer.

3. Choose your printer's ColorSync profile from the CMYK Default pop-up menu if you use a four-color printer.

4. Leave the Preferred CMM option in automatic unless you have a device that has a specific CMM profile.

5. Close the control panel.

Outputting Electronic Documents

In today's environment, you are likely to have to produce documents that will be distributed over the Net or via email. One of the most common formats for electronic documents isAdobe's *Portable Document Format* (PDF). A PDF file can be read with the freeware Adobe Acrobat Reader. PDF documents have a number of good features. All of the fonts needed for that document are included in the document. If the recipient's computer does not have the same fonts installed, Acrobat Reader will create a very close approximation of the fonts used in the document. The page setup for your PDF documents is set by the driver that you use to create that document. Acrobat Reader maintains the page layout of your documents no matter what driver the recipient has chosen. This means that your document looks the same on all the major platforms as long as the recipient has a copy of Adobe Acrobat.

In order to create a PDF, you need a copy of Abode Distiller. Distiller provides a print driver that writes the output to a PDF file rather than a printer.

For most applications, after you have installed Distiller, it is as easy to create a PDF as it is to print one.

Page setup and the printer driver

When an application creates a page of a document, it determines the dimensions of that page from the print driver that is currently selected in the Chooser. That is why you see the warning about selecting Page Setup in all open applications when you change printer drivers. By opening Page Setup, you force the open application to reformat its pages according to the dimensions set in the printer driver.

Where do you get Distiller?

You can get Adobe Distiller in several ways. It is included with some of Adobe's applications, such as PageMaker. You can also purchase a copy of Abode's Acrobat Exchange, which enables you to create and modify PDF documents.

Creating a PDF with PageMaker

1. Open the Chooser.

2. Select the PSPrinter driver. You will see the Virtual Printer in the Type pop-up menu (see Figure 19.6).

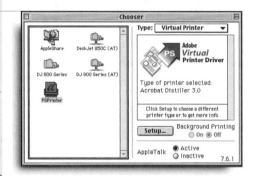

FIGURE 19.6

Once Distiller is installed, you can choose the PSPrinter driver to print to the virtual printer.

3. Close the Chooser.

4. Open the application that you will use to create your document and prepare your document.

5. Choose Export PDF from the File menu (see Figure 19.7).

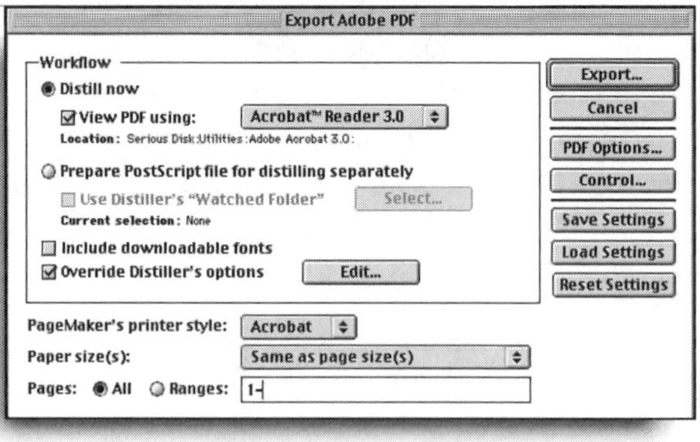

Virtual printer?

Distiller requires a PostScript printer driver in order to work. If you do not have a PostScript driver available, the virtual printer performs the same function. You can also choose a PostScript printer from the Type pop-up menu.

FIGURE 19.7

This dialog enables you to print to a PDF document.

6. Set the options you want to use.

7. Click Export.

8. Name the PDF file and save it. The application will print the file and Distiller then creates the PDF (see Figure 19.8). When it is done, you can open the document.

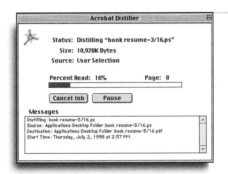

FIGURE 19.8
Distiller "distills" a PDF document from your file.

One of the great things about creating PDFs is that you can configure the options such that all of your Table of Contents entries can be links so that when the reader clicks on a section title, he moves to that section. Plus, it is easy to create other links in a PDF document to enable the reader to quickly move within the document, go to Web sites, or even to send email to you. You can also create very nice graphical outlines for your documents so that a reader can quickly navigate to the relevant parts of it. Another advantage is that recipients cannot easily alter your PDF documents, unlike some other methods.

PDF files are only one way to distribute electronic documents. Other methods include providing a document in HTML (which makes your document into a Web page) and via common file types that popular applications can work with (for example, you can provide Microsoft Office files if you are sure that your audience has Microsoft Word, or you can send graphics in common formats such as JPEG or TIFF).

Understanding and Using Networking Devices

Using modems

Using AppleTalk serial and Ethernet networks

Using other networks

Connecting to the World

In today's world, no Mac is an island. If you aren't connecting with other people, you aren't making the most of your Mac. Collaboration is the name of the game, and the information, resources, and tools you need are "out there."

If you and your Mac are located with other computer users, you really need to be networked with them in order to share files, applications, and other resources, such as printers, back-up drives and so on. You can also communicate with people on your network via e-mail, and you can set up a local Web to make important information available to everyone in the office. And transferring files via sneakernet (using floppy disks) is no longer acceptable. Many files that you need won't even fit on a single disk anymore.

However, just because your Mac is the only one in your office or home is no reason not to connect with others. With a modem, you can connect with people all over the world, not to mention the vast sources of information, tools, and even entertainment that are waiting for you.

Working with Modems

A modem (short for MODulator DEModulator, not that it matters) enables you to network with other users via the phone lines. A modem converts the analog language that phone lines speak into the digital language that your Mac speaks. This enables you to communicate over a modem and phone lines as you do when you are connected to other computers over a network.

Understanding Modems

There are various manufacturers and models of modems available for your Mac. And there are different styles— some modems are internal to your Mac while others are external. The most important characteristic of a modem is speed. Speed affects everything that you do with a modem from sending email to surfing the World Wide Web. And one rule always applies, *faster is better*.

Intranet versus Internet

A local network that provides Web and other resources is called an *intranet* as opposed to the Internet.

It takes two to tango

Realize that your capabilities are only half of the equation. The speed of the modem receiving your call also contributes to the speed of your connection, and speed always defaults to the *lowest* common denominator. If you have a 56K modem, but the modem that you are calling (at your Internet Service Provider perhaps) supports only a 33.6K connection, 33.6K is what you experience. Many Internet Service providers and online services (such as AOL) have multiple lines, some of which have differing speed capabilities (for example, there may be 56K, 33.6K, and even 28.8K lines available). Sometimes, you can use different phone numbers for different modem speeds. Whenever you configure your modem to connect to another modem or service, make sure that you use the fastest line in.

In a few short years, modem speed has improved exponentially. A few years ago, a typical modem communicated at 1,200 bps (bauds per second, don't worry about what means, just realize that a higher number means a faster modem). Today's modems are rated at 56,000 bps. There are other speeds available as well. The most common of these are 33.6 (short for 33,600 bps) modems, and there are a few 28.8 modems lingering about. Anything less than 28.8 is unacceptable.

Since speed is the most important factor, why would anyone use a 33.6 or 28.8 modem? There are several possible reasons. One possible reason may be that the receiving end of your connection cannot handle 56K speeds. Another reason is that the phone lines that connect to the modem are older and can't support the faster 56K speeds. Although 56K modems are fast, they are also more "finicky" than the slower modems. There is no reason to pay the additional cost of a 56K modem if you aren't going to be able to achieve speeds close to the maximum possible anyway.

Knowing beforehand if you will be able to achieve 56K speeds is not easy. There are some tests that you can run, but these will likely result in inconclusive results. In all likelihood, you will simply have to try a 56K modem and see what it can do in your environment. Of course, before you buy a 56K modem, make sure that the other end of your connection (such as your Internet Service Provider) supports 56K connections and that there are plenty of 56K lines available.

SEE ALSO

➤ *To learn about Internet Service Providers, see Chapter 23, "Connecting Your Mac to the Net"*

If you have purchased your Mac in the last year or so, you might have received either a 56K or 33.6K modem with it. Or perhaps you purchased one on your own. If you don't have a modem at all and you can't use a local network of some sort, you should purchase one immediately. Using the Internet and other online services is one of the best and most productive things you can do with your Mac.

Why 56K modems aren't really 56K modems

Although they are called 56K modems, you should realize that 56K is the theoretical maximum that these modems can achieve. Because of the noise in phone lines, as well as government restrictions, the fastest speed that you can hope to communicate is about 53K. And you will be lucky to get speeds that high. More realistic speeds are in the 45-51K range. Should this stop you from using a 56K modem? Not at all. They are still a lot faster than any other kind of analog modem available for your Mac.

When not to even try 56K

If you live in a home in which the phone lines have not been installed or updated in the last 20 years, the odds of you being able to support a 56K connection are pretty small. Ditto if you live in a rural area where the local phone company is somewhat behind the times. In order for 56K modems to actually get high-speeds, everything needs to be "just right."

Buying a modem

When you look at modems, you may be overwhelmed by the number of them that are available. The fact is that most modems will work just fine for you. Once you decide if you want a 33.6 or 56K modem and if that modem will be internal or external, you will probably be able to choose from a couple of brands. Check your favorite Mac magazine (such as *Macworld*) for modem reviews to see which you should buy. Or if you can access the Internet (perhaps through a friend's computer), there are lots of sources of information about modems, as well as great places to buy them.

PowerBooks and external modems

Most PowerBooks have at least one serial port so that you can use an external modem with them. Of course, external modems don't run on battery power, and you will have to lug one around with you, but if you usually don't connect until you are in a working area with power, a good external modem may not be a bad choice. They are a lot cheaper than PC card modems.

Combo cards

Some PC modem cards are combo cards. Combo cards offer both the modem function and some other networking function, usually Ethernet, in one form or another. Some internal modems are also combo modems. Combo modems are excellent choices when you need to connect via a modem at times and at other times, you need to physically connect to an Ethernet network (and the PowerBook's built-in Ethernet support is not sufficient).

The other basic factor that you need to understand when purchasing or configuring a modem is whether it will be internal or external. Internal modems are nice because there isn't any separate hardware to mess around with (for example, you never have to turn it on separately). External modems are nice because you can easily move them to another computer, and it is often easier to tell what is going on with an external modem. External modems are also easier to upgrade should you decide that you need a faster one.

If you use a desktop Mac that is not equipped with an internal modem, I suggest that you not bother with an internal modem and just go with an external one. Installation is trivially easy and external modems are easier to work with.

If you use a PowerBook, you have two "mobile" choices: internal modems or PC card modems. Some PowerBooks come with internal modems already installed, and if yours did, well, use it as long as it works for you. Internal modems for PowerBooks are difficult to upgrade and unless you have a relatively new PowerBook, you are probably stuck with a 28.8, or even worse, a 14.4 modem. A PC Card modem is the size of a credit card, and it is installed in the PowerBook's PC card expansion bay. PC card modems are easy to work with, and are the better choice. Be aware that PC card modems are still a bit more expensive than external modems.

If you have an internal modem, you can simply connect your phone line to the phone jack on the back of your Mac. If you have an external modem, you will need to connect its power supply, connect its communication cable to the modem port on your Mac, and connect the phone line to the back of the modem. If you have a PC card modem, you can insert it into the PC card slot on your PowerBook and connect a phone line to it.

Using a Modem

After a modem is connected to your Mac, you really don't work with it directly. All modem activity is controlled through the communications software that your Mac uses. Before you can use a modem to connect to the Net or to another computer, you need to configure it.

There are two control panels that you can use to configure your modem. The Modem control panel is pretty basic, and it requires only a few steps. You use the DialAssist control panel to set particular aspects of the way you need to dial phone numbers from your location.

If you are going to use your modem to connect to the Internet, you can configure it with the Internet Setup Assistant, and you don't have to deal with either control panel directly. However, you need to know how to use them both so that you can make adjustments to your configuration after you have used the Internet Setup Assistant.

SEE ALSO

➤ *To learn more about the Internet Setup Assistant, see Chapter 23, "Connecting Your Mac to the Net"*

Configuring a modem with the Modem control panel

1. Open the Modem control panel (see Figure 20.1).

2. Choose the location where your modem is attached with the Connect via pop-up menu. Your choices are Modem Port or Printer Port for an external modem, Internal for an internal modem, or one of the PC card slots if you are using a PC card modem.

3. From the Modem pop-up menu, choose your modem. This setting determines the initialization string that is sent to your modem to prepare it for use. You don't need to know anything beyond that (initialization strings are simply a series of commands sent to your modem that in effect tell it to get ready to dial). If your modem is not listed (it probably will be), contact the manufacturer or look in the software that came with the modem to see if there is a modem scripts file for your modem. If there is, place it in the Modem Scripts folder that is in the Extensions folder. If you can't find one, try one of the installed modems to see if you can use its settings (one of the Hayes modem files may be a good start).

Connecting an external modem to a Mac with an internal modem

Some Macs come with internal modems already installed. If this modem is not acceptable, for example, you want a 56K modem and the one that is installed is only 33.6, you will have to disable the internal modem in order to be able to use an external one. How you do this depends on the particular model of Mac that you are using. Check the user manual for your model or talk with a knowledgeable representative when you purchase another modem. They will often be able to tell you if and how you can disable or replace an internal one with an external one.

Windows and modems

Modem handling is one of the few areas in which Windows computers are superior to Macs. With Windows, you can support several modems on the same computer, and it is easy to switch between them. And it is easier to find and install internal modems for Windows machines.

Bulletin Boards and online services

In the olden days (the early 1990s), lots of Mac users were connected to small services, called *Bulletin Board Services (BBS)*. These Mac users used a terminal emulating program to connect to these BBSes in order to download files or communicate with others. Often, software companies had a BBS from where you could download updates and bug fixes. BBSes have gone the way of the dinosaur; they have been replaced by the Internet.

FIGURE 20.1

You use the Modem control panel to configure your modem.

Online services

There are some online services that you may want to use, the primary example being America Online (AOL). With AOL, you can do everything that you can do on the Internet, and it is easier to configure. For total beginners to the online world, AOL is often a good choice. However, once you are comfortable with being online, you should move to an Internet Service Provider. They are usually cheaper, and you can use better software to browse the World Wide Web and to send email.

No configuration required

If you use AOL or another online service, the software you use will handle all your modem and dialing configuration for you. Once you have the modem installed on your Mac, simply run the online service's software to get started.

G3 modems

If you are lucky enough to have a G3 PowerBook, and it has an internal modem, that modem may have its own software built in to the OS. If so, your PowerBook will autosense the modem and will configure the modem for you.

4. If you want to hear the sounds of the modem dialing and connecting, use the Sound radio button to turn the sound on. If you don't want to hear the sound, click the Off button. It is a good idea to leave the sound on until you are sure that you can connect reliably. Then you can turn it off if the sounds annoy you.

5. If your phone system uses Tone dialing (which it probably does), ensure that the Tone radio button is checked. If you use Pulse dialing (a rotary phone system), check the Pulse radio button.

6. If you want your Mac to dial regardless of the dial tone, check the "Ignore dial tone" check box. This can be useful if your voice message system uses a "beeping" or other odd dial tone to indicate that you have messages waiting. If this check box is not checked, such a dial tone will prevent your Mac from being able to dial out.

7. Close the control panel.

Once your modem has been configured, you need to set any special dialing options that you want to use.

Customizing your dialing settings with the DialAssist control panel

1. Open the DialAssist control panel (see Figure 20.2).

2. Enter your area code in the City/Area Code field and choose your country from the Country pop-up menu.

3. If you need to dial a prefix to get an outside line when you dial the phone, choose it from the Prefix pop-up menu.

FIGURE 20.2

Using DialAssist, you can set any special prefixes or suffixes that you want to be dialed (when you have to use a calling card for example).

4. If you need to use a prefix to dial a long distance number (such as 1 or to use Sprint for example), choose it from the Long Distance Access pop-up menu.

5. You can add a suffix to a phone number by choosing it from the pop-up menu.

6. You can use the buttons at the bottom of the DialAssist control panel to modify any of the choices in the pop-up menus. For example, to change the Prefix choices you have, click the Prefix button. You will see a dialog that enables you to add to, edit, or delete choices from the Prefix pop-up menu (see Figure 20.3).

FIGURE 20.3

You can add to, edit, or delete any of the choices in the pop-up menus in the DialAssist control panel.

7. When you are done setting the configuration, close the control panel.

After your modem is connected and configured, you can use software to access it. For example, to connect to the Internet, you can use Remote Access.

SEE ALSO

➤ *To learn how to connect to the Net using Remote Access, see Chapter 23, "Connecting Your Mac to the Net"*

Understanding the Future of Modems

While modems are a lot faster than they used to be, they are still too slow. It takes too long to download a Web page or to transfer large files. Conventional modem technology has topped out at 56K. Eventually, changing a Web page should be as fast as changing channels on a TV. Plus, full-screen video will eventually be transmitted over the Web, too. This requires that even more data be transmitted even faster. There are several initiatives to make data transmission faster, and they include the following:

- **Cable modems**. Computer data can be transmitted via a cable that is similar to that used by cable TV. Cable modems offer the highest speed of any current or in-development technology; cable modem's speed is, in order of magnitude, faster than a conventional modem. Plus, there is no connecting. A cable modem is always ready to send and receive information. Cable modems are deployed in limited test areas. In a few years, cable modems should be widely available.

- **ISDN**. Integrated Services Digital Network (ISDN) is a digital service that combines voice and data transmission. You also need an ISDN modem to use it. ISDN is two to three times faster than a 56K modem. It is available in many locations (contact your local phone company to see it if is available in your area). The costs of ISDN are still prohibitive for most users. Unless you have a business for which speed is critical, IDSN will probably be too expensive for you. ISDN costs continue to decrease though, so it may not be long before ISDN is a viable choice.

■ **ADSL/VDSL**. Asymmetric Digital Subscriber Line (ADSL) and Very High Speed Digital Subscriber Line (VDSL) are new technologies to transmit more data over regular phone lines. Eventually, ADSL/ADSL technology will enable very high speed connections, probably faster than ISDN, but not as fast as cable modems. ADSL/ADSL are still in their infancy and can't be expected to be in place for most users until well into the next century.

Working with AppleTalk Networks

Since its inception, the Mac has always been "network-ready." That is because AppleTalk support has always part of the Mac. While AppleTalk is a relatively slow networking scheme, it is also very easy and inexpensive to set up and use. You can quickly connect any AppleTalk-compatible devices to form an AppleTalk network. Once you create an AppleTalk network, you can use it to enable File and Web sharing, and you can also share network resources, such as printers.

Setting Up an AppleTalk Network by Using Serial Connections

Setting up an AppleTalk network by using serial connections is simple. Each AppleTalk device needs an AppleTalk connector box, also called a *phonet box*. This box has a serial connector on one end and two phone jacks in the other. These boxes cost about $15 per box (you need one box for each device that is to be on the network).

To connect an AppleTalk-compatible device to the network, you simply plug the serial connector on the phonet box into the serial port of the device (the Printer or Modem port on the Mac). Then you connect the various phonet boxes with regular phone cable. That is all there is to it.

All Macs are AppleTalk-compatible, as are many printers, so it is easy to create a fully-functional network that will enable users to share files and folders and network printers. You can even set up a local Web by using Mac OS 8.5's Web Sharing abilities.

SEE ALSO

➤ *To learn how to use File sharing, see page 465*

➤ *To learn how to connect Windows PCs to an AppleTalk network, see page 490*

Setting Up an AppleTalk Network by Using Ethernet

Using an Ethernet network makes AppleTalk much faster, usually 10 or more times faster. Connecting an Ethernet network is a bit more complicated and expensive than using a serial, connection-based network, but the speed improvement can easily make the additional cost and complexity worthwhile. Explaining the details of setting up an Ethernet network is beyond the scope of this book; however, it may help you decide if that is what you need to do if you learn about the general ways such a network is set up.

Each device that will be on the network must support Ethernet. Most Macs have built-in Ethernet support so that it is not a problem (unlike Windows PCs to which you have to add an Ethernet card). Most laser printers also support Ethernet connections. If the Mac or other device that you want to connect to an Ethernet network doesn't have built-in Ethernet support, you need to install an Ethernet card in that device.

On each device on the network, you must install an Ethernet transceiver. The transceiver manages the information flow to and from that device. A transceiver costs about $50.

An Ethernet cable connects the transceiver of each device to an Ethernet hub (or router). This device acts like a network traffic cop and ensures that information flows properly. The information from all devices must flow through a hub so that it can be routed to the appropriate device. A small hub can cost a couple hundred dollars.

After the devices are all connected and the hub is configured, information can flow across the network.

Building a bridge

You can use a device with a serial connection, but no Ethernet port, on an Ethernet network by installing a bridge to connect the serial port on the device to the Ethernet network. These kind of bridges are fairly expensive, usually about $200. Unless the device that you want to use is really expensive or is one-of-a-kind, bridges don't make much sense.

Ethernet for two

If you have two devices that you want to connect to an Ethernet network, you can do so without an Ethernet hub. You use a special cable, called a *crossover cable*, to connect the transceivers that are connected to each device. The devices will then be able to communicate with each other by using Ethernet. This is an excellent choice when you want to connect two computers or perhaps a single computer and a printer. Using a crossover cable saves you money because you don't need an Ethernet Lab.

Configuring an AppleTalk Network

In addition to being easy to set up, AppleTalk networks are also easy to configure.

Configuring AppleTalk

1. Open the AppleTalk control panel (see Figure 20.4).

FIGURE 20.4

Using the AppleTalk control panel, you can set the port that will be used for an AppleTalk network.

2. From the Connect via pop-up menu, choose the port to which the network is connected (Printer, Modem, Ethernet, or Remote). The Mac will search for the network, and will report the zone it is in.

3. Close the control panel.

Using Other Networks

There are lots of other networking schemes around, especially for non-Mac based networks (such as those that use Windows NT servers). These schemes are based on Novell, Windows NT, or similar technologies. You can connect Macs to these networks (for example, Mac support is built into Windows NT). Setting up a network using one of these technologies is a complex and expensive proposition, and you really need to know what you are doing. Usually, these networks are set up by certified technicians and then administered by a network or system administrator. If you want to connect your Mac to such a network, you need to see the system

Zones?

Networks can be configured in zones, where each zone is sub-network. This improves the speed of the network as compared to having all the networked devices on a single network. If you have a network complex enough to benefit from having zones, you should have a network administrator who can help you set up the zone for your Mac.

Connect via remote

You can connect to an AppleTalk network via a modem if the network supports Remote Access. This enables you to log onto your network from other locations just as if you were physically connected (albeit with a slower connection). Talk to your network administrator to see if your network will support remote connections.

Using Your Mac to Work with Others

21   **Working with Other Macs 463**

22   **Working with Windows PCs 489**

Working with Other Macs

Working with other Macs

Sharing files with other Macs

Using files, folders, and volumes that are shared with you

Working with files that you receive from others

Sharing applications

Understanding How You Can Work with Other Macs

The odds are that you use your Mac to work with other people. Whether you work with files that other people create or you send the files you create for others to work with, there are very few activities that do not involve information flowing among a group of people. If you are fortunate, most of the people with whom you work also use Macintoshes. If they use Windows PCs or another platform, that is OK too, because you can work with just about every computer platform out there.

There are four major ways in which you can use the Mac's capability to work with other Macs:

- **Transferring files**. Sometimes you need to provide someone with a copy of a file or to provide a file you have created to someone else. Moving files from Mac-to-Mac is about as easy as moving a file from your Mac's hard disk to a floppy disk. Mac OS 8.5 enables you to easily transfer files to other Macs as well as to Windows PCs.

- **Sharing files**. There are a million ways that sharing files can help team members work together on a project. For instance, if you're a writer, you probably want to share your file with your editor. (Actually, you probably don't, but editors are insistent.) Your editor probably wants to share files with proofreaders and production folks. If you're a project manager putting together a spreadsheet, you may need to get numbers or other data from a variety of team members. If you're a digital artist, you want to share your images with the designer or art director who puts the image into a layout. You can probably think of three or four ways that sharing files can save you (and someone else) a lot of time and trouble. Mac OS 8.5 includes tools and features that make it easy for you to share files with others. The great thing about Mac OS 8.5 is that you don't need to be a computer or networking expert to get a lot out of sharing files.

- **Sharing applications**. Sometimes, it's nice to be able to run applications that reside on other Macs. Suppose that you

File servers versus workstations

Sometimes files that are shared by a number of different users are stored on a dedicated machine called a file server. A file server isn't a workstation with a user sitting in front of it; rather, it's a fast, high-storage machine that shares its files with the Macs on the network. A file server provides faster performance over a network, and it is easier to keep properly backed up than sharing files among workstation Macs on the network. Once a network grows larger than just a few users, a file server is the best solution for sharing files.

Macs can also work with file servers that are other computer platforms, such as Windows NT machines. You will learn more about this in Chapter 22, "Working with Windows PCs."

have software that you use only occasionally—say, an application that helps you create org charts —but you use the application on all of the Macs on the network. Rather than installing a copy of the network on every computer on the network, you can save some disk space by installing a single copy on a single machine. Using Application Sharing, you can run the application from any Mac on the network. Be aware that sharing an application over a network results in very poor performance, and if the application crashes, it can take down the entire network. Still, for occasional use, sharing an application can be beneficial.

- **Using a local Web**. With Mac OS 8.5's Web sharing feature, you can set up and use a local Web for the other computers on your network. There are lots of uses for a local Web site; for example, you can create a Web site containing information for specific projects that other users can view with their Web browsers.

Sharing and Transferring Files

No matter what you use your Mac for, you will need to work with files created by others. You will also need to provide files that you create to coworkers for them to work with. The Mac makes it easy to share with and transfer files to and from other Mac users.

SEE ALSO

➤ *To learn how to share and transfer files with Windows PC users, see Chapter 22, "Working with Windows PCs"*

When you transfer a file, you move the file from its original location onto another Mac. When you share a file with someone, the file remains where it is and you open the file from your Mac, or someone else opens a file on your Mac from his. The fundamental difference between transferring and sharing a file is that when you transfer a file, there is no further connection with the original version. When a file is shared, that version remains for others to use.

Transferring Files Among Macs

When you want to transfer a file to another Mac user, there are a couple of basic ways that you can do so:

- **Sneakernet**. The term *sneakernet* refers to using a floppy disk, Zip disk, or other removable media to move a file from one Mac to another. The idea is that you copy the file to a disk, carry the disk to another Mac, and insert the disk in the other Mac. As long as the person with whom you want to transfer files is relatively close, sneakernet is actually a pretty good way to transfer files. (Of course, you can always mail disks to another Mac user, but that can be time consuming.) Using disks to transfer files is simple, and you have control over how and when files are transferred.

What is small?

When considering a file transfer via email, what is a small file? It all depends on the way in which the involved people are connected. For someone using a slow modem, a 2 or 3 MB file might be large. For someone connecting to email with a high-speed direct network connection, a file as large as 200 MB may not be a big deal. When transferring files via email, you need to keep the capabilities of your recipient in mind.

- **Email**. You can transfer files to other people by attaching them to email. This method has one primary advantage over sneakernet: you can transfer files to and from other Mac users wherever they are located. You can transfer files via email with almost any Mac user who has an email account. There are a few disadvantages to the email method. First, large files can be problematic to send via email. If the recipient has a slow or unreliable connection, the file may take a long time to transfer, or it may be interrupted and not make it at all. Second, some email accounts are behind various gateways that will not properly handle email attachments. But for relatively small files, using email can be the best way to transfer files to other Mac users. Third, files need to be encoded when they are attached to email, and they are usually compressed as well. This may be a problem for some recipients if they do not have the knowledge or tools to properly handles encoded or compressed files.

SEE ALSO

➤ *To learn about attaching files to email, see page 587*

- **Web/FTP**. You can also transfer files by uploading them to Web or FTP sites. People can then connect to these sites to download your files. This method has similar advantages and disadvantages as using email does; the person downloading your files from the Web or an FTP site is not likely to have any problems with a gateway.

SEE ALSO

➤ *To learn how to download files from Web and FTP sites, see page 646*

■ **Network**. Using file sharing on a network, you can transfer files to and from your Mac as easily as if they were stored on your own hard drives. You will learn about this option in the next section.

Once you transfer files to your Macs, you can work with them just as if you created them on your own disk. See the section called, "Working with Files You Share or Receive" later in this chapter to learn more about working with files that you have transferred to your Mac.

Sharing Your Files with Others

After you have your Mac connected to an AppleTalk or other network, you can easily share your files and folders with other Mac users on the network.

SEE ALSO

➤ *To learn about networking your Mac, see Chapter 20, "Understanding and Using Networking Devices"*

Here are the four tasks you need to use to share your files with other Macs on your network:

1. Set up file sharing on your Mac.

2. Share folders and files that live on your Mac.

3. Set up users and groups to control who has access to the files and folders on your Mac, and apply those security settings to the items you want to share.

4. Monitor the file sharing activity on your Mac.

Setting Up File Sharing

Before you can use file sharing, you have to turn it on and configure your Mac's identity on the network.

Using Non-AppleTalk networks

If your Mac resides on a network that doesn't use AppleTalk as its protocol, you may or may not be able to use the techniques described in this section. Some non-AppleTalk networks (such as those using Windows NT servers) provide services for Macintosh that are just like those you can use with other Macs. Other networks may not support AppleTalk, and you will have to learn how to work with those networks from the network administrator who set up and administers that network.

Mac OS Setup Assistant

If you used the Mac OS Setup Assistant when you first started your Mac after installing Mac OS 8.5, the Owner name, Owner Password, and Computer Name fields will already be filled in. You can change them in the File Sharing control panel if you want to.

Setting up File Sharing and configuring your Mac's network identity

1. Open the File Sharing control panel (see Figure 21.1).

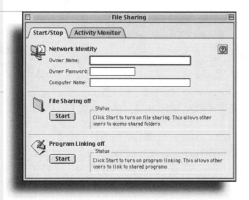

FIGURE 21.1

The File Sharing control panel enables you to configure File Sharing on your Mac.

2. Enter an Owner Name—this should be your name. Keep in mind that this is the name that will be used to track your activity on the network, so be careful about creating a name for yourself such as "Master of the Universe."

3. Enter an Owner Password. This is important because this enables anyone with your Owner Name and Password to modify *anything* on your Mac. If someone on your network knows your Owner Password, they can access your machine as if they were you. The Owner Password is case sensitive; for example, "Master of the Universe" is not the same as "master of the universe."

4. Name your Mac by entering a name in the Computer Name field. This is the name that other users will use to log onto your machine. If you are on a large network, try to keep it something meaningful even to people who don't know you very well.

5. Click Start. You will see a status message telling you that File Sharing is starting on your Mac (see Figure 21.2). The start-up process may take a little while, depending on your Mac and the network to which you are connected.

Disappearing password

After you enter an Owner Password and move out of that field, your password will change to a series of bullets. This protects your password from prying eyes.

The button tells you

Once File Sharing is running on your Mac, the Start button changes into a Stop button.

FIGURE 21.2
After you click the File Sharing button, it may take a moment for File Sharing to start.

6. Close the control panel. Once File Sharing has finished starting up, your Mac is ready to share its treasures with the world.

Sharing Files and Folders

After File Sharing is active, you can share individual items that are on your Mac with the people on your network. For each item, you will assign one of four privileges levels to it.

These privileges are the following:

- **Read & Write**. When you assign someone to have Read & Write privileges to an item, they can do anything to the item they want.

- **Read only**. This level means that they can read the item, but can't make any changes to it.

- **Write only (Drop Box)**. When you choose this level, users can place things in the folder, but cannot see anything that is contained in it.

- **None**. When you choose None, users will not be able to see the item.

You can assign these items to three categories of user:

- **Owner**. This is the person who controls the item. For most of the items to be shared that exist on your Mac, this should be you.

Sharing folders and files

Before you can share any folders or files on a volume, you have to share the volume that contains those items first. If you don't, users won't be able to share any contents of that volume.

- **User/Group**. These are specific users or a group to whom you assign privileges for an item. You will learn more about these in the next section.

- **Everyone**. Everyone means everyone on the network shares these privileges.

Sharing folders on your Mac

1. In the Finder, select the item that you want to share (see Figure 21.3).

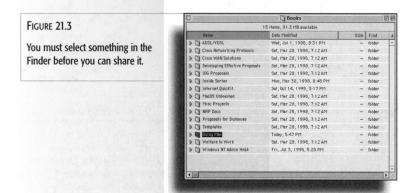

2. From the Finder's File menu, choose Get Info and then Sharing from the hierarchical menu. You will see the Sharing pane of the Get Info window for that item (see Figure 21.4).

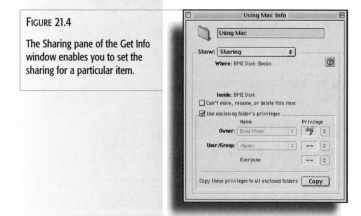

3. If you haven't shared the volume or folder that contains the item you want to share, uncheck the "Use enclosing folder's privileges" check box. If you check this check box, the item assumes the same settings as the folder or volume that contains this item. This makes it easy to set sharing for all the contents of a volume or folder. When the check box is unchecked, the controls for setting the privileges for this item will become active.

4. Check the "Can't move, rename, or delete this item" check box if you don't want users to be able to do any of these things. Usually, you should check this box so that people can't hide (even unintentionally) your own folder from you. The icon at the top of the pane will have a lock on it to indicate that it can't be renamed, deleted, or moved (see Figure 21.5).

FIGURE 21.5
When the icon at the top of the Sharing pane has a lock next to it, the item cannot be renamed, moved, or deleted.

5. Ensure that your name appears in the Owner pop-up menu, and choose the level of access you want the owner to have; normally, this will be Read & Write access (see Figure 21.6).

6. Skip the User/Group pop-up menu for now (you will learn about that in the next section).

7. Set the level of sharing privilege for Everyone on the network.

8. If you want to copy all of the sharing settings for this item to each item within it, click Copy. The control panel will display the sharing privileges you have set for this item (see Figure 21.7).

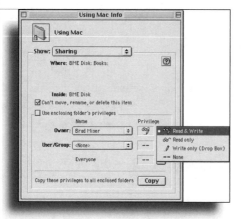

FIGURE 21.6

You can choose from the four levels of sharing privileges from the
pop-up menu next to each user
category.

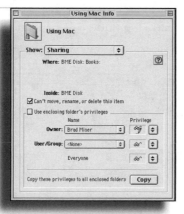

FIGURE 21.7

This folder can be read by everyone (the glasses icon), but only
the Owner can change it (the
pencil).

9. Close the control panel. The icon of the item will change to
reflect the sharing privileges that you have applied to it (see
Figure 21.8). The item will be able to be accessed by others
on the network as you have indicated; in this case, everyone
on the network will be able to see what is in the folder, but
they will not be able to change its contents.

Setting Up Users and Groups

If you are on a small network, perhaps an office of two or three
people, or your PowerBook and desktop Mac are networked
together, you probably don't need to worry about security.
However, if you're dealing with a bigger network, you should
only provide selective access to files. For example, you might

want to allow an employee into a folder that contains procedure documents, but you may not want that same employee to have access to a folder that contains the office budget spreadsheets.

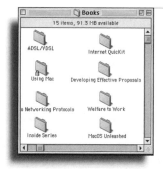

FIGURE 21.8

The Using Mac icon has a lock to indicate that it can't be changed.

Mac OS 8.5 provides substantial security features that you can use to control with whom and how files on your Mac are shared.

Fortunately, the Mac's File Sharing security system is pretty darn flexible as well as being easy to use. You can set up any number of authorized users for your Mac and set the security privileges on a folder-by-folder—or even file-by-file—basis. Furthermore, you can set up different levels of security clearance for each folder. For example, you might set up a folder so that users can read files but not delete them, or create a drop-box folder so that users can submit files, but can't open the folder that contains the submitted files.

Just to make things a little easier, you can also set up groups of users. For instance, you don't need to set up privileges for Andy, Betty, and Charles from the accounting department separately; rather, you can set up a group called "accounting," add them to the group, and set the privileges for everyone in the group all at once.

First, you'll need to create user accounts for people to share items on your Mac. The following two user accounts are created automatically:

- **Yours**. Your account was created automatically when you added your name and password to the File Sharing control panel earlier in this section. This is the Owner account.

Are guests welcome?

When configuring your Mac for File Sharing, you can set up usernames and passwords that enable individuals or groups of individuals to log onto your Mac. You can also enable "guests" to log onto your Mac if you want to. A Guest is anyone who has access to your network. With a large network, you may not know everyone on your network so providing guests with many privileges is not a good idea.

Be careful

Remember that when you share your Mac, or even parts of it, you are giving permission for people to access your Mac. If you give people write access to your Mac, they can add files to your machine. If they have delete privileges, they can remove files from your Mac. Be very careful about giving permission to people to write to or delete from your Mac. People who are untrustworthy, or perhaps simply don't know what they are doing, can cause all kinds of problems for you.

■ **The Guest**. The account called "guest" does not require a password. (You'll learn how to give privileges to the guest account, if you chose to do so, in a few pages.) This is the same as Everyone, which means everyone on the network.

You can create user accounts that specific people who can access your Mac.

Creating a user account

1. Open the Users & Groups control panel (see Figure 21.9).

FIGURE 21.9

The Users & Groups control panel enables you to apply sharing privileges to items based on who you want to be able to access those items.

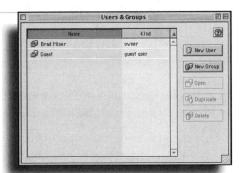

2. Click the New User button on the right side of the control panel's window. You will see the New User dialog (see Figure 21.10).

FIGURE 21.10

Using the New User dialog, you can create users to whom you will be able to assign access privileges to items on your Mac.

3. Give the New User a name and password—anything's fine, but it's a bad idea to give the new user the same password that *you* use.

4. If you want the user to be able to change her own password, check the "Allow user to change password" check box. It's up to you to decide whether or not to allow the user to change her password. (If it helps you decide, remember that you can always change it back whenever you like.)

5. Select Sharing from the Show pop-up menu at the top of the New User's window. You will see the Sharing pane of the new user's dialog (see Figure 21.11).

FIGURE 21.11
You set general sharing preferences for a particular user with the Sharing pane of the New User's dialog.

6. Make sure that the "Allow user to connect to this computer" check box is checked. (Otherwise, why are you setting up an account for the user?)

7. If you want the user to be able to link programs that are on your Mac, check the Program Linking check box (you will learn about this is in a later section of this chapter).

8. Close the window. The user you created can now be assigned sharing privileges to an item on your Mac. You will see the user listed in the Users & Groups window (see Figure 21.12).

9. Tell the user for whom you created an account what his username and password are and what you will be allowing him to access on your Mac.

Creating group accounts is very much like creating individual user accounts. You create user accounts, then group accounts, and then you place users in the appropriate groups. This makes it easy to assign sharing privileges for multiple users to an item.

FIGURE 21.12

The Users & Groups control panel
shows all of the users and groups
whom you have defined.

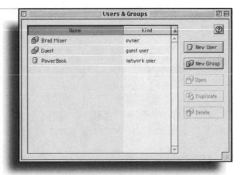

Creating a user group and assigning users to it

1. Click New Group. You will see the New Group dialog (see Figure 21.13).

FIGURE 21.13

The New Group dialog enables
you to create groups of users to
whom you can quickly assign
access privileges.

Other options

In the Users & Groups dialog, you
can edit a user or group by double-
clicking its icon or by selecting the
icon and clicking Open. To quickly
copy a user or group, select its icon
and click Duplicate. To remove a
user or group, select its icon and
click Delete.

2. Give the new group a name.

3. Drag any user's icon from the main Users & Groups window into the new group's window. (You might need to drag the New Group window to one side if it's covering the control panel window.) Repeat, as necessary, to move all of the group member's icons into the group's window (see Figure 21.14).

4. Close the open windows.

After you have user and group accounts set up, you can use them to control access to shared items on your Mac.

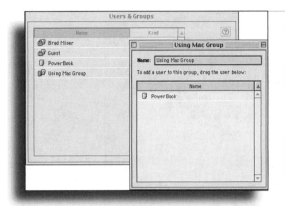

FIGURE 21.14
You can add users to a group by dragging their icon from the Users & Groups window into the group's window.

It takes time

It may take a while for your Mac to set all of the necessary sharing privileges, especially if you're sharing a folder that holds a lot of files. Try to ignore the unholy clanking of your hard drive as the privileges are updated. The performance of your Mac with File Sharing on it will also be slower while File Sharing is starting up.

Using user and groups accounts to control access to shared items

1. Select the item that you shared in the earlier step-by-step.
2. Choose Get Info and then Sharing from the show pop-up menu.
3. Click the User/Group pop-up menu. You will see all of the users and groups that you defined with the Users & Groups control panel (see Figure 21.15).

FIGURE 21.15
The User/Group pop-up menu shows all of the users and groups whom you have defined with the Users & Groups control panel.

4. From the User/Group pop-up menu, choose the user or group to whom you want to give sharing privileges for this item.
5. Use the Privilege pop-up menu to set the privileges that that user or group will have for this item.
6. Set the privileges for the Owner and Everyone if you need to. The window will reflect the sharing settings for this item (see Figure 21.16).

Another warning

Be aware that users with write or delete privileges can delete files inside a shared folder, even if they can't delete the folder itself. They can also fill up the volume containing the items that they can share. Be careful who you give access to.

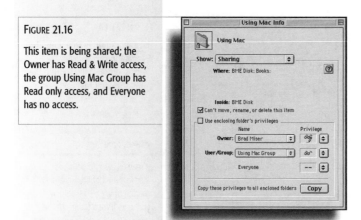

File Sharing costs you

Even if nobody is accessing your Mac's files through File Sharing, it still consumes RAM and slows down the performance of your machine. If you don't need to share files with others on your network, turn off File Sharing.

7. Close the window. The sharing privileges will take effect.

Monitoring Sharing Activity

You can use Mac OS 8.5 to monitor who is accessing files on your Mac. This is a good practice so that you can understand how often people are accessing your Mac. Remember that any time someone accesses a file from your Mac, the performance of your machine will suffer, depending on the speed of your system and the activity of people accessing your files.

Monitoring sharing activity on your Mac

1. Open the File Sharing control panel.

2. Click the Activity Monitor tab. You will see the Activity Monitor pane (see Figure 21.17). You can use this pane to monitor all of the sharing activity on your Mac. The Sharing Activity bar shows you how much activity is happening at any moment. The Connected Users section shows you the users who are connected to your Mac (you can use the Disconnect button to disconnect a user). The Shared Items section shows you each item that is shared from your Mac. If you select one of the Shared Items folder and click the Privileges button, you will move into the Get Info window for that item.

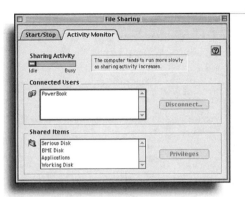

FIGURE 21.17
You can use the Activity Monitor pane of the File Sharing control panel to monitor the sharing activity for your Mac.

3. When you are done, close the control panel.

Accessing Files That Others Share with You

You can also access files that others on your network make available to you. Using someone else's files is even easier than sharing your files with others. The process you use to access shared files is the following:

1. Use the Chooser or the Network Browser to select a drive containing the files that you want to use.

2. Enter your username and password to log onto that shared volume.

3. Mount the volume on your desktop.

4. Use the files that you want to share (what you can do will depend on the permissions you have been assigned).

In previous versions of the Mac OS, you used the Chooser to mount shared volumes on your desktop. In Mac OS 8.5, you can still use the Chooser, but you can also use the new Network Browser to mount shared volumes.

Managing Your Connections with the Chooser

The Chooser enables you to sign onto any volumes to which you have been given sharing privileges.

Accessing shared files by using the Chooser

1. Open the Chooser.

You don't need to use File Sharing to access network volumes

Be aware that you don't need to have File Sharing on for you to be able to access shared volumes on the network. You only need to use File Sharing when you are sharing files on your machine with the network. You can mount network volumes on your Mac while File Sharing is off–assuming that the volumes you want to use allow you access privileges, of course.

Transferring instead of sharing

If you want to transfer a folder or file to your Mac instead of sharing it, simply drag it to one of your volumes just as you would from a floppy or other removable media. The folder or file will be copied to the volume to which you drag it.

2. Click AppleShare. You will see a list of the currently available volumes that you can mount on your desktop (see Figure 21.18).

FIGURE 21.18

This Chooser window shows two volumes that can be shared.

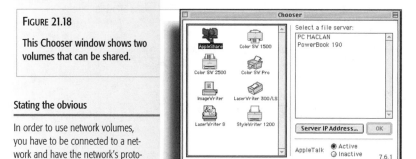

Stating the obvious

In order to use network volumes, you have to be connected to a network and have the network's protocol enabled on your Mac. In this step-by-step, the protocol is AppleTalk, which must be turned on before you will be able to access any network volumes.

3. Click a file server in the Chooser window and click OK (or double-click a file server). You will see the Connect to dialog (see Figure 21.19).

FIGURE 21.19

The Connect to dialog enables you to log onto a file server.

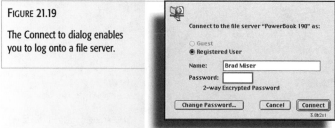

4. Enter the Name and Password that the person who set up File Sharing on that machine provided to you and then click Connect. You will see the items that are available on that file server (see Figure 21.20).

FIGURE 21.20

This filer server has one volume available for file sharing.

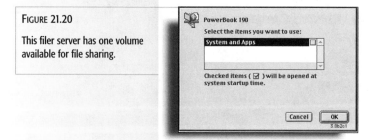

5. Select the volume that you want to mount on your Mac.

6. If you want this volume to be mounted each time you start your Mac, check the box next to the volume you have selected. When you do, you will see some options at the bottom of the window. If you click the Save My Name Only radio button, you will have to enter your password each time your Mac tries to mount the shared item. If you check the Save My Name and Password radio button, your Mac will automatically log on each time you start. The second option is a bit more insecure, but if you are the only one who has access to your Mac, you may want to use it.

7. Click OK. You will move back to the Chooser window. You can continue to mount other volumes if you would like.

8. When you are done, close the Chooser.

9. Move to your desktop, and you will see the volume that you just mounted (see Figure 21.21).

Zones

If there are zones on your AppleTalk network, you will see a Zones window at the bottom of the Chooser window. The Chooser automatically selects your zone when it opens, but if you're curious, you can click around to other zones to see what life is like on the other side of the tracks.

FIGURE 21.21

The System and Apps volume is a shared volume; you can tell by its icon (the cables running out of it indicate that it is a shared item).

You can treat a mounted server just like you'd treat a mounted floppy, Zip disk, or whatever. Double-click on the server's icon to open its window. When you want to terminate your connection to the remote machine, just drag the server's icon into the Trash (or use Command-=).

Managing Your Connections with Network Browser

The Network Browser, which is new to Mac OS 8.5, enables you to connect to various machines on your network. You can also use it to create favorites for quick access to servers, and it presents a consistent interface for network devices.

Using shared files and folders with the Network Browser

1. From the Apple menu, choose Network Browser. The window will open, and you will see all the volumes that are available for sharing (see Figure 21.22).

Putting away shared volumes

You can also "unmount" a shared volume by selecting it and pressing Command-Y (the Put Away command).

AppleShare

When you select a driver in the Chooser, you use AppleShare. AppleShare is the underlying technology that enables your Mac to share files on it, as well as access shared files on the network.

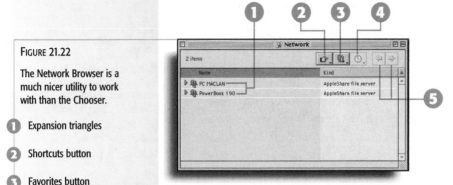

FIGURE 21.22

The Network Browser is a much nicer utility to work with than the Chooser.

1 Expansion triangles

2 Shortcuts button

3 Favorites button

4 Recent button

5 Backward and Forward buttons

2. To log onto a file server, double-click its icon. You will see the Connect to dialog.

3. Enter the name and password that you were assigned by the owner of the shared item and click OK. You will see a window representing the file server that shows all of the volumes of that server that are available for you (see Figure 21.23).

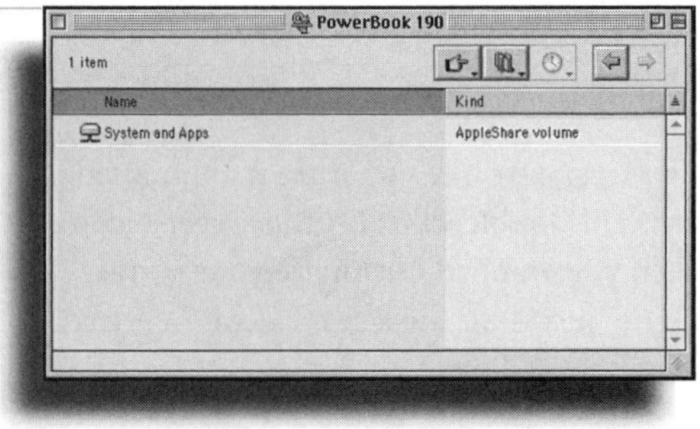

FIGURE 21.23

The Network Browser shows that the System and Apps volume is available on the PowerBook 190 file server.

Aliases to shared items

You can create an alias to any shared item. To access that item, simply double-click its alias. If you haven't saved your name and password for that item, you will be prompted for your password before the item opens. If you have saved your name and password in the Chooser, it will open immediately.

Double-clicking

You can also double-click a shared volume in the Network window to display its contents.

4. Select the volume that you want to mount and close the file server's window. You will see the shared volume on your desktop.

The Network Browser has some nice features, including the following:

- **Expansion triangles**. If you click the expansion triangles next to a file server or volume in the Network window, the item will be expanded (if you aren't logged on, you will have to do so before the item will expand). This works just like a Finder window.

- **Shortcuts button**. This button enables you to access the Network window and the Connect to Server command. The Connect to Server command enables you to connect to an AppleShare server with an Internet Protocol address or a Uniform Resource Locator address.

- **Favorites button**. The Favorites button enables you to add an item to your Favorites folder (on the Apple menu) for quick access. You can also access your favorites by selecting them from this menu.

- **Recent button**. This button enables you to move back to recently used AppleShare volumes.

- **Back and Forward buttons**. These buttons move you back to or forward to previously viewed items.

Working with Files You Share or Receive

Once you have accessed a shared file, you need to determine how to best use the file. There are four options for using files that you share (listed from most likely to result in a usable file to least likely to result in a usable file):

1. If the file was created by an application that you have installed on your Mac, use that application to work with it.

2. If you can share the application that created the file from the network, you may be able to use that shared application to work with the file (you will learn how to do this in the next section).

3. If you have an application that is similar to the one that created the file (for example, WordPerfect for a Word file), try to open the file from within a similar application. Many applications can open files created by other applications in their category (for example, most word processors can open files created by other word processors).

4. If none of the first three options work, your Mac will try to automatically identify the file type of the document and will

---

Changing shared files

Be careful about changing files that you are sharing. If you change a shared file into another file type, other users who need to use the file may have trouble. For example, if you change a WordPerfect file into a Word document, people who don't have Word may have trouble with the file. Before you translate a file or even save it from an application that is different than the one that created it, check with the other users of that file before you change it.

Generic icons

If a shared file has a generic icon (a plain rectangle), that means that the application that created it is not recognized by your Mac. To see which application created the file, open Find from the Finder's File menu. Use the Criteria pop-up menu to choose Creator. Drag the unknown file onto the Find window. You will see the creator code in the Find window. If it is something recognizable, you can get some clues about which application you should try to open that file with. If it isn't, well, at least you tried. You will have to experiment to get it open.

try to open it in an application that you do have. If it can't decide which application to use to try to open the file, you will see a dialog box asking you to choose an application to try to open the file with. That application will be used for all files of that type that you try to open in the future.

Mac OS 8.5's automatic translation might work some of the time, but you are better off trying the first three options first. Those are more likely to result in a usable file.

You can configure how the Mac tries to translate files with the File Exchange control panel.

SEE ALSO

➤ *To learn how to use File Exchange with PC files, see page 497*

Setting translation preferences with File Exchange

1. Open File Exchange.

2. Click the File Translation tab to move to the File Translation pane (see Figure 21.24).

FIGURE 21.24

You use the File Translation pane of the File Exchange control panel to set how your Mac tries to translate files.

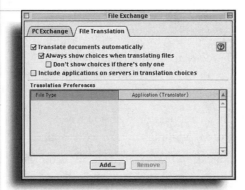

3. Ensure that the "Translate documents automatically" check box is checked.

4. If you want your Mac to always show you choices when it attempts to translate files, check the check box with that title. I recommend this option since you are more likely to pick a good choice than your Mac is.

5. If you want the Mac to automatically proceed with the translation if there is only one possible application that can accomplish it, check the "Don't show choices if there's only one" check box.

6. If you want the Mac to use applications that are shared from a file server on the network, check the "Include applications on servers in translation choices" check box.

7. You can set the translation application that the Mac uses by working through the following steps.

8. Click the Add button in the Translation Preferences area. You will be prompted to select an example file.

9. Choose a file of the type for which you want the Mac to automatically attempt a translation. For example, if you want the Mac to translate a Zip file (a file compressed for the PC) with StuffIt Expander (the Mac's decompression utility), find a Zip file and click Continue. Your Mac will search for all possible applications that it believes may be able to translate this file type (see Figure 21.25).

FIGURE 21.25

This list shows the applications that your Mac thinks it can use to open the file type you selected as an example.

10. Select the application that you want the Mac to use to translate files of this type in the future and click OK. When you return to the File Translation window, you will see that this file type is now associated with the translator application that you selected. From now on, the Mac will use that application to try to open files of that type.

11. Repeat for other files types that you need to translate.

12. When you are done, close the control panel.

Copying an application rather than sharing it

If you can access an application's files over your network, you can copy those files to your hard disk and run the application from there. You have to make sure that you copy all the files associated with the application, especially those stored in the System Folder of the machine on which the application is stored. If you do this, make sure that you remove the application from your machine as soon as you are done with it. Also make sure that you are not violating the license agreement for that application by copying it to your drive. If your network is entitled to only one copy, running more than one at the same time is illegal.

Network email

Another advantage of having a local network is that you can set up an email system for that network. This enables you to easily communicate with all of the people on that network. Of course, if everyone on the network already has an Internet or email account, there is not much value to setting up an additional email system.

Sharing Applications

If you are on a network, you can use applications that you don't have, but that reside on other machines on the network. This is called *sharing an application*. The application that you share uses the RAM and system resources of your machine, but the preference settings of the network copy the other machine (for example, if you share Word, the toolbars and other customizations would reflect the settings used on the volume containing the copy of Word you are running).

There are a few disadvantages to sharing an application. First of all, the application runs more slowly, much more slowly, in fact. Depending on the speed of the network and the amount of traffic on the network, the application may slow down a little, or it may become impossibly slow. Second, only one Mac can use the remote application at any time; you can't have five different users all running the same copy of Microsoft Word. Third, using shared applications places an additional load on the network. If your network is on the edge of stability already, the additional load can push it over the edge and result in network crashes and other problems.

To share an application, simply locate it on a server and double-click it to run it or drag it to your hard drive to run it locally.

Sharing the Web

In addition to sharing files and folders, Mac OS 8.5 enables you to set up and share Web pages on your network, as well as on the Internet. On your local network, you can post a Web site for particular projects, post your company procedures, provide resources that your coworkers need, and so on. Using a local Web is an excellent way to provide access to resources and information to groups of people.

You can also use your Mac to serve Web pages on the Internet.

Mac OS 8.5 provides all the tools you need to set up your Mac as a Web server. The Mac's Web sharing capability is analogous to its File Sharing capability, and you can use the Web Sharing control panel to set up your Mac as a Web server.

Using your Mac as a Web server is more complicated than using it as a file server, though. You need to understand the Web, as well as some of the intricacies of the Internet. This subject is beyond the scope of this book. If you want to explore this on your own, you can use the Mac's Help System to get started.

Working with Windows PCs

Transferring and sharing files among PCs and Macs

Working with PC files

Running Windows applications

Living in a Windows World

As a Mac user, you are no doubt aware that a lot more people use computers that aren't Macs than there are who use Macs. That is unfortunate for them (not to show my pro-Mac bias too much!), but it also means that you need to know how to work with other platforms, especially Windows PCs. Windows PCs dominate the computing world, for better or worse, and that isn't going to change anytime soon. Fortunately, your Mac provides the tools you need to live peacefully in a Windows-dominated world.

Working with Windows PCs basically involves moving files to and from PCs, using Windows files, or running Windows applications.

Moving Files from PCs to Macs and Back Again

The most common interaction that you will have with Windows PCs is using files that were created or modified on a PC. Before you can work with PC files, you have to get those files onto your Mac, and you may also need to provide files to PC users. There are several ways to do this.

Using Sneakernet to Transfer Files

Hush puppy networks

Sneakernet refers to a "network" on which files are moved by carrying a disk from one computer to another.

PC Exchange

In the previous versions of the Mac OS, the PC Exchange control panel enabled your Mac to work with PC-formatted disks. Under Mac OS 8.5, the function of PC Exchange has been incorporated into the File Exchange control panel.

Since the Mac can mount and use PC-formatted disks, including floppy disks, Zip disks, and other removable media, you can use good old sneakernet to transfer files to and from your Mac. With previous versions of the Mac OS, you had to configure your Mac to recognize PC disks. With Mac OS 8.5, this function is built into your system and is always "on." You can work with a PC-formatted disk just like you work with Mac-formatted disks.

Since you will also be providing Mac files to PC users, you need to be able to format a disk in the PC format so that Windows machines can read them.

Formatting a PC disk on the Mac

1. Insert the disk that you want to format in your Mac. If it has been formatted previously, it will be mounted on your desktop. If it hasn't, you will be prompted to format it (if so, skip to step 4).

2. Select the disk.

3. From the Special menu, choose Erase Disk. You will see the erase disk dialog (see Figure 22.1).

It is not just for floppies anymore

You can format other removable disks such as Zip and Jaz disks as well as floppy disks.

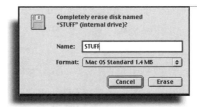

FIGURE 22.1

This erase disk dialog enables you to erase and format a floppy disk.

4. Name the disk if you want to.

5. Choose the format that you want to use to format the disk from the Format pop-up menu. For Windows disks, choose DOS 1.4 MB.

6. Click Erase. You will see a progress window telling you that your Mac is erasing the disk. When it is done, you will see the disk that you named on the desktop. If you formatted the disk with the DOS 1.4 MB format, the disk's icon will indicate that it is a PC disk (see Figure 22.2). You can now use this disk to provide files to PC users.

FIGURE 22.2

This floppy has been formatted to be a PC disk.

Using Email to Transfer Files

Attaching files to email is also an excellent way to exchange files with PC users. There are only a couple of things you need to keep in mind when sending files to and from a PC: the first is encoding and the second is compression.

When a file is attached to an email message, the file is actually converted into a plain text file for transmission over the Net. When the file is received by the recipient, it is converted back into a usable file. This process is called *encoding*. You need to be aware that PCs use different encoding schemes than Macs do. Macs primarily use the encoding method called *binhex* ,while PCs use *uucode* and *base64* encoding. You don't need to understand the details of how these encoding techniques work, you simply need to know how to use the encoding method that is appropriate for the person to whom you are sending the file. Fortunately, Mac email applications enable you to choose the encoding method you use for email attachments.

SEE ALSO

➤ *To learn about attaching files to email for PC users, see page 587*

The other thing you need to understand when sending files to and receiving files from PC users with email is that most files sent over the Net are *compressed*. When a file is compressed, it becomes smaller, and thus takes less time to send over slow connections. PCs and Macs use different compression techniques to compress and decompress files. Macs use the StuffIt format to compress and uncompress files while PCs use the Zip format. There are tools on each platform to enable them to work with the other platform's compression formats.

SEE ALSO

➤ *To learn how to uncompress zipped files, see page 587*

Using a Network to Transfer Files

Macs and PCs can be networked together in a variety of ways. For the purpose of this book, however, I will focus on two general ways of networking Macs and PC—one is non-Mac based and the other is Mac-based.

Macs can be added to non-Mac based networks in a variety of ways. For example, the fastest growing networking strategies are based on Windows NT servers. Windows NT provides services that enable a Mac to connect and use a Windows NT network (these services are called, cleverly enough, *Services for Macintosh*, or SFM). SFM enables Mac clients on a Windows network to

---

Using the Internet to network Macs and PCs

One of the easiest ways to network Macs and PCs is to use the Internet. On the Internet, you can work with PCs (and other platforms for that matter) as easily as you can with other Macs because all the machines speak the same language (TCP/IP). For example, you can easily transfer files by using the Web. There are some differences in the details, such as how files are compressed and what file formats are used, but you can usually handle almost anything you run into with the basic Mac tools.

use the Mac's File and Print Sharing capabilities to share network resources with Windows machines. These networks can also use add-on tools to provide Mac services if the network administrator does not want to use SFM. If you are connecting your Mac to a non-Mac based network, see the system administrator for that network to learn how to get your Mac on the network.

PCs can also be added to Mac-based networks. In order to do so, the PC must have the hardware and software needed to connect to and use a Mac-based network.

PCs can also use Ethernet or LocalTalk to connect to an AppleTalk network. One difference between Macs and PCs is that PCs require additional hardware to be able to network with other computers, while all Macs have LocalTalk networking hardware built-in. You can add an Ethernet card to a PC's PCI card slot to enable it to connect to an Ethernet network. To enable a PC to connect to a LocalTalk network, you need to add a LocalTalk adapter to it; some LocalTalk adapters attach to the PC's parallel port while others are installed in a PC's PCI slot.

After the PC is connected to your AppleTalk network, you need to install software to enable your PC to "speak" AppleTalk. The best solution for this is Miramar System's PC MACLAN Connect. PC MACLAN Connect enables the PC to do the following:

- Share files with the Macs—Mac users can mount PC drives just like they mount other Mac drives.
- Use files shared by Macs on the network—PC users can mount Mac disks on their desktops.
- Print to printers on the network.
- Use tape drives and other network resources.

Using PC MACLAN Connect is straightforward and works very similarly to the Mac's native File Sharing capability.

LocalTalk adapter

Apexx Technology's PCTalk Adapter installs onto a PC's parallel port and enables your PC to connect to an AppleTalk network. This costs less than $160 and can be installed in less than five minutes.

Getting PC MACLAN Connect

You can download a demo version of PC MACLAN Connect from Miramar's Web site at `http://www.miramarsys.com/`.

Groups

PC MACLAN enables you to create groups of users just like Users & Groups on the Mac does.

Using PC MACLAN Connect to share PC files on a Mac network

1. Install PC MACLAN on the PC that is attached to the AppleTalk network.

2. Launch PC MACLAN. You will see the PC MACLAN console (see Figure 22.3).

FIGURE 22.3

You can set up file sharing on the PC by using the PC MACLAN console.

3. From the Configure menu, choose Users & Groups. You will see the Users & Groups dialog (see Figure 22.4).

FIGURE 22.4

You use PC MACLAN's Users & Groups dialog to define users and groups that can share files on your PC.

4. Click New. You will see the User dialog (see Figure 22.5).

5. Set the Attributes that you want this user to have when he signs onto the network. Use the check boxes to do this (see Figure 22.6).

6. Enter the user's network name.

7. Click Set Password.

8. In the Set password dialog, enter the password twice and click OK.

FIGURE 22.5
The User dialog enables you to define a new user for file sharing on the PC.

FIGURE 22.6
PC MACLAN's User dialog enables you to set privilege attributes for a new user.

9. Click OK to close the User window.

10. Click Done to close the Users & Groups dialog.

11. From the Configure menu, choose Share Directories. You will see the Share Directories dialog (see Figure 22.7).

FIGURE 22.7
You use the Share Directories dialog to set which volumes or folders on the PC will be shared on the network.

12. In the top pane of the window, choose the drive that contains the items that you want to share.

13. In the middle pane, select the particular folders that you want to share and click Share. You will see the Shared Directory dialog (see Figure 22.8).

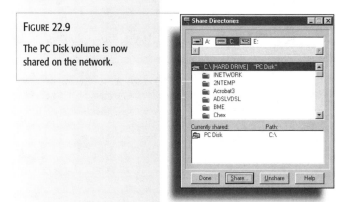

14. In the Seen As field, enter the name that will be shown when the item is mounted on a Mac user's machine.

15. Use the Privileges pane to set the sharing for the Owner, Group, and Everyone. This works just like the Sharing pane of the Get Info window on the Mac.

16. When you are done, click OK. The shared items will be shown in the bottom pane of the Share Directories window (see Figure 22.9).

17. Click Done to close the Share Directories window. You will return to the PC MACLAN Console.

18. From the Server menu, choose Start Server. After a few moments, PC MACLAN will begin serving the shared items to the network and Macs will be able to mount the shared volumes (see Figure 22.10).

FIGURE 22.10
The PC Disk volume is actually on a PC on the network, but it can be used just like it is a Mac disk.

As this simple example shows, PC MACLAN enables PCs on your network to act just like the Macs on your network. The PCs will also be able to share printers and other network resources (such as tape back-up drives), as well as the Macs on the network do.

Using Windows Files

Once you have a PC file on your Mac, you need to know what to do with it. That requires that you understand the fundamental differences between Mac and PC files.

Understanding Windows Files

When you double-click a file on the Mac, it uses the desktop database and the file's File Type and Creator code to know which application should be launched to work with that file; the File Type and Creator codes are stored in the Resource fork of every Mac file. This is elegant because you don't have to do anything to tell your Mac about the application it should use to work with a particular file. That means less work and complexity for you. That is good.

SEE ALSO

➤ *To learn more about the Mac's desktop database and the structure of Mac files, see page 715.*

File icons

Your Mac also uses its desktop database to apply an icon to a file. Your Mac looks at the File Type and Creator for a file and then uses its desktop database to know what kind of icon to apply to that file based on the application that created it. If you don't have the application that created the file installed on your Mac, your Mac doesn't have an icon to apply, and you get the famous generic file icon.

Extensions don't have to be valid

Windows assumes that the last three characters of a file's name are the extension, whether it actually is or not. You can use anything as an extension. Of course, if you use an extension to which Windows does not have an application mapped, the PC won't know what to do with a file when you try to open it.

Windows files, on the other hand, do not have anything equivalent to a Mac file's resource fork. And Windows does not use a desktop database to keep track of the link between files and their applications. Windows links a file to its application by the three-character *filename extension*, more commonly referred to as simply the *extension*, that is appended to the end of every Windows file's names; the extension is separated from the filename by a period (as in filename.ext). When you open a file on a Windows PC, the OS looks at the extension on the file and uses the association map it has to figure out which application it should use to open the file. If there is no extension on a file, Windows doesn't know what to do with the file.

Table 22.1 shows some examples of Windows file extensions and what they mean.

Windows and file icons

Windows applies icons to files also based on the file's extension. As you change a file's extension, Windows will change the file's icon. This doesn't actually change anything about the file, though. For example, if you change the extension on an Excel file to *.doc*, which is the extension for Word files, the file's icon will change to a Word icon. The file is still an Excel file, but if you open it, Windows will try to use Word.

TABLE 22.1   Some Examples of Windows Filename Extensions

Extension	What it means
.exe	Application file
.doc	Word file
.xls	Excel spreadsheet
.htm	HTML file (viewed with Web browser)
.ppt	PowerPoint file
.mpp	Project file
.pdf	Portable document format (viewed with Acrobat Reader)
.tif	Tagged Image File format
.gif	Graphic Interchange Format
.fp3	FileMaker Pro database
.zip	File compressed in the Zip format
.pm6	PageMaker document

Providing Mac Files for the PC

When you create a file that you will provide to PC users, you need to ensure that the appropriate extension is added to the filename. This can be problematic for you if you don't use

Windows yourself since you don't have to worry about extensions on the Mac, and it is hard to remember to add them sometimes. But if you don't, the recipient of that file may not be able to work with it. When you save a file that will at some point be used by a PC user, ensure that you add the appropriate file extension before you pass it to a PC user. The best time to add the extension is when you are naming the file for the first time. If you regularly collaborate with PC users, you should get in the habit of adding extensions to all your filenames so that it becomes a habit for you that you don't even have to think about.

Being a Mac user, you probably aren't all that familiar with many of the PC filename extensions that are out there. That can make it hard to apply the appropriate extension to your files. There are several sources of information on file extensions. You can check the manual and online help system with the application that you are using; if the application has a Windows version, you will probably find information on which extensions to use for that application. If you don't find the information you need, you can search for it on the Web.

SEE ALSO

➤ *To learn about searching the Web, see page 639*

For example, the site at `http://wwwf.rrz.unikoeln.de/themen/Graphik/ImageProcessing/fileext.html` provides an extensive list of filename extensions (see Figure 22.11).

Working with PC Files on Your Mac

When you receive a file from a PC user, you need to open it with an application. Since the file is not a Mac file, and thus won't have a Creator code, your Mac won't be able to tell what application it needs to use to open the file in the same way that it can for Mac files. Mac OS 8.5 recognizes the most common PC file extensions and automatically opens the correct application to work with them. And if your Mac comes across an extension that it doesn't recognize automatically, you can use the File Exchange control panel to associate a file extension with a particular application.

You may not see the whole thing

Under Windows 95/98, you can set the views so that you don't see the filename extensions when viewing files. If a Windows PC is set up this way, the filenames *look* just like they do on the Mac. You see just the text name of the file without the period or filename extension. However, the file extensions are still there and are part of each file's name. The same thing is true within Windows applications. When you name a file, you don't have to add the extension. The application will add it for you, based on the format in which you save the file.

FIGURE 22.11

This Web site provides an extensive list of filename extensions for PC files.

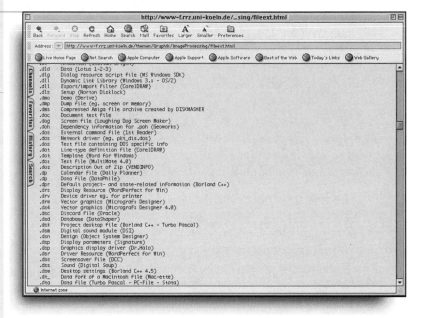

Change mappings

To change a current map, select it and click Change. You will see the Change Mapping dialog, which works just like the Add Mapping dialog does.

Configuring File Exchange to enable your Mac to work with PC files

   1. Open the File Exchange control panel and click the PC Exchange tab so that you see the PC Exchange pane (see Figure 22.12).

FIGURE 22.12

The PC Exchange pane enables you to map PC filename extensions to Mac applications.

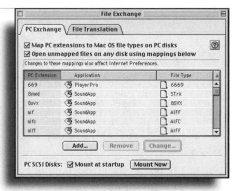

   2. Leave the "Map PC extensions to Mac OS file types on PC disks" and "Open unmapped files on any disk using mappings below" check boxes checked. These settings enable

your Mac to automatically recognize PC files by their extensions.

3. If you come across an extension for which your Mac does not recognize the correct application, click Add. Your Mac will search for all of the applications on all the disks mounted on your Mac. You will see the Add Mapping dialog (see Figure 22.13).

FIGURE 22.13
The Add Mapping dialog enables you to map Mac applications to PC file extensions.

4. Enter the extension that you want to map in the Extension field.

5. From the Application pane, select the application that you want to use to open this file type (see Figure 22.14).

FIGURE 22.14
I have used the Add Mapping dialog to map Zip files to StuffIt Expander.

6. Click Add. Your mapping will be shown in the mappings window (see Figure 22.15).

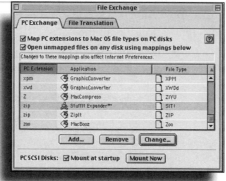

7. If there is already an extension map for the extension (notice that there are two maps for the Zip extension in Figure 22.15), select the old map and click Remove; then click OK in the warning dialog.

8. Close the control panel. From now on, when you try to open a file with the extension that you mapped, the Mac application to which you mapped the extension will be used to open the file (in this step-by-step, the application StuffIt Expander will be used to open files that have *.zip* as their extension.)

When you receive a PC file from any source, try the following in order to use it:

1. Double-click the file. If the file opens in one of your Mac applications and it looks OK, you are all set to work.

2. If the file doesn't open at all or doesn't open properly, try opening it from within the appropriate application.

3. If that doesn't work, try opening it from within another similar application.

4. If you aren't able to successfully open the file with any of your applications, try translating it with a translation utility such as DataViz's MacLinks Plus.

5. If all else fails, ask the person who created the file to try saving it in another format and try again. It sometimes takes a little experimentation to get the file to open properly, especially if you haven't worked with that type of file before. For the most popular applications, though, double-clicking will usually work.

Running Windows Applications

In addition to working with PC files, you may need to work with PC applications. There are several situations in which you may need to run a PC application:

- The application may not have a Mac version available or the Mac version may be out-of-date.

- The Windows version of an application may offer a feature that you need but that is not yet part of the Mac version of the application.

- Your client or boss may insist that you use the Windows version of the application.

There are three basic ways to run Windows applications.

Using Windows Emulators

A *Windows emulator* is an application that you install and run on your Mac that creates a Windows environment in which you can run Windows applications. There are two Windows emulators currently available. One is Insignia Solutions SoftWindows. The other is Connectix Virtual PC. Both of these work similarly to enable you to run Windows applications.

While being able to use a software-based solution has the advantage of being inexpensive and easy to install and use, Windows emulators suffer from a significant problem: speed (or more clearly, the lack thereof). Because Windows emulators are software-based, everything they do is done in software. And software is slower than hardware. Plus, the Windows emulator is stacked on top of everything else that is happening on your Mac. This

Emulator Web sites

You can learn more about SoftWindows by visiting the Insignia Web site at `http://www.insignia.com/`.

You can learn more about Virtual PC by visiting the Connectix Web site at `http://www.connectix.com/`.

Copy and paste

You can copy text and graphics from the Windows desktop to your Mac applications and from Mac applications to Windows applications running in SoftWindows.

makes Windows emulators fairly slow. In fact, unless you have the latest and most powerful Mac, you may find the speed at which Windows applications run under an emulator to be almost unusable. Still, if you need to run a Windows application only occasionally, or if you have a fairly new and powerful Mac, an emulator may be your most cost-efficient choice.

Insignia Solutions SoftWindows is an excellent Windows emulator and is easy to install and run on your Mac. The following step-by-step shows you how SoftWindows works.

Running Windows applications on a Mac with SoftWindows

1. Install SoftWindows on your Mac. The installer creates a single file that is used to store all of the software that relates to Windows (you need at least 170 MB of room, but you should use more if you want to install additional applications, which is the point after all).

2. Run SoftWindows. After the application launches, you will see a Windows desktop (see Figure 22.16).

FIGURE 22.16

Is it Windows or a Mac–the answer is Yes (notice the Mac desktop and menu bar peaking out behind the Windows desktop).

3. Install the Windows applications that you want to run just as you would if you were using a real PC. Things will work a bit more slowly than they would on a real PC, but they *will* work, and you will be able to use Windows applications.

Installing a PC Card in Your Mac

In order to run Windows applications on your Mac with the speed of a "real" PC, you may be able to add a PC card to your Mac. A PC card contains all of the major hardware subsystems of a PC. You can run this card simultaneously with Mac OS 8.5 so that you can run Windows applications right on your Mac's desktop. You can easily switch between the Windows environment and the Mac.

PC cards are much faster than a Windows emulator, but they are also considerably more expensive. And depending on your Mac, you may or may not be able to install a PC card in your Mac. Orange Micro makes a relatively affordable line of PC cards (beginning at $499) that enable you to have both a PC and a Mac inside your Mac. Apple has made PC compatibility cards, but the Apple cards had very limited applicability and were also expensive (a bad combination in my book). A few Mac models came with the PC card installed.

Most of the Orange Micro PC cards can be installed in the PCI slots in your Mac. You can visit the Orange Micro Web site to learn if your Mac can support an Orange Micro PC card.

Buying a "Real" PC

One of the reasons that Windows PCs have dominated the computing world is that PCs cost less than Macs. While you have to add components to most PCs to match the equivalent Mac models, they still are less expensive. In fact, you can buy a complete PC system (including a monitor) for $1,000. If you need to run Windows applications regularly and you can afford the additional cost, buying a separate PC may make the most sense. Not only will you get excellent performance, but you will also have the benefit of a separate system so that you can work on the PC

More on Orange Micro PC cards

You can visit Orange Micro's Web site at `http://www.orangemicro.internet/`.

An example of Mac and PC bliss

A good example of accomplishing a project by using a PC and a Mac at the time same time is this book. I wrote the book on a PC using Microsoft Word while I was using my Mac to run Mac OS 8.5. I have these machines on an AppleTalk network along with a PowerBook, printer, tape drive, and so on.

and the Mac at the same time. You will have the best of both worlds. When a Windows application is the best tool for the job, you can use it. When the Mac application is the best tool, you can use it. You can even work on them simultaneously. Plus, the systems will back each other up. If one goes down, you can work on the other until the down machine is up and running again. As you learned earlier in this chapter, you can network your PC to your Mac network so that you can easily move files back and forth, and you can use your Mac's printer and other resources.

Fighting PC Viruses

Just as there are lots more PCs than there are Macs, there are also lots more PC viruses than there are Mac viruses.

PC viruses that affect documents or macros stored with documents (such as the infamous Word macro viruses) will infect your Mac if you use the Mac version of the application to open the infected file. For example, if a Word document created on the PC is infected with the Concept macro virus, and you open it on your Mac using Word, you get infected (unless you are taking the proper precautions of course). You need to follow the same anti-virus strategies for PC files that you do for Mac files.

SEE ALSO
➤ *To learn how to protect your Mac against viruses, see Chapter 30, "Fighting Viruses"*

PC viruses that are in PC applications (called executables on Windows machines) can't affect your Mac because your Mac can't run a PC application.

If you use an emulator or a PC card to run Windows on your Mac, PC viruses can affect your Windows files just as if you were running a real PC. If you are going to be receiving files on the PC side of your Mac, you also need to install and use a good anti-virus program in your Windows environment.

PART

V

Using Your Mac to Surf the Internet

23 **Connecting Your Mac to the Net 509**

24 **Using Email: The Basics 543**

25 **Using Email: Advanced Techniques 573**

26 **Browsing the Web: The Basics 597**

27 **Browsing the Web: Advanced Techniques 627**

28 **Reading Newsgroups 661**

Connecting Your Mac to the Net

Understanding the Internet and how it works

Understanding Mac OS 8.5 Internet software

Connecting your Mac to the Net through a network

Connecting your Mac to the Net with a modem by using an existing Internet account

Connecting your Mac to the Net with a modem and obtaining a new Internet account

Connecting to and disconnecting from the Net

Understanding the Internet—It's Not Just a Lot of Hype

The Internet is one of the most significant social and economic movements—it is a movement as much as it is technology—in human history. In just a few years, the Internet (or more simply, the Net) has moved from an obscure scientific and government computer network to become a dominant means of global and local communication, commerce, entertainment, and information management. The Net empowers individuals to act on a global basis by interacting with other individuals, as well as governments, businesses, and other organizations. The Net has already become integrated into many people's daily lives; for example, you can hardly read or hear anything without seeing an Internet address connected to it. For many people, the Internet has become the first stop whenever they are looking for information, products, or relationships. It doesn't take Nostradamus to predict that the Net will continue to be more and more intertwined with our daily lives.

Fortunately, your Mac is an ideal vehicle for you to use to put yourself on the Net.

Net equals Internet

Throughout this book, I'll use the term Net interchangeably with Internet. They mean the same thing.

Connecting to the Net with the Mac's Internet Setup Assistant

You can use the Internet Setup Assistant to set up an Internet account on your machine (see Figure 23.1). If you do not have an Internet account, the Assistant can help you get one and configure your machine for it. If you already have an account, you can use the Assistant to help you configure Mac OS 8.5 to work with your existing account.

Understanding Email

One of the best things about the Internet is electronic mail (email). With email, you can communicate your thoughts, ideas, and feelings just as you do with regular mail. But, unlike regular mail, email is transmitted almost instantly.

FIGURE 23.1
The Internet Setup Assistant can help you configure your Mac to surf the Net.

Email has several other advantages that make it an indispensable part of the Internet. For example, through email you can send all sorts of files directly from one computer to another, regardless of the distance. Plus, it's more convenient than regular mail (and cheaper!). You can send email from your computer with a click of the mouse for a lot less than the price of a stamp. And the Internet is always open. So there's no worrying about holidays or mail delivery times.

You can also send multiple messages as easily as you can send one. Want to send a message to your whole project team? Write one message and send it to everyone at the same time.

SEE ALSO
➤ *To learn how to use the basics of email see Chapter 24, "Using Email: The Basics"*
➤ *To learn more about email, see Chapter 25, "Using Email: Advanced Techniques"*

Newsgroups are electronic discussions among Internet users on any topic under the sun (and some that are better left in the dark). Newsgroups are similar to a radio talk show—you can be a participant or merely an eavesdropper. These newsgroups include discussions about politics, religion, news events, entertainment, music, education, computers, and much more. In fact, there are literally tens of thousands of active newsgroups!

SEE ALSO
➤ *To learn how to read and post to newsgroups, see Chapter 28, "Reading Newsgroups"*

Mac OS 8.5 includes Microsoft's Outlook Express as its default email program (see Figure 23.2). With Outlook Express you can create, send, read, and organize your email. You can also use Outlook Express to read newsgroups.

Another one bites the dust

Before the $150 Million dollar deal between Apple and Microsoft, Claris Emailer was the default email program for the Mac OS. Claris no longer exists (the company formerly known as Claris now focuses exclusively on FileMaker Pro and is called FileMaker Inc.). At press time, the future of Emailer is uncertain, but many Mac users continue to use it anyway.

FIGURE 23.2

Outlook Express is an excellent email program that also enables you to read Internet newsgroups.

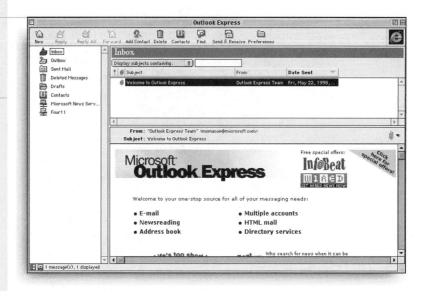

Understanding the World Wide Web

The World Wide Web (referred to simply as the Web) is the biggest and fastest growing part of the Internet. It is the most difficult to describe—although it is also the easiest to use. The Web enables you to access seemingly unlimited information in a variety of formats, including text, graphics, sound, and video. This information is all linked together so that you can move easily from one point to another via a weblike structure (thus the name). The best part is that all you have to do to move around is to click on well-marked links. For example, while you are reading something or looking at an image, you may come across an underlined word. Click on that word, and you will be taken to a different place on the same site, or to another Web site entirely, that has information related to the item you clicked on. Of course, you can also move directly to specific sites if you want to.

A few examples of the types of Web sites you can find are the following:

- **Company Web sites**. Find out what is happening with specific companies, place orders, get help, and so forth.

- **Government Web sites**. Access information that is gathered by the government (using your tax dollars, of course). Some of the best of these are NASA sites where you can see all kinds of fantastic images from space.

- **Educational Web sites**. Get information from some of the largest and most well-known academic and scientific institutions in the world.

- **Magazines**. Access articles and exhibits online.

- **Topical Web sites**. Explore a variety of topics, such as aviation, history, biology, and much more.

- **Personal Web pages**. Read and enjoy these sites, which are created by people like you who have something that they want to say to the world.

This list only scratches the surface of the Web, but hopefully you get the idea.

FTP (File Transfer Protocol) may be one of the most compelling reasons to be on the Net; FTP is the electronic transfer of computer files over the Internet. There are thousands of FTP sites around the world that you can access on the Web and that enable you to access millions of files that you can download (transfer) to your computer and then use.

SEE ALSO

➤ *To learn the basics of how to use the Web, see Chapter 26, "Browsing the Web: The Basics"*

➤ *To learn even more about the Web, see Chapter 27, "Browsing the Web: Advanced Techniques"*

Mac OS 8.5 comes with Microsoft's Internet Explorer version 4.01 as the default Web browser. Internet Explorer is one of two major Web browsers available on the Mac (the other is Netscape Navigator). Internet Explorer is a full-featured browser that offers a number of powerful features to make your Web browsing a great experience (see Figure 23.3).

Jargon Ho!

By the way (commonly abbreviated BTW on the Internet), you've probably noticed that there is some jargon associated with the Internet. Many of these terms, such as BTW, are easy to understand. Others are more confusing. Don't worry, though, you'll catch on quickly. Here are a few more to get you started. FWIW is For What It Is Worth. LOL is Laughing Out Loud. ROTFL is Rolling On The Floor Laughing. IMHO is IN MY Humble Opinion.

Remember when…

With Mac OS 8 and earlier versions, Netscape Navigator was the default Web browser. Internet Explorer replaced it as one part of the famous $150 Million Microsoft investment in Apple in the summer of 1997.

Using Navigator

While Netscape Navigator is no longer the Mac's default Web browser, it is still included on the Mac OS 8.5 installation CD. There is no reason that you can't install it from the CD and try it for yourself. To install Navigator, run the Install Mac OS 8.5 application, use the Customize option, and then choose the Customized Installation option for the Internet Access software. Check the Netscape Navigator check box and continue with the install. Netscape Navigator version 4.05 will be installed on your Mac. See Appendix A, "Installing and Maintaining the Mac OS," for more information on running the installer to install components.

FIGURE 23.3

Microsoft's Internet Explorer is a full-featured Web browser that comes with Mac OS 8.5.

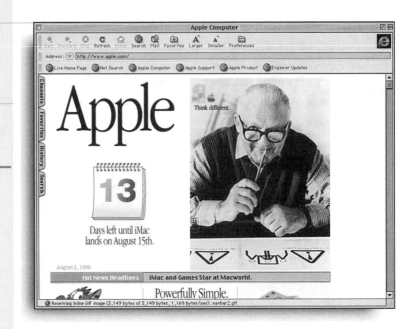

FIGURE 23.3

Microsoft's Internet Explorer is a full-featured Web browser that comes with Mac OS 8.5.

Choosing the browser that is right for you

Since you have a choice of browsers, which should you use? That depends on your personal preferences. Frankly, they both work similarly. The differences between them are relatively minor, and if you can use one, you can use the other with just a little exploration. You may end up using them both at certain times. After you are comfortable using Internet Explorer, I suggest that you give Navigator a try and see which browser you prefer.

Hey, let's be careful out there!

You need to know that, for now at least, the Internet is not regulated. Just like many things in life, that's good and that's bad. It's good because nobody can tell you what you can see, say, or do on the Net. That's also bad because there are a lot of things that aren't worth the electrons they use. Fortunately, it is easy to avoid the things in which you don't want to participate. If you stumble on a site you don't like, don't go there again.

For adults this is not a big problem, assuming that we can control ourselves. There is some danger for children, though, so please be careful about giving your kids unmonitored access to the Net. Just like television or movies or any other material, it's up to us parents to protect our kids as we see fit.

Understanding How the Internet Works

Although you don't need to understand the technical aspects of the Net in order to use it, you do need to have a grasp of the basic processes involved. Think of using the Internet as driving a car; you don't need to understand the inner workings of the engine, but you do need to know how to put the key in the ignition to start it. In the following sections, you will learn everything you need to know to become part of the Net.

Using a Computer and Modem (or Network)

In order to use the Internet, you need a computer and a modem (or a network connection). Yes, this may be obvious to you, but it is the place to start.

If you can run Mac OS 8.5, your computer is capable of doing most of the things you will find to do on the Net. The faster machine you have, the faster certain actions will happen, but your processor and graphics systems are not the limiting factor when it comes to speed. You will need plenty of RAM to run Internet applications. You will also need a fair amount of disk space to store all of the files that you will download.

You also need a modem. If you bought your computer fairly recently, you probably got a modem with it. If not, you can buy one separately.

The only real question you need to think about modems is how fast they are, or more importantly, how fast yours is. Speed is an essential factor in your enjoyment of the Internet, particularly when you are using the Web and FTP. If you have to wait a long time between activities, you aren't likely to enjoy it very much.

If you just bought your modem (or it came with your new Mac), it is probably a 56K modem (short for 56,600 bits per second). If your modem is just fairly new, it will probably be a 28.8 (short for 28,800 bits per second) or 33.6 (33,600 bits per second) modem. These numbers indicate how fast the modem communicates. For example, a 33.6 modem is faster than a 28.8.

How fast does your modem have to be to use the Internet? It depends on your tolerance for waiting. I don't enjoy waiting so I find my 28.8 modem to be barely acceptable. A 33.6 modem is better, and a 56K modem makes you feel as if you are flying.

If your Mac is wired into a business' Local-Area Network (LAN) or a Wide-Area Network (WAN), you won't need a modem. You more than likely will connect through a direct connection of some type such as a T1 line. If so, consider yourself lucky. Data will download for you almost instantaneously.

Understanding Internet Service Providers

The Internet is big. Millions of computers located all over the planet. You'd think with something this big, it would be easy to get to it, right? Wrong. There are only certain points through which you can enter the Internet; you have to get on the Internet through specific kinds of hardware and software.

Fortunately, there are many *Internet Service Providers* (ISPs) around. An ISP provides a place for you to connect to the

Modem?

The modem—MOdeulator DEModulator just in case you were wondering—acts like a translator between your computer and the telephone line. Your computer doesn't speak "telephonelinese" which is an analog signal. Your telephone line doesn't speak "computerese" which is digital. The modem helps your computer speak "telephonelinese" and your telephone line speak "computerese."

If your Mac is on a network

If your Mac is part of a Local-Area Network or a Wide-Area Network that is directly connected to the Net, much of the setup and configuration information in this chapter will not apply to you. You should rely on your network administrator to make sure that your Mac can get on the Net. Continue reading this chapter until you finish the section called, "Connecting Through a Network." Then skip the rest of this chapter and move on to the next chapter, which covers email.

Internet. This makes it possible for you to connect via your Mac and modem instead of having to be directly connected to the Internet.

In order to access the Net, you need an account with an ISP. You, and you alone, connect through this account. In exchange for this service, you must pay the ISP a fee of one sort or another—usually a monthly fee for a certain number of hours of connect time or perhaps for unlimited access time. It can be complicated to find an ISP and get an account. But the Mac OS contains software that will help you find a provider if you don't have one already.

If you are on a network that has direct Net access, you won't need an ISP either. You will get access through your organization.

Username and Password

Your Internet account is controlled by a username and password. The username is your identification while you are on the Internet. The password is a code that makes it much more difficult for someone other than you to access your account through your username.

Understanding Connection Software

After you have an account with your ISP, you need software that calls your provider and logs in to your account. Think of this step as connecting wire between your telephone and the jack in the wall. After this is connected, you can use the phone. In this case, the phone is your computer/modem, the wall jack is the ISP, and the wire is the connecting software.

This software is built into the Mac OS. It is called Open Transport PPP, and you use the Remote Access control panel and Remote Access Status to connect to and disconnect from the Net.

Understanding Internet Software

When you are connected to the Internet, you need software to use the services available, such as email, the Web, FTP, and so on.

Mac OS 8.5 also comes with all of the software you need to email, browse the Web, read newsgroups, and other Net activities.

Understanding Mac OS 8.5's Internet Software

There are a lot of different Mac OS 8.5 components that are used to set up and connect to an Internet account. If the Internet Assistant is able to configure your account, which is the most likely scenario, you won't need to bother with many of these pieces of software directly. Still, you should know that they are here in case you have trouble or want to modify your account later. The Net software that your Mac uses to connect to the Net is the following:

- **Internet Setup Assistant**. This software walks you through the process of configuring your Mac for Net access. If you don't have an Internet account, you can get one through the Assistant. The Setup Assistant is located in the Internet Setup folder that is within the Internet Utilities folder that is in the Internet folder on your startup disk. There are a couple of aliases to this application on your Mac. These are located in the Internet folder and in the Assistants folder.

- **Configuration Manager control panel**. This control panel stores all of the configuration information that you use to work on the Net with the Microsoft applications (Internet Explorer and Outlook Express) after you are able to connect. It contains all of your configuration information for the Microsoft Internet applications that you will use (see Figure 23.4). This configuration information is shared among all the Internet applications so that you don't have to enter it more than once. The Internet Setup Assistant configures all of the information you need to get started, but you can always use the Configuration Manager to check or change any aspect of your configuration.

- **DialAssist control panel**. This control panel will help you when you have some special options that you need to set when you dial. For example, you can specify different phone carriers and credit cards to use. Or you can set any codes that you need to dial to get an outside line. The Assistant

Internet Config

If you have used the Net on a Mac before, you may remember a utility called Internet Config. The purpose of this utility was to store all of your Internet information in one place so that you only had to enter it once. Then applications could use this information to configure themselves. Internet Config was included with earlier versions of the Mac OS, but now has been replaced by the Internet application (which is actually based on Internet Config).

will configure this for you. Or you can configure it yourself.

- **Internet application**. This is similar to the Configuration Manager. Why are there two of them? Well, Microsoft's applications use its Configuration Manager while other applications use the Internet application. You only need to configure the Internet application, and most of this configuration is done for you if you use the Internet Setup Assistant. You'll learn how to configure it later.

- **Modem control panel**. You use this control panel to tell your Mac what modem to use.

- **Remote Access control panel**. With this control panel, you can manage the Internet accounts on your Mac, and you can use it to connect to and disconnect from the Net (see Figure 23.5). You can also use Remote Access to connect to

other networks beside the Internet, for example, to your companies local network.

- **Remote Access Status**. This application (located on the Apple menu) also enables you to connect to and disconnect from the Net. You use it similarly to how you use the Remote Access control panel, except that it only enables you to use one account. You have to use the Remote Access control panel to change accounts.

- **TCP/IP control panel**. This control panel contains the settings you use to connect via a PPP account, through an Ethernet network, or via AppleTalk. When you use the Internet Assistant, it configures this control panel for you.

- **Internet Access extension**. These extensions enable your Internet access account to function.

- **Internet Config Extension**. This extension enables the Internet Application, which is a utility that stores all of your configuration information in one place. When a Net application needs it, it can look up the required info via this extension.

- **Modem Scripts folder**. This folder is located in the Extensions folder and contains the various modem initialization scripts that you choose in the Modem control panel.

- **Open Transport extensions**. The Open Transport extensions (all being with OpenTpt or Open Transport) provide the basic communication technology that your Mac uses to connect to the Net.

Finding Your Own Path to the Net

Now that you understand how the Internet works, as well as the Mac OS 8.5 software that enables you to connect to it, it is time for you to get your Mac online.

There are three basic ways that you can connect your Mac to the Net:

Bye bye PPP

Remote Access replaces the PPP control panel of previous versions of the Mac OS. It works similarly, though, so if you are familiar with the PPP control panel, you will know how to use the Remote Access control panel.

Internet Config lives

As you can see, Internet Config hasn't really gone away, but has simply been folded into the Mac OS 8.5. The name of the extension hasn't been changed.

Duality

The dual Net configuration systems, Configuration Manager and the Internet application, might be a bit confusing. As long as you use the Internet Setup Assistant to configure your Mac for the Net, you only need to deal with one of them. The Mac will keep both updated with any changes that you make.

- **Connecting through a network**. If you use your Mac from a company or other organization that uses a Local-Area Network (LAN) or Wide-Area Network (WAN) and that network is connected to the Net, you can connect to and use the Net through your organization's network. If that is your situation, read the section called, "Connecting Through a Network."

- **Connecting through a modem by using an existing account**. If you already have an Internet access account and will be connecting to it with your modem, read the section called, "Connecting Through a Modem by Using an Existing Internet Account."

- **Connecting through a modem and obtaining a new access account**. If you haven't been on the Net before or don't have a current Internet access account, read the section called, "Connecting Through a Modem and Obtaining a New Internet Account."

Connecting Through a Network

If you are connecting to the Net through a LAN or WAN, congratulations. A network connection offers lots of advantages. You will likely have a very fast connection so Web pages will download almost instantly. You will be connected all the time, no need to sign on and off like poor modem users do. Plus, you have a network or system administrator who can handle all of the complicated setup for you. Yes, you have it made.

Hopefully, your network administrator has, or soon will, take care of configuring your Mac for Net access. If so, you can skip the rest of this chapter. You get to move ahead to the good stuff—doing things on the Net. In case your administrator wants you to configure your own machine, you can use the following step-by-step to do so. But first, make sure that you have all of the information that you need. Your administrator should provide you with the following information:

- **IP Address**. The IP (Internet Protocol) address is your machine's identification to the rest of the Internet. It will be a series of four numbers separated by periods. In some cases, you may not be assigned a permanent IP address, but rather you may use a *dynamic* IP address, which means that your IP address will be assigned each time you go on to the Net. If you use dynamic IP addressing, you will need to know the protocol that you are going to use (MacIP or something else).

- **Subnet mask and router address**. Don't worry about what these mean; just get the appropriate information from your administrator.

- **Domain Name Server (DNS) and domain name**. The DNS is a computer that translates IP addresses into somewhat regular English so that we mere humans can better understand and use addresses. The domain name will likely be your company or service provider's name followed by a .com or .org.

- **Email address and password**. Your email address will probably be some permutation of your name followed by @your company.com. You will need a password to be able to access your email.

- **Email account**. This is the machine that receives your mail. It is different than the address; just use whatever your administrator tells you to.

- **Email host address**. The email host is the computer that actually sends your mail.

- **News server**. This is the computer that provides newsgroups to your Mac. You may or may not have one, just ask your administrator.

- **Proxy servers (firewalls)**. If your company network uses a firewall to provide security, you need to know that. A firewall acts as a barrier between your network and the Internet. A firewall prevents computers outside the firewall (on the Net) from accessing your network and usually prevents you from being tracked as you move about the Net. You will need a host and port to access each service that you will use (Web, FTP, and so on). You will also need a username and password to get through your firewall and onto the Net. If you have a firewall, you will need your system administrator's help to configure your Mac for Net access.

Once you have all of the information in this list, you are ready to configure your Mac. Don't worry, it won't take long. And the Internet Assistant will be there to help you each step of the way.

Using Internet Assistant to configure a network Internet connection

1. Launch Internet Setup Assistant (an alias is located in the Assistants folder on your startup disk), and you will see a window asking if you want to get on the Internet (which is probably the reason you are using the Assistant, right?). Click Yes to proceed with the configuration. (If you click No, the Assistant will quit.)

2. Since you are using a network connection to access the Internet, click Yes to answer the question asking you if you already have an account (your system administrator has to have set an account up for you). You will see the Introduction screen (see Figure 23.6).

FIGURE 23.6

Welcome to the Internet Setup Assistant!

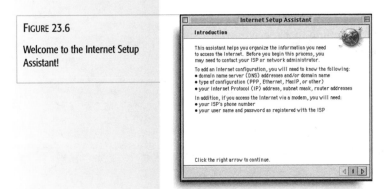

3. Read the text in the next Introduction screen and click the right arrow.

4. Name your configuration, click the Network button, and then click the right arrow. You will see the Apple Remote Access dialog. This is used to enable you to log into your network from a remote location (your home computer or a

laptop, for example). If you need to do this, you will have to get help from your system administrator. For now, I assume that you are going to use your direct network connection.

5. Click the No radio button and click the right arrow.

6. If your administrator provided an IP address to you, click the Yes radio button in the IP Address screen, click the right arrow, and then skip to step 8. If you are going to use a dynamic address, click the No radio button and then click the right arrow.

7. Select the protocol that you are going to use by clicking the appropriate radio button (MacIP or other). If you use MacIP, you will select your zone and then move to step 8. If you select Other, click the right arrow and move to step 10.

8. Enter the IP address provided by your administrator and click the right arrow.

9. Enter the subnet mask and router address, and then click the right arrow.

10. Enter your DNS addresses and domain name, and then click the right arrow.

11. Enter your email address and password. You may want to leave your password blank if you want to be more secure. Then click the right arrow.

12. Enter your email account, mail server address, and click the right arrow.

13. Enter your news server address and click the right arrow. You will see a question asking if you use a proxy server to connect to the Internet.

14. If your company doesn't use a firewall, click the No radio button, click the right arrow, and skip to step 16. If it does, click Yes and then the right arrow.

15. Check the boxes for the services you will use, enter the host and port number, and then enter your FTP username and password. When you have it all in, click the right arrow.

16. To save all of your settings, click Go Ahead. Your Mac should now be able to access the Net.

The system administrator

You probably have guessed by now that if you are connecting to the Internet through a LAN, that your system administrator is a very important person. You won't be able to connect to the Internet without that person's assistance because the folks supporting your company's network are the only ones who have the information you need. They might even do all of the configuration for you, in which case you are ahead of the game.

Connecting and disconnecting is a no-brainer for you. Your Mac is always connected so that you can just launch Net applications and go to it. The most you will have to do is to go through your firewall by entering a username and password.

Test your connection by going to the next chapter and trying to get your email. If that works, you are all set. If not, contact your system administrator for help.

Connecting To an Existing Internet Account

When you signed up for your Internet access account, your ISP provided you with configuration information for your account; you might have used this information to set up your account on another machine. Gather this configuration information so that you can easily refer to it during the configuration process. The following data are what you need to have ready:

- **Domain Name Server**. A Domain Name Server (DNS) is a computer that simply (it isn't really so simple) translates the numbers that the computers really use as addresses into English that we humans can usually understand. The DNS makes it possible for you to use an address such as www.companyname.com rather than having to deal with a series of numbers such as 233.453.22.345. The DNS number you need from your provider will be something that looks like 234.45.234.563.

- **Type of configuration**. This information tells your computer what protocol to use to connect to the Net. If you are using a modem, this is likely to be either Point-to-Point (PPP) or Serial Line Interface Protocol (SLIP).

- **Your IP address, subnet mask, and router addresses**. These numbers help the machine that you connect to when you call your ISP to identify you to the rest of the Internet while you are connected. Most modem-based connections use dynamic IP addressing, which simply means that your Mac will have an IP address assigned each time it connects

TCP/IP

You may have seen the term *TCP/IP* which stands for Transmission Control Protocol/Internet Protocol. All you really need to know is that this is the "language" that a computer must be able to speak to be on the Internet.

rather than having a static address. Should you think any more about this? No. Just get the numbers you need or the fact that you will be using dynamic addressing.

- **Phone Number**. You need to have the phone number that you need to dial to reach your ISP. Some ISPs offer different numbers for different modem speeds so make sure you get the phone number for your modem's speed (for example, 33.6). Also make sure that you use the connection phone number and not the one for technical support.

- **Username and password**. These are the two pieces of information that will uniquely identify you and enable you to access your account. You probably chose your own user- name when you established your account. Your password may or may not have been assigned by the ISP.

   You may have more than one username or password. Sometimes, your ISP will give you one username and pass- word that enables you to connect to the Net and another set (or maybe just one of the them) to let you use your email account. Make sure that you know which is which and use the right ones in the right setting fields.

- **PPP Connection scripts**. If your provider requires that you use a PPP connection script, make sure that you get a copy of it from your provider. If you get a connection script, it will be a file that you need to store in the PPP Connect Scripts folder that is within the Extensions folder. Most providers don't require you to use a PPP connection script so you probably won't need one.

- **Email addresses**. You will be given your email address (probably something like username@isp.net). You will also need an address for the server that receives your mail (this often has a "pop" in it, such as in pop.isp.net). The third piece of information you need is the address of the server that sends your mail (this usually has "smtp" in it, such as smtp.isp.net).

- **News server**. You should also be provided with a news- group server (this enables you to read newsgroups). It might look something like, news.isp.net.

The Internet Setup Assistant by another name...

As you are using the Internet Setup Assistant, you may notice that the name displayed at the top of the Application menu is Internet Editor Assistant. Does this application have an identity crisis? Not really. Once you have used it to configure your account, you can also use it to modify (or edit) an account.

If you need to dial special codes

If you need to dial any special codes before you dial your ISP's phone number, such as an access code (usually 9) or a credit card number, you must use the DialAssist control panel to configure the way your modem will dial before you can successfully connect to the Net. You also need to disable call waiting if you have it before you dial up your Internet account. See the "Using a Modem" section of Chapter 20, "Understanding and Using Networking Devices," to learn how to configure DialAssist.

Once you have all of the information handy, you are ready to configure your account.

Using the Internet Assistant to connect to the Internet through a modem and an existing account

1. Launch Internet Setup Assistant (open it from the Internet Access folder that is under the Apple menu).

2. Answer Yes to the question asking if you want to get on the Internet (see Figure 23.7).

3. Answer No to the question asking you if you already have an account. You will see an Introduction screen that explains the Assistant will help you find and register with an ISP.

4. Read the text and click the right arrow. You will see the

FIGURE 23.7

This screen lists the information you need to have on hand to configure your Internet account.

Modem Settings screen. Configure the screen for you modem, including any special codes that you need to dial to reach an outside line. When you finish, click the right arrow.

5. Read the Disclaimer screen and click the right arrow.

6. In the next screen, select your country from the Country pop-up menu, enter your area code, and then enter your phone prefix. Click the Register button.

Your Mac will dial out and connect to the Apple Referral Server. A list of potential ISPs will be downloaded to your

What modem?

If you have an external modem, just look at it to see what type it is. If you have an internal modem, look at the configuration information that came with your machine to see what kind of modem was installed. See Chapter 20, "Understanding and Using Networking Devices," for information on setting up a modem on your Mac.

If your modem is external, it is probably connected to the modem port on the back of your machine. The modem port is identified by an icon of a phone receiver. If your modem is internal, choose the internal port.

Mac. When the list is done, you will be asked to confirm the ISP server phone number that your Mac will call next. Check the number, and add any codes to the number that you would need to dial to connect to it (such as a 9 to get an outside line). When you are done, click the right arrow.

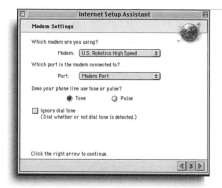

FIGURE 23.8

This is my Modem Settings dialog.

Ignoring dial tones

If your phone system uses the dial tone for different purposes, you may want to check the "Ignore dial tone" check box so that your Mac will dial out without checking to make sure that there is a dial tone first. For example, some voice mail systems use a "beeping" dial tone to indicate that you have messages waiting for you. If your Mac is looking for a dial tone before it dials out and it "hears" this beeping dial tone, it will think that there is a problem with the phone line and so won't try to dial. If your phone system uses such dial tones, check the "Ignore dial tone" box.

7. In the next screen, you will be told that the Assistant is ready to connect to the ISP registration server. Click Details to see the ISP that has been located for you. If that looks OK, click the Hide Details. Then click Go Ahead.

Your Mac will dial the selected ISP and the assistant will prepare to configure your Mac to connect to that ISP. Internet Explorer will open and you will see additional information about the ISP that has been selected for you. I can't give you specific instructions since they depend on the particular ISP you are using, just follow the directions you see on the Web pages you see. Note that you will have to provide a credit card in order to register with an ISP.

When the process is complete, the Assistant will configure your Mac to use that provider.

8. Try connecting to your account to make sure that it works ok.

SEE ALSO

➤ *To learn how to configure the DialAssist control panel, see page 452*

9. If it does, move to the section called, "Finishing Your Configuration," to do the final configuration of your account. If it doesn't, go to the "Troubleshooting Your Connection Through a Modem," section to get some help solving your problems.

10. If your ISP uses dynamic IP addressing (most do), click No and the right arrow to move to the DNS dialog. If your ISP provided you with an IP address, click Yes, the right arrow, enter the IP address, and click the right arrow.

11. In the Domain Name Servers dialog, enter the DNS (which will be a number that has four sets of digits all separated by periods) and Domain Name for your account; then click the right arrow (see Figure 23.9).

FIGURE 23.9

You use the Domain Name Servers screen to set the DNS for an Internet access account.

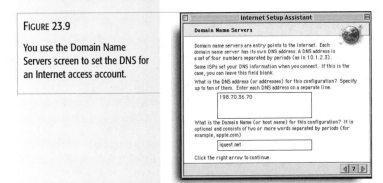

12. In the email address and password dialog, enter your email address and password; your email address should be something like yourname@yourisp.xxx. Make sure that you enter your email password and not your access password (if they are different). Then click the right arrow.

13. Enter your email account and SMTP information in the next dialog box. Make sure that you use your email account and not your email address here. Your email account will have some additional information in it that your address doesn't have. It will look something like yourname@pop.yourisp.xxx. Email is received via one protocol, usually POP (Post Office Protocol), while mail is sent via another, usually Simple Mail Transfer Protocol (SMTP). When you have completed these settings, click the right arrow.

14. Enter your newsgroup server name and click the right triangle.

15. Answer "No" to the question about proxies (if you know what they are, you don't need these steps!) and click the right arrow. You will see the Conclusion screen that tells you that you are finally done entering information (see Figure 23.10). If you want to review the details of the configuration that you have entered, click Show Details.

Passwords

In the dialogs that prompt you to enter your passwords, you can leave the password fields blank. If you do, you will have to enter your password each time you connect or check for mail. If other people have access to your Mac, this is a good security measure. If you are the only one who can use your machine, it will probably be OK to enter the passwords in the dialogs so that you don't have to type them each time you do something on the Internet.

FIGURE 23.10
All done—finally.

16. When you are ready to connect, click Go Ahead. You will see the Assistant finishing the configuration and then begin dialing (see Figure 23.11). In a few moments, you should hear the modems talking. If your Mac is able to connect, the Assistant window will go away, and you will see your desktop. Look in the upper-left corner, and you will see a flashing Mac/telephone pole icon; this means that you are connected to the Net. Congratulations!

FIGURE 23.11

In this screen, you can see that your Mac is dialing your ISP and connecting you to the Net.

If there was a problem and you weren't able to connect for some reason, see the "Troubleshooting Your Connection Through a Modem" section later in this chapter.

Now skip ahead to the section called, "Finishing Your Configuration," to do the final steps of the configuration process.

Connecting Through a Modem and Obtaining a New Internet Account

If you don't already have an Internet access account, you need to get one before you can connect to the Net. You have two basic choices. One is to go ahead and find an account on your own and then use the Internet Setup Assistant to help you configure it. The other option is to let Microsoft's Internet Connection Wizard find and configure an account for you. The benefit of finding your own account is that you can shop around and look for the "best" provider for your area, and you will have more choices than you will with the Connection Wizard. Another advantage is that you will understand what you are doing a bit better than you might if you use the Connection Wizard. The disadvantage to finding your own provider is that this is a bit more complicated than using the Connection Wizard to help you find and configure an account. If you feel confident about selecting a provider, go ahead and try and find your own provider.

The benefit of using the Connection Wizard is that it is easy to obtain and configure your account. The software will find an account and do all of the configuration for you. The disadvantage of using the Wizard is that you are limited to using providers that have a business agreement with Apple and Microsoft. This means that you may not be able to find the best possible provider for your area. That said, if you want to get an account the easiest and fastest way, the Connection Wizard is for you. If you want to use the Wizard, see the previous section called, "Connecting Through a Modem and Obtaining a New Internet Account."

Finding an Internet Service Provider

As you learned earlier, an Internet Service Provider enables you to connect to the Net with your Mac and a modem. The most complex part of getting on the Net is figuring out which provider to use. There are local providers that service just your local area, and there are national providers that provide service the entire country (with local phone numbers or 800 numbers).

When setting up a new Net account, you can either find an ISP on your own, or you can let the Connection Wizard find one for you. Finding one on your own can be a bit intimidating, but you may end up with a better provider than the one that the Internet Assistant will find for you.

Whichever method you choose, *cost* and *reliability* are the most important factors to consider when choosing an ISP. Cost is important because you probably don't like to spend money, and if your access is expensive, you aren't likely to use the Net as much as you would like to. Look for a provider that you can call

Finding a provider

One of the best sources of information about local Internet service providers are the people you know. There are probably several people in your immediate circle who have Internet access through a local provider. You should ask these folks if they are happy with their providers. You can also find out if the provider provides good technical support, how much the service costs, and so on. Using your personal network is an excellent way to find a provider for yourself.

Finding a local provider

One way to find a local provider is to check out the local news broadcasts in your area. Almost all local TV stations have Web sites that are maintained by a local ISP. At the end of the broadcast, you will see a credits screen saying that Internet services are provided by XYZ Company. XYZ Company might be a good choice for you to check out.

Beat the clock

One of the most important things to look for is an account that offers you unlimited access (or at least a very large number of hours per month). This means that you pay the same amount whether you are on the Net one hour or 100. That is good. If you pay on some sort of time basis (such as so many dollars per hour), then you will spend all your time worrying about how much time you have spent online instead of enjoying the Net. Fortunately, it isn't hard to find an unlimited account these days. This wasn't always the case.

ISPs and your company

If the company you work for has a Web site that is administered by an outside ISP or an outside ISP provides access to your company, check with that ISP to see if it offers a discount for employees of your company (this means you). Often, an ISP will provide inexpensive Internet access to the employees of a company to which it provides service. I have heard of some cases where the ISP offers rates as low as $8 per month for unlimited access. So it is worth a few minutes to see if your company has such a relationship with an ISP.

with a no-toll local phone call. Also look for a provider that charges you a reasonable *flat* fee for unlimited access—this means that you can use your account as little or as much as you would like, and you will pay the same amount. If you can't find one that will provide an unlimited access account, look for one that lets you use a lot of hours for a flat fee (typically, the limit will be 100 or more hours). Avoid a provider that charges a per hour fee rather than a flat fee. If you are paying by the hour, you will be watching the clock all of the time every moment that you are surfing the Net.

There are some providers that enable you to use an 800 number to access your Net account. If you can't find a local provider, these can sometimes be your lowest cost option, but 800 number access is usually fairly expensive. Providers that use 800 number access are good for those who travel a lot because you can easily access your account from wherever you happen to be with only minor changes to your settings.

A reasonable fee for unlimited Internet service is about $20-$25 per month. You may have to pay more if you live in a remote area; you may pay less if you live in an area with a lot of competition.

The other factor, reliability, refers to how easy it is for you to connect. If your provider is overloaded (doesn't have enough modems for all of its customers), you will get lots of busy signals when you try to dial in. Or if the provider has flaky equipment and systems, you are likely to have trouble getting and staying connected. Lastly, if the provider has poor technical support, you won't be able to count on getting any problems you encounter fixed quickly. Unfortunately, there really isn't any way to judge reliability before you get an account, beyond talking to other customers of that ISP. Just be aware that if the provider you choose first doesn't prove to be reliable, you can always cancel the account and try another one.

Once you have your account (no matter how you get it), go back to the earlier section called, "Connecting Through a Modem by Using an Existing Internet Account," to learn how to configure your Mac to use that account.

Using the Internet Connection Wizard

You can use the Internet Setup Assistant's Register option if you need to obtain an Internet access account (in other words, if you do not have an existing Internet access account).

Using the Internet Assistant to connect to the Net if you don't have an account

1. Launch Internet Setup Assistant (open it from the Internet folder that is under the Apple menu).

2. Answer Yes to the question asking if you want to get on the Internet.

3. Answer No to the question asking you if you already have an account. At this point, you will move into the Microsoft Internet Connection Wizard that will help you find and configure your account.

4. Follow the directions on the screen to locate a provider. When the process is complete, your Mac will be set up for Internet access.

5. Try connecting to your account to make sure that it works OK.

6. If it does, move to the section called, "Finishing Your Configuration," to do the final configuration of your account. If it doesn't, go to the "Troubleshooting Your Connection Through a Modem," section to get some help solving your problems.

Use the Net to find a provider

If you have some access to the Net, perhaps through a friend or work, use the Web to locate a provider. Go to `http://thelist.internet.com/` which enables you to find local access providers for just about every location in the world.

Microsoft?

You may wonder why a Microsoft application is part of the Apple Mac OS. In July of 1997, Steve Jobs and Bill Gates made an agreement for Apple and Microsoft to work more closely together on Macintosh-related products. Microsoft gave Apple about $150 million. Apple gave Microsoft the right to be the default Net software for Mac OS 8.5, including the Internet Connection Wizard, Outlook Express, and Internet Explorer.

The Internet application

Configuring the Internet application means that Internet applications, such as Outlook Express and Netscape Navigator, will be able to access your configuration and you won't have to enter it within each application.

Finishing Your Configuration

There are just a few more steps that you need to do to double-check and finish off your configuration. To do these steps, you will use the new Internet application.

Finishing your Internet configuration

1. Choose the Internet application from Control Panels on the Apple menu. The control panel will open.

2. Make sure that the account name you used in Internet Setup Assistant appears in the Active Set pop-up menu (if it doesn't, select it from the Active Set pop-up menu); then click the triangle next to Edit Sets so that you can see the details (see Figure 23.12).

FIGURE 23.12

You configure the Internet application so that Internet applications can get your configuration information from it.

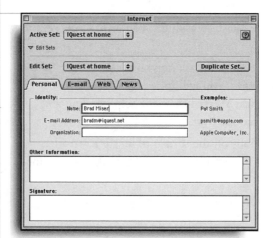

Some data may be complete

The fields should already be filled in based on the data you entered in the Internet Setup Assistant. If you haven't used the Assistant, you will have to enter this information yourself.

3. Click the personal tab; your name and mail address should be already be entered for you.

4. If you want to have a signature that you can have your email application add to your messages (you'll learn about this in the next chapter), enter it in the Signature block.

5. Click the Email tab.

6. In the User Account ID field, enter your username (your email username in case it is different from your email access name).

7. In the Incoming Mail Server field, add your email server name (probably something like pop.isp.net).

8. Check for your password in the Password field (unless you want to have to enter it each time you check your email).

9. Check the outgoing mail server address in the Outgoing (SMTP) Mail Server field (probably something like smtp.isp.net).

10. Using the check boxes, choose an action that should happen when you receive new mail (for example, a sound or flashing icon).

11. Make sure that the Default Email Application pop-up menu shows Outlook Express. If not, select Outlook Express. When you are done, the window should look something like Figure 23.13.

This will make sense later

The settings you enter in the Internet application will make more sense to you once you read the email and Web chapters. For now, just follow the steps and don't worry if you don't understand what you are entering.

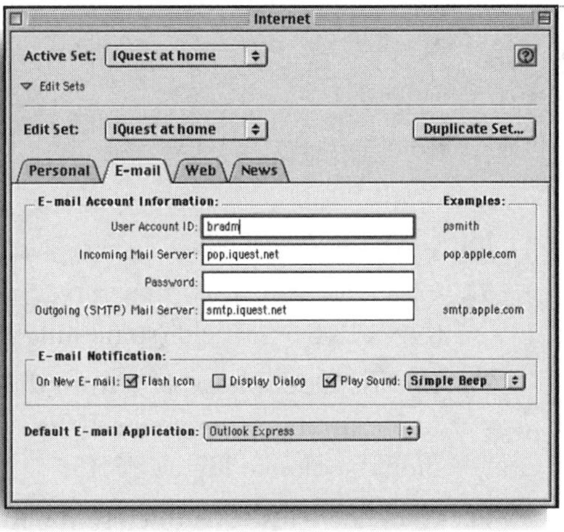

FIGURE 23.13
The Email tab enables you to set various settings for your email applications.

12. Click the Web tab, check that the Home Page radio button is selected, and type http://www.apple.com in the text box.

13. Click the Search Page radio button and enter http://www.yahoo.com.

14. Click the Select button, choose the Desktop from the pop-up menu at the top of the Select a Folder dialog, click New, enter Downloaded Files, and click Create. Then click Select again when you move back into the Select a Folder dialog.

This step creates a folder into which files you download are placed. Having a single folder makes it easy to find all of the files you receive.

15. Make sure that Microsoft Internet Explorer appears in the Default Web Browser pop-up menu. When you are done, the screen should look something like Figure 23.14.

FIGURE 23.14

Using the Web tab, you can set defaults for your Web browsers.

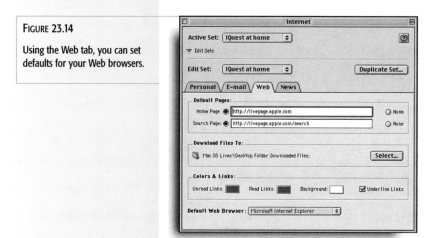

16. Click the News tab.

17. Check for your ISP's new server address in the News (NNTP) Server field (something like news.isp.net).

18. Choose Outlook Express from the Default News Application pop-up menu. When you are done, this screen should look like Figure 23.15.

19. Click the Close box to close the Internet application making sure that you save your changes.

20. Open the Remote Access control panel. You should see Remote Access (account name) window (where account name is the one you gave your account at the beginning of the process).

21. Click the Setup triangle to open the setup part of the window.

22. Click Options. You will see the Options window (see Figure 23.16).

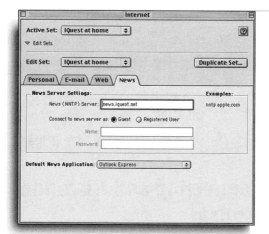

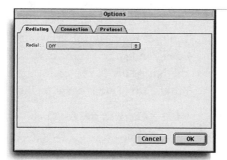

FIGURE 23.16

The Options tab of Remote Access enables you to set your access preferences..

23. Click the Redialing tab and choose the Redial main number only from the pop-up menu. Enter a number in the Redial times box; this is the number of times your Mac will redial the number in case it is busy the first time. Try entering 5. Leave the time between retries at 5 seconds.

24. Click the Connection tab. In this window, check the "Flash icon in menu bar while connected" check box. This will flash the telephone pole icon in the upper-left corner of your screen while you are connected to the Net. Check the "Disconnect if idle for" check box and enter 10 minutes. This will cause your connection to be disconnected if no data has been transferred for at least 10 minutes. This is a good idea so that you don't tie up phone lines in case you forget to disconnect.

Multiple Net accounts

You can set up multiple Net accounts on one Mac. Just go back to the beginning of the configuration steps and use the same process. Give the accounts different names and enter the information for each account.

25. Click the Protocol tab.

26. Check the "Connect automatically when starting TCP/IP applications" check box if you want your Internet applications to be able to automatically connect to the Net when they need to.

27. Click OK.

28. Close the Remote Access dialog and save changes.

Connecting and Disconnecting with a Modem

Using the Internet is always a three-step process. First, connect to the Internet. Second, after your connection is established, run the programs for the services you want to use (for example, Internet Explorer for browsing the Web, Outlook Express for email, and so on). Third, when you are finished, disconnect from the Net. This can be confusing if you are new to the Net so here are the three steps again:

1. Connect to the Internet.

2. After you are connected, run the applications for the services that you want to use. If you want to use the Web, launch Internet Explorer. If you want to send or receive email, launch Outlook Express. If you want to read Usenet news, launch Outlook Express.

3. When you are done, disconnect from the Internet.

Think of the connection program—the part that connects you to the Net—as an electronic version of the cord that attaches your phone to the wall jack. To use the phone, you have to plug the cord into the wall. When you are done, you remove the cord from the wall to disconnect the phone (OK, it doesn't really work like this, but I think you get the point). So, in our little analogy, your computer is the phone. The connection software is the phone cord. The Internet (actually your access provider) is the wall jack. To make a call, you plug the phone cord (you run the connection package). After the connection is made, you can start talking (running Internet Explorer or Outlook Express).

A quiet modem?

In the Modem control panel, you can turn the speaker for your modem off so that you don't have to listen to the annoying sounds of your modem connecting to your ISP's modem. However, until you are sure that your connection works reliably, you should leave the sound on so that you can hear what is happening with your modem during the connection process. For example, with the sound on, you can hear your modem dialing, the ISP modem answering, and the negotiation process. This can be helpful in troubleshooting any problems.

Once you can connect reliably, you can turn the sound off.

One of the great things about the Mac is that most Internet applications can be configured so that they can automatically connect to the Net when you need to do something (browse the Web, for example). So you can simply start an application or do a command (such as checking your email). After a certain period of inactivity, you will automatically be disconnected. Most of the time, you don't need to bother connecting and disconnecting. But you still need to understand the process.

You will learn how to use Internet applications in the following chapters. For now, practice connecting and disconnecting from your Net account.

Connecting to and disconnecting from the Net

1. From the Apple menu, choose Remote Access Status (see Figure 23.17).

2. Click Connect. You will hear your modem dialing out, and you can watch the progress of your connection in the Remote Access window. When the connection is complete, the Remote Access window enables you to monitor the activity of your connection (see Figure 23.18). At this point, you can launch an application to get your email or browse the Web.

3. For now, click Disconnect to break your connection. The Remote Access window will return to the Connect state.

4. Close the window.

Using multiple accounts

To change the account that your Mac uses to connect to the Net, open the Remote Access control panel. From the File menu, choose Configurations. In the Configurations window, choose the account that you want to use and click Make Active. The Remote Access window will change to reflect the name of the account that you choose. It will also be the one the Remote Access Status uses to connect.

FIGURE 23.17

Remote Access Status will connect you to the Net.

FIGURE 23.18

This Mac is on the Net; notice that my account has unlimited access (indicated by the word "unlimited").

More than one way to connect

You may have noticed that the Remote Access control panel also has a Connect button. You can connect and disconnect by using the Remote Access control panel in the same way that you use Remote Access status. Use whichever way you prefer. They do the same thing. If you need to change the account you use, you will have to use the Remote Access control panel though.

You can also let your Internet applications connect for you when they need to.

If this process has worked, you have successfully configured your Mac for the Net, and you are ready to start experiencing the Net for yourself (you can skip the rest of this chapter).

Once you are sure that the connection works properly, you really don't have to connect manually if you checked the "Connect automatically when starting TCP/IP applications" check box in the Remote Access control panel. With this check box checked, your Net applications can connect when they need to.

If you haven't been able to connect, move to the next section for some troubleshooting suggestions.

Troubleshooting Your Connection Through a Modem

You probably wouldn't be reading this section if everything went well, and you are able to connect and disconnect from the Net. Unfortunately, troubleshooting connection problems can be difficult because there are so many variables involved. These include: your modem, your configurations, the phone lines, your ISP's system, and so on. While I can't list every problem that you may have, this section will give you some ideas of where to look for the most common problems. Unless you find a simple error, such as incorrect data in the configuration, you will probably have to call your ISP for help. But work through these ideas before you do. Even if they don't solve your problem, they will save you time with your ISP when you do call.

The following list includes the typical problems that you may be experiencing. After each problem, you will see the general things you can try to solve your problems. The problems are listed first in bold, and then some steps that you should try are described.

You don't hear or see any activity with your modem when you try to connect. The problem may lie with your modem setup.

Checking modem problems

1. Check the Modem and DialAssist control panels to make sure that you have installed and configured your modem properly.

2. Test the modem with another application (such as a commercial online service or by connecting to a BBS). If the modem works with another application, you know the problem is related to your configuration. If your modem still doesn't work at all, see the manual that came with the modem for troubleshooting help.

3. Make sure that the modem selected during your Net configuration is the right one—it should be the modem that you set up with the Modem control panel.

4. If none of these steps result in your modem dialing, try the modem with another computer. If it still doesn't work, contact the modem manufacturer for troubleshooting help. If it does work with another computer, you know the problem is with your installation or configuration. Reinstall the modem and double-check the Modem control panel.

You hear the modem dialing, but you never hear the call being answered. This can happen when your ISP is offline for some reason or it may be simply overloaded. It can also happen if your configuration is not properly set.

Checking answering problems

1. Open the Remote Access control panel.

2. Check the phone number to make sure that it is the right one for your ISP.

3. Make sure that any codes you need to dial before a phone call are reflected in the number. For example, if you need to dial a "9" before making phone calls, make sure that there is a "9," before your ISP's phone number.

4. Try again. Sometimes the phone lines are busy.

5. If you still can't get an answer, call your ISP for help.

You hear the modem dialing and you hear your ISP's phone answering, but you never connect. You may see various error messages in the Remote Access Status window, such as, "Authentication failed." This is probably the result of an incorrect configuration.

Checking your configuration

1. Open the Remote Access control panel.

2. Make sure that your username, password, and the phone number are correct. If not, correct them and try again.

3. From the RemoteAccess menu, choose Modem. In the Modem control panel, verify that the correct modem is chosen in the pop-up menu. Close the control panel.

4. From the RemoteAccess menu, choose TCP/IP. Make sure that PPP is selected in the Connect via pop-up menu, Using PPP Server is connected in the Configure pop-up menu, the name server add block contains the DNS from your ISP, and that the search domain is the right one for your ISP. Close the control panel.

5. Make sure that if your ISP requires that you use a PPP script, that the proper script is installed.

6. Try working through the configuration steps again. Give the account another name and make sure that you enter the correct information.

7. If all of the information is correct, but you still can't connect, call your ISP for help.

Troubleshooting connection problems can be tough, but the odds are that you will connect just fine. If not, the problem is most likely an incorrect configuration information that you can fix in the Remote Access control panel or by redoing the configuration with the Internet Setup Assistant. Your ISP will also be able to help you. Once you get your connection working and start using the Net, you will find that your work getting online was worthwhile.

Activity log

By the way, you can choose Activity Log from the RemoteAccess menu to see a log of your recent Remote Access activity. This log is sometimes helpful. Have it ready when you call for help.

Using Email: The Basics

Understanding how email works

Using Outlook Express to send email

Using Outlook Express to read email

Using Outlook Express to reply to email

Understanding Internet etiquette

Understanding Outlook Express features

Using Email Is Excellent

Today, email has become the communication medium of choice for many people. Using Internet email, you can communicate with anyone in the world who has access to any email service. Not only can you reach out and touch these people, but email is also easy, convenient, fast, and inexpensive. It's also more interactive than regular mail (also known as snail mail) because you can get a reaction to your mail almost immediately.

You can use email in a number of different ways. The most obvious way is to communicate with another individual. That individual may be your next door neighbor, a business associate who lives across town, or a friend who lives across the ocean. Through email, you can form and maintain relationships with other people; that's what it is all about.

In addition to one-on-one communication, email also makes it easy to communicate with groups of people. Unlike regular mail, it's as easy to send a message to 20 people as it is to send a message to one person.

E-mail also enables you to participate in mailing lists. Mailing lists are ongoing electronic discussions on a wide variety of topics, each installment of which is automatically delivered to your electronic mailbox. Let's say you are interested in playing the guitar. You might get on a mailing list that discusses a particular style of guitar music. As people communicate about this topic, you are automatically sent messages generated by other members of the mailing list. These messages may be new information on the hot guitar released last week, tips for achieving a certain sound, or reviews of a famous performer's recent concert. You can respond to these messages and participate in a dialogue with other members of the list.

In addition to messages and mailing lists, email enables you to send just about anything that you can store on your Mac. You can send files (text, images, sounds, movies, or whatever) as attachments to your email messages. For example, you can send a text file to a colleague for her review. The possibilities are almost endless.

One of the best things about email is that it is very convenient. You can send and read your email at your discretion. Likewise, the recipient can open it at his or her convenience. You don't have to worry about interrupting an important meeting or being a nuisance.

Before you can use email, however, you need to understand some of its basic components.

Understanding Addresses

Understanding addresses is key to being able to use email. Internet email addresses look something like *username@someplace.xxx*.

The first part of the address, the *username*, is an identifier for the person to whom the mail is being sent. It may be some part or parts of the person's name. (You chose your own username when you signed up for your Internet access account.) Each username must be unique within a specific Internet access provider; however, usernames are not unique outside of particular providers. For example, there could be a *johns@nowhere.com* and a *johns@somewhere.net*, but there cannot be two *johns@nowhere.com*.

The next item, the @ symbol, is translated as "at." It separates the username from the location of that user, and says, "Look for this person *at* this location."

The *someplace* identifies where on the Internet the electronic mailbox is located; this is sometimes the access provider. Other times, it is a company name. It is usually a machine or a company name.

Someplace is also a domain

Often the "someplace" in an address is also the domain. You configured your domain when you set up your Mac for Net access in the previous chapter.

Finally, the *xxx* is a code that represents the type of organization or location that *someplace* is. Common codes include *.com* for a commercial organization, *.edu* for an educational institution, *.net* for an ISP, and *.gov* for government. You may also see a two-letter country code at the end of an address, such as *.us* (USA) or *.ca* (Canada).

Saying your address the Net way

Your email address will be *user-name@someplace.xxx*, where *user-name* is the username that you selected. For example, my email address is *bradm@iquest.net*. When giving your address verbally, you should follow certain conventions that make your address easier to understand. Pronounce the @ as "at." Pronounce the period as "dot." So, I would say that my email address is, "brad em at iquest dot net." Of course, if you have an unusual word, or an unusual spelling of a normal word, be sure to spell out your address.

When you see an address, it may have more than three parts or fewer than three parts, but each part will be separated by either a period or the @. The basic thing to remember is just to use addresses as you find them.

Finally, you usually address mail to people who don't have Internet accounts (but do have email accounts on some service) by tacking an *@someplace.xxx* to the end of their user name on that service. The *someplace* is the name of the service that has the person's email account. The *xxx* is the code for that service (most of the time this will be commercial or *com*). For example, let's say that you are writing to a friend who has a CompuServe account, and his CompuServe number is 76350,3014. To send email to him from your Internet account, just address the message to *76350.3014@compuserve.com*—you have to replace the comma with a period because the Internet can't handle commas in addresses. Then let's say that you want to write to another friend who uses America Online (pretend her username is JaneD). You address the message to *janed@aol.com*.

Now that you understand addresses, how do you find someone's email address to use? If that someone writes to you first, it's easy to get his address from the email message; just look in the From block. What if he doesn't write to you first? Just ask for it. You should also keep your eyes peeled for addresses as you browse the Web, read newsgroups, and so on.

Understanding the Anatomy of an Email Message

Every email message has two basic parts that you need to understand, which are the *header* and the *body*. Some email software also enables you to use a third part, called the *signature*. Different email software programs construct these parts differently, but they all have the same information more or less.

Understanding the Header

The header comes at the top (or head) of a message. The header is the area that is used to handle the actual sending of the message. The header looks a bit different on mail that you send than it does on mail that you receive, but the information contained is the same. For example, the header contains the following information:

- **The date the message was sent**. You can use this to get an idea of when the message was sent. Depending on what kind of network and software was used to generate the message, it may be off by quite a bit, but you can at least get a general idea of when the message was sent.

- **Address of the recipient (the To block)**. This is the address of the person (or persons) to whom the message is being sent.

- **Address of the sender (the From block)**. This tells you who sent the message.

- **The subject of the message (the Subject block)**. This should be a short, but explanatory sentence or phrase that gives the recipient an idea as to what the message is about.

- **Addresses of people who get copies of the message (the Cc block)**. Each person who is listed in the Cc block will get a copy of the email message. Technically, there is no difference between the To and the Cc blocks; in practice, the person the mail is To is supposed to do something with it, while the Cc people just get the message for their information.

Headers are usually more important to you when you are preparing a message than reading one. When you receive a message, you will probably only look at the sender, subject, and sometimes the Cc line. These tell you almost everything you need to know.

Understanding the Body

The body of the message is the most important part and is also the easiest to understand. The body comes below the header, and this part is where you read—or type—the message.

Going in blind

There is also a Bcc (Blind Carbon Copy) block on mail you send. This lists addresses that will receive the message, but that will not be listed in the other recipient's Cc fields. This is useful if you want to copy someone on your message, but don't want other recipients to know that you have sent a copy to that person.

Gobbledygook central

Sometimes, especially when dealing with bounced email (which you will learn about in a later section), you will see a lot of almost incomprehensible "stuff" in the header of a message. This is usually the path that the email traveled in its way to its final destination. While you normally only see the originating address of a message and the destination address of a message, email actually travels through lots of different servers in between. Normally, you have no need to see all of the intermediate stops. However, that information is provided to you when your email is unable to reach its destination so that you can use it to figure out what has happened to your message. You will learn more about that in the section called, "Working with Bounced Email."

More on signatures

Of course, even if an application doesn't support automatic signatures, you can always type one in yourself. You can also use an automation program, such as QuickKeys or OneClick, to be able to add a signature with a keyboard shortcut.

Setting a signature

You can set a signature in the Email tab of the Internet application (see the previous chapter for details on using the Internet application).

AKA

Email applications are also called email *clients*. That is because email is actually a client/server process. You use an email client to connect to an email server to read and send email.

Understanding the Signature

Some email applications enable you to use a signature block. A signature is a set group of text that the email program automatically pastes onto outgoing mail. Signatures can save you from typing your name or some special message every time you send email. It's considered to be good form to place your email address in your signature, just in case your email address is difficult to decipher. Many people put clever—and not so clever—messages in their signatures.

Understanding Email Applications

In order to use email, you need several things. First, you need a computer (like you couldn't have figured that out on your own). Second, you need an email account and a way to access that account (you learned how to get this in Chapter 23, "Connecting Your Mac to the Net"). Third, you need an email application.

There are several email applications for the Mac available, but really only three are worth considering. These are the following:

- **Claris Emailer**. Emailer, originally created by Fog City Software and then purchased by the company formerly known as Claris (now known as FileMaker), is an excellent email application that boasts a number of powerful features (see Figure 24.1). In fact, it was the first email application to offer features such as multiple email accounts, scheduling, and easy filtering. Emailer Lite used to be included as the Mac OS' email program. Since the demise of Claris, the future of Emailer is uncertain.

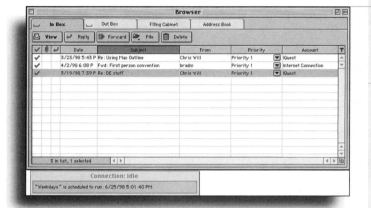

FIGURE 24.1

Claris Emailer is a powerful email application that is, alas, in limbo due to the demise of Claris.

- **Qualcomm Eudora Pro and Eudora Lite**. Eudora was one of the first Mac email programs that looked like a Mac program (see Figure 24.2). It was easy-to-use, had lots of good features, and it had an excellent interface. Plus, it was free. It was the dominant Mac email program until Emailer arrived on the scene; these two programs duked it out for the claim to be the number one Mac email program. The basic version was renamed Eudora Lite and was left as freeware. A more capable version was named Eudora Pro and was sold commercially. Both versions are available for Mac and Windows; they have continued to be updated and are still widely in use today.

- **Microsoft Outlook Express**. While it has produced email clients for Windows for some time, Microsoft appeared not to be interested in the email Mac market. However, when it did decide to get in the game, Microsoft wasted no time in producing an excellent Mac email application called Outlook Express. Outlook Express boasts all of the features of commercial email programs, and it is included as part of Mac OS 8.5 as its default email program.

Getting Eudora

You can purchase a copy of Eudora Pro from your favorite software retailer.

You can download a copy of Eudora Lite from http://www.eudora.com.

Outlook Express and Mac OS 8.5

Mac OS 8.5 ships with version 4.01 of Outlook Express. If you are using a different version, some of the screens may look slightly different than they do in this chapter, but the steps will probably work with just some minor deviations.

FIGURE 24.2

Eudora Lite is an excellent, and free, Mac email program.

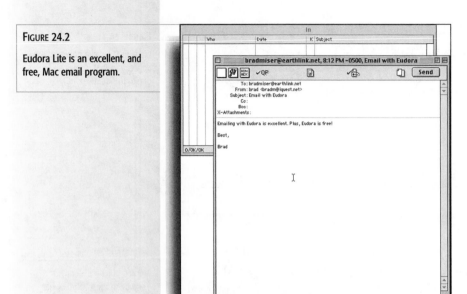

Using Microsoft's Outlook Express

Outlook Express is a full-featured email program—not a scaled down or light version with few features. It offers many powerful features, including the following:

- **Address book**. The Contacts feature lets you store all of your commonly used addresses so that you can easily address email.

- **Spell checker**. Outlook Express enables you to check the spelling in your messages. This feature is usually only found on email applications for which you must pay extra.

- **Styled text**. With Outlook Express, you can apply formatting styles to your email (such as bold and italics). (Note that if the recipient of your email doesn't use a program that supports styled text, she will see plain text).

- **Newsgroup reader**. Outlook Express is also a full-featured newsgroup reader.

SEE ALSO

➤ *To learn more about using Outlook Express to read newsgroups, see Chapter 28, "Reading Newsgroups"*

- **Multiple mail folders**. You can set up multiple folders that you can use to organize your mail. You can also have sub-folders within folders.

- **Multiple email accounts**. Outlook Express enables you to use a single program to manage multiple email accounts.

SEE ALSO

➤ *To learn how to use multiple email accounts, see page 582*

- **Filters**. Filters enable you to automatically sort mail according to rules that you define. For example, you may want all the mail from a particular person to be stored in a specific mailbox.

SEE ALSO

➤ *To learn how to use filters, see page 582*

- **HTML support**. Outlook Express supports HTML mail so that you can receive messages that have the formatting and other features of Web pages.

SEE ALSO

➤ *To learn more about HTML support, see page 575*

- **IMAP support**. Outlook Express supports *Internet Message Access Protocol (IMAP)*.

SEE ALSO

➤ *To learn more about IMAP, see page 576*

Experiencing Outlook Express—a Quick Look

When you launch Outlook Express, you will see a three-pane window (see Figure 24.3). The left pane contains all of the email folders that you set up, as well as the standard folders that Outlook Express uses. The Inbox is where all the mail you receive is deposited (unless you set up a filter to send it to another folder). The Outbox is used to hold mail that you've created until you send it. The Sent Mail folder contains all of the messages that you have sent. The Drafts folder is a folder for drafts of mail messages on which you are working that aren't ready to send yet.

FIGURE 24.3

Outlook Express is a full-featured
email client—it uses a three-pane
window to make it easy to get to
various areas.

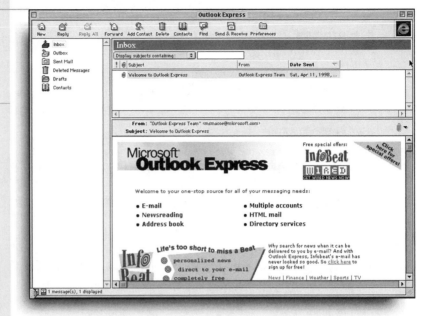

Across the top of the window, there are buttons for tasks that
you will frequently do; for example, New for creating a new
message and the Trash button for deleting messages or folders.

The top pane on the right side of the window contains a list of
all of the messages in the folder that is selected in the left pane.
To view the contents of a message, click it in the top pane and
the message body appears in the lower pane, which is where you
will read the text of your messages.

Configuring Outlook Express

When you configured your Mac to connect to the Net, you
entered all of the information that Outlook Express needed to
receive and send email. Your email account should already be
properly configured. However, just in case you ever need to
reconfigure Outlook Express manually, or when you need to add
another email account, the following step-by-step shows you
how to do it.

Manually configuring Outlook Express

1. Open Outlook Express and from the Edit menu, choose
    Preferences (the first time you launch Outlook Express, you
    will be taken to the Preferences window automatically. You
    will see the Configuration Manager.

Configuring Outlook Express

When you used the Internet Setup
Assistant and the Internet application, all the necessary information
should have been entered in the
proper places to configure Outlook
Express. However, if Outlook
Express doesn't seem to be working
for you, manually check the configuration and correct any settings that
aren't right for your account. You
can also force Outlook Express to
reload your Internet preferences to
configure it.

2. Make sure that Email is selected in the left pane.

3. Click New Account. If you want to edit an existing account, select it by using the Mail Accounts pop-up menu and skip to step 6.

4. Name your account and click the POP or IMAP radio button, depending on what type of account it is (your ISP or system administrator will tell you this, but if there is a pop anywhere in the mail server address, you should click POP).

5. Click OK. You will see a mostly blank Preferences window. If you choose a POP account, you will see a field for POP Server; if you choose an IMAP account, this field will be labeled IMAP Server instead.

6. Complete the fields with the information that was provided by your ISP or by your system administrator (such as email address, SMTP server, POP or IMAP account, and so on. Be especially careful with the "Save password" check box. If you have Outlook Express and save your password, then anyone who can access your machine can get your email.

SEE ALSO

➤ *To see a list of the information that you need to have, see page 530*

➤ *To learn how to add another email account to your configuration, see page 502*

7. Click Message Composition in the left pane.

8. Click the Plain text option in the Mail sending format box, unless you are sure that most of the people with whom you will be emailing have an HTML capable mail program.

9. Click OK, and you will return to the Outlook Express window.

You can also force Outlook Express to reload your Internet preferences. You might want to do this if you have previously opened Outlook Express or perhaps incorrectly configured it. One warning, though, if you follow the next step-by-step, you will remove *all* configuration information from Outlook Express, so think carefully before you do this.

Forcing Outlook Express to reload your Internet preferences

1. Quit Outlook Express.

The same as Configuration Manager

Working through the step-by-step to configure Outlook Express does the same thing as configuring the email part of the Configuration Manager (which you can access through Control Panels under the Apple menu). It also uses the same email information that you entered via the Internet Setup Assistant. It is all the same data stored in the same place—you just get it in different ways.

2. Open the Outlook Express folder that is within the Internet Applications folder that is on your startup disk.

3. Open the Outlook Express User(s) folder and then open the Main User folder.

4. Select the Outlook Express Prefs file and move it to the Trash.

5. Restart Outlook Express. When it opens, you will be asked if you want to import messages and contacts from other applications. Answer No. You will see the Welcome to Outlook Express message.

6. Click OK to clear the welcome message. You will see the New Account window.

7. Name the email account, click the POP or IMAP radio button, and click OK. You configuration will be loaded as the default account. The Preferences pane should show the configuration information that you entered in the Internet Setup Assistant and the Internet application.

8. Click OK to close the Preferences window. You are now ready to use Outlook Express.

Writing and Sending Email

No subject or message required

While you can't send an email message without an addressee, you can send one without a subject or message. If you wanted to send an attachment to someone, but no explanation was needed, you might choose to do this. (You will learn about attachments in the next chapter.)

I'll bet that you are excited about sending your first email message. Who should you send it to? If you know someone's address, go ahead and send it to her—just replace the address, subject, and text I'm using in the following step-by-step with information that is appropriate for your recipient. If you don't know any of your friends' or family's email addresses, try writing to me just so you get the hang of using Outlook Express (and you can tell me what you think about this book at the same time!).

Creating and sending email with Outlook Express

1. Click the New Message icon at the top of the window or press Command+N. You will see the new message window, ready for you to create a piece of email (see Figure 24.4).

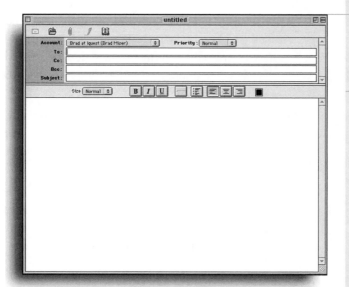

FIGURE 24.4

When you create a new message, you will see a new window like this one.

2. The cursor will be in the To box, so type the email address of the person to whom you want to send mail to (if you want to send a message to me, use bradm@iquest.net).

3. If you want to copy someone on this message, press Tab and enter another address in the Cc box.

4. Press Tab again, and you will be in the Bcc box; enter an address here if you want to copy someone whose address won't be seen by other recipients of your message.

5. Press Tab again and enter a subject. Try to use meaningful subjects when you send email so that the recipient has a good idea of what the message is about. For example, if you write to me, use something like, "Feedback on your Using Mac OS 8.5 book."

6. Press Tab again, and you will move into the body of the message.

7. Type your message. Notice any red wavy lines underneath words as you type them? That is Outlook Express telling you that the word you typed is not recognized and that it may be a misspelling.

8. When you are done typing, select the account from which you want the message sent from the Account pop-up menu at the top of the window. If you only have one account configured, it will be selected automatically.

Auto connections to the Net

If you have configured Remote Access to do so, you can have your Net applications automatically connect to the Net. If you don't have this configured, you will need to open Remote Access Status or Remote Access and manually connect before you will be able to send or receive email. See the "Finishing Your Configuration" section in Chapter 23, "Connecting Your Mac to the Net" to see how to set up the automatic connection feature.

If you chose not to configure the automatic connection feature, you will need to add the connection and disconnection steps to the step-by-steps in this chapter, which you need to use to connect to the Net because I assumed that this feature was enabled.

9. When you are done with your message, it will be ready to send (see Figure 24.5). In Figure 24.5, you can see that I have a misspelling in my message (look for the word with the wavy line under it). Outlook Express makes correcting spelling mistakes easy.

10. Hold down the Control key and click any misspelled words. You will see a contextual menu with suggestions for correct spelling of the unrecognized word (see Figure 24.6). Choose the correct spelling from the contextual menu.

11. When you are done with your message, click the Send Message icon or choose Command+M. If you aren't connected to the Net, the software will tell your connection to activate and will log onto the Net and send your email.

FIGURE 24.5

Don't make emailing to yourself a habit!

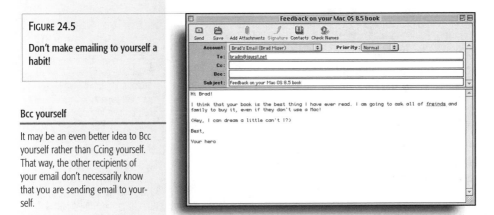

FIGURE 24.6

Outlook Express has a full-featured spell checker; just press Control and click a misspelled word, and you will see Outlook Express' suggestions.

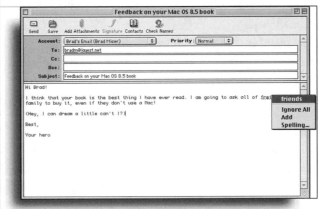

Congratulations! You've just sent your first email message! Easy wasn't it?

If you are using a modem, it is usually a good idea to set Outlook Express to store messages until you connect rather than sending messages right away. That way you can stay offline and write all of your messages. When they are all ready to go, you can send them all at once. Also, many people that you will email do not use programs that are capable of receiving HTML mail, so you should set Outlook Express to use plain text instead. Setting this behavior is also a good exercise to show you how you can set various other preferences to your liking.

SEE ALSO

➤ *To learn more about HTML mail, see page 575*

Setting Outlook Express to send messages only on your command

1. Choose Preferences from the Edit menu or click the Preferences button (the folder with dots on it). You will see Outlook Express' Preferences dialog that you use to determine how Outlook Express operates (see Figure 24.7). The groups of preferences that you can set are shown in the left pane of this dialog. When you click on a group, the options that you can choose appear in the right pane. In Figure 24.7, General preferences are selected in the left pane and the options are shown in the right pane.

2. Click General. You will see the Mail and News Settings window.

3. Uncheck the "Send messages immediately" box. Notice that there are other options that you can set, such as the sounds that you want to play when various things happen.

4. Click Message Composition in the left pane.

5. Click the Plain text radio button under "Mail sending format." If you know that your recipients are using an HTML capable email program, you can leave this set to HTML.

Checking Spelling

You can also launch Outlook Express' spelling checker by choosing Spelling from the bottom of the contextual menu.

Email offline

It is usually a good idea to write your emails while your computer isn't connected to the Net. That way you don't waste valuable bandwidth while your Mac isn't transferring data to the Net. When you are ready to send your messages, you can connect to the Net, send them, and then log off again.

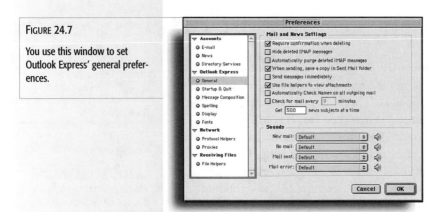

6. Click OK. From now on, when you click Send, the outgoing message will be stored in the Outbox rather than being sent immediately. The next time that you tell Outlook Express to send and receive mail, the mail in your Outbox will be sent. This is good because you won't waste online resources while composing messages if you stay connected only while sending and receiving your mail. And your mail will be in plain text, which means that everyone will be able to read it easily.

You should explore the Preferences options on your own. You will learn how to set a few more later in this chapter and in the next one, but you should customize Outlook Express to work the way you want it to.

Before I leave the topic of sending mail, you need to understand something about how Outlook Express works. In a new message window such as that in Figure 24.4, you can see formatting tools across the top of the body part of the window (they look just like formatting buttons in your other applications). You can use these to format the message you write, but be aware that not everyone's email servers and applications can receive formatted email.

While it won't hurt anything to send formatted email to someone whose email can't show formatting, you may waste a lot of your time if you format mail without being sure that your recipient can view it. On the Internet, you usually should work to the lowest common denominator unless told otherwise. While most

Sending multiple copies of the same message

If you want to send multiple copies of your message, you can add multiple addresses to the To, Cc, or Bcc lines. To use multiple addresses in any line, just separate them with a comma as in *johns@nowhere.com*, *johns@somewhere.com*.

email programs and servers are heading towards formatted mail, for the time being email's bottom line is plain old boring, unformatted text (tabs won't even work; you have to use spaces instead). However, you can always try formatting some messages and sending them to people; then check to see if they see any formatting when they receive the message. If a recipient can't see the formatting, don't bother. If he can, you can make all your messages to him look better.

Retrieving and Reading Email

It is better to give than to receive, but with email you get to do both. Reading email is as important as sending it. Reading email requires the following three basic steps:

1. Connect to the Net and tell Outlook Express to Send & Receive your email (if you use the automatic connection feature, Outlook Express will connect when you tell it to Send & Receive).

2. Wait for the email to be downloaded to your Mac.

3. Read the messages that have been downloaded.

4. Disconnect from the Net.

Reading email is just that simple.

Reading your email with Outlook Express

1. Choose Send & Receive All from the Send & Receive menu command on the Tools menu (or press Command+M). If you use a modem, but are not already connected to the Net, you will see the Remote Access Status window as your Mac signs on to the Net. After the connection is complete, you will see the mail downloading progress window as Outlook Express logs into the email server and gets your mail (see Figure 24.8). (If you use a network to connect, you will move directly to the downloading progress window since you are always connected to the Net.) If you have email, you will see new messages in your Inbox (click on the Inbox to display its contents).

IMAP is slightly different

If you use IMAP, you don't actually download email messages to your computer. They stay on a server on which you can read and manipulate them as if they were on your computer. This can be beneficial in a number of situations, which you will learn more about in Chapter 25, "Using Email: Advanced Techniques."

Another way to receive

You can also receive your mail by pressing the Send & Receive icon on Outlook Express' toolbar.

FIGURE 24.8

Outlook Express' progress dialog box shows you the progress of your mail delivery.

2. To read a message, click on it in the upper right pane. You can read the message in the lower right pane (see Figure 24.9).

FIGURE 24.9

To read a message, click on it in the upper right pane, and the text will be displayed in the lower right pane.

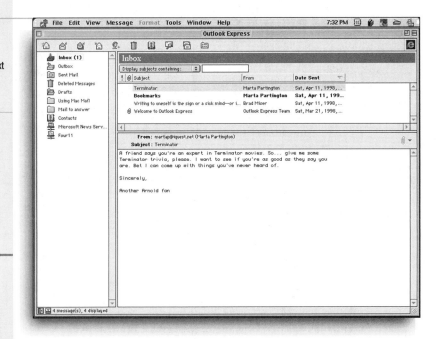

Deleting email that has been read versus leaving it on the server

Usually when you download your email, it is deleted from the mail server as soon as it is successfully downloaded to your Mac. However, you may want to leave that mail on the server so that you can download it again. This can be useful when you are checking your email from a remote computer or from another person's computer. To avoid deleting your email as it is downloaded, open the Preferences window, click Email, click Advanced, and then check the "Leave a copy of message on server" check box. Click OK twice to exit Preferences. With this setting, your email will be left on the server, and you will see the messages each time you check your mail until you delete them.

3. To read the next message in your Inbox, click it or simply press the Down arrow key.

4. Continue reading your messages until you have seen them all.

5. If you want to delete a message after you have read it, click on the Trash can button while you have the message open or selected.

Replying to Email

One of the great things about email is that you can carry on extended conversations by replying to email messages. When you reply to a message, Outlook Express creates a new message for you and automatically addresses it to the person from whom it came. The subject is also modified by the addition of "Re:" to the front of it. After you send your reply, the recipient can reply to your reply, and so on.

Before you learn how to do this, though, you need to understand one of the most important things about replying to email: quoting.

When you reply to email, it is a good idea to quote the message to which you are replying. Quoting means that you paste the relevant part of the original message into your reply so that your reply can be understood in the context of the original message. This enables the recipient of your reply to better understand your reply. For example, pretend that you just received a long message about the latest developments in the Mac OS saga. You are all excited about the fact that the Mac OS comes with a new Corvette (just kidding of course, it only comes with a Yugo). So you fire off a reply that says, "That's great." If that is all that is in your reply, the recipient may have no idea what you think is great. But if you quote the part about the Yugo, the recipient of your reply will understand exactly what you are talking about.

When you reply to a message, Outlook Express automatically copies all of the original message into your reply. To differentiate the original message from your reply, you need to make sure that Outlook Express is set so that the quoted material is marked with the > symbol. If the person you sent the reply to replies to your reply, the original message is marked with two symbols like this: >>. Your reply will be marked with one >. And so it goes.

Figure 24.10 shows an original message, while in Figure 24.11 you can see the reply. Notice that text from the original message is marked by >. Quoting really helps the person who receives your mail to put a context around what you have said. Quoting is one of the most important ways you can make your email communication clear.

Double-clicks work too

In Outlook Express, anything on which you double-click will open into its own window. This works for messages and folders. Double-click an email message, and it will open into its own window.

Email delivery settings

Remember that you can set Outlook Express to play various sounds when you receive mail or even when it finds that you don't have any mail. Use the Preferences icon or the Preferences command on the Edit menu to set this behavior.

FIGURE 24.10

This is the original email message.

FIGURE 24.11

This is a reply; notice that the text that was in the original message is marked with the > symbol.

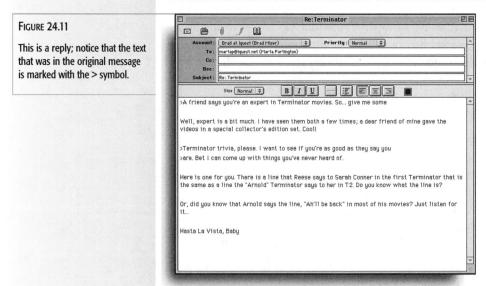

Quoting is useful, but you should be selective about what you quote. Outlook Express automatically pastes the entire message into your reply. If you are only replying to a portion of what is in the original message, delete everything but the portions to which you are replying. If you don't, your reply will be longer and less clear.

Ensuring that the quote character is set in Outlook Express

1. Click on the Preferences icon (small folder with dots on it), or choose Preferences from the Edit menu.

2. In the left pane of the window, choose Message Composition.

3. Ensure that the "Quote plain text message using" check box contains the > symbol.

4. Click OK.

Other than quoting, replying to an email message is even easier than creating a new one.

Replying to a message

1. Open a message that you have received (in any mailbox). You will see the text in the lower right pane of the Outlook Express window (see Figure 24.10).

2. Click the Reply to Sender icon (single open envelope with a red arrow pointing to it) or choose Reply to Sender from the Message menu. The message will open in a new window (see Figure 24.12). You will see that the text from the previous message has been pasted into the window and that the reply is already addressed. The quoted message text is pasted below a dashed line and is marked with the quote character, >.

3. Type your reply, editing the quoted material as necessary so that any replies you make to specific items are clear (see Figure 24.13).

4. When you are done with your reply, click on the Send message icon. If you are connected to the Net, the reply will be sent. If not, it will be stored in your Outbox.

FIGURE 24.12

This is a reply to a message; notice how the original message text has been pasted in and how the message is already addressed.

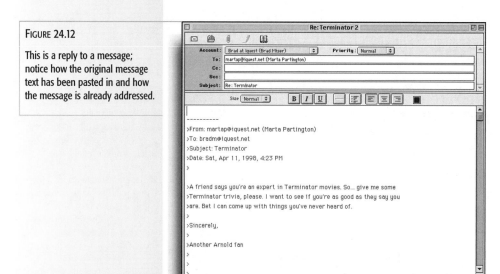

FIGURE 24.13

This is the completed reply, ready to mail; take a look at how the quoted material is used to provide context for the reply.

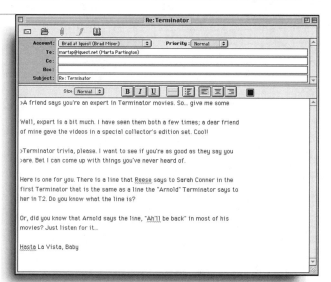

Working with Bounced Email

Occasionally, email that you send won't reach its intended address. This can happen for a number of reasons, including the following:

- **Bad address**. The most common reason is that you used the wrong address. You may have made a typo when you entered the address or you used the wrong address entirely. If you send mail to an account that doesn't exist, you can't expect it to get there, can you?

- **Canceled account**. If the email account to which you are sending mail has been closed for some reason, your mail will not be delivered.

- **Failed server**. If the server needed to get your mail to its destination goes down (quits working) and stays down for a period of time, your mail may not get delivered.

In all these cases, when email is not delivered to the correct address, it is said to have bounced. That's because the undeliverable email will be returned to you again—it bounces back to you. You will receive your original message back, normally with a new header that provides some explanation of the bounce, as well as the entire path that the mail followed until it went as far as it could (this is the gobbledygook I referred to earlier). If an email of yours bounces, use the following step-by-step to handle it.

Dealing with bounced email

1. Open the bounced mail and read the header. Sometimes, it will explain exactly why the message bounced. Sometimes, it won't. If the reason was that the account or username doesn't exist, then you probably have an addressing problem (move to step 2). If it is some other reason, you have to try to send the message again (move to step 4).

2. In the header of the bounced message, locate the address to which the message was actually sent.

3. If it is the address that you intended to send the mail to, you need to contact the recipient and determine if that address is still valid. If it isn't, get another address or find some other way to communicate with that person. If the address is incorrect (a typo), then you need to resend the message.

4. Open the message in your Outbox and copy the text, or copy the text from the body of the bounced message.

Correct address, wrong person

Occasionally, the address you enter will be a valid address, but not for the person to whom you intended to send email. When this happens, you will have no notice that your mail was delivered to the wrong person (the message won't bounce since it was delivered) unless that person contacts you to ask you why he received a message from you. This can be embarrassing so double-check your addresses before you send a message. The safest way to avoid this is to define a contact for everyone to whom you send mail and use that to address your e-mails so that you don't type addresses each time (you will learn how this works in a later section of this chapter).

5. Create a new message and address it.

6. Paste the text from the previous try in the body of the new message.

7. Add a subject.

8. Send the message.

Using Contacts

The contacts feature of Outlook Express is an excellent way to avoid retyping addresses (and mistyping them) where you regularly send mail. With contacts, you can create an email address book to make it extremely easy to address mail.

Using contacts to create an email address book

1. Click the Open contacts button (the open address book). You will see the Contacts window (see Figure 24.14).

FIGURE 24.14

Contacts makes it easy to send email because you don't have to retype addresses–this is the Contacts window.

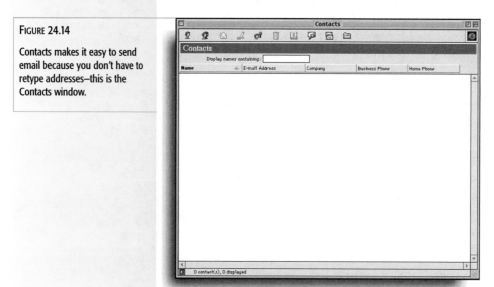

2. Click the Create a new contact button (the profile of a single person). You will see a new Contact window containing lots of fields for contact data.

3. Enter information for the contact—make sure that you enter an email address (see Figure 24.15).

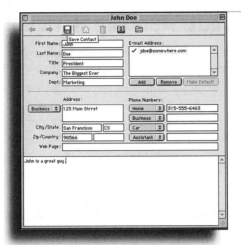

FIGURE 24.15
You can store lots of data for each of your contacts, including email addresses, "real" addresses, and phone numbers.

4. Click the Save Contact button (the floppy disk icon).

5. Close your contact's window. You will see the new contact entry in the Contacts window.

6. Close the Contacts window.

The purpose of creating contacts is to be able to quickly address email.

Addressing a mail message by using the contact information

1. Create a new message.

2. Click the Open contacts button (the open address book icon). You will see the Contacts window with all of the information your have entered.

3. Click on the name of the person to whom you want to send mail.

4. Hold down the mouse button and drag the name to the To block in the new message's window.

5. Release the mouse button. The message will be addressed. Much easier than typing an address, isn't it?

Understanding Netiquette

Just like other areas of life, the Net has its own set of customs and traditions. Fortunately, most of these idiosyncrasies are pretty obvious, and you can understand them by using a little common sense. However, some things will seem pretty bizarre to you at first. Keep these two things in mind as you use the Net: no one can see your face and no one knows your name. And although I have included this etiquette discussion in the email chapter, it is equally applicable to all of your Net activities.

Remembering That No One Can See Your Face

When you are communicating over the Net, remember that other people can't see you (unless you are video conferencing, of course). Most of the time, they can't hear you either. This makes effective communication a bit difficult since how you communicate is dependent upon body language and modulations in your voice. So remember: on the Net, these clues are absent. Here are some things to remember while you are using faceless/voiceless communication:

- Because there are no other sources of information (body language and voice tones), the words and sentences you use to communicate are even more important. So take the time necessary to make your writing as clear as possible. Be precise.

- Information in writing tends to have more impact than verbal communication. The bad news seems worse. The good news seems better. It is often necessary to understate things just a bit to convey the correct level of feeling.

- To help you communicate feelings, you can use smileys which are symbols that look roughly like someone's face (on its side) expressing emotion. Some common ones are: **:-)** happy or kidding, **;-)** sarcasm or joking, **:-0** surprise, and of course, **:-(** unhappy or angry. There are lots more that you will see, but these are enough to get you started.

  To see how these work, try reading this:

I don't see how you could say such a thing.

Now read it again with a suitable smiley added:

I don't see how you could say such a thing. **;-)**

In the first case, the reader may presume that the writer was truly offended. By adding the smiley, the same sentence takes on a much less harsh tone.

Realizing That Nobody Knows Your Name

On the Net, the only thing you have to make an impact on someone else is the power of your communication. Unless you are someone famous, people are unlikely to have a clue as to who you are. So if you are giving an opinion on something, it is a good idea to give some amount of justification for that opinion if you can. For example, a comment about a software program from someone who has used it for years may carry more weight than from someone who just started using it.

On the Net, there exists a certain informality and equality. Because poor and rich, young and old, men and women, and so forth, can access the Net, it is hard to draw boundaries based on economic or physical characteristics. You can communicate with the president of a major corporation or a 9-year-old child in the same way. What really counts on the Net is how effective that communication is.

Related to this is the fact that you should have a certain skepticism about information that you get from individuals on the Net. Just because someone says something is so does not mean it is so. Some people like to exaggerate their own value and may indicate they are more knowledgeable than they actually are. Also, there a few nuts who may actually enjoy misleading you. Just be careful to really evaluate any information you get before you act upon it.

Understanding Some Dos and Don'ts

The following is a short list of dos:

- **Use your manners!** The people you deal with on the Net are real people and deserve to be treated as such. You should not say anything to someone via the Net that you wouldn't say in person.

- **Give as well as receive**. If you can help other folks on the Net, do so. If you have the urge to provide some resource on the Net, do it. Much of the Net is done on a volunteer basis, so join in.

- **Explore and learn**. There is a lot to do on the Net so jump in with both feet.

- **Understand that resources are limited**. Be considerate of the fact that although the Net is huge and appears to be unlimited, there are real resources being consumed. Be careful to sign off when you aren't using your account. Avoid busy sites during working hours if you are just playing around.

- **Keep the topic of mailing lists and newsgroups in mind**. Don't clog up these areas with inappropriate material—for example, if you are reading a mailing list on Elvis, don't start a discussion of Bach (unless Bach and Elvis are somehow related, which I doubt).

Now some don'ts:

- **Don't be intimidated**. There are a few know-it-alls who will jump on you for asking a silly question. Your question may be silly, but everyone asks a silly question now and then. Besides, even some silly questions need to be answered.

- **Don't expect to be spoon fed**. If you need help, ask for it, but give the information people require in order to help you. Since you know you can search for information on your own, try that before asking a specific person.

- **DON'T USE ALL CAPS**! It looks like you are shouting and is irritating to read.

- **Don't trust a person without good reason**. There are creeps on the Net just as there are in real life.

- **And last, but certainly not least…don't be a jerk**. The fact that you can't see or touch the people you interact with on the Net doesn't give you justification to "take the gloves off."

Understanding More About Outlook Express

Outlook Express is a very powerful email program, and in this chapter you have learned how to use its basic features. In the next chapter, you will learn about some of Outlook Express' more advanced features. But before you go there, read the following list to learn about some of Outlook Express' other features:

- Mail that you haven't read appears in bold within a mailbox. Mailboxes that contain mail that you haven't read are also in bold.

- Messages that you haven't sent that are in the Outbox or the Drafts folder are also shown in bold. Ditto the folders that contain them.

- If you want to hide the left pane of the Outlook Express window, click the small icon with the left facing triangle in the bottom left corner of the Outlook Express window.

- If you want to hide the bottom right pane, click on the small icon with the downward pointing arrow in the bottom left corner of the Outlook Express window.

- The Trash button deletes whatever you have selected—messages or folders.

- You can forward a message to someone by choosing the message and clicking the Forward this message button (front view of an open envelope with a red arrow pointing to it).

- If you receive a message that has more than one recipient (in the To or Cc blocks), you can reply to all recipients by clicking the Reply to all recipients button (back view of two envelopes with a red arrow).

- To expand a folder, simply click on the Finder-like triangle that appears next to it.

- You can sort mail within folders by priority, subject, sender, or date. Simply click the item at the top of a mailbox's window by which you want the mailbox sorted. You can change the order by which a window is sorted by clicking the triangle that appears in the column heading.

- You can resize the subject, sender, and date sent columns by dragging the right edge of the column head box (Date Sent for example).

- Check the Outlook Express help for lots of tips and other information about Outlook Express.

Email is a great thing. You can use it to keep in touch with people around the world. If you have read this chapter and have worked through the step-by-steps, you know everything you need to know to handle lots of email. However, Outlook Express is a powerful program; you will be better off if you learn more about it. That is where the next chapter comes in.

Using Email: Advanced Techniques

Understanding email protocols and formats

Organizing, filtering, and searching email

Using public mailing lists and creating your own mailing lists

Using multiple email accounts

Viewing, saving, and attaching files to email and working with files that you receive

Moving Ahead with Email

Once you have a grasp of email basics, such as sending and receiving email, you will probably find it to be an indispensable tool for home and work. And while knowing the basics is good enough to get by, you can get even more out of it if you learn some of email's more advanced features. Fortunately, Outlook Express is packed with excellent features so that it will be able to handle just about anything that you want to do.

Understanding Email Protocols and Formats

In the previous chapter, I intentionally skimmed over the various protocols and formats with which you must deal when you use email. The reason I did this was because you really don't need to know much about the various format and protocol options that you have available to you in order to understand the basics of email.

Understanding Email Formats

Formatting with plain text

When you are creating a plain text email and want to add a table or other element, make sure that you are using a nonproportional font. With a nonproportional font, each character takes up the same amount of space and things will line up properly. If you try to use a proportional font, in which each character takes up space in proportion to its width, there will be no way to line up columns.

You learned before that on the Net, it is best to work to the lowest common denominator. In the case of email, this enables your email to be appropriate for the largest possible audience. When it comes to email, that lowest common denominator is plain, old text—no bold, italics, tabs, or formatting of any kind. You know, text like you used to have available on the most basic of typewriters. However, there are a couple of other possibilities that you can use to "jazz" up your email if you are sure that your recipient has the capability to see the "jazz."

Understanding Plain Text

Well, there isn't much to understand about plain text. It is simply plain. There are no special characters, no fancy outline styles, nor anything like you have in the most basic of work processors. Plain text is just that, plain text characters. If you want to have a table, you have to use spaces to make the table columns line up. If you want to include graphics, you have to use *regular* keyboard characters to draw them, which is no easy feat. Still, with all of its limitations, *every* email application and protocol can handle plain text. And since the content of your email is the really important part, that makes it just fine. Unless you are *sure* that your recipients (all of them on cc messages) can use the other type of email format, use plain text for your email.

Setting plain text as the default email format

1. Open Outlook Express.
2. From the Edit menu, choose Preferences.
3. Click Message Composition.
4. Click the Plain text radio button.
5. Click OK. From now on, all of the messages you send will be in plain text.

Understanding HTML

Unless you have been living in a cave for the past three years, you have probably heard of *HyperText Markup Language* (*HTML*). HTML is a way of coding text so that a program can read that coding and interpret the kind of text it is. This coding can contain style information, links, or other such information. HTML is the language that makes the Web work.

With Outlook Express, you can send messages that are encoded with HTML. This enables you to use some basic formatting tools to add some zest to your email messages. Outlook Express is set by default to use the HTML format (this, the step-by-step in the previous section).

If you know that your recipient uses an HTML capable email program (such as Outlook Express), then you can use HTML to format your emails. When the recipient receives the message, she will see your formatted masterpiece.

Even if you aren't sure about your recipient's email capability, you can use the HTML format. If your recipient has an HTML capable email program, he will see your formatted message. If he doesn't, he will still see the text of the message, but he will also see the raw HTML code. Or he will receive the message as an

Where did the buttons go?

You may notice the next time that you create a new message, that the formatting buttons just above the body are gone. That is because you now create messages by default in the plain text format, so there is no need for formatting buttons. If you change the default back to HTML, the formatting buttons will return.

Your HTML greeting

The email that is automatically in your Inbox when you first launch Outlook Express is an example of an HTML email message. As you see, you can get very sophisticated. But it is not likely that you will spend that much time formatting an email message. Email is supposed to be somewhat "down and dirty," although you can receive Web pages as email, which is a nice feature. Some mailing lists give you the option of receiving the mail as an HTML document rather than a plain text file (an example is CNN's excellent quick news bulletin that you can receive each morning—visit `http://www.cnn.com` to sign up).

Setting HTML as the default

You can set HTML as the default type by choosing HTML instead of Plain text in the Message Composition Preferences window. See the step-by-step in the previous section.

HTML attachment that can be opened in a Web browser. Both of these are a bit of a pain, though, so unless you are sure, I recommend that you use plain text.

Creating an HTML message

1. Create a new message.

2. From the Format menu, choose Rich Text (HTML). A formatting tool bar will be added to the new message window (see Figure 25.1).

FIGURE 25.1

You can create a formatted mail message by using the formatting tool bar.

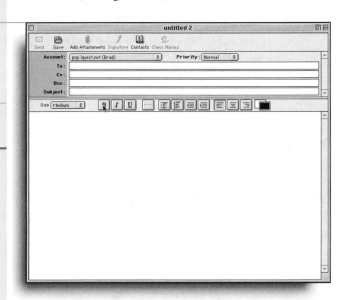

Try as hard as they can

Some email programs that aren't HTML capable, such as Eudora Light, will do their best to interpret the HTML the best that they can. The basic text formatting will come through, although there will be artifacts and leftovers from the HTML code. To set this behavior in Eudora Light, choose Special, Settings, and select the Styled Text preference. You can then select which styles Eudora pays attention to.

Reply in like format

Notice that in the Message Composition Preferences window, there is a "Reply to messages using the format in which they were sent" check box. If this is checked, when you create a reply, you will automatically use the format of the message to which you are replying. For example, if you reply to a message in HTML, your reply will also be in HTML. This is a good option to leave on.

3. Write the text and apply formatting by using the buttons on the tool bar and the commands on the Format menu.

4. Send the message as you normally do.

Being Aware of Email Protocols

There are two email protocols that you might use with your email account: POP or IMAP. POP, or *Post Office Protocol*, is the more widely used on the Net. The other major protocol is IMAP, or *Internet Message Access Protocol*. The most important difference between them is that with POP, when you check your mail, your messages are transferred from the mail server to your computer (they are normally deleted from the server unless you set a preference so that they are not). With IMAP, messages are left on the server, and you can read them from there. The advantage of this is primarily for people who read their mail from different computers. Each time you check your mail with an IMAP email account, you see the same Inbox because it is stored on the server rather than on your computer. So if you work on a computer at work and another one at home, you don't have to bother sending important messages to yourself at home. You can just sign onto your mail from home, and it will be the same as it was when you checked it from work.

The kind of email account you have determines whether you use POP or IMAP—you can't change from one to the other without changing your email account. And since there isn't much difference in using them, it doesn't matter all that much. The only case in which you should try to get an IMAP account is if you frequently check your mail from different computers. IMAP is particularly handy if you use a laptop and a desktop Mac.

Since IMAP email remains on the server, you may be wondering how you can ever get rid of email with an IMAP account. After you marked it for deletion, the mail moves into the Deleted Messages folder. Then you can purge the mail, which removes it from the server. The best way to do this is to check the "Automatically purge deleted IMAP messages" check box from the General Preferences window. You can also do it manually by choosing Purge Deleted Messages from the Edit menu.

Organizing Your Email

As you start sending and receiving lots of mail, keeping it all in the Inbox will become a pain as you scroll through tons of messages looking for the one you want. Fortunately, Outlook Express provides you with tools to keep your email nice and tidy. The most important tool is the capability to create folders in which you can store your email.

Outlook Express provides a number of standard folders by default. These are the following:

Appealing to the commoner

It is a good idea to leave the Plain text formatting button selected since you can always create an HTML message by using the Format menu. That way, you have to take an action to create an HTML message since it is likely to be the exception rather than the rule.

Outlook Express and Mac OS 8.5

Mac OS 8.5 ships with version 4.01 of Outlook Express. If you are using a different version, some of the screens may look slightly different than they do in this chapter, but the steps will probably work with just some minor deviations.

Outlook Express and Mac OS 8.5

Mac OS 8.5 ships with version 4.01 of Outlook Express. If you are using a different version, some of the screens may look slightly different than they do in this chapter, but the steps will probably work with just some minor deviations.

The point of no return

The Outbox is email's point of no return. If a message is still in the Outbox, you can open and change it. If it is no longer in the Outbox and you have sent your mail, it is too late to make any changes.

Sent Mail folder

If you do have Outlook Express save all the mail that you send, it is a good idea to open up the Sent Mail folder every so often and delete any messages you no longer need. Otherwise, this folder can grow very large.

- **Inbox**. This is where all of your incoming email is stored.

- **Outbox**. This is the folder in which Outlook Express stores mail that you have created and put in the queue, but that has not actually been sent yet.

- **Sent Mail**. After you send a message, Outlook Express stores it in the Sent Mail folder. This is a nice way to have a history of the email you have sent. You can turn this off by unchecking the "When sending, save a copy in the Sent Mail folder" check box in the General Preferences window.

- **Deleted messages**. When you delete a message, it is moved into the Deleted Messages folder, which works much like the Mac's Trash. By default, this folder is emptied of all messages when you quit Outlook Express. You can change this by unchecking the Empty Deleted Messages folder in the Startup & Quit Preferences window.

- **Drafts**. When you have created a message, but haven't yet put it in the queue, Outlook Express stores it in the Drafts folder.

You can add your own folders to Outlook Express, and it is easy to move messages from one folder to another. Here are a few pointers on how Outlook Express folders work:

- New folders are created by choosing New and then Folder from the File menu. When the folder is created, its name is selected, and you can name it whatever you would like.

- Folders in Outlook Express work just like folders in the Finder (for example, you can rename them by selecting the folder's name).

- Subfolders within folders are created by selecting a folder, choosing File, New, and the Subfolder. Name the subfolder, and it will appear within the selected folder.

- The contents of a folder can be expanded or collapsed by clicking the triangle next to its name.

- Messages can be moved from one folder to another by drag-and-drop.

Filtering Your Email

You can use filters to perform actions on mail that meet criteria that you define. For example, you can create a folder for mail from your best friend and set up a filter to automatically move mail from that person into that folder. Another use may be that you want all mail from particular people or groups to be placed in a folder dedicated to a specific project.

In the following step-by-step, I will create a mail action that places all the email I receive from my pal, Jane, into a single folder. For this example, pretend that Jane's email address is jane@someplace.net. You can use the same steps to set up a mail action for mail from any address. Just use a real address instead of my fictional one.

Creating a filter to place mail from Jane Jones into the Mail from the Jane folder

1. Create a folder into which you want the mail moved.

2. From the Tools menu, choose Mail Rules. You will see the Mail Rules window (see Figure 25.2).

3. Click New Rule. You will see the Define Mail Rule dialog that you use to create your rule (see Figure 25.3).

FIGURE 25.2
You can develop mail rules, more commonly called filters, to perform certain actions on mail that meets your criteria.

4. Name your rule.

5. Check the "Apply to incoming" check box.

6. In the Criteria area, choose From and Is from the pop-up menus.

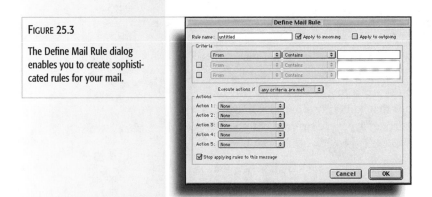

FIGURE 25.3

The Define Mail Rule dialog enables you to create sophisticated rules for your mail.

7. Enter Jane's address in the text field.

8. From the Action 1 pop-up menu, choose Move message.

9. Select the folder that you created in step 1 from the pop-up menu. When you are done, your rule should look something like Figure 25.4.

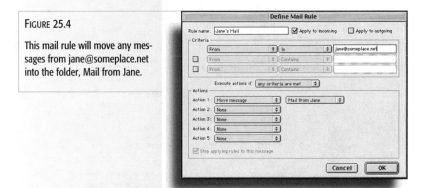

FIGURE 25.4

This mail rule will move any messages from jane@someplace.net into the folder, Mail from Jane.

10. Click OK.

11. Close the Mail Rules dialog. Now, whenever you get mail from jane@someplace.net, it will automatically be moved into the Mail from Jane folder.

Mail rules are very powerful, and the step-by-step only scratches the surface of what you can use them for. Open one of the Action pop-up menus in the Define Mail Rules to get a better idea of the variety of mail actions that are possible. For example, you can set a mail action to automatically add people from whom you receive mail to your Contacts. You can also automatically redirect or forward mail to or from certain people.

Note that you can have multiple actions for a single criteria, and you can have multiple criteria for a single rule. Rules are very powerful and once you create one or two of them, you will see how easy they are to create and use.

Searching Your Email

After you build up many folder with lots of messages, you won't be able to remember the contents of each message that you have stored. Fortunately, Outlook Express provides a Find tool that you can use to search your email.

Searching your email

1. Click the Find button. You will see the Find dialog (see Figure 25.5).

FIGURE 25.5

You can use Outlook Express' Find command to search your email.

2. Enter the text for which you want to search.

3. Use the Headers check boxes to determine which parts of messages that you want Outlook Express to search (From, To, Subject, or Body).

4. Use the Location radio buttons to set the locations in which you want Outlook Express to search (Current Message, All folders, or choose a folder from the pop-up menu).

5. Click Find. You will see a Search Results window containing all of the messages that contained your search text.

6. Click a message to read it.

7. When you are done, close the Search Results window.

Of POP and IMAP

There is no reason that all of your email accounts have to use the same protocol. You can use a combination of POP and IMAP accounts at the same time.

Using Multiple Email Accounts

You may find that you end up with more than one email account. For example, you may have a work email account and a personal email account, while your spouse has yet another account. With Outlook Express, you can access each of these accounts by using the same program. This makes working with multiple email accounts easy.

Configuring Multiple Email Accounts

Before you can work with additional email accounts, you have to configure Outlook Express to use each account.

1. From the Edit menu, choose Preferences. You will see the by-now-familiar Preferences window.

2. Click on Email in the left pane.

3. Click New Account. You will see the New Account dialog (see Figure 25.6).

FIGURE 25.6

Using the New Account Dialog, you can set up multiple new email accounts.

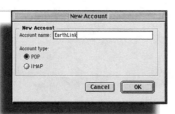

4. Name the new account, set the account type, and click OK. You will return to the configuration window.

5. Complete the fields in the dialog, just as you would if you had to reconfigure your first account.

6. If you want the new account to be the default account, click Make Default. The default account will always be the one selected when you perform any action that requires you to select an account.

7. Click General to move to the Mail and News Settings Preferences.

8. If you are using a modem to connect, uncheck the "Send messages immediately" check box. Adjust any other settings in this dialog to suit your preferences. For example, if you are using an IMAP account, check the "Hide deleted IMAP messages" check box if you do not want to see deleted messages before they are purged.

9. Click Message Composition.

10. Set the Mail sending format (either plain text or HTML).

11. Click OK. This account will be enabled, and you can work with it by using Outlook Express.

Working with Multiple Email Accounts

There isn't all that much to working with multiple email accounts after you have them configured. Mostly, it is a matter of choosing the account that you want to use for a particular action. Here are some points of which you should be aware:

- When sending mail, you can choose which account it is from by using the Account pop-up menu. When you choose an account from this menu, the return address for that account will be on the mail the recipient receives. Your default email account will be selected automatically.

- When you send and receive email, you can choose to use either or both accounts (see Figure 25.6). If you choose Send & Receive All (Command-M), mail from all accounts will be sent and received.

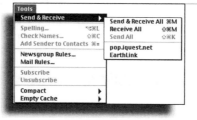

> **Auto checking mail**
>
> If you want Outlook Express to automatically check your email at specified intervals, go to the General Preferences window and check the "Check for mail every ___ minutes" check box. Enter the number of minutes between email checks. When this amount of time passes, Outlook Express will automatically check your mail in all accounts. If you connect through a modem and the connection is down at the time, Outlook Express will be unable to check your mail.

FIGURE 25.7

Using the Send & Receive command, you can choose to send and receive email for any or all of your email accounts.

- Remember that your email account is separate from the account through which you connect to the Net. This enables you to use multiple email accounts with one access account. However, occasionally, some email accounts will not let you send mail through a mail server if you are logged on from an account not originating from that server's operator. For example, if I am logged on through my IQuest ISP and try to send email through my EarthLink mail account, I will get an error message (I can read email from it, however). If this happens to you, you will need to configure an access account that corresponds to that mail account and use that to connect to send mail.

- If you want email from different accounts to automatically go into different folders, set up mail actions that move mail addressed to each account into specific folders.

Using Mailing Lists

Mailing lists are email discussions about almost any topic you can imagine. There are two basic types of mailing lists: public and private. *Public mailing lists* enable anyone to sign up for, read, and send messages to the mailing list. You can find public mailing lists on such diverse topics as games, music, fan clubs, computers, stock market reports, sports, comics, aviation, arts, jobs, pets, news, jokes, juggling, climbing, reviews, fractals, classifieds, and much more.

Private mailing lists are a way for you to send mail to multiple recipients at the same time. These are particularly useful for team projects. You can set up a mailing list for each member of the team and use that to send out important announcements (such as meeting notices) or any other information that is relevant to the project. Believe it or not, a lot of families also use mailing lists to keep in touch with each other and transmit family news all over the world.

Using Public Mailing Lists

Here's how public mailing lists work. First, you send an email message to a specific address for each mailing list that interests you; your message contains a command that requests that you be added to the mailing list (you will be *subscribed* to the list). Then you receive confirmation that you have been added to the mailing list along with instructions on how to do various things with the list (such as *unsubscribe*). From that point on, all you have to do is read the messages as they are automatically sent to you. You can reply when you are so moved; your reply goes to every person on the mailing list.

One mailing list that you should subscribe to is the Mac EvangeList mailing list. This list is for all things Macintosh. And it is a very pro Mac list—it was started by Guy Kawaski, (Apple's first evangelist).

Subscribing to the Mac EvangeList mailing list

1. Create a new email message.

2. Address the message to majordomo@public.lists.apple.com.

3. In the body of the message, type *subscribe EvangeList-Digest* (you can leave the subject line blank).

4. Send the message. After a time, you will receive a confirmation message from the mail server. You need to reply to this message. You will also receive a message telling you the results of your mailing list command (which was subscribe).

5. Open the confirmation message that you receive and reply to it.

6. In the reply, delete everything but the line of text that is "auth <auth_key> subscribe **listname** your_address"—make sure that you remove the > symbol as well.

7. Send this reply. You will receive a welcome message and after that you will start receiving the mailing list messages. Enjoy!

Be careful if you decide to send mail to a mailing list. Make sure that you send mail to the correct address. There are usually two addresses for each list: one is an administrative list, and the other is the address to which you send messages that you want everyone on the list to see. Check the information that is mailed to you when you subscribe to a list to learn which is which.

You can read mailing list messages just like you do any other email. If you subscribe to a digest version, you will see multiple messages combined into one. When you don't want to continue receiving the mailing list anymore, you will need to send the

Digest?

Digests are compilations of messages sent to a mailing list. Instead of receiving lots of separate messages each day, you will receive a single message that contains all of those sent to the list that day. Digests are more efficient, especially if the mailing list is very active.

Keep the addresses straight

Whatever you do, make sure that you use the administrative address to send subscribe and unsubscribe commands. If you post these to the mailing list, you will receive lots of mail asking you not to do that again (some of it in a rather rude way, too).

proper command to the mail server to unsubscribe from it. Make sure that you save the welcome email you receive from all the lists to which you subscribe. Then you will always have the instructions you need to unsubscribe from that list.

If you have something to contribute to the list, you can *post* a message to the list. Your message will be sent to all the members of that list. Be careful and consider what you post to a list. A lot of people will be reading your message, and if you send something inappropriate to the list, you may get a lot of nasty email back in response.

Some lists are *moderated* ,which means that all mail to be posted goes to a person or a group who screens the message to make sure that it is appropriate for the list. (The Mac EvangeList is a moderated list). In an *unmoderated list*, it is a free-for-all, and all messages are immediately posted to the list. Unmoderated lists tend to have more traffic, but much of it is a waste of time. Still, if you like more free-flowing discussions, you may refer to unmoderated lists.

Creating Your Own Mailing List

Adding people to contacts

A great way to add people to your contacts is to select a message and from the Tools menu, choose Add Sender to Contacts (Command-=). The sender's address will be placed in your contacts list for easy use.

Public mailing lists can be good, but you may find that personal mailing lists are as useful to you. You can create personal mailing lists that contain one or more of your contacts. When you want to send mail to the people on your mailing list, drag the mailing list to a new message window. The mail will then be addressed to everyone whose address is part of the mailing list.

Creating a personal mailing list

1. Click Contacts to open your contacts.

2. Click the Mailing List button.

3. Name your mailing list. The Contacts window will change to show the contents of that list, which will be nothing immediately after you create it (see Figure 25.8).

4. Click the Find People button.

5. In the Find People window, enter the name of the person who you want to add to your mailing list.

6. Drag the name from the Find People window onto the new mailing list's window.

7. Repeat steps 5 and 6 until you have added everyone that you want to add.

8. Close the list window by clicking the Inbox.

Sending mail by using a personal mailing list

1. Expand the Contacts by clicking the triangle next to it.

2. Select the mailing list to which you want to send email.

3. Click the Mail to button. A new message window will appear with the mailing list in the To field.

4. Create and send your message as you normally do. It will be sent to each address in the mailing list.

Working with Email Attachments

One of the best features of email is that you can send and receive files with your email. This makes email one of the most convenient ways to transfer files to other people.

Understanding File Encoding

The steps involved in attaching and receiving files are easy; however, sometimes getting a usable file to its destination is not so easy. There are lots of different file types, email packages, networks, and computer platforms involved. Plus, because only

Changing attachment coding

To change how files are coded
when they are attached, use the
Attachment encoding preference
under the Message Composition
preferences.

plain text can be sent across the Net, files are *encoded* before they
are sent; when a file is encoded, it is converted into a plain text
file. When you receive a file, it is *decoded* and becomes a usable
file again.

Sometimes the files you attach will get messed up (computer
geeks say the file gets *munged*) when the recipient receives them.
There are lots of ways this can happen, but if you do a little
investigation first, you can prevent some problems. Most of the
time, attachments work fine. If not, you can often experiment
until you make them work.

You usually don't have to worry about decoding a file that you
receive because Outlook Express will do that for you. Sending
files is another matter, however.

Before you send an attachment, try to figure out what kind of
computer and network the recipient is using. Here are some
general guidelines on attachments:

What's MIME?

MIME stands for *Multipurpose
Internet Mail Extensions*. Basically, it
is a set of standards for files that
enable MIME compliant email packages to transfer files easily and successfully. Outlook Express on the
Mac and on the PC are both MIME-
compliant.

- If the recipient is using a Macintosh, set the Encoding
  method to BinHex—this is the default. This ensures that
  both *forks* of Mac files are transferred

- If the recipient is using a PC, choose another encoding
  option, such as *Base64*. Base64 is a MIME-compliant encoding format.

- If the recipient is using a local area network of some kind
  instead of connecting directly to the Internet—this is the
  way a lot of companies connect—go ahead and try to send
  the attachment. But be sure to check with the recipient to
  make sure that he was able to use the file. Often, the gateways to these local networks will trash attached files,
  although email messages themselves generally get through
  just fine.

- If you are sending the file to another Mac user, you should
  compress the file before you attach it—make sure that you
  attach the compressed file rather than the uncompressed
  version. By compressing the file, you are making it smaller
  and thus much faster to send and receive. The StuffIt format
  is the most common compression format on the Mac. You
  will learn more about compression in the next section.

- If you are sending files to a PC user who is using Windows 3.1, stick with the 8.3 naming convention. This means that you should name the file with eight characters or less and add a three-letter extension that is appropriate for the type of file that you are sending (.doc for a Word file for example).

SEE ALSO

➤ *To learn more about PC file naming conventions, see page 497*

- In fact, unless you are 100 percent sure that the recipient is using a Mac, you should try to name files that you will send with the three-letter extensions that are used on the Windows platform (such as .xls for an Excel file). This is a pain, but it will make the file easier to use for the PC user receiving it.

When you attach files to mail, you need to set the encoding used (if you want to use something other than the default) and make sure that you have named it appropriately for the recipient.

Understanding File Compression

In order to make attachments as small as possible (and thus faster to download), it is a good idea to compress any files that you send. You are also likely to receive compressed files.

On the Mac, almost all files are compressed by using the StuffIt format; these usually have .sit appended to the file's name. On the PC, files are compressed by using the Zip format (the extension is .zip). Mac OS 8.5 comes with the utility you need to both compress and uncompress files.

While it is a good idea to compress files before you send them, if you aren't sure that your recipient will be able to uncompress them (if they are using a PC for example), you can send them without compression. The files will take a lot longer for you to send and for your recipient to receive, but at least you are more sure that the file will be usable once it reaches its destination.

Bravo AOL

PC files are usually compressed by using the zip format. America Online software doubles as an excellent decompression program for zip files. You can open zip files from within AOL, and it will decompress them for you. You can use the AOL software for this even if you don't have an AOL account. You are likely to receive a disk or CD with the AOL software on it, or you can download it from http://www.aol.com.

It's two tools in one!

StuffIt Expander will also decode a number of encoding formats as well. If you receive a file with an extension that you don't recognize, try using StuffIt Expander on it; if it is an encoded file, StuffIt Expander may be able to decode it for you.

Double-clicking to unstuff

If you double-click a stuffit archive, StuffIt Expander will uncompress it for you.

Aladdin Systems

Aladdin Systems can be contacted at `http://www.aladdinsys.com`.

Enhanced Expander?

The Enhanced version of StuffIt Expander, that is part of the DropStuff application, will decode and uncompress lots more formats than the free version. If you plan on downloading files from the Web or using email to send and receive attachments, you should definitely register DropStuff.

Uncompressing Files

When you receive a .sit file, you need to uncompress it before you can use it. Fortunately, Mac OS 8.5 comes with an excellent uncompression utility from Aladdin Systems called StuffIt Expander. StuffIt Expander is freeware so you can use it without any cost. Plus, it is easy to use.

To use StuffIt Expander, create an alias for it on your desktop. Using it is just a matter of drag-and-drop.

Preparing and using StuffIt Expander

1. Open the Aladdin folder that is within the Internet Utilities folder that is within the Internet folder on your startup disk.

2. Open the StuffIt Expander folder.

3. Select StuffIt Expander and hold down the Option and Command keys as you drag it to your desktop. An alias will be created on your desktop.

4. Close the folders.

5. Drag a compressed file (one with the .sit extension) onto the StuffIt Expander icon on your desktop. You will see a brief progress window as StuffIt Expander uncompresses the file. When it is done, the uncompressed files will be in the same folder as the compressed file was.

Compressing Files

Mac OS 8.5 includes Aladdin Systems' excellent DropStuff for compressing files. DropStuff is easy to use and is quite powerful. Note that the version of DropStuff included with Mac OS 8.5 is shareware. If you continue to use it for more than 15 days, you need to register it with Aladdin. At $30, it is a bargain. You must first install Drop Stuff before you can use it.

Installing DropStuff

1. Open the Internet Utilities folder that is within the Internet folder on your startup disk. Then open the Aladdin folder.

2. Double-click the DropStuff w/EE 4.0 Installer icon to launch the installer.

3. Click Continue.

4. Read the Welcome message and click Continue.

5. Click Install.

6. Tell DropStuff where to install the DropStuff folder and click Install.

7. If you have not registered any Aladdin products, click Cancel in the dialog prompting you to locate a personalized Aladdin product. If you have registered an Aladdin product, find it, and the installer will transfer the information to the DropStuff installation.

8. Click OK in the "Installation was successful" window.

9. Hold down Option and Command and drag the DropStuff icon onto your desktop to create an alias there.

10. Close the folders.

Using DropStuff is also easy with drag-and-drop.

Compressing a file or folder with DropStuff

1. Drag the folder or file that you want to compress onto the DropStuff icon. If you haven't registered it, you will see the registration dialog.

2. To use it in the demo mode, click Not Yet. Then you will see a progress window as the file or folder is stuffed. (After you register DropStuff, you move straight to the progress window.) The compressed file will be located in the same folder as the file or folder that you are compressing. It will have the .sit appended to its name.

Viewing Attachments

You can choose to view attached files from within Outlook Express rather than downloading them. Outlook Express uses helper applications to enable you to view the files. Because you are more likely to want to use help applications while you are using the Web, you will learn more about them in the Web chapters. For now, just know that you can set the helpers that Outlook Express uses by choosing the File Helpers preference in the left pane of the Preferences window.

Multiple versions of compressed files

If you uncompress a file or folder into a folder with a file of the same name, DropStuff will append a .1 onto the duplicate's name.

SEE ALSO

➤ *To learn about configuring and using helper applications, see page 651*

Receiving Files Attached to Email Messages

You will probably want to receive files attached to email messages that are sent to you as well.

To receive a file attached to a message

1. When you see a new message that has a paper clip symbol next to its subject, the message has a file attached to it (see Figure 25.9).

2. Open and read the message.

3. Click on the Get attachments button (the paper clip with the downward arrow). You will see a pop-up menu showing all of the files attached to that message (see Figure 25.10).

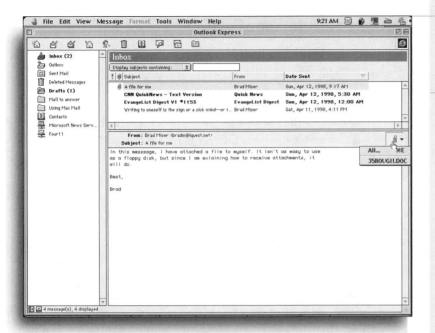

FIGURE 25.10

The Get attachments pop-up menu shows you the files that are attached to a message.

4. Choose the file you want to open from the pop-up menu. The file will launch just as if you had double-clicked it in the Finder. The file will be opened by using the helper file that is set for the file type.

You may want to save files you receive rather than opening them right away. If you are working on a project, for example, you might want to collect all of the files in a particular folder instead of opening them from the emails to which they are attached.

Saving files when you receive them

1. Open the message that has a file attached.

2. Hold down the Option key, click the Get attachments button, and select the file. You will be prompted to save the file with a standard Save dialog box.

3. Maneuver to where you want to save the file and click Save.

4. If the file is compressed (it has a .sit or .zip extension), you will have to uncompress it before using it.

Saving files

You can make the save function the default (instead of viewing the file) by unchecking the Use file helpers to view attachments preference (in the General preferences window). If you do this, you will be prompted to save files rather than view them with a helper. Then when you hold down the Option key, you will view the file instead of saving it.

Attaching Files to Your Email

To send a file with an email message, you can create a message and then attach your files to it.

Attaching a file to an email message

1. Compress the file you are going to send by using DropStuff; if you aren't sure that the recipient can deal with a .sit file, skip this step.

2. Create a new message or reply to a message in the usual way, but don't send it yet.

3. Click the Add Attachments button (the paper clip).

4. In the standard file dialog box, move to the file you want to send (choose the stuffed version if you compressed it), highlight it, and click Add. The file will appear in the Attached Files section of the window (see Figure 25.11).

Drag-and-drop

You can also attach a file to a message by dragging the file onto a message window. Once you do, the file will be attached just as if you had followed the steps.

Add them all at once

If you click on the Add All button, all of the files in the opened folder will be attached to the message.

FIGURE 25.11

The file called Archive.sit is now attached to the email message.

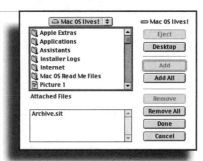

Automatic compression

You can set Outlook Express to automatically compress your attachments by going to the Message Composition Preferences dialog and checking the Compress Attachments check box. When you send a message with a file attached, Outlook Express will automatically use DropStuff to compress the file when it sends it. This prevents you from having to manually stuff the file. The down side is that all the files you send will be compressed and if you some of your recipients can't deal with stuffed files, they won't be able to use them. Sometimes, it is better to have to think about compressing files for this reason.

5. If you want to add additional files, repeat step 3 until they are all attached.

6. When you have added all of the files that you want to attach, click Done. The file will now appear in the bottom of the email message to which it is attached (see Figure 25.12).

7. Send the message.

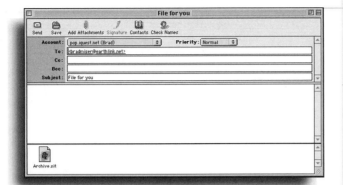

FIGURE 25.12
This message has a file attached;
it appears in the bottom pane of
the window.

Updating Outlook Express

The version of Outlook Express that comes with Mac OS 8.5 is
4.01. As with all other applications, Microsoft periodically
updates it. To get the latest version of Outlook Express as well as
for information and support, use your Web browser to go to
`http://www.microsoft.com/ie/ie40/oe/`.

Browsing the Web: The Basics

Understanding the Web and URLs

Understanding the anatomy of a Web page

Surfing the Web

Touring and configuring Internet Explorer

Working with the history of the Web sites you have visited

Using great Web sites

Understanding the Web

You are about to experience a revolutionary form of communication, which also happens to be a revolutionary form of entertainment, commerce, the arts, *and* education. The World Wide Web is evolving into a phenomenon, the likes of which have rarely been seen before.

The World Wide Web enables you to virtually explore the world from your computer. And the world is only as big as your imagination. Just imagine being able to tap into some of the finest university libraries in the world to do research on a paper. It's possible. But there's more. You can buy and sell goods and services, watch movie clips of upcoming feature films, hear fantastic sounds, visit art galleries, experience different types of imagery, and read about any topic under the sun. Are you a news junkie? The Web enables you to browse through newspapers and magazines from all over the world.

But the best thing about the Web is the people you'll meet there. You can visit personal Web pages of individuals whom you could never hope to meet in any other way. Visiting the Web is truly an amazing experience.

It's time for the wonderful World Wide Web. Weady?

Understanding URLs

URLs (*Uniform Resource Locators*) are fundamental to exploring the Web; URLs are a standardized way of identifying places on the Internet. They function just as street addresses do, and they also tell your Web browser what kind of Internet service you will be accessing when you move to that URL.

URLs look like the following:

code://xxx.somewhere.zzz/document

Each of the elements of a URL are explained in the following list:

- **The service code**. This is the type of Internet service that you will be using when you move to the URL. Table 26.1 lists *some* of the codes you may see. Although there are a number of different codes, those in Table 26.1 are the most common. Once you get the hang of these codes, any others you see won't cause you any trouble.

Table 26.1 URL codes and the services they represent.

Service Code	Service	Comment
http	World Wide Web	The http code indicates a World Wide Web site. You'll use URLs with this code frequently.
https	World Wide Web	The https indicates a secure Web site; when you transmit data to and from an http site, it is encrypted for security purposes.
ftp	File Transfer Protocol	You'll use ftp URLs when downloading files from the Internet.
mailto	Email	You'll use mailto when sending email via a Web browser and some email programs.
news	Usenet News	You'll see news URLs when reading Usenet News.
file	A file	This code indicates that what you are looking at is a file on your Mac.

SEE ALSO

➤ *To learn about newsgroups, see Chapter 28, "Reading Newsgroups"*

- **The domain name**. The next part is the address of the server that is hosting the Web site. For example, *xxx.some-where.zzz* stands for a particular Internet service on a specific computer somewhere on the Net. The domain *xxx.some-where.zzz* can refer to many different kinds of machines located all over the world, everything from large computers at major universities to a PC in someone's home. Usually, the *xxx* will be the service code that you are using—*www* for the World Wide Web, *ftp* for file transfer protocol, and so

Codes and syntax

You should know that of the codes listed in Table 26.1, the *mailto* and the *news* don't use the two slashes (*//*) after the *code*. So a mail URL may look like this:

mailto:bradm@iquest.net

Sometimes a URL will end with a slash (*/*) and sometimes it won't.

on. The *somewhere.com* identifies the particular computer; it is the computer's Internet name. This part is very similar to everything after the @ in an email address.

- **The document.** The last part, *document*, is the specific item to which you're moving; it can represent anything from a Web page to a file that you want to download, to a newsgroup message, and so on. However, *document* won't be part of every URL you see. Sometimes, you'll see a URL to a specific server rather than a document. In this case, the URL will end with *xxx.somewhere.zzz/*.

Usually, you don't have to worry about these details as you'll either be entering URLs as you find them or just clicking the mouse button to indicate where you want to go. When you do type a URL, just type it as shown and you'll be fine.

You primarily use URLs in a Web browser such as Internet Explorer, although you can also use them in service-specific applications, such as email clients. Of course, they are superfluous in single-purpose applications since there is only one place that the address can point to (an email address in an email program, for example).

Do you hate to type? I do. I personally am waiting for the day when voice recognition becomes a *practical* reality, like in "Star Trek." *Computer do this, computer do that.* But, until then, typing is a way of life and URLs are long, ugly beasts. Unfortunately for all of us, we just have to deal with them.

Fortunately, you don't have to type many URLs you use. Often, you can use a URL by clicking on something with your mouse or by copying and pasting it. And with favorites (which you will learn about in a later section), you really only have to type a URL once.

That's enough about URLs. It's time to get on the Web.

Introducing Microsoft's Internet Explorer

Mac OS 8.5 includes an excellent Web browser, Microsoft's Internet Explorer, as its default Web browser (see Figure 26.1). In addition to basic Web surfing, Internet Explorer provides many excellent features that you can use to get the most out of your Web experiences.

FIGURE 26.1

Internet Explorer is an excellent Web browser.

Using Navigator

While Netscape Navigator is no longer the Macís default Web browser, it is still included on the Mac OS 8.5 installation CD. There is no reason that you canít install it from the CD and try it for yourself. To install Navigator, run the Install Mac OS 8.5 application, use the Customize option, and then choose the Customized Installation option for the Internet Access software. Check the Netscape Navigator check box and continue with the install. Netscape Navigator version 4.05 will be installed on your Mac. See Appendix A, ìInstalling and Maintaining the Mac OS,î for more information on running the installer to install components.

Previously, Netscape Navigator was the default Mac Web browser. The two programs are fairly similar and have been battling it out for market dominance. Netscape Navigator is also an excellent application (see Figure 26.2). Each program excels in certain areas, but you are likely to prefer one over the other for aesthetic or other reasons. Since Netscape Navigator is also free to use, there is no reason that you shouldn't try it for yourself to see which you prefer, especially since Netscape Navigator is also included on the Mac OS 8.5 CD-ROM.

FIGURE 26.2

Netscape Navigator is also a very powerful and easy-to-use Web browser.

FIGURE 26.2

Netscape Navigator is also a very powerful and easy-to-use Web browser.

Choosing the browser that is right for you

Since you have a choice of browsers, which should you use? That depends on your personal preferences. Frankly, they both work similarly. The differences between them are relatively minor, and if you can use one, you can use the other with just a little exploration. You may end up using them both at certain times. After you are comfortable using Internet Explorer, I suggest that you give Navigator a try and see which browser you prefer.

For the remainder of this chapter and the next, you will be learning how to use Internet Explorer, but you can do the same tasks similarly in Netscape Navigator. The terminology and commands are slightly different, but once you can use one, you can use the other.

Understanding the Anatomy of a Web Page

Web pages, just like email messages, have a certain structure. With a Web page, the structure is even simpler because there really isn't much to them, from the user's point-of-view anyway (see Figure 26.3). The Web page itself is within the inside borders of the window. Everything else you see is part of Internet Explorer (which you will learn about in a few pages). Within Web pages, you will see text, graphics, and links. Text and graphics you'll no doubt understand. Links are the only thing that really makes a Web page different from many other documents that you view. Links are simply pointers to someplace else.

That place may be another Web page, a different part of the current Web page, a larger view of a graphic, a file, and so on. Most links are shown by underlined text, but many graphics also contain links. Using a link is simple—click a link and move to wherever it points.

FIGURE 26.3

Your basic, everyday Web page (not really, CNN is more useful than your everyday Web page).

1. Text links

2. Search box

3. TOC links

4. Advertising banner

5. Link buttons

Some Web sites use frames, which simply divide the page into different sectors (see Figure 26.4). Usually the frame on the left contains a live list of contents of the site. To move to a particular area, you simply click it in the left frame. Sometimes, you can resize frames and sometimes you can't. It depends on how the page is designed. Frames were in vogue for a while, but once everyone who used them figured out that they were harder for both Web page creator and viewer to work with, they were not used as much anymore.

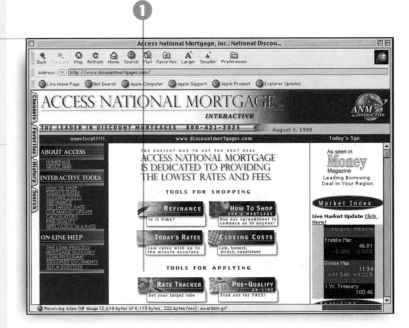

FIGURE 26.4

Access National Mortgage's Web site (www.someplace.com) uses frames.

1 Frames

That is about all you need to know about how a Web page is constructed —for now anyway.

Surfing the Web

Before you get into more complicated information, take your first cruise on the Web. There are three basic ways to move around. You can use links, enter a URL directly, or set and use favorites.

Just like email, there are three basic steps in order to use the Web. These are the following:

1. Connect to the Net (as with email, if you configure Remote Access to allow it, Internet Explorer will automatically connect to the Net for you).

What is this little thing called hypertext?

As you use the Web, you'll hear a lot of words and phrases that begin with "hyper." These terms sound complicated, but all you really need to know is that "hyper" usually indicates that there are links among the information presented. Hypertext means that certain words are linked to other words in the same document, and in the Web's case, words on other documents. You usually activate these links by clicking on a word, words, or a graphic. (You can also see hypertext in many Mac online help systems when you click on certain terms to move to detailed explanations of those terms or related terms.)

2. Launch Internet Explorer and use the Web.

3. When you are done, disconnect from the Net.

Browsing the Web

The method that really makes the Web "the Web" involves moving by using hypertext links. These links are "gateways" to other sites. You can spot links by looking for underlined words, different colored text, and graphics. Each of these links can indicate a link to another site. You simply activate the link and move to the site it links with by clicking on the link. Go ahead and try it.

Browsing the Web

1. Connect to the Net (from the Apple menu, choose Remote Access Status, when the window appears click Connect, and wait for the status information to appear).

2. Launch Internet Explorer (an alias to it is located in the Internet folder that is on your startup disk). If you configured your Home page to Apple's Web site as described in Chapter 23, you will see Apple's Web site (see Figure 26.1).

3. Click on links to move to other pages.

4. When you are done browsing, move back to Remote Access Status and click Disconnect.

Amazing isn't it? The Web is one of the few things in life that does live up to its media hype. But wait. What if you want to go to a specific Web page for which you don't see a link?

Using URLs

You will see URLs for Web sites all over the place including television, newspapers, magazines, advertisements, and so on. How do you visit a site when you have its URL? It's not any more difficult than following a link.

A networked Mac

If your Mac has access to the Internet because it is part of a "hard-wired" network (it is physically connected to the network), you don't need to connect and disconnect. You are always on the Net.

Letting Internet Explorer do the work for you

If you have Remote Access configured to allow automatic connections, you can just open Internet Explorer, and it will connect for you. See the "Finishing Your Configuration" section of Chapter 23, "Connecting Your Mac to the Net," for details.

Watch for the hand

When you are moving your cursor around a Web page, watch for it to change to a hand. When the cursor changes to a hand, it means you are over a link. Click on the left mouse button to move to the site that the link points to.

Or watch for the URL

Another way for you to tell that your cursor is over a link is to watch the lower left-hand part of the screen. When you are over a link, you'll see the URL of the site to which the link points. If you are not over a link, you won't see a URL there.

And follow your links!

Also notice that links you have followed change color to indicate that you have followed those links. This can be useful when you are really roaming far and wide because you can avoid going places that you have already been. You can set the colors that are used to track links in Internet Explorer's Preferences window.

No need to close Internet Explorer

You don't have to quit Internet Explorer just because you disconnect from the Net. If you leave it open, you can see the last page that you visited. In fact, you can use this page just as you could when you were online, except that links won't work (although you may have some pages stored on your hard drive, see the next chapter for details on how this works).

Using a URL to move to a Web page

1. Connect to the Net if you disconnected since the previous step-by-step.

2. Move back to Internet Explorer.

3. Choose Open Location from the File menu or press Command-L. You will see the Open Internet Address window (see Figure 26.5).

FIGURE 26.5

You can enter a URL in the Open Internet Address dialog to move to that site.

4. Enter the URL to which you want to move. After a few moments, the Web site will begin downloading, and you can read text and graphics on the page that you are downloading.

5. When you are done browsing, move back to Remote Access Status and click Disconnect.

Another way to do the same thing

Instead of using the Open Location command, you can enter the URL directly in the Address box that is just below the tool bar. You can even modify the URL that is already in the box–this may save you some typing. When you have the URL the way you want it, press Return to move there.

URL tips

There are some shortcuts you can use when you enter URLs. When the URL contains www, you can skip the http:// part. If the server address for a site is www.something.com, you can just type the something (for example, to move to Apple's Web site at http://www.apple.com, just type apple).

Although entering URLs is easy enough, they can be long and a pain to type. Fortunately, using Internet Explorer favorites, you really have to enter a URL only once.

Setting and Using Favorites

The third way to navigate is to use favorites. Favorites are an easy way to store URLs to which you may want to return; they make going back to sites extremely easy. All you have to do is select a favorite to quickly move back to that site.

Setting and using favorites

1. Connect to the Net and launch Internet Explorer.

2. Press Command-L, type *cnn* in the Open Internet Address dialog box, and press Return. You will move to the excellent CNN Interactive Web site from which you can get more news than anyone could possibly use.

3. From the Favorites menu, choose Add Page to Favorites (or press Command-D).

4. Now press Command-L and this time enter *weather* and then press Return. This will take you to The Weather Channel's Web site.

5. Press Command-D to create a favorite since you are probably going to want to come back to this site.

6. Select the URL in the Address bar and type *macworld*, then press Return. This takes you to the *Macworld* magazine site (see Figure 26.6).

FIGURE 26.6
This is the Web home of
Macworld magazine.

7. Press Command-D.

8. Now move to the MacFixIt site at `http://www.macfixit.com`.

9. Press Command-D to add a favorite for this site.

10. Now move back to the CNN Interactive site by opening the Favorites menu and choosing CNN Interactive (see Figure 26.7).

A head start on your favorites

In Figure 26.7, you can see that there are already some folders that contain favorites on the Favorites menu. These are pre-installed and are ready for you to use. They are mostly Mac related sites that you will find very useful.

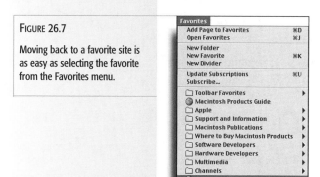

FIGURE 26.7

Moving back to a favorite site is as easy as selecting the favorite from the Favorites menu.

11. Now click on the Favorites tab on the left side of the Internet Explorer window. You can see your favorite sites listed (see Figure 26.8).

FIGURE 26.8

You can use the Favorites tab in the Internet Explorer window to quickly move to a favorite Web site.

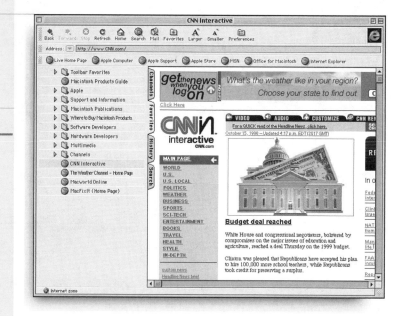

Facts of Web Life

Here's a fact that you can hang onto as a certainty: *Internet resources are always changing.*

Sites are becoming available; sites are disappearing; and sites are changing their URLs. Some locations are popular and hard to get on. The bottom line is that you may try to move to a site and not be able to log on. You may even get a message saying that the site is no longer available. Or you may see a message that the site is too full for you to enter.

If any of this happens to you, you can do one of two things. You can throw up your hands in disgust, yell that this Internet thing doesn't work, and put your modem in the trash. Or you can just try the site again later. If you're going to use the Internet, you have to be a bit flexible. So, recognize right now that the Net, just like life itself, isn't perfect.

12. Click a favorite in the Favorite pane that opens to move to that site.

13. Click the Favorites tab again to collapse the Favorites pane.

14. You can move back to any of the other sites for which you created favorites just as easily.

Organizing Favorites

Adding and using favorites is so easy that you are bound to pile up a lot of them as you move about the Web. Internet Explorer provides tools that you can use to keep your favorites organized so that they remain easy to use.

Organizing favorites

1. Click the Favorites button at the top of the Internet Explorer window. You will see the Favorites window (see Figure 26.9). You can use this window to manage and organize your favorites. You will see the favorites that you created in the previous step-by-step.

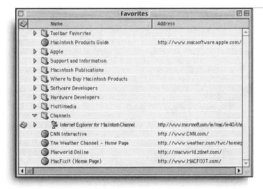

FIGURE 26.9

You can use the Favorites window to manage your favorites.

2. From the Favorites menu, choose New Folder. A new folder will appear in the Favorites window.

3. Name the folder; in this case, name it News & Weather.

4. Drag the CNN and The Weather Channel favorites into the new folder.

5. Create another new folder called Mac Support Sites and put the MacFixIt site into it.

6. Create another folder, call this one Mac News Sites, and put your Macworld favorite into this folder. Your Favorites folder should now look something like Figure 26.10.

Favorite folders

Favorite folders act just like Finder folders do. You can rename them, place other folders inside them, expand or collapse them, and so on. You can also drag them to change their order.

Using the predefined favorites

Donít forget to explore the folders of favorites that were installed when you installed Internet Explorer. For example, the Macworld site is already part of the Macintosh Publications folder. But add it to the Mac News Sites folder just so you get the hang of it.

FIGURE 26.10

These favorites are now a bit
more organized.

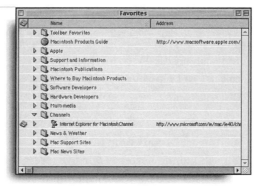

7. Close the Favorites window.

8. Open the Favorites menu and choose one of the Favorites folders that you just created. It will be a hierarchical menu from which you can choose the favorites in the folder (see Figure 26.11).

FIGURE 26.11

The Favorites menu becomes a hierarchical one based on the folders that you created within the Favorites window.

Yet another way to view favorites

The bar just below the Address bar is the Favorites bar. You can add your favorites to those already installed in this bar and move to one by clicking its button on the bar. To do this, open the Favorites tab and drag a favorite onto the Favorite bar. You will then see the favorite on the bar.

To remove a favorite from the bar, open the Favorites window and delete the favorite from within the Toolbar Favorites folder that is created as soon as you add a favorite to the Favorites bar. Deleting a favorite from this folder does not remove the favorite from its other locations, so it will still be accessible from the Favorites tab.

9. Click the Favorites tab. This pane is also organized according to the work you did in the Favorites window (see Figure 26.12). Just click a favorite to move to that site.

You can see that it is simple to keep your favorites organized. There are a few more things that you can use to work with favorites. These are the following:

■ You can add a divider between favorites or between the Favorite folder by using the New Divider command on the Favorites menu. The divider will be added below the folder that you have selected when you choose the command.

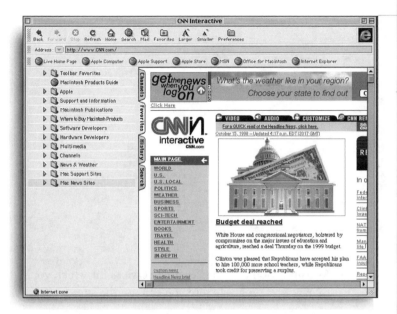

FIGURE 26.12
The Favorites tab is also based on how you have organized your favorites in the Favorites window.

■ You can sort the favorites items by clicking the newspaper icon in the upper left corner of the Favorites window. The favorites will be sorted according to item name.

■ You can use the New Favorite command to manually add favorites and to subscribe to Web sites (you'll learn more about this in the next chapter).

Manually creating favorites

If you manually create a new favorite by choosing the New Favorite command (or Command-K), you will see an empty info dialog into which you can manually enter all the information needed to create the favorite.

Getting Info on Favorites

If you select a favorite in the Favorites window nand then do a Get Info (from the File menu or by pressing Command-I), you will see the Info dialog for that favorite (see Figure 26.13).

The Info dialog contains a number of tabs, which are the following:

■ **Info**. With the Info tab, you can see the name, address, and comments for the site that the favorite represents. You can modify any of the fields shown by editing them.

■ **Subscribe**. This tab enables you to work with subscriptions (you'll learn about subscribing to sites in the next chapter).

FIGURE 26.13

The Get Info command works on favorites, and you have a number of options with which to work.

- **Account**. Some Web sites offer services for which you have to have an account before you can use the site. Sometimes, you have to pay for such an account, while other times it will be free. In either case, you can store your username and password for that site in this tab's window, and Internet Explorer will automatically enter that information for you. You also can enter your domain into this tab as an additional security check. Be careful, though, because if you use this tab, anyone who can access your computer and get onto the Net can use the site with your account on it. Only use this feature if your Mac is secure (there aren't a lot of people using it).

- **Schedule**. This is used to set a time at which Internet Explorer will update your subscription to a site. You will learn how to use this in the next chapter.

- **Notify**. This is another subscription related function.

- **Offline**. You can have Internet Explorer download a site to your Mac so that you can browse it while you are not connected to the Net. Why would you want to do this? If you have an account that is hard to access during peak hours, you might want the site to be downloaded to your Mac at a less busy time, and then you could explore it from your Mac whenever you wanted to. Also, the site will be much faster to use from your Mac than it is from the Net. The down side is that a site will consume a *lot* of hard disk space. You will learn how to use this in the next chapter.

Touring Internet Explorer

You have already used a number of Internet Explorer's features, but now let's take a few minutes to explore some of the commands and interface elements that you will be using.

Using the Tool bar

Just under the menu bar is the tool bar. You can activate these buttons by clicking on them. Not much explanation is required, but just in case they don't make sense to you instantly, here's the *Reader's Digest* version of what each one does.

- **Back and Forward**. These buttons take you either back to the last page you visited or forward to the next page in the list of sites you have visited.

- **Stop**. This one stops everything Internet Explorer is doing. If you try to move to a site and it is taking forever and a day, click on this to make Internet Explorer stop what it is doing. You will probably use this button quite a bit.

- **Refresh**. This button refreshes the current page, which makes Internet Explorer go get the page again. Occasionally, a page will have problems when you try to load a page to your machine. Other times, such as with weather maps or stock quotes, the data on the page may have changed. This button tells Internet Explorer to reload the page to clear any errors and get any new data.

- **Home**. This button takes you back to your Home page. You will learn about this in a later section.

- **Search**. The Search button takes you to your default search site. If you configured the default search site in the Internet application to be `http://www.yahoo.com` as in the step-by-step in Chapter 23, you will move to the Yahoo site when you click this button.

SEE ALSO

➤ *To learn how to search the Web, see page 639*

- **Mail**. This button opens Outlook Express (if it is configured to be your default email program).

- **Favorites**. This one opens the Favorites window in which you can organize your favorites.

- **Larger and Smaller buttons**. These buttons increase or decrease the size of the fonts used to display a Web page.

- **Preferences**. This one opens the Preferences window that you use to configure Internet Explorer. You'll learn about this in a later section.

Using the Address Bar

Sometimes when you're crawling around the Web, you can get lost. If you want to see your present URL, just look in the Address bar that is just underneath the tool bar. It always shows your present location. As you have already learned, you can also move to a URL by entering it in this box and pressing the Return key.

Http?

The http that you see at the begin-ning of Web URLs stands for *HyperText Transfer Protocol*. This is the language, or set of standards, that enable Web servers to provide Web pages in a standard and consistent format that your Web browser understands.

The downward facing arrow next to the Address bar is used with the Autocomplete feature. With this feature, Internet Explorer tries to select a site from the history list (you will learn about this in a later section) to fill in URLs as you type them in the Address bar. When Autocomplete finds matches, the arrow becomes active. You can click on it to choose a URL from the pop-up menu that appears.

Using the Explorer Bar

You have already seen how the Favorites tab works. There are three additional tabs on the Explorer bar. These are the following:

- **Channels**. Channels are Web sites that you view regularly because you find the information useful or at least entertaining. A channel is downloaded to your Mac from where you view it. As the site changes, the update is downloaded to your Mac according to a set schedule. You can view these channels by clicking the Channel tab to open the Channel area and then clicking the channel that you want to view. Since channels are so similar to subscriptions, you can read about subscriptions, and then you will also be able to use channels.

- **History**. As you visit sites, Internet Explorer keeps track of the sites you visit and maintains a history of your Web travels. You can use the History tab to quickly move back to any site that you have visited. You will learn how to work with the History feature in a later section of this chapter.

- **Search**. The Search tab enables you to perform a search in the tab's window while you are exploring the results of your search in the main Internet Explorer window. You will learn more about searching the Web in the next chapter.

Lose the tabs

You can turn off the Explorer bar with the Browser Display Preferences.

Using Status and Security Information

And last, in the bottom left corner of the Internet Explorer window, is the status display area. Here you see messages from Internet Explorer telling you what it is doing or what is happening with the current Web page. One of the most useful things you see here is the status of a Web page as it downloads into your computer. From this, you can get an idea of how long the page will take to fully load. Keep your eyes on the status area as you move around because it will help you know what is going on.

Another important feature of the status area is that it will show you when you are dealing with a secure Web site. This is indicated by a lock icon as well as a text message (see Figure 26.14). You'll learn more about Web security in the next chapter.

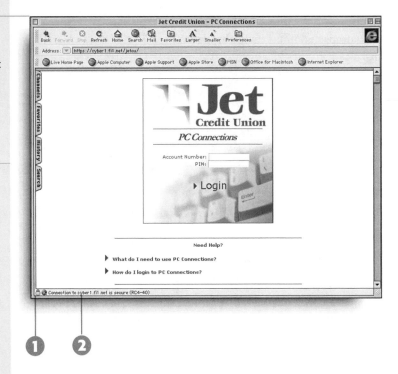

Using the Menu Bar

Internet Explorer also has a menu bar that contains lots of commands. You have used some of these and many are replicated by the buttons in the tool bar. You will learn about some additional commands in the other sections in this chapter as well as the next chapter.

Configuring Internet Explorer Preferences

Internet application

You can also use the Internet application (in the Control Panels folder) to set your Home page. Setting it there will cause all your Web browsers to use it. Configuring it within Internet Explorer will only cause that Home page to be used in Internet Explorer.

Just like any other application, there are a number of preferences for Internet Explorer that you can set to make Internet Explorer work better for you. There are lots of preferences that you can configure, and you will learn about some of them in the sections about particular topics (for example, you will learn about the security preferences in the security section in the next chapter). In this section, you will learn about some of the more basic preferences that you may want to configure.

Setting Your Home Page

In Web-speak, the Home page is the term used for the page that your Web browser automatically goes to when you launch it. You can set your Home page to be any page you want it to be. In Chapter 23, you configured Internet Explorer to go to Apple's Web site as your Home page (see Figure 26.1).

But the Home page you choose is up to you. Use the following steps to change your Home page—just in case the mood ever strikes you.

Changing your Home page

1. Move to the site that you want to use for your Home page. In this step-by-step, I'll use the CNN page as an example, but you can use any site that you choose.

2. Move into the Address bar and copy the URL for the site that you want to be your new Home page.

3. Click the Preferences button.

4. In the Internet Explorer Preferences window, click the Home/Search tab. You will see preferences you can use to set your Home page and the default search site (see Figure 26.15).

5. Move into the Address field and select the current address of your Home page.

6. Paste the URL you copied earlier over the current URL.

7. Click OK. From now on, this page will open when you open Internet Explorer and when you click the Home button.

Home Pages Everywhere

There are really two "kinds" of Home pages. I'm talking about the first one here: the page that Internet Explorer automatically loads when you start it. The other kind is the Home page on every Web server (a Web server is a computer on which Web pages are presented for your browsing pleasure). In this context, the Home page is the base upon which all the pages at a particular Web site are built.

How can you tell that you are on the Home page of a server? Just look at the URL. If it ends with the server portion of the address, you're visiting the Home page of that site. Want an example? The URL for the publisher of this book is `http://www.mcp.com/`. Anytime that you see a URL like this—without any document title after the last `/`—then you know you're at that site's Home page.

Finding Home

Here's a related browsing tip. You can move to the Home page of any Web site by deleting everything in the URL after the server address. For example, pretend that you moved into the Weather page of the CNN site, the URL is `www.cnn.com/WEATHER/`. To quickly move back to that site's Home page, you can delete */WEATHER/* from the address in the Address bar and press the Return key. This will move you back to www.cnn.com, which is the Home page of the CNN site. Try this when you move to various URLs to explore a site's Home page.

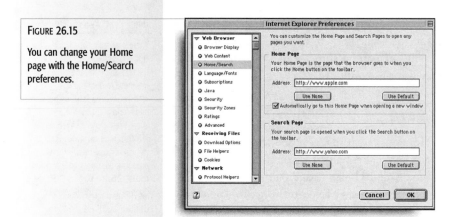

Here are a few more Home page related tips:

- The Use None button will blank out the Home page so that you see a blank screen when you start Internet Explorer. This can be useful if there isn't a Web page that you like to see each time you open Internet Explorer and connect to the Net. There is no use wasting time downloading a Home page that you don't want to see anyway.

- The Use Default button resets your Home to Microsoft's page at `http://home.microsoft.com`.

- When checked, the "Automatically go to this Home Page when opening a new window" check box applies your Home page to any new Web browser windows that you open (you can have multiple Internet Explorer windows open at the same time). If you uncheck this box, a new window will be blank when you open it.

If you want your Home page to be in your Favorites folder, you can make it so.

Setting your Favorites folder to be your Home page

1. From the File menu, choose Open File.

2. Maneuver to the Favorites.html file. This will be located within the Explorer folder that is in the Preferences folder.

3. Select the Favorites.html file and click Open. Your favorites will open into a Web page.

4. Copy the address shown in the Address bar.

5. Move back to the Home Page Preferences and paste this address into the Address field.

6. Click OK. Now your Home page will be in your favorites (see Figure 26.16). This is good because the page takes almost no time to load, and it gives you quick and easy access to all of your favorite sites.

FIGURE 26.16
This Home page contains the favorites I have set.

Opening HTML files

You can use the steps that you used to set your favorites as your Home page to open any HTML files on your Mac. You can browse for them with the Open File command just as you can with any other application. You can also set any HTML file to be your Home page.

Internet Explorer's help system is really a set of HTML pages stored on your Mac. Choose Internet Explorer Help from the Help menu and take a look at the URL. You will see file:/// at the beginning. This means that the address is a file on your Mac. The rest of the address will be the path to that file, with the last part being the name of the file itself.

Setting the Internet Explorer Window Display

There are lots of ways to change how the Internet Explorer window looks and what tools and bars that you see on it. Open the Internet Explorer Preferences window and click Browser Display (see Figure 26.17). You will see the following options:

- **Colors**. These options enable you to change the appearance of the text and links that you see on a page. You can change the color of text, the background, links you have viewed, and links that you haven't viewed by clicking the color bars next to each option. When you do, you will see the familiar Color Picker. You can use this to customize the colors used for each item.

FIGURE 26.17

Internet Explorer enables you to customize the appearance of and controls in its window.

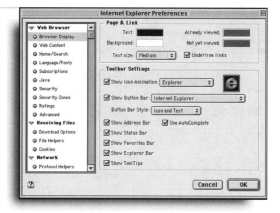

■ **Text size**. You can use this pop-up menu to set the relative size of text.

■ **Underline links**. By default, links are underlined so that you can easily distinguish them from regular text. You can uncheck this box to remove the underline.

■ **Toolbar settings**. You can use these settings to change the appearance of the tool bars that you see and to see if particular tool bars are present or not. You can also change the appearance of the spinning Internet Explorer icon.

Setting Web Content

You don't have to take Web pages as they come. You can determine how pages are displayed by Internet Explorer, including if some content is displayed at all. The Web Content Preferences enable you to do this. Access them by clicking Web Content in the Internet Explorer Preferences window (see Figure 26.18). The content options are the following:

■ **Page Content**. These settings determine how particular kinds of content are handled by Internet Explorer. For example, the show pictures preference determines whether graphics are displayed at the highest possible quality or with the highest possible speed. The Animated GIFs preference determines if animations loop continuously or play only once per page loading.

FIGURE 26.18
You can determine how the content of Web pages is handled by IE.

- **Active Content**. Active content is content with which you interact with controls. This area enables you to set how active content is used. Unless you really understand this, you should leave these preferences set to their default values.

- **Progressive Formatting**. As Web pages load, not all items are loaded at the same time. Usually, text loads first. Then individual graphics and files (such as movies) load. This enables you to read text while the related graphics are still loading onto your computer. As the graphics load, the page is refreshed so that it looks its best. If you use a modem (which is a slow connection), you want this refreshing to happen as each image is loaded so that the page looks as good as it can while the other images are loading. If you use a network, there is no reason to have the refresh done after each image. Pages load so quickly that the refresh just wastes resources. If you use a network, set the "Refresh after all images are loaded" radio button. If you use a modem, leave the default radio button selected.

Exploring Your Web History

As you travel the Net, Internet Explorer diligently makes a list of each site you visit. This list makes it easy to get back to any site that is still on the History list.

There are a couple of ways you can use the History list.

Visiting the past with the History list

1. From the Explorer bar, click the History tab. You will see a list of all the sites you have visited (see Figure 26.19).

FIGURE 26.19

Using the History tab, you can quickly move back to any site that you have recently visited.

Changing History

To set the number of sites that Internet Explorer remembers that you have visited, choose the Advanced pane of the Internet Explorer Preferences window. Change the amount shown in the "Remember the last ___ sites visited" field. The default value is 300.

Autocomplete

If you leave the Autocomplete option on (it is on by default), Internet Explorer will try to complete URLs as you type them into the Address bar. It uses the History list to do this. As you type, Internet Explorer finds all of the sites that match what you have typed and puts the closest match into the address field for you. As you keep typing, Internet Explorer refines the matches until there is only one left.

Day by day

Internet Explorer creates folders into which it places the sites you have visited on previous days. To move back to a site you visited on a particular day, open the folder with that day's date and click the site.

2. To move to a site, click it.

3. Click the History tab to close the Explorer bar.

4. Open the Go menu. You will see the History list on the menu (see Figure 26.20).

5. Choose a site from the list to move to it.

6. To see the full list of sites on the History list, choose Open History from the Go menu.

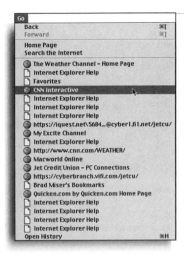

FIGURE 26.20
The History list also shows up on
the Go menu.

Erasing the past

If you want to clear the History
list, set the number of sites that
Internet Explorer remembers to
zero. After you click OK, Internet
Explorer will forget its past. You
can reset the number it remembers if you want to create
another History list.

Exporting History

You can export the History list
as an HTML file by opening the
History window (open History
from the Go menu) and then
choosing Export from the File
menu.

Using Great Web Sites

After you have used the Web for a while, you will develop quite
a list of sites that you use regularly. Until then, you can explore
some of the sites listed in Table 26.2. They provide a good starting point for your Web adventure.

TABLE 26.2   **Good Web sites for Mac users**

URL	Description	Comments
Mac Sites		
www.apple.com	Apple Computer's Web site	You can shop in the Apple Store as well as get support and read the latest Apple and Mac news.
macworld.zdnet.com	*Macworld* magazine's Web site	You can read the latest Mac news as well as search for information on specific topics.
www.macaddict.com	Web page of MacAddict magazine	More Mac news from a very pro-Mac site.
www.machome.com	Web home of *MacHome* magazine	Read the magazine, down load files, and more.

TABLE 26.2   Continued

URL	Description	Comments
Mac Sites		
www.evanggelist. macaddict.com	Web home of the Mac EvangeList mailing list	All things pro-Mac.
www.macintouch.com	Ric Ford's MacInTouch site	An outstanding source of Mac news, especially for troubleshooting and update news.
www.macfixit.com	Ted Landau's MacFixIt site	Another excellent site for help with Mac problems.
www.maccentral.com	Home of MacCentral Online	More Mac news.
www.outpost.com	Home of Cyberian Outpost	Cyberian Outpost is an excellent source for all Mac software and hardware.
www.cdw.com	Home of Computer Discount Warehouse	CDW offers some of the best prices on Mac-related hardware and software
www.macdownload.com	ZDNet's site for Mac software	Good source from which to download shareware and freeware software.
Other Sites		
www.mcp.com	Home of Macmillan Computer Publishing	
www.cnn.com	CNN Interactive	An excellent news site.
www.weather.com	Home of The Weather Channel	All the weather information you would ever need.
www.loc.gov	U.S. Library of Congress Web site	An amazing collection of important documents, all available on the Web.
www.quicken.com	Quicken's Home page	All the financial news and tools that you need to keep your finances in top condition.

URL	Description	Comments
Other Sites		
www.dvdexpress.com	An expensive source for DVD movies.	
www.reel.com	Home of Reel.com	An excellent source for videos and DVDs; if it is available, reel.com will have it (you can also rent videos).
www.netflix.com	Home of Net Flix	You can buy or rent DVDs here.
www.musicblvd.com	Music Boulevard	If you want some music, this is the place to go.
www.amazon.com	Home Amazon.com	This is the ultimate book store.

This list is relatively small compared to the list you will build up on your own. Still, it gives you some great sites to visit. Between these and your preconfigured favorites, you have a lot of sites that you can visit already!

Browsing the Web:
Advanced Techniques

Understanding how the Web works

Subscribing to Web sites

Browsing offline

Searching the Web

Downloading files

Working with plug-ins and helper applications

Speeding up browsing

Understanding How the Web Really Works

In the previous chapter, you learned much of what you need to know to move around the Web. But why stop with just the basics? Internet Explorer is extremely powerful, so why not take advantage of that power?

Before you learn how to do more advanced things on the Web, you should understand a little more about how the Web works.

Web creation tools

There are lots of programs that enable you to create your own Web pages. These include Microsoft's FrontPage, Adobe's PageMill, and many more. There are also lots of tools devoted to specific items on Web pages such as graphics and animation.

Understanding HTML

The fundamental thing that makes the Web work is *HyperText Markup Language*, or *HTML*. HTML is the language that is used to create Web pages. Web pages are actually just a bunch of text marked up with HTML codes. Each element on a Web page (headlines, captions, links, and so on) is marked with a specific code that tells your Web browser what to do with the item marked by that code.

Unless you intend to create your own Web page, you really don't need to know any more than that about HTML.

However, after you use the Web for a while, you may want to create your own Web page. There are many different tools you can use to do so, and this topic is beyond the scope of this book. Just go to your local bookstore (or better yet use the Web itself) to learn more about creating your own Web pages.

Many of the items that make up the code for a Web page are actually links, or pointers, to files. For example, each graphic that you see on a page is actually a separate file somewhere. The HTML code for that item is a pointer that tells your Web browser to display that file at that location. So a Web page is made up of the file containing the HTML code for that page as well as all of the files that are linked to that page.

If you want to see what the HTML code looks like for any page that you're looking at, just choose Source from the View menu while you are visiting that page. In the resulting HTML window for that site, you can see the HTML that created that page.

Understanding How a Browser Really Works

When you visit a Web page, Internet Explorer downloads and reads the HTML code for that page and interprets the code accordingly. For example, it displays the regular text with a font and point size that you set in the Preferences dialog. It follows links to other files, such as graphics, and downloads all those too. It then displays all of this information on your screen.

When you are looking at a Web page, you are really looking at files that are stored on your own computer. That is why the Web is relatively slow because you have to download every file that is used on a page.

All of these files, and there are usually lots of them, are stored on your Mac in Internet Explorer's *cache*. This cache contains all of the files that make up a Web page, or *site*, that you have visited. You can look at a site that has been downloaded from the cache; there is no need to connect to the Net to look at it again. The more files you have cached, the less your Mac has to download from the Web and the faster you can browse pages. Your Mac accesses files stored in it many times faster than those files you have downloaded from the Net.

The cached files are stored in the folder MS Internet Cache that is located in the Preferences folder. Within that folder, there is a single file called cache.waf. This file contains all of the files in Internet Explorer's cache.

You can control the size of the cache. Having a large cache is good because that means that Internet Explorer can store more information on your hard drive and will have to download fewer files from the Net, thus speeding things up for you. The down side is that the larger the cache file is, the more disk space it consumes. After a certain point, a very large cache file becomes so big that Internet Explorer will slow down while using it.

Configuring Internet Explorer's cache

1. Open Internet Explorer.
2. Open the Internet Explorer Preferences window and click Advanced. You will see the Cache section of the Advanced preferences window (see Figure 27.1).

FIGURE 27.1

You can use the Advanced Preferences to set Internet Explorer's cache.

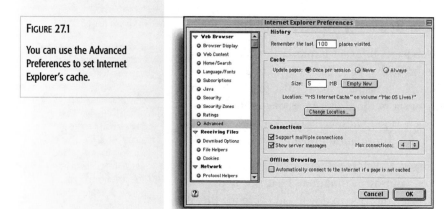

3. You can have Internet Explorer update the pages in the cache once per session, never, or always. Unless you have a very long browsing session, you should leave this set to the default.

4. You can increase or decrease the size of the cache by changing the number in the Size field. The default is 5 MB. If you can spare disk space, increase this to 10 or 15 MB.

5. To clear the cache, click the Empty Now button. This will force Internet Explorer to reload each page that you want to visit.

6. Use Change Location to change the location of the cache file. You will learn how this can be useful in a later section in this chapter.

7. Click OK.

The Java theory

The theory behind Java is that all of the major players will agree to standardized Java commands, features, and programming syntax. This would make it possible for a programmer to implement the Java architecture once and create a program that can run on any computer.

Understanding Java

Java is a technology that, ideally anyway, enables programmers to create programs that will run a *Java virtual machine* on any computer platform. The Java machine translates standard Java commands into the appropriate action on each computer platform. Ideally, the same Java program can run the Mac, Windows 95/98, Windows NT, and UNIX. Each of these platforms has its own Java virtual machine and should be able to run the Java program equally well. Alas, it doesn't really work that way, and probably never will.

The place where Java has found a home is on the Web. Java programs, called *applets*, can be embedded into the HTML code for Web pages. When you browse a page containing a JAV applet, the applet runs and does what it is supposed to do. This enables Web page creators to add a single application (an applet) to a page and each browser (whether it is running on a Mac, Windows PC, or UNIX machine) will be able to run the applet. Many of these applets create moving elements, such as animations and banners. Others create fairly sophisticated controls and interface elements that you can use to cause something to happen on the Web site. Lots of games that you play on Web sites are actually Java applets.

Mac OS 8.5 includes a Java virtual machine, called *Mac OS Runtime for Java*, or *MRJ*. Mac OS 8.5 also provides an Applet Runner, as well as some sample applets with which you can play. These are stored in the Mac OS Runtime For Java folder that is located in the Apple Extras folder installed on your startup disk. If you want to see some Java applets in action, use the following step-by-step.

Using Java applets

1. Open the Mac OS Runtime For Java folder and then open the Apple Applet Runner folder. You will see the Apple Applet Runner, as well as a folder called Applets, that contains sample applets.

2. Open the Applets folder.

3. Open one of the applet folders. It doesn't matter which one (I used the TicTacToe applet for this example).

4. Open the example1.html file (each applet has one). The applet will begin to run (see Figure 27.2).

5. When you are done, close the applet or quit Apple Applet Runner.

Internet Explorer also includes Microsoft's version of its Java virtual machine, called *Microsoft Virtual Machine*. You can set which virtual machine Internet Explorer uses through the Java Preferences window.

Java's harsh reality

Of course, reality has been quite different than theory. The major players have formed different teams with slightly different implementations of Java. Currently, one group is led by Sun Systems that claims to have the "pure" Java. The other group is led by, you guessed it, Microsoft that claims to have a better implementation of Java. Of course, there are sufficient differences between the two to cause users all kinds of problems.

As with most of these sorts of disputes, there are major court battles going on. In the end, it is doubtful that Java will ever have reached its original purpose. That would simply require too much cooperation among vicious competitors.

Running applets

You can also launch the sample applets by launching the Apple Applet Runner and choosing an applet from the Applets menu.

FIGURE 27.2

With the TicTacToe applet, you can challenge your Mac to a game (don't ask who is x and who is o!).

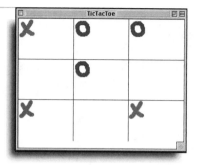

Configuring Java on Internet Explorer

1. Open the Internet Explorer Preferences window.

2. Click Java.

3. To disable Java, uncheck the "Enable Java" check box. You might want to do this if you don't want to run any applets from within Internet Explorer. Java applets do present some security risk, so to be absolutely safe from them, you can disable Java.

4. Choose the Java virtual machine that you want Internet Explorer to use to run applets that it encounters. The default is the Microsoft Virtual Machine, but you can select Apple MRJ to try that. Which should you use? You can try both of them and see if you notice any difference. You probably won't.

5. If you are familiar with Java, you can work with the other options; otherwise, the defaults will probably be fine.

6. Close the Preferences window.

Of course, for programmers and Web page creators, Java is much more complicated than this. But as a user, that is all you really need to know.

Subscribing to Sites

When you subscribe to a page, Internet Explorer monitors that page for changes. When the page changes, Internet Explorer automatically downloads it to your Mac so that you can browse it. You can subscribe to a page manually, or you can do it on-the-fly while you are browsing a page online.

When you subscribe to a page, a favorite for that page is automatically created. The difference between a Favorite site and one to which you have described is that you have to tell Internet Explorer to update a Favorite page by selecting it to browse. Pages to which you have subscribed will be automatically updated as they change.

Manually Subscribing to a Web Site

In the following step-by-step, you will learn how to subscribe to the CNN Interactive site so that you can monitor news as it changes. However, the steps for subscribing to any page for which you already have a favorite are similar. Just replace CNN with the page to which you want to subscribe.

Subscribing to a Favorite Web site

1. Open the Favorites window (Command-J).

2. Choose the CNN site favorite.

3. Press Command-I. You will see the info window for that site.

4. Click the Subscribe tab. You will see the Subscribe window (see Figure 27.3).

FIGURE 27.3

With the Subscribe window, you can subscribe to your favorite Web sites.

5. Check the "Check this site for changes" check box. This will cause Internet Explorer to check this site for changes once per day. If it finds that the site has changed, it will download it to your Mac.

6. If you want to set a custom schedule for this site, click the Schedule tab. You will see the Schedule window (see Figure 27.4). If you want to have the site checked once per day, skip step 7.

FIGURE 27.4

You can use the Subscribe window to modify the interval at which IE will check your subscribed sites for changes.

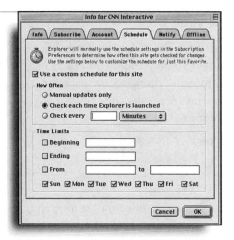

Look for the stars

If a site to which you have subscribed has changed since you last viewed it, its icon will be marked with a star in the Favorites tab of the Explorer bar, as well as in the Favorites bar. This star will change back to the globe icon as soon you view the updated site.

7. Check the "Use a custom schedule for this site" check box and set the interval at which you want this site checked check box. One useful setting is the "Check each time Explorer is launched" option. This causes Internet Explorer to check your subscribed sites every time you launch it.

8. Click OK to close the info window.

9. From the Favorites menu, choose Update Subscriptions. If the site has changed, Internet Explorer will show you a window as it downloads the site and will play a sound. You can browse the updated site. Each time you launch Internet Explorer, it will check this site and notify you if it has changed.

Subscribing to a Web Site While Browsing

You don't have to have a favorite for a site in order to subscribe to it. Ric Ford's MacInTouch site is a good one to subscribe to since he provides excellent information on the latest developments in the Mac world.

Subscribing to a site while browsing

1. Open Internet Explorer and move to www.macintouch.com.

2. Choose Subscribe from the Favorites menu. You will see a dialog box that asks you if you want to use the standard subscription settings for this site or create a custom subscription (see Figure 27.5).

FIGURE 27.5

You can choose to create a standard or custom subscription to a Web site.

3. Click Customize. You will see the info window for that site.

4. Check the Schedule tab.

5. Check the "Use a custom schedule for this site" check box.

6. Set the interval at which you want the site checked for changes.

7. Click the Notify tab. You will see the Notify window (see Figure 27.6).

8. Click the "Use a custom notification for this site" check box.

9. Choose the options that you want Internet Explorer to use to notify you of changes to this site. These options include the following: a sound, an alert, a flashing icon, or even an email message.

10. Click OK.

Subscribe to a site, and make a favorite

When you subscribe to a site, a favorite for that site is automatically created.

11. From the Favorites menu, choose Update Subscriptions. You
    will see a progress window as Internet Explorer checks all of
    your subscribed sites. If they have changed, you will see the
    star icon and will hear any notification sounds that you set.

12. Click the favorite for the site to browse it.

Setting Subscription Preferences

As you have already seen, you can subscribe to a site by using
standard settings, or you can customize the settings for each site
to which you subscribe. The standard settings are controlled by
the Internet Explorer Preferences.

Setting standard subscription preferences

1. Open the Internet Explorer Preferences window.

2. Click Subscriptions. You will see the available subscription
   preferences (see Figure 27.7).

3. Set the standard interval at which you want Internet
   Explorer to check for changes. The option "Each time
   Explorer is launched" is a good choice for you if you con-
   nect to the Net with a modem.

4. Set the standard notification that you want Internet
   Explorer to use when your sites have changed.

5. Click OK.

FIGURE 27.7
Using the Subscriptions preferences, you can change the
standard settings that are applied
to subscriptions.

Browsing a Site Offline

There may be times when you want to browse sites while you
are not connected to the Net. For example, you may want to do
most of your browsing in the early evening. This also happens to
be the busiest time on the Net, and you may have trouble connecting and the Web may be slow because of heavy use.

You can set Internet Explorer to download your favorite sites to
your Mac, where you can browse them at another time. This has
the advantage of making the browsing fast since you are loading
the site from your hard drive rather than the Net. The disadvantage is that storing a site on your hard drive requires lots of hard
drive space and downloading an entire site can take a long time.

For best results, use offline browsing with a site to which you
have subscribed or that is a channel.

Browsing offline

1. In the Favorites window, choose a site that you want to
browse offline (you can do this from a favorite).
2. Press Command-I to get info for that site.
3. Click the offline tab. You will see the offline window (see
Figure 27.8).
4. Check the "Download site for offline browsing" check box.
5. Click Options. You will see the Options dialog (see Figure
27.9).

FIGURE 27.8

Using the offline settings for a Favorite site, you can set Internet Explorer to download that site to your Mac for offline browsing.

FIGURE 27.9

With the Options dialog, you can determine which parts of a site are downloaded to your Mac.

Subscribe and browse offline

If you subscribe to a site that you have set for offline browsing, it will be downloaded to your computer when the subscription is updated. This is the most convenient way to use offline browsing.

6. Check the check boxes for those elements that you want to have downloaded to your Mac. You can choose to have the following elements downloaded to your Mac: images, sounds, and movies. These all require lots of disk space, especially sounds and movies, so it is best to leave these unchecked unless you are sure that you will want to see any movies and hear any sounds that are on this site.

7. Check the "Download links" check box and set the level of links that you want to have downloaded. Be careful with this. If you set this to happen, at least the first level of every link on this site will be downloaded. That may be an enormous amount of information. Also make sure that the "Skip links to other sites" check box is checked. If it isn't, links on all of the sites linked to the one you are downloading will be downloaded as well.

8. When you are done setting options, click OK.

9. Set the location where you want all of the files stored on your Mac with the Change Location button. If you leave the default setting, it will be stored in the Explorer folder that is on your startup disk.

10. Click OK.

11. If you want Internet Explorer to automatically connect to the Net to download a site when it is not stored on your Mac, open the Internet Explorer Preferences window, click Advanced, check the "Automatically connect to the Internet if a page is not cached check box," and click OK. The next time that your subscription is updated, the site will be downloaded to your Mac.

12. To browse offline, choose Offline Browsing from the File menu and select the site that you set for offline browsing. You can then browse the site from your hard drive rather than the Net. If you browse beyond the links that have been downloaded, you will be connected to the Net and those pages will be transferred to your Mac.

Searching the Web

Although the Web is a great thing, it does have its problems. One of them is that there is so much information of every conceivable kind that the Web appears to be a jumbled mess of pages and links going back and forth with no overall organization or order. And you know what? That's exactly what it is. The power of the Web is that anyone—assuming that he cares to

Search engine?

Don't worry about the term search engine. It just means "a way of looking for things." There are different search engines because there is more than one way to find things on the Net.

For example, one search engine may only catalog the subjects of Web pages, while another may search through the actual text of Web pages. In these examples, the engine looking at the subjects would be faster, but the one that searches the text might be more helpful in finding what you are looking for.

In practice, the details of a particular search engine don't matter very much. You just try different ones to see which works best for you.

Add a favorite

Yahoo! is a site to which you will return again and again so add a favorite for it. You can also configure Internet Explorer so that you move to it when you click the Search button (not the Net Search button which actually takes you to the excite search site). You can do so in Internet Explorer's Preferences dialog as well as the Internet application in the Control Panels folder.

The (numbers)

By the way, the numbers in parentheses after a topic are the number of site links within that topic.

learn how—can put his own pages on the Web, and any Web page can be linked to any other Web page. Combined with the millions of Web sites available—with thousands being added each week—this makes for quite a jumbled morass of information.

This arrangement is fine if all you want to do is click around and follow the links provided on various pages. It also works if you have specific URLs to visit.

Often, however, you may want to find Web pages relating to specific topics or even certain keywords. Fortunately, there are resources available (called *search engines*) on the Web to help you sort through the tangled web of Web pages and find what you are looking for. In this section, you'll learn a few of the ways that you can find information on the Web about specific topics.

Searching with Yahoo!

This site wins the award for having the best name *and* being one of the most useful areas from which to search for information on particular topics. After you use it, you'll agree that its name is appropriate.

The Yahoo! site enables you to find Net resources related to a wide variety of topics (see Figure 27.10). These topics run the gamut from art to society and culture.

Not only is the Yahoo! site very powerful, but it is as easy to use as the Web itself. Want to see more about some topic? Just click on it. As you continue to click through the links, you will move further down into the Yahoo! hierarchy until you start moving to individual Web pages that contain the information for which you are looking.

You can also search for specific information with Yahoo! In the following step, I'll search for information on contextual menus. The process works similarly for any search that you want to do.

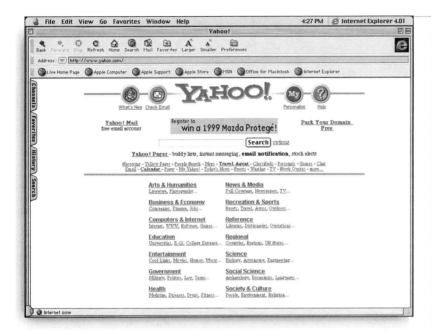

FIGURE 27.10

Yahoo!—a site by any other name
would not be half as good.

Conducting a basic search with Yahoo!

1. Move to the Yahoo! page at www.yahoo.com.

2. Enter the text for which you want to search in the field next to the Search button (see Figure 27.11).

3. Click Search. Yahoo! will search for sites that contain your search text. When it finishes, you will see the results window that contains the matches with your text (see Figure 27.12).

4. To move to a site to see if it has the information for which you are looking, simply click its link.

5. Click back to move back to the Yahoo! results page or use your history list to move back.

6. You can continue to explore the links Yahoo! found until you find the information for which you are looking.

Most of the time, these simple searches will yield what you are looking for. If a basic search doesn't work, try an advanced search.

Yahoo! as default

In Chapter 23, you learned how to use the Internet application to configure your default search engine to be Yahoo!. If you did so, all you have to do to move to it is click the Search button in Internet Explorer and you will move there.

FIGURE 27.11

You can search for Web sites on a topic by entering text in the Search field, in this case contextual menu.

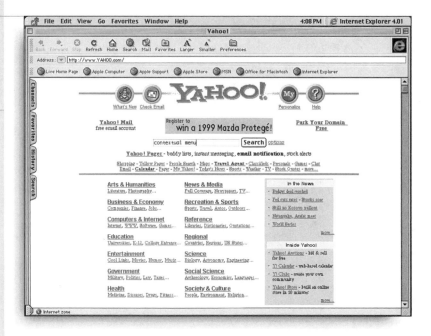

FIGURE 27.12

Yahoo! found a lot of sites containing information about contextual menus.

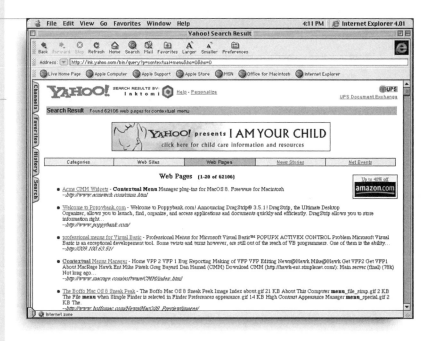

Conducting a more advanced search with Yahoo!

1. Move to Yahoo!

2. Click the options link that is next to the Search button. You will see the Search Options page (see Figure 27.13).

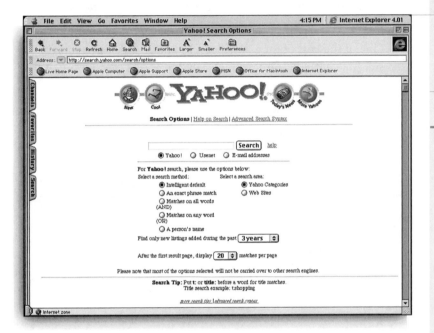

FIGURE 27.13

The Search Options page on Yahoo! enables you to conduct more sophisticated searches.

Boolean expressions

When you use a word in your search such as *and*, *or*, and so on, you are using a Boolean expression. Most search engines enable you to use Boolean expressions in your searches, but not all of them do it in the same way. While Yahoo! provides radio buttons, some sites require that you use the words themselves; for example, you might have to enter the words "contextual" *and* "menu" in the search field.

Sherlock Mac

With Mac OS 8.5, the Finder's Find command can now search the Web (this features is called Sherlock). You can set Sherlock to search several different search engines at the same time. To learn how to use this feature, see the "Finding Information on the Internet" section of Chapter 4, "Working with the Finder."

3. Use the options on this page to refine the search text. For example, use the Matches on all words to search for Web pages that contain all the words in the search phrase. For example, to search for contextual *and* menu.

4. When you have set all of the options that you want to use for your search, click Search. You will see the results of your search in a new window.

There's more to Yahoo!, but this is enough to keep you busy for a while. If you need more information about Yahoo!, just click the Help link on the Yahoo! Home page.

There are more search engines out there

Yahoo! is certainly not the only great search engine available; there are plenty of other excellent search sites that you can use. Some examples are the following: excite at www.excite.com, infoseek at www.infoseek.com, Lycos at www.lycos.com, and AOL Net Find at http://www.aol.com/netfind/.

Searching with Hotbot

Yahoo! is an individual search engine; that means it only searches the resources that it has available to it. There are other search engines that also search all search engine resources, resulting in even more information. These engines are called *metasearch engines*.

One of the best of these is called Hotbot. It will search more sites that a single search engine can, but it isn't much more difficult to use.

Searching with HotBot

1. Move to the HotBot site at www.hotbot.com (see Figure 27.14).

FIGURE 27.14

HotBot is a metasearch site—it searches other search engines.

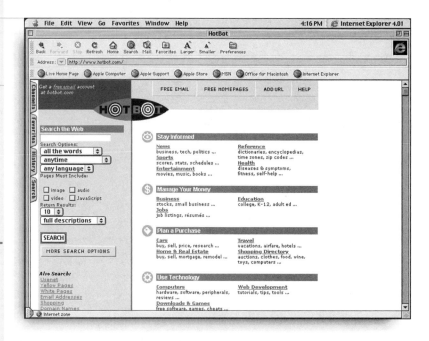

There's more than the Web

In many of the searches you will do, the results will contain more than just Web sites. You will also see FTP sites, newsgroups, and more. Fortunately, Internet Explorer enables you to access all of these services.

Hit me

When you do a search, a hit means an item in which your search word was found. In context of a search, hit and match mean pretty much the same thing.

2. Enter your search text in the search field.

3. Choose your search options by using the check boxes and pop-up menus.

4. Click Search. HotBot will perform its search and display the results in a new window (see Figure 27.15).

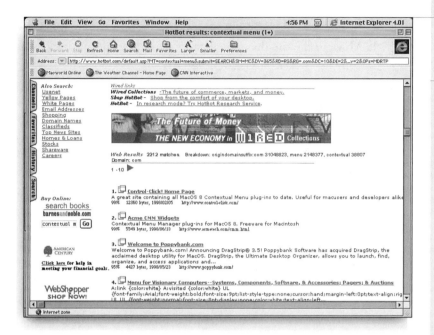

FIGURE 27.15
HotBot also found a lot of information on contextual menus.

5. Click on the links to move to the sites that HotBot found.

6. You can revise the search by clicking the Revise button.

There are many search engines available, and you can use them to do much more sophisticated searches than the ones that you have seen here. With most search engines, help is also provided, so be sure to look for it if you are having trouble. Most of the time, you will find what you are looking for with a simple search and a few clicks. You will find searches to be easy, productive, and yes, even fun. As you do your own searches, you will certainly pick up additional techniques to help you find what you want even faster.

Setting Your Default Search Page

When you click the Search button, you move to the search engine that is set as the default. Unless you have used the Internet application or Internet Explorer's own Preferences to change it, the excite search engine that has been customized for Mac users (www.excite.com/apple/) is set as the default. If you find a search site that you like better than this, it is easy to change the default search site.

Another metasearch site

Just as there is more than one search engine, there is also more than one metasearch engine. For example, you'll find another called the *Alta Vista metasearch engine* at `altavista.digital.com`.

Another way to default

You can also use the Internet application (in the Control Panels folder) to set your default search engine (see the "Finishing Your Configuration" section of Chapter 23, "Connecting Your Mac to the Net," for details). If you use Internet Explorer's Preferences to set it, the settings in Internet Explorer also change those set with the Internet application.

Setting your default search site

1. Move to the site that you want to use as your default and copy its URL from the Address bar.

2. Open Internet Explorer Preferences.

3. Click Home/Search.

4. Paste the new URL over the one currently shown in the Address field in the Search Page section of the window.

5. Click OK. From now on, when you click the Search button (not the Net Search button in the Favorites bar which is actually a favorite for the excite search site), you will move to the site you set as the default.

Using the Search Tab to Search

The Explorer bar provides a Search tab that you can use to search. Here's how.

Using the Search tab to search

1. Click the Search tab and choose a search engine from the Chooser Provider pop-up menu.

2. Perform your search. The results will appear in the Explorer bar.

3. When you click a link, you will see the linked page in the right pane of the Internet Explorer window (see Figure 27.16). This is a great way to search because your search page is always available. This makes trying multiple links much faster.

4. When you are done searching, close the Search window by clicking the Search tab.

Downloading Files

One of the best things about the Web is that you can download files from it. These files may be applications, graphics, text files, updaters, or whatever. Downloading files is simple once you get the hang of it.

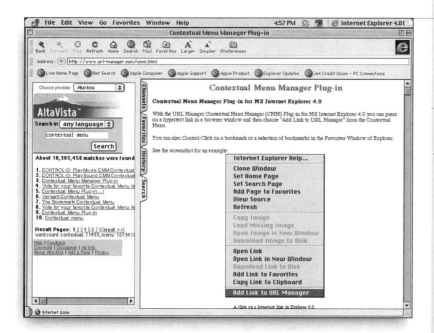

FIGURE 27.16

Using the Search tab in the Explorer bar enables you to see the search page and the results at the same time.

Another way to set a folder for downloaded files

Similarly to the default search engine, you can also set a default downloads folder by using the Internet application (see the "Finishing Your Configuration" section of Chapter 23, "Connecting Your Mac to the Net," for details). If you followed the steps in that section, you already have a download folder (called Downloaded Files) on your desktop and don't need to create another one for this step-by-step. At press time, Internet Explorer was not using the download folder you set in the Internet application. If you have already created a download folder, you can skip step 1.

Multiple download folders

You may want to have separate folders for downloading. In that case, choose a different folder that you selected in the Internet application. In the step-by-step, I used a folder called DOWNLOADS to differentiate it from the folder I selected in Chapter 23 using the Internet application. If you created a downloads folder in Chapter 23, you can skip this step-by-step.

Before you get started, though, it is a good idea to create a folder and have Internet Explorer always download files into that folder. That way, you will always know where your downloaded files are.

Creating a Downloads folder

1. On your Desktop (or on whatever volume that you want your downloaded files to be stored on), create a new folder called DOWNLOADS.

2. In Internet Explorer, open the Preferences window.

3. Click Download Options. You will see the Download Options window (see Figure 27.17).

4. Click Change Location.

5. Move to and select the folder that you created in step 1.

6. Click Select DOWNLOADS (this will be the name of the folder you selected) to select the folder. Any files that Internet Explorer downloads will be stored in this folder.

FIGURE 27.17

You can control how Internet Explorer downloads files with the Download Options preferences.

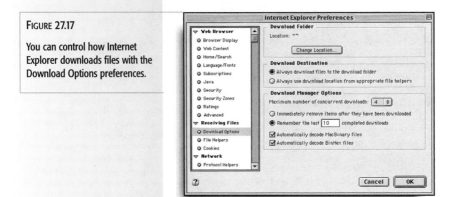

Multiple downloads

You can download multiple files at the same time. Start one; then move back to the Web windows and move to the next. Start it downloading and move to another if you want to.

You can also continue to browse the Web while your files are downloading. The speed will decrease a bit, but at least you can do something while the file is downloading.

7. Look at the other options and set them if you need to; the defaults are usually OK.

8. Click OK to close Internet Explorer Preferences.

Internet Explorer uses its Download Manager window to work with files that you are downloading.

Downloading files with Internet Explorer

1. Move to the file that you want to download (you can find lots of files to download at www.zdnet.com/mac/download. html).

2. Click the file's link. Sometimes this will take you to additional information about that file. If so, there is usually a Download button. Click that button to begin the download. As the download begins, the Download Manager window will open (see Figure 27.18). The Download Manager provides information about the download, such as the file name, its status, the time required to download it, and how much data has been transferred.

FIGURE 27.18

The Download Manager provides a status on files that you are downloading.

3. When the file has been downloaded, move to your DOWN-LOADS folder to use it.

Most files are encoded and compressed. These are the same processes that are applied to email attachments. Internet Explorer will handle the decoding for you, and it will automatically unstuff files that are in the .sit format. When it finishes, you will see both the compressed and uncompressed versions of the file in your DOWNLOADS folder (see Figure 27.19). You can work with the uncompressed version and throw the compressed version away.

FIGURE 27.19
Internet Explorer automatically uncompresses files for you.

SEE ALSO

➤ *To learn more about file encoding and compression, see page 587*

Working with Plug-ins

There are lots of file types that are on the Internet. In addition to HTML, gif, jpeg, cgl, and other files that are used to present a Web page, there are graphics, movies, sounds, and lots of other file types that you can open and view. Internet Explorer can't work with all of these file types directly, and fortunately, it doesn't have to. Internet Explorer uses plug-ins to expand its capabilities for those files that it doesn't natively support.

Internet Explorer comes with some plug-ins; these are stored in the Plug-ins folder that is in the Internet Explorer 4.01 folder that is within the Internet Applications folder. The plug-ins installed in the folder by default include QuickTime and Shockwave (which is Macromedia's multimedia Web technology).

QuickTime

To use the QuickTime plug-in that came with Internet Explorer, you must have QuickTime version 3.0 installed as part of Mac OS 8.5. If you used the Easy Install option to install Mac OS 8.5, QuickTime 3 was installed on your machine. If you used a Customized installation and did not install QuickTime, you need to install QuickTime to use the Internet Explorer QuickTime plug-in. See Appendix A, "Installing and Maintaining the Mac OS," for help installing Mac OS components.

Using Internet Explorer Plug-ins

Once a plug-in is installed in the Plug-ins folder, it works with Internet Explorer to provide its capabilities. When you click on a file that requires the plug-in to be used, the appropriate plug-in activates and enables you to do whatever it is designed to do.

Using the QuickTime plug-in

1. Move to a site that has QuickTime movies on it (try www.apple.com/quicktime).

2. Click on a QuickTime movie. The QuickTime plug-in will activate, and you will be able to view the QuickTime movie (see Figure 27.20). The controls that the QuickTime plug-in provides are the same as those provided by MoviePlayer.

FIGURE 27.20

The QuickTime plug-in enables you to watch QuickTime movies on the Web.

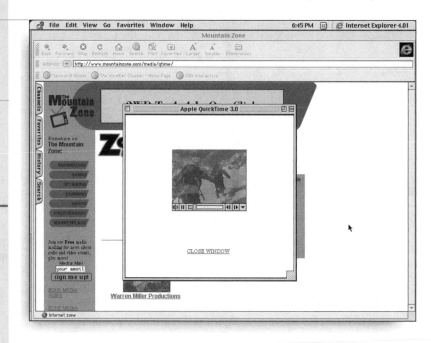

Streaming

With QuickTime version 3.0, QuickTime movies can stream, which means that you can watch them while they download to your Mac.

If you upgrade to the Pro version of QuickTime 3.0, you can also save movies to your Mac so that you can watch them again without being online.

SEE ALSO

➤ *To learn more about working with QuickTime, see page 201*

Installing Internet Explorer Plug-ins

As you travel around the Web, you may encounter files types for which you do not have the required plug-in. In that case, you need to find and install the plug-in you need. Usually, sites will have links to places from which you can download the plug-ins needed for the file types on the site. After you have downloaded the plug-in, simply place it in the Plug-ins folder that is within the Internet Explorer 4.01 Folder, and it will be available to Internet Explorer the next time that you launch it.

Working with Helper Applications

The purpose of helper applications is similar to that of plug-ins—they enable Internet Explorer to present files of types with which it can't work on its own. The difference is that helper applications are stand-alone applications that can be used outside of Internet Explorer, while plug-ins only work from within Internet Explorer.

Installing and Using Helper Applications

Like plug-ins, you usually will find links to needed helper applications on the sites that contain files that require those helper applications. One of the best helper applications is RealPlayer. This application enables you to listen to streaming audio and watch streaming video.

Downloading, installing, and using the RealPlayer helper application

1. Move to www.realplayer.com.
2. Scroll down the Web page and choose Download RealPlayer from the pop-up menu.
3. Click the link to download RealPlayer.
4. Complete the download form and then click Download Free RealPlayer.
5. Choose a sight to download the file from and click it. You will see the Download Manager, and it will tell you how long the download will take.

6. When the file is done, move to your DOWNLOADS folder.

7. Double-click the RealPlayer Installer icon. You will see a warning that your browser needs to quit for the installation process to proceed. Click Continue.

8. Follow the instructions provided in the installer. When the installer is done, you will see the RealPlayer application (see Figure 27.21).

FIGURE 27.21

RealPlayer enables you to hear audio and see video files on the Web.

9. Move back to Internet Explorer and go to www.realplayer.com.

10. Find the best clips link and follow it.

11. Click on a clip. When you do, Internet Explorer will open the helper application for that file type, in this case, RealPlayer (see Figure 27.22). From now on, whenever you click on a RealPlayer file, Internet Explorer will launch RealPlayer so that you can view (and hear) the file.

Configuring the Helper Applications that Internet Explorer Uses

You can set Internet Explorer so that it uses certain helper applications with specific file types.

FIGURE 27.22
Using RealPlayer to watch a video
clip on the Web.

Configuring Internet Explorer helper applications

1. Open Internet Explorer Preferences.

2. Click File Helpers.

3. To change the application for a file type, select the file type
(by its extension) and click Change. You will see the Edit
File Helper window (see Figure 27.23).

FIGURE 27.23
Using the Edit File Helper dialog,
you can change the application
that is used for various file types.

4. Click the Browse button and move to the application that
you want to be the helper application for that file type.

5. Select the application and click OK. The Application shown
at the top of the File Type window will change to be the
application that you just selected.

6. Close the Edit File Helper window by clicking OK.

Adding helpers

You can add helpers for new
files types by using the Add
button.

7. Continue changing helper applications or click OK to close Internet Explorer Preferences. The next time you open that file type from Internet Explorer, the new helper application will be launched.

Understanding Something About Web Security

Security on the Internet is a very important, complicated topic. Because this is not an Internet book, you won't find much detail in this section. But, there are really only two things that you need to know.

If you are looking at an unsecured page, everything you see and everything that you provide via forms can be intercepted by a third party. Unsecured pages do not have the lock icon in the bottom left corner of the Internet Explorer window.

If you are visiting a site and don't see the lock, don't provide any data that you don't want someone else to see—such as credit card information, your Social Security number, and so on. In fact, this is a general principle that you should follow while you are on the Net. Unless you are *sure* that the service you are using is secure, don't provide any information that you don't want transmitted to the world.

This sounds pretty dramatic, and it is a bit overstated. I believe that the chances of anyone intercepting any particular data on the Net are pretty small, but if the potential loss is great, even that small risk may be too much. It's up to you to choose how much risk you want to assume.

Fortunately, by using Internet Explorer, you can provide data via a secure connection to sites that are running the proper server software. A secure connection is one in which the data transmitted is either scrambled, encrypted, or both. This data may still be intercepted, but the person intercepting it won't be able to do anything with it. All he'll get is an electronic mound of goo. Only the server receiving the data will be able to decode and unscramble it. While this system isn't perfect, it's about as close to perfect as you'll get. After all, the only way to be perfectly safe is to never do anything at all.

How do you tell that you are using a secure connection? Look for the lock at the bottom of the window. If it is there, you are using a secure connection. You can also tell by looking at the URL. If it begins with an *https* instead of just *http*, you are visiting a secure location.

You can usually find secure sites in places where you have the opportunity to buy things and need to transmit your credit card information to do so.

Of course, how *you* want to deal with sensitive data is up to you. Some people can accept more risk than others. However, here is the guiding principle that I use.

Do not transmit—via an unsecured means—any data for which you can't accept the risk of a third-party intercepting that data.

You, like me, may find shopping via the Web extremely convenient, easy, and inexpensive, but I suggest that you only transmit credit card data via secure sites. And always remember to judge what you do on the Net not against a perfect world (where there is no chance of your data being misused), but consider the risks you are willing to accept in the non-Net world. For example, you probably think nothing of using your credit card in one of those gas pumps with an integrated card reader. That is certainly no more secure, and may be much less secure (especially if you get a paper receipt), than using your credit card on a secure Web site.

Internet Explorer has lots of security features, and you configure them with four panes of the Internet Explorer Preferences window. These are the following: Security, Security Zones, Ratings, and Cookies. You can explore these settings on your own if you want, but the default settings are likely to be acceptable for you.

Speeding Up the Web

You will love the Web, but you may not like the speed at which it works sometimes. Unless you use a fast network to connect or only connect during off-peak times, you are sometimes going to

---

Security warnings

As you move around the Web, Internet Explorer will present various warnings when you change from a secured to an unsecured site (or vice versa), or when you do anything that Internet Explorer judges to be a security risk. Pay attention to these dialogs, and you will learn quite a bit about security on the Web.

Baking cookies

On the Web, cookies are small text files that Web sites use to track information about you. When you visit a site that uses cookies, the site can check the cookies it previously installed on your machine in order to serve you or to capture more information about you. For example, a cookie may contain areas of interest so that you are automatically taken to spots on the site that are more likely to generate a sale from you.

If you don't like the idea of spreading your cookies all over the Web, you can control how Internet Explorer deals with cookies by using the Cookies Settings Preferences. You can refuse to accept any cookies, or you can choose to accept or reject them on a case-by-case basis.

You can only control your end

There are two sides to every connection, and you can't do anything about the "other side" of your Net connection. This includes the phone lines you are using, your ISP, and the Web servers that you are visiting. If these resources are overloaded, your browsing will slow to a crawl. There isn't much you can do about that except to use the offline browsing feature of Internet Explorer and download pages during off-peak hours. What you will learn in this section is how to work more efficiently with your end of the connection so that you get the most speed possible.

be frustrated by slow Web pages. In this section, you will learn a few things you can do to make your Web surfing move a bit more quickly.

Using Contextual Menus

While you are in Internet Explorer, hold down the Control key and click the mouse button. You will see an extremely useful contextual menu (see Figure 27.24). This menu enables you do a lot of what you may want to do without ever taking your hand off the mouse.

FIGURE 27.24

Using Internet Explorer's contextual menus can speed up your Web surfing.

Some options will not be selectable until you are in a position where selecting that option makes sense (in other words, you can't choose the image commands unless your cursor is over an image). As you use this contextual menu, you will become familiar with the situations in which it can be helpful.

Turning Off Images

Why would you want to do this? After all, isn't one of the great things about the Web the images that you see? Yes, but if you have a slow connection, you may not want to wait to see images. Perhaps you're looking for some specific information and want to see only the text of pages until you find what are looking for. In any event, you should know how to do this in case you want to see the text-only Web.

Turning off images

1. Open Internet Explorer Preferences.

2. Click Web Content.

3. Uncheck the "Show pictures" check box.

4. Click OK. Your pages will load more quickly, but they won't look as nice (see Figure 27.25).

5. To load a particular graphic, click its icon. That graphic will be downloaded and displayed.

Loading all the graphics at once

You can load all of the graphics on a page by choosing Load Images from the View menu.

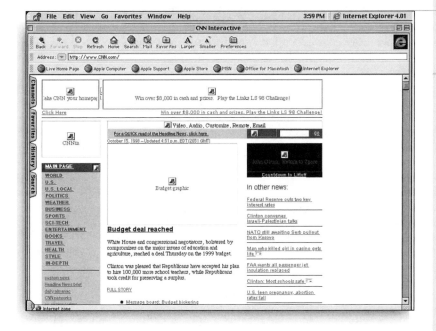

FIGURE 27.25
A Web page without graphics is not a pretty picture.

Because Internet Explorer enables you to see pages while they load, you can see a partial page during the loading process. This means that you can read the text on a page while the graphics are downloading. Thus, turning the automatic downloading of graphics off may not make all that much difference for you. But if you are trying to squeeze every bit of speed out of the Web that you can, foregoing the graphics will help.

Using More Windows on the World

You can have multiple Web windows open at the same time. What's so great about this? The windows in Internet Explorer are *independent*. That means that you can do different things in each—simultaneously. You can load related pages and see them side-by-side (this is great for comparison shopping). You can be loading one page while you are reading another. You can browse a page in one window while you are doing a search in another. You will find this to be very useful, and once you use this technique, it will quickly become indispensable. The number of windows that you can have open is only limited by your computer's processing power and memory and your screen's real estate (see Figure 27.26). To open Web windows, choose New Window from the File menu. You can use the new window just like any other one; enter a URL or click a link to move to a Web page.

While opening a new window and moving to a different site is useful, using multiple windows really shines when you are searching or when you are following multiple links from the same page. Try it a few times, and you will find that this technique will dramatically improve the speed at which you use the Web.

Using multiple windows to accelerate the Web

1. Connect to the Net and move to a Web page.

2. When you find a link that you want to follow, point to it, hold down the Control key, and click.

3. From the contextual menu, choose Open Link in New Window. A new Web window will open, and the page will begin to download in it.

More windows means more data

The more windows you have open, the more RAM Internet Explorer needs to work with all of that data. You can experiment to see how many windows you can have open on your machine and still maintain acceptable performance.

Sharing bandwidth

The down side to using multiple windows is that each must share the total bandwidth that you have available because they all download at the same time (you can only fit so much data through your connection). With multiple data streams being downloaded, each stream will slow down somewhat compared to its speed if it was the only stream being transferred to your Mac. This isn't a big deal for two reasons. One is that your connection is used much more efficiently since data is constantly being downloaded to it (as opposed to when you are using a single window and much of the time no data is being transferred). The second is that *you* are doing something while the data is being downloaded (such as reading a page that already has been downloaded) and so your time is not being wasted staring at a partial page while it is being downloaded.

FIGURE 27.26
Lots of Web windows can make
your surfing go faster.

4. While the Web page is downloading, move back to the first page and continue to read it (you can click on the page or choose it from the Window menu).

5. When you find another link that you want to follow, repeat steps 3 and 4. As pages finish downloading, you can jump to them to read them. This keeps you from wasting time staring at a page while it is downloading.

Caching It In

In an earlier section, you learned that Internet Explorer stores all of the files that it downloads in a cache on your hard drive. While your hard drive is a lot faster than downloading something from the Web, there is another way to make Web browsing even faster. Rather than storing the Web files on your hard drive, you can have them stored on a RAM disk instead. Loading files from the RAM disk is even faster than loading them from a hard drive.

Multiple windows and searches

The multiple window technique is especially useful when you are searching. First, open the search engine in a window and perform your search. From the results page, open a new window for every link you follow. By doing so, you can always quickly jump back to the results page in order to follow more links. This will significantly decrease the time it takes for you to find things on the Web.

Setting the Internet Explorer cache to use a RAM disk

1. Create a RAM disk.

SEE ALSO

➤ *To learn how to create and use a RAM disk, see page 332*

2. Open Internet Explorer Preferences.

3. Click Advanced.

4. In the Cache area, click Change Location (see Figure 27.27).

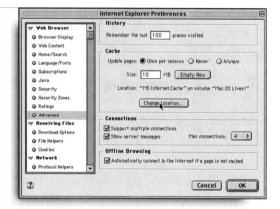

5. Move to your RAM disk and click Select RAM Disk (or whatever your RAM disk is called).

6. Click OK. When Internet Explorer needs to load a file from its cache, it will be able to do so much faster than from your hard drive.

Updating Internet Explorer

Microsoft is continually updating and improving Internet Explorer. You should periodically check Internet Explorer's Web site at www.microsoft.com/ie/ for updates as well as support.

You can also subscribe to this site so that you are notified whenever it changes. This will keep you informed of all the latest Internet Explorer developments as they happen.

Reading Newsgroups

Understanding what newsgroups are and how they work

Finding newsgroups

Subscribing to newsgroups

Reading and posting to newsgroups

Newsgroups versus mailing lists

Newsgroups are very similar to mailing lists. The main difference is in how you receive the information. With a mailing list, the discussion is delivered to your Inbox, one message at a time. With a newsgroup, you have to retrieve the messages, and you will see a lot of individual messages at one time.

A newsgroup by any other name

Most online services have areas that function similarly to newsgroups. For example, if you've used forums on CompuServe or message boards on AOL, then you pretty much know what newsgroups are all about.

A whole lotta noise

Before you get any further into newsgroups, you should know something about them. Many newsgroups have extremely poor signal-to-noise ratios. What I mean by this is that in many groups, you have to wade through a whole lot of messages that you find to be a waste of time before you read some that you find worthwhile. If you can accept this, you'll be fine. If you want to find information in a hurry, another Internet service (such as the Web) may be a better choice.

Understanding Newsgroups

Usenet newsgroups are one of the oldest parts of the Internet. Although newsgroups are a little tough to explain, they are easy to use. You may find newsgroups to be an extremely valuable source of information and entertainment, or you may find them to be a waste of time. Try a few groups and decide for yourself.

Basically, newsgroups are electronic discussions; the topics of these discussions are as varied as the people who participate in them. There are so many topics, in fact, that it is impossible to provide a list that will give you any idea of how vast the range of newsgroup topics is. Suffice it to say that there are newsgroups on more topics than you will ever need or want. There are groups on just about every computer-related topic. There are groups discussing all facets of entertainment. There are groups devoted to the two taboo topics of regular conversation: politics and religion. There are even a few groups devoted to hating Barney the dinosaur. There are so many groups, that it seems like every topic anyone has ever thought about has a newsgroup devoted to it.

Each newsgroup is devoted to the discussion of a specific topic. This topic can be narrow or broad. For example, there may be a newsgroup that discusses the TV show, "Star Trek: The Next Generation." There might be another newsgroup that discusses the impact of TV on the global culture.

One thing you need to keep in mind is that anyone can write anything on a newsgroup so beware of all information that you get via newsgroups. Many people try to be as truthful as they can be. Others like to give out bogus information just for the fun of it. Still others only think they know what they are talking about.

The trouble with newsgroups is that there is no way to tell what kind of person posted a message. It may be an expert in the topic area, or it may be someone who wouldn't know the topic from a hole in the ground, but thinks he does. Just be careful and you'll be all right.

Given its problems, why read newsgroups? Because sometimes you *do* hear from experts and *can* converse with them. Or you can have the chance to interact with people around the world who share interests similar to yours. Or you can tune in just for laughs. There are as many reasons to read newsgroups as there are newsgroups.

Understanding How Newsgroups Work

In order to use newsgroups, you must have some idea of how to get to the groups you want. You can do this through the newsgroup name. Each newsgroup has a unique name that looks sort of like an email address without the @.

Understanding Newsgroup Names

Newsgroup names look something like this:

category.topic1.topic2.topic3

Generally, as you move to the right in the newsgroup name, the topic words become more specific. Here's an example:

comp.sys.mac.digest

In this case, the category is computer—the *comp* tells you this. The second level is *sys*, which stands for system. The next level is *mac*, the best operating system in the world. And last, but not least, is the *digest*, which means this group is a digest (a collection of digest messages).

You can generally decipher newsgroup names in this way, and that's good because the name is all you have to go by when you are figuring out the newsgroups in which you want to participate. Of course, sometimes the name you decipher has nothing whatsoever to do with the newsgroup, but that's OK because it's also easy to unsubscribe from newsgroups. Sometimes, you won't be able to decipher the name at all; you just have to try the group to see what it is about.

The *category* part of the name is used to organize newsgroups so that you can sort through them in some reasonable fashion. Don't laugh—there are a ton of newsgroups! (BTW, a ton of newsgroups is more than 12,000.) Here are some of the major categories of newsgroups:

- **alt**—Alternative newsgroups are groups that cover topics that don't fit into other categories. Some of these groups are truly bizarre.

- **clari**—Clarinet newsgroups carry a variety of commercial information, such as news feeds from the major news services.

- **comp**—Computer newsgroups discuss each and every computer platform and just about every piece of hardware and software.

- **loc**—Local newsgroups are dedicated to issues impacting local regions.

- **rec**–Recreation newsgroups cover various hobby and sports topics.

- **sci**—Science newsgroups discuss, amazingly enough, science topics.

- **talk**—Talk newsgroups are devoted to general discussions.

Understanding Newsgroup URLs

You might have guessed from our URL discussion in Chapter 26, "Browsing the Web: The Basics," that you can move to a newsgroup by using its URL. Newsgroup URLs look like this:

news:category.topic1.topic2.topic3

In the case of the Mac newsgroup I mentioned earlier, the URL is the following:

news:comp.sys.mac.digest

If you enter this URL in your Web browser, however, your newsgroup reader will open and move to the group whose URL you entered. The default newsgroup reader for Mac OS 8.5 is Outlook Express. You will learn how to read newsgroups with it later in this chapter.

Subscribing and Unsubscribing to Newsgroups

First, you must select which newsgroups you want to read. You can do this by scrolling through a list of available groups in each category and selecting those that interest you. When you select a group, you, in effect, "subscribe" (become a member) to that group. The obvious benefit of this is that you can see only those groups that interest you.

These groups are downloaded to your machine, where you can read them. Each message that you read is called a *posting*. Postings look just like email messages, but they're sent to a newsgroup instead of an individual.

Within the newsgroup, the postings are organized into various *threads*. Threads help you follow a specific discussion within the general newsgroup topic. The thread is shown in the Subject block of the message. Some threads will interest you and some won't. (Go ahead and skip anything that doesn't interest you— that's the purpose of a thread.)

While you are reading a thread, you may have a question you want to ask, an answer to someone else's question, or just a thought or opinion that you want to share. You can do these things in two ways, either by posting your message to the newsgroup or by responding to an individual by email.

Posting to the newsgroup places your message in the particular thread that you post in. When other people read the group, they'll see your message. So be careful that you are posting something germane to the group. Remember that thousands of people may read your posting so don't embarrass yourself by saying something inane or stupid. When you first start using newsgroups, it's better not to post unless you are really sure what you have to say will interest others. After you read newsgroups for a while, you'll know what is appropriate and what's not.

You can also reply directly to the person who made the posting via email. Only the person to whom you reply sees this message, and it does not impact the newsgroup at all. Replying by email is better if your response is not relevant to the rest of the group (such as a personal greeting or a thank-you for a posting). If you have something very critical to say or you are trying to correct someone's behavior, reply by email.

Lurkers unite!

When you only read a newsgroup and don't post messages to it, you are lurking. On the Net, lurking is actually a good thing, especially if you are just getting started. It is often a good idea to just read a newsgroup for a while until you know the lay of the cyberland. Once you understand what the group is about, you can feel free to post messages without fear of getting a royal *flame* job—flames are nasty messages from people who don't appreciate what you have to say. Or you can continue to just lurk.

After you are finished reading the groups you have subscribed to, you can mark the threads you have read so that you will not see them again. The next time you read news, you will see only those messages you haven't already read.

The last thing you should know about newsgroups is that some are moderated and some are not.

In moderated groups, every posting is sent to a moderator who decides if the posting is really appropriate for the group. If it is appropriate, he posts it to the group. If he feels the message isn't suitable, he does not post it. Sometimes, the rejected message will be returned with an explanation of why it was rejected. This sounds a bit like censorship, and it is. But it can prevent groups from becoming filled with inappropriate messages that waste everyone's time and frustrate people in the group. (Plus, you always know whether a group is moderated or not, so it's not as though someone is doing something behind your back.) When you subscribe to a group, you agree to abide by the moderator's decision. If you don't like it, you can always drop the group.

In an unmoderated group, what you post is automatically posted to the group. No censoring, no filters, nothing. This allows for free-flowing discussion, but it may also waste time because you may read messages that really don't belong in the group.

That's all there is to it. It may sound a bit confusing, but after you get the hang of it, newsgroups are pretty straightforward.

Reading Newsgroups

Before you can read newsgroups, you have to find some that you want to read, and then you have to subscribe to them. After you have subscribed, you can download the messages in that group and begin to read, post, and reply. If you tire of a group, you can always unsubscribe from it.

Finding Newsgroups

First things first—find a list of newsgroups to which you can subscribe. You can use Outlook Express to read newsgroups. But before you can do that, you need to add the news server to your Outlook Express configuration. (A news server is simply a server that feeds your newsgroups to you.) When you obtained your Internet access account, you should have been told what the news server was for your ISP—it is probably something like news.isp.net (where the isp is the name of your ISP).

Configuring a News Server

When you used the Internet application to configure your Mac for the Net, you should have entered a news server. If you didn't, use the following step-by-step to configure your news server.

Configuring a news server

1. Launch Outlook Express.

2. Open the Preferences window.

3. Choose News in the left pane. You will see the News server configuration window (see Figure 28.1). You probably will see that the Microsoft news server is already configured on your setup. If you used the Internet application to configure your Mac, you may see your news server instead. I'll show you how to add another news server in case yours isn't already set up or in case you want to add another one.

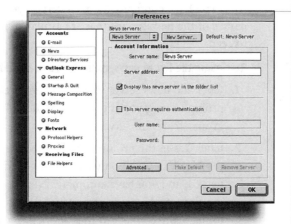

4. Click the New Server button.

5. In the New Account dialog box, enter a name for the news server and click OK.

Multiple news servers

You can have multiple news servers configured in Outlook Express. You will then be able to choose a particular server in order to be able to access the newsgroups on that server. If you want to add a news server rather than replacing one, click the New Server button, enter a name, and click OK. Then enter its address in the Account Information dialog.

FIGURE 28.1
The news server preference screen enables you to configure a news server.

6. When you return to the Preferences window, enter the news server address that your ISP provided you with.

7. When you are done, click OK. You will now see the news server in the left pane of the Outlook Express window (see Figure 28.2). Your news server is now configured.

FIGURE 28. 2

You can see the IQuest news server (called News Server) that I just added in the left pane in Outlook Express.

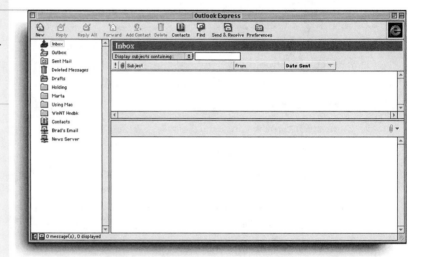

Multiple news servers

If you have more than one news server configured on your Mac, you need to download the list of available newsgroups for each server. Some of the newsgroups will be the same, and some will be different. Different news servers carry different newsgroups.

In the future

After you have downloaded the full list, use the Get New Newsgroups command on the View menu to update your list with any groups that have been added to those available on the news server since you last checked the list.

Retrieving the Newsgroup Lists

After you have configured a news server, you need to retrieve the names of the newsgroups that are available on that server for you to read.

Retrieving the list of newsgroups that are available to you

1. Click the news server that you configured. You will see a prompt asking you if you want to download the list of newsgroups from this server.

2. Click Yes in the prompt. Outlook Express will connect to the Net. (This will only happen if you aren't already connected, and you have automatic Net connections enabled in the Remote Access control panel. If you don't, you will have to manually connect to the Net before you can get the list of newsgroups.) The full list of newsgroups that are available to you will download to your Mac. The list of available newsgroups is likely to be huge—probably 10,000 or more

groups. If Outlook Express is strapped for RAM in which to run, you may have trouble and may need to allocate more RAM to Outlook Express. Downloading the entire list of newsgroups may take several minutes. When the list has been downloaded, you will see the list in the right pane of the Outlook Express window (see Figure 28.3). Fortunately, you only have to do this step the first time that you retrieve the list from a news server. From this point on, you can simply retrieve new groups as they are added to the server.

SEE ALSO

➤ *To learn how to allocate more memory to an application, see page 327*

But wait, there's more

You should know that the newsgroups available to you are not necessarily all the newsgroups in the world. You can only see the groups that flow through your news server. But don't be alarmed, there are still a lot more than you will ever need. And if you can't find a particular one, you can always add another news server if you can find one you are able to access.

FIGURE 28.3

I told you that there are a lot of newsgroups; in this case the full newsgroup list contains 24,000 newsgroups.

Subscribing to Newsgroups

The idea behind subscribing is to develop a set of newsgroups that you like to read; remember that subscribing to a group means that it will be downloaded to your computer so that you can read the messages in it.

Winnowing the field

In the "Display newsgroups containing" field, you can enter as much of the newsgroup name as you like and Outlook Express will winnow the list down to all items that match the text you enter. In this example, you can enter *comp.sys.mac.digest* to move to the comp.mac.sys.digest newsgroup, assuming that it is on your particular news server.

Subscribing to newsgroups

1. At the top of the window that displays the list of newsgroups you just downloaded, enter a word that you might be interested in reading about (in this example, I will look for Mac-related groups, but you can use anything you like). The newsgroups that contain that word are now shown in the window (see Figure 28.4). In this example, you can see that a lot of the groups are not Macintosh related, but simply contain the three letters "mac."

2. Scroll through the list until you find a group that you might like to try; in this example, I chose comp.sys.mac.digest. You may or may not have this group available to you. If not, use any other group for this step-by-step.

FIGURE 28.4

I found the groups that had the word "Mac" in the name, which only narrowed the field down to 237 groups!

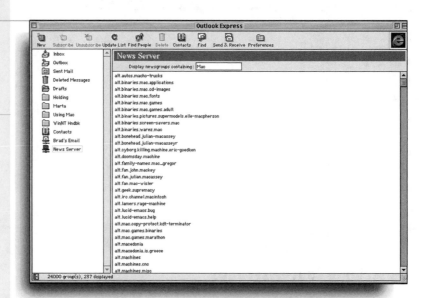

3. Select the list to which you want to subscribe (you can hold the Shift key and select multiple groups if you want to).

4. Click the Subscribe button (newspaper with a green check mark). The newsgroup name will become bold and will now appear underneath the news server icon (see Figure 28.5). This indicates that you have subscribed to this group.

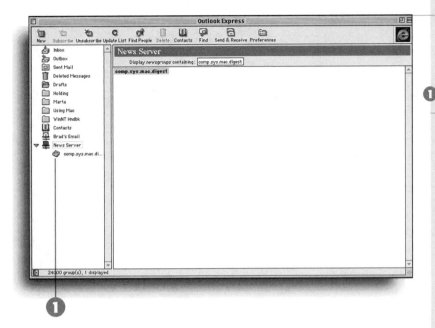

FIGURE 28.5

This figure shows that I have subscribed to the comp.sys.mac.digest newsgroup.

1 Subscribed newsgroup

5. Repeat steps 1-4 until you have subscribed to as many groups as you would like to try.

Reading Newsgroup Messages

After you have subscribed to newsgroups, you can download messages and read them.

Reading a newsgroup

1. Click the newsgroup that you want to read from the list of subscribed newsgroups under the news server icon in the left pane of the Outlook Express window. The messages that have been posted to that group will appear in the top right pane of the Outlook Express window in Figure 28.6.

2. When you see a message that you want to read, click it. The text of the message will be downloaded to your machine, and you can read it in the lower pane of the Outlook Express window (see Figure 28.7).

FIGURE 28.6

The messages that have been posted to a newsgroup appear in the top pane of the Outlook Express window.

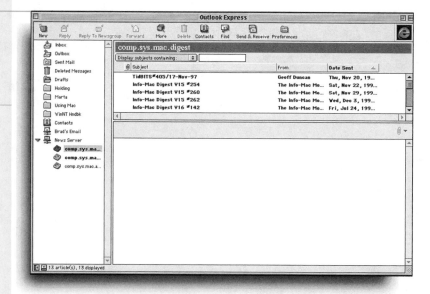

FIGURE 28.6

The messages that have been posted to a newsgroup appear in the top pane of the Outlook Express window.

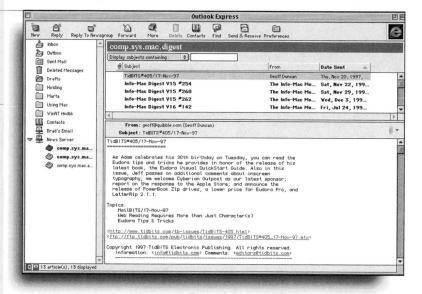

FIGURE 28.7

This newsgroup posting is selected in the top pane and can be read in the lower pane of the Outlook Express window.

3. Continue reading other messages in the group. As you read messages, they will become unbolded, which means that they are marked as read. The next time you download messages from this group, the messages marked as read will not be downloaded since you have already read them.

4. When you have read all of the messages in which you are interested, press Command-A to select all the messages in the group.

5. Choose Mark as Read from the Message menu. It is a good idea to do this so that you see only new messages from now on—especially during the first time that you read a group since you will be so far "behind."

Some messages are files

Files can be posted to newsgroups so that others can download them. This is particularly popular with graphics files, but other files get uploaded as well. I'll leave figuring out how to handle files via newsgroups to you.

Here are some quick and easy things to know about reading newsgroups.

- To read to the next message in a thread, press Command-].

- To move to the preceding message in the thread, press Command-[.

- Threads are shown in the top pane of the Outlook Express window with expansion triangles next to them. To see a list of all the messages in that thread, click the arrow to expand the thread.

- To move to the next thread, press the down arrow key—to move to the previous thread, press the up arrow key.

Posting and Replying to Newsgroups

OK, it's time to learn how to add *your* pearls of wisdom to a newsgroup, but first a warning.

Warning: *If you post something on a newsgroup, your address appears on a posting so everyone knows "who done it." If you do something stupid (or perhaps juvenile), thousands of your closest friends may take note of it and gently point out your error to you.*

That said, when should you post?

If you have a question or just want to share your thoughts with the readers of the group, you can post a new message to the newsgroup—you will be starting a new thread.

If you can answer somebody's question or if you have something significant to say on a topic, you can post a reply. You should only post a reply if you want everyone in the newsgroup to see it.

If you want to just reply to the author of the posting (which is often a better idea), reply via email.

Posting a Message to a Newsgroup

After you lurk for a while, you may be ready to ask your own questions or share your thoughts with everyone who reads the newsgroup. You can do this by posting a new message. Before you do, make sure that your posting is appropriate to the group.

Posting a message on a newsgroup

1. Select the newsgroup to which you want to post a message.

2. Click the New button (newspaper with a green line on it). You will see an untitled message window with the address of the newsgroup in the Newsgroups field.

3. Enter your subject in the Subject field.

4. Move to the body and type your message.

5. Review your message to make sure that you aren't saying something you shouldn't (see Figure 28.8).

FIGURE 28.8

The window that you use to post to a newsgroup looks very similar to an email message.

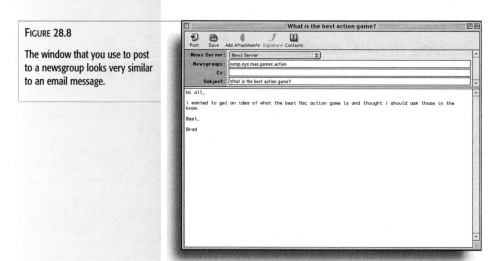

6. When you are ready to post to the group, click the Post button (paper with a push pin in it). Your message will be posted to the group for others to read.

Replying to Posts

You are probably more likely to reply to existing messages than to post new ones. There are two ways to do this. You can reply to the message in the newsgroup so that everyone will see your reply, or you can reply to just the author of a message via email.

You should reply to the group if your response is likely to be useful to many people. Reply via email if your response is intended only for the author of the message.

Posting a reply to the group

1. With the message that you want to reply to displayed in the bottom pane of the window, click the Post reply to newsgroup button. The message will appear in a new window with quotes added to show that it is a reply.

2. Type your reply.

3. Click the Reply to Newsgroup button. You will see a message window with the text from the message to which you are replying pasted in it.

4. Edit the quoted text until the message contains only the text to which you will be replying.

5. Type your reply.

6. When you are ready to post your reply, click Post. You reply will be posted to the group.

If you want to reply only to the person who posted a message, do the following steps.

Replying via email instead of posting to the group

1. With the message that you want to reply to displayed in the bottom pane of the window, click the Reply button. A new message window will appear with the email of the message's author already entered along with the quoted text of the message.

2. Type your reply.

3. Click the Send message button. Your reply will be seen only by the person who posted the original message.

Unsubscribing from Newsgroups

If a newsgroup turns out to be a dud for you, you can unsubscribe from it so that you don't have to see it any more.

Unsubscribing from a newsgroup

1. Select the news server that contains the group from which you want to unsubscribe.

2. Choose Subscribed Only from the View menu. The right pane will show the list of groups to which you have subscribed.

3. Highlight the group from which you want to unsubscribe.

4. Click the Unsubscribe button. The group will become unbolded and will disappear from the list that appears under the news server in the left pane. You can always subscribe to it again later.

Using Newsgroups

Some newsgroups are great for beginners, and some can be pretty rough. The following paragraphs provide some tips about newsgroups.

Sometimes, if you post an inappropriate message, a stupid one, or merely an unpopular one, you may get flamed. Mild flames will gently point out your error and helpfully suggest that you don't do it again. Other times, you get nuked; lots of nasty email burying you alive (your email address is on the posting, remember?). In either case, try to learn from any mistakes you may have made.

Of course, if you get flamed just for having an unpopular opinion, that's cyberlife (at least that's what people say).

Some folks can get nasty in a hurry. Don't worry about it too much, though. After all, flames don't really harm you. Just remember what a flaming feels like so that after you are a Net expert and are tempted to unleash a volley of your own on some rank beginner, perhaps you'll think twice about it.

Remember that just subscribing to a newsgroup doesn't mean that you have to post to the newsgroup. In fact, you shouldn't post anything unless you truly think that it will add something positive to the discussion. Although you can't see them, there are many more people who simply browse the newsgroups than ever post anything on them. In fact, you should lurk for a while until you get the hang of newsgroups.

When you do post, remember the 2 C's of writing: clarity and conciseness. Be clear, particularly if you ask a question. Don't post a question such as, "I have a problem with my Mac." No one will have a clue as to what your problem is. If you post something like this, you'll be lucky if you are simply ignored—you may get flamed for a message like that. Be as specific as you can.

The other C, conciseness, makes it more likely that people will actually read your posting. Shorter messages are better—given that you keep the first C in mind.

Also, the third C, politeness, always helps.

When you begin reading, be sure to check out the Frequently Asked Question (FAQs). Almost all newsgroups have them. This may save you the embarrassment of asking a question that has already been answered a hundred times.

The FAQs will also point you to the Web, mailing lists, and FTP sites, as well as all sorts of other places on the Internet where you can find more information on any given topic.

Maintaining, Fixing, and Upgrading Your Mac

29   **Backing Up 681**

30   **Fighting Viruses 701**

31   **Preventing Mac Problems 713**

32   **Fixing Mac Problems 745**

33   **Maintaining Your Mac Through Upgrades 773**

Backing Up

Understanding why you should back up

Developing your own backup strategy

Obtaining and using backup hardware

Obtaining and using backup software

Learning tips for effective backups

Backing up is not only for crashes

You need a good backup for more than just catastrophic failures of your hardware. I'll bet that you have accidentally deleted a file right before you needed it. If you have a backup, you can quickly recover a document that you accidentally delete. Or, perhaps you edited a document and discovered that all of your changes were actually worse than the original. You can use your backup to bring the file back to the way it was. If your Mac is ever stolen or destroyed, your backup enables you to recover from the disaster.

Consider yourself warned

You may be thinking that this backup stuff is a waste of time, and that you have more important things to do. If that is your attitude, OK, you might as well skip the rest of the chapter. Hey, you may get lucky and never need a backup. However, when the day comes that you suddenly have a sick feeling in the pit of your stomach because you realize that you have lost something that will take you hours and hours to re-create, remember this chapter. Once you are done reinventing the wheel, you may change your mind and decide that having a backup would be a good thing after all.

Backing Up Can Save You

If you use a computer, at some point, your system will crash and you will lose information that you would rather not lose—maybe not today or tomorrow, but it *is* the inevitable nightmare. Think of the information that you have on your Mac at this very moment that would be difficult—if not impossible—to reconstruct if your computer bombed and destroyed it. This data might be a report for work, a school project, your tax information, a complex spreadsheet, or even the blockbuster novel that might make you the next John Grisham. Whatever the information, rest assured that some day, somewhere, somehow, you will suddenly lose it. You want to be able to restore all of the information on your Mac so that when something bad happens, you can quickly re-create your work. Backing up is the means by which you ensure that you are always able to preserve most of your work, no matter what happens to your Mac.

Backing up your Mac simply means having a copy of the data (including documents, applications, utilities, system software, and other software) on your computer; a backup is analogous to having a photograph of the data on your computer at a particular point in time. You can use a backup to recover everything from a single file to the entire contents of your hard drives.

While backing up your data is strongly recommended by computer authors, experts, and support personnel, it is a task that many Mac users never do for a variety of reasons. Some people don't back up data because they think their systems are infallible and won't crash. Still others are confused about how to make a backup of their system, or they lack the hardware and software necessary to maintain good backups. And then there are always those who simply don't believe that protecting their data is enough of a priority to waste the time on it.

But, trust me, all of these people are wrong. It is absolutely imperative that you back up your Mac, no matter who you are and how you use your computer. You can use fairly sophisticated schemes and hardware to back up your system, or you can keep it simple. Whichever way you decide to go, having backups of your critical data can be a life saver.

In this chapter, you'll learn techniques to back up your Mac successfully, what hardware and software to use, and also develop a backup strategy to make the plan work on a consistent basis.

Understanding Backups

There are four steps to create and implement a solid backup plan. These steps are the following:

- **Define a strategy**. You need to define your own backup strategy; your strategy should define the types of data that you will back up and how often you will back up your data. These choices will guide you as you decide on the kind of hardware and software that you use.

- **Obtain and learn to use backup hardware**. You need some kind of hardware on which to store the backedup data. There are many types of hardware that you can use including tape drives, removable media drives, additional hard drives, or CD-Recordable drives.

- **Obtain and learn to use backup software**. Ideally, you should use some sort of software to automate the backup process. The easier you make it on yourself, the more likely it is that your backup system will work reliably.

- **Maintain your backup system**. Like all other systems, you need to maintain your backup system and make sure that your data is safe.

Defining a Backup Strategy

One of the first things you need to decide is what data on your machine will be backed up.

Deciding What to Back Up

There are three general categories of data that you should consider backing up:

A backup by any other name is an archive

An archive is similar to a backup, but the difference is the intended purpose for duplicating the data. For example, a backup is used to recover information that has been lost from some kind of calamity, and backups are usually overwritten as time passes so that the backup contains only recent data. An archive is usually done to save data permanently that has long-term value. You should archive data when you want to remove data from your hard disk because you don't use it often.

Back up the archive

Backup techniques can also be used to create archives. Remember that once you remove the data from your computer, the archive becomes your only copy of that data. Unless your archive is reliable and will hold up over time, you should maintain a backup of your archive (by that I mean that you keep more than one copy).

What is a document?

The word document may bring an image of a text document to your mind. But remember that on the Mac, everything you create is a document. A document can be a text file, graphic, tax return, digital video, or anything else.

- **Documents and other important data that you create**. These documents are, after all, the reason you use a Mac in the first place. You will probably want to back up all of your documents since they exist no place besides your computer. If you lose important documents, it may be impossible to re-create them. Even if you are able to re-create them, you will be wasting a lot of valuable time redoing what you have already done.

- **System files**. You probably have a CD-ROM that contains your Mac OS software, so you usually don't risk losing the Mac OS software itself. What you do risk losing is any customization you have done. If you have adjusted any settings or added any third-party software, all of the settings you have changed will be lost in the event of a major failure.

  It can take a lot of time and effort to re-create your tailored system configuration; a full backup of your system will make restoring your customized OS configuration much easier and faster.

  Additionally, don't forget about all of the configuration information you have on your machine. For example, if you lose your system for some reason, you may lose all of the configuration you have done to make your Mac connect to the Internet. You may also lose all the serial numbers of your software, which you will have to re-enter if you need to reinstall it.

- **Applications and other third-party software**. As with the OS software, you probably have floppy disks or CDs containing all of your third-party software. What you lose if you have a failure without a backup is all of the customization of those applications. Plus, you will have to reinstall all of that software—not an easy task for many large applications. In any case, it can be very time consuming to reinstall your applications.

Deciding What Kind of Backup to Make

In conjunction with the kind of files you will back up, there are also several different types of backups you can make:

- **Full backup**. In a full backup, you back up each and every file on your system. The advantage of doing full backups is that it is easy to restore your entire system as well as just particular parts of it. You can restore all of your customization so that you can quickly and easily get your system back to the way it was. The disadvantages of full backups are that you need a large amount of storage space on your backup drive, and it can take quite a long time to complete the backup.

- **Selected files only**. Using this scheme, you select particular files to back up; usually these are your important documents and some of your customization files (for example, the preferences files). The advantage of this scheme is that you can make a backup quickly while protecting the most important files on your computer. The disadvantage of this approach is that you may have to spend lots of time and effort restoring your system and applications.

- **Incremental backup**. This scheme combines the first two techniques in that all files are backed up the first time, but after that only files that change are backed up until the next full backup. Often, you can have your backup software select all files that have changed since the last backup so that you always have a current backup for every file. This scheme protects all your files, but avoids the time and space requirements of doing a full backup each time. The disadvantage is that you need backup software and capable hardware to make this technique feasible.

Choosing a Backup System

What you decide about the type of data that you will back up and how you will back it up should determine the type of backup system that you develop and use. For example, if you decide that you don't mind having to reinstall applications and reconfigure settings or you mainly use small document files, you might be able to simply copy your document files onto a floppy disk. If you have lots of data to protect, you will need to implement a more sophisticated system.

If you can assemble the hardware and software to do incremental backups, you should use this approach. It is the only one that is both practical for frequent backups and also protects all of your data.

Choosing Backup Hardware

The hardware that you use for your backup system is important because having hardware that doesn't match the kind of backups you want to make will doom your backup plan to failure. For example, if you go with a tape drive, then you will be able to do frequent, incremental backups, but if you rely on a floppy disk, you will have to be very selective about the files you back up because of the limited storage space on each disk. ref _Ref415736106 * Mergeformat Table 29.1 summarizes the advantages and disadvantages of the major types of hardware you can use to back up your data. In the sections following the table, you'll learn some details about each type of hardware.

TABLE 29.1   Hardware That You Can Use to Back Up Your Mac

Drive Type	Back Up Capability	Advantages	Disadvantages
Tape	Can handle large amounts of data for full and incremental backups	Large storage capability is perfect for unattended backups	Tape can't be mounted (drive can't be used or work); a tape drive is a single purpose device
		Low cost per MB of storage	Tapes can be affected by magnetic fields and will degrade over time
		Tapes are inexpensive	Relatively slow
		Backups can be stored away from your Mac	Drives can be expensive
		Can be used for archival of data	

Drive Type	Back Up Capability	Advantages	Disadvantages
Removable media (Zip, Jaz, SyQuest, and so on)	Depending on the drive type, can handle medium to large amounts of data for full and incremental backups	Drives can be mounted and used for work as well as for backups	Unlikely that a single disk will hold all the data on your Mac so full, unattended back ups won't be possible
		Low cost per MB of storage	Magnetic storage devices can be affected by magnetic fields and will degrade over time
		Can be used to easily share data with others	Multiple lower capacity disks (such as Zip disks) will be required for large amounts of data
		Fast	Disks are too expensive for archiving data
		Zip drives have become standard on newer Mac hardware	
		Backups can be stored away from your Mac	
CD-R and CD-RW	Can handle large amounts of data for full and incremental backups, but full unattended backups are not probable	Drive has multiple uses (mastering CDs for distribution, mounting CD-ROM discs, and so on)	Unlikely that a single CD will hold all the data on your Mac so unattended, full back ups won't be possible
		Data is easy to share and recover since almost all computers have CD-ROM drives	CD-R discs cannot be reused (CD-RW discs can be)
		Provides nearly permanent storage; this is the best choice for archival purposes	Relatively slow

continues...

TABLE 29.1   Continued

Drive Type	Back Up Capability	Advantages	Disadvantages
		Backups can be stored away from your Mac	Higher cost per MB of storage
			Drives are expensive and more difficult to use than other types
Hard drive	Depending on size, can handle large amounts of data for unattended full and incremental backups	Very fast	High cost per MB of data storage
		Data is easily accessible	Data is harder to share
		Drive can be mounted and used for other tasks	Unlikely to have sufficient storage space to make full backups
		Drive can be used for other purposes in a pinch	Backup drive likely to be used for other purposes and thus not be available for backing up
			Difficult to store backups away from your Mac
			Backup subject power surges and other outside causes of failure
			Can't be used for archival purposes
			Capacity can't be expanded
Floppy disk	Suitable only for backing up very small documents	Data is easy to share	Small storage capacity makes unattended backups impossible
		Low cost per MB of storage (free if you can collect enough AOL disks!)	Very slow, especially with frequent disk changes

Drive Type	Back Up Capability	Advantages	Disadvantages
		Very accessible since all computers have a floppy drive	Very cumbersome to use, unlikely to maintain good backups
			Poor reliability
			Can be difficult to restore data and keep the backups organized

Backing Up with Tape Drives

Tape drives use a magnetic tape to store data (similar to a music cassette tape, only larger). There are a variety of tape drives available including Digital Audio Tape (DAT) drives, one-quarter inch tape drives, and several others. These drives are not intended to be mountable (you can't mount a tape on your desktop like you can a hard or removable media drive), thus you won't be able to access individual files directly from the tapes. Remember that you can use tape drives only to *store* data. Data has to be restored back to a hard drive or some other bootable drive before it can be used.

A tape drive suitable for backups will cost anywhere from $300 to $700 dollars, with a good, fully capable drive costing about $500. The primary variable with these drives is the kind of tape they use. Individual tapes can hold from 250 MB to 8 GB or more of data. The cost of tapes varies from about $15 to $40 per tape.

The size of tape you use depends on the amount of hard drive storage available on your system (include all drives). You should choose a tape that is at least as large as the maximum amount of information that you can store plus a little extra. This will enable you to perform unattended backups since you won't have to change the media in the middle of a backup. For example, if you have a 2 GB internal hard drive plus a 500 MB external hard drive, you should choose a tape with at least 3 GB (for a tape, this is on the small side!).

A good tape drive

An excellent tape backup drive is the APS HyperQIC Drive. While the tapes are a bit pricey (around $30), they hold so much data (4 GB) that you are likely to only need one or two.

Expanding a tape

Some drive and software combinations will enable you to choose to compress the data as you do the backup. This usually doubles the amount of data that you can store on a tape. The drawback is that the backup takes longer to create (but if you are doing unattended backups, who cares?).

Mounting a tape drive

Although tape drives are not really designed to be mounted, there is software available that will enable you to mount a tape. Tapes drives are too slow to be practical as working drives though.

Recommendation: If your Mac has a lot of data on it that you can't afford to lose, you always want your backup to be current, you want to be able to do unattended backups, and you can afford to have a dedicated backup drive, a tape drive is the best option. Tape drives are the ultimate backup hardware.

If you also need more working space, and you can't afford to add two devices to your system, consider a removable media drive.

Backing Up with Removable Media Drives

Removable media drives use a removable disk to store data. They work on the same principle as the floppy disk, but hold hundreds of times more data. Plus, they are also many times faster than a floppy drive, which is important when you need to back up a lot of data. There are a wide variety of these drives now available including Zip, Jaz, SyQuest SyFlyer, traditional Syquest drives, and so on. The distinguishing feature of these drives is that they perform almost as well as a hard drive, but have an infinite storage capacity because you can swap disks.

Each drive uses a specific type of disk. Disk storage capacity ranges from 40 MB (on the older SyQuest drives) to more than 2 GB (Jaz II disks hold 2 GB, there are other kinds that hold even more). The cost of the disks vary with the amount of storage they provide.

Two of these drives seem to be the most popular: the Zip drive and the Jaz drive (both invented by Iomega, but compatible drives are also manufactured by other vendors, such as APS). These two drives hit the market first in each category (around 100 MB per disk and around 1 GB per disk, respectively) and seem to be more widely used—which is important if you need to share your data with others. Both drives have undergone recent improvements that increased the storage space while decreasing the cost. Even better, the Zip drive is now standard on many Macintoshes.

These drives are advertised as being ideal for backups, and in some ways they are. They are relatively inexpensive, fast, and have unlimited storage capacity. Plus, you can work off the drive since they can be mounted on your desktop and their performance is almost as good as a hard drive.

The down side is that even with the 2 GB cartridges, such as Jaz drives use, you may not have enough room to make a full backup on a single disk. This means that you won't be able to do unattended backups—you will physically have to swap out a disk at some point.

As long as you can live with the possibility of having to change a disk or two during the backup process, these drives are an excellent choice—especially since they are so useful in other ways (for example, sharing your data with others). Obviously, if your Mac already has a Zip drive, you should work with it first to see if it will be adequate.

Recommendation: If you already have a Zip drive in your Mac, give it a try for backup purposes. You will not likely be able to do a full backup (unless you want to spend a lot of money on Zip disks), but you may be able to back up your important documents and system software.

If you need more disk working space in addition to backup functions, consider a Jaz or equivalent drive. If you have less than 2 GB of hard drive space on your system and you want more working space, a Jaz drive may be your best option.

For backup purposes only, a tape drive is a better choice if you don't need the additional working space.

Backing Up with CD-R and CD-RW Drives

Compact Disc-Recordable (CD-R) and Compact Disc-Rewritable (CD-RW) drives enable you to make your own CDs. These drives range in price from $300 to around $1,000. The difference between these drives is that CD-R discs can only be written to only once, while CD-RW discs can be erased and reused, much like a removable media disk. Individual CD-R media is about $2 per disc while CD-RWs are about $10 per disc.

Compatibility

If you frequently need to share data with others, a removable media drive has the advantage of being widely available. For example, many print shops accept input on Zip disks. Before you purchase a drive, make sure you have a good idea of what kind of drives the majority of people with whom you share data use so that you make it as easy as possible to swap disks with them.

CD-R drives provide good service as a backup drive; however, they do have some serious limitations. One limitation is that a CD will hold only 650 MB of data—not nearly enough for unattended backups. Also, CD-Rs are not reusable so once you fill a disc, it can't be used for any additional backups. Thus, keeping a drive backed up with incremental backups will eat up lots of CD-R media.

CD-RW drives share the same 650 MB limitation, but at least the CD-RW media is reusable. Of course, you will pay for that; both the drives and the media are more expensive than for CD-R technology.

The benefits of both drives are that you can easily share data with others (since most computers have CD-ROM drives), and you can easily use the backedup data since the disc can be mounted by any Mac with a CD-ROM drive. The down side is that creating a CD (called burning a CD) is not as easy as using one of the other options. There are lots of pitfalls that you may encounter.

Recommendation: Consider a CD-R or CD-RW drive only if it will serve a dual purpose for you—for example, you need to distribute files via a CD for other purposes in addition to creating a backup and you can't afford to add two devices to your system.

Otherwise, a tape drive or removable media drive is a better choice, primarily because of the 650 MB limitation of a disc and the intricacies of burning CDs.

DVD is on the way

Digital Versatile Discs (DVD) drives are on the way. These drives will be able to store more than 17 GB (that is not a typo!) on a disc the same size as a CD. Within the next few years, there will also be DVD-RW drives. After the cost of these drives comes down, they may be an excellent choice for creating backups.

Backing Up with Hard Drives

If you have lots of money, you can use another hard drive (or two or three!) to keep your primary drives backed up. While enabling you to instantly access your data, this solution is relatively expensive and you are unlikely to want to pay for enough hard drive space to keep all your data and software backed up. You need more storage space at least equal to that of all of your primary drives. For example, if your Mac has a 4 GB drive, you would need a second 4 GB drive.

Mirror, mirror on the Mac

If you use a hard drive as a backup drive, you can set it up as a *mirror* to your working drives. This simply means that your backup drive can contain duplicates for every file on your working drives.

Hard drives are definitely the fastest option, and if you can afford to have multiple hard drives, you can keep your backups continually up-to-date. For example, you can use a mirror strategy whereby your backup is updated every hour or even every few minutes.

Although the cost of a hard drive is somewhat prohibitive, these drives suffer from two main drawbacks. The first and most important is that they are subject to the same potential causes of failure as your Mac (especially if the hard drive is internal). For example, if you have a power surge that is strong enough to damage your Mac (thus, requiring you to use your backup), there is a good chance your backup hard disk will be taken out too. Whereas, with a removable media (such as tape drive), your backup is protected from system problems. The second major drawback is that the storage capacity of a hard drive is fixed. This makes a backup hard drive limited in what you can use it for (you can't use it to archive your data for example).

Recommendation: As a mirroring backup device, a hard drive is an excellent option because of the speed at which it works. If you can afford to have two backup devices, a hard drive for mirroring and a tape drive for long-term backups, a backup hard drive is an excellent choice.

Because of the potential for a backup hard drive to be taken out with a catastrophic event that may also take out your Mac (such as a power surge or theft), you should not rely on a hard drive as your only backup device. Tape or removable media drives are better options.

Backing Up with Floppy Drives

While using a floppy drive is very simple and inexpensive, it is impractical unless you only have a few MB of important data on your computer; you won't have the inclination to keep your backups in good shape using floppy drives because it takes a long time to copy data to a floppy and you have to be there for all of it (to change disks). Plus, floppy disks are not very reliable. I don't recommend relying on floppy disks for backup purposes.

Recycling drives

Don't forget about older hard drives that you might have, but that you might not use because of system upgrades. You may be able to use these as backup devices.

If money is less important than keeping your data safe

The ultimate backup system would have all the hard drives on your system mirrored with backup hard drives and also protected with a tape backup on a daily or more frequent basis. This provides the most protection that you can get. Of course, you may not be able to afford all that hardware. It all depends on how important your data is to you. If your income depends on your data, it might be worth spending $1,000 to $1,500 on a backup system.

Backing up over a network

Just because a device isn't physically connected to your Mac doesn't mean that you can't use it to backup your data. You can use any device that is connected to the same network as your Mac as a backup device. For example, if your network has a server on it, it may also have a tape drive that you can use to create and maintain your backups. Even if your network does not have a server, you can attach a backup device (a tape drive is probably the only one that will provide enough capacity for this purpose) to one of the Macs and then back up all of the Macs on the network to that single drive.

The lazy man's way

As you can probably tell, unattended backups are the way to go. What this means is that after you configure your hardware and software, you don't have to do anything else. Which make them perfect for the lazy (or busy) among us. Even though tape drives are ideal for unattended backups, you can manipulate other drive types to make unattended backups easier. For example, you can make a full backup on a set of Jaz disks and then use a single disk for unattended incremental backups until that disk is full. Then you make another full backup and start the cycle over again.

However, one of the key things with backups is making them as simple and as "hands off" as possible. For my money, that means a tape drive.

External drives make sense

Consider getting an external drive for your backup needs, rather than an internal one. Since external devices are easy to take to another machine, you can use the same backup drive after you replace your current computer, and the same drive can service multiple Macs even if they aren't on a network. Plan on keeping your backup drive for a long time—it will probably outlast your current as well as your next, several computers.

Practice what you preach

Just in case you are wondering, I use a backup hard drive to mirror my working drives and a tape backup to maintain daily backups. This system supports a desktop Mac, PowerBook, and PC that are networked. Since I use my computers to make money, it is very important to me not to lose any data.

Recommendation: Don't rely on floppy disks unless you absolutely cannot afford anything better. If you do end up using floppies, make sure you are religious about keeping them up-to-date.

Deciding Which You Should Use

If you are serious about protecting your data—which you should be—you should invest in some backup hardware. My favorite choice is a tape drive because of the capability to simply do unattended backups and their infinite storage capacity (by adding more tapes). However, a Jaz or Zip drive (especially if you already have one in your Mac) is also an excellent choice, especially since you can do so much more with them than just make backups. While the other options can work for you, you will be better off with a tape or removable media drive as your primary backup device.

Choosing Backup Software

While you can manually copy files from your hard drives to the backup device, this quickly becomes impractical for more than a few MB of data. A better solution is to use a backup program that manages your backups for you. Backup software enables you to define which files will be backed up and how often the backup will be updated. It also enables you to restore your data when the time comes. The software should enable you to automate the process as well.

While on the hardware side, you have lots of choices, there is only one serious option for Mac backup software: Dantz Corporation's Retrospect and Retrospect Remote.

Retrospect only does one thing: it helps you create, implement, and maintain backups. While limited in scope, Retrospect excels in function; it is a "must-have" piece of software. It is easy to use, yet it includes all the functions you need to establish and automate your backup strategy. If you intend to back up your Mac, you simply must use Retrospect.

Creating a Backup

While I don't have the space to show you all of the great things that Retrospect does, it is worthwhile to show you how to set up and automate a backup using Retrospect. While there are a number of steps in the following example, each step is easy to do.

Using Retrospect to define and automate a backup

1. Launch Retrospect. After the program opens, you will see the main window, which has tabs and buttons that enable you to use all of Retrospect's features (see Figure 29.1).

2. In the main window, click the Automate tab. Retrospect automates the backup process by enabling you to create scripts. These scripts perform the actions that you indicate at the specific times that you want them to be done. The result is that backups can be made with little or no action on your part.

3. In the Automate window, click the Scripts button.

4. In the Scripts window, click New.

5. At the "Create what kind of script" prompt, make sure that Backup is highlighted and then press the Return key (or click OK).

6. Enter a name for your script and click on New (or press Return). For this example, I will create a script that backs up an entire startup disk, so I named my script, "Mac OS Lives!" because that is the name of the drive; you can use whatever is meaningful to you (see Figure 29.2).

FIGURE 29.1
Retrospect's well-designed main window is where you start the backup process.

FIGURE 29.2

Defining a backup script enables you to perform unattended backups.

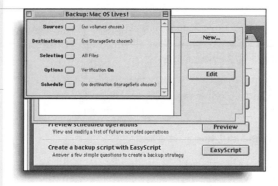

Flavors of Retrospect

There are several versions of Retrospect. Retrospect provides the software you need to back up over a server. For each computer on the network that you want to back up, you need to add the client software (one license is required for each machine). Thus, the Retrospect Network Backup Kit. There is also Retrospect Express, which is designed for an individual machine.

Backing up folders

If you want to choose individual folders rather than an entire disk or volume, highlight the volume or drive, click the Subvolume button, choose the folder you want to add, and then in step 8, highlight that folder rather than the disk or volume.

7. Click the Sources button. You will see a window containing all of the drives and volumes mounted on your desktop.

8. Highlight the drive or volume that you want to back up and click OK. You will see that the Sources window now shows the drive or volume that you just selected. If you have other sources that you want to add to this backup, click on the Add button and repeat step 8. Continue this process until you have selected all the sources that you want to back up.

9. When you have chosen all the sources that you want to include in this backup, click OK.

10. Back in the Script window, click on the Destinations button.

11. Click Create New. Retrospect will look for all the potential drives on which you may want to store the backup. When it is done, you will see the StorageSet Creation window (see Figure 29.3).

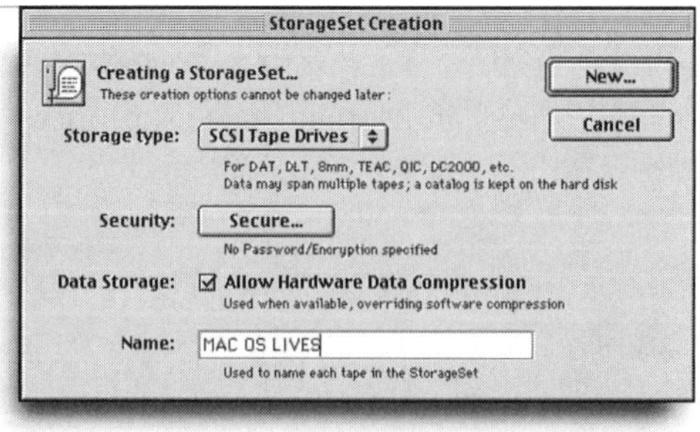

FIGURE 29.3

A storage set contains the data for all of the files that you are backing up.

12. Choose the drive type that you want to use (for example, a SCSI Tape Drive or a Macintosh Disk).

13. Give the storage set a name and click New.

14. In the resulting Save dialog box, tell Retrospect where you want the storage set saved and click Save.

15. Click OK in the next two windows.

16. In the Script window, click Schedule.

17. Click Add.

18. Choose the interval at which you want the backup done and click OK.

19. In the next dialog, set the particulars for your script (for example, the days of the week and times that you want the script to run).

20. Click OK; then click OK in the next window you see (see ref _Ref415809112 * Mergeformat Figure 29.4). In this example, the script will back up my startup disk at 10 PM every Monday, Wednesday, Friday, and Saturday. As long as I have room on my tape, this script will make sure that all of my files are backed up—I don't have to do anything else.

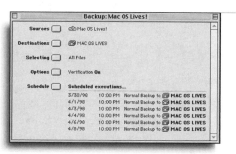

21. When you are done with your script, click the Script window Close box and save your changes.

Creating a Storage Set

A storage set is simply the file in which Retrospect stores all the information about a particular backup.

FIGURE 29.4

This script will back up my startup drive every other day.

Learning more about Retrospect

Retrospect is the ultimate backup software. To learn more about it, visit Dantz's Web site at `http://www.dantz.com`.

Using Other Backup Software

Some disk drive maintenance programs and other utilities provide a backup module. While you should own such programs for maintenance and other purposes, the backup modules tend to be pretty weak. Invest in Retrospect rather than using one of these other applications.

However, if you decide to play it risky and only back up a few of your key files via floppy disks, you might be satisfied with one of these programs as your backup software.

Backing Up Isn't Hard to Do

I can't emphasize enough how important it is to maintain good backups for your data. Here are a few tips to keep in mind:

- Develop your own strategy based on the hardware and software you have or can afford to purchase. At the least, make sure that your critical data files are protected.

- Make sure that backing up is easy. If you have to do a lot of work to back up or if it takes a lot of your time, you won't end up keeping up-to-date backups. Ideally, you want to be able to do unattended backups. Using Retrospect will help.

- Be consistent. Whatever strategy you decide upon, keep up with it. Old, out-of-date backups are not much better than no backups.

- Always refresh your backups before you install any new software or make major changes to your system. This will enable you to recover data should the changes you make to your system cause problems.

- Make sure that you test your backups regularly. Try to restore a file or two to make sure that everything is working properly. If you don't, you may get a nasty surprise when you really need to restore some data.

- Maintain your equipment. Almost all equipment needs some kind of maintenance now and again, so follow the manufacturer's guidelines to keep your system in top condition.

- Maintain more than one set of backups. Create multiple copies of your backups in case something happens to one set.

- Keep a backup off-site. Keep a copy of your backups in a different location than your Mac is in. This will save you in the event of a catastrophic event such as fire or theft. (This is a primary reason that you shouldn't rely on a hard drive as your only backup system.)

If you never have a hardware failure, major software problem, virus attack, accidental deletion, or other calamity, using these tips and the information presented earlier in the chapter may never make a difference in your life. You may find backing up to be a waste of time and money. However, if you don't back up, you may experience that sick feeling in the pit of your stomach when you suddenly realize that a file that is very important to you is gone forever. The risk you want to take with your valuable data is up to you.

30

Fighting Viruses

Understanding what viruses are and what they do

Knowing how to protect yourself from viruses

Learning about two popular Mac anti-virus programs

Knowing and using anti-virus tips

Macs Versus PCs

This is another area where using a Mac is better than using a PC. There are proportionally far fewer viruses for the Mac than there are for the PC. And those on the PC tend to be more destructive.

Protecting Your Mac from Viruses

No matter what level of computer user you are, you have probably heard of computer viruses. Viruses are programs that make it on to your computer without your knowledge and do everything from harmless pranks (some silly message) to major damage (erasing your hard drive). What makes a virus different from an application program or utility is that viruses are hidden and do things of which you're not aware. Many viruses are malicious, many are not. But all of them are bad because they do things to your computer that you didn't want done.

Part of practicing smart computing is understanding viruses and taking appropriate steps to protect your machine from them.

Understanding How Your Mac Might Get Infected

The first thing you need to understand about viruses is how a virus can get into your Mac. A virus can only infect your Mac through a file. Potentially infected files may be documents, applications, control panels, extensions, and so on. The key characteristic of files that may infect your Mac is that they have to have some executable code (a set of instructions) associated with them. All applications have executable code, as do control panels and extensions. Some documents can also have executable code in them, such as when the document contains macros (for example, Word files can have macros). Plain text files, however, cannot introduce a virus to your Mac.

Although not all files that you add to your Mac can infect you, you should act as if any file may infect you. It is better to be safe than sorry.

You can add files to your Mac in the following ways:

- Copied from any removable disk (floppy, Zip, Jaz, CD-ROM, and so on)
- Downloaded from Internet Web or FTP sites, online services, or bulletin boards
- Attached to email messages

You need to be careful when you add files to your Mac from any of these sources.

Understanding the Types of Viruses

While there are many types of individual viruses, there are only two major groups of viruses of which you need to be aware:

- **Application viruses**. These viruses are small applications that do *something* to your computer. It may be as harmless as displaying a silly message, or as harmful as corrupting particular files on your hard drive. Anything is possible with a virus. Application viruses can be hidden in many ways, such as within another application (such as Trojan Horse), as an extension or control panel, or other software that you add to your Mac.

- **Macro viruses**. A macro virus is a macro (a miniprogram) that can be created by any applications that support macros (such as the Microsoft Office applications). This kind of virus is attached to documents that you may receive. Instead of using a macro to do something useful, a macro virus does damage to your computer, or at the very least makes it behave strangely—the most notorious of these are the Word 6 macro viruses. When you open a file that has been infected by a macro virus, that virus (the macro) runs and performs its dirty deed.

> **Viruses are always bad**
>
> Even when viruses are relatively benign, they still use valuable storage space and RAM; they may eventually cause problems that were not even intended by their creators.

Viruses are called by many names (for example, nVIR, scores, and MDEF) and also come in different flavors, such as worms and Trojan Horses (yes, these work just like the original, you think you are getting a gift that turns out to be more than you bargained for).

Covering the multitude of viruses that are out there is beyond the scope of this book, and besides, there is no real need to become an expert on the viruses that exist. It is more important that you understand how to protect yourself from these viruses and be able to recover from an infection should one occur.

Preventing Infection

I hate to use this cliché, but when it comes to viruses, an ounce of prevention is indeed worth a pound of cure. The main way to avoid viruses is to avoid files that are likely to have viruses in them. Here are some tips to help you "stay clean":

- Find and use a good anti-virus software program (I cover some in this chapter).

- Make sure that you keep your anti-virus software up-to-date.

- Be careful of any floppy disks that you receive or find lying around.

- Be wary when you download files from any source.

- Never run programs or use files that are attached to email messages from someone you don't know.

- Be especially careful of files that offer promises that seem too good to be true. They may contain a Trojan Horse.

- When you do download files, download them from reputable sites, such as magazine sites or directly from a software publisher's site. These sites scan files for viruses before making them available so your chances of getting an infected file are lower. Remember the expression, "Consider the source."

- After you download a file, run your anti-virus software on it to make sure that it isn't infected. Most programs let you designate the folder into which you download files and will automatically check files in this folder.

Identifying Infection

Even with good preventive measures, you may occasionally become infected. Hopefully, you will find out that you have been infected by being notified by your anti-virus software—that means it is doing its job. But if you suddenly notice that your computer is acting peculiarly, it may be that you have become infected. What does acting peculiarly mean? Viruses can have many different effects on your computer; some of the more common effects are the following:

Viruses and email

One of the ways you can't get infected is by reading an email message. There have been numerous hoaxes claiming that certain email messages contain nasty viruses that will destroy the world. But since viruses are executable code, a virus must be activated by either an application or a macro, which an email message cannot contain.

If you receive an email message warning you of some other email message that supposedly contains a virus, please don't forward it to everyone you know. If it claims that you can be infected by reading a particular message, it is a hoax. However, you should be very leery of attachments to email messages. They can contain viruses.

- Weird messages, dialog boxes, or other interface elements. Sometimes viruses make themselves known by presenting something odd on the screen. So if you suddenly see a strange dialog box, you may have stumbled across a virus (for example, one of the Word macro viruses causes a happy face to appear in Word's menu bar).

- Loss in speed. Viruses often make your computer work more slowly. So if certain tasks seem to be taking longer than they used to, a virus may be the culprit.

- Disappearing files. Some viruses cause files to be deleted or hidden. If this happens, you need to take action immediately or you may find that all of your files have been erased.

- Errors. Many viruses will cause various errors on your computer and will prevent programs from working properly. If you haven't changed anything on your machine for a while, and you suddenly start experiencing errors, you should check your computer for a possible infection.

Using Anti-Virus Software

You usually will not be able to remove a virus without a software tool of some kind. You can remove infected files, but the virus may have spread beyond the original file through which it infected your machine. Once you think that your Mac is infected, you will need some help to "cure" it.

For every problem there is a solution, and for most viruses, there is an anti-virus application. These applications generally perform the following functions:

- Monitor activity on your computer to identify potential infection

- Periodically scan your drives to look for infections

- Notify you if an infection is discovered

- Repair the infected files and eliminate the virus

- Delete infected files if it is not possible to repair them

- Provide a way to update itself

Virus definition files

Most viruses are identified by their code. The anti-virus software knows about the virus' code through its virus definition file that, amazingly enough, defines all known viruses. As new viruses appear, this virus definition file needs to be updated so the new viruses will be recognized as being viruses. You can usually obtain an updated virus definition file from the Web site of the manufacturer of your anti-virus software. Most programs automate this process and can update the virus definition at intervals that you set.

Watching for viruses

Many organizations that are interested in the Mac keep track of viruses, and there are lots of good sources for news about viruses on the Internet. Symantec maintains a good virus information site at `http://www.symantec.com/avcenter`. You can also download updates to Symantec's Anti-virus for Macintosh here.

There are several major anti-virus applications available for the Macintosh including Symantec Anti-virus for Macintosh (SAM), Virex, and others. Most of these will do an adequate job of protecting your Mac from the virus plague. In this section, you'll get an overview of two anti-virus programs—the others work similarly.

Using Symantec Anti-virus for Macintosh (SAM)

SAM is one of the oldest anti-virus programs on the Mac—it has been around a long time, but Symantec updates it regularly so that it will do anything that the "new kids on the block" will do.

There are two phases of SAM's activities:

- **Protection**. SAM monitors suspicious activity on your computer. SAM watches what is happening on your Mac and alerts you when it detects a possible virus. You can also set SAM to scan floppy drives. For even more protection, you can identify a SafeZone folder into which you download files. SAM automatically scans files as they are downloaded into this folder so that you can avoid infecting your system.

  SAM will also scan your disks to check for infection, either automatically according to a schedule you set, or manually from within the application.

- **Repair**. SAM will attempt to repair any infected files. It will do this automatically, or you can start the repair process manually.

When Sam is launched, you will see the main window which shows all the mounted drives SAM detects (see Figure 30.1).

To determine the kind of protection you want, click the Preferences button and the Preferences window appears (see Figure 30.2). The various protection areas are shown in the left pane, and the options for those areas are selected in the right part of the window.

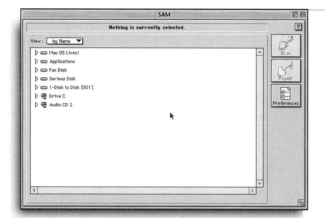

FIGURE 30.1

SAM's main window provides the tools you need to manage and protect your Mac from viruses.

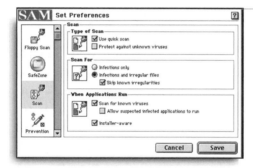

FIGURE 30.2

You can set SAM's preferences to determine the level of protection that it provides for your Mac.

SAM provides a *SafeZone* feature that lets you set a folder that SAM always monitors; usually, you should have a specific folder into which all of your downloaded files are placed. SAM's SafeZone feature will monitor this folder so that any files you download are immediately checked for viruses.

SEE ALSO

➤ *To learn how to work with attachments to email messages, see page 587*

➤ *To learn about downloading files from the Web, see page 646*

As an example of how easy SAM is to use, I will show you how the SafeZone feature is activated.

Creating a SafeZone with SAM

1. Click the SafeZone button in the Preferences window.

2. Check the box next to the Enable SafeZone (see Figure 30.3).

FIGURE 30.3

Any files you place in a SafeZone are automatically scanned for viruses.

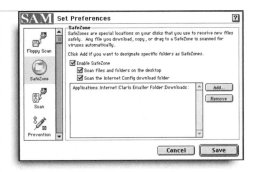

3. Check the box next to "Scan files and folders on the desktop" if you want all of these items scanned automatically.

4. Check the box next to "Scan the Internet Config download folder" if you have a download folder identified in Internet Config.

5. Click the Add button and maneuver to any other folders you want to be a SafeZone (for example, the folder into which all of your downloads are placed).

6. Select the folder and click the Select button.

7. Click Save. Now, whenever you download a file into this folder, SAM will automatically scan the file for viruses. This is a great way to protect yourself from infection.

SAM has lots of other great features that you can explore through its Help system (see Figure 30.4). If you are concerned about viruses, SAM is a great choice for you.

Using Disinfectant

One of the best known anti-virus applications for the Mac was John Norstad's freeware application called Disinfectant (see Figure 30.5). This application offers protection against viruses as well as the ability to repair infected files. It was updated as often as new viruses were discovered.

Macro viruses

One of the important things to look for in an anti-virus program is that it can detect and repair macro viruses. Macro viruses can infect your system through the macro capability that many programs provide to enable you to automate tasks. There has been a rash of these viruses in Microsoft Word files so they are fairly common. SAM does handle macro viruses.

By the way, Microsoft provides a set of macros that can detect and repair files infected with Word 6 macro viruses. Check out `http://www.microsoft.com/` to obtain them.

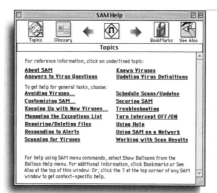

FIGURE 30.4

SAM provides lots of help for you.

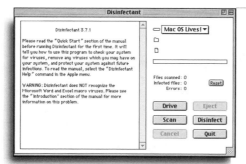

FIGURE 30.5

Disinfectant provides minimal protection against some of the older viruses, but since it is free, you can't complain.

I said *was* updated because after version 3.7 was released, the program was moved into the commercial arena as part of a commercial product. So Disinfectant is no longer updated; however, it is still available on the Internet as well as in other places. While it won't protect you against some of the newer viruses—it does not protect against Word macro viruses, for example—it is free. If you can't afford one of the commercial applications, Disinfectant is better than nothing.

Disinfectant comes with an extensive help system to guide you through the wonderful world of viruses (see Figure 30.6). You can get a copy of Disinfectant at your favorite Mac software file site, or you can search the Web to locate a copy to download (look for version 3.6 or 3.7).

Getting anti-virus protection for free

Since Disinfectant doesn't protect you against macro viruses, you should not rely on it alone. However, if you download the free Word anti-virus package from Microsoft (assuming that you use Microsoft Word, of course) and use it in combination with Disinfectant, you will have a fair amount of protection at no cost. However, you will be better off buying and using a commercial package.

FIGURE 30.6

Disinfectant comes with a lot of free help.

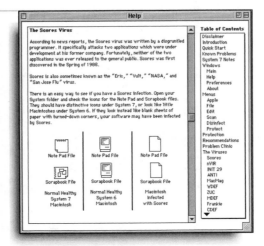

Viruses and backups

If you backed up your system after you were infected, the virus will be part of your backup. The only hope in this case is to use your anti-virus program to clean things up. Then make a fresh backup with disinfected files.

Using Anti-virus Tips

Viruses are hyped by the media now and again, and although the seriousness of them is often blown out of proportion, they do exist, and you need to take suitable measures against them. Here are some tips to keep your Mac pure and clean:

- Get good anti-virus software and use it properly.

- Be wary of files from unknown sources. Try to download files only from reputable sites. Also, be wary of floppy disks that you find or that are handed to you by coworkers or friends.

- Keep your system backed up in case you do get infected with a damaging virus—you will have to get rid of the virus before restoring your files, though, or the virus will remain.

- Create an anti-virus floppy disk; this enables you to have a clean system to start from and enables your software to be able to clean all the files on the startup disk. Most anti-virus software will do this for you; see the manual that came with your software for details.

- Don't worry too much; viruses are a problem, but they can be managed without too much hassle.

Once you have an anti-virus program and keep it updated regularly, you shouldn't have to think about viruses very much. If you don't practice safe computing, however, you may find yourself having to think about them a lot.

CHAPTER

31

Preventing Mac Problems

Maintaining your drives

Keeping your System Folder in top condition

Being prepared for problems

Building a Mac tool kit

Preventing Problems Is Easier Than Solving Them

The old cliché that an ounce of prevention is worth a pound of cure holds true even in the digital age. While your Mac doesn't require as much maintenance as other complex devices (your car for example), there are some relatively simple things you can do to keep your Mac in top operating condition. In addition, you can prepare yourself and your Mac so that if problems do occur, you will have the confidence and resources you need to be able to solve them on your own. Here are some activities that you can do to prevent—and since no prevention is perfect, to prepare for—Mac problems:

- Maintain your drives
- Maintain your System Folder
- Maintain backups
- Watch out for viruses
- Maintain your hardware
- Prepare for trouble

In this chapter, you'll learn about each of these tasks in detail. But remember that your goal here should be to minimize potential problems rather than eliminate them entirely. Even the best prevention can't account for all the variables that your Mac deals with—eventually, you will have problems of one sort or another. Don't worry, though, in Chapter 32, "Fixing Mac Problems," you'll learn how to recover from Mac problems when they do occur.

Maintaining Your Drives

The heart of any Macintosh is its hard drives; I say *drives* rather than drive because many Macintoshes have more than one internal hard drive as well as external hard drives. In addition to hard drives—also known as *fixed drives*—your Mac also has a floppy drive and CD-ROM drive. You may also have drives of other types such as Zips, SyQuests, and other *removable media drives*.

Most drives are simple to use; like all things Macintosh, you can simply point and click to use them. However, there is a lot of complexity behind the simple icons that you see on your desktop. The file structures of drives are fairly complex, and they are described with confusing terminology such as b-trees, nodes, directories, and so on. While you don't really need to understand all the details of drive technology, you do need to be prepared to use tools to perform maintenance (both preventive and corrective) on your drives. As thousands of files are written and rewritten to a drive, the structure of that drive can become corrupted, or at least disorganized. This can result in everything from system slowdowns and minor annoyances to severe crashes that prevent you from using the disk.

There are several software tools that can enable you to perform preventive and corrective maintenance on your disks—one of them is even included as part of the software that came with Mac OS 8.5. However, before you learn how to use those tools, I'll discuss a relatively simple task for which you don't need any additional software.

Rebuilding Your Desktop File

One of the great things about a Macintosh is that you don't have to worry about which application you use to open a particular file. To open and edit a file, you simply double-click it. The Macintosh knows which application it should use to open the file, and if you have a copy of the application that created that file, it opens the right application for you. Your Mac knows all of this because each disk (hard disk, Zip disk, floppy, and so on) has a desktop database (also called the desktop file).

SEE ALSO

➤ *To learn how to work with Mac files when you don't have the application used to create them, see page 483*

➤ *To learn how to work with PC files when you don't have the application used to create them, see page 497*

All Mac files consist of two parts—more correctly called *forks*. One fork, called the *data fork*, is where all of the data in the file is stored. The other fork is called the *resource fork*. Among the information stored in the resource fork of the file is the *type* and *creator* of that file. Both the type and creator are four letter codes. The type identifies the general kind of file it is; for example, a SimpleText Read Me file is type ttro, while an Excel spreadsheet file is type XLSB, and so on (I never said the codes made sense). The creator indicates which application was used to create a file; for example, a file created by Microsoft Excel has XCEL as its creator code, while a file created by Word has creator code MSWD, and on they go. Each application has its own unique creator code.

The Mac's desktop database keeps track of all of the file types and creators that are on your disk. When you try to open a file, the Mac gets the file type from the resource fork of the file and uses its database to find and open the creator application for that file type. The file is then opened in the correct application, and you can get to work.

The desktop database is also how the Mac knows what kind of icon to use to represent a file on your desktop. When your Mac looks at a file and identifies its creator, it uses its desktop database to figure out what kind of icon it should display to represent the file (for example, the QuickTime movie icon for QuickTime movies).

Each disk and volume that you mount on your desktop has its own desktop file. This includes all your hard disks, floppy disks, removable media drives (such as a Zip disk), and so on.

If something happens to your Mac's desktop databases, various problems can result. These include your icons suddenly becoming "generic" and looking like plain rectangles instead of a custom icon or one that resembles the creating application's icon.

Rather than waiting for the desktop database to become corrupt and suffer these problems, you can have your Mac *rebuild* its desktop. When it does this, it searches through all of the files on a disk and reconstructs the database so that it will have references for all types and creators.

No creator application found

If the Mac can't find a suitable creator application when you open a file, it will use the settings in the File Exchange control panel to try to translate the file so that you can work with it by using an application that you do have. See Chapter 21, "Working with Other Macs," to learn how to configure this control panel.

Icons and more

In addition to the type and creator, the resource fork also contains any custom icons by which the file is represented on the screen. There can be icons for each setting of your monitor (black-and-white, millions of colors, and so on). Version information for applications is also stored in the resource fork along with lots of other data about the file.

Rebuilding a disk's desktop database

1. From the Finder, choose Restart from the Special menu (if your Mac is turned off, just turn it on instead of using the Restart command).

2. As your Mac begins to start up, hold down the Option and Command keys.

3. During the start-up process, you will see a dialog box asking you if you are sure that you want to rebuild the desktop file on your startup disk (see Figure 31.1).

FIGURE 31.1

Do you want to rebuild this disk's desktop?

4. Click OK. Your Mac will begin the rebuilding process and will keep you informed of its progress (see Figure 31.2). If the disk is large and you have lots of files on it, it may take a minute or two for the process to be completed. When the Mac is done rebuilding the desktop on your startup disk, it will attempt to rebuild the desktop on each hard disk and volume that it mounts on the desktop. To rebuild each desktop, click OK in each dialog box that asks you if you want to rebuild the desktop. If you want the rebuilding process to stop, click Cancel. When all the desktop files have been rebuilt, you will see your normal Mac desktop and you are done with the rebuilding process.

Rebuild them one, rebuild them all

If you rebuild your startup drive's desktop, you should also rebuild the desktops on all of the disks you use, whether they are hard drives or not.

Rebuilding the desktop on a removable disk is as simple as it is to rebuild a hard drive's desktop.

Rebuilding a removable disk's desktop

1. Hold down the Option and Command keys and insert the disk in the drive. When the disk mounts, you will see the dialog box in Figure 31.3.

FIGURE 31.2

This Mac is working to rebuild its desktop file.

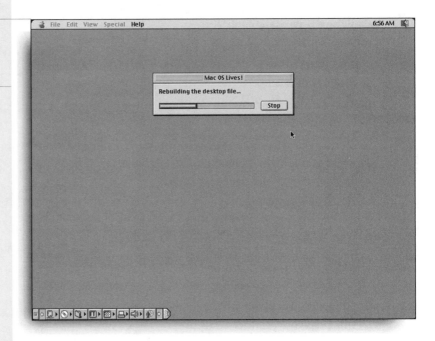

FIGURE 31.3

When you rebuild the desktop on a removable drive, you will see this dialog.

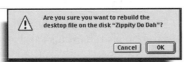

2. Click OK to rebuild the disk's desktop. Depending on the size of the disk, it may take a few moments to complete the rebuild. You will see a progress bar just like the one in Figure 31.2. When the disk's desktop has been successfully rebuilt, it will be mounted on the desktop and will be ready to use.

You may be wondering how often you should rebuild your desktop files to prevent problems with them. Some experts recommend that you rebuild your desktop about once a month. I don't think it is necessary to do it that often, "once in a while" is good enough. You should rebuild the desktop after you install lots of new software or do a major reorganization of your Mac's files.

Rebuilding your desktop files can also help you solve certain problems on your machine.

SEE ALSO

➤ *To learn when to rebuild a desktop to solve problems you are experiencing, see page 754*

Maintaining the Structure of Your Disks

As you use your Mac, it constantly writes data to disks and reads data from them. After lots and lots of this, the underlying structure of your disks (the b-trees, directories, and so on) can become disorganized and the drive will not work as well as it should. Your Mac may begin to work more slowly and applications may begin to crash more frequently. Fortunately, you don't need to understand the complexities of a disk's structure to keep it working properly. There are disk maintenance applications that can help you maintain your disks—as well as repair them when you run into trouble.

As is the case for most software, there are several different disk maintenance applications including Disk First Aid, Norton Utilities for Macintosh, and others. In this section, you'll learn how to use a couple of these tools so that you will know how to maintain the structure of your disks.

Using Disk First Aid

Apple's Disk First Aid can detect and repair a large number of problems (including problems that you haven't noticed yet) with the disks on your Mac (it also works on floppies and other removable disks). Even better, Disk First Aid is provided free as part of the Mac OS 8.5 installation (it is in the Utilities folder that is installed on your startup disk). Using Disk First Aid, you can scan disks for problems and then try to correct any problems it finds.

Checking a disk by using Disk First Aid

1. Move to the Utilities folder and launch Disk First Aid. At the top of the main window, you will see all of the drives that are mounted on your system (see Figure 31.4). In the lower part of the window, you can read about how to use Disk First Aid.

Disk First Aid and HFS+

If you use the newer HFS+ disk structure, Disk First Aid can detect and repair problems with the disk, unlike the current version of Norton Utilities for Macintosh, which was version 3.5 when I wrote this chapter. To learn more about HFS and HFS+ see Chapter 5, "Working with Hard Disks, Partitions, and Volumes."

Disk First Aid and improper shutdowns

If your Mac crashes or you donít shut it down properly, Disk First Aid will automatically run when you restart it. Disk First Aid will fix any problems that it finds on your startup disk (such as may have been caused by the crash).

Disk First Aid on the Mac OS 8.5 CD-ROM

Disk First Aid is also located in the Utilities folder on the Mac OS 8.5 CD-ROM. If you need to start up from the CD-ROM, you can run Disk First Aid from it to correct problems that you may be having.

FIGURE 31.4

Disk First Aid is a powerful addition for your Mac tool kit—even better, you get it for free as part of Mac OS 8.5.

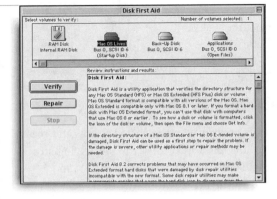

The worst case scenario

If nothing you try can repair a problem with a disk, you may need to reformat the disk, which involves deleting all the files on it. Of course, you have to make sure that you back up all the files on a disk before you reformat it. To learn how to reformat a disk, see Chapter 5, "Working with Hard Disks, Partitions, and Volumes."

2. In the top pane, select the drive you want to check. You can select multiple drives and volumes by holding down the Shift key while you are making a selection.

3. Click the Verify button. In the bottom pane, you will see the software working. If the disk is OK when the process is done, you will see a message saying so in the lower pane of the window. If Disk First Aid finds a problem, you will see something like Figure 31.5. In this figure, you can also see some examples of some of the terminology relating to the drive's structure. Mostly you can ignore these terms, which only the disk gurus among us understand.

FIGURE 31.5

Disk First Aid checked the disk Applications and found that it needed to be repaired (in this case, it was a very minor problem with a missing icon).

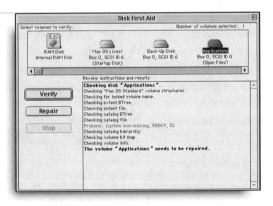

4. To try to repair a problem, click Repair. The software does the rest. If the identified problems can be repaired, they will be and the program will tell you so. If it can't fix the problems, it will tell you that as well. If this is the case, you need to try some other utilities (such as Norton Utilities for Macintosh) to see if they can repair the problem.

You should use Disk First Aid to check your disks every so often to make sure that things are OK with your drives. I strongly recommend that you also purchase a second disk maintenance application, the best of which is Norton Utilities for Macintosh.

Using Norton Utilities for Macintosh

Symantec's Norton Utilities for Macintosh is a collection of modules that can perform various kinds of maintenance on your disk drives. The tasks Norton can do for you include

- Drive structure repair
- Defragmentation and optimization (covered in the next section)
- Recovery of files that you accidentally delete
- Recovery of initialized or crashed disks
- Data protection when your Mac crashes
- Analysis of your system's configuration and performance

I've used Norton Utilities for a long time (it is now in version 3.5), and it has saved my bacon on more than one occasion. Although Norton Utilities performs some very sophisticated functions, it is an easy-to-use application. In this section, you'll learn how to use it for drive structure maintenance. In the next section, you'll see how to use it for defragmentation and optimization. In Chapter 32, Fixing Mac Problems," you'll learn how to use it to correct problems

One limitation removed

In previous versions of Disk First Aid, it could not repair your startup disk. Now it can.

Why verify rather than repair?

Once you have selected a disk to work on, you can either click the Verify or Repair button. In most cases, you should click Repair so that Disk First Aid will automatically try to fix any problems that it finds. Why are there two buttons then? In case you don't want Disk First Aid to correct problems. Mostly, it is a leftover from earlier versions that could not repair the startup drive.

A major limitation

With version 3.5 and earlier versions of Norton Utilities for Macintosh, you can't diagnose or repair problems with disks that use the HFS+ format. If you use HFS+ on any of your disks, you will need to find another utility for your tool kit (in addition to Disk First Aid). One good choice is Tech Tool Pro which you will learn about in the next chapter.

Norton startup disk

The Norton Utilities CD-ROM disc can also serve as a startup disk when you are having problems starting your Mac. While you will be using an older version of the Mac OS when you start up from the Norton CD (Mac OS 7.5.5 with Norton version 3.5), it is sufficient while you correct any problem you have.

Using Norton Utilities to check a disk

1. Launch Norton Utilities. You will see the main menu (see Figure 31.6). From this menu, you can launch each of Norton's modules. Norton Disk Doctor is the module that performs disk maintenance tasks.

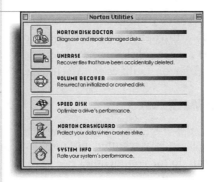

2. Click Norton Disk Doctor. You will see the Disk Doctor window that shows the disks that are mounted on your system.

3. Highlight the disk that you want to check and click the Examine button. You will see a progress window (see Figure 31.7). In the upper window, you will see all of the tests that the disk doctor performs. The progress bar will let you know how each test is progressing. When a test is complete, a green check mark will appear next to the test's name. If the doctor finds a problem with your disk, you will see a Diagnosis Report dialog box that tells you about the error (see Figure 31.8).

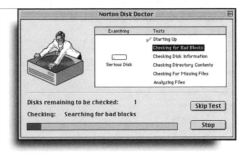

FIGURE 31.8
This disk has a problem.

4. Read about the problem, and the doctor does provide some explanation of what the "problem" area does. Near the bottom of the window, you will see the Disk Doctor's recommendation as to what needs to be done about this problem. You have three options: stop the process, don't fix the problem, or fix the problem. For most problems the doctor finds, you should choose Fix.

5. Click Fix or press Return. Norton will try to fix the problem. If it can, you will see a dialog telling you that the problem is fixed. Disk Doctor will then continue the testing process until it finds another error. This loop continues until all errors have been fixed. When the process is done, you will see the "report" dialog box (see Figure 31.9). You can either read about what tasks the program performed or you can quit the process.

Why is there a choice?

Frankly, I don't know of any situations in which you would not choose to have a problem fixed. It would seem like this choice must be allowed for some reason, although I have yet to see one. In my opinion, it would better if Norton went ahead and fixed all the problems it found without you having to tell it to do so.

FIGURE 31.9
This windows shows you that the doctor is done.

6. To read a detailed report about what happened with your disk, click the Show Report button. You will see a text window that shows the results of each test (see Figure 31.10). This information includes each error that was found, as well as if that error was successfully repaired. If you scroll down the page, you will also see a report on your system configuration.

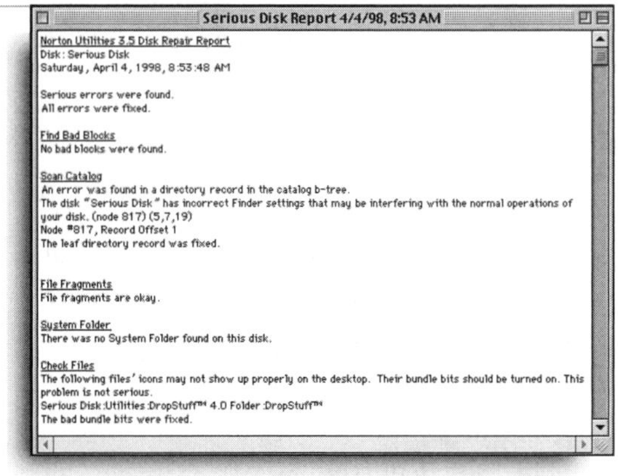

FIGURE 31.10

Reading a disk report can be useful.

```
Serious Disk Report 4/4/98, 8:53 AM

Norton Utilities 3.5 Disk Repair Report
Disk: Serious Disk
Saturday, April 4, 1998, 8:53:48 AM

Serious errors were found.
All errors were fixed.

Find Bad Blocks
No bad blocks were found.

Scan Catalog
An error was found in a directory record in the catalog b-tree.
The disk "Serious Disk" has incorrect Finder settings that may be interfering with the normal operations of
your disk. (node 817) (5,7,19)
Node #817, Record Offset 1
The leaf directory record was fixed.

File Fragments
File fragments are okay.

System Folder
There was no System Folder found on this disk.

Check Files
The following files' icons may not show up properly on the desktop. Their bundle bits should be turned on. This
problem is not serious.
Serious Disk:Utilities:DropStuff™ 4.0 Folder:DropStuff™
The bad bundle bits were fixed.
```

7. When you are done reading the report, close the window. You will move back to the Disk Doctor window.

8. Choose another disk to check or quit the program.

As with the other preventive maintenance tasks, it is a good idea to run the Disk Doctor on your drives periodically to make sure that they are in good condition.

Defragmenting and Optimizing Your Disks

As you save files to a disk (again, this means any kind of disk that you have mounted on your Mac, except for CD-ROMs and locked disks from which you can only read data), data is written to the disk. The Mac is also frequently writing other sorts of data (such as preference changes and other system-level data) to the startup disk. As data is written to a disk, it is written in the next available space (called a *block*). Once the data is "laid down," the Mac returns to what it what was doing. When it is time to save more data, the next batch is written in the next open space and so on. Think of this as the Mac putting all the data down in a straight line (yes, the disk is round, but it is easier to think of it this way), one chunk after another.

As files are opened and closed, data from different files is laid down in the next available space so that instead of all the data from one file being in a continuous block, it can be stored in blocks located in various spots around the disk. In this state, the data is *fragmented*. While fragmentation is a normal part of the way disk drives function, excessive fragmentation can slow down the disk. Things slow down because the drive head must read data from all the blocks that make up a particular file. As those blocks become more numerous and are spread out around the disk, it takes longer and longer to read all of the data for that file.

You use a process called *defragmentation* to correct this condition. You need a disk maintenance program to do this, such as Norton Utilities for Macintosh (in particular the Speed Disk component of Norton Utilities for Macintosh). What the defragmentation process does is to "pick up" all of the data blocks for each particular file and write them in a continuous block. It does this for every file on the disk. After the data is laid out nice and neat, the drive will perform faster because it doesn't have to move as far to read and write the data for a particular file.

Chevette or Corvette?

Faster is a relative term. Defragmenting your hard drive will make it operate faster, but don't expect the difference to seem like moving from a Chevette to a Corvette. It will be more like moving from a Chevette needing a tune-up to one that has been tuned-up.

Since a hard drive is made up of a round disk that spins at a constant speed, it takes longer to read and write data to various parts of the disk. Data near the center is read more quickly than data out near the rim. Data can be written to the disk in such a way that the access speed of the drive is *optimized*.

To do this, the data that is used constantly, but not changed much—such as the system software and applications—is stored near the center of the disk. The documents and other data that are infrequently used are stored out towards the edge of the disk. This arrangement speeds up the disk because access to the most frequently used data is faster, and keeping the static data together means that it will not become fragmented. Thus, the data is read and written in an optimized (for speed) fashion. You also need a disk maintenance application to optimize a disk.

Enter Norton Utilities for Macintosh (again). The Speed Disk module will both defragment and optimize a drive at the same time.

Speed Disk options

Speed disk has a fair number of options; for example, you can optimize the disk based on various uses such as for CD-ROM Mastering or for multimedia. You can also get additional information about the disk and create a report showing the fragmented files. For now, though, just proceed with the defragmentation and optimization based on "general use." You can explore other options on your own if you are so inclined.

Defragmenting and optimizing a drive by using Norton Utilities

1. Launch Norton Utilities for Macintosh.

2. Click Speed Disk. You will see a warning dialog box that tells you that you should run Disk Doctor on the disk and have it backed up (of course!) before running speed disk.

3. If you have run Disk Doctor on this disk, click OK; otherwise stop the process and run Disk Doctor first to make sure your disk is in good condition (since you read Chapter 29, you are backing up regularly, I don't need to tell you to do that, right?). You will see the Speed Disk window (see Figure 31.11). The large pane on the left shows you a representation of the fragmentation on the drive. The more white spots and lines that you see within the black "data," the more fragmented the drive is.

FIGURE 31.11

Norton's Speed Disk window shows you a graphical representation of the fragmentation of a drive.

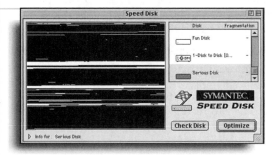

Check Disk

If you click Check Disk instead of Optimize, the program will recolor the data in the left pane to indicate what kind of data it is (applications will be one color, data files another, blank space will be white, and so on). To see the types of data on the disk, choose Show Detail View from the Explore menu. You will see a Detail View window. As you move your cursor over the data in the Speed Disk window, you will see what kind of data is in the Detail View window (for example, it will show you the specific application for application data). This doesn't do anything to the data, but it is kind of interesting.

4. Select the disk that you want to defragment and optimize and click Optimize. The disk will be unmounted, and the data in the left pane will be recolored to indicate what kind of data it is. The disk checking process will continue until the program is sure that the disk is ready to be defragmented and optimized. After the check is complete, defragmentation and optimization begins. The program joins all of the data scattered about in separate blocks into contiguous blocks with specific data being stored in certain locations on the disk (system files and applications being stored towards the center of the disk). When the process is complete, you will see that the data is now in neatly layered blocks (see Figure 31.12). The files on your drive are no longer fragmented, and they have been arranged so that the drive operates as quickly as possible.

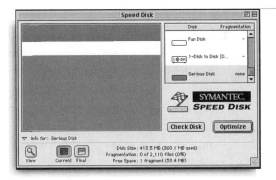

FIGURE 31.12

All of your data in nice, neat layers; this disk is ready to rock.

5. Select another disk to work on or quit the program.

While you may not notice huge speed gains when you defragment and optimize your disks, it is a good idea to do so every now and then because every little bit of speed helps when you are working with large files or complex applications. Do it more frequently if you move lots of data around on the disk. Do it less frequently if you don't notice much improvement in speed.

Cleaning Up Your Drives

You can do a lot for the performance of your disks by simply keeping them cleaned up. The more data that is on your drive, the less room you have to store new files. If your disks get too full, their performance will slow down significantly. More data means that there is more information for your Mac to manage, and thus it has to work harder than it does with less data. You can also run into all kinds of problems if you try to save files to disks that are full to the brim; how full this is depends on the size of the files with which you are working. If you are using small text files, say around 100 KB or less, then a disk with a MB or two has enough free space. If you are working with 20 MB QuickTime files, you may need to have 100 MB or more free. A good general guideline is to ensure that every disk on your system has at least ten percent or more of its space free.

Startup disks

Just as with Disk Doctor, you can't defragment or optimize a disk on which the active System Folder is located. That is because files cannot be moved while they are open. So all the files on a disk must be closed before they can be defragmented. You can start up from the Norton Utilities CD-ROM and then run Speed Disk from there to defragment your startup disk.

Optimizing CD-ROMs

When using certain software to create a CD-ROM, it is very important that the disk you use to master the CD is optimized. Since data can't be written to most CDs that you will distribute, recipients of your discs will be stuck using what you give them. If the files on the CD are heavily fragmented, the disc will perform slowly. Defragmenting and optimizing a disk immediately before you burn a CD from it, will ensure that the CD operates as quickly as possible. Some CD-creation software takes care of this for you, but it doesn't hurt anything to optimize a disk before creating a CD from it anyway.

Running on full

Just because your drives are full doesn't mean that you have a lot of files that you can delete. You simply need more storage space than you have available. If this is the case, you will need to add more storage space to your system. You can do this by adding internal or external hard drives or adding a ZIP, Jaz, or other removable media drive.

Archiving instead of trashing

If you find files that you don't currently use, but want to keep for future reuse or maybe even for sentimental value, you may want to archive them before you throw them out. Archiving is very similar to backing up. See Chapter 29 for the details on archiving.

Cleaning up your drives

1. On your desktop, create a folder called "Trash this *(date)*." Make *date* about a week or so in the future. The purpose of this folder is to provide a temporary storage space for files that you are planning on deleting. You will drag all of the "trash" files that you find into this folder.

2. Look for old versions of documents that you are working on, documents that you don't need any more, and other documents that are of no value.

3. Drag these files into the Trash this *(date)* folder.

4. Look for applications that you no longer use. Look especially for older versions of applications that you have upgraded (for example, do you really need Microsoft Word version 5, 6, and 98 all installed at the same time?).

5. Drag these applications to the Trash this *(date)* folder. Be careful to make sure that you have the original disks or discs for any applications that you trash. If not, make a backup or archived copy of these applications

6. Open application folders that you do want to keep to look for useless folders and files within them. Examples are sample documents and tutorial files that are not useful to you once you have learned how to use an application. Other likely candidates for deletion are AppleGuide files that you never use, templates that you don't need, and so on.

7. Drag these files and folders to the Trash this *(date)* folder.

8. Use the Finder's Find command to locate duplicate files; one likely culprit is the application SimpleText that is included with just about every application you have.

SEE ALSO

➤ *To learn to use the Finder's Find command, see page 88*

9. From the Finder, choose Find from the File menu.

10. In the Find File window, type "SimpleText" and press Return (make sure that the "on local disks" item is on the Find Items pop-up menu). You will see more than one copy of good old SimpleText (see Figure 31.13). There may also be duplicate support files (in the figure you can see duplicates of the SimpleText Guide file as well as the application).

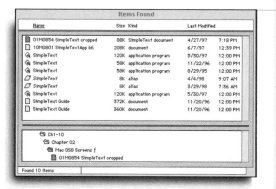

FIGURE 31.13
Guilty as charged—more copies of SimpleText than you can shake a stick at.

11. Compare the duplicates to see which can be deleted (usually you should just keep the newest version).

12. Drag the duplicate files from the Items Found window to the Trash this *(date)* folder. You may have to rename some of the files to move them because there can't be two files within the same folder that have the same name. You can also drag them straight to the Trash. (In this example, I recovered more than .5 MB just by trashing duplicate SimpleText files).

13. Keep looking until you have moved all of the chaff into the Trash this *(date)* folder.

14. After the *(date)* has passed and you haven't needed any files in the Trash this *(date)* folder, drag the contents of this folder into the Trash and empty it.

You may be amazed at how much junk you have accumulated on your Mac. Keeping your drives cleaned up will go a long way toward preventing "out of room" and other disk problems.

Maintaining Your System Folder

Your System Folder is the heart of your Mac and to keep your Mac operating in top form, you should keep your System Folder tuned up.

As you use your Mac, install new software, and customize your Mac, lots of stuff is stored in the System Folder. Some of this is useful to you and some isn't. Just as you now know the value of keeping your disks neat and tidy, you should know that it is especially important to keep your System Folder trim and in fighting condition.

Now, this gets a bit trickier than cleaning off old files from your drive. That is because the function of some of the files in your System Folder will remain a mystery. You will see files that have odd names, and you may have no idea what they are supposed to do. And since we are talking about the System Folder, you know that the software in this folder makes your Mac work like it does. So you need to be a bit careful about removing files from it.

You will also see more profound benefits from cleaning out your System Folder than you did by just cleaning up your drives. That is because some of the software in the System Folder consumes valuable RAM. Increasing the RAM available to your Mac by deactivating extensions and control panels that you don't use will free up RAM for applications, as well as the system, to use.

There are two areas that you should clean up in the System Folder. The first area is extensions and control panels. The second is some of the other files in your System Folder.

Cleaning Up Control Panels and Extensions

Rather than deleting extensions and control panels, you can use software to turn them off so they aren't loaded and thus don't consume any system resources (other than a small amount of drive space). Your purpose here should be to turn off every extension and control panel that you don't use. No need to worry either because it is easy to simply turn them back on again.

You can turn off extensions and control panels by using the free Extensions Manager that is provided by Apple as part of OS 8.5.

SEE ALSO

➤ *To learn about using Extensions Manager to disable control panels and extensions that you aren't using, see page 350*

Extensions Manager is a good tool, especially since it is free, but as with some parts of the Mac OS, there is a third-party application that is much more powerful. This is Cassady and Greene's Conflict Catcher. Conflict Catcher provides much more control over the parts of the system software that load, and it also can better help you figure out what individual files do.

Using these tools, you can keep your system trimmed down to be as minimal as you like it. A smaller system is good because it frees up RAM and at the same time reduces the likelihood for conflicts between various parts of the system. Both benefits make Mac problems less likely.

Cleaning Up Other System Files

In addition to extensions and control panels, there are other files in the System Folder that you should clean up. These include the following:

- **Fonts**. Fonts require RAM since they are loaded when you have one or more applications open. You should remove fonts that you don't use.

SEE ALSO

➤ *To learn how to remove fonts from your system, see page 158*

- **Preferences**. Preference files store customization information (for example, the default font in an application) for applications, as well as the OS. You should periodically delete the preference files for applications that you no longer use.

- **Apple Menu Items**. Check through the Apple Menu Items folder and delete anything that you don't need.

- **Other stuff you don't use**. Look through other folders to see if there are items that you don't use. For example, if you don't use the Launcher (and who does?), throw out the

Trashing extensions and control panels

In the previous section, I told you that you should trash any files that you don't use. After you are sure that you aren't using extensions and control panels, you can delete them if you want to (you can always reinstall them from the OS 8.5 CD or the other floppy disks or CDs on which the software came to you). But since they are usually small files, it might be better to leave them installed and just turn them off. That way, it will be very easy to turn them back on again should you need to do so later.

An exception to the "don't delete extensions" rule, is the boatload of printer extensions that the OS installer placed in your Extensions folder. You should delete all of those for which you don't have the printer (for example, Color SW 1500, if you don't have a Color Style Writer 1500).

Going hog wild

When you clean out your System Folder, use the "buffer" technique that you learned about earlier. Create a folder to store files that you are going to throw away. If you can still do everything that you need to do with these files removed from the system, then it is probably safe to permanently delete them.

Launcher Items folder (you should throw out the related control panel, too). The same goes for the Control Strip Modules folder. Also look for support folders for applications that you have removed from your Mac. Look for old, broken aliases as well.

Maintaining Backups

Backups are a critical part of preventing problems. If you have a good backup, you will be able to recover from even the most severe problem, which prevents the biggest problem (losing some of your previous data).

SEE ALSO

➤ *To learn about the fine art of backing up, see Chapter 29, "Backing Up"*

Keeping an Eye Out for Viruses

Viruses can cause lots of problems for you, some severe, some not. A good anti-virus strategy can keep you safe from these nasty digital bugs.

SEE ALSO

➤ *To learn about preventing and curing virus infections on your Mac, see Chapter 30, "Fighting Viruses"*

Maintaining Your Hardware

Most of the problem prevention you do is on the "inside" of your Mac via software. There are a few simple "exterior" tasks you should do, too. These include the following:

- **Clean the machine**. You should periodically clean the dust from the monitor, CPU, keyboard, and other components. The best way to do this is to use a blowing device to remove the dust, especially on the keyboard that has lots of nooks and crannies. You can also use a soft cloth on the exterior, but never spray dusting solutions or sprays directly onto the hardware; on the monitor face, put a small amount of glass cleaner on a soft cloth and lightly rub the face with it. Liquid going inside any part of your system can ruin your day.

- **Check cables**. Be careful with the cables that run between the various devices that are part of your system. If cables get pinched or pulled on, you can break the internal wires or bend connecting points. If that happens, something is likely to stop working. Try to keep cables neatly out of the way and make sure that nothing slides across or sits on top of them.

- **Watch the environment**. Make sure that the external temperature of your Mac and its peripheral equipment stays relatively low. High temperatures make electronic equipment unreliable. It is likely that any temperatures that are bad for your Mac will be uncomfortable for you, but also watch out for equipment jammed close together where the heat from one will increase the temperature of something else. Never block the ventilation holes on any device.

  Lastly, some devices emit certain kinds of radiation that will affect other devices (or maybe even you). Monitors are the most likely culprits; try not to sit too close to yours. Large speakers can emit magnetic interference that can do nasty things to magnetic storage media (your disks!). As long as you don't try to cram too much equipment into too little area, you should be fine.

Preparing for Trouble

Even with the best preventive maintenance, you are bound to have a little trouble now and again. If you consistently do what I have suggested in the first part of this chapter, you will minimize the problems that you experience, but even so, problems are inevitable since you can't control all aspects of the hardware and software that you use.

When (or should I say if?) a problem happens, you will be able to solve it more quickly and easily if you have a plan and the tools you need in place before the problems occur. In this section, you will learn what you can do to prepare for trouble.

Looking for Trouble

If you think you are immune to problems because you chose a Mac, you are mistaken. You will have fewer problems than a PC user, and those problems will be easier to solve, but nonetheless, solving problems is an inherent part of computing, whether you use a Mac or PC.

Here are some things you can do to plan for trouble:

- **Keep track of what you do**. Whenever you install new software or make major changes to your system, take the time to jot down some notes about what you do. You don't need to be extremely detailed; you mainly need to record the actions you took and when you took them.

    You might want to consider keeping a calendar next to your Mac. When you install software or make a major system change, you can jot a quick note on the date that you made the changes. This information can be extremely helpful if you have to troubleshoot problems. Sometimes, the timing of events (for example, you installed the GreatProgram 3 upgrade and two weeks later your system started crashing) can quickly lead you to a solution. If you rely on your memory, you may not be able to re-create events accurately.

- **Read and learn**. Take advantage of the plethora of information available on the Mac. You can find this information in books, magazines, mailing lists, and, of course, Web sites. You will be ahead of the Mac game if you spend some time reading about the Mac. You will often come across some tidbit of information that may not make a big difference when things are going well, but may be just the bit you need when you are having trouble.

- **Build a Mac tool kit** (see the next section). A good tool kit can easily make the difference between spending minutes or hours solving a problem.

- **Become friends with a Mac expert**. Somewhere in your sphere (at work, school, clubs, and so on) there is likely someone who lives and breathes Macintosh. Make friends with this person. She can teach you lots of vital information and may even be there when you need help.

Building a Mac Tool Kit

A large part of preparing for trouble is making sure that you have the tools you need to solve any trouble when it happens. While there are a lot of tasks you can do manually (moving files, changing settings, rebuilding the desktop, and so on), most problems will require some kind of tool to be solved. It is better if you have the tools you need before you need them. When a problem occurs, you can concentrate on fixing it rather than acquiring the tools you need to fix it while at the same time you are working on the problem.

In the following sections, I'll describe a capable Mac tool kit that will enable you to solve problems. Some of the tools are free, some will cost you a bit of money (but those do double duty and are very useful in preventing problems as well fixing them). Having most or all of these tools at your disposal will make it much more likely that you will be able to handle any problems that come up.

Knowing Your System Configuration

One of the most helpful things you can have in your tool kit is a complete description of your system. This information is vital if you have to ask anyone for help. If you have this information on hand, the probability of you being able to get successful help from someone is much, much greater. I'll show you one way to create this configuration report, but there are other tools that will help you do this as well.

Remember that you need to create a configuration report now, while you are not having problems. If you try to wait until you are troubleshooting a particular problem, you may not be able to collect the required data (if you can't start up your Mac, for example).

Apple includes Apple System Profiler as part of OS 8.5. This utility will enable you to create a customized configuration report for your Mac.

Using Apple System Profiler to create a system configuration report

1. From the Apple menu, choose Apple System Profiler. You will see the Apple System Profiler window (see Figure 31.14). This screen provides you with information about your hardware, including the machine ID number, what version of the system you are using, the kind of processor in your machine, memory information, and the disk you are using as your startup disk.

FIGURE 31.14

Apple System Profiler will enable you to understand the hardware and software components of you Mac.

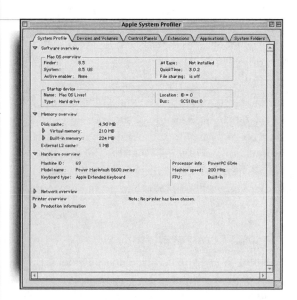

2. From the File menu, choose New Report. You will see the Create Report dialog (see Figure 31.15). This dialog enables you to choose which areas of your system that you want included on your report.

3. Check as many of the boxes as you would like—I suggest that you include all of the areas, so go ahead and check all of the boxes.

4. Click OK. Your Mac will scurry off and begin creating the report. It will seem to be jumping all over the place, and you will see all sorts of data pop on the screen. When it is finished, you will see an ASP Report window (see Figure 31.16).

FIGURE 31.16
Apple System Profiler creates a customized configuration report for your Mac.

5. Print the report and save it on your Mac.

The configuration report created by the Apple System Profiler provides lots of extremely useful information. The information includes the following:

Norton Utilities and Conflict Catcher

I've mentioned these applications quite frequently in this and other chapters (and will do so again). Each of them has the capability to produce reports similar to that of the Apple System Profiler. See their manuals and AppleGuides to see how to do so.

Installation log

Earlier I recommended that you keep a log of major changes that you make to your Mac. The ASP report is a perfect log. Simply run and print the report after each major upgrade or software change. The report is dated; all you will need to do is highlight the items that you changed.

- **System overview**. This section tells you all about the hardware in your Mac, including processor type and memory configuration.

- **Networking information**. This section tells you which printers you are connected to, what networking software you are using, and whether file sharing is active.

- **Volume information**. In this section, you will see all of the drives and volumes that are currently mounted on your Mac.

- **Device information**. This listing tells you lots of detailed information about all of the devices within and connected to your Mac. You will see information on all of your hard drives, Zip drives, CD-ROM drives, and so on. This information includes the SCSI location, manufacturer, and capacity.

- **Control panel information**. This gem of a section provides a list of all the control panels active on your system, as well as the version number of each.

- **Extension information**. This is similar to the control panel report, except that it covers extensions.

- **System Folder information**. This tells you where your system folder lives.

- **Application information**. This lists all of the applications installed on your system, as well as the version number of each.

If you haven't done much troubleshooting, you may not appreciate how great this report is. You will just have to trust me for now. This report can really help you solve problems yourself, and it is even more helpful when you need someone else's help to solve a problem.

The report is also useful for things in addition to troubleshooting. For example, if you are considering buying a new piece of software, a quick glance at this report will tell you if your machine is capable of running it. You can also easily tell if you need any patches or upgrades that you happen to come across. This simple report is a very important part of your tool kit. Remember to rerun the report whenever you make major changes to your system.

Preparing Software Tools

You will most likely solve any problems that you encounter through software. Here is a list of software tools that should be part of every Mac user's tool kit:

- **Dantz Retrospect**. This is the premiere Mac program for backing up your Mac.

SEE ALSO
➤ *To learn about Retrospect, see page 694*

- **Symantec Norton Utilities for Macintosh**. I have already shown you how useful Norton Utilities is; you simply must have a copy.

- **Conflict Catcher**. Now in version 4, this essential utility provides industrial strength tools for troubleshooting software conflicts. In addition to its troubleshooting prowess, you can use it to keep your Mac's performance at its maximum potential.

- **Symantec Antivirus for Macintosh (SAM)**. There are several anti-virus applications for the Mac, and they all work well. SAM has been with the Mac for a long time, and has proven itself.

SEE ALSO
➤ *To learn about SAM, see page 705*

- **Mac OS 8.5**. Mac OS 8.5 comes with a number of features and utilities that you will use during your troubleshooting efforts. These include tools for RAM management, as well as lots of help via AppleGuide, the Mac OS Info Center, and even the mostly unread ReadMe files.

- **ResEdit**. ResEdit is a tool that Apple provides to help you edit the resource forks of the files on your Macs. While there are a tremendous amount of things you can do to customize your Mac with ResEdit, it's usefulness in the troubleshooting process is fairly limited. But in those situations where you need it, it is vital. And since Apple provides ResEdit for free, there is really no reason not to have it available when you need it.

SEE ALSO

> *To learn about RedEdit, see page 373*

I suggest that you obtain all of these tools as soon as you can. Assuming that you already have Mac OS 8, the total cost of these tools will be less than $375 (much less if you get a copy of Retrospect bundled with your back-up drive). When the time comes when you need to solve problems, you don't want to obtain—and learn to use—new software at the same time that you are trying to solve your problems. Plus, most of these tools will help you in your day-to-day use of the Mac.

Preparing Emergency Disks

Some problems prevent you from being able to start up your Mac. When that happens, you will need another disk that contains valid system software from which you can start up. This disk can be a floppy, but you will be better off with a CD or Zip disk to use. Here are four options for a back-up startup disk:

- **Mac OS 8.5 CD-ROM**. You can start up from the Mac OS installation CD. Check your Mac's manual to see what keys you need to hold to make your Mac start up from a CD. (For example, on a Power Macintosh 8600, you hold down the c key while the machine is starting.)

- **Norton Utilities CD-ROM**. The Norton CD has a System Folder on it that you can use to start up your Mac. In the 3.5 version of Norton Utilities, this was version 7.5.5 of the Mac OS, but that is sufficient to start the machine and fix problems that prevent you from starting your OS 8.5 system.

Other uses for a startup disk

There some tasks that you will want to do on your startup disk, but that can't be done while it is being used for the active system software. These include defragmenting and optimizing a disk, repairing a disk, and so on. A second startup disk enables you to start the Mac from another disk so that you can do these tasks on your primary startup disk.

- **Zip or other removable drive disk**. You can use the Mac OS installer to install the system software on a Zip or other disk. Or you can drag a copy of your System Folder onto a removable disk and make your Mac start from that. (No need to hold down keys, the Mac will check the Zip disk before it boots from the hard drive.)

Using Information Sources

When you get into trouble (or want to stay out of it), it is good to have information sources to which you can turn. Again, it is not a good idea to wait until you need them to find them. There are many good sources of Mac information, including the following:

- **ReadMe files**. Most software comes with one or more ReadMe files. These files are provided to give you information that could not be included in the printed documentation that came with the software. These files often provide vital information that will help you avoid problems.

- **The manual and online help**. Most applications come with a paper manual, online help (AppleGuide or Balloon Help), or both. You should peruse this information to help you understand what you are doing and help you prevent problems.

- **People**. There are lots of people you can ask to get help. You can ask people you know or the tech support group for the "problem" application.

- **The Internet**. You can also use the Internet to look for help via email, Frequently Asked Questions (FAQs), newsgroups, and of course, Web sites. There are also lots of good mailing lists that you can join.

- **Books and magazines**. There also are lots of books and magazines that contain information that will help you prevent problems.

If you develop a "pool" of information sources that you are accustomed to using, it will become second nature to try this pool when you need help or when you are considering a change to your system.

ReadMe?

You really should read the ReadMe files before you install new software. You might be able to prevent some problems from ever occurring. And all for only a few minutes of your time. What a deal.

Passwords and paper

Should you write down your passwords? All the security experts say that you shouldn't. But if you have a poor memory, this is a risky policy. Especially if you have multiple passwords to remember, and with the rise of the Internet, who doesn't? Whether you write your passwords down is a personal choice, but if you decide to write them down, don't make them too obvious. You might want to consider encoding them in some way, such as adding extra characters or reordering them in some fashion.

Maintaining Your Records

While you have already learned about backing up your data, you also need to back up all of the usernames, passwords, Internet settings, software serial numbers, and so on that you will end up collecting as you add software to your system and register at various Internet sites. Some of these items will be captured in your data backups, but much of it is difficult to retrieve from this source. Here are some important data that you should also back up in some other way:

- **Software information**. This includes serial numbers and versions. If you have to reinstall an application, sometimes you will need the serial number to do it. You also may need the serial number to upgrade the software or get tech support. Sometimes, the serial number is printed on a sticker attached to the manual or registration card so be sure to hang onto these items.

- **Internet/online settings**. There are lots of usernames, passwords, phone numbers, and other data you need to connect (remember those you use to enter Web sites also). If you lose your system for some reason, you want to be able to easily reconfigure it. You don't want to have to figure what all this is at the same time that you are reconfiguring your system.

There are several ways you might choose to keep this kind of data backed up:

- Keep a folder on your computer that contains text files with this information. You can also use clippings or stickies to quickly record and retrieve this kind of data. Since you will be backing up your computer regularly, the data will automatically get backed up as well. You can also print the text files so that you have a paper copy.

- Keep a folder in your email system with various usernames and software registration information in it.

- Go low-tech and use paper. This one is the most risky in terms of security. Make sure that you either encode the data somehow or make sure that no one has access to it but you.

It may seem kind of silly to you to keep all of this information backed up, especially because a lot of it (such as the serial numbers for your software) is usually provided in other places already. Trust me, having all of this information in one place can literally save you hours in the event that you ever have to reinstall your system—which is not as unlikely an event as it should be.

Fixing Mac Problems

Knowing the general types of Mac problems you may face

Troubleshooting your system

Solving common problems yourself

Getting help

Facing Your Problems

Even though you practice all of the smart computing techniques that you learned in Chapter 29, "Backing Up," Chapter 30, "Fighting Viruses," and Chapter 31, "Preventing Mac Problems," eventually something may not work correctly. You may experience *crashes* or *hangs*, or a program just may not work the way it is supposed to. You might even experience minor annoyances, such as having to do something in several steps that should require only one. In any case, one of these days, you will run into a situation that requires you to troubleshoot and solve a problem.

Dealing with a problem, especially related to your computer, can be intimidating because there is so much going on that you may not understand. Fortunately, you don't need to be a computing expert to be able to troubleshoot and solve problems. Mostly, what is required is the ability to carefully observe what is happening and to be able to follow logical trails. Being able to communicate clearly to others is also important when you need to get help from someone who knows more than you do.

In short, when you need to solve a Mac problem, you need to think of yourself as a detective working on a case. You will assess the crime scene (your Mac's behavior), interview witnesses (talk to tech support or other Mac users), construct a theory as to "who done it" (use your Mac tools to identify the problem), and then capture the perpetrator (fix the problem).

Most troubleshooting and problem solving material focuses on listing specific problems and their solutions. This works fine if your specific problem happens to be part of the listing. If not (which is more likely the case), then such lists aren't much help. The most important thing is to understand the principles of troubleshooting so that you know how to discover the solutions to your specific problems on your own—even if they don't show up on a list somewhere.

Why bother?

I spent a lot of time in the previous chapters telling you how to prevent problems. Now I'm telling you that you are likely to have problems anyway. You may be wondering why you should bother with the techniques described in those chapters if they won't prevent all problems anyway? Here's the answer: because with those techniques, you will have fewer problems, and you will be able to solve any problems that *do* happen more quickly and easily.

Understanding What Could Go Wrong

The Mac OS is one of the most stable and reliable operating systems around. Mac and Mac clone hardware are usually very high quality machines. Likewise, Mac software is usually very well crafted. Nonetheless, Macs are sophisticated systems with technology that is always changing, thus creating a fertile ground for problems.

On the Mac, the problems you experience will be one—or a combination—of five general types of problems.

Being Your Own Worst Enemy

The results of many investigations into aviation accidents can often be summed up with the phrase, "pilot error." Similarly, this is often the case with an "accident" in the Mac world. Many problems are the direct result of a user (this means you) doing something improperly—or not doing something properly.

Some of the things that a user might do to cause problems are the following:

- **Not following instructions**. This is the big one. Many times, you will cause your own problems simply because you fail to follow the instructions provided with software or hardware. Believe it or not, sometimes these steps are written for a specific reason, so that not following them is asking for trouble. Remember the old adage, "If all else fails, follow the instructions."

- **Operating a machine past its limits**. If you know that a particular application requires a computer with a PowerPC 604 processor, but you try to run it on a 68040 Mac, you are bound to have troubles. If you live to the edge of your machine's capabilities, you will have more problems than you might with a more capable machine.

- **Not meeting minimum hardware or software requirements**. For example, if a program requires 16 MB of RAM to operate, and you try to run it knowing that you only have 8 MB available, there is no one to blame but yourself for problems you experience.

- **Not doing proper maintenance on your system**. For example, if your tape drive manual says that you should clean the heads every month, but you never do, whose fault is it if you find that your back-up system has failed due to a dirty head?

- **Not keeping enough free space on a drive**. This is a fairly common cause of problems. All drives need to have free space in order to be able to store files, sometimes temporarily. If a drive is full, or very close to being full, you will have problems as you try to store more data on it.

Fighting Bugs

Sometimes the cause of a problem is a "bug" inherent in the design of the products involved. The bug can be a design flaw, a manufacturing problem, or a conflict with some other part of your system. While companies often do the best they can to prevent bugs, there is usually no way to prevent all the possible bugs in a product. Many bugs aren't revealed until a piece of software or hardware is combined with some other pieces of hardware or software.

Bug-induced problems are usually solved by a maintenance/bug fix release of software. Even if a bug is part of a piece of hardware, it can often be fixed by a bug fix release of the software that drives that hardware.

Battling Software

One of the most common cause of problems is conflicting software. Some programs just don't play well with others. Conflicts are often associated with control panels and extensions since they modify the low level operations of the system. However, applications can also conflict with one another and cause you headaches.

If you call for technical support, this is likely to be the cause that the support person tries to identify first. Unfortunately, unless a conflict between software is known, it can be hard to identify the exact causes of the conflict. Sometimes, the applications that are affected are the problem, but other software is the reason for the conflict and somehow affecting another application.

Software conflict problems can usually be solved by shutting down or removing the software that is responsible for the conflict. When this particular software is something you must have, you may need to remove the software that it is conflicting with instead, or you can often obtain an upgrade or a patch that will cause the problem to go away.

If the conflict is between software that is fairly popular, the companies involved will usually issue bug fixes that eliminate the conflict. If the conflict happens only in isolated circumstances, you may be out of luck.

Fighting Viruses

Although fairly rare—especially if you use a good anti-virus strategy as I discussed in Chapter 30—your computer can sometimes get infected by a virus. Viruses can cause all sorts of problems from simple and silly messages appearing to strange dialog boxes to major system crashes and even hard disk deletions or failures.

The best cure is to prevent infections, but if you do get a virus, you will have to rely on your anti-virus program to get rid of it.

Suffering Hardware Failures

The most unlikely cause of problems is a hardware failure. While hardware does fail now and again, it doesn't happen very often. Hardware failures are most likely to occur immediately after you start using a new piece of hardware or close to the end of its useful life. Sometimes, you can induce a hardware failure when you upgrade a machine or perform some other kind of maintenance on it; for example, if you install new RAM in a machine, but fail to seat a RAM chip properly.

Unfortunately, the solution to most hardware failures is to have the hardware repaired by a professional or to simply replace it.

Fax conflicts

By the way, fax software is one of the most notorious causes of software conflicts. If you are having trouble with anything related to communication programs (such as an Internet connection) and you have fax software installed and active, try deactivating the fax software first.

Disk failures are bad

If you do have a major hardware failure, such as a disk drive failure, and you don't have a good backup, you will be in big trouble. You can usually kiss all of your data good-bye, although there are services that will try to recover your data—at a high price.

Troubleshooting Techniques

If you understand the general techniques you should use when troubleshooting, you will be able to handle almost all of the problems you are likely to encounter. Having a good understanding of what you need to do will also make you more confident, which in turn will help you be more effective.

One of the tough things about troubleshooting is that you usually have to do it at an inconvenient time; for example, in the middle of a big project. At times like these you are likely to feel lots of stress, which can lead to frustration, which in turn often leads to hasty actions. Haste will often drive you down the wrong path.

Effective troubleshooting requires a cool head. The best approach when you are working on a deadline is to find a quick workaround for the problem that will enable you to complete the job you need to get done immediately. Then you can come back and really fix the problem later when you are more in a "troubleshooting" frame of mind.

This is also the reason I emphasize not waiting until you need to solve a problem before learning how to solve problems. In the heat of battle, it is hard to learn.

When you experience a problem, there are certain groups of tasks that you need to do to get past that problem. In this section, you'll learn about these groups so that you have a good top-level understanding of the troubleshooting process.

Preparing to Troubleshoot

As you leaned in the previous chapter, you should always be prepared to troubleshoot.

SEE ALSO

➤ *To learn how you can be ready for trouble, see page 733*

Looking, Listening, and Learning

When a problem occurs, you need to use your observation skills to obtain the information you will need to solve that problem. The following sections explain how you can be more aware of what is happening on your Mac.

Looking at What You Just Did

Many problems are triggered by something you do. When a problem happens, think about what you were doing immediately before the problem occurred. Here are some questions you need to answer:

- What applications were you running (not only the particular one with which you were working)?

- What specifically were you trying to do (print, save, format, and so on)?

- Have you made any changes to the computer recently (installed software, changed settings, and so on)?

The answers to these questions provide significant clues to help you figure out what is causing the problem.

Trying to Repeat the Problem

When a problem occurs, you should recover the best you can, and—as crazy as it seems—try to make the problem happen again. Try to re-create everything that was happening when the problem popped up. Obviously, you shouldn't intentionally re-create a problem in such a way that you will lose data. Make sure that your data is safe by having a good backup before you do much troubleshooting.

If you can re-create the problem, it will be much easier to figure out what is happening. The hardest problems to fix are those that only occur occasionally or intermittently. A "repeatable" problem is much easier to troubleshoot.

Knowing your system

As you learned in the previous chapter, you can use the Apple System Profiler to have a good understanding of your system configuration. The configuration report that the Apple System Profiler will generate for you can be very helpful in figuring out exactly what the components of your system are.

Intermittent problems are hard to solve

What do you do about an intermittent problem? If you can't figure out what happens to trigger it, you may just have to live with it until you do figure it out.

Being able to Describe Your Problems

If you need to get help to solve the problem, it is vitally important that you be able to accurately describe the situation and the symptoms of the problem. The help other people will be able to provide will only be as good as the information you provide to them. (Recreating the problem will also help you be able to accurately describe it.) Make sure that you understand what is happening when the problem occurs, and also that you can describe what the problem is (i.e., "When I print, the application crashes and gives me the 'you're out of luck' error message" rather than, "This stupid printer doesn't work!").

Solving the Problem

After you have a good understanding of the problem, you can try to fix it. In this section, I'll give you an overview of the major tasks you need to do to get your Mac back into action.

Getting it Fixed—Now!

Have you heard the one about the guy who goes to the doctor and says, "Doctor, if I bend my elbow like this, it hurts." The doctor looks at him and says, "Well, then don't bend your elbow like that."

If you are in the midst of a project and don't have time to troubleshoot, you can try to work around the problem by not doing whatever it was that you were doing when the problem happened. Try using an alternate application or an alternate way of completing a particular task. Avoid the situation that led to the problem and perhaps you can avoid the problem. This is a short-term solution, but if you need to get back in the game quickly, this may be your best choice.

Getting Good Help Is Sometimes Hard

Unless you can instantly see how to solve your problem or one of your tools takes care of it, the odds are that you will need to get help. There are lots of sources for troubleshooting help, including the following:

- Technical support from the manufacturer
- The manual and online documentation (such as the AppleGuide) that comes with the software
- Web sites
- Newsgroups
- Magazines
- Troubleshooting software
- Mailing lists
- Coworkers, families, and friends

When asking for help from people—regardless of the means you use, such as the telephone or email—be sure that you keep the following in mind:

- **As your Mom probably told you, "Use your manners!"**
  You have no call to be rude to people who are trying to help you, even if they happen to work for the publisher of software or hardware that is giving you trouble. Besides being the right thing to do, using good manners will likely get you better help. Manners are equally important when making requests via email or other online sources. "Please" and "Thank you" go a long way towards encouraging people to be willing to help you.

- **Give accurate, specific, and complete information**.
  Provide a complete description of your problem, as well as what you were doing when the problem occurred. Unless you give the person who is trying to help you a good idea of what is really going on, that person is unlikely to be able to help.

  An ineffective request for help goes something like this, "I was printing, and my stupid computer crashed. What's wrong?" This kind of question—which happens more than you might imagine—is just about impossible to answer.

  A more effective question might be something like this, "I am using a Power Mac 8600 running system 8.5 that is connected to an HP DeskJet 855C via LocalTalk. While trying to print from Microsoft Word 6.0.1, Word quit and gave me

There are no "know it alls"

Sometimes, it will become clear that a person you are asking doesn't really know how to help you. Even the local "computer expert" has limitations. Don't assume that because someone knows more than you, that he knows everything. If it becomes clear that someone is struggling to even figure out where to start, you should tactfully bow out and find someone else to help you.

the following error message, 'The application unexpectedly quit because of a Type 11 error.'" You might also need to provide the extensions and control panels you are using, but this question would probably get you headed in the right direction.

- **Don't wear out your welcome with someone who is only trying to help you**. You need to be careful not to impose on people who are trying to help you only out of the goodness of their hearts. If you are asking a friend or coworker to help with a problem, use their time efficiently. Be prepared to describe your situation. Be specific. And if the person can't help you after a reasonable amount of time, go to someone else. It is not fair to ask a "volunteer" to spend large amounts of time trying to solve your problems.

Trying to Solve Your problems

After you have identified the problem and sought help, you should have some ideas of what to try to correct the problem. This may involve running troubleshooting software or installing a bug fix release of the problem software.

Try your solution to see if it works. If it does, you are done. If not, you need to go back to the initial steps and begin the troubleshooting process again—except this time you have one less solution to think about.

It is not unusual for the first solution that you try to fail. Troubleshooting is often an iterative process. You will need some patience and endurance, but if you keep working through the process, you will eventually solve the problem.

Solving Problems

Now that you understand the general sources of problems, it is time to learn how to solve them. Each general kind of problem has its own section. Within those sections, you'll learn how to recognize the symptoms of that problem type, and you'll see some ideas on how to solve those problems.

Solving Problems You Create

Let's face it. Most of the time, when you get new software, you pop the CD or floppy disks in your Mac, double-click, and go. Fortunately, most Mac hardware and software is so well designed, that this approach works much of the time. Occasionally, though, you will do something that you aren't supposed to do, or you won't do something that you were supposed to do. The result in either case: user error.

User errors typically result in "things just not working like they are supposed to." A program may or may not be crashing, but whatever it is that you want to do just isn't happening. Often, there isn't any indication of a problem—for example, a program quitting unexpectedly—you just can't seem to get the job done. Other times, you will run into problems when you are installing a new piece of software. Usually, these problems happen because you have failed to follow proper installation procedures.

When you run into a problem that is not clearly a hardware or software problem (see the following sections for symptoms of those problems), one of the first things you should think about is what you are doing or maybe what you *weren't* doing that you should have been. If you take a close look, you may discover that you are sometimes your own worst enemy.

If you are having problems that don't seem to be clearly hardware or software related, the best thing to do is to look for information that will help you figure out if you are doing something you shouldn't—or not doing something you should. There many sources for this information, including the following:

- **ReadMe files**. Most software comes with one or more ReadMe files. These files are provided to give you information that could not be included in the printed documentation that came with the software. If you have trouble with a particular application, you should read through the ReadMe files. They will often provide essential information.

- **The manual and online help**. Most applications come with a paper manual, online help (AppleGuide or Balloon Help), or both. You should peruse this information to help you understand what you are doing and help you prevent problems.

RTFM

If you don't check the manual and ask a question somewhere, you may get a terse response "RTFM." This stands for "Read The Fudgy Manual" (OK, so it isn't really fudgy, but, hey, this is a family book!). Anyway, the point is that sometimes the information you need is right in front of you; people often don't make a decent effort to find information on their own before asking a question. If this is standard practice for you, don't be surprised if people get snippy with you when you ask a question that you could have easily answered on your own.

Great Mac troubleshooting Web sites

The best place to look for troubleshooting help is sites dedicated to the software with which you are having trouble (usually the manufacturer's Web site). However, there are lots of general Mac troubleshooting Web sites that you can visit to look for help. These sites provide lots of help for you.

Ted Landau's excellent Mac Fix It site is at `http://www.macfixit.com`.

Ric Ford's MacInTouch site is at `http://www.macintouch.com`.

The Mac Central site is at `http://www.maccentral.com`.

The Mac Resource Page is at `http://www.macresouce.com`.

You should also visit the Mac magazine sites such as `http://www.macweek.com` and `http://www.macworld.com`.

Autosave

If the application you work with doesn't have an autosave feature, you should consider adding a utility that will issue a save command at predetermined intervals so in the event of a quit, you won't lose much work.

Most modern applications have an autosave feature. You really should use it.

- **Ask around**. There are lots of people you can ask for help. You can ask people you know or the tech support group for the "problem" application. You can also use the Internet to look for help via email, Frequently Asked Questions (FAQs), newsgroups, and of course, Web sites.

- **Books and magazines**. There also lots of books and magazines that contain information that will help you prevent yourself from causing problems.

It may take a little while to find the information for which you are looking, but once you do, correcting "user error" problems is usually straightforward. Just follow the recommendations or instructions you find.

Fixing Software Problems

As you add and use software, you are going to run into software that doesn't work properly. There can be several causes for software problems, and there are different tools for resolving the various kinds of problems you will encounter.

There are lots of individual symptoms that indicate a software problem, but they usually fall into one of the following kinds:

- **Quits and Type Whatever Errors**. Sometimes, the application you are using will suddenly quit. You may or may not get an error message saying something like, "The application has unexpectedly quit because of an error." When this happens, you lose all of the changes that you made to the open document since the last time that you saved it. This is not a good thing.

- **Hangs and freezes**. Sometimes software errors will cause your application—or Mac—to *freeze* ,also known as a *hang*. When this happens, your machine will seem to lock up, and you won't even be able to make the pointer move on the screen. This is also very bad if you haven't saved your work lately.

- **Won't do what it is supposed to do**. Many times, errors will occur that prevent you from doing what you want to do—be it using a particular function of the software, printing, saving files, and so on. These kind of errors are a bit more subtle than the others, but they can still be a big problem for you.

- **Error messages during startup**. Software conflicts can cause various error messages and other problems to occur during startup.

Unfortunately, software problems are unpredictable. And once they happen, there isn't usually much you can do to recover from them. You simply save and restore as much of your data as you can, reboot your machine, and begin the task of figuring out how to *prevent* future occurrences of the problem. The bulk of your troubleshooting efforts for software problems thus revolve around the prevention of future problems rather than the treatment of problems that have already occurred.

Fixing Quits

When an application quits unexpectedly, there isn't much you can do about it—except try and prevent future quits. The program is simply gone. Sometimes, you can recover your data; sometimes, you can't. Usually, you will need an additional piece of software that captures your keystrokes to be able to recover your work. For example, Casady & Greene's excellent Spell Catcher will capture and save all of your keystrokes in its GhostWriter function. You can go back to the GhostWriter file for the application that quit and restore the keystrokes you made since the last save. This is helpful to recover some of the work, but all formatting and graphics are lost. Plus, this process records all keystrokes, even command keys. Still, it can help you recover a substantial portion of your data.

The most likely way to prevent future quits is to give the problem application more RAM to figure out if there is a software conflict.

Unhanging Hangs

When an application hangs, you can attempt to shut it down by pressing Command-Option-Esc. This is a force quit and will sometimes shut down the hung application. When you attempt this, you will see a dialog asking you if you want to force the application to quit. You will also see Force Quit and Cancel buttons. If you click Force Quit, the Mac will attempt to shut down the problem application. If it works, you will be returned to the desktop. You need to immediately save all the work in other open applications and restart your Mac. A force quit is only a last resort measure and will cause problems for the system.

If the Force Quit doesn't work, then you will need to reboot your Mac. You can do a *soft* restart by pressing Control-Option-Power key (the key in the upper-right corner of the keyboard that has a small triangle on it). You can turn the power switch off and then on again, but this should be a last resort.

If you use a PowerPC Mac and have Norton Utilities for Macintosh, you can use Norton's CrashGuard feature. CrashGuard enables you to quit the problem application or try to fix it so you can save your data, and CrashGuard also maintains a record of crashes and other problems. If CrashGuard is able to help you save your data, you still need to reboot your Mac immediately so that other parts of the system are affected.

Until you have a fully protected memory structure, CrashGuard is about as close as you can get.

Solving Miscellaneous Problems

If your application is "acting up," save your work and begin preventive troubleshooting as soon as you can.

After you have recovered from the immediate problem, you need to figure out what to do to prevent future occurrences of that problem. The following bullet points, provide some things to try:

- **Error messages during startup**. Use Conflict Catcher or Extensions Manager to help you resolve startup conflicts.
- **Not enough RAM**. One of the most frequent causes of software problems is not having enough RAM in which the application can run. Likely symptoms of a RAM problem are either unexpected quits (some blather about a type xx error) or certain functions of the application not working. Often,

---

Memory protection

If Mac OS 8.5 were a fully capable multitasking and memory-protected OS, then one application crashing would not affect the other applications running at the time. Unfortunately, you won't get such an OS until a later version, probably Mac OS X. Mac OS 8.5 offers more memory protection than previous versions, but it does not offer full memory protection.

increasing the RAM allocation for a particular application will solve its problems.

SEE ALSO

➤ *To learn how to manage an application's RAM allocation, see page 326*

If the problem does not recur, then you have found the culprit. You can adjust the program's RAM allocation downward again to get to true minimum levels, but that isn't necessary unless you have a system that is strapped for RAM.

If you continue to have trouble, try increasing the RAM allocations to ridiculously large amounts. If the problem persists, it is not likely a RAM problem. Reduce the RAM allocations to more reasonable levels and look for other solutions.

Bring Peace to Your Battling Software

The more extensions, control panels, and applications that you use, the more likely it is that some of this software will conflict. What happens when software battles it out? You lose. You can experience startup errors when conflicting software tries to load into the system, or you may experience quits, hangs, and performance problems. The most likely source of conflicts are extensions and control panels, but applications can occasionally conflict with each other as well.

There are two ways to root out conflicting control panels or extensions. One is hard, the other is easy. First, let's take a look at the hard way to do it.

The basic technique to root out extension and control panel conflicts is to systematically remove items until the problem goes away. Then the removed items are returned until the problem recurs. The last item added back to the system is the likely source of the conflict.

The primary tool you can use for "the hard way" is Apple's own Extensions Manager. Extensions Manager enables you to turn various extensions, control panels, and other items off or on. You can also save sets of these items so that reconfiguring your system is simply a matter of selecting the appropriate Extensions Manager set.

It may be the best money you will ever spend

Adding RAM to your Mac is probably the best single thing that you can do to improve its performance *and* make it less likely to have problems.

This is ridiculous

How much RAM is ridiculously high? It all depends on the particular application. If you increase the Minimum and Preferred Sizes by 50 percent or more and the problem doesn't go away, it is probably not related to insufficient RAM allocation.

Military intelligence

Known conflicts will often be listed in ReadMe files and on Web sites for software you install. It is a good idea to check these sources for known conflicts before purchasing or installing new software.

Using Extensions Manager for this is no fun. If you have lots of control panels and extensions, it can take a long, long time. But since Extensions Manager is part of OS 8.5, it may be the only option you have.

Using Extensions Manager to search for extension and control panel conflicts

1. Choose Extensions Manager from the Control Panels folder from the Apple menu. Extensions Manager will open (see Figure 32.1).

FIGURE 32.1

Extensions Manager—it takes a long time to find conflicts with it, but at least it is free.

2. Choose New Set from the File menu, enter a name for your set (try something like Set1), and click OK.

3. Scroll through the lists of control panels, extensions, and other items, clicking the On/Off check boxes for those that might be related to your problems.

4. Continue this process until you have turned off about half of the items you see in Extensions Manager.

5. Restart the computer by choosing Restart.

6. After the machine is running, try to duplicate the problem. If the problem doesn't happen again, you know that the problem item is one that you turned off. If it does happen again, you know that the problem item is still on.

7. If the problem is gone, go back to Extensions Manager and turn on about half of those items that you turned off the first time. If the problem still happens, turn off about half of those items that are still on. Save this group of settings.

Stay focused

Try to focus on items that are related to the application or function you were using at the time of the problem. For example, if you were having problems with a communications program, choose the items that are related to modems.

Restarting by any other means

If you press the Power key (the key in the upper-right corner of the keyboard that has a triangle on it) on most Macs, a dialog box will pop up that will let you click Shutdown, Restart, Sleep, or Cancel. Each of these buttons does just what it says.

8. Restart the computer to see if the problem occurs again. If it doesn't happen, you know the problem isn't caused by one of the items you turned back on, and the culprit is still off. If it does happen, you know that the culprit is still on.

9. Repeat steps 7 and 8 until the problem happens again. Continue turning items off and on until you finally have isolated the piece of software causing trouble.

If this process sounds difficult and time consuming, that's because it is. It can be hard to keep track of all the items that you turn off or on. You have to be very disciplined about keeping things straight. And it takes lots of time.

Eventually, you will identify the software that is causing the problem. To correct the problem, you can do one of the following:

- **Live without it**. If you can do without the problem software, you can solve the problem by leaving the item off.

- **Get an upgrade**. You can try to get an upgrade for an item to see if the conflict has been solved.

- **Change the loading order**. You can rename items to change the order in which they load into the system. (Try adding z's or spaces to the item's name.) Sometimes, conflicts can be eliminated by changing the loading order.

In Chapter 31, I said that Conflict Catcher is an essential part of your software took kit. Once you see how it can help you troubleshoot conflicts, you will probably agree.

Conflict Catcher provides a complete management tool for your system extensions, control panels, plug-ins, and other items. In addition to what the extremely powerful, troubleshooting Conflict Catcher can do for you, it also offers the following features:

- **Displays information on your startup files**. After you install a few dozen or more extensions, control panels, and other startup files on your computer, it is easy to forget what they all do. With Conflict Catcher, you can easily get very detailed information on almost all the startup files on your system.

Conflict Catcher demo

You can download a demo version of Conflict Catcher from the Casady & Greene Web site located at `http://www.casadyg.com`.

The starting team

Conflict Catcher also identifies start-up files by grouping them in functional groups (for example, the Apple CD-ROM group that contains all the startup files needed to use a CD-ROM drive). This makes it easy to identify all of the startup files associated with a particular technology.

- **Provides contact information for important vendors**. It also gives you contact information for the vendors of the startup files in your system. This is a great help when you need to contact the vendor for support or to obtain an upgrade.

- **Enables you to create custom groups**. With Conflict Catcher, you can make custom sets of startup files to maximize the performance of your computer for specific tasks.

Once Conflict Catcher is installed, it can be launched in a variety of ways. The simplest way is to choose Open Conflict Catcher from the custom Conflict Catcher menu installed next to the Application menu. The control panel will open (see Figure 32.2). The right pane of the Conflict Catcher windows lists all of the startup files in your system. These can be sorted in various ways by using the pop-up menus at the top of the pane. In the lower-right corner, the Group Links area can be used to quickly turn all the startup files associated with a particular technology on or off. The left pane of the window is the area where Conflict Catcher displays detailed information about individual files. The Set pop-up menu at the top of the left pane enables you to quickly select a particular set with which to work. At the bottom, you'll see buttons that enable you to start the conflict testing process and to generate a report on your system configuration.

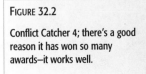

FIGURE 32.2

Conflict Catcher 4; there's a good reason it has won so many awards—it works well.

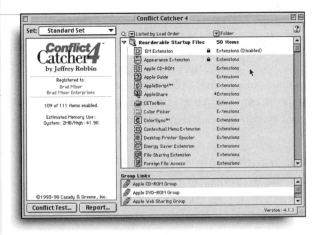

If you read the section about finding a conflict with Extensions Manager, you saw that it is no easy task. Now I'll do the same thing with Conflict Catcher to see how it works.

Using Conflict Catcher to isolate problem software

1. Open Conflict Catcher and click the Conflict Test button. You will see the Conflict Test Checklist (see Figure 32.3).

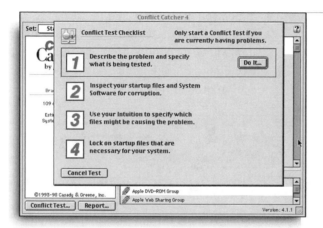

FIGURE 32.3
Conflict Catcher works through a very disciplined test process—automatically.

2. Click the Do It button.
3. In the resulting window, enter a description of the problem and choose the area you want to test from the Conflict Test pop-up menu (you can test startup files, everything, or particular plug-ins).
4. Click OK. You will return to the Checklist window.
5. Click Do It if you want Conflict Catcher to inspect your system software for corrupted files or Skip it if you don't. If you have Conflict Catcher inspect your startup files, you will see a progress box. If it finds problems, it will prompt you to have it fix them, which of course you should. When the inspection is complete, you will return to the Checklist window.
6. If you have an idea where the problem originates, you can use the Intuition function to tell Conflict Catcher where to start. If you don't have an idea, you can skip this by clicking Skip.

7. If you want to put a lock on the files that are necessary to start your system, click on Do It. If not, click on Skip. This function enables you to keep certain files always on. For example, you don't want Conflict Catcher to disable files that are necessary for your machine to start up. Normally, Appearance Manager is the only item that needs to be locked.

8. When you have completed the checklist, click on Start Conflict Test (see Figure 32.4). The Conflict Catcher window will change to the Conflict Test in Progress window (see Figure 32.5). Conflict Catcher will begin to turn sets of startup files off and on.

FIGURE 32.4

When you click Start Conflict Test, Conflict Catcher will begin to systematically test your system to isolate software conflicts.

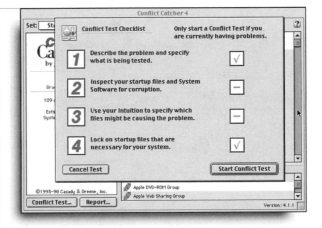

FIGURE 32.5

When you see this screen, Conflict Catcher is in the process of turning system items off and on in order to find out what is causing your troubles.

9. Restart your Mac to begin the first round of testing. Conflict Catcher will continue the testing cycles as you indicate whether or not the problem was solved. Each time the computer is restarted, a different set of startup files will be active. You simply look for the problem to occur—remember to do the same things you were doing when the problem first appeared so that you don't miss it by "luck." As you restart the computer, you will tell Conflict Catcher if the problem has been resolved. If not, Conflict Catcher will start another round of testing. Conflict Catcher will require no more than eight text cycles; usually, it requires even fewer.

Eventually, you will find the culprit—it will take no more than eight cycles and probably less. At that point, Conflict Catcher will also help you figure out what to do about the problem file; for example, remove it or try to reorder the loading sequence. If Conflict Catcher cannot identify the problem file, you will be notified via a dialog box.

Conflict testing with Conflict Catcher is elegant and effective. Having to use it even one time will make the purchase more than worthwhile.

SEE ALSO
➤ *To learn how to use Conflict Catcher to manage your system and to get information on items within in, see Chapter 15, "Managing Your System Folder."*

Fixing Buggy, Poorly Designed, and Conflicting Applications

Some applications are just plain buggy. There may be plenty of RAM, no conflicts, and no other system-level problems. Software may just not work very well. Symptoms of these problems can include quits, hangs, and odd performance.

In the case of a buggy application, the only real solution is to get a bug fix release of the application, assuming that the publisher will issue one, of course. You may just have to live with the problem or live without the application. If it conflicts with another application you also need, one of them may have to go.

SEE ALSO
➤ *To learn about obtaining bug fixes for your software, see page 774*

Conflict Catcher makes it easy to find help

When you run Conflict Catcher, you will see a Web menu item. This makes it extremely easy to move to Web sites related to troubleshooting and problem solving sites. Simply select the site you want to visit. Conflict Catcher will automatically open your default Web browser and take you to that site. This is another example showing why Conflict Catcher is such a great program.

Web browsers can be buggy

Web browsers and other Internet applications are notorious for being extremely buggy. These applications are upgraded frequently and are often pushing the envelope of technology. So don't be surprised if you have more trouble with Internet applications than you do with other types.

The bottom line is that there are some things you won't be able to fix. If an application is basically flawed, there probably isn't much you can do about it. The best bet in this case is to either get a bug fix or get an alternate application.

Killing Viruses

Viruses can also cause software problems for you. Again, problems caused by a virus may be quits, hangs, or poor performance. You should suspect a virus if something particularly strange is happening; for example, weird messages or strange dialog boxes appearing on your screen.

SEE ALSO

➤ *To learn how to combat viruses, see Chapter 30, "Fighting Viruses"*

Solving "General Weirdness" Problems

Sometimes, your Mac will do weird things that don't seem to be related to any specific applications. These kinds of problems are usually either very easy to solve or darn near impossible. In either case, they won't take much of your time because if you are able to solve them, it won't take long. If you can't solve them, you won't need to waste much time trying.

There are several problems that can be lumped under the "general weirdness" category. These include the following:

- **Generic icons**. One of the great things about the Mac is that it keeps track of which applications can be used to edit specific documents so that you don't have to worry about it yourself. You open a document by simply double-clicking it. Each icon has a distinctive look based on the type of file it is (for example, Word documents have the Word document icon). Sometimes, the Mac will seem to lose its mind and all of the icons will suddenly become generic (just a plain looking rectangle).

- **Lost time or date**. Your Mac always—almost always anyway—keeps track of the time and date. This is important for many reasons, the most significant of which is date and time stamping the files you create and modify. Once in a while, your Mac may seem to lose its watch and won't know what time it is.

- **Lost preferences**. You make your Mac your own by setting various preferences that tell your Mac how you want it to work and look. Occasionally, you will find all of your preferences gone.

These problems are almost always solved by one of three things.

Rebuilding the Desktop

The Mac associates documents with applications through its desktop database, which links particular files with the applications that create those files. This linkage is indicated by the custom icon on the document file. When these icons go generic—they lose the custom icons and become plain rectangle—you need to rebuild the desktop database. This helps the Mac "remember" which files go with which applications. This also restores the custom icons. As with most things on the Mac, there is more than one way to rebuild the desktop.

In Chapter 31, you learned an easy way to rebuild the desktop database on your startup disk by holding down the Option and Command keys and then restarting your Mac. There are other, more complicated ways to do it, but this easy way should work for most situations.

Zapping the PRAM

Parameter RAM (PRAM) is an area of your Mac where the information that needs to be retained when the power to the computer is turned off is stored. These settings include time and date, system preferences, and so on. Occasionally, your Mac will start acting oddly and will seem to lose its mind every time you restart it. If you have problems with your date and system preferences, try zapping the PRAM.

To zap the PRAM, hold down Command-Option-P-R while you restart your Mac. When it starts back up, the PRAM is cleared. You will then have to reset the Date and Time as well as all of your other custom settings.

ResEdit fun

The desktop database consists of invisible files on each of your volumes—in fact, every disk you mount on your machine has these files. To do the most thorough job of rebuilding these files, you can use ResEdit to help you delete the two invisible desktop database files. This forces the Mac to rebuild them (actually it has to create new ones). This technique can be helpful when you are preparing a disk to master a CD.

Warning about zapping the PRAM

Note that if you zap the PRAM, you will lose all of your system settings and will have to reconfigure everything that you changed from the defaults.

Batteries and your monitor

Losing the battery can also affect your monitor. If you restart your Mac, but the monitor won't come back on, it may be due to a failed battery. Weird things can happen when good PRAM goes bad.

Hardware burn-in and wear out

Strangely enough, hardware failures are the most likely when your computer is brand new. This is a result of something called "*burn-in*." This is the result of minor quality defects or design problems that lead to premature failures of hardware components. Fortunately, almost all hardware is warranted past the burn-in period so these failures—while annoying—are not likely to cost you money.

The odds of hardware failure also increase as the device approaches the end of its useful life and "wears out." For most hardware, you can expect to replace it because it won't do what you need it to do long before it wears out. This is just one of the "benefits" of the rapidly changing world of computer technology.

The sound you should hope that you never hear

If you haven't ever heard the chimes of death, be glad. You know that pleasant sound your Mac makes when you restart it? The chimes of death are just about the worst sound you can hear. Although they are tough to describe, you will know them if you ever hear them. They are usually accompanied by a sad Mac face. Both clues mean the same thing: trouble for you.

All RAM requires power to store data, PRAM is no exception. So how does PRAM maintain data when the machine is powered down? Simple. Your Mac has a battery in it that provides power to the PRAM so that certain settings will be maintained even when the power to your Mac is turned off. Most important of these are the time and date.

Sometimes, these batteries fail. When that happens, your Mac will forget the time and date and most of the preferences you have changed after every time you turn the power off and on again. If this happens, try zapping the PRAM. If that doesn't help, you will need to replace the battery in your machine. See the manual that came with your Mac to learn how to do that.

Solving Hardware Problems

Hardware problems are quite different from software problems. While software problems can be very tough to troubleshoot, hardware problems often are not—hardware failures usually make themselves abundantly obvious. While software problems usually can be solved by you with a minimal cost, major hardware problems often require a service technician and a fair amount of money. Fortunately, hardware problems are fairly rare, especially when compared to software problems.

The major symptoms of a hardware failure are usually pretty obvious. Your system won't work. It is usually that simple. It may be that your Mac won't boot up, or you might hear the dreaded chimes of death, or you may not be able to mount a drive. In all these cases, it will be very clear that you have a problem, and you will also know what the nature of that problem is.

While many hardware failures require a trip to a service technician, there are several hardware problems that you can troubleshoot and fix on your own.

When you have a hardware problem, start simple. Check all the cables that connect various components to your system. Turn the power off and check each cable to make sure that it is properly plugged in. Sometimes, a loose cable will prevent the system from operating properly.

Another good idea is to strip the system down to its basic components. Disconnect everything except what you need to start the machine up. If the machine boots in the stripped condition, you know that the problem lies in one of the peripherals. If the machine still doesn't boot, you know that is where your problem lies.

As you use your disk drives, the constant writing and reading of data to the drive can lead to the data structure of the disk becoming corrupted. When this happens the disk may not mount, or if it does, you may get disk errors when you try to write data to it. There are a variety of tools that you can use to check and repair a disk's data structure.

SEE ALSO
➤ *To learn how to maintain your disks, see page 714*

Often, your system won't operate properly because you are trying do things of which the hardware is simply not capable. You may not have enough RAM, the processor may be underpowered, or your video system may not be capable of supporting the number of colors or resolution needed. You can avoid this by paying attention to hardware requirements that are listed on all the software and hardware that you buy. If the hardware requirements are greater than your system, then you can expect to have troubles if you try to use the device or software. And the minimum requirements are usually optimistic, so if your system just barely meets the requirements, you may have trouble.

Each SCSI device on your system must have a unique ID number in order to be recognized by the system. If you attach two devices with the same ID number, your system won't boot. Usually, this is pretty obvious. When you connect an additional device and the system won't start, but it does start when you remove the device, then you have a SCSI ID conflict. You will have to change the ID number on one of the conflicting devices in order to get your system to boot up.

Be careful of external devices

Never plug or unplug SCSI (disk drives, tape drives, scanners, and so on) or ADB (mice, keyboards, joysticks, and so on) cables while your system is powered up. If you do so, you run the risk of destroying your motherboard, which means that you will need to make major repairs. It is OK to do so with the serial cables (modem and printer), however.

SCSI ID

Remember that all SCSI devices have an ID number, even the internal devices such as hard drives and CD-ROM drives. Usually, the internal drives have low SCSI ID numbers (0 or 1) or high numbers (6). There are various utilities that will let you see the SCSI ID numbers of the devices on your system. You can use the System Info function in Norton Utilities for Macintosh to tell you this information. You can also run an Apple System Profiler to see which SCSI ID numbers your devices use.

When you install new hardware in your system—such as RAM or VRAM chips, a new drive, or a PCI card—you always run the risk of not installing the item correctly or moving something that is already installed. If these devices are not seated properly, you will hear the chimes of death, and your system will not start. If this happens, open the case again and make sure that everything is installed properly. If you find no problems, the new device may be bad. Remove it and see if the system will start without the new hardware. If it does, either the new device was bad or you installed it improperly. Try again in that case.

Sometimes hardware fails due to it wearing out or even during the initial period of operation (usually due to quality problems). In this case, you usually have to replace the item or have it repaired.

Solving the Startup Problem

One of the worst problems you can have is when your Mac won't start. This can be caused by lots of things, including software conflicts, buggy software, failed hardware, or a combination of all of these. This problem is the failure of your Mac to boot to the desktop. When instead of loading the system, it just sits there and flashes a disk icon with a question mark in the center, that means that your Mac can't find a suitable System Folder to use to start up the machine. (If the system doesn't try to start up at all, but you just hear the chimes of death, that means you definitely have a hardware problem.)

There are several things that can cause your Mac to be unable to find a usable System Folder. One is that there is a problem with the system software that is installed. Another may be a faulty disk with a corrupted disk structure. Or the hardware itself may have failed. In any case, you must provide the Mac with a different startup disk for it to start up. If you have the emergency disks that were discussed in Chapter 31, this isn't as hard as it may sound.

Hearing is believing

You can often tell when hard drives and other rotating devices are on the way to failure. Usually, you will hear louder than usual noises from these devices before they fail. If you start hearing unusual noises from your equipment, make extra sure that your data is backed up. Unusual noises are never good news.

Starting your Mac from an emergency disk

1. Turn off the power to your Mac.

2. Insert your emergency startup disk into the appropriate drive (if you are using a CD-ROM, you will have to turn the power back on first).

3. Power the Mac back up.

4. While it is starting up, hold down any special keys needed to make your machine start up from that drive (for example, you need to hold C down to startup from the CD-ROM drive). If the Mac finds a valid system, the machine will start up. You should notice a different set of extensions and control panels loading—the desktop pattern might be different as well. You can tell what disk is being used as the startup disk by looking in the upper-right corner of the desktop. The startup disk is always the one closest to the top of the screen. If the startup continues and you eventually see a desktop, that is good news. That means that you only have a software problem. If the machine just sits there or you hear the chimes of death and see a black screen, you have a hardware problem.

5. Run Norton Utilities on the disk that you used to start up your machine.

6. Fix any problems that it finds.

7. Try to restart the machine from that disk (don't hold down any special keys). If it starts up successfully, your problem is solved, and you can get back to work. If not, move to step 8.

8. If the disk checks out OK, but your Mac still won't start up from the original disk, you will have to reinstall your system from the Mac OS installation CD (which you won't be able to do if you are starting from the Norton or other CD).

9. Start up from the Mac OS 8.5 installation CD and reinstall the system software for your Mac (see Appendix A, "Installing and Maintaining the Mac OS" for help with this).

Hard drives as startup disks

If you have multiple hard drives installed on your Mac, you can have a valid System Folder installed on one or more of them. If your Mac can't find a valid System Folder on the drive you have set to be your startup disk (using the Startup Disk control panel), it will search your drives to locate a system that it can use to start up. It will start up from the first valid System Folder that it finds.

Other startup disks

As discussed in Chapter 31, your emergency disk can be the Mac OS 8.5 installation CD-ROM, a floppy disk, a Zip or other removable disk with system software installed, or the Norton Utilities for Macintosh CD. The Norton disc is an excellent choice because it also contains the tools you need to check the disk that your failed System Folder is installed on.

Startup options

You can use any disk on which you can install, or which already has, a valid System Folder. If you use a CD-ROM as a startup disk, you will need to use a special code during the startup sequence to tell your Mac to use that disc (you hold down the C key). Check the manual that came with your Mac to find out what to use. You can also use a Zip disk or other removable media drive. You can also use a floppy disk, although the system has grown so large, you will only be able to have minimal functions when starting from a floppy. You don't need a code to start up from a floppy; the Mac checks the floppy drive first.

Here is where a backup comes in

If you have a backup of your System Folder when it was working OK, you can restore that version instead of reinstalling a new one. The advantage of this is that you won't have to reinstall your third-party software. See? Backups are good.

10. Now reinstall any third-party software that you had in your System Folder (for example, Conflict Catcher).

11. Restart your Mac. You should be back in operating condition.

The "won't startup" problem is one of the more stressful problems you will face. But if you have the appropriate tools, and the knowledge you gained in this chapter, you can solve even this daunting problem without too much difficulty.

Maintaining Your Mac Through Upgrades

Knowing how and when to upgrade software

Understanding types of Mac OS and other software upgrades, and how to get them

Evaluating potential hardware and software upgrades to see if they make sense for you

Learning about hardware upgrades for your Mac

Understanding why and when to upgrade your Mac's hardware

Improving Your Mac's Software and Hardware

You have no doubt heard the expression, "Progress marches on!" This expression is doubly true in the world of Macintosh where something new is developed every time you turn around. Mac users are faced with a bewildering myriad of sales pitches for new products or improved versions of products that they already own.

This confusion can be particularly intense when it comes to upgrading the software and hardware you use on your Mac. Should you upgrade to the latest version of Myfavoriteapp 6.3? Do you need more RAM? Should you get a removable media drive?

Upgrade to the wrong product and you may end up wasting your money and causing all kinds of headaches for yourself. If you don't ever upgrade, you may be missing out on features that can help you work faster, smarter, and more reliably. The "upgrade" question is not an easy one to answer.

In this chapter, you'll figure out how to answer the "upgrade" question for yourself. This chapter is divided into two major sections. In the first, you'll learn about software upgrades. In the second, you will get an overview of hardware upgrades.

Upgrades upon upgrades

Some software upgrades, particularly an upgrade to the OS itself, will require that you upgrade other parts of your system to maintain compatibility. The better you understand the upgrade that you are considering, the more you will be aware of these potential "domino" effects.

Upgrading Software

Upgrades are "new and improved" versions of software that will (supposedly) do things better, faster, and more reliably than the previous versions. Software companies tend to make a large portion of their incomes from upgrade sales so they turn out upgrades to their products as often as is feasible, and that usually turns out to be around once per year.

To be fair, though, many upgrades do provide significant new features or improved reliability that easily justify the upgrade price.

As with all things on which you spend your money, you need to understand and be able to evaluate upgrades so that you spend your computing dollars wisely. Additionally, you need to be wary because sometimes upgrades can actually cause more problems for you than they solve—especially when they are first released.

Understanding Software Upgrades

There are several different types of upgrades that are produced by software publishers. These include the following:

- **Major releases**. Major upgrades usually add lots of new features and capabilities to an application. They usually offer improved reliability and compatibility as well. At least those are the claims. Sometimes they are true and sometimes they aren't.

  The cost of major upgrades is usually some percentage of the full package price. That percentage can be fairly high or quite low depending on the software publisher.

- **Bug fixes/minor releases**. These type of upgrades are made to fix the problems that were created in the last major upgrade. Software companies do at least some testing to try and catch all the errors and incompatibilities in their software, but it is impossible to prevent all problems, given the incredible variety of computers and circumstances in which software is run.

  Usually, there is a flurry of problems discovered just after an upgrade is released as all of the early adopters scramble to keep up with the latest and greatest version. As problems are reported, software companies scramble to fix them, and typically issue one to three bug fix upgrades in the few months following the release of a major upgrade.

  Bug fix releases are generally free or provided at a minimal cost (usually to cover the cost of the media and mailing). While you should carefully evaluate major releases before upgrading to them, you should almost always upgrade with minor releases so that you have a more stable and reliable application.

To upgrade or not, that is the question

There is a tremendous temptation to automatically purchase every upgrade of every piece of software that you own. You frequently receive mailings telling you about the new version of your favorite applications that sport tons of new features, so why wouldn't you upgrade? Especially at the super special upgrade price you are offered. The answer is that often—dare I say more frequently than not?—you may not need the extra features of the upgrade and can wait for the next "must have" upgrade.

Be careful about upgrading, and evaluate each upgrade as you would when purchasing new software.

Timing is everything

When it comes to buying software, timing is important. Usually, if you purchase a software package and a major upgrade is released within a few weeks to a month, the publisher will give you the upgrade for free. Sometimes, you can find the older version for a very low price and then upgrade it for less cost than buying a full copy of the new version. This works particularly well if you can buy the older version right before or right after the upgrade is released (at which time prices are usually at rock bottom since retailers will be trying to "dump" all of the old inventory).

Alpha, then beta

Prior to the beta version is the alpha version, which is usually a very rough version of the software that is being developed. Companies usually don't issue alpha releases to the outside world; they keep the release of that version for its employees or related developers.

Using betas

Remember that if you do use beta release software and discover problems, it is helpful if you report those problems to the publisher. Otherwise, you may get to face that same problem in the "real" version.

However, even with a bug fix release, it is possible to introduce new bugs. Occasionally, the bug fix version will actually be more buggy than the version that it is supposed to fix.

■ **Beta releases**. Most software goes through a rigorous development process that includes several major phases. One of these is the "beta" test phase during which a selected group of users receive the upgrade in a prerelease (beta) version to test. The beta testers use the software and try to identify all the problems it has. They report these back to the publisher who is supposed to fix as many as it can before releasing the product to the market.

Some beta releases are very limited—you have to have special permission by the company to obtain them. Other beta releases are more general and anyone can get a copy (this is usually the case with most Internet-related applications).

Generally, you won't want to use the beta releases for more than evaluation purposes because they tend to be quite buggy. But for that purpose, beta releases are excellent because they are usually free, and you can evaluate most of the functions that will eventually end up in the released version. Many beta releases are programmed to expire after a certain date so that you can't continue to use them indefinitely.

Understanding Software Version Names

All these types of upgrades can be confusing, and the naming schemes can add even more confusion to the mix. However, publishers usually follow some general trends when naming software versions. Almost all software has some number associated with its name to indicate the version it is; for example, Microsoft Word 6.0.1 or Claris FileMaker Pro 4.0.

The first number usually indicates a major release of the software. Thus, you should expect that Yourfavoriteapplication 2.0 will have more features than version 1.0 did.

The next one or two places in the numbering scheme can be a bit more confusing. Sometimes, the second number indicates a minor release (bug fixes), while other times it may indicate a release that is somewhere between a major and minor release (some bug fixes and a few new features).

The third number—if there is one, which is certainly not always the case—almost always is used for bug fix releases only.

Confused? Perhaps looking at an example will help. Take Apple's naming schemes for the Mac OS. Version 7.0 was released in the early 1990's and was a major upgrade. Version 7.5 was released in 1994, and contained quite a few new features, but didn't warrant the status of a major upgrade. Then there was version 7.6 (there were bug fix releases between 7.5 and 7.6), which was merely a consolidation of the many bug fix releases for 7.5. And then we had 7.6.1, which was a big fix release for version 7.6. Then we moved to Mac OS 8, which again was a major upgrade. The current version is 8.5, which has a few more features than did 8.0, and it also has a number of big fixes in it.

If that naming scheme makes sense to you, I would recommend that you seek professional help!

At any rate, a publisher is usually fairly consistent in naming its own versions, but you can't really compare naming schemes between different publishers.

Finding Out About Upgrades

How do you know when upgrades are issued? There are several ways:

- **Application mailing lists**. If you register your application (either via the paper card or via email or the Web), you will be added to the lists of users that software companies keep for each application. When an upgrade becomes available, you will usually receive one (and usually more) notices in the mail or via email. These notices usually claim to offer you a special upgrade price.

- **The publisher's Web site**. Almost all software publishers maintain a Web page that provides a variety of information related to their products. Usually, this includes information about available upgrades. You can also download bug fix and minor upgrades from the Web site (see Figure 33.1).

Version letters

You may also see letters thrown into the mix, but thankfully only two are typically used. A "b" usually indicates a beta release while an "a" indicates an alpha release.

Warranty cards

Most registration cards seem to imply that you need to return the card to "activate" the warranty. This is not the case. It is illegal for a company to require that you
do something to legitimize its warranty—other than purchase its product, of course. A warranty is a legally created instrument that cannot be used to discriminate against users who don't submit the warranty card.

The real reasons for warranty cards

There are two "real" reasons that software and hardware companies want you to return the registration card (or register by email). The first is that the company wants to know who is using its product. This helps in developing and supporting the product, and it also helps the company know the demographics of its customers (how many, interests, and so on). The second purpose, hopefully a very minor one, is that some companies sell their application mailing lists to other organizations that might want it—usually for direct advertising purposes.

While companies cannot make the warranty dependent on you completing and returning the card, they can make technical support available only to registered users. So before you toss that card in the trash, be sure that you don't need to register for technical support.

FIGURE 33.1

The Casady and Greene Web site offers minor and big fix upgrades that you can download for free.

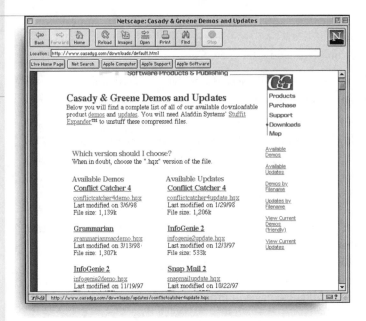

- **Mac magazines**. Most Mac magazines provide coverage of new versions of the major applications. They typically have a "news" area where upgrades are also mentioned.

- **Newsgroups and mailing lists**. Many of the major Mac applications have newsgroups or mailing lists dedicated to them. You can monitor these to find out about upgrades.

- **Mac Web sites**. You can (and should) find some good Mac Web sites that you visit regularly for upgrade news, as well as bugs that have been discovered, user tips, and other good information. For example, check out the MacAddict site at `http://www.macaddict.com/` (see Figure 33.2).

Understanding How to Upgrade

Different types of upgrades can be delivered to you in different ways:

- **New installation**. Most major upgrades look very similar to a new purchase in that you receive a full set of disks or a CD as well as the manual and other documentation. Occasionally, there will be a special package provided for upgrades that contains only the material that has changed for the upgrade (for example, a manual supplement rather than a full manual).

You can purchase major upgrades through the usual sources: mail order, the publisher, the Internet, computer stores, and so on.

Recently, it has become possible to download full or upgraded versions directly from a Web site. The manuals and support information are provided via PDF or other electronic

Upgrade means upgrade

Some upgrade packages will search your hard drive for a copy of a previous version of the software so don't remove the earlier version until you have successfully installed and used the new version. Plus, you may want to use the older version in certain situations.

documentation method. You never receive a physical package so you need to make sure that you back up such software since you won't have disks or a CD.

- **Updaters or patches**. Minor releases and bug fixes are usually issued as an updater or patch. These are applications that modify the code of the application that you have installed on your computer. Updaters and patches are widely available via the Internet for a free download (see Figure 33.3).

FIGURE 33.3

You can usually download an updater to applications that you own by simply clicking a link on a Web page (in this figure, I am downloading an updater for the Spell Catcher application).

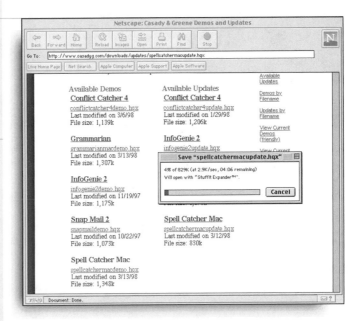

Understanding Mac OS Upgrades

Upgrades of the Mac OS are a special case of software upgrade because making changes to the operating system can have an effect on other parts of your system, such as the third-party control panels and extensions you use.

Apple releases upgrades to Mac OS in the same way that other software publishers do.

Understanding Mac OS Minor Releases

Apple regularly issues bug fixes and system enhancements for the Mac OS. These typically solve problems that have appeared with the OS and occasionally add some minor new features or make minor improvements to system performance. Apple has said that it will release one minor upgrade of the Mac OS per year, plus one major upgrade. Since the release of OS 8, it has done so.

The best place to get a minor release of Mac OS is right from the horse's mouth: the Apple Web site at `http://www.apple.com/` `support/` (see Figure 33.4). Minor upgrades are usually available here for you to download.

FIGURE 33.4

Apple's Web site at `http://` `www.apple.com/support` is an excellent source of information on Mac OS updaters and upgrades.

Once you choose Software Updates from the pop-up Destination menu, you will move to the Software Update page (see Figure 33.5). You can read about all of the update news and other information from this site.

You should also regularly check this site for upgrades for any other Apple software you have, such as monitor drivers or upgrades for particular technologies.

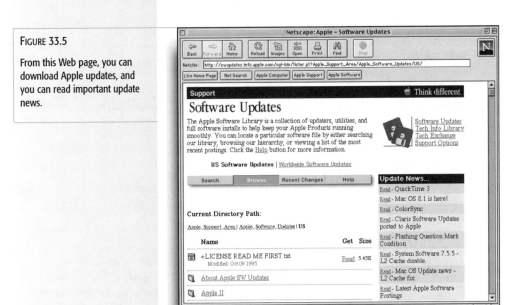

FIGURE 33.5

From this Web page, you can download Apple updates, and you can read important update news.

To download an updater, simply click on the appropriate links. Most Apple updates are provided as a disk image or a series of disk images. You can use Disk Copy, which is provided as part of the OS package, to mount these images on your desktop, or you can use it to copy the updater to a floppy disk. To mount the image, simply double-click it.

If you don't have access to the Web, you can usually order minor upgrades from Apple for less than $15.

It is almost always a good idea to update your system software when minor upgrades are released. I added the "almost" because once in a while, a minor upgrade is released that will cause you more problems than it solves. In that case, upgrading is not a good idea.

How can you tell the difference? Simply wait a few days to a week before upgrading. If there are any significant problems with the release, you are likely to hear about them within that time (by checking your favorite Mac sites, newsgroups, and mailing lists). Then you can determine if the new problems will affect you or not (problems are usually related to a specific machine or configuration).

Besides which, after an upgrade is announced, Apple's Web site is usually so busy that you will likely be forced to wait to get the upgrade anyway.

Major Releases

If you are using Mac OS 8.5 (or 8.0 or 8.1), you have experienced the result of one of Apple's major releases of Mac OS. Mac OS 8 added a large number of features and other improvements over Mac OS 7.6 and earlier versions. Unlike updaters, you have to purchase major system upgrades. You can obtain copies from the usual sources (including Apple), and they usually cost less than $100.

Whether you should upgrade to a major release is usually not a major issue. Apple normally makes major upgrades worthwhile by including new features and reliability improvements.

However, when to upgrade to a major release is a more complicated question. It is often a good idea to wait for a little while (two weeks or a month) before you do. This waiting period allows some of the more major bugs to be discovered (and fixed!) before you actually install the upgrade. (Remember to look for any updaters immediately after installing the upgrade.) Also, major OS upgrades sometimes are not compatible with the current versions of applications; if that is the case, the application may not run (or it may be buggy if it does run). If you wait a little while before upgrading the OS, you will also be able to get updaters for any incompatible applications from the publishers of those applications so that you are never without the applications that you need.

SEE ALSO

➤ *To learn how to install the Mac OS 8.5 upgrade, see Appendix A, "Installing and Maintaining the Mac OS"*

Knowing That Software Upgrades Aren't Always Good for You

To this point, I've written about the kinds of upgrades available and the mechanics of upgrading. Equally—perhaps more—important is the question of whether you *should* upgrade.

Apple's online store

You can purchase Apple hardware and software directly from the Apple online store by visiting `http://www.apple.com/` and clicking the Apple Store link.

Upgrading is definitely not a "no-brainer," and you should always carefully evaluate any upgrade to make sure it provides value to you.

First, let's look at the reasons you might want to upgrade.

Understanding the Reasons Why You Should Upgrade

There are basically four reasons you might want to upgrade a particular piece of software:

- **New Features**. Many upgrades offer significant new features that will make you more productive or make your computing life easier.

- **Compatibility with others**. If you share files with others—and these days just about everyone does—you may want to upgrade so that you will be using the same version as the people with whom you collaborate. This makes exchanging files easier and saves everyone work.

- **Compatibility with hardware and software**. Sometimes, you will have to upgrade software so that it is compatible with hardware and software you use. Usually, you will find this out immediately after you install new or upgraded software or hardware when something doesn't work properly.

- **Bug fixes**. This can be one of the most important reasons to upgrade, particularly if an application is crashing regularly or is causing you problems. Fortunately, most big fix upgrades are free or can be obtained at a minimal cost.

Understanding Why You Shouldn't Upgrade

As I said earlier, upgrading is not always a cut-and-dried situation. Here are some reasons you may not want to upgrade:

- **Cost**. Many major upgrades cost a significant amount of money, sometimes as much as 60 or 70 percent of the "full" application's price.

- **System Requirements**. As software increases capability, the hardware requirements to run that software also increase. The upgrade may simply be too much for your current computer to handle.

The upgrade domino

Sometimes the upgrade process results in the domino effect. You upgrade a piece of software or hardware that forces you to upgrade a different piece of software, which in turn forces you to upgrade another piece of software and so on. If this happens, you don't have much choice but to either go back to the way things were or keep upgrading until you reach the end of the chain.

- **Potential for conflicts and problems**. With every upgrade you get, you run the risk of introducing problems with that software conflicting with other parts of your system. Plus, you always run the risk that the upgraded software will introduce its own set of bugs into your life.

- **Features you don't need**. Most of us only use a subset of the capabilities of the software we have. Perhaps an upgrade will provide new features that you simply won't end up using anyway. So why pay for them?

Answering the Upgrade Question

Here is the key question regarding upgrading, "Are the additional features and bug fixes worth the cost and potential trouble you may incur by upgrading?"

If the answer to this question is clearly "Yes," life is good. If the answer is clearly "No," life is also good. But unfortunately, the answer is usually "Maybe."

Using Sources of Information on Upgrades

There are many sources of information on upgrades. You should check as many of these as you can before making the decision to upgrade:

- **Demos**. Many publishers have developed demo versions of applications that you can download from the company's Web site (you can also call and ask that the demo be mailed to you for a nominal fee). Demos are an excellent way to evaluate how an upgrade will actually work in your specific situation—especially if the demo is close to fully-functional.

- **Magazines**. The various Mac magazines will usually publish a review of major upgrades shortly after they are released.

- **Internet**. There are many sources of good information on upgrades on the Internet including FAQ lists, newsgroups, Web sites, and mailing lists.

Knowing What to Do If You Do Upgrade

If you decide to upgrade, there are several steps you should take to ensure that your upgrade is as painless as possible.

Upgrading software

1. Get the complete upgrade package. Make sure that you get the entire upgrade package from a legitimate source. Download it yourself or only use the original disks. If you get it from a friend or other source, you may not have all the pieces you need. And you may be stealing.

2. Back up your system, you may need to go back! Before you install the upgrade, make sure that you have an up-to-date backup—one that includes the current version of the application, as well as any documents that were created by it. If you have a major problem when you upgrade, you need to be able to restore your system to the "pre-upgrade" condition. See Chapter 29, "Backing Up" for details.

3. Check the requirements—twice. Read through the documentation that came with the upgrade to make sure that it is compatible with your system. Look carefully for any "ReadMe" documents that may contain late-breaking information.

4. Install the upgrade. Follow any instructions provided with the upgrade.

5. Pass judgment. As you use the upgraded application, keep an eye out for problems it may be causing. If you suddenly start having a problem after installing an upgrade, it is likely that something that happened during the upgrade may have caused the problem. Don't automatically assume that the upgrade itself is causing the problem. It could be something else that happened at the same time that you upgraded. For example, you might have accidentally changed a system setting or removed some piece of software that you need. You should also evaluate the upgrade to see if the decisions you made based on the information you had turned out to be good ones. Plus, certain companies release better upgrades

than others. It may be that you discover that company X's major upgrades are worth every cent while you can safely skip every other major upgrade released by company Y.

Knowing What to Do If You Don't Upgrade

You may decide that a particular upgrade is not worth the cost or potential hassles it may introduce. In that case, you can continue on as you have been. Just keep your eye peeled for developments relating to that application. At some later time, you may discover additional information that will lead you to upgrade.

Understanding Hardware Upgrades

Although you will usually maintain your Mac with software upgrades, from time to time you may need or want to improve the hardware in your system. Hardware upgrades can provide significant improvements to your system's capabilities and performance. Hardware upgrades are usually fairly expensive, and they can be somewhat difficult to install, so you need to consider them even more carefully than you do software upgrades. Plus, keep in mind that your Mac's hardware expansion is limited in one way or another. You simply can't keep upgrading hardware indefinitely. You will eventually run out of slots or expansion bays.

Before getting started, though, there is one caveat. This chapter will not prepare you to understand and implement the wide variety of hardware upgrades that are available. What it will do is to give you "the big picture" of hardware upgrades so that you are aware of what is out there. The solution to specific problems, or the specific upgrade for a certain function, is beyond the scope of this book. But you will understand the most likely upgrades that you may need to implement to keep your Mac in tip-top condition.

Basic to any upgrade that you consider is understanding the hardware configuration that you have now. So that is where I'll start.

Hardware upgrades can be dangerous to your Mac

Here's a warning before moving on. Installing hardware upgrades can damage or destroy your computer if you damage any of the internal components of the machine. If you take some relatively simple precautions, though, you can easily avoid causing any damage. Just be a bit careful, and you will be OK.

Understanding the Hardware Upgrades Your Mac Can Handle

Before you undertake any hardware upgrade, you must understand the current configuration of your computer as well as its expansion capabilities. This understanding goes beyond simply knowing what model you have; you also need to know things such as the machine's RAM configuration, how many and what type of PCI slots are available, the VRAM configuration, and so on.

Discovering this information can be a bit frustrating, depending how good the manual and other information that came with your computer is. Some manuals are better than others. No need to worry, though. There is a lot of information available from other sources, including the Internet, books, and magazines. Understanding the expansion capabilities of your Mac will help you to evaluate, obtain, and install hardware upgrades.

Using the Receipt

One place to look for configuration information is the receipt and invoice that came with your computer. From these you can usually get the following information:

- **The manufacturer and model number**. Examples: Apple Power Macintosh 8600 or Power Computing Power Center 210.

- **RAM installed**. When you ordered the machine, you probably chose a RAM configuration, which should be identified on the receipt. You will usually see 16, 32, or 64 MB as the base configuration.

  One thing to keep in mind about RAM configurations is that even though your machine may have the same amount of RAM as another, the configuration of that RAM can be quite different. For example, one machine may have 32 MB of RAM composed of two 16 MB chips while another may have a single 32 MB chip. The RAM configuration of your computer will be important to know if you need to upgrade the RAM.

- **Hard drive size**. This will hopefully be a very large number, probably 2 GB or more. You may also have some additional specifications, such as the drive speed or AV compatibility.

- **CD-ROM speed**. Assuming that your Mac is equipped with a CD-ROM, you should see the speed of the drive as 8x, 12x, or even faster.

- **Other features**. You may also see other options that you selected, such as an internal Zip drive or special graphics card.

Using the Manual

Hopefully, the manual that came with your system is a good one and will serve you well as you begin to upgrade your computer. You should take some time to review the manual, particularly looking for sections that discuss hardware upgrades. At the least, there should be sections that cover removing the case, installing RAM, and other basic hardware tasks. There should also be a diagram of the internal configuration of the machine, including the location of the PCI slots, the VRAM chips, and other important areas.

Using Online Resources

There are numerous online resources that will help you identify the hardware configuration of your computer. These include Web sites and Mac magazines sites (*MacAddict*, *Macworld*, and such).

A good way to explore your machine is to go to the magazine Web sites and search for reviews on your machine that are invariably written when new machines are released. Even if your machine is fairly old, it is likely that you will be able to find reviews on it. These reviews almost always include a thorough description of the hardware configuration of the model being reviewed.

SEE ALSO
➤ *To learn about some great Web sites for Mac resources, see page 623*

Look, but don't touch

Remember how your Mom always told you to look, but don't touch when she took you into an expensive store? Well, that is also a good rule when exploring your Mac. The most obvious danger that you present to the machine is the discharge of static electricity. That can ruin your whole day. So don't touch anything that you don't have to. And make sure that you are properly grounded before opening the case. Leave your Mac plugged in and touch the power supply case every so often to safely discharge any static electricity that may be building up on you.

Using Your Mac Itself

There are a couple of ways your computer can tell its own story. The first requires you to do some manual labor (but not much), while the second way is as easy as clicking the mouse button.

One of the best things you can do is to go ahead and open the case of your computer. Use the manual's instructions and the configuration diagram to see what the "guts" of your Mac are like. Don't worry—no need for surgical gloves, just follow the precautions mentioned in the manual. Have a look around and see if you can identify the locations of the following: RAM, VRAM, PCI slots, empty drive bays, and so on. Get comfortable with the innards of your Mac so that you will be comfortable when it comes time to upgrade.

The best way to explore your Mac is with the Apple System Profiler. All you have to do is to choose it from the Apple menu and away you go.

SEE ALSO

➤ *To learn more about the Apple System Profiler, see page 735*

Understanding Active Memory Upgrades

Next to processor power, one of the most important factors that determines how well your machine performs is the active memory that is available to it; active memory consists of the memory that is "active" during computations of the main processor. I'll discuss three types of active memory in this section: RAM, VRAM, and second-level cache. You can make major improvements to the performance and reliability of your computer by upgrading its active memory.

If you have a relatively new processor, but your machine seems sluggish and you can't open many applications before getting "out of memory" messages and errors, it is very likely that adding active memory will make your Mac life much better.

Upgrading RAM

As you have learned throughout this book, RAM is probably the most important factor that determines how well your Mac will perform in everyday—as well as special— situations. If you take a Mac and equip it with the bare minimum amount of RAM, it will perform, well, barely. With a minimum amount of RAM, you will more than likely experience system slowdowns, errors, crashes, hangs, and other associated problems. Even if you don't experience problems that cause your system to fail, your system will not be operating up to its full potential.

Take that same Mac and equip it with more RAM, and suddenly the machine will perform like it is a different computer. Tasks will be completed faster, there will be fewer errors, and system crashes will be less frequent. With additional RAM, you can also provide more "working room" for your applications so that they also perform better.

As technology progresses, there is no doubt that RAM requirements will continue to grow as the capabilities of application and system software continue to increase.

In the past, people kept the bare minimum of RAM because additional RAM chips were very, very expensive. By just adding a few megabytes of RAM, you could have easily spent more than the Mac cost in the first place. However, in the past few years, RAM prices have fallen dramatically, and you can add 64 MB of RAM or more for only a couple hundred dollars.

So should you add RAM? The answer in almost all cases is, "Yes." Add as much as your system can handle and you can afford. Most Macs should have at least 64 MB of RAM if you are going to do anything beyond basic word processing.

The hardest part of upgrading RAM is to know exactly which chips you can use and how many you need to add. Fortunately, many vendors that sell RAM chips also have extensive databases on the RAM chips and configurations used in all Mac models. You can simply call such a retailer and tell them what kind of Mac you have and how much RAM you want it to have. They will tell you what kind of chips you need to buy.

After you have your RAM chips, installing them in most Macs is pretty easy. You simply remove the case and install the new RAM chips in the open RAM slots (your manual will tell you where those slots are located). You may have to remove some existing chips before you can install new ones if all of the slots are full.

Multitasking

Plenty of RAM also enables you to keep several applications running at the same time. This alone can make the expense of the additional RAM worthwhile since you can save lots of time that you might otherwise waste waiting for applications to open.

An excellent RAM source

One of the best RAM dealers is The Chip Merchant at `http://www.thechipmerchant.com`. I have purchased lots of RAM through The Chip Merchant and have always been impressed with the excellent service I have received.

RAM installation tips

When you call to order your RAM, ask the person you speak to for tips on installing that RAM in your particular Mac model. They will usually know if there is something unusual about installing RAM in your model.

Upgrading Video RAM (VRAM)

If you can't display as many colors as you would like or if you want to try to improve the resolution of your monitor, you may want to see if you can add VRAM to your machine.

The graphics subsystems on your computer use a special kind of RAM to provide the graphics capabilities of your system—this is called Video RAM or VRAM. Your system has a certain amount of VRAM installed in the base configuration. Sometimes, there are additional slots in which you can add more VRAM to improve the graphics performance of your machine (enabling you to display more colors for example). Or you may be able to replace the existing VRAM with larger chips.

VRAM chips, just like RAM chips, can also be purchased and installed in your Mac (assuming that you have available VRAM slots). They come in smaller capacities, however, with the most common ones being 256K, 512K, 1 MB, and 2 MB.

Upgrading your computer's VRAM is a similar process to upgrading the RAM. Again, the most important part is understanding the configuration of your computer before you consider adding VRAM. Use your system documentation to determine how to upgrade the VRAM.

Upgrading Cache

Most modern Macs use a second-level cache. Basically, this is memory located on a separate (second level) card that the main processor can use to temporarily store (or cache) data. This speeds up the processing process because the main processor does not have to spend as much time waiting for the data to come in from the data bus (the bus tends to be a drag on system performance). Thus, the computer works more quickly.

Most modern Macs have a second level cache slot; however, not all Macs come with a cache card installed. If this is the case with your machine, you should definitely install some cache memory. If you do, the machine will perform much faster.

As with the other kinds of active memory, you need to understand the configuration of your computer to see if you can add a

---

Max VRAM

Many Macs come with the maximum amount of VRAM already installed. Be sure to check the configuration of your machine before ordering any VRAM upgrades.

Boosting video output

You may be able to increase your Mac's video output by adding a PCI graphics card to it. In addition to enabling your Mac to display more colors, these cards will often accelerate 3-D graphics and provide special features, such as a TV tuner.

Where to buy VRAM

Most retailers (including The Chip Merchant) that carry RAM chips also carry VRAM chips.

second level cache card to your machine. If you can, you need to also identify the amount of memory that can be installed.

Even if your machine already has second level cache memory installed, you may be able to upgrade that to provide even better performance (for example, increasing the cache to 1 MB from 256K).

Obtaining and installing a second level cache is similar to installing other kinds of active memory.

Understanding Storage Memory Upgrades

The other major kind of memory that your computer uses is "storage" memory. The main purpose of this memory is to store data for the long term, rather than just for more temporary needs of the processor and graphics system.

While upgrading your storage memory may not result in as dramatic performance improvements as upgrades of the active memory can provide, having enough storage space available to you will play a large part in how effective your total system is (for example, when you need to store new files on your disk, do you spend lots of time deleting files to make room, rather than working?).

You also need to consider upgrading the storage memory of your system for maintaining good backups.

Upgrading with Hard Drives

Hard drives are fixed storage devices (meaning that you can't remove the disk), and they tend to be the location where you store most of your files. Hard drives are very fast, and you don't have to bother with loose disks. This is also one of their disadvantages because you cannot expand their storage capability beyond what they came with.

Most new machines came with at least a 4 GB drive, but sizes of 8 GB and more are not uncommon. As with all things computer-related, performance of hard drives continues to improve while prices decrease.

Drives have grown

For some perspective, early Macs, such as the Mac SE, came with a whopping 20 MB hard drive. This wouldn't even contain half of the System Folder for most modern Macs!

More on access time

Access time refers to the time, on average, it takes for data to be retrieved from this disk. Access time is measured in ms (milliseconds). Access times of 9 to 11 ms are common.

There are a couple of instances where access time of the hard drive is very important. One is for recording and playing digital video and audio. Faster drives, often called AV (Audio Visual) drives, have faster access times and greater spin rates so that they can keep up with demanding digital and audio streams.

Managing heat

There is a characteristic called thermal recalibration that can also be important. Most hard drives stop for a small instant to manage their internal heat. For most applications, this minor pause is irrelevant. However, when digitizing video or audio, or recording CDs, this pause can cause problems. AV drives do not pause during operation for this thermal recalibration, so the data stream is not interrupted.

If you are running into storage limitations on your machine, you may want to consider adding additional hard drive space. When evaluating a hard drive, there are several factors you need to consider:

- **Size**. Hard drives come in a wide variety of capacities, ranging from 500 MB to 8 GB and larger. In this case, bigger is better, although bigger is also harder on the wallet.

- **Speed**. Hard drives spin at different speeds and also have different access times. Faster (higher spin rate and lower access time) is better, although most drives that you can buy will have adequate spin rates and access times.

- **Internal or external configuration**. Hard drives can either be internal to your Mac or external to it.

  Internal drives are nice because they are out of the way and no external cables are needed. Internal drives are also less expensive than external drives (because they don't have a power supply or case). Internal drives tend to have better performance since the bus through which they communicate with the processor is usually faster.

  External drives are contained in a separate case with its own power supply. They connect to your Mac through the SCSI port. External drives are good because they are very easy to take from computer to computer as you upgrade.

- **Bus type**. There are three types of data buses that support hard drives. The type the Mac has used since its inception is SCSI. This technology has continued to improve and provides greater speed and expansion capability than other technologies currently in use. SCSI drives are also more expensive. The second type is IDE. This type was created on the PC and continues to be the most common type on Windows machines (although PCs can be upgraded to use SCSI dries as well). IDE drives are slower than SCSI drives, but they are considerably less expensive. The newest interface for external drives is USB.

  In the past few years, some Macs have been equipped with internal IDE drives as a means to make Macs less expensive.

If you are replacing or adding an internal drive, you need to know if your Mac uses a SCSI or an IDE drive. If you use an external drive, you need a SCSI or USB drive because that is how the Mac interfaces with external components.

Upgrading the hard drive on your machine is usually a case of adding more capacity by adding a new drive rather than replacing a drive. The type of drive you need often depends on whether or not you have any free internal drive bays in your computer.

Even if you do have a free drive bay, you may choose to add an external drive. Installing an external drive is easier than installing an internal drive—you simply plug the power cord in, attach the cable to the appropriate port on your Mac, and format the disk (if necessary). Plus, external drives are much easier to "carry" with you to your next Mac.

In either case, check the usual sources for reviews of hard drives and to purchase a drive.

Upgrading with Removable Media Drives

Removable disk drives have a mechanism that is very similar to fixed hard drives except that the platter is contained in a removable cartridge. There are various types of these drives including: Zip (100 MB per disk), Jaz (1 or 2 GB per disk), SyQuest (various sizes of disks including 40 MB and 230 MB), Bernoulli (230 MB), and others.

While there is clearly no industry standard for these removable disk drives, the Zip and Jaz drives (both created by Iomega) seem to be gaining wide popularity. Apple offers the Zip drive on most of the Macs it sells.

Which drives are best for you depends largely on what you want to spend and if you plan on sharing disks with anyone. Cost is largely determined by the storage capacity of the disks. Currently, the Zip drive costs about $120 with a 100 MB cartridge being available for about $15. The 1 GB version of the Jaz drive currently costs about $399 with 1 GB disks costing about $100. There are many more options than these two. Check your favorite Mac news sources to see what is available and how much it costs.

If you will be using the disks to transport data to other computers, you need to make sure that the drive you choose is compatible with those computers you intend to share your data with.

Removable disks drives also come in internal and external configurations, just as hard drives do.

Upgrading with CD-Recordable and CD-Rewritable

CD-Recordable(CD-R) and CD-Rewritable (CD-RW) drives enable you to store data on a CD. While you could use these drives similarly to a hard drive, they are more appropriate for archival or back-up purposes. Writing data to a CD is a relatively slow process and is more complicated that using other types of media.

You should consider adding a CD-R or CD-RW drive for backing up your system or for making CDs to distribute to other users. These drives are still somewhat expensive and will cost much more than hard or removable media drives. However, if you need to distribute data to others, these drives are ideal. Another advantage of CD media is that it will not degrade over time as all magnetic-based media does (hard or removable media disks).

Upgrading with Tape Drives

Tape drives are intended more for backing up and archiving rather than to be used as a mounted drive. There are various types of tape drives, including Digital Audio Tape (DAT), quarter inch, and other tape formats. Tapes tend to have large storage capacities, including 4 GB, 8 GB, and even larger.

Consider adding a tape drive as your primary back-up drive. You can get a good tape drive for $500 or less. Tapes range in price from $10 to $40, but the tapes can be used over and over again.

Understanding Processor Upgrades

Perhaps the ultimate upgrade is to replace the main processor of your computer with a later and greater one. The theory is that you get most of the performance of a new machine equipped with the latest and greatest processor at less cost than a new machine. Unfortunately, the cost of these upgrades is usually quite high relative to a new machine with which you also get faster and bigger drives, more RAM, and other updated components.

Generally, I don't think you will find upgrading your processor to make economic sense. You can usually purchase another Mac for only a slightly higher cost, and then you have two systems to use. The one case in which upgrading a processor may make sense is when there isn't a new Mac that offers a specific feature that you have to have. For example, the most PCI cards you can add to current Macs is three. Some older models allow you to add six. If you need more than three PCI cards, you may have no choice but to upgrade your current Mac.

However, if you feel that a processor upgrade will be the right choice for you, Apple offers a few upgrade cards for certain models of Macs. Several third parties also provide processor upgrade cards. Just make sure that any processor upgrade that you purchase is compatible with your particular computer (and any other upgrades that you have installed in it).

Upgrading PCI Cards

Apple has used an expandable architecture in its Macs for a number of years. In the past, this architecture was based on NuBus technology, which was only used on the Mac. Consequently, Mac NuBus cards were produced in relatively low quantities and were quite expensive when compared to similar expansion cards available for the PC. Shortly after the introduction of the PowerPC-based Macs, however, Apple switched to a PCI-based architecture—the standard in the PC world—which dramatically lowered the cost of adding capability to the Mac.

PCI cards are circuit boards that plug into PCI slots in the computer. There are two types of PCI cards used in Macs. The first type is the "standard" length cards, which are similar to those used on the PC. The second type is "short" (seven inch) card slots that can only accommodate shorter, nonstandard PCI cards.

Turning up the clock

There also are ways to improve the performance of the existing processor in your computer. These include various kinds of accelerators and clock speed boosters. You must match these types of upgrades with your specific computer model and processor type.

Some of these upgrades can cause the computer to operate differently than it was designed to operate. For example, increasing the clock speed at which your processor operates can make it run hotter, which can be a bad thing if it runs too hot. Unless you are very comfortable with the details of how your hardware works, I don't recommend "clocking" your processor.

Making movies

A number of Macs come with the capability to digitize video built into the system. Examples are the AV Macs and the Power Mac 8600, as well as some of the Power Mac 6500 configurations. There are optional G3 Mac configurations that come with AV capabilities also.

DVD-ROM is here

Soon, Macs will be equipped with DVD drives (DVD drives are already an option on G3 PowerBooks). To use DVD-ROM technology, your computer will need two major components: the DVD-ROM drive itself (which will be similar to a CD-ROM in size and hardware) and the Apple CD/DVD extension. The DVD-ROM drive works just like a CD-ROM drive, except that a DVD disc holds 10 times more data.

So is DVD-Video

DVD is also the next generation of home theater movie viewing. DVD movies offer superb picture and sound quality as well as lots of special features. You may want to be able to play DVD movies on your Mac (imagine playing a movie on your PowerBook while you are traveling!). In order for a Mac to play a DVD movie, it has to have a means to decode the MPEG-2 encoding with which DVD movies are produced. To upgrade existing Macs to be able to play DVD movies, you will have to add the DVD-ROM drive and, most likely, a PCI card to handle the decoding function. So keep an open PCI slot if you can!

G3 PowerBooks users can obtain a PC card that enables your PowerBook to play DVD movies.

Generally, Apple's mid-to-high end Macs have three full-length PCI slots. The lower end machines tend to have one or two short PCI slots. Mac clone makers often provided more expansion capability for their machines and provided as many as five or six PCI slots.

PCI cards can expand the capabilities of your Mac in several areas, including the following:

- **Graphics**. There are a variety of PCI cards that can improve graphics capabilities of your Mac. These cards can make your Mac be able to display more colors at higher resolutions, and they also provide 3D and 2D acceleration for improved graphics performance in many types of applications. There are also add-on TV tuner cards so that you can display TV on your Mac monitor while you are supposed to be working.

  Another benefit of an additional graphics card is that you can have two monitors connected to your Mac. There are several ways you can use multiple monitors; for example, you can display all the tool bars and palettes on one monitor, leaving the other dedicated to your document.

- **Capturing video**. There are several professional-level and hobbyist-level video capture boards. These PCI cards enable you to connect a video source to your Mac so that you can digitize your own videos.

- **Networking**. There are several different types of networking cards that can provide additional networking capabilities beyond the AppleTalk and Ethernet that are built into most Macs.

- **Running a PC**. There are also PCI cards that contain fully functional PCs so that you can have the best of both worlds: a Mac and a PC in the same box.

- **Connecting to peripherals**. Some cards enable you to make high-speed connections to peripheral devices. These include FireWire cards, which are primarily designed for very high-data requirements, such as digital video.

- **Other Functions**. There are other more specialized PCI cards that can be added to expand your Mac's capabilities.

There are a myriad of cards out there, and once you have identified the need for some additional capability, it may be a bit tough to sort through the available cards. As with other upgrades, you can go to the usual sources for reviews and other information to help you determine which card to purchase.

Evaluating Hardware Upgrades

As you evaluate potential hardware upgrades, there are several questions that you need to answer:

- What additional capabilities or features do I want to add to my computer?

  There can be at least two primary reasons for hardware upgrades: one is to provide your computer with capabilities it does not currently have (for example, the capability to display full-screen QuickTime movies or to capture digital video), and another is to improve an existing aspect of your machine (for example, increase the RAM available for faster and more stable applications).

  The answer to this question will determine the type of hardware upgrade that you will consider.

- What is the potential for expansion of my computer?

  Some models have lots of RAM and PCI slots, empty drives bays, and so on. Other models are already packed to the gills; in order to expand those models, you will have to add an external upgrade or replace some internal components. On other models, items such as RAM may already be "maxed out," in which case you will be unable to improve the machine via a hardware upgrade.

  This is the most important question to answer when considering hardware upgrades because the answer will determine whether it is even possible to accomplish the upgrade you are considering.

- What is the internal design of my computer?

  Many Mac and Mac clone models are designed for easy upgrades and anyone with basic skills can perform simple upgrades. Other models require a contortionist to be able to install upgrades.

The answer to this question will help you decide if performing the upgrade yourself is feasible, or if you will need an expert to do it for you.

- Can I take the upgrade with me when I change models?

There are certain upgrades, especially external drives, that you can attach to just about any Macintosh compatible computer. There are other upgrades (such as VRAM and RAM) that are likely to remain with the computer for which you purchase them.

If you are coming close to the time when you will replace your computer, it is often a good idea to delay internal hardware upgrades since they are often incompatible with new machines. Exceptions to this rule are PCI cards, which should be compatible for the foreseeable future.

- How much will the upgrade cost?

Some hardware upgrades can be expensive while others are relatively inexpensive. The cost will largely depend on the type of expansion you are considering. For example, adding a new drive will cost you several hundred dollars while upgrading the VRAM could cost less than $20.

- Should I upgrade my computer or replace it?

When you are considering a hardware upgrade, the machine for which you are considering is usually a year or two old. In the accelerated world of computer technology, this is considered ancient. Often, the type of capability that you are seeking with the upgrade will already be part of the latest and greatest Mac models. Most of the time, it is much more economical to purchase this capability as part of a new system than it is to purchase an upgrade (of course you have to factor in the entire cost of the new system rather than just comparing the cost of the upgrade as part of the new system).

This can be a very difficult question to answer. Some upgrades (such as processor upgrades) just don't make financial sense. Why pay around $1,000 for a new processor card when you could get the same processor, new drives, more

RAM, and so on for $1,500? Similarly, if you need multiple upgrades, say more RAM, more storage space, and a PCI card, the sum of the costs of the upgrades may be in the same ballpark as the cost of a new system.

When considering hardware upgrades, it is best to have a longer term view than just looking at the immediate future.

Upgrading your Mac's hardware, while it isn't the easiest proposition to contemplate, can significantly improve the capabilities and performance of your Mac. Just take your time figuring out what you need, and the rest of the process will probably go quite smoothly.

Using Mac OS 8.5
Appendices

A **Installing and Maintaining the Mac OS 805**

B **Working with PowerBooks 817**

C **Speaking Essential Mac Lingo 837**

Installing and Maintaining the Mac OS

Preparing to install Mac OS 8.5

Installing Mac OS 8.5 with the Easy
Install option

Installing Mac OS 8.5 with the
Custom Install option

Updating your System Folder

Installing system components

Installing the Mac OS

Mac OS 8.5 is made up of literally thousands of files. Despite
the number of files involved, it's easy to install Mac OS 8.5 on
your Mac. You can install everything you'll ever need (and then
some) with just a few clicks, customize your installation on a
file-by-file basis, or strike a balance between ease and customization.

Before you get started, there are a few steps that you can take to make it less likely that you'll find yourself tossing your Mac out of the nearest window. Again, it's not hard to install the Mac software, but it's a lot easier if you do a little preparation.

Making Sure That Your Mac Has Adequate Resources

Your Mac needs to have a powerful enough processor, enough RAM, and enough disk space to be able to run Mac OS 8.5. And a Mac that you thought was pretty snazzy might not have the resources to run Mac OS 8.5 and useful application programs at the same time. Before you crack the license-agreement seal on the Mac OS CD-ROM envelope, make sure that Mac OS 8.5 is for you by considering the following:

- **CPU requirements.** Your Mac must use a PowerPC chip in order to run Mac OS 8.5. If your Mac says PowerPC on the front, you're all set. If you have a G3 Mac or iMac, you are in even better shape.

- **RAM requirements.** Apple recommends at least 32 MB of RAM for Mac OS 8.5, but that is pushing it in my opinion (your Mac will run just fine on 32 MB, but you won't be able to run that many applications at the same time). I suggest that you make sure that your Mac has at least 64 MB of RAM before you consider Mac OS 8.5. RAM is currently inexpensive so you can upgrade your Mac to 64 MB of RAM or more for just a little money.

- **Disk Space Requirements:** A complete installation of all of the packages included in Mac OS 8.5 requires a huge amount of disk space—depending on the size of the disk that you install it on, you'll need at least 150 MB of free space.

Mac OS 8.5 floppies

Obviously, if your Mac does not have a CD-ROM drive, which is only the case for older PowerPC PowerBooks, you will have to either get Mac OS 8.5 floppies from Apple, or connect your PowerBook to a desktop Mac as a SCSI drive and run the installer from the desktop Mac. See Appendix B, "Working with PowerBooks" to learn how to use your PowerBook as an external SCSI drive.

Gathering Resources

Next, get all of your essential resources together:

- **System 8.5 CD-ROM.** Obviously, you'll need a copy of the system software. If you have a new Mac, a System 8.5 CD-ROM should have come with your machine; if your machine came with older system software, you'll need to buy the commercial distribution of Mac OS 8.5.

- **Alternate startup disk.** It's a good idea to make an emergency startup disk when you're installing the system—otherwise, you'll probably put it off until it's too late. If you have a ZIP or other removable media drive, copy your current System Folder on a Zip or other disk to use as an alternate startup disk. If you have multiple hard drives or partitions, you can install a System Folder on one of them. If you have a CD-ROM with a bootable System Folder on it, you can use that.

SEE ALSO

➤ *To learn how to use an alternate startup disk, see page 740*

- **System backup.** Make sure that you have the proper storage media—tape, removable disks, or whatever—for your backup system.

SEE ALSO

➤ *To learn how to create and maintain a backup, see Chapter 29, "Backing Up"*

Plugging in Your PowerBook

If you're installing your system on a PowerBook, be sure to plug it in so that it doesn't fall asleep or run low on batteries during the installation. (The installation will probably take at least half an hour, and it's disk- and CD-intensive, and hence battery-intensive.)

Recording MacTCP Info, if Necessary

If you're moving from a System 7.x to Mac OS 8.5, you may need to record information from the MacTCP control panel. Mac OS 8.5 uses a new control panel, called TCP/IP, and the installer will not migrate the settings from MacTCP to TCP/IP.

Recording MacTCP info

1. From the Apple menu, choose Control Panels.
2. If the Control Panels folder contains a TCP/IP control panel, you're done. Skip the rest of these steps.

3. If there is a MacTCP control panel, double-click it to open it.

4. Click the More button at the bottom of the control panel.

5. The Mac displays the MacTCP more info window. Press Command-Shift-3 to take a screen shot of this window.

6. Find the file called Picture 1 on your hard disk. (If you've taken more screen shots and haven't renamed them, the new screen shot may be called Picture 2 or Picture 5 or Picture 50 or whatever—look for the Picture file with the most recent modification date.

7. Rename the file *MacTCP settings* and save it where you can find it again—preferably on a floppy or a removable disk.

Restarting from an Alternate Startup Disk

You can't install system software on a disk that's currently being used as your startup disk. If you're installing Mac OS 8.5 on the disk that holds your current operating system—and that's the most likely case—it's easiest to start up from the Mac OS 8.5 installation CD-ROM.

Starting up from Mac OS 8.5 CD

1. Make sure that the Mac OS 8.5 CD is in your CD-ROM drive.

2. Restart your Mac.

3. As the Mac starts, hold down the C key. (After you see the "Welcome to MacOS" splash screen, you can let go of the C key.) When the desktop appears, you will see the Mac OS 8.5 CD as the startup disk.

Updating System Software

Chances are, your Mac will have *something* on it—Apple ships Mac with the operating system installed, so at the very least, your Mac should have operating system software. If you're using a machine that can support Mac OS 8.5, I assume that it's running System 7.x or 8.x, since System 7 is older than the oldest machines that can support 8.x.

Basically, it's OK to simply install Mac OS 8.5 over your current operating system. The installer does not erase files willy-nilly, and the basic rules are pretty simple:

- If the installer wants to create a file that doesn't already exist, it creates the new file without asking.

- If the installer want to create a file, but there's already a file in your System Folder with the same name, in a folder (or set of folders) with the same name(s), the installer compares the creation date on the old file with the creation date on the new file. If the file that it wants to install is newer, it replaces the old file without asking. If the file that it wants to create is older than the file that it replaces, the installer asks you (via a dialog box) which file you'd prefer to keep.

- The installer leaves alone files whose names don't compete with the names of the new files that it installs. Thus, if you have stuff of your own in your current System Folder (like commercial fonts or third-party extensions such as Retrospect Remote or Adobe Type Manager), your stuff will remain unmolested.

If you're updating to a new version of Mac OS 8.5 from the original MacOS 8.0 or 8.1, you can use the Update to Mac OS 8.x application (rather than the Install Mac OS 8.x application) on the Mac OS 8.5 installation CD-ROM. The updater application is much faster than the installer.

If you're updating to Mac OS 8.5 from System 7.x, you'll need to use the Install Mac OS 8.5 application, rather than the updater. (The updater application only works if an earlier version of Mac OS 8 has been installed.)

Installing Mac OS 8.5

You will use the Mac OS 8.5 Installer for the following tasks:

- **Installing a new operating system (System Folder).**
  When you do this, you end up with a brand-new System Folder. This is also called a *Clean Install*.

- **Installing an update**. If you choose to update your current System Folder, rather than replace it, you can use the Installer to install or update only those files that are needed (see the previous section for an explanation of how this works).

- **Install system components**. You can use the Mac OS 8.5 Installer to install specific parts of Mac OS 8.5. This is useful if you choose to do a custom install and later decide that you should have installed a particular technology. It is also useful because the Easy Install option may not install everything you need.

Performing a Clean Install

When you want to start from scratch, you should perform a clean install. This results in an "untarnished" System Folder for you to work with. After tweaking your System Folder when you add software, play with settings, and so on, you may find that it is easier to do a clean install than to try to undo things you have done. Other times, you may want to do a clean install when you are having lots of trouble with your system.

When you are doing a clean install, you have the following two options:

- **Easy Install**. With this option, the installer picks the software it thinks is best for your particular Mac. This is the option to use if you aren't very comfortable with individual technologies.

- **Custom Install**. When you have done a custom install, you select the software components that are installed. You should use this option if you feel comfortable with most of the Mac OS 8.5 technologies. Using a custom install, you can install only those resources that you are going to use.

You can perform a clean installation with either of these options.

Performing a clean install using the Easy Install option

1. Launch the Install Mac OS 8.5 Installer. You will see the Welcome screen that explains the four steps needed to install Mac OS 8.5 (see Figure A.1).

2. Click Continue.

3. Choose the disk on which you want the clean install performed. This does not have to be a hard disk. You can install Mac OS 8.5 on removable disks, such as ZIP or Jaz disks. When you choose a disk, the Installer will tell you if there is a system currently installed, how much disk space is available on that disk, and how much disk space will be required to install the options currently selected (see Figure A.2).

4. Click Options. You will see the Perform Clean Installation dialog.

5. Check the Perform Clean Installation check box and click OK.

6. Click Select when you return to the Select Destination dialog.

7. In the Important Information screen, read the text and when you are done, click Continue.

8. In the Software License Agreement window, read the license agreement and click Continue.

9. If you agree with the terms of the license, click Agree. (If you don't agree, you will exit the installer.). You will see the Install Software dialog (see Figure A.3).

FIGURE A.3

You begin the installation in earnest when you see the Install Software dialog.

Choosing options

If you click the Options button in the Install Software dialog (see Figure A.3), you can stop the Installer from updating the Apple hard disk drivers. If you uncheck the Create Installation Report check box, the Installer won't create a report explaining what files were installed. You should generally use both of these options.

10. Click the Start button. You'll see a dialog warning you that all applications except the Installer must be quit to continue the installation.

11. Click Continue. The Installer will quit all open applications. The drive will check the drive that you choose to install the software on. It will also update the disk drivers. You will also see an estimate of the time it will take to complete the installation. Then it will complete the installation. When the installer finishes the installation, you will need to restart your Mac. If the disk you installed Mac OS 8.5 on is your startup disk, it will start up from the new startup disk.

If you want to customize your system, you can use the custom option. This enables you to choose which parts of the system that are installed.

Performing a clean install by using the Custom Install option

1. Complete steps 1-9 in the previous step-by-step.

2. Click Customize. You will see Custom Installation and Removal dialog (see Figure A.4). On the left side of the window, you will see the components that you can install. For

each component, you can choose the Installation mode pop-up menu. Your choices are Recommended Installation, Customized Installation, or Customized Removal. If you choose Customized Installation, you will see a list of features that you can install for that component (see Figure A.5). Wherever you see the button with an "i," you can click it to see additional information about that item (see Figure A.6).

Removing components

You can remove particular components from your system by choosing the Customized Removal option and then selecting each component and feature that you want to remove.

FIGURE A.4

You can use the Custom Installation and Removal dialog to choose which components are installed in your system.

FIGURE A.5

You can select custom options from within the installer when you choose the Customized Installation option from the Installation mode pop-up menu.

FIGURE A.6

You can press the "i" buttons to read information about an item.

3. Check each box next to the software component that you want to install. Choose Customized Installation from the Installation mode pop-up menu.

4. In the Features Installation dialog, check the check box next to the feature that you want to install. If the feature has an expansion triangle next to it, there are subfeatures that you can choose to install (see Figure A.7). These work just like the component install options, so check the check box next to an item to install it. If you want to install all of the sub-features for a feature, check the check box next to it. If you want to install particular subfeatures, expand the feature and check the check box next to each subfeature that you want to install.

FIGURE A.7

Some features that you choose to install have subfeatures that you can choose from.

5. Continue choosing software components and customizing them until you have selected all the options that you want to have installed.

6. Click Start. The installer will check the destination disk and then update its drivers. After that, it will begin to install the software you have selected. You will see an estimated time remaining in the bottom of the progress dialog.

7. Click the Start button. You see a dialog warning you that all applications except the Installer must be quit to continue the installation.

8. Click Continue. The Installer will quit all open applications. The drive will check the drive that you choose to install the software on. It will also update the disk drivers. You will also see an estimate of the time it will take to complete the installation. Then it will complete the installation. When the installer finishes the installation, you will need to restart your Mac. If the disk from which you installed Mac OS 8.5 is in your startup disk, it will start up from the new startup disk.

Performing an Update to Your System

The steps to perform an update to your existing System Folder are similar to those needed to perform a clean install.

Updating your System Folder

1. Launch the Mac OS Installer.
2. Click Continue in the Welcome screen.
3. In the Select Destination dialog, choose the disk that contains the System Folder that you want to update and then click Options.
4. Uncheck the Perform Clean Installation check box and click OK.
5. Click Select. You will see a dialog from which you can choose to Reinstall or Add/Remove software. Click Add/Remove.
6. Use the step-by-steps for the Clean Install options to do the update. Instead of adding a new System Folder, the Installer will add the appropriate files to the existing System Folder. (See the earlier section explaining how this works.)

Installing System Components

If you find that you need to install a component or feature after you have installed your System Folder, you can use the Mac OS Installer to add only that item to your system.

Adding a component to your system

1. Launch the Mac OS Installer.
2. Click Continue in the Welcome screen.

3. In the Select Destination dialog, choose the disk that contains the System Folder to which you want to install components and then click Options.

4. Uncheck the Perform Clean Installation check box and click OK.

5. Click Select. You will see a dialog from which you can choose to Reinstall or Add/Remove software. Click Add/Remove.

6. Use the steps after step 3 for the Custom Clean Install to install the components. Instead of adding a new System Folder, the Installer will add the appropriate files to the existing System Folder. After you restart your Mac, the components and features you added will be available on your system.

You won't need to use the Mac OS 8.5 Installer very often, but being familiar with the different ways you can use it will help you keep your Mac in top operating form, and you can expand its capabilities as you need to add system components.

Working with PowerBooks

Managing your PowerBook's energy

Using the PowerBook Control Strip

Using the track pad

Using Location Manager to set up
and use different PowerBook
configurations

Synchronizing files

Protecting your PowerBook

Computing on the Run

PowerBooks give you the power to be productive no matter where you are; Mac OS 8.5 running on a PowerBook is pretty much the same thing as Mac OS 8.5 on a desktop Mac. Most of the Mac's features are exactly the same, and you can use the techniques and technology that were described in the earlier parts of the book to get the most out of your mobile Mac. However, there are a few areas in which using a PowerBook is different than using a desktop Mac. In this appendix, you will learn about the differences between using a PowerBook and a desktop Mac.

Managing Energy

The biggest difference between using a PowerBook and a desktop Mac is that with a PowerBook you do not have to be connected to a power source since the PowerBook has its own internal power supply (its batteries). While this is excellent in terms of freeing your Mac from having to be close to a power supply, it presents some problems as well. As much as battery technology has improved over the past few years, batteries still don't last all that long. If you want to maximize the amount of working time on your Mac while you are on the move, then you need to be able to make your Mac's energy supply last as long as possible. Making your Mac's energy last isn't something that you can ignore; you have to think about it and take the steps needed to reduce your Mac's power usage to the minimum amount needed to do what you need to do.

There are several areas of Mac OS 8.5 on a PowerBook that will enable you to manage its energy use:

- **Energy Saver control panel**. You use the Energy Saver control panel to put your PowerBook to sleep whenever it is not doing work. You also use this control panel to reduce the amount of processing power your PowerBook uses while it is operating on battery power.

- **Control Strip modules**. There are several PowerBook-specific Control Strip modules that provide battery information, enable you to spin down your hard disk, and so on.

- **Desktop display**. When you run Mac OS 8.5 on a PowerBook, the condition of the battery is indicated by the icon on the right side of the menu bar and in the PowerBook's Control Strip (see Figure B.1).

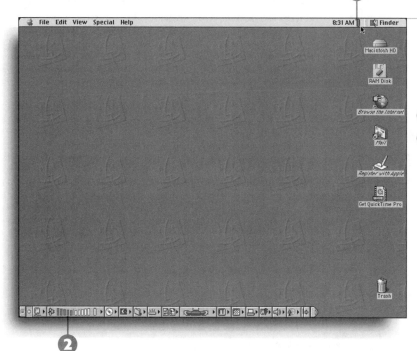

FIGURE B.1

The PowerBook's battery icon and the Battery Monitor Control Strip module tell you how you are doing power-wise.

1. Battery icon
2. Battery Monitor Module

- **Memory control panel**. You can use the Memory control panel to set up a RAM disk. This helps you conserve power by reducing the amount of time that your hard disk is being used.

- **Battery Reconditioning utility**. This utility exercises your batteries to prevent them from developing a memory and thus not being able to hold a full charge.

More good reasons to sleep

Another benefit of putting your PowerBook to sleep (as opposed to shutting it down) is that it wakes up a lot faster than it starts up. Also, when you start your Mac, it uses a lot of power. Putting it to sleep instead of shutting it down will help you squeeze a few more minutes of work out of it.

Power used during Sleep mode

In the Sleep mode, about the only thing going on that requires power is the RAM. In order to store information, a small amount of electricity has to be applied to the RAM chips. Information in RAM is retained during sleep; this requires a very small amount of power.

Putting Your PowerBook to Sleep

Using the power-conserving Sleep mode on a desktop Mac is pretty much an option. It is good for the environment as well as for your electric bill, but if your desktop Mac never goes to sleep, you won't have any problems. However, on a PowerBook, sleep is an essential power conservation tool.

The Sleep mode causes almost all activity on your Mac to cease, thus almost all power consumption is stopped. You should be conscious of those times that you are not using your PowerBook and put it to sleep as soon as you can (one of the fastest ways is to hold down the Command and Option keys while you press the Power key). Just about every minute that your PowerBook is in Sleep mode is another minute that you will have it available for work.

Like the desktop Mac, you can set your PowerBook to go to sleep after a defined period of inactivity passes. And just like a desktop Mac, you use the Energy Saver control panel to define the period of inactivity. The Energy Saver control panel on a PowerBook has additional controls that you can use to manage your battery usage.

On a PowerBook, there are three sleep items to consider:

- **Sleep**. This is the same as the sleep option on a desktop Mac. It causes all activity on the Mac to cease.

- **Display dimming**. This option causes the display on your PowerBook to dim. This saves a considerable amount of energy so you may want to have your screen dim after a small period of inactivity.

- **Hard disk spindown**. This option causes the hard disk to stop turning. You can't use a disk while it is not turning, but you can use a RAM disk to work off in order to keep your hard drive spun down.

Another difference is that you can have different energy saving settings for different situations. For example, you probably aren't as concerned with saving energy when your PowerBook is plugged in; however, when you are running off your batteries, you need to save all the energy you can. The PowerBook Energy

Saver control panel enables you to set different energy saving properties for each condition. Your PowerBook will automatically switch between them (for example, when it senses that you are connected to the power adapter, it uses the Power Adapter energy saving settings).

Setting energy saving options

1. Open the Energy Saver control panel (see Figure B.2). You will see some additional features of the PowerBook's Energy Saver control panel, including the Advanced Settings button and the Settings for the pop-up menu.

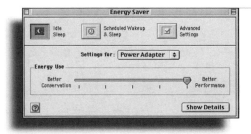

2. Choose the condition for which you want to set the energy saving features from the Settings for pop-up menu. If you want to have the whole system go into the Sleep mode at the same time, set the Energy Use slider at the sleep interval you want to use.

3. If you want the display and hard disk to have a different sleep period, click Show Details. You will see separate sliders for the display and the hard disk.

4. Check the "Separate timing for display dimming" check box and set the slider to the period of inactivity after which you want the monitor to dim.

5. Check the "Separate timing for hard disk spindown" check box and set the slider for a period of inactivity after which the hard disk will go into its sleep mode.

6. Close the control panel. When the specified time periods pass, the monitor will be dimmed and the hard disk will spin down. You can wake the PowerBook up by moving the mouse or pressing the spacebar.

Where is the PowerBook control panel?

Under Mac OS 8.5, most of the features that were previously part of the PowerBook control panel are in the Energy Saver control panel.

FIGURE B.2

The Energy Saver control panel enables you to have your Mac sleep after a predefined interval of time.

Unplugging PC cards and external drives

When you are using a PowerBook with battery power, you should get in the habit of unplugging anything from it that you aren't using. For example, if you have a PC card networking card, remove it from the slot if you are not connected to a network. If you have an external drive that draws its power from your PowerBook's batteries, disconnect the drive when you aren't using it (shut down your PowerBook when connecting or disconnecting a drive).

Any peripheral that uses your PowerBook as its power supply has the potential to use its battery power, even if you aren't using the peripheral. It is good practice to ensure that such peripherals can't use your PowerBook's power by disconnecting them when not in use.

Reducing Your Processing Power and Other Advanced Energy Saving Techniques

Your PowerBook's process requires more power at its peak performance so performance and power use are always a trade-off. In order to have your PowerBook use less power, you can also have it use less of its processor's capability. You can also have your PowerBook conserve energy by shutting down PC cards and turning off the display among other things. You use the Advanced Settings button to access these options.

Changing your PowerBook's advanced energy saving settings

1. Open the Energy Saver control panel.

2. Click Advanced Settings. You will see the Advanced Settings pane of the control panel (see Figure B.3).

3. Choose the condition for which you want to set the advanced options by using the "Settings for" pop-up menu (choose Battery or Power Adapter).

4. If you connect your PowerBook to a network, the connections will be terminated when the PowerBook goes to sleep; check the "Reconnect to servers on wakeup" check box if you want your PowerBook to automatically reconnect to the network when it wakes up.

5. Check the "Remember my passwords" check box if you do not want to have to enter the password you need to reconnect to the network. If you are the only one who can access

your PowerBook, use this option. If other people may be able to access your PowerBook, leave this unchecked, and you will have to manually enter your passwords in order to reconnect to the network.

6. If you use your PowerBook for telephony functions (such as an answering machine), check the "Wake up when the modem detects a ring" check box.

7. Check the "Allow processor cycling" check box if you want the processor to run in a reduced power mode when you are not using it. The disadvantage of using this setting is that it will take your PowerBook longer to wake up.

8. Check the "Turn off the PowerBook display instead of dimming it" check box if you want the display to shut off rather than being dimmed, but it does save more energy than having the display only dim. The disadvantage of this option is that it takes longer for the PowerBook to wake up if the display is turned off rather than dimmed.

9. Any installed PC cards (such as a modem card) require power from the PowerBook to operate; check the "Turn off power to inactive PC Cards" check box to cut off power to PC cards when they are not in use. This will slow down tasks that involve a PC card because it will have to be turned on, but you should use this option when you are running on the battery.

10. Check the "Reduce processor speed" check box if you want to run your PowerBook's processor at a slower speed. This causes your PowerBook to require less power, but it also slows down your PowerBook's speed.

11. Use the Settings for pop-up menu to select the other operating condition (Battery or Power Adapter) and repeat steps 4 through 10.

12. Close the control panel. Your energy saving settings will take effect.

You need to evaluate your own PowerBook use to determine which advanced settings to use, but I can make two generalizations. When running on the Power Adapter, consider leaving all of the advanced settings off, except for the "Reconnect to servers on wakeup" option (also use the "Remember my passwords" option if your PowerBook is in a secure location). Since you are plugged into a power source, there is no real reason to use the other options, and since they reduce the speed at which your PowerBook works, they do have a penalty associated with them. When running from battery power, use most or all of the advanced options to maximize battery life.

Dimming the Screen

Control panel?

Depending on the model of PowerBook you use, you may also be able to use a control panel to adjust the brightness and contrast of your screen. But if you have hardware controls, there is no reason to mess around with a control panel.

Contrast

As you adjust the brightness of your screen, you can also adjust the contrast to see if you will find a dimmer screen easier to see with a different level of contrast.

One of the largest users of power on your PowerBook is the screen. The brighter the screen, the easier it is to read, but the more power it uses. When you are operating on battery power, you should keep your screen's brightness as low as is comfortable for you to see what is on the screen.

To turn down your screen's brightness, use the rocker switch on the face of your PowerBook. The Brightness button usually is marked with an icon that looks like the sun (a ball with rays coming off it).

Spinning Down the Hard Disk

Another large drain on your batteries is your hard disk. It takes a significant amount of energy to spin the hard drive and to read data from it and write data to it. However, there is no need to have the hard disk spinning when you are not using it. You can cause it to spin down (in other words, to be turned off) when you are not writing data to it or reading data from it. This works because your Mac stores most of the information it uses in RAM; it only reads from and writes to the hard disk when a program is opening or when it is accessing some information from the disk and when you save or open a file. You can spin the drive down whenever you aren't using it to save energy. When your Mac needs it, it will spin up again.

Causing the hard drive to spin down is easy—just click the HD Spin Down button on the Control Strip and choose Spin Down Hard Disk from the pop-up menu (see Figure B.4). No need to restart the hard disk because your PowerBook will restart it when it is needed. One thing to keep in mind is that it does take a few seconds for the hard disk to become usable after it has been spun down. So you should only spin it down when you aren't likely to be using it for a little while. You can use a RAM disk to keep your hard disk spun down as long as possible (see the next section for details).

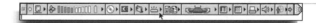

FIGURE B.4

You can use the HD Spin Down control on the Control Strip to shut your hard disk down to save energy.

Using a RAM Disk

You can use a RAM disk to greatly reduce your PowerBook's energy consumption while you continue to work. A RAM disk is an area of RAM that is used to store data just like a hard drive. Rather than reading data from and writing data to your hard disk, your PowerBook uses its RAM to store the data instead. Since your PowerBook doesn't have to store data on the hard drive, it can remain in the spun-down condition in which it uses almost no energy. You should consider using a RAM disk whenever you are using your PowerBook on battery power.

SEE ALSO

➤ *To learn how to set up and use a RAM disk, see page 332*

Conditioning Your Batteries

Some types of rechargeable batteries have a *memory*. This is a physical phenomenon that happens when a battery is recharged before it has fully discharged. After this happens a number of times, the battery is unable to receive a full charge, and thus doesn't last as long as it did when it was new. If the memory is severe enough, the battery may become unusable.

Fortunately, newer PowerBooks that use Lithium Ion batteries do not suffer from memory problems. Only older PowerBooks that use Nickel Cadmium (NiCad) batteries are affected. With PowerBooks that have NiCad batteries that are affected by memory problems, Apple provides the Reconditioner utility that fully discharges the battery and then recharges it again. You should use this utility on your battery every month or so.

Check the documentation that came with your PowerBook to see which type of batteries it uses. If you purchased the PowerBook within the last year or so, you probably have Lithium Ion batteries.

Using the Battery Recondition to recondition your PowerBook NiCad battery

1. Plug your PowerBook into a wall outlet.
2. Find and open the Battery Recondition application.
3. Read the explanatory text screen and click OK.
4. Read the text in the next information screen, and if you are ready to proceed, click Recondition.
5. Click OK in the warning screen. The screen will change to a battery symbol that will bounce around your screen. The PowerBook will exercise itself until it runs the battery all the way down. Then it will recharge your battery for you.

Using the PowerBook's Control Strip

There are certain Control Strip modules that are only installed on PowerBooks; you have already seen one of them (to spin down your hard drive). Your PowerBook Control Strip may have all or only some of the following controls (see Figure B.5):

FIGURE B.5

The PowerBook Control Strip contains some modules that are specific to PowerBooks.

1 Battery Monitor

2 Energy Settings

3 HD Spin Down

4 Media Bay

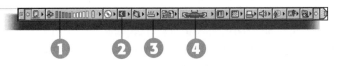

- **Battery Monitor**. This module shows you the status of your batteries; for example, if they are being charged and how much power is left in them.
- **Media Bay**. If your PowerBook has bays that can support different components, this control enables you to manage the device that is installed in the bays. For example, if you have a battery in your left media bat and a CD-ROM drive in the right bay, you can replace the CD-ROM drive in the

right bay with a second battery. You can use the Media Bay button to determine the status of the devices installed in your PowerBook.

- **Energy Settings**. You can use this button to quickly manage the energy use of your PowerBook. The options you see are the following: Sleep Now (puts your PowerBook to sleep immediately), Better Performance (maximizes the processor speed and other settings), Better Conservation (reduces processor speed and other settings), and Open Energy Saver Control Panel (which you learned about earlier in this chapter).

- **HD Spin Down**. You can use this control to cause your hard disk to spin down.

- **Video Mirroring**. If you hook your PowerBook to an external monitor, you can use this control to display the same information on two monitors. It is used for the same purpose as the PowerBook Display control panel.

Using the Track Pad

Apple PowerBooks use a track pad as the primary control device. Using a track pad is straightforward—just place your finger on the pad and move it to move the cursor. You can also set the track pad so that you can "click the mouse button" by tapping on the track pad. This makes working with a track pad more efficient.

Configuring a track pad

1. Open the Trackpad control panel (see Figure B.6).

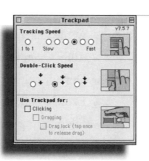

What you see may not be what you get

You may or may not see all of the Control Strip modules listed here on your PowerBook because you will see only modules that can be used on your particular PowerBook. For example, if your PowerBook does not have a media bay, you won't see the Media Bay control.

Moisture and the track pad

Track pads are somewhat sensitive to moisture. If your skin is extremely dry, the track pad may not register your finger movements very accurately. If your finger is moist, the track pad may be uncontrollable (this can happen if you are drinking a cold beverage while you are working with your PowerBook).

FIGURE B.6
The Trackpad control panel enables you to configure your track pad.

2. Set the Tracking Speed with the radio buttons. This determines how fast the cursor moves relative to your finger movements.

3. Set the double-click rate of the buttons (not the track pad itself) with the Double-Click Speed radio buttons.

4. If you want to be able to tap your track pad to "click" the mouse button, check the Clicking check box.

5. If you want to be able to drag things by pressing your finger on the track pad, check the Dragging check box. When you point to something and tap your finger twice rapidly (once to select the item, once to start the drag), it will be selected and placed in the drag mode. It will move with your finger. When you release pressure, the item will be dropped.

6. Check the Drag lock check box if you only want the item to be dropped when you tap the track pad again (rather than having to continue to press your finger on the pad).

7. Close the control panel.

Managing Your Location

It's not just for locations

You can also define configurations for different people who use your Mac. For example, you can have a configuration for you, one for your spouse, and one for your children. Each person's preferences and settings can be quickly restored by choosing his or her configuration in the Location Manager.

Some of your settings are dependent upon your location. These include the phone numbers that you dial to connect to the Internet, your time and date settings, and so on. Using the Location Manager, you can define sets of configurations for many areas of Mac OS 8.5 and then switch between those configurations easily. This is extremely useful when you are traveling with your PowerBook, especially if you visit the same places repeatedly.

You can have any or all of the following as part of a location set:

- AppleTalk and TCP/IP
- Auto-Open Items (in the Startup Items folder)
- Default Printer
- Extension Set (using Extensions Manager)
- File Sharing State (all of your File Sharing settings)
- Internet Set

- Remote Access (such as the number Remote Access calls)
- Sound Level
- Time Zone

Before you configure a location, you need to configure your PowerBook as you want it to be when it uses that location. Set any item in the previous list that you want to be part of the location.

Configuring locations with Location Manager

1. Open the Location Manager application that is in the Control Panels folder (you can also use the Location Manager button on the Control Strip).

2. Choose New Location from the File menu.

3. Name your location and click Save. You will return to the Location Manager window and will see the various settings that you can configure as part of a location (see Figure B.7).

FIGURE B.7
The Location Manager enables you to save the setting shown in the Settings pane as part of each location.

4. Click the check box next to an area of settings that you want to be part of the location. You will see information relating to those settings in the Values pane.

5. Click Edit if you want to change the settings for that area. If you have to use a control panel for that area, you will be able to open it from within Location Manager. Some areas require that you edit them from outside of Location Manager.

6. When you are finished editing the settings, click Apply to apply them to the location (they will overwrite the current settings).

No Control Strip?

If you don't use the Control Strip, you can open Location Manager and choose a location from the Current Location pop-up menu.

7. To learn more about an area, select it and click Get Info. Click OK when you are done reading about it.

8. Repeat steps 4-7 for each area that you want to be set by the location.

9. When you are done defining a location, press Command-S to save it.

10. Quit Location Manager.

After you have your configurations established, it is simple to switch among those applications.

Changing configurations with Location Manager

1. Click the Location Manager control on the Control Strip.

2. Choose the location that you want to use from the pop-up menu. You will see a window showing you the progress of all the settings being changed to the location's values.

3. If the location change involves extensions, control panels, or other components loaded into the system, you will have to restart your PowerBook by clicking Restart. If not, click the OK button to close the window.

Synchronizing Files

You will often transfer files from your desktop Mac to your PowerBook before you go on a trip. While you are away, you can work on those files and create other ones. When you return to your desktop machine, you have to manually drag files from one machine to the other to make sure that you have the latest versions where you need them. If you use more than a few files, it can be very confusing trying to remember which versions of which files need to be moved where. That is where Mac OS 8.5's File Synchronization utility comes in. With it, you can identify folders on your desktop Mac and PowerBook that should be kept in synch. The Macs will handle making sure that each folder contains the latest and greatest versions of your files. No more having to hunt around for the files you need to move from one machine to the other.

Synchronizing folders

1. Open the File Synchronization application that is in the Control Panels folder (see Figure B.8).

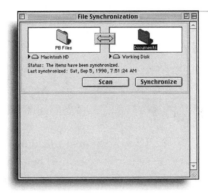

FIGURE B.8

Using the File Synchronization application, you can keep two folders synchronized; this is very useful when you have the same files on a PowerBook and a desktop Mac.

2. Double-click the folder icon in the upper-left pane of the window.

3. Maneuver to a folder that you want to synchronize; you can choose a folder on your PowerBook and click Select. You will see the folder you selected in the upper left pane of the window.

4. Double-click the folder icon in the upper right pane of the window.

5. Maneuver to a folder that you want to synchronize with the folder in the left pane; you can choose a folder on your desktop Mac (assuming that you are networked in some way) and click Select. You will see the folder you selected in the upper right pane of the window. The double arrow in the center of the window will become active, as will the Scan and Synchronize buttons.

6. Click the Scan button. You will see a list of items in the folders that are not the same (see Figure B.9).

7. Click Synchronize. The files will be copied between the folders until they both contain the same versions of the files. (You don't have to scan the folders first; you can jump straight to this step if you want to.) When the process is complete, you will see a message saying so (click OK to clear it).

Drag and drop

You can also drag a folder onto either pane to select it.

Removable disks

The folders you used can be on a removable disk as well. Can you say back up?

The folder on the right contains a file with the left-facing arrow next to it; this needs to be moved to the folder on the left to synchronize the two folders.

The arrow

You can click on the large arrow between the folders to set the direction of the synchronization.

Help

Use Balloon Help to learn more about File Synchronization.

8. Use the Synchronize menu to define how you want the synchronization to be done. For example, if you want files to only be moved from one folder to the other, choose Left to Right or Right to Left.

9. Use the Preferences command on the Edit menu to set other Synchronization preferences, such as when an error should be generated (see Figure B.10).

FIGURE B.10

You can use the Preferences command to configure File Synchronization

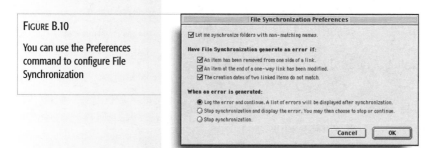

10. Quit File Synchronization when you are done.

Protecting Your PowerBook

Since you will often be using your PowerBook in areas that you don't control, it is a good idea to protect your PowerBook. You need to protect your PowerBook in two ways: physical security and data security.

Regarding the physical security of your PowerBook, there is one paramount rule: keep your eyes on your PowerBook. If you aren't looking at it, it may grow legs and walk away. Let's face it, PowerBooks are really cool precisely because they can be moved around. That makes them prime targets for theft. You may be able to use various locks and cables when your PowerBook is at a working location, but when you are on the move, make sure that you have a good grasp on your PowerBook at all times. For example, if you carry your PowerBook in a bag, when you sit down, wrap the shoulder strap of the bag around your leg so that no one can move it without your knowledge.

You also need to be concerned with the data that is on your PowerBook. You probably have information on it that you need to protect. You can use the Password Security control panel to add a password to your PowerBook.

Protecting your PowerBook with a password

1. Open the Password Security control panel (see Figure B.11).

> **Learn from someone who carries a purse**
>
> Carrying a laptop bag around is about like carrying a purse. If you know people who carry purses, ask them for tips on how they keep their purses safe.

FIGURE B.11

You can protect the data on your PowerBook with the Password Security control panel.

2. Click Setup.

3. Type the password you want to use in the "Type new password" field.

4. Verify it by typing it again in the "Retype new password" field.

5. If you want to see a hint to help you remember your password, type it in the "Hint for remembering the password" field.

6. If you want the password to be required each time your Mac wakes up from sleep, check the "Also ask when waking from sleep" check box. This is a good idea if you will be working in an area where other people might access your PowerBook when you step away from it.

7. Click OK. You will have to enter your password and click OK to enable the protection.

8. Close the control panel. The next time you restart your PowerBook, you will have to enter the password to get it to start up.

Using Your PowerBook as a Hard Disk

Installing software

One good use for a PowerBook as a SCSI drive is to install software on it, especially if you don't have a CD-ROM on your PowerBook. You can select the PowerBook drive from installer applications just as you can any other SCSI drive connected to your desktop Mac. If there are system components installed, they will be installed in the startup drive's System Folder, rather than the PowerBook's. You will need to manually install any system software in the PowerBook's System Folder.

No security

To use a PowerBook as a SCSI device, you have to disable the Password Security feature first.

To get the maximum speed of data flow between your desktop Mac and your PowerBook, you may want to be able to connect the PowerBook to your desktop Mac as a SCSI disk. When you do this, the volumes on your PowerBook are mounted on your desktop just like the other devices that are part of your system. The advantage of this is that you can move data between the devices *fast*. The disadvantage is that you can't use the PowerBook while it is a SCSI drive; it acts just like an external drive.

To connect your PowerBook to a desktop Mac as a SCSI drive, you need a special cable, called an *HD-30 cable*. It has a square connector that fits into the PowerBook's square SCSI port. There are several different PowerBook SCSI cables available, so make sure you ask specifically for the one that enables you to use your PowerBook as a SCSI drive when you order it.

Once you have the cable, you need to set the SCSI drive number of the PowerBook. Open the PowerBook SCSI Disk Mode application in the Control Panels folder (see Figure B.12). Use the ID radio buttons to set the ID number of your PowerBook when it acts like a SCSI drive. Make sure that you set a number that is not already in use on your desktop Mac. If you do, you won't be able to start up with the PowerBook attached. (You can use the Devices and Volumes of the Apple System Profiler to see what SCSI ID numbers are being used.) Close the application when you are done.

Using a PowerBook as a SCSI disk

1. Shut down your Mac and all SCSI devices connected to it.

2. Connect the HD-30 cable to the PowerBook and your desktop Mac (or SCSI chain).

3. Turn on all SCSI devices connected to your Mac, including the PowerBook.

4. Start up your Mac. As the Mac starts, the PowerBook screen will have the SCSI symbol bouncing around it. After your system starts, you will see the PowerBook's drives mounted on the desktop Mac's desktop. You can use the PowerBook's drives just like any other SCSI drive.

5. When you are done using the PowerBook as a drive, shut everything down again (you will need to use the reset button on the PowerBook to shut it down).

6. Disconnect the PowerBook's SCSI cable from the PowerBook and the desktop Mac.

7. Restart everything. Your PowerBook will become a PowerBook again.

Networking without Wires

Most PowerBooks are capable of using Infrared networking. This makes it possible to connect to networks, printers, and other computers by simply setting your PowerBook next to the Infrared receiver on the device to which you want to connect. To use Infrared networking, you must have the following components:

- **Infrared capable PowerBook**. Many, but not all, PowerBooks are capable of infrared networking. Some require an upgrade to be able to use Infrared networking though. Check the documentation that came with your PowerBook to see if Infrared is supported on yours.

- **Infrared receiver**. You need to have an infrared receiver installed on the device to which you want to connect. This may be a networked computer, printer, or other device.

Viva iMac!

The iMac has a built-in Infrared port which makes it an ideal compliment to your PowerBook.

- **Infrared control panel**. This control panel is installed by default on Mac PowerBooks.

After all of the components are installed, you can use the Infrared control panel to configure the way the connection works (see Figure B.13). To connect your PowerBook to the network, you simply need to be in the line of sight of the receiver, no wires needed!

FIGURE B.13

The Infrared control panel controls how your PowerBook connects to other infrared capable devices.

Speaking Essential Mac Lingo

Understanding Mac and computer terms

A

Acrobat　Adobe Acrobat is an application/technology that enables you to publish electronic documents so that people can view those documents as you designed them—without having to have the same applications, fonts, or even the computer platform that you use. All that is required to view Acrobat files is the free Acrobat reader. Acrobat files are very common on the Internet and have the extension .pdf.

Active (application or window)　The active application or window is the one that is frontmost on the screen and is the one with which you are currently working. Active windows have horizontal lines in their title bars. Only one window can be active at a time.

ActiveX　Active X is Microsoft's technology that enables applications to be run from remote sites independent of the type of computer on which it is run. ActiveX is a competitor to JAVA. ActiveX is an underlying technology for many of Microsoft's applications, especially its Internet applications.

ADB   (Apple Desktop Bus) This is the type of connection that you use to attach a mouse, keyboard, and other input devices to the computer. The Mac is the only platform that uses ADB technology. ADB will be replaced by USB; the iMac is the first Macintosh that does not have an ADB port.

Alias   An alias is a "pointer" file that you can create to help you organize your computer. An alias acts just like the "real" file; for example, when you double-click on an alias, the original file is opened. The advantage of using aliases is that you can make files easily accessible without moving them from their original locations; you can also have several aliases that point to the same file. Alias files are very small, so having lots of them is not likely to consume much space.

Aliasing   Aliasing involves creating the jagged edges associated with a bitmapped image.

Allocated memory   Allocated memory is that portion of your computer's RAM that is set aside for a particular application (including the system software). When the application is launched, the allocated memory block is opened and can only be used for that application.

Alpha release   A version of software that is used during its development. Alpha versions are produced very early in the development process. You usually will not use alpha versions—access is frequently limited to the software publisher and to a target group of developers.

Anti-alias   This technique involves smoothing out the rough edges of an image or font.

Appearance control panel   A control panel that enables you to customize certain aspects of your Mac's interface including the desktop, interface elements, and sounds. The Appearance control panel also enables you to set up and use desktop themes.

Apple Applet Runner   This enables your Mac to run JAVA applets.

Apple menu   The Apple menu is an organizational tool for you to use to make your most commonly accessed files easy to open. There are also certain items available on the Apple menu as a default condition (for example, an alias to the Control Panels folder).

AppleGuide   The technology that your Mac uses to provide online help. In addition to providing information, AppleGuide can also show you how to perform tasks and even do some of those tasks for you.

AppleScript   The Mac's built-in scripting language that can be used to automate many processes and tasks. AppleScript is very powerful, but its language does take a bit of effort to learn (even though it is perhaps the most English-like scripting/programming/language around). Most Mac users will be better off running the AppleScripts that are provided as part of the Mac OS and using a macro utility such as QuicKeys to create their own macros.

Applet   An Applet is a program written in an independent language, for example, JAVA, that executes within an HTML document displayed by a World Wide Web browser without requiring the application and/or language that created it.

Application   An application is software that enables you to perform some task (e.g., word processing, Web browsing, and so on). It is the same thing as a program.

Application heap   This is the amount of memory consumed by an application.

ASCII   (American Standard Code for Information Interchange, pronounced ask-ee) Computers don't know what letters or numbers are; they recognize only bits of information, such as zeros and ones. ASCII is a binary code that represents characters. It enables computers to display, transmit, and print textual information.

AV Macs   AV Macs are Mac or clone computers that have additional audio-visual capabilities. Usually, this means that you can digitize video on the computer. The first AV Macs were the Centris/Quadra 660AV and 840AV, two of the most popular models ever.

B

Balloons   Balloons are an online help feature, enabling you to see balloons that contain helpful information on an item to which you are pointing with the cursor.

Beta release   A beta release is a version of an application that is being used for development. Companies use the beta version of software to perform testing. Some beta versions are widely available while others are tightly controlled.

Binhex   Binhex is the encoding scheme that is used to prepare most Mac files which are sent over the Internet.

Bitmapping   Bitmapping is the process by which information (bits) are translated and appear on the monitor (they are mapped to the monitor).

Bitmapped images   Bitmapped images are images that are created by mapping data to individual pixels on the computer screen. Individual objects in a bitmapped image cannot be edited, as opposed to vector based images in which individual objects can be manipulated.

Bug fixes   Bugs are unforeseen flaws in applications that lead to errors and other problems. Bug fixes are minor releases of applications that are supposed to fix the bugs.

Bus   Bus refers to the interface to which devices are attached in order to be able to communicate with the rest of your Mac. You can have more than one bus. For example, some Mac models have an internal SCSI bus that is separate from the external one. Every component uses a bus of one sort or another to transfer data.

C

Cache   A cache is a storage area to which data is written. There are lots of places on your Mac that are used to cache data (cache is both a noun and a verb). These include a cache card that may be part of your Mac's architecture and the cache to which Web browsers store data downloaded from the Web.

Cable modem   This is a modem that uses a fiber-optic cable to connect to the Internet. Cable modems are the fastest technology available and offer performance that is many times faster than "regular" modems. The availability of cable modems is quite limited, but it can be expected to increase rapidly over the coming years.

Carbon   This is the name for Mac OS X technology that will make it possible for many applications to be run on Mac OS X while requiring only minor updates instead of major overhauls.

CD-ROM   (Compact Disc-Read Only Memory) CD-ROM drives use digital data to store audio, video, and other data. CD-ROM discs are widely used to distribute software, especially multimedia applications. CD-ROMs are widely used now, but will be replaced in the not-too-distant future by DVD drives.

Character set   This is the set of individual characters that can be recognized by a computer. For example, the ASCII character set consists of the basic alphanumeric characters. The Mac recognizes a wider character set that includes lots of special characters.

Clipboard   This is the place to which your Mac stores any information that you cut or copy. You can view the contents of the clipboard from the Finder.

Clone   Clones are computers that run the Mac OS, but are not produced by Apple. After a short trial period, Apple killed the clone market so there are no longer any Mac clones being produced.

Codec   (COmpression DECompression) Codecs are algorithms that compress video data. There are a number of codecs available; each has its own advantages and disadvantages.

Color depth   This is the number of colors a device can display or output. The number of colors is determined by raising 2 to the power of the number of data bits that can be displayed on each pixel. For example, 8-bit color results in 256 colors (2 raised to the power of 8).

ColorSync   ColorSync is Apple's color management technology. The purpose of ColorSync is to provide consistent color across all of the devices attached to your Mac (for example, monitors, scanners, and printers). You can install ColorSync profiles for each device, and the Mac uses those profiles to make colors match, no matter what device is displaying them. ColorSync could be very important to the Mac's survival because color consistency is one of the most challenging tasks faced by publishers and artists (the Mac's largest user group).

Compression   This is a scheme that makes files smaller, usually by finding a pattern and substituting shorthand for the pattern. Most files that you download from the Internet or receive via e-mail are compressed to make them transfer more quickly. You need a decompression utility to use the files. The dominant compression scheme on the Mac is the StuffIt format, which is identified by the extension .sit. Aladdin Systems' StuffIt Expander is freeware that enables you to decompress .sit files.

Conflict Catcher   Conflict Catcher is a utility that enables you to manage your System Folder and to automate a method of identifying and solving software conflicts. Conflict Catcher is a replacement for Apple's Extensions Manager. You should consider adding Conflict Catcher to your Mac as soon as you can.

Contextual Menus   These are pop-up menus that appear when you Control-click an item, whether it be on the desktop or in an application. The menu you see depends on the context in which you access it. You can also add and removed contextual menus for the desktop and applications.

Control panel   This is a piece of software that provides your Mac with specific capabilities that can be adjusted via the control panel. There are a number of control panels that are part of the Mac OS. There are also many third-party control panels that can be added to your machine to increase its capabilities.

Control Strip   The Control Strip is a bar across your desktop that enables you to quickly access certain controls. You can add or remove modules from the Control Strip to customize the controls it offers.

CPU   (Central Processing Unit) The CPU is the heart of your computer, which contains the main processor and data buses. It also refers to the main "box" that houses the motherboard, disk drives, and other parts of the computer.

Crash   When an application suddenly and unexpectedly stops working, it is called a *crash*. A crashing application can also cause the OS to crash or sometimes the OS can crash on its own. Operating systems that have protected memory structures will prevent an application crash from causing the system to crash.

Creator   This is the application that creates a specific type of document. Every Macintosh file contains information on its "creator;" when the file is double-clicked, the Mac looks for the creator application to use to open the file. If it can't be found, the Mac's built-in file translator will help you locate an application that can be used to open that file.

D

Data fork   This is the part of a Mac file that contains the data in a file (the text or graphic information). Mac files contain two forks; the other one is the resource fork.

Defragmenting   Defragmenting involves the process of rewriting all of the files on a disk so that they are in contiguous blocks rather than pieces scattered across the disk. This makes a disk work more quickly, as well as more reliably.

Desktop   The desktop is the main interface of the Mac OS where you see all of the drives, the Trash, and so forth. The desktop is controlled by the Finder.

Disk cache   This is an area of a disk where data is temporarily stored for quick access. Virtual memory strategies use a disk cache.

Distributed applet   It is an applet that is run remotely by referencing the applet (calling its URL) in the Apple Applet Runner. Distributed applets are often run from the Web.

Driver   A driver is a piece of software that enables a piece of hardware to work with your Mac. Whenever you add a peripheral to your Mac, you will also need a driver, unless the Mac OS supports the peripheral natively (external hard disks, for example).

DVD   (Digital Video Disc—when the term was first created, now it doesn't really stand for anything specific but is its "own" term) DVD is similar to CD-ROM except that DVD discs can store up to 17 GB on a single disc (compared to a paltry 650 MB on a CD). DVD technology will provide yet another revolution in multimedia. This will include the capability to display full-screen, full-motion video on your computer. Player DVD drives are already available; DVD drives for the Mac have been available for the Mac since mid-1998. Most Macs will require a PCI board to provide translation and decompression capabilities for DVD data. G3 PowerBooks use a PC Card decoder for MPEG-2 encoded files (such as DVD movies).

E

Encoding   When you send a file over the Internet, it is converted into a plain ASCII text file (which consists of a seemingly incomprehensible string of characters) so that it can be transmitted across the Net. This process is called encoding. There are different encoding schemes, the Mac uses binhex, while Windows uses uucode. E-mail applications and Web browsers will do the necessary encoding and decoding for you, but you have to know which encoding scheme you should use.

EPS   (Encapsulated PostScript) For more information, see PostScript.

Extension   An extension is a piece of software that adds additional functionality to your Mac. You cannot adjust the operation of an extension as you can with a control panel. An extension is either on or off.

Extensions Manager   This control panel enables you to turn various parts of the operating system off or on in order to troubleshoot or tailor the Mac's performance.

F

FAQ   (Frequently Asked Questions) FAQs are often seen as sections of Web sites or as updated files posted to newsgroups or servers. They answer the most common questions on a certain topic. It's considered poor form to ask a question that is covered in a FAQ.

Favorites   A new feature for Mac OS 8.5, favorites are folders, files, volumes, and other items that you use regularly. You can add items to your Favorites folder with the Add to Favorites command. You can access your favorites in several places, including the Apple menu and the new Navigation Services window that you will see when you save or open files.

File extension   All PC files have a three-letter, file extension appended to their names. Windows uses the file extension to determine which application opens when a file is opened. Your Mac also uses extensions when you open a PC file.

File format   This is the way in which data is stored in a file. There are many, many file formats. Fortunately, you will usually only deal with a few main types. The Mac makes dealing with file formats simpler than it is on other computers.

File Type   This is one of the two codes associated with all Mac files (the other is the Creator code). The File Type code indicates what kind of file the file it is attached to is—for example, a text document or a jpeg image.

Finder   This is the main application that controls your Mac; it provides the desktop and manages all activity on your computer.

FireWire   This is a very high-speed connection technology that is used for data intense media, such as digital video and other technologies, where it is necessary to move large amounts of data at a high rate of speed. In order to use FireWire, you have to add a FireWire card to your Mac and install the appropriate system software (which is included in Mac OS 8.5).

Flame   A flame is a newsgroup or e-mail message in which the recipient is attacked, usually in response to a message that was inappropriate or offensive.

Floating window   This is a window that "floats" on top of all other windows. AppleGuide uses floating windows so that you can always see the help it provides.

Font   A font is a definition of how characters will appear on-screen and in print. Mac OS comes with many font families, and there are hundreds more available.

Font family   This is a collection of character sets that share a similar design. The Font menu actually lists font families rather than just fonts. Most people refer to what appears on the Font menu as a "font."

Fork   All Mac applications, control panels, and other files that contain code, as well as many document files, consist of two forks. One is the resource fork that contains icons and other resources used by the file. The other fork, the data fork, is where the file's data is stored.

G

Get Info   This is the command that provides information on files which you select, including the amount of memory allocated for applications. Under Mac OS 8.5, you also can access a file's sharing privileges through its info window.

GIF   (Graphics Interchange Format) This is a file format commonly used with graphics or photos displayed on Web documents. It is the most supported and popular graphics format on the Web. It was originally developed by CompuServe.

Groups   Groups are sets of users that are defined to enable other users to be assigned privileges to access files and folders on your computer.

Guest   A guest is a user who can sign onto your machine, but will only be able to access files that have guest access permissions.

H

Hang   When an application or the operating system "freezes" and won't respond to anything you do (move the mouse, use the keyboard, curse, etc.), it is called a *hang*. You can sometimes recover from a hang by pressing Control-Command-Esc.

Hierarchical File Structure   Also known as HFS, this is the system that the Mac uses to store and organize files on a drive. When Mac OS 8.1 was introduced, it included the HFS+ architecture, which stores files more efficiently than HFS, but is not backwards compatible. You can choose to use either system with any hard disks under Mac OS 8.5.

HTML   (HyperText Markup Language) HTML is the set of commands used to mark up documents with standard elements so they can be displayed and read on the World Wide Web by different browsers on different computers. It is a subset of SGML (Standard Generalized Markup Language).

I

IDE   (Integrated Drive Electronics) IDE is the standard interface on the PC for hard disk drives. Some Macs also use IDE drives. They are cheaper than SCSI drives, but don't offer as good a performance.

iMac   This is another revolutionary Mac industrial design. The iMac is a one-piece unit that has several advanced features such as USB and a powerful processor. The iMac is also noteworthy for what it does not have, including ADB ports and a floppy disk. The iMac is designed for lower-end users and is priced at less that $1,300.

Inkjet printer   An inket printer is a printer that uses small particles of ink to produce output. Inkjet printers are low cost, and they produce output that is sufficient for most uses.

Internet   The Internet is the worldwide conglomeration of various networks that provide various services, such as e-mail, the World Wide Web, and so on.

Internet Explorer   This is Microsoft's Web browser. It is free, and features are continually being added to it. It requires less RAM and hard drive space than its only real competitor, Netscape Navigator (part of Netscape Communicator). Internet Explorer is the Mac's default Web browser.

IP   Internet Protocol (IP) is part of the language that computers on the Internet use to talk to each other.

IP Address   The IP address is your machine's identification to the rest of the Internet.

Internet Service Provider   An Internet Service Provider (ISP) provides a place for you to connect to the Internet. This makes it possible for you to connect via your Mac and modem instead of having to be directly connected to the Internet.

Intranet   A Local-Area Network (LAN) that is used to provide services similar to the Internet except that access is usually limited to members of the organization that created the intranet.

ISDN   (Integrated Services Digital Network) ISDN is a communication technology that uses digital technology and combines voice and data transmission. To use ISDN, you need an ISDN line and an ISDN modem. ISDN provides speeds up to twice that of a 56K modem.

J

JAVA   JAVA is Sun Microsystems' programming language that is platform independent. It enables programmers to create one set of code that can be used on various computer platforms.

JAVA Beans   These are the components of a JAVA application that provide specific functions (dialog boxes and other features).

JAVA Script   It is the scripting language that is used by JAVA.

Jaz drive   It is a removable media drive that uses 1 or 2 GB cartridges.

JPEG   (Joint Photographic Expert Group) JPEG is a compression technology for graphics. The extension for JPEG documents is .jpg. JPEG files are very common on the Internet and commercial services. JPEG View is one of the best JPEG file viewers for the Mac.

K

Kernel   A kernel is the lowest level of an operating system that interfaces with the hardware. All operating systems are built on top of a kernel. The next generation operating system for the Mac platform, Mac X, will be built on the Mach kernel.

Kerning   Kerning is the space between letters. Most word processing and desktop publishing applications enable you to adjust the kerning of text.

Key Caps   This is the application that shows you particular symbols associated with a font family.

L

LAN   (Local-Area Network) A LAN is a network usually associated with a single office, building, or organization.

Laser printer   This is a printer that uses a laser to produce text and graphics. Laser printers are more expensive than inkjet printers, but they also produce higher quality output.

Leading   The leading is the space between baselines in text. Most word processing and desktop publishing applications enable you to adjust the leading of paragraphs.

Lossless compression   These are compression schemes that don't "lose" any data. While the output of a lossless compression scheme is higher quality than that of a "lossy" compression scheme, the compressed files are larger in size.

Lossy compression   These are compression schemes that lose some data during compression. The compressed file is of lower quality than lossless compression, but the file sizes are smaller as well.

Lurking   You're considered to be lurking when you Read newsgroups or chat sessions without contributing any messages. On the Internet, lurking is a good thing.

M

Mac OS   This is the collection of software that enables Macintosh or clone hardware to operate.

Mac OS X   Mac OS X is the next evolution in the Mac OS. Mac OS X is based on Rhapsody/NeXT technology and will be a modern OS that offers excellent features such as preemptive multitasking, protected memory, and more PowerPC code. Mac OS X will run applications designed for previous versions of the OS, but in order to take advantage of the Mac OS X's advanced features, applications will need to be updated (see Carbon).

Mach kernel   This is the core of the Mac OS X operating system.

MacinTalk   This is the technology that enables your Mac to speak.

Macintosh Runtime JAVA   This is the JAVA engine built into Mac OS 8 that enables your Mac to run JAVA applets.

MacsBug   MacsBug is an application that can be used to debug programs. Most Mac users don't need it because it is primarily intended for programmers.

MacTCP   MacTCP is the technology that enables your Mac to "speak" TCP/IP, which is the "language" of the Internet.

Metasearch engines   "Regular" search engines search Web pages while metasearch engines search the other search engines so that they can access information from lots of different sources, including the Web and newsgroups.

Microsoft   The company that produces software that dominates several markets including spreadsheets and word processing. Microsoft also produces the most widely used operating system, Windows. Many of the features that the Mac pioneered have appeared in Windows as well. For many years, Apple and Microsoft were bitter rivals, but in the past year or so, the companies have formed a closer relationship, which has benefited Mac users (primarily because of Office for Macintosh 98).

MIDI   (Musical Instrument Digital Interface) This is the technology that plays music by interpreting code rather than replaying digitized/recorded sound.

MIME   (Multipurpose Internet Mail Extensions) MIME is a standard used for transmitting varying file formats across computing platforms.

Minimum size   This is the smallest amount of RAM that has to be available for an application to open.

Modal   A modal is a dialog box or window that requires that you do something in it before you can do anything else, such as switch to another application.

Monospaced font   A monospaced font is a font that uses the same amount of space for every character; for example, the space required for a "W" is the same that is required for an "i."

Motherboard   This is the main circuit board in your computer. It contains the main processor, data buses, and RAM among other things.

Movable windows   These are windows that you can move around the screen.

MPEG-2   MPEG-2 is a compression scheme for digital video; it is used for all DVD movies. A computer must have a DVD drive and some sort of MPEG-2 decoder for it to be able to play DVD movies.

Multi-threaded   This is an architecture that can run many processes simultaneously in different threads. Each thread is handled independently by the processor. Multi-threaded processes are good because a single process does not consume all of the system resources and many tasks can take place at the same time. The Finder became multi-threaded in Mac OS 8.0, which enables it to copy different files to different locations at the same time for example.

Multitasking   Multitasking is the ability to do two or more things at once. The Mac currently has some multitasking (cooperative multitasking) capabilities, but the actions of open applications affects the other open applications. In a true multitasking environment, each application is provided with resources by the OS so that both performance and stability are better. Mac OS X will feature true multitasking.

Munge   When you munge a file, you mess up the file so that it doesn't work properly anymore.

N

Netscape Navigator   This is a Web browser that dominated the market until Microsoft decided to produce Internet Explorer. Netscape Navigator has pioneered many Web technologies, and it continues to be innovative.

Newbie   A newbies is a person who is new to the Internet.

NeXT   NeXT is the OS software created by Steve Jobs' company after he left Apple. It is a respected OS for many reasons and will form the basis of the next generation of Mac OS, Mac OS X, etc.

Non-modal   This is a window or dialog box that enables you to move to another window without closing it first.

O

Oblique   This is a substitute for true italic style in which the character is simply angled to the side.

Open Transport   This is the networking component of Mac OS 8.5.

Optimizing   Optimizing is the process of writing files to a hard disk in such a way that access to that disk is made the fastest it can be.

P

Patch   A patch is a piece of software that fixes a bug in a specific application. Usually, a patch application is provided by the software manufacturer. You run the patch and the bug is squished (hopefully).

PDF   (Portable Document Format) This is a portable document format in which documents created with Adobe Acrobat portable document software are presented. Acrobat documents end with the suffix .PDF. PDF files can be viewed with Adobe's free Acrobat Reader.

PICT   A PICT is the basic graphic file format used on the Mac.

Picture Element   See Pixel.

Pixel   (Picture Element) This is the smallest block of data displayed on a monitor or captured by an imaging device, such as a digital camera. All digital images are made up of dots. On a monitor, digital camera, or scanner, these dots are called pixels. The more pixels that a device can work with, the higher its resolution and the more detail it can provide.

PlainTalk   This is the technology that uses MacinTalk to enable your Mac to speak to you and uses Speech Recognition to enable your Mac to respond to your verbal commands. PlainTalk was in danger of becoming extinct for a while, but it has been revived with Mac OS 8.5.

Plug-in   Plug-ins are software components that extend an application's capabilities—giving you, for example, the capability to play audio samples or view video movies from within a Web browser. Generally, plug-in installation requires you to save the plug-in to your hard drive and then double-click the saved file to start the installation. You tell your application which type of plug-in you have installed, and it knows from then on what to do when it comes across this type of file.

Point   A point is a measurement for type size; there are 72 points to an inch (each point is 0.0138 inches).

Pop-up Windows   This is the view of a window in which it appears as a tab at the bottom of the screen. When you click a window's tab, the window pops up and you can work within it. When you move out of the window, it collapses back to the tab again.

Posting   Posting involves sending a message to a newsgroup for the other members of the group to read.

PostScript   PostScript is a page description/programming language developed by Adobe Systems, Inc. It describes a page in a way that is device-independent so that the quality of the output depends on the resolution of the device on which it is printed.

PPP   (Point-to-Point Protocol) PPP is one way to connect to the Internet (another is SLIP).

PRAM   (Parameter RAM) PRAM is the area of memory in which your Mac stores various information that is retained even when the power to the computer is turned off (e.g., date and time settings, mouse configuration, and so on). PRAM is maintained by a battery installed in your Mac. Occasionally, you may need to reset the PRAM on your computer.

Preferred size   This is the maximum amount of RAM that will be allocated to an application.

Proportional font   This is a font that adjusts the spacing between letters based on the width of characters; for example, a "W" uses more space than an "i."

Publish and subscribe   This is the technology the enables you to publish parts of a document so that they can be included in another document by subscribing to those parts. The subscription parts automatically reflect any changes made to the original.

Push technology   Push technology occurs when data is "pushed" from the Web onto your Mac (rather than you downloading [pulling] it) to provide continuous information or to enable you to run applets.

Q

Quantizing   This is the process of measuring the intensity of the signal in each sample of a sound and assigning a numeric value to that sample.

QuickDraw   This is the technology that the Mac uses to display information. Some printers (non-PostScript) use QuickDraw as well.

QuickDraw 3D   This is the software that maximizes your Mac's capability to display and manipulate 3D data.

QuickDraw GX   This is a technology that provides high-level graphics and text capabilities for your Mac. It was never widely adopted, but is still an option with the Mac OS 8.5 installer.

QuicKeys   QuicKeys is an excellent macro/scripting utility that enables you to easily automate repetitive tasks. QuicKeys is an essential add-on for your Mac.

QuickTime   QuickTime is the technology that enables your Mac to display time-synchronized data, such as digitized video and animations. Unlike many other technologies developed by Apple, QuickTime has been widely adopted on the PC as well.

QuickTime VR   This is the QuickTime technology that enables you to see and explore virtual worlds on your Mac.

R

RAM   (Random Access Memory) RAM is the place where your Mac stores any information with which it is currently working. The RAM available to software on your Mac is one of the major determinants of the way your Mac will work. If the RAM you are using is not sufficient, you will experience a lot more problems and the capabilities of your Mac will be limited. Fortunately, RAM prices have been drastically reduced so that you can add more RAM to your machine for a relatively small amount of money,

RAM allocation   This is the amount of RAM that is set aside for a particular application or for the system.

RAM disk   This is a scheme whereby RAM is used to store information that usually would be written to a hard drive. This speeds up the operation of the computer. RAM disks can also be useful for laptop computers as a means of saving battery power.

Rastering   Rastering is the process whereby an outline font is converted into a series of pixels for use by an output device.

Remote Access   Remote Access is the software that enables your Mac to communicate with remote computers via a modem. You can use Remote Access to connect to the Internet as well as to other networks. In Mac OS 8.5, Remote Access replaced the PPP control panel that was used for Internet access.

Removable media   These are storage media that can be removed (for example, floppy disks, Zip disks, and so on) from the respective drive.

Resolution   Resolution is the number of pixels that can be displayed by a device in specific color depths (for example, 480 pixels x 600 pixels with millions of colors). Resolution is a key measurement of the output of monitors, printers, digital cameras, and other devices. Different devices are capable of displaying graphics with different resolutions. Some devices also enable you to set the resolution, depending on what you are doing.

Resource fork   This is the fork in a Mac file where resource data is stored (for example, the File Type and Creator of the file).

Restart   This is the process of shutting down the computer and starting it again. It is best done with the Restart command on the Finder's Special menu.

Rhapsody   Rhapsody is an operating system that is based on Steve Jobs' NeXT technology. Rhapsody runs on Mac hardware and Intel-based hardware, and it can run applications written for either platform (via its boxes, such as the Blue Box), as well as applications written for Rhapsody. For a period of time, Apple was planning on replacing the Mac OS with Rhapsody, but has since come to its senses and developed the Mac OS X strategy instead—Mac OS X is partially based on Rhapsody technology. Rhapsody will be available, but Apple's resources will be focused on the Mac OS.

ROM   (Read Only Memory) The information on your Mac that is permanent is stored in the ROM. For example, the information stored in ROM tells your Mac how to look for an operating system to use.

RTF   (Rich Text Format) This is a word processing file format that contains formatting information, but is not specific to any individual application.

S

Sans Serif   Sans serif fonts are font families without the little "hooks" attached to the letters. The lines that compose font families of this type are straight. Sans serif font families are good for headlines and other short blocks of text. They are also useful for numerals and numerical data. Some examples are Helvetica and Geneva.

Scrapbook   This is a utility that stores clippings that can be easily re-used.

SCSI   (Small Computer Serial Interface) SCSI is the bus structure that manages the data flow between the motherboard and various devices (both internal and external devices). SCSI devices include drives, scanners, tape drives, and so on. SCSI is a fairly fast architecture and is also used in the PC world, although hardware upgrades are required for PCs to use SCSI devices. There are also various "flavors" of SCSI devices, such as wide-SCSI, SCSI-2, and so on. Each offers improved levels of performance over plain-old SCSI.

Search engine   This is an Internet site that helps you search for specific information on the Web.

Serif   Serif characters are composed with little "hooks" that make the characters seem more elaborate. Serif font families are usually good choices for large amounts of text. Examples include Palatino, New York, and Times.

Server-bound applets   These are Applets that reside on your computer rather that existing on a remote server.

Set   A set is a group of extensions, control panels, and other system files that you can define and select within Extensions Manager or Conflict Catcher to quickly and easily switch between custom configurations.

Services for Macintosh   Windows NT, destined to become the most popular OS for network servers, provides Services for Macintosh so that Mac users can connect and use an NT-based network very similarly to how they would use a Mac-based network.

Sherlock   This is Apple's code-name for the Finder's new ability to search the Internet. Because this feature works well, this name is certainly appropriate!

SimpleText   This is the free Apple text editor that provides basic word processing capabilities and is used for most ReadMe files.

Sleep   Putting the computer to sleep powers down the hard drive and blacks out the monitor. This is done to conserve power.

SLIP   (Serial Line Interface Protocol) This is another protocol that enables your Mac to use TCP/IP to connect to the Internet.

Sneakernet   When you use sneakernet, you use a floppy disk or other removable media to move files by physically carrying the media to the next computer (in other words, you carry the disk to another machine).

Speech recognition   This is the technology that enables your Mac to respond to verbal commands.

Spring-loaded folders   This is a feature that automatically opens folders when you drag a file onto them.

Sticky menus   These are menus that stay open without you having to hold the mouse button down.

Stroke   These are the lines of which a typographic character is made.

Style   Style involves the various formatting features applied to text (bold, underline, outline, and so on).

Suggested size   This is the minimum amount of RAM required for an application, according to the application's manufacturer.

Suitcase   This is a special folder type that contains items used by the system. For example, fonts are stored in suitcases. The Mac also uses a System suitcase to store alert sounds and keyboard maps.

System Folder   This is the folder that contains all the software your Mac uses to run. You should understand what is in the System Folder so that you can tune your Mac to your personality and so that you have a better idea of how to solve problems you may experience.

System heap   This is the amount of RAM used by the operating system.

T

TCP/IP   (Transmission Control Protocol/Internet Protocol) TCP/IP is the protocol (or language if you will) that enables the Internet to function. Your computer has to be able to "speak" TCP/IP in order to access the Internet.

Themes   Themes are a new feature for Mac OS 8.5 and are collections of interface customizations, such as the desktop pattern or picture, menu appearance, fonts used in menus, and even sounds. You can define themes to include many of these customizations and then easily switch among "looks" by choosing a different theme.

Thread This is a series of newsgroup postings that are related to the same original message.

TIFF (Tagged Interchange File Format) This is a widely used graphics file format.

Trash You can drag files and folders that you want to delete to the Trash. It is also used to eject disks and remove volumes.

Typeface A typeface is a particular style of character. There are two primary types: serif and sans serif. Members of the same font family have different weight strokes and other aspects, for example, plain, italic, bold, and bold italic.

U

Unattended backup This is a backup that is done without any action on your part (such as changing disks). It is a good idea to be able to do unattended backups.

Updater This is a program that "updates" an application to a newer version. It is similar to a patch except that updaters usually solve multiple problems or add new functions.

Upgrade An upgrade involves the process of replacing an older version of an application with a newer one to get more features, better stability, and for other reasons. Most software companies make a large portion of their income from upgrades. You can also upgrade hardware by adding RAM or VRAM chips, larger hard drives, and other items.

URL (Uniform Resource Locator) This is a standard address for a file or location on the Internet. URLs always begin with an Internet protocol (FTP, Gopher, HTTP), an Internet host name, folders, and the destination file or object.

USB (Universal Serial Bus) USB is a modern interface that enables you to connect all sorts of peripherals (mice, keyboards, scanners, hard disks, tape drives, and so on) to the same port. The Mac determines what kind of device is connected to the USB port and configures itself appropriately. In addition to making life simpler for the user, USB ports also offer better performance than many of the ports they replace (SCSI still has better performance however and is likely to be used when high performance drives are needed). You can also chain multiple USB devices through a single hub (similar to SCSI). The iMac was the first Mac to use USB ports; they are widely used in the PC world.

Uucode   This is an encoding strategy used to prepare Windows files to be transmitted over the Internet. You can also use uucode to encode Mac files, but it is more appropriate for Windows files.

V

Video RAM   See VRAM.

Virtual memory   This is the technology that enables your Mac to use a hard drive as it would RAM. While this enables you to do things for which you may not have enough physical RAM, virtual memory is slower than physical RAM.

Volume   This is a disk space that can be mounted on your Mac. A volume may be a partition on a drive connected to your machine, or it may be a drive that is connected to your Mac via a network of some sort.

VRAM   (Video Random Access Memory) Your Mac uses VRAM to display information. The amount of VRAM that your Mac has, in conjunction with its video hardware, determines the color-depth and resolution at which it can display images.

W

Warm start   This is the process of restarting your Mac without turning off all power to it.

Webmaster   This is the person who manages a Web site.

Windows 95   Windows 95 is the "other" graphical operating system.

Windows 98   Windows 98 is the latest version of the "other" graphical user interface operating system.

Windows emulator   A Windows emulator is a program that provides the Windows operating system that you can run on your Mac. Using a Windows emulator, you can run Windows applications on your Mac without adding hardware. Emulators work, but they are also quite slow relative to a real PC, but for occasional use of Windows applications, Windows emulators are a good choice. There are two emulators available: Insignia SoftWindows and Connectix Virtual PC.

Windows NT   This is a higher-end version of Windows 95/98. Currently, it is mostly used on servers, but eventually Windows 95/98 will be replaced by versions of Windows NT. Windows NT is a very stable operating system, and it is perhaps the most modern OS that can be used on a personal computer (until Mac OS X).

WSIWYG   (What You See Is What You Get) If you have been using a Mac for a long time, you may not appreciate this, but the Mac introduced a revolutionary way of computing—what appears on-screen appears as it will when you print it or distribute it electronically. Before WSIWYG, you had to guess what the final version would look like.

Z

Zip drive   These are Iomega's removable drives that store 100 MB of data on a 3.5 inch disk.

Index

Symbols

56K modems, 451

@ (at), 545

A

About this Computer command (Apple menu), 241, 243, 321

About This Computer dialog box, 14, 241, 243, 321

accelerating Web searching, 656-660
contextual menus, 656
opening multiple windows, 658-659
RAM disk, 659
turning off images, 657

access time, 794

accessing
Favorites folder, 101
shared files, 479-481

accounts
email
canceled, 565
Internet configuration information, 521
multiple, 583-584
multiple, 582-583
Outlook Express, 551
Internet, 516, 539
users, 473-475

ACTION files, 265-266

ACTION files download Web site, 266

activating. *See* enabling

active memory

RAM, 790-791
second-level cache, 790, 792-793
VRAM, 790, 792

ADB (Apple Desktop Bus), 424-425

Add Mapping dialog box, 501

Address bar (Internet Explorer), 614

address book, 550, 566-567

addresses (email), 545-546
@ (at) symbol, 545
bad, 565
finding, 546
location type, 545
mailbox location, 545
multiple, 558
username, 545

adjusting
audio parameters, 306-307
monitor settings, 293
RAM allocation, 328-329

Adobe
Distiller, 445
Photoshop, 183-184
Adobe Type Manager (ATM), 152

ADSL (Asymmetric Digital Subscriber Line), 457

Advanced preferences window, 629

Aladdin Systems Web site, 590

alert sounds
adding non-recorded, 310-311

creating
AppleCD Audio Player, 224-225
MoviePlayer, 215
recording, 309-310
setting, 308
window, 309

alert windows, 37

aliases, 97
adding
Apple menu, 402
Items folder (Apple menu), 130
benefits, 97
broken, 97
creating, 98, 129, 482
original file, 98

alt newsgroup category, 664

alternate startup disk, 807

Amazon Web site, 625

animation file formats, 197

anti-aliasing, 156, 305

anti-virus applications, 705-706
Disinfectant, 708-709
macro viruses, 708
SAM (Symantec Anti-virus for Macintosh), 706-708, 739

AOL (America Online) Web site, 589

AOL Net Find Web site, 644

APIs (Application Programming Interfaces), 348

appearance, 302-303

Appearance control panel, 292
desktop themes, 313, 315
fonts, 304-305
setting
appearance, 303
highlight color, 303
sound effects, 307

Appearance folder (System Folder), 337

AppleCDAudio Player, 14, 220
alert sounds, 224-225
audio CDs, 225-227
components, 220-221
functions, 221-222
keyboard shortcuts, 223

Apple Desktop Bus (ADB), 424

AppleGuide, 115, 276, 280-281, 283-284
AppleScripts, 400
file folders, 281
getting help, 284
modes, 281-282

Apple menu, 72, 81, 124-125
adding
aliases, 402
items, 129
Calculator, 132
Chooser, 130-131
control panels, 126-127
customizing, 127
deleting items, 129
folders, 125
Graphing Calculator, 132
axes, 135
demos, 134
graphs, 133-134
help, 134
keypad window, 133
opening, 133
panes, 135
hierarchical view, 56
Items control panel, 128
Items folder, 125, 130
Jigsaw Puzzle, 140
Key Caps, 135

Note Pad, 136
Options control panel, 126
organizing, 129-130
overview, 13-16
recent documents, 127
Recent Items folders, 125, 127-128
Scrapbook, 136, 139
opening, 137
placing items, 138
storing items, 137-138
Stickies, 139-140

Apple menu commands
About this Computer, 241, 243, 321
Apple System Profiler, 324
Automated Tasks, 129
Add Alias to Apple Menu, 129
Favorites, 100
Network Browser, 481

Apple Menu Items control panel, 128

Apple Menu Items folder, 125, 337

Apple Menu Options control panel, 126

AppleScripts, 130, 398
adding (Apple menu)
aliases, 402
items, 129
application support, 403-404
as applications, 400
Automated Tasks and More Automated Tasks folders, 400
commands, 406
creating, 403, 405-406, 408-409
extension, 399
folder, 399
Guide, 400
Help, 400
launching, 401
library file, 399
limitations, 400
predefined, 401
QuicKeys, compared, 413
Script Editor, 399

Scripting Additions folder, 343, 399
Scripts folder, 343, 399
Speakable Items and More Speakable Items folders, 399
Speech control panel, 399
syntax, 406
Web site, 406

AppleScriptsLib, 399

AppleShare, 12, 481

Apple System Profiler, 14, 115

Apple System Profiler command (Apple menu), 324

Apple System Profiler dialog box, 324

AppleTalk, 457
configuring, 457-459
control panel, 459
phonet box, 457
setting up, 457-458
software (PCs), 493

Apple upgrades Web site, 781

Apple Video Player. *See* AVP

Apple Web site, 357, 405, 535, 623

applets (Java), 631

Application menu, 75-77
customizing, 76-77
Finder, 82
Hide command, 76
Hide Current Application command, 76
Show All command, 76
switching applications, 75

Application Programming Interface (APIs), 348

Application Switcher, 76-77

applications. *See also* software
anti-virus, 705-706
Disinfectant, 708-709
macro viruses, 708

SAM (Symantec Anti-virus for Macintosh), 706-708, 739
AppleCD Audio Player. *See* AppleCD Audio Player
AppleScripts as, 400
AVP. *See* AVP
bringing to front, 75
bugs, 765
contextual menus, 68
copying to networks, 486
Custom installer, 249-250
Digital Color Meter, 181
Disk First Aid, 719-721
disk maintenance, 719
Easy installer, 248-249
Edit menu (standard commands), 260
email, 548-550
Extension Manager. *See* Extension Manager
File menu (standard commands), 258-259
Finder. *See* Finder
force-quit, 273
Get Info command, 84
getting general information, 85-85
graphics
    images resolution, 171
    raster-based, 184-185
    disadvantages, 185-186
    vector-based, 184, 186
helper
    configuring, 653-654
    plug-ins, compared, 651
    RealPlayer, 651-652
Installer, 247-248, 250
Internet, 534-538
keyboard shortcuts
    adding, 381, 383
    creating, 368, 378
    disadvantages, 378
    predefined, 371
launching, 48, 255-257
mailing list, 777
mapping PC file extensions, 501
moving information
    between, 267-268,
    270-271

Norton Utilities for Macintosh, 721-724
OCR, 185
preferences, 267
RAM, 83
    allocation, 320, 328-329
    managing, 328
Remote Access Status, 519
running multiple, 9-10
Script Editor, 399
sharing, 464, 486
support
    AppleScript, 403-404
    extensions, 348
unstuffing compressed files, 257
viruses, 703
windows, 38, 258
Windows operating system. *See also* Soft Windows/Virtual PC
    emulators, 503-504
    running on Macs, 504-505

Applications menu, 9-10

archives, 683. *See also* **backing up, 683**

assigning user groups, 476

Assistants, 276, 286
    Internet Setup, 286, 510, 517
        connecting to Internet, 526-530, 533
        modems, 453
        network Internet connection, 522-523
    Mac OS Setup, 286
        configuring Mac, 287
        File Sharing control panel, 467
    Monitor Calibration, 440

Asymmetric Digital Subscriber Line (ADSL), 457

at (@) symbol, 545

ATM (Adobe Type Manager), 152

attachments (email), 492, 588, 594

receiving, 592-593
saving upon receipt, 593
sending, 588-589
viewing, 591

audio. *See also* **sounds**
    AppleCD Audio Player
        alert sounds, 224-225
        audio CDs, 225-227
        components, 220-221
        functions, 221-222
        keyboard shortcuts, 223
    CDs, 146, 225-227
    digital, 196
    parameters, 306-307
    music (QuickTime), 197-198
    sound effects, 307

auto connections (Internet), 555

Automated Tasks and More Automated Tasks folders, 400

Automated Tasks, Add Alias to Apple Menu command (Apple menu), 129

automating
    startup and shutdown, 109
    tasks, 14, 22

AutoPlay (QuickTime) virus, 198

AV drives, 230

avoiding infected files, 704

AVP (Apple Video Player), 14, 228
    capturing
        still images, 232
        video, 233
    components, 230-231
    hardware and system requirements, 228-230
    movie quality, 234
    watching TV/movies, 231-232

axes (Graphing Calculator), 135

B

back to front printing
option, 442

background printing, 442

backing up, 682, 698-699,
732. *See also* saving
   categories, 683-684
   data, 114
   hardware, 686
   Internet/online settings, 742
   online settings, 742
   overview, 30
   plan, 683
   software, 694, 742
   startup disk, 740-741
   tools for
      *CD-R (Compact Disc-
      Recordable) drives,
      691-692, 796*
      *CD-RW (Compact Disc-
      Rewritable) drives,
      691-692, 796*
      *DVD (Digital Versatile
      Discs) drives, 692*
      floppy disks, 693
      hard drives, 692-693
      *removable media drives,
      690-691*
      Retrospect, 695, 697
      tape drives, 689-690
      Zip and Jaz drives, 690
   types, 684-685
   system, 807
   unattended, 686

backside caches, 324

backup disk, 771-772

Balloon Help, 146, 276,
285-286

batteries (PowerBooks),
825-826
   icon, 819
   monitor (Control Strip),
   826
   reconditioning, 819, 826

BBSes (Bulletin Board
Services), 453

beta software upgrades, 776

binhex, 492

bit depth (color palette),
175-176

bitmap fonts, 152, 155
   advantages, 155
   disadvantages, 156
   TrueType fonts, compared,
   158

bitmap images, 184-186

bitmaps, 155

blocks, 724

bookmarks. *See* favorites

Boolean expressions, 643

booting (from)
   backup disk, 771-772
   Mac OS 8.5 CD, 808

bounced email, 564-566

broken aliases, 97

browsers
   images, 171
   Internet Explorer, 601
      Address bar, 614
      cache, 629-630
      downloading files, 648-649
      Explorer bar, 614-615
      *helper applications,
      653-654*
      History list, 622
      installing plug-ins, 651
      Java, 632
      menu bar, 616
      plug-ins, 649
      QuickTime plug-in, 650
      secure connection, 654
      security features, 615, 655
      setting cache location, 660
      status display area, 615
      subscribing, Web sites, 633
      tool bar, 613-614
      updating, 660
      *Web pages display, 620-
      621*
      window display, 619-620
   Internet Explorer 4.01, 513
   Netscape Navigator, 513,
   601
   Network, 481-483

browsing (Internet)
   favorites, 605-608
   links, 605
   offline, 637-639
   subscribing, 635-636
   URLs, 606

bug fixes (software
upgrades), 775-776

bugs, 748, 765

Bulletin Board Services
(BBS), 453

burn-in (hardware), 768

buses, 114, 426, 794

Button view (folder
windows), 45, 47

buttons
   AppleCD Audio Player, 222
   Extensions Manager, 359
   Launcher, 48

buying
   PCs, 506
   scanners, 433

C

cable modems, 456

caches, 323
   backside, 324
   determining if installed,
   324-325
   disk, 325-326
   inline, 323-324
   Internet Explorer, 629-630,
   660
   second-level, 792-793

Calculator, 132

calibrating monitors, 440

cameras (digital), 434-435

capturing
   devices, 163
   still images, 232
   video, 233

Casady & Greene (Conflict
Catcher) Web site, 761,
359, 360

categories (newsgroups),
663-664

Cathode Ray Tube (CRT), 438

Cc block headers (email), 547

CD Remote programs (AppleCD Audio Player), 221

CD-R drives (Compact Disc-Recordable), 691-692, 796

CD-RW drives (Compact Disc-Rewritable, 691-692, 796

CDs
audio, 146, 225-227
Mac OS 8.5, 808

Change Mapping dialog box, 500

characters
special, 135
voice recognition, 410

checking
disks
Disk First Aid, 719-721
Norton Utilities for Macintosh, 722-724
Internet
answering problems, 541
configuration, 542
modem problems, 541

Chip Merchant Web site, 318, 325, 334, 791

Chooser, 15, 130
opening, 131
printers, 131
shared files, 479-481

clari newsgroup category, 664

clean install (Mac OS 8.5), 810
custom install, 810, 812-815
easy install, 810-812

Clipboard, 338

clippings (desktop), 270-271

clock, 82, 104
configuring, 104-105, 107
correcting dates, 767-768
Network Time Server, 106-107

clocking processor, 797

close boxes (windows), 40

CNN Web site, 575, 624

coachmarks (AppleGuide), 283

collapse boxes (windows), 40, 43

color laser printers, 441

Color Picker, 17, 176-177
highlight color (desktop items), 179-180
HTML Picker, 179

colors, 173
black-and-white mode, 173
components, 174
decreasing displayed amount, 177
depth
changing, 145
games, 177
QuickTime movies, 196
setting, 177
highlight, 302
matching, 180, 183-184. *See also* ColorSync
palettes, 173, 175-176
spaces, 173-174
systems
palette-based, 174-175
true, 174
variation, 302

ColorSync, 180-181, 439
Adobe Photoshop components, 181-182
control panel, 181, 445
Extras folder, 182
matching colors, 183-184
monitors, 440
overview, 16
plug-ins for Adobe Photoshop, 183
printers, 182-183, 443, 445
profiles, 181

Profiles folder, 182
System Folder, 339
System Profile control panel, 181
Web site, 180, 183

combo modems, 452

commands
Apple menu
About this Computer, 241, 243, 321
Apple System Profiler, 324
Automated Tasks, 129
Favorites, 100
Network Browser, 481
AppleScript, 406
Application menu, 76
Contextual menu, 658
Edit menu
Paste, 138
Preferences, 102
Show Clipboard, 338
Edit menu (Graphing Calculator), 134
Edit menu (Outlook Express), 552, 557
Equation menu (Graphing Calculator), 133-134
File menu
Find, 89, 91-92, 484, 728
Put Away, 73
File menu (Note Pad), 136
File menu (Stickies), 140
Functions menu, 119
Get Info, 84-85
Help menu, 278, 286
Help menu (Graphing Calculator), 134
Note menu (Stickies), 140
Special menu
Eject Disk, 73
Empty Trash, 73, 108
Erase Disk, 74, 491
Restart, 74, 717
Shut Down, 74
Sleep, 74
Tools menu (Outlook Express), 559
voice, 411-412

comp newsgroup category, 664

Compact Disc-Recordable (CD-R), 691-692, 796

Compact Disc-Rewritable (CD-RW) drives, 691-692, 796

compressed files, 492, 589-591

Computer Discount Warehouse Web site, 624

Configuration Information dialog box, 527

Configuration Manager (Outlook Express), 552

Configuration Manager panel, 517

configuration report (Mac tool kit), 735-738

configuring
  AppleTalk, 457-459
  cache
  clock, 104-105, 107
  ColorSync (monitors), 440
  energy saving, 108-109
  File Exchange, 500-502
  File Sharing, 468-469
  Internet connection, 534-538, 542
  Internet Explorer
    cache, 629-630
    helper applications, 653-654
    Java, 632
  keyboard, 369-370, 428-429
  location sets (PowerBooks), 829-830
  Mac, 287
  modems, 453-454
  multiple email accounts, 582-583
  network
    identity, 468-469
    Internet connection, 522-523
  news servers, 667-668
  Outlook Express, 552-553
  QuickTime, 197-198

track pad (PowerBooks), 827-828
  voice recognition, 410-411

Conflict Catcher, 359, 731, 739, 761-762
  customizing, 365
  files, 364-365
  finding software problems, 763-765
  launching, 360, 762
  Mac related Web sites, 365
  sets, 361-362, 365
  system files
    disabling, 360
    enabling, 361
    information, getting, 363
  window, 360

Conflict Catcher's Create Set dialog box, 361

conflicting software problems, 748-749, 759, 761

Connect to dialog box, 120, 480, 482

conserving PowerBook energy
  advanced energy saving options, selecting, 822-823
  batteries, 825-826
  energy saving options, 820
  energy saving options, selecting, 821
  RAM disk, 825
  reconditioning batteries, 826
  screen dimming, 820, 824
  Sleep mode, 820
  spinning down hard drive, 820, 824-825

Contents menu (SimpleText), 414

contextual menus, 67-68
  add-ons, 71
  adding items, 68, 70
  applications, 68
  commands, 658
  desktop, 69
  displaying, 68-69
  extension, 69

files, 70
  icon, 69
  Items folder, 69, 339
  overview, 8
  Web searching, 656
  windows, 70

control devices, 425

control panels, 347
  ACTION Utilities, 265
  Appearance, 292
    creating and saving desktop themes, 315
    customizing fonts, 304-305
    selecting desktop themes, 313, 315
    setting appearance, 303
    setting highlight color, 303
    setting sound effects, 307
  Apple menu, 126-127
  Apple Menu Items, 128
  Apple Menu Options, 126
  AppleScripts, 399
  AppleTalk, 459
  ATM, 152
  ColorSync, 181, 445
  ColorSync System Profile, 181
  Configuration Manager, 517
  conflicts with extensions, 759-761
  Control Strip, 144, 147
  DialAssist, 453-455, 517
  disabling and enabling, 350, 352-353
  Energy, 83
  Energy Saver, 108
    PowerBooks, 818, 820
    Scheduled Startup & Shutdown, 109, 396-397
  extensions, compared, 347
  Extensions Manager. *See* Extensions Manager
  File Exchange, 500
  File Sharing, 467-468, 478
  Finder, 80
  folder, 339
  getting information, 355-357
  Infrared, 836

Items, 128
Keyboard, 369-370,
    428-429
Memory (PowerBooks), 819
Modem, 453-454, 518
Monitors & Sound, 440
    *adjusting audio parame-
        ters, 306-307*
    monitor settings, 166, 169
    setting alert sounds, 308
Mouse, 428
Numbers305
overview, 15
QuickTime Settings, 192,
    220
Remote Access, 518, 540
Speech, 312
TCP/IP, 519
third-party, 348
turning off, 730, 731
Users & Groups, 474
windows, 38

Control Panels folders, 339

Control Strip, 144
audio CDs, 146
Balloon Help, 146
CDStrip, 220
collapsing and expanding,
    145
color depth, 145
control panel, 144, 147
extension, 144
modules
    deleting, 148
    finding, 148, 150
    installing, 149
    moving, 147
Modules folder, 144, 148,
    339
Modules Web sites, 149
overview, 16
PowerBook modules, 819,
    826
    battery monitor, 826
    energy settings, 827
    hard drive spin down, 827
    Media Bay, 827
    video mirroring, 827
Preferences file, 144
resizing and moving,
    146-147

cookies (Web), 655

**Copy Graph command (Edit
    menu, Graphing
    Calculator), 134**

**copyright Web information,
    270**

correcting
conflicting software
    problems, 761
generic icon problems, 767
hardware problems,
    768-769
lost date and time problems,
    767-768

**CrashGuard feature
    (Norton Utilities), 758**

creator files, 716

Creator columns, 358

crossover cable, 458

**CRT (Cathode Ray Tube),
    438**

**current configuration
    information (Mac), 788**
Mac (itself), 790
manual, 789
online resources, 789
receipt and invoice, 788-789

custom icons, 299, 301-302

**custom install (Mac OS 8.5),
    810, 812-815**

**Custom Installation and
    Removal dialog box, 812**

**Custom Setup dialog box,
    116**

**custom views (folder
    windows), 54-56**

customizing
Apple menu, 127
Conflict Catcher, 365
desktop, 293
fonts (desktop), 304-305
Mac, 19-20
modem dialing settings,
    454-455
mouse, 428

cutting and pasting, 267

**Cyberian Outpost Web site,
    624**

D

Dantz Retrospect, 739

Dantz Web site, 697

data forks, 373, 715

data storage, 113. *See also*
    hard drives

date and time, *See* clock

debugging (MacsBug), 344.
    See also troubleshooting

**Define Mail Rule dialog box,
    579**

defining sets
Conflict Catcher, 361-362,
    365
Extensions Manager,
    353-354

**defragmenting drives,
    725-727**

**Delete Note command (File
    menu, Note Pad), 136**

**Deleted messages folder
    (Outlook Express), 578**

deleting
Apple menu items, 129-130
control panels, 731
Control Strip modules, 148
email, 560
extensions, 731
fonts, 159
locked Trash items, 108
Note Pad notes, 136
software, 253-255

desktop, 81
clippings, 270-271
contextual menu, 69
customizing, 293
fonts, 304-305
highlight color, 179-180
overview, 5
patterns, 294-297
pictures, 297-300, 302

printing, 442
size, 168
themes, 313, 315
watching TV/movies

desktop database, 716-719, 767

DialAssist control panel, 454-455, 517

dialing settings (modems), 454-455

dialog boxes, 37
About This Computer, 241, 243, 321
Add Mapping, 501
alert window comparison, 37
Apple System Profiler, 324
Change Mapping, 500
Configuration Information, 527
Conflict Catcher's Create Set, 361
Connect to, 120, 361, 480, 482
Custom Installation and Removal, 812
Custom Setup, 116
Define Mail Rule, 579
Domain Name Servers, 528
Erase Disk, 491
Features Installation, 814
Find, 89, 91-92, 581
Find by Content, 93
Index, 93
Info, 611, 613
Initialize, 116
Internet Explorer Preferences, 617
Microsoft Word 98 Customize, 379
Modem Settings, 526
Navigation Services, 18, 101, 263, 265
Navigation Services Choose a File, 101
New Account, 582, 667
New Group, 476
New User, 474
offline, 637

Open and Save, 265-266
Open File, 261
Open Internet Address, 606
Outlook Express Preferences, 557
Perform Clean Installation, 811
Preferences, 102
Print, 389, 442-444
QuicKeys, 391
QuicKeys Editor, 390
QuicKeys Repeat Extension, 391
QuicKeys Sequence Editor, 389-390, 393
Remote Access, 522
Search Internet, 95
Select a Folder, 535
Select Destination, 815-816
Server Options, 106
Share Directories, 495
Shared Directory, 496
standard, 261-263
User, 494
Users & Groups, 494
View Options, 55
Views Preferences, 53

digests, 585

digital audio, 196

digital cameras, 434
advantages, 434-435
resolution, 163, 171

Digital color Meter, 181

digital images, 197

Digital Versatile Disc (DVD) drives, 234, 692, 798

digital video, 196

digital video cameras, 435

Digital Video Disc (DVD), 234, 692, 798

digitizing/video input board, 228-229

dimming PowerBook screens, 820, 824

disabling
Balloon Help, 286
control panels, 350, 730-731
extensions, 350, 730-731
fonts, 159
images (Internet), 657
items, 352-353, 358
system files, 350, 360

Disinfectant (anti-virus application), 708-709

disk cache, 325-326

disk drives, 769, 795-796. *See also* **hard drives**

Disk First Aid, 103, 719-721

disk information (windows), 40

disks
alternate startup, 807
backup, 693, 740-741, 771-772
blocks, 724
checking
    Disk First Aid, 719-721
    Norton Utilities for Macintosh, 722-724
defragmentation, 725
ejecting, 73
erasing, 74
fragmentation, 725
maintenance applications, 719, 721
PCs, 490-491
problems, 721, 723
RAM, 332
    creating, 332-333
    PowerBooks, 825
    setting as Internet Explorer cache location, 660
    Web searching, 659
shared volumes, 120-121
startup, 114, 740-741

display. *See* **monitor**

Distiller, 445

DNS (Domain Name Server), 521, 524

document windows, 36, 45-46

documents
electronic
HTML files, 447
PDF files, 445-447
general information, 86
Get Info command, 84
opening, 127, 268
previewing before printing, 443
Text-to-Speech, 414-416

domain name
Internet, 521
URLs, 599

Domain Name Servers dialog box, 528

dot pitch (monitors), 439

dots per inch (dpi), 165

downloading
Internet files, 648-649
QuickTime movies, 202
RealPlayer, 651-652

Downloads folder, 647-648

dpi (dots per inch), 165

Drafts folder (Outlook Express), 551, 578

drag-and-drop
between applications, 268
launching applications, 256-257
unstuffing compressed files, 257

Drive Setup
Guide, 115-116
initializing and partitioning hard drives, 115-118
mounting volumes, 119-121
non-Apple drives, 115

drives
AV, 230
CD-R, 796
CD-RW, 796
cleaning up, 728-729
defragmenting, 726-727
disk, 769, 795-796
DVD, 234

hard, 112
access time, 794
as backup hardware, 692-693
buses, 794
connecting, 114
Drive Setup, 115-118
external, 794
IDE (Integrated Drive Electronics), 112
initializing, 114-118
installing, 114
internal, 794
overview, 12
partitioning114-118
PowerBooks, 820, 824-825, 827
SCSI (Small Computer Serial Interface), 112-113
size, 794
size, 115
speed, 794
thermal recallibration, 794
upgrading, 793-795
initializing, 112
mounting, 112, 384, 392-394
non-Apple, 115
optimizing, 725-727
partitioning, 113, 115
removable disk, 795-796
removable media, 13, 795-796
SCSI (Small Computer Serial Interface), 834-835
tape, 796
USB (Universal Serial Bus), 113
volumes, 112-113, 119

DropStuff, 590-591

Duplicate Set button (Extensions Manager), 359

DVD (Digital Versatile Discs) drives, 234, 692, 798

DVD Movie Source Web site, 625

dye-sublimation printers, 441

dynamic data, 190

E

easy install (Mac OS 8.5), 810-812

Edit menu
applications, 81, 260
Finder
Paste, 138
Preferences, 102
Show Clipboard, 338
Graphing Calculator commands, 134
Outlook Express commands, 552, 557

editing
file information, 364
QuickTime movies, 207, 209
sets, 365
tracks (QuickTime movies), 210, 212
user accounts and groups, 476

Eject Disk command (Special menu), 73

ejecting disks, 73

electronic documents
HTML files, 447
PDF files, 445-447

email (electronic mail), 510, 544-545. *See also* **Outlook Express**
accounts
canceled, 565
Internet configuration information, 521
Outlook Express, 551
addresses, 545-546
@ symbol, 545
bad, 565
finding, 546
Internet configuration information, 521, 525
location type, 545
mailbox location, 545
multiple, 558
username, 545
advantages, 511
applications, 548-550

attachments, 492, 588, 594
receiving, 592-593
saving upon receipt, 593
sending, 588-589
viewing, 591
bounced, 564-566
contacts (address book),
566-567
default format, 575
filters, 579-580
formatting, 558
headers, 546-547
host address, 521
HTML messages, 575-576
leaving (on servers), 560
mailing lists, 544, 585-586
messages
body, 546-547
Cc block, 547
creating, 554-556
date sent, 547
deleting, 560
formatting, 558
From block, 547
headers, 546-547
reading, 559-560
replying, 561, 563
sending, 556-558, 587
signatures, 546, 548
Subject block, 547
To block, 547
multiple accounts, 582-584
overview, 27
passwords, 521
plain text messages, 575
private mailing lists, 584,
586-587
protocols, 576-577
public mailing lists, 584-585
quoting, 561-563
searching, 581
transferring files, 466, 491
viruses, 704

Emailer, 548

emergency disk, 771-772

**Empty Trash command
(Special menu), 73, 108**

emptying Trash, 73, 108

enabling
control panels, 350
extensions, 350
installed items, 359
items, 353, 358
QuickTime plug-in, 650
SafeZone feature, 708
sets, 362
Speakable Items, 411-412
startup items, 359
system files, 350, 361

encoding, 588, 492

energy
PowerBooks
*advanced saving options,
822-823*
Control Strip settings, 827
saving options, 820-821
supply, 818
saving, 108-109

Energy control panel, 83

**Energy Saver control panel,
108**
PowerBooks, 818, 820
startup and shutdown times,
396-397

**Equation menu (Graphing
Calcualtor) commands,
133-134**

**Erase Disk command
(Special menu), 74, 491**

Erase Disk dialog box, 491

erasing disks, 74

error sounds. *See* **alert
sounds**

Ethernet, 458, 493

Eudora Lite, 549

Eudora Lite Web site, 549

Eudora Pro, 549

Exchange (QuickTime), 198

Excite Web site, 644

**Expansion triangle
(AppleCD Audio Player),
222**

Explorer bar, 614-615, 646

extensions, 347
application support, 348
conflicts with control
panels, 759-761
control panels, compared,
347
ColorSync, 182
Control Strip, 144
disabling and enabling, 350,
352-353
Finder, 80
getting information,
355-357
hardware drivers, 348
Internet Access, 519
Internet Config, 519
Open Transport, 519
PC files, 498-499, 501
QuickTime, 192
Startup (AVP), 231
System software, 348
technology enablers, 348
third-party, 348
turning off, 730-731

Extensions folders, 339

**Extensions Manager,
350-351, 731**
Creator columns, 358
Duplicate Set button, 359
finding
*control panel and extension
conflicts, 759-761*
*software problems,
760-761*
installed items, 359
items
*disabling and enabling,
352-353, 358*
*getting information,
355-357*
opening, 352-353
Package column, 352
Revert button, 359
sets, 353-355
startup items, 359
text list (System Folder
contents), 357
Type columns, 358
window, 352, 357

external drives
 hard drives, 794
 mounting volumes, 119
 PowerBooks, 821
 USB (Universal Serial Bus)
  drives, 113

external modems, 452

**Extras folder (ColorSync),
 182**

F

**faceless/voiceless communi-
 cation, 568**

**Favorites command (Apple
 menu), 100**

Favorites folder, 15, 99
 accessing, 101
 files, 100
 folders, 100
 Internet
  browsing, 606-608
  displaying, 610
  Info dialog box, 611, 613
  organizing, 609-611
  subscribing, 633-634
 Home page, 618-619
 items, 100
 System Folder, 340

**Features Installation dialog
 box, 814**

File Exchange
 configuring, 500-502
 control panel, 500
 translation preferences,
  484-485

**file folders (AppleGuide),
 281**

File menu, 81
 applications, 258-259
 Finder
  Find, 89, 91-92, 484, 728
  Put Away command, 73
 Note Pad commands, 136
 Stickies commands, 140

**file name extensions Web
 site, 499**

file server, 464

File Sharing
 access, 476-478
 activity, 478-479
 configuring, 468-469
 control panel, 468, 478
 Mac OS Setup Assistant,
  467
 security system, 473
 user accounts, 474-476
 user groups, 476

**File Synchronization utility,
 830-832**

**File Transfer Protocol
 (FTP), 466, 513, 599**

files, 715
 adding, 703
 aliases, 98
 attaching (email), 594
 comments, 48
 compressing, 492, 589-591
 data (Help Center), 278
 data forks, 715
 dates, 48
 decoding and encoding, 588
 downloading (Internet),
  648-649
 finding, 88
  ACTION Files, 266
  aliases (belong to), 98
  attributes, 89-91
  content, 92-94
  *Find by Content featuer,
   88*
  Find File feature, 88
  Find Similar Files, 94
  *name and similarity,
   91-92*
  searches, saving, 91
 infected, 702, 704
 information
  editing, 364
  *General Information
   command, 83*
 labels, 48
 Macs, PCs, compared,
  497-498
 moving between
  PowerBooks and Macs,
  830-832

 opening
  ACTION Files, 266
  Favorites folder, 100
  Launcher, 48
 order, 365
 PCs
  extensions, 498-499
  Macs, compared, 497-498
  opening, 499
  running, 502-503
  sharing, 25, 494-497
  transferring to Macs, 490
 PDF, 445-447
 QuickTime formats, 192,
  196
 ReadMe software, 239
 resource forks, 715
 service code, 599
 sharing, 483-484
  access, 476-478
  activity, 478-479
  changing, 483
  *File Sharing control panel,
   468, 478*
  generic icons, 484
  *Mac OS Setup Assistant,
   467*
  Network Browser, 481-482
  other Macs, 464
  overview, 24
  privileges levels, 469
  security system, 473
  setting up, 468-469
  user accounts, 474-476
  user categories, 469-470
  user groups, 476
 size
  calculating, 54
  images, 170
  viewing, 48
 synchronizing, 830-832
 transferring
  email, 466, 491
  network, 467
  other Macs, 464, 466
  sneakernet, 466
  Web/FTP, 466
 type and creator, 48, 716
 uncompressing, 72, 257,
  589-590
 versions, 49

Find (Apple menu), 15

Find by Content dialog box, 93

Find by Content feature, 88

Find command (File menu), 89, 91-92, 484, 728

Find dialog box, 89, 91-92, 581

Find File feature, 88

Find Similar Files command, 94

Finder, 80-81
  Application menu, 82
  clock, 82, 104
    configuring, 104-105, 107
    correcting dates, 767-768
    Network Time Server, 106-107
    testing, 107
  Edit menu, 81
  Energy control panel, 83
  File menu, 81
  Find command (Sherlock), 643
  functionality, 80
  menus, 72
    Apple, 72
    Application, 75-77
    Help, 82
    Special, 73-74
  overview, 11-12
  preferences, 102-103
  Special menu, 81
  tools, 82
  Trash, 82, 107-108
  View menu, 81
  window preferences, 42-44

Finder file (System Folder), 340

finding
  control panel and extension
    conflicts, 759-761
  Control Strip modules, 148, 150
  email addresses, 546
  files, 88
    ACTION Files, 266
    aliases (belong to), 98

  attributes, 89-91
  content, 92-94
  Find by Content feature, 88
  Find File feature, 88
  Find Similar Files command, 94
  name and similarity, 91-92
  searches, saving, 91
  help
    AppleGuide, 284
    Balloon Help, 286
    Help Center, 278-280
  Internet Service Providers, 531-532
  newsgroups, 666
  software problems
    Conflict Catcher, 763-765
    Extensions Manager, 760-761
  software upgrade informa-
    tion, 777-778
  special characters, 135

firewalls (proxy server), 524

FireWire, 114, 427

fixed drives. *See* **hard drives**

flames, 665

floating menus, 67

floating toolbars, 67

floating windows, 43

floppy disks, 693

folders
  adding, Apple menu, 125
  Apple menu, 125, 130
  Apple Menu Items, 125
  AppleScripts, 399-400
  ColorSync Extras, 182
  ColorSync Profiles, 182
  Control Strip Modules, 144, 148
  Downloads, 647-648
  expanding, 50
  Favorites, 99, 100
  Fonts, 153
  Get Info command, 84
  Help, 278
  icons (windows), 40

  information, 83
  Items, 130
  Modem Scripts, 519
  opening, 100
  Outlook Express, 551, 577-578
  overview, 6
  Recent Items, 125, 127-128
  sharing, 470-472
    access, 476-478
    information, 87
    Network Browser, 481-482
    privileges levels, 469
    user categories, 469-470
  size, 54
  Speakable Items, 410
  spring-loaded, 8, 61
  Startup Items, 397
  synchronizing, 831-832
  System. *See* System folder

folder windows, 36, 45
  features, 62-64
  icons, 45
  management, 45
  views, 45
    Button, 45, 47
    custom views, 54-56
    hierarchical views, 56-57
    Icon, 45-47
    List, 45, 47-52
    preferences, setting, 52-53
    Standard Views, 53-54

fonts, 135, 152
  adding, 158-159
  changing, 158-159
  Control Strip control panel, 147
  defaults, 159
  deleting, 159
  desktop, 304-305
  folder, 153, 340
  installing, 158-159
  menus, 304-305
  overview, 16
  PostScript, 153, 156-158
  screen, 152, 155-156, 158
  smoothing (anti-aliasing), 305
  suitcases, 153-154
  TrueType, 153, 157-158

force quit, 273

forks (files), 373, 715

forums (CompuServe). *See* newsgroups

fragmentation, 725

frame rate (movies), 177, 196

freezes, 756-758

FTP (File Transfer Protocol), 466, 513, 599

full backup, 685

full color, 174

Functions menu commands, 119

G

General Information command, 83

generic icons, 766-767

Get Info command, 83-84
applications, 84-86
documents, 84, 86
folders, 84, 87
subcommands, 83
Trash, 85
volumes, 84

Graphing Calculator, 132
axes, 135
demos, 134
graphs, 133-134
help, 134
keypad window, 133
opening, 133
panes, 135

Graphing Calculator Help command (Help menu), 134

graphs (Graphing Calculator), 133-134

grayscale printing, 442

H

hangs, 348, 756

hard drives, 112
access time, 794
as backup hardware, 692-693

buses, 794
connecting, 114
external, 794
IDE (Integrated Drive Electronics), 112
initializing
cautions, 114-115
Drive Setup, 115-118
installing, 114
internal, 794
overview, 12
partitioning
cautions, 114-115
Drive Setup, 115-118
size, 115
PowerBooks, 820, 824-825
SCSI (Small Computer Serial Interface), 112-113
size, 794
speed, 794
spinning down (PowerBooks), 827
thermal recalibration, 794
upgrading, 793-795

hardware
AVP requirements, 228-230
backing up (tools), 686
Compact Disc-Recordable (CD-R) drives, 691-692, 796
Compact Disc-Rewritable (CD-RW) drives, 691-692, 796
floppy disks, 693
hard drives, 692-693
removable media drives, 690-691
tape drives, 689-690
drivers, 348
failures, 749
maintenance, 732-733
overview, 22-23
problems
burn-in, 768
correcting, 768-769
disk drives, 769
installations, 770
SCSI ID conflict, 769
symptoms, 768
wear out, 768

software requirements, 244-245
upgrades, 787, 799-801

headers (email), 546-547

help
AppleGuide, 280-281, 284
coachmarks, 283
file folders, 281
index mode, 282
modes, 281-282
search mode, 282
topic mode, 282
underlining, 283
windows, 284
Assistants, 286-287
Balloon Help, 146, 285-286
getting
AppleGuide, 284
Balloon Help, 286
Help Center, 278-280
Graphing Calculator, 134

Help Center, 276
capabilities, 277
data files, 278
getting help, 278-280
Help folder, 278
Help Viewer, 278
overview, 18
quitting, 280

Help Center command (Help menu), 278

Help folder, 278, 340

Help menu commands, 82, 278, 286

Help menu commands (Graphing Calculator), 134

Help Viewer, 278

helper applications
configuring, 653-654
plug-ins, compared, 651
RealPlayer, 651-652

Hertz (Hz), 168

HFS (Hierarchical File Structure), 113

Hide command (Application menu), 76

Hide CurrentApplication command (Application menu), 76

Hierarchical File Structure. *See* HFS, 113

highlight color (desktop items), 179-180, 302-303

History list (Internet Explorer), 622

Home page, 617-619

hot keys, 147

HotBot, 644-645

HotBot Web site, 644

HSB (Hue Saturation Brightness) color space, 174

HTML (HyperText Markup Language), 447, 575, 628
  code, 628
  email, 551, 575-576
  Picker (Color Picker), 179

http (HyperText Transfer Protocol), 599, 614

Hue Saturation Brightness color space (HSB), 174

hypertext, 604

HyperText Markup Language. *See* HTML

HyperText Transfer Protocol (http), 599, 614

Hz (Hertz), 168

I

Icon view (folder windows), 45-47

icons
  battery (PowerBooks), 819
  changing, 300-301
  contextual menus, 69
  copying and pasting, 300-301
  custom, 299, 301-302
  folders, 45
  generic, 766-767
  pop-up windows, 58, 60

IDE (Integrated Drive Electronics) drives, 112, 114, 426

images, 162, 169
  applications, 171, 184-186
  bit depth (colors), 176
  bitmap, 184-186
  colors
    matching, 183-184
    palettes, 176
  creating, 165-166
  desktop pictures, 297-300, 302
  digital, 197
  dithering, 175
  editors, 171
  higher/lower pixel-to-inch ratio, 171
  resolution
    browsers, 171
    details, 169
    determining, 170
    displaying on monitors, 171
    file size, 170
    graphics applications, 171
    image editors, 171
    imaging devices, 172
    layout applications, 171
    managing, 165
    measuring, 169
    printing, 172
  slide show, 216, 218-219
  still, 232
  viewing, 203-204
  Web, 657

IMAP (Internet Message Access Protocol), 576-577, 551, 559

Inbox (Outlook Express), 551, 577

incremental backup, 685

Index dialog box, 93

index mode (AppleGuide), 282

indexing volumes, 93-94

infected files, 702, 704

Info dialog box, 611, 613

information sources, 741, 755-756

Infoseek Web site, 644

Infrared control panel, 836

Infrared networking (PowerBooks), 835, 835-836

initialization strings, 453

Initialize dialog box, 116

initializing
  drives, 112
  hard drives
    cautions, 114-115
    Drive Setup, 115-118

inkjet printers, 441

inline caches, 323-324

Installer (Mac OS 8.5), 809-810
  clean install, 810, 812-815
  system components, 815-816
  updating, 815

installer applications, 247
  Custom, 249-250
  deleting software, 254
  Easy, 248-249
  Minimal, 250
  running, 247-248
  Typical, 250

installing
  contextual menu add-ons, 71
  Control Strip modules, 149
  DropStuff, 590-591
  fonts, 158-159
  hard drives, 114
  Mac OS 8.5
    clean install, 810
    custom install, 810, 812-815
    easy install, 810-812
    over existing operating system, 809
    PowerBook, 807
    updating System Folder, 815

Netscape Navigator, 513, 601

plug-ins, 651

printer drivers, 443-444

RealPlayer, 651-652

software

disk space requirements, 242-243

hardware requirements, 244-245

RAM requirements, 241-242

troubleshooting, hardware problems, 770

Integrated Drive Electronics drives (IDE), 112, 114, 426

Integrated Services Digital Network (ISDN), 456

interfaces, 424

ADB (Apple Desktop Bus), 424-425

bus, 426

Firewire, 427

IDE (Integrated Drive Electronics), 426

RCA jacks, 427

S-video, 427

SCSI (Small Computer Serial Interface), 426

serial ports, 425

sound input, 427

USB (Universal Serial Bus), 426-427

internal hard drives, 794

internal modems, 452

Internet. *See also* **Web sites; Web pages**

account, 516, 539

applets (Java), 631

application, 518

auto connections, 555

browsing, 88, 95-96, 605-608

configuring

finishing, 534-538

information, 521-525

connecting, 519-520, 539

account, 539

components, 517-519

existing account, 526-530

Internet Setup Assistant, 510

Open Transport PPP, 516

software, 516

without an account, 533

default search site, 646

disconnecting, 539

downloading

files, 648-649

QuickTime movies, 202

email. *See* email

etiquette, 568-570

favorites. *See* favorites folder

FTP, 513

Images, 657

Mac current configuration information, 789

metasearch engines, 644

network connection

configuring, 520-523

Macs and PCs, 492

newsgroups, 511

non-regulation, 514

opening new window, 658-659

overview, 26-28

reloading preferences, 553-554

searching, 640

accelerating, 656-660

HotBot, 644-645

Search tab (Explorer bar), 646

Yahoo!, 641, 643

security, 654-655

Service Providers, 515, 531-532

settings, 742

system requirements, 514

transferring files, 466

troubleshooting, 540-542

Yahoo!, 640

Internet Access (Apple menu), 15

Internet Access extension, 519

Internet Config extension, 518-519

Internet Connection Wizard, 530-531, 533

Internet Editor Assitant. *See* **Internet Setup Assistant**

Internet Explorer, 601

Address bar, 614

Cache, 629-630, 660

downloading files, 648-649

Explorer bar, 614-615

helper applications, 653-654

History list, 622

Home page, 617-619

Java, 632

menu bar, 616

plug-ins, 649, 651

Preferences dialog box, 617

QuickTime plug-in, 650

security information, 615, 654-655

Setup Assistant, 286, 510, 517

Internet connection, 526-530, 533

modems, 453

network Internet connection, 522-523

status display area, 615

subscribing (Web sites), 633

subscription preferences, 636

tool bar, 613-614

updating, 660

Web pages display, 620-621

Web site, 660

window display, 619-620

Internet Explorer 4.01, 513

Internet Message Access Protocol (IMAP), 576-577, 551, 559

Internet search feature, 88, 95-96

Internet Search Sites folder, 340

Internet Setup Assistant, 286, 510, 517

Internet connection, 526-530, 533

modems, 453

network Internet connection, 522-523

intranet, 450

IP (Internet Protocol) address, 521, 524

ISDN (Integrated Services Digital Network), 456

ISPs (Internet Service Providers), 515, 531-532

J - K

Java, 630
    applets, 631
    Internet Explorer, 632
    virtual machine, 631

Jaz drives, 690

joysticks, 431

Key Caps, 135

keyboard
    configuring, 369-370, 428-429
    control panel, 369-370, 428-429
    Power key, 74, 371
    scroll keys, 41

keyboard shortcuts, 368, 378
    adding (applications), 381, 383
    AppleCD Audio Player, 223
    creating, 372-373
        applications, 378
        applications tools, 368
        keyboard/macro utility, 383-384
        macros, QuicKeys, 387-391
        Microsoft Word 98, 379-380
        QuicKeys, 368, 384-386
        ResEdit, 368, 375-377
    predefined, 370-372

keypad window (Graphing Calculator), 133

L

labels
    audio CDs, 225-227
    files, 48, 51-52

LAN (Local-Area Network), 515

laser fonts, 153, 156, 157-158

laser printers, 441

Laser Writer driver, 443

Launcher, 48, 103, 341

Launcher Items folder, 341

launching. *See also* opening
    AppleScripts, 401
    applications, 48, 255-257
    Calculator, 132
    Chooser, 131
    Configuration Manager (Outlook Express), 552
    Conflict Catcher, 360, 762
    control panels, 126-127
    Control Strip, 147
    Control StripModules folder, 148
    Drive Setup Guide, 116
    Extensions Manager, 352-353
    Graphing Calculator, 133
    items at shutdown and startup, 397-398
    Key Caps, 135
    Launcher, 103
    Mac, 109, 396-397
    Note Pad, 136
    Outlook Express Preferences dialog box, 557
    PC files, 499
    recent documents, 127
    Scrapbook, 137
    Simple Finder, 103

LCD (Liquid Crystal Display), 438

links, 605

Liquid Crystal Display (LCD), 438

list information (windows), 41

List view (folder windows), 45, 47
    columns, 48-50
    expanding folders, 50
    labels, 51-52
    sorting lists, 51

loc newsgroup category, 664

local access providers Web site, 533

local Web, 465, 486

Local-Area Network (LAN), 515

LocalTalk, 493

Location Manager (PowerBooks), 828-830

lost preferences, 767

low-level formatting, 118

lurking, 665

Lycos Web site, 644

M

Mac Central Web site, 756

Mac EvangeList mailing list Web site, 624

Mac magazines, 756, 778

Mac OS
    major upgrades, 783
    minor upgrades, 781, 783
    versions, 243

Mac OS 8.5 CD, 808

Mac OS Extended (partition), 118

Mac OS Runtime for Java (MRJ), 631

Mac OS Setup Assistant, 286-287, 467

Mac OS Stanadard (partition), 118

Mac Resource Page Web site, 756

Mac tool kit, 735
    configuration report, 735-738
    software tools, 739-740

MacAddict magazine Web site, 623, 778

MacCentral Online Web site, 624

MacHome magazine Web site, 623

Macmillan Computer Publishing Web site, 624

macros, 383
  creating
    QuicKeys, 384, 388-389
    Text-to-Speech, 416-419
  keyboard shortcuts, 387-391
  naming, 390
  positioning, 394
  sequence control, 390-391
  testing, 390
  viruses, 703, 708

Macs
  configuring, 287
  current configuration information, 788-790
  customizing, 19-20
  maintenance, 30-32
  restarting, 74
  startup sound, 214-215
  shutting down, 74

MacsBug, 344

MacTCP DNR file, 341

MacTCP information, 807-808

Macworld magazine Web site, 623

Mail rules (Outlook Express), 581

mailing lists, 544, 585
  digests, 585
  moderated, 586
  newsgroups, compared, 662
  posting messages, 586
  private, 584, 586-587
  public, 584-585
  software upgrade information, 777-778
  unmoderated, 586

mailto, 599

maintenance
  applications, 719
  hardware, 732-733
  Mac, 30-32, 247

mappings, 500-501

Media Bay (PowerBook Control Strip), 827

Media Keys (QuickTime), 198

memory (RAM), 240, 318-320
  allocation
    adjusting, 328-329
    applications, 320, 328
    assessing, 321-322
  amount, 321-322
  available, 349
  awareness, 322-323
  command, 83
  control panel (PowerBooks), 819
  disk, 332-333
    PowerBooks, 825
    setting as, 660
    Web searching, 659
  increasing, 330-331
  managing, 326-328
  overview, 20
  Parameter, 320, 767-768
  physical, 318
  plug-ins, 242
  software requirements, 240-242
  substitues, 330-332
  upgrading, 333-334, 791
  virtual, 318, 330-331

menu bar (Internet Explorer), 616

menus
  Apple, 72, 81, 124-125
    adding aliases, 130
    adding folders, 125
    AppleScript (adding items), 129
    Calculator, 132
    Chooser, 130-131
    control panels, 126-127
    customizing, 127
    deleting, items, 129-130

    folders, 125, 130
    Graphing Calculator, 132-135
    Items control panel, 128
    Items folder, 125
    items, 14-16
    Jigsaw Puzzle, 140
    Key Caps, 135
    Note Pad, 136
    Options control panel, 126
    organizing, 129-130
    overview, 13
    recent documents, 127
    Recent Items folders, 125, 127-128
    reordering, 130
    Scrapbook, 136-139
    Stickies, 139-140
    volumes, 130
  Application, 9-10, 75-77
  contextual, 67-68
    add-ons, 71
    adding items, 68, 70
    applications, 68
    desktop, 69
    displaying, 68-69
    extension, 69
    files, 70
    icon, 69
    items folder, 69
    overview, 8
    Web searching, 656
    windows, 70
  Edit, 81
  File, 81
  Finder, 72, 82
  fonts, 304-305
  Help, 82
  pop-up, 66
  pop-up windows, 58
  pull-down, 66
  Special, 73-74, 81
  sticky, 68
  tear-off, 67
  unique, 67
  View, 81

messages (email)
  body, 546-547
  Cc block, 547
  creating, 554-556

date sent, 547
deleting, 560
formatting, 558
From block, 547
headers, 546-547
reading, 559-560
replying, 561, 563
sending, 556-558, 587
signatures, 546, 548
Subject block, 547
To block, 547

metasearch engines, 644

microphones, 410, 431

Microsoft Office 98 for Macintosh, 248

Microsoft Virtual Machine, 631

Microsoft Web site, 708

Microsoft Word 98, 379-380

Microsoft Word 98 Customize dialog box, 379

Miramar Web site, 121

modal windows, 41

modems, 450
56K, 451
ADSL (Asymmetric Digital Subscriber Line), 457
cable, 456
combo, 452
configuring, 453-454
connecting, 452
control panel, 453, 518
dialing settings, 454-455
external, 452
faster data transmission, 456-457
initialization strings, 453
internal, 452
ISDN (Integrated Services Digital Network), 456
PC Card, 452
PowerBooks, 452
problems, 541
Scripts folder, 519
Settings dialog box, 526
sound, 538

speed, 450-451, 515
VDSL (Very High Speed Digital Subscriber Line), 457

moderated mailing lists, 586

moderated newsgroups, 666

modulator demodulator. *See* modems

monitors, 438
bit depth (colors), 176
Calibration Assistant, 440
color depth, 145
colors, 177
ColorSync, 439-440
display size and type, 168, 438-439
dot pitch, 439
higher/lower pixel-to-inch ratio, 171
multiple, 439
name, 169
physical screen size (pixels), 163-164
resolution, 172
changing, 168
determining, 168-169
displaying images, 171
Hz (frequency), 168
measuring, 163
settings, 166, 293
sizes and resolutions (common), 169

Monitors & Sound control panel, 440
adjusting audio parameters, 306-307
alert sounds, 308
monitors, 166, 169

More Automated Tasks folder, 400

More Speakable Items folder, 399

Motion Picture Experts Group (MPEG), 192

Mount Volumes command (Functions menu), 119

mounting
drives, 112, 384, 392-394
shared volumes, 479-481
volumes, 119-121, 384, 392-394

mouse, 427-429

Mouse control panel, 428

movable windows, 42

MoviePlayer (QuickTime), 193, 202
creating alert sounds, 215
editing movies, 207, 209
saving movies, 209
transitions, 209
upgrade message, 202
watching movies, 202-203

movies
color depth, 196
creating, 233
creating startup sound, 214-215
downloading (Internet), 202
editing, 207, 209
frame rate, 196
multiple tracks, 196
playing, 202-203
quality, 234
resolution, 195
saving, 209
specifications, 194-196
streaming, 191
tracks, 210, 212, 214
transitions, 209

MPEG (Motion Picture Experts Group), 192

MRJ (Mac OS Runtime for Java), 631

MS Preference Panels folder, 341

multimedia, 190
AppleCD Audio Player, 14, 220
audio CDs, 225-227
components, 220-221
creating alert sound, 224-225
functions, 221-222
keyboard shortcuts, 223

AVP, 228
  capturing still images, 232
  capturing video, 233
  components, 230-231
  *hardware and system
    requirements, 228-230*
  movies quality, 234
  *watching TV/movies,
    231-232*
  DVD, 234
  features, 190-191
  platform, 17
  QuickTime 3 Pro. *See
    QuickTime 3 Pro*
  QuickTime VR, 192,
    204-205
  QuickTime. *See QuickTime*
multitasking, 9, 74
music (QuickTime), 197-198
**Music Boulevard Web site,
  625**

N

names
  finding files, 91-92
  macros, 390
  newsgroups, 663
  PostScript fonts, 157
  versions software upgrades,
    776-777
  voice commands, 412
**Navigation Services dialog
  boxes, 18, 101, 263, 265**
Net Flix Web site, 625
**Netscape Navigator, 513,
  601**
**Network Browser, 15,
  481-483**
**Network Browser command
  (Apple menu), 481**
**Network Time Server,
  106-107**
networks
  AppleTalk, 457-459
  applications, 486
  identity, 468-469
  Infrared (PowerBooks),
    835-836

  Internet connection, 520,
    522-523
  LAN, 515
  Macs and PCs, 492-493
  non-AppleTalk, 467
  overview, 24
  PCs with Macs, 121
  sharing Web pages, 486
  transferring files, 467
  WAN, 515
**New Account dialog box,
  582, 667**
New Group dialog box, 476
**New Note command (File
  menu), 136, 140**
New User dialog box, 474
news servers, 521
  adding (multiple), 667
  configuring, 667-668
  Internet configuration
    information, 525
**newsgroups, 511, 662-663,
  676-677**
  categories, 663-664
  finding, 666
  flames, 665
  mailing lists, compared, 662
  moderated, 666
  names, 663
  news servers
    adding (multiple), 667
    configuring, 667-668
    *Internet configuration
      information, 525*
  overview, 28
  posting messages, 674
  posting replies, 675
  postings, 665
  reader (Outlook Express),
    550
  reading, 671-673
  replying via email, 675
  retrieving lists, 668-669
  software upgrade
    information, 778
  subscribing, 665, 669-671
  threads, 665
  unmoderated, 666
  unsubscribing, 676
  URLs, 664

non-Apple drives, 115
**non-AppleTalk networks,
  467**
non-modal windows, 41
**non-recorded alert sounds,
  310-311**
**Normal button (AppleCD
  Audio Player), 222**
Norton Utilites, 721, 739
  checking disks, 722-724
  CrashGuard feature, 758
  defragmenting drives,
    726-727
**Note menu (Stickies)
  commands, 140**
Note Pad, 136
numbers format, 305
Numbers control panel, 305

O

**OCR (Optical Character
  Recognition) applications,
  185**
off line dialog box, 637
**Open dialog boxes, 261-262,
  265-266**
Open File dialog box, 261
**Open Internet Address
  dialog box, 606**
**Open Link in New Window
  command (Contextual
  menu), 658**
**Open Transport extensions,
  519**
**Open Transport PPP
  (Internet connection
  software), 516**
opening
  documents (another
    application), 268
  files, 48, 100, 266
  folders, 100
  multiple Web windows,
    658-659
  new Web window, 658
  pop-up windows, 57, 61

Optical Character Recognition applications (OCR), 185

Orange Micro Web site, 505

organizing
    Apple menu, 129-130
    favorites folder (Internet),
      609-611

Outlook Express, 549-550
    address book, 550
    configuring, 552-553
    contacts, 566-567
    default format, 575
    Deleted messages folder,
      578
    Drafts folder, 551, 578
    email accounts, 551
    email messages
      creating, 554-556
      deleting, 560
      leaving (on servers), 560
      quoting, 561-563
      reading, 559-560
      replying, 561, 563
      sending, 556-558
    features, 571-572
    filters, 551, 579-580
    folders, 551, 578
    HTML mail, 551, 575-576
    IMAP (Internet Message
      Access Protocol) support,
      551
    Inbox, 551, 577
    Internet preferences,
      553-554
    Mail rules, 581
    mulitple accounts, 582-584
    news servers, 521
      adding (multiple), 667
      configuring, 667-668
      Internet configuration
        information, 525
    newsgroup reader, 550
    Outbox, 551, 577
    overview, 27
    Preferences dialog box, 557
    quoting, 563
    searching, 581
    Sent Mail folder, 551, 578
    spell checker, 550
    text, 550
    Web site, 595
    windows, 551-552

P

Package column (Extensions Manager), 352

PageMaker PDF files, 445-447

pages (Web). *See* Web pages

palette-based color systems, 174-175

palettes, 173
    colors, 175-176
    Launcher, 341

panes (Graphing Calculator), 135

Parameter RAM (PRAM), 320, 767-768

partitioning
    drives, 113
    hard drives
      cautions, 114-115
      Drive Setup, 115-118
      size, 115
    size, 117, 119
    types, 118
    viewing, 115

passwords (PowerBooks), 833-834

Paste command (Edit menu), 138

pasting, 267

patterns (desktop), 294-297

PC cards, 505
    modem, 452
    PowerBooks, 821

PC MACLAN, 494-497

PC MACLAN Connect, 493

PCI cards, 792, 797-799

PCs
    adding (Mac-based
      networks), 493
    applications, 504-505
    buying, 506
    cards, 505
      modem, 452
      PowerBooks, 821
    connecting, 493
    disks, 490-491
    extensions, 498-499, 501
    files
      Mac files, compared,
        497-498
      opening with Macs, 499
      running on Macs, 502-503
      sharing, 25, 494-497
      transferring to Macs, 490
    networking with Macs, 121
    SCSI drives, 113
    software, 493
    viruses, 506

PDF files (Portable Document Format), 445-447

Perform Clean Installation dialog box, 811

personal mailing lists, 584, 586-587

phonet box, 457

physical RAM, 318

physical security (PowerBooks), 833

picture elements (pixels), 162-164

PictureViewer (QuickTime), 193, 203-204

pixels, 162-164

pixels-to-inch ratio, 171

plain text (email), 575

PlainTalk, 410

play buttons (AppleCD Audio Player), 222

playing
    applets (Java), 631
    audio CDs, 146
    QuickTime movies,
      202-203

plug-ins
    ColorSync, 183
    helper applications, com-
      pared, 651

Internet Explorer, 649-651
QuickTime, 193
RAM, 242
**POP (Post Office Protocol),
576-577**
pop-up menus, 66
pop-up windows, 57-59, 61
closing, 59, 61
creating, 58-59
dragging files onto, 57
expanding files, 60
icons, 58, 60
menus, 58
opening, 57, 61
overview, 6, 8
placing files/folders within,
61
resizing, 58-59
views, 60
**Portable Document Format
(PDF), 445-447**
**Post Office Protocol (POP),
576**
posting, 665
messages
mailing lists, 586
newsgroups, 674
replies (newsgroups), 675
**PostScript fonts, 153, 156,
157-158**
Power key, 74, 371
PowerBooks
as SCSI drive, 834-835
batteries, 819, 825-826
Battery Reconditioning
utility, 819
Control Strip modules, 819,
826-827
data security, 833-834
Energy Saver control panel,
818
energy saving options,
820-821, 822-823
energy supply, 818
external drives, 821
hard disk spindown, 820,
824-825

Infrared networking,
835-836
installing Mac OS 8.5, 807
location sets, 828-830
Memory control panel, 819
modems, 452
passwords, 833-834
physical security, 833
RAM disk, 825
screen dimming, 820, 824
Sleep mode, 820
synchronizing files, 830
synchronizing folders,
831-832
track pad, 827-828
unplugging PC cards, 821
PPP connection script, 525
**PRAM (Parameter RAM),
320, 767-768**
**predefined keyboard
shortcuts, 370-372**
preferences
AppleCD Audio Player, 221
applications, 267
AVP, 231
Control Strip, 144
dialog box, 102
Finder, 102-103
folder, 342
Internet, 553-554
lost, 767
QuickTime, 192
spring-loaded folders, 61
subscription (Internet
Explorer), 636
translation, 484-485
windows
documents, 46
Finder, 42-44
folder views, 52-53
**Preferences command (Edit
menu), 102**
**Preferences command
(Outlook Express Edit
menu), 552, 557**
**preventing virus infections,
704, 710**

previewing documents
(before printing), 443
**Print dialog box, 389,
442-444**
printers, 441
back to front option, 442
color laser, 441
ColorSync
applying, 182-183
profiles, 445
settings, 443
connecting, 442
dialog box, 442-444
drivers, 131, 442-444
dye-sublimation, 441
fonts, 153, 156, 157-158
grayscale, 442
image resolution, 172
inkjet, 441
laser, 441
preview, 443
quality, 442
selecting, 131, 384
**PrintMonitor Documents
folder, 343**
**private mailing lists, 584,
586-587**
privileges (sharing)
controlling, 476-478
files and folders, 473
levels, 469
problems. *See* troubleshooting
processor
caches, 323
clocking, 797
slow, 349
upgrading, 796-797
ProDos (partition), 118
**Profiles folder (ColorSync),
182**
**Prog button (AppleCD
Audio Player), 222**
proxy servers, 521
public mailing lists, 584-585

Publisher's Web site (software), 239

pull-down menus, 66

Put Away command (File menu), 73

Q

QuickDraw 3D, 219

QuickDraw GX, 158

Quicken Web site, 624

QuicKeys, 384
  AppleScript, compared, 413
  Editor, 390
  keyboard shortcuts, 368, 384-386
  macros
    creating, 384, 388-389
    keyboard shortcuts, 387-391
    naming, 390
    positioning, 394
    sequence control, 390-391
    Text-to-Speech, 416-419
  mounting drives and volumes, 384, 392-394
  Mounty, 392
  Repeat Extension dialog box, 391
  scripts, 419
  selecting printers, 384
  Sequence Editor, 389-390, 393
  Web sites, 385, 392, 413, 418

QuickTime, 191-192, 194
  AutoPlay virus, 198
  configuring, 197-198
  Exchange, 198
  extension, 192
  file formats, 192, 196-197
  Media Keys, 198
  MoviePlayer, 193, 202
    creating alert sounds, 215
    editing movies, 207, 209
    saving movies, 209
    transitions, 209
    upgrade message, 202
    watching movies, 202-203
  movies
    color depth, 196
    creating, 233
    downloading (Internet), 202
    frame rate, 196
    multiple tracks, 196
    quality, 234
    resolution, 195
    specifications, 194-196
    streaming, 191
    tracks, 210, 212, 214
    watching, 202-203
    Web site, 202
  MPEG extension, 192
  music, 198
  Musical Instruments extension, 192
  overview, 17
  PictureViewer, 203-204
  plug-in, 650
  PowerPlug extension, 192
  Preferences, 192
  Settings control panel, 192, 220
  viewing tools, 193
  VR extension, 192, 204-205
  Web site, 196, 204

QuickTime 3 Pro, 194
  MoviePlayer
    editing movies, 207, 209
    saving movies, 209
    transitions, 209
  slide show, with soundtrack, 216, 218-219
  startup sound, 214-215
  tracks, 210, 212, 214
  upgrading to, 199-201
  Web site, 199

QuickTime VR (Virtual Reality), 192, 204-205

quitting applications, 273, 280

R

RAM (Random Access Memory), 240, 318-320
  allocation
    adjusting, 328-329
    applications, 320, 328
    assessing, 321-322
    amount, 321-322
    available, 349
    awareness, 322-323
    disk, 332-333
      PowerBooks, 825
      setting as, 660
      Web searching, 659
    increasing, 330-331
    managing, 326-328
    overview, 20
    Parameter, 320, 767-768
    physical, 318
    plug-ins, 242
    software requirements, 240-242
    substitues, 330-332
    upgrading, 333-334, 791
    virtual, 318, 330-331

raster-based images, 184-186

RCA jacks, 427

Read Only Memory (ROM), 319

reading
  email, 559-560
  newsgroups, 671-673
  SimpleTextdocuments, 414-415

ReadMe files, 239

RealPlayer, 651-652

RealPlayer Web site, 651

rec newsgroup category, 664

Recent Items folders, 125, 127-128

rechargeable batteries (PowerBooks), 825-826

recording
  alert sounds, 309-310
  MacTCP information, 807-808

Recycling Bin (Windows 95, 98), 82

Red Green Blue color space (RGB), 174

Reel.com Web site, 625

Remote Access
control panel, 518, 540
dialog box, 522
Status, 16, 519

removable media drives
as backup hardware,
690-691
disk drives, 795-796
overview, 13
upgrading, 795-796

removing. *See* **deleting**

**Repeat button (AppleCD
Audio Player), 222**

requirements
AVP hardware and system,
228-230
software, 239
disk space, 242-243
hardware, 244
RAM, 240-242
sources, 239-240

ResEdit, 368, 374, 740
books, 303, 373
custom icons, 303
keyboard shortcuts
*adding (applications), 381,
383*
creating, 375-377
Web site, 373

resizable windows, 42

resizing
Control Strip, 146-147
Graphing Calculator
graphs, 134
panes, 135

resolution, 162
determining, 170
digital cameras, 171
images, 164-166
browsers, 171
details, 169
*displaying on monitors,
171*
file size, 170
graphics applications, 171
*higer/lower pixel-to-inch
ratio, monitor, 171*
image editors, 171

imaging devices, 172
layout applications, 171
managing, 165
measuring, 169
printing, 172
Mac, 166
managing, 165
maximum, 165-167
measuring, 163, 165
monitors, 172
changing, 168
common, 169
determining, 168-169
Hz (frequency), 168
QuickTime movies, 195
scanners, 171

resource fork, 373, 715

**resources (Mac OS 8.5),
806-807**

**Restart command (Special
menu), 74, 717**

restarting Mac, 74

Retrospect, 694-695, 697

Retrospect Remote, 694

**Revert button (Extensions
Manager), 359**

reviews (software), 239

**RGB (Red Green Blue) color
space, 174**

**Ric Ford's MacInTouch Web
site, 624, 756**

**ROM (Read Only Memory),
319**

**router addresses (Internet),
521, 524**

running
installer applications,
247-248
Custom, 249-250
Easy, 248-249
multiple applications, 9-10
PC disks on Macs, 490
PC files on Macs, 502-503
Windows applications,
504-505

S

S-video interfaces, 427

**SafeZone feature (SAM),
707-708**

**sales information (software),
239**

**SAM (Symantec Anti-virus
for Macintosh), 706-708,
739**

**Save dialog boxes, 263,
265-266**

saving
desktop themes, 315
email attachments, 593
energy, 108-109
QuickTime movies, 209
searches, 91

scanners, 432
buying, 433
functions, 432-433
photographs, 434
resolution, 163, 171

**Scheduled Startup &
Shutdown button (Energy
Saver control panel), 109**

**scheduling startup and
shutdown times, 396-397**

sci newsgroup category, 664

Scrapbook, 136-139
file, 343
items, 137-138
opening, 137

screen (PowerBooks)
battery icon, 819
dimming, 820, 824

screen fonts, 152, 155
advantages, 155
disadvantages, 156
TrueType fonts, compared,
158

**Script Editor (AppleScripts),
399**

**Scripting Additions folder,
343, 399**

scripts, 384. *See also* macros

Scripts folder, 343, 399

scroll arrows, 41-42

scroll bars, 41

scroll boxes, 41-42

scroll keys, 41

SCSI (Small Computer Serial Interface) drives, 112, 426
  benefits, 426
  bus, 114
  ID conflicts, 769
  PCs, 113
  PowerBooks as, 834-835

Search Internet dialog box, 95

search mode (AppleGuide), 282

search site, 646

Search tab (Explorer bar), 646

searching
  email, 581
  Web, 640
    accelerating, 656-660
    files, 91
    HotBot, 644-645
    Search tab (Explorer bar), 646
    Sherlock, 643
    Yahoo!, 641, 643

second-level cache, 792-793

secure connection, 654

security
  File Sharing, 473
  information, 615
  Internet, 654-655
  Internet Explorer, 655
  PowerBooks
    data, 833-834

Select a Folder dialog box, 535

Select Destination dialog box, 815-816

selected files only backup, 685

selecting
  alert sounds, 308
  appearance, 303
  color palettes, 176
  default search site, 646
  desktop
    patterns, 294-295
    pictures, 297-300, 302
    themes, 313, 315
  disk cache, 325-326
  energy saving options (PowerBooks), 821-823
  highlight color, 303
  monitor color amount, 177
  Network Time Server, 106-107
  numbers format, 305
  plain text (default email format), 575
  preferences (Finder), 102-103
  printers, 131
    ColorSync profiles, 445
    QuicKeys, 384
  RAM disk, 660
  random desktop pictures, 302
  sites stored amount (History list, Internet Explorer), 622
  sound effects, 307
  sound input source, 410
  startup disk, 346
  subscription preferences, 636
  translation preferences, 484-485
  virtual RAM, 330-331
  Web pages display, 620-621
  window display, 619-620

Send & Receive, Send & Receive All command (Outlook Express Tools menu), 559

sending
  email
    on command, 557-558
    Outlook Express, 556-557
    private mailing lists, 587
  email attachments, 588-589

Sent Mail folder (Outlook Express), 551, 578

sequence control (macros), 390-391

serial connections (AppleTalk), 457

serial ports, 425

Server Options dialog box, 106

servers
  email, 560
  failure, 565
  news, 521, 525
  proxy (firewalls), 521
  Windows NT, 492

service codes (URLs), 599

Services for Macintosh (SFM), 492

sets, 353
  creating, 359
  defining
    Conflict Catcher, 361-362, 365
    Extension Manager, 353-354
  editing, 365
  enabling, 362
  System Folder, 354-355

setting. *See selecting*

SFM (Services for Macintosh), 492

Share Directories dialog box, 495

Shared Directory dialog box, 496

sharing
  activity, 478-479
  applications, 464, 486
  controlling access, 476-478
  disks, 120-121
  files
    accessing, 479-481
    changing, 483
    generic icons, 484
    Network Browser, 481-482
    other Macs, 464
    overview, 24

privileges levels, 469
working with, 483-484
user categories, 469-470
folders, 470-472, 481-482
access, 476-478
privileges levels, 469
user categories, 469-470
libraries, 337
PC files
Mac network (PC MACLAN), 494-497
overview, 25
privileges, 473, 476-478
volumes, 479-481
Web pages, 486

Sharing Information command, 83

Sherlock, 96, 374, 643

shortcuts. *See* aliases

Show All command (Application menu), 76

Show Balloons command (Help menu), 286

Show Clipboard command (Edit menu), 338

Show commands (Graphing Calculator, Equation menu), 133

Shuffle button (AppleCD Audio Player), 222

Shut Down command (Special menu), 74

Shutdown Items, 398

Shutdown Items folders, 344

shutting down (Mac), 74, 109, 396-397

signatures (email), 546, 548

Simple Finder, 103

Simple Text, 414

SimpleSound, 309-310

SimpleText, 414-415

sites (Web)
ACTION files download, 266
Aladdin Systems, 590

Amazon, 625
AOL (America Online), 589
AOL Net Find, 644
Apple, 357, 535, 623
AppleScript, creating (go to), 405-409
upgrades, 781
browsing
offline, 637-639
subscribing, 633-636
Cassady & Greene (Conflict Catcher), 360, 365, 761
Chip Merchant, 318, 325, 334, 791
CNN, 575, 624
ColorSync, 180, 183
Computer Discount Warehouse, 624
Control Strip modules, 149
Cyberian Outpost, 624
Dantz, 697
DVD movie source, 625
Eudora Lite, 549
Excite, 644
Favorite, 633-634
file name extensions, 499
HotBot, 644
Infoseek, 644
Internet Explorer, 660
local access providers, 533
Lycos, 644
Mac EvangeList mailing list, 624
Mac magazines, 756
Mac Resource Page, 756
MacAddict magazine, 623, 778
MacCentral Online, 624, 756
MacHome magazine, 623
Macmillan Computer Publishing, 624
Macworld magazine, 623
Microsoft, 708
Miramar, 121
Music Boulevard, 625
Net Flix, 625
Orange Micro, 505
Outlook Express, 595

PC MACLAN Connect (demo version), 493
Quicken, 624
QuicKeys, 385, 392, 413, 418
QuickTime, 196, 204
QuickTime 3 Pro upgrade, 199
movies, 202
RealPlayer, 651
Reel, 625
ResEdit (free copy), 373
Ric Ford's MacInTouch, 624, 756
software upgrade information, 778
SoftWindows (Insignia), 503
subscribing, 633-636
Symantec virus information, 706
Ted Landau's MacFixIt, 624, 756
types, 512-513
U.S. Library of Congress, 624
Weather Channel, 624
Yahoo!, 535, 641
ZDNet's Mac software, 624

size
desktop, 168
display, 168
hard drives, 794
monitors, 169
partitions, 115, 117, 119
pop-up windows, 58-59

size boxes (windows), 41

Sleep command (Special menu), 74

Sleep mode, 83
PowerBooks, 820, 824-825
starting, 109

slide show (with soundtrack), 216, 218-219

Small Computer Serial Interface drives. *See* SCSI drives

smoothing fonts, 305

sneakernet, 466, 490

software. *See also* applications

backing up, 742

backup tools, 694-695

conflicting, 748-749, 759, 761

Custom installer applications, 249-250

deleting, 253-255

demo versions, 239, 785

disk space requirements, 242-243

documentation, 240

Easy installer applications, 248-249

freezes, 756

hangs, 348, 756

hardware requirements, 244-245

installer applications, 247-250

Internet connection, 516

newly installed, 251-252

packaging, 240

PC MACLAN, 494-497

PC MACLAN Connect, 493

PCs, 493

Publisher's Web site, 239, 777

RAM requirements, 241-242

ReadMe files, 239

registering, 252-253

requirements, 239

disk space, 242

hardware, 244

RAM, 240-241

sources, 239-240

reviews, 239

sales information, 239

Speech Recognition, 410

Spell Checker, 757

system extensions, 348

tools (Mac tool kit), 739-740

troubleshooting, 756

finding errors, 760-761, 763-765

freezes, 757-758

symptoms, 756-757

unexpectedly quits, 757

upgrades, 253, 774-775, 783, 786-787

beta releases, 776

bug fixes/minor releases, 775-776

information, 777-778

major releases, 775

new installation, 779-780

patch, 780

reasons for and against, 784-785

sources of information, 785

updaters, 780

version names, 776-777

SoftWindows, 504-505

SoftWindows (Insignia) Web site, 503

sorting lists (List view), 51

sounds. *See also* audio

alert

adding (non-recorded), 310-311

creating, 215, 224-225

recording, 309-310

setting, 308

Finder windows, 44

effects, 307

input, 427

input source, 410

modems, 538

source, 412

startup, 214

stereo, 46

soundtracks (QuickTime movies), 210, 212

sources

information

Mac, 741

software upgrades, 785

troubleshooting, 752-754

Speakable Items

activating, 411-412

disadvantage, 412

folder, 410

QuicKeys scripts, 419

Speakable Items and More Speakable Items folders, 399

speaking

commands, 411-412

Mac, 312

special characters, 135

Special menu commands, 73-74, 81

Eject Disk, 73

Empty Trash, 73, 108

Erase Disk, 74, 491

Restart, 74, 717

Shut Down, 74

Sleep, 74

Speech control panel

AppleScripts, 399

controlling speech (Mac), 312

Speech Recognition software, 410

speed

accelerating Web searching, 656-660

hard drives, 794

modems, 450-451, 515

spell checker

Outlook Express, 550

software, 757

spinning down hard drive (PowerBooks), 820, 824-825, 827

spring-loaded folders, 8, 61

standard application commands

Edit menu, 260

File menu, 258-259

standard dialog boxes, 261

Open, 261-262

Save, 263

Standard Views (folder windows), 53-54

starting. *See* launching

starting up. *See* booting

startup and shutdown times, 396-397

startup disk, 114
back-up, 740-741
desktop database, 717
setting, 346

Startup folder, 344

Startup Items, 397

Startup Items folders, 344, 397

startup sound, 214-215

status display area (Internet Explorer), 615

stereo sound, 46

Stickies, 139-140

sticky menus, 68

storage memory
hard drives, 793-795
removable media drives, 795-796
upgrading, 793

storing
data, 113, 323. *See also* hard drives
Scrapbook items, 137-138

streaming QuickTime movies, 191

structure (Web pages), 603-604

StuffIt, 589

StuffIt Expander, 257, 590

StuffItCMPlugin, 71-72

subnet mask (Internet), 521, 524

subscribing
Favorite Web sites, 633-634
newsgroups, 665, 669-671
preferences (Internet Explorer), 636
public mailing lists, 585
Web sites, 633, 635-636

substitutes (RAM), 330-332

suitcase fonts, 152, 155
advantages, 155
disadvantages, 156
TrueType fonts, compared, 158

suitcases, 153-154, 344

surfing (Internet), 88, 95-96
favorites, 605-608
links, 605
offline, 637-639
subscribing, 635-636
URLs, 606

Symantec Anti-virus for Macintosh (SAM), 706-708, 739

Symantec virus information Web site, 706

symbols, 135

synchronizing files and folders, 830-832

syntax (AppleScript), 406

system
adding components, 815-816
Extensions (Disabled) folder, 344
fonts, 152, 155
advantages, 155
disadvantages, 156
TrueType fonts, compared, 158
hardware. *See* hardware, 787
RAM, 327
requirements
AVP, 228-230
Internet, 514
running Mac OS 8.5, 806
resources, 349

System 8.5 CD-ROM, 807

system files, 344
disabling
Conflict Catcher, 360
Extensions Manager, 352-353
manually, 350

enabling
Conflict Catcher, 361
Extensions Manager, 353
manually, 350
information
getting, 363

System Folder, 336-337, 345
changing sets, 354-355
cleaning up, 730-731
Clipboard file, 338
Finder file, 340
folders
Appearance, 337
Apple Menu Items, 337
Application Support, 338
ColorSync Profiles, 339
Contextual Menu Items, 339
Control Panels, 339
Control Strip Modules, 339
Extensions, 339
Favorites, 340
Fonts, 340
Help, 340
Internet Search Sites, 340
Launcher Items, 341
MS Preference Panels, 341
Preferences, 342
PrintMonitor Documents, 343
Scripting Additions, 343
Scripts, 343
Shutdown Items, 344
Startup Items, 344
System Extensions (Disabled), 344
Text Encodings, 344
MacTCP DNR file, 341
overview, 21
Scrapbook file, 343
System file, 344
text list, 357
updating, 815

System Profiler, 736-737

talk newsgroup category

T

talk newsgroup category, **664**

talking. *See* speaking

tape drives, 689-690, 796

tasks (automating), 22

TCP/IP (Transmission Control Protocol/Internet Protocol), 341, 524

TCP/IP control panel, 519

tear-off menus, 67

tear-off tool bars, 67

technology enablers, 348

Ted Landau's Mac Fix It Web site, 624, 756

testing
  clock configuration, 107
  macros, 390
  newly installed software, 251

text
  fonts, 135
    adding, 158-159
    changing, 158-159
    Control Strip control panel, 147
    defaults, 159
    deleting, 159
    desktop, 304-305
    folder, 153, 340
    installing, 158-159
    menus, 304-305
    overview, 16
    PostScript, 153, 156-158
    screen, 152, 155-156, 158
    smoothing (anti-aliasing), 305
    suitcases, 153-154
    TrueType, 153, 157-158
  formatting, 550
  plain, 575
  symbols, 135

Text Encodings folder, 344

text list (System Folder contents), 357

Text Style command (Stickies, Note menu), 140

text tracks (QuickTime movies), 210, 212, 214

Text-to-Speech, 414. *See also* voice recognition
  macros, 416-419
  non SimpleText documents, 415-416
  SimpleText documents, 414-415

themes (desktop), 313, 315

thermal recalibration, 794

third-party control panels and extensions, 348

threads (newsgroups), 665

time. *See* clock

title bars (windows), **40**

tool bar (Internet Explorer), 613-614

tool bars, 67

Tools menu (Outlook Express) commands, 559

topic mode (AppleGuide), 282

trackballs, 429

trackpads, 429, 827-828

transceiver, 458

transferring
  files
    email, 466, 491
    network, 467
    other Macs, 464, 466
    sneakernet, 466
    Web/FTP, 466
  PC files to Macs, 490

transitions (QuickTime movies), 209

translation preferences, 484-485

translators, 268

Transmission Control Protocol/Internet Protocol, 341, 524

Trash, 82, 107
  empty warning, 107
  emptying, 73, 108

Get Info command, 85

locked items, 108

moving items into, 108

Trojan Horses (viruses), 703

troubleshooting, 750
  answering (Internet), 541
  bugs, 748
  conflicting software, 748-749, 759, 761
  descriptions, 752
  disks, 721, 723
  generic icons, 766-767
  hangs, 348
  hardware
    correcting, 768-769
    disk drives, 769
    installations, 770
    SCSI ID conflict, 769
    symptoms, 768
  hardware failures, 749
  Internet connection, 540-542
  lost preferences, 767
  lost time or date, 767-768
  Mac, not starting, 770
  miscellaneous, 758-759
  modem, 541
  observation, 751
  planning for, 734-735
  preventing, 31
  recreating problems, 751
  software, 756
    finding, 760-761, 763-765
    freezes, 757-758
    newly installed, 251-252
    symptoms, 756-757
    unexpectedly quits, 757
  solutions, 754
  solving, 752
  sources, 752-754
  unexplained crashes, 348
  user related, 747-748, 755-756
  viruses, 749
  Web sites, 756

true color (color system), 174

TrueType fonts, 153, 157-158

turning Macs on and off, 74, 396-397

TV Tuner Guide Additions (AVP), 230

TV/movies (watching), 231-232

Type columns (Extensions Manager), 358

types
files, 716
partitions, 118
Web sites, 512-513

U

U.S. Library of Congress Web site, 624

Unallocated (partition), 118

unattended backups, 686

uncompressing files, 589-590

undeliverable email. *See* bounced email

underlining (AppleGuide), 283

Uniform Resource Locators. See URLs, 598

uninstalling
fonts, 159
software, 253
installer, 254
manually, 254-255

unique menus, 67

Universal Serial Bus (USB), 113, 426-427

unmoderated
mailing lists, 586
newsgroups, 666

unplugging (PowerBooks), 821

unstuffing
compressed files, 257
files, 72

unsubscribing (newsgroups), 676

updaters (software upgrade), 780

updating
Internet Explorer, 660
System Folder, 815

upgrading
drives
CD-R drives, 796
CD-RW drives, 796
hard drives, 793-795
removable disk drives, 795-796
removable media drives, 795-796
tape drives, 796
hardware, 787
evaluating, 799-801
PCI cards, 797-799
processor, 796-797
QuickTime 3 Pro, 199-201
RAM, 333-334, 791
second-level cache, 792-793
software, 253, 774-775, 786-787. See also Mac OS
beta releases, 776
bug fixes/minor releases, 775-776
information, 777-778, 785
major releases, 775
new installation, 779-780
patch, 780
reasons against, 784-785
reasons for, 784
updaters, 780
version names, 776-777
storage memory, 793
VRAM, 792

URLs (Uniform Resource Locators), 598
documents, 600
domain names, 599
newsgroups, 664
service codes, 599
Web browsing, 606

USB (Universal Serial Bus), 113, 426-427

User dialog box, 494

usernames
email addresses, 545
passwords (Internet configuration information), 525

users (file sharing)
accounts, 473-474
creating, 474-475
editing, 476
categories (files and folders), 469-470
groups, 476
problems, 747-748, 755-756

Users & Groups control panel, 474

Users & Groups dialog box, 494

utilities. *See also* applications
Battery Reconditioning
PowerBooks, 819
reconditioning batteries, 826
Conflict Catcher. *See* Conflict Catcher
File Synchronization, 830-832
Internet Config, 518
Key Caps, 135
MacsBug, 344
QuicKeys, 368
drives and volumes, 384, 392-394
keyboard shortcuts, 383-386
keyboard shortcuts (macros), 387-391
macros, 384
printers, 384
StuffIt Expander, 257

V

variation color, 302

VDSL (Very High Speed Digital Subscriber Line), 457

vector-based graphics, 184, 186

versions (software upgrades), 776-777

video
capturing (AVP), 233
digital
digital cameras, 435
QuickTime file formats, 196
increasing output, 792
sources (AVP), 229

video cards, 166

video mirroring (PowerBook Control Strip), 827

Video RAM (VRAM), 165, 792

View menu, 81

View Options dialog box, 55

viewing
email attachments, 591
files
as buttons, 45-47
as icons, 45-47
comments, 48
dates, 48
in lists, 45, 47-52
labels, 48
size, 48
type, 48
versions, 49
partitions, 115
QuickTime
MoviePlayer, 193
PictureViewer, 193, 203-204
plug-in, 193

views
folder windows
Button, 45-47
custom views, 54-56
hierarchical views, 56-57, 125
Icon, 45-47
List, 45, 47-52
preferences, 52-53
Standard Views, 53-54
Extensions Manager window, 357
pop-up windows, 60

Views Preferences dialog box, 53

virtual RAM (memory), 240, 318
setting, 330-331

viruses, 749, 766
anti-virus applications, 705-706
Disinfectant, 708-709
macro viruses, 708
SAM (Symantec Anti-virus for Macintosh), see SAM
application, 703
AutoPlay (QuickTime), 198
common effects, 704-705
email, 704
infected files, 702
identifying, 704-705
preventing, 704, 710
macro, 703
overview, 30
PCs, 506
Trojan Horses, 703
worms, 703

voice recognition
characters, 410
commands, 410
names, changing, 412
speaking, 411-412
configuring, 410-411
overview, 22
voice, changing, 410

volume (AppleCD Audio Player), 222

volumes, 112-113. *See also* partitioning
Apple menu, 130
AppleShare, 12
Get Info command, 84
indexing, 93-94
mounting
drives, 119
QuicKeys, 384, 392-394
shared, 479-481
shared disk, 120-121
overview, 12

VRAM (Video RAM), 165, 792

W

WAN (Wide-Area Network), 515

warranty cards, 777

watching
QuickTime movies, 202-203
TV/movies, 231-232

wear out (hardware), 768

Weather Channel Web site, 624

Web pages. *See also* **Internet; Web sites**
browsing offline, 637-639
display, 620-621
Favorite, 633-634
HTML source code, 628
sharing, 486
structure, 603-604
subscribing, 633-636

Web sharing feature, 465

Web sites
ACTION files download, 266
Aladdin Systems, 590
Amazon, 625
AOL (America Online), 589
AOL Net Find, 644
Apple, 357, 535, 623
AppleScript, creating (go to), 405-409
upgrades, 781
browsing
offline, 637-639
subscribing, 633-636
Cassady & Greene (Conflict Catcher), 360, 365, 761
Chip Merchant, 318, 325, 334, 791
CNN, 575, 624
ColorSync, 180, 183
Computer Discount Warehouse, 624
Control Strip modules, 149
Cyberian Outpost, 624
Dantz, 697
DVD movie source, 625
Eudora Lite, 549

Excite, 644
Favorite, 633-634
file name extensions, 499
HotBot, 644
Infoseek, 644
Internet Explorer, 660
local access providers, 533
Lycos, 644
Mac EvangeList mailing list, 624
Mac magazines, 756
Mac Resource Page, 756
MacAddict magazine, 623, 778
MacCentral Online, 624, 756
MacHome magazine, 623
Macmillan Computer Publishing, 624
Macworld magazine, 623
Microsoft, 708
Miramar, 121
Music Boulevard, 625
Net Flix, 625
Orange Micro, 505
Outlook Express, 595
PC MACLAN Connect (demo version), 493
Quicken, 624
QuicKeys, 385, 392, 413, 418
QuickTime, 196, 204
    QuickTime 3 Pro upgrade,
        199
    movies, 202
RealPlayer, 651
Reel, 625
ResEdit (free copy), 373
Ric Ford's MacInTouch, 624, 756
software upgrade information, 778
SoftWindows (Insignia), 503
subscribing, 633-636
Symantec virus information, 706
Ted Landau's MacFixIt, 624, 756
types, 512-513

U.S. Library of Congress, 624
Weather Channel, 624
Yahoo!, 535, 641
ZDNet's Mac software, 624

Wide-Area Network (WAN), 515

windows, 36. *See also* **dialog boxes**
    About this Computer, 321
    Advanced preferences, 629
    alert, 37
    Alert Sounds, 309
    Apple System Profiler, 324
    AppleGuide, 284
    application, 38
    applications, 258
    close boxes, 40
    collapse boxes, 40
    Conflict Catcher, 360
    contextual menus, 70
    control panel, 38
    differences, 41
    disk information, 40
    display (Internet Explorer), 619-620
    document, 36, 45-46
    Extensions Manager, 352, 357
    Finder, 42-44
    floating, 43
    folder, 36, 45
        features, 62-64
        icons, 45
        views, 45-46
        window management, 45
    folder icons, 40
    keypad (Grpahing Calculator), 133
    list information, 41
    modal, 41
    movable, 42
    nonmodal, 41
    Outlook Express, 551-552
    overview, 6
    pop-up, 57-59, 61
        closing, 59, 61
        converting windows to and
            from, 58-59
        creating, 58-59

        dragging files onto, 57
        expanding files, 60
        icons, 58, 60
        menus, 58
        opening, 57, 61
        overview, 6, 8
        placing files/folders within,
            61
        resizing, 58-59
        views, 60
    resizable, 42
    scroll arrows, 41
    scroll bars, 41
    scroll boxes, 41
    scroll keys, 41
    size boxes, 41
    title bars, 40
    Web (opening), 658-659
    WindowShade, 45
    zoom boxes, 40

Windows platform
    emulators, 503-504
    Recycling Bin, 82
    PCs
        adding (Mac-based
            networks), 493
        applictions, 504-505
        buying, 506
        connecting, 493
        disks, 490-491
        extensions, 498-499, 501
        files, 490, 497-498
        opening files, 499
        running PC files, 502-503
        sharing files 494-497
        software, 493
        transferring files, 490
        viruses, 506
        Windows NT servers, 492

WindowShade, 45

wizards (Internet Connection), 530-533

worms (viruses), 703

WWW (World Wide Web), 28. *See also* **Internet, Web**

X - Y - Z

Yahoo!, 640
    advanced searches, 643
    basic searches, 641
    Web site, 535, 641

zapping (PRAM), 767-768
ZDNet's Mac software Web
    site, 624
Zen and the Art of Resource
    Editing, 303
Zip drives, 690
zoom boxes (windows), 40